Microsoft® Office SharePoint® Server 2007: A Beginner's Guide

ABOUT THE AUTHOR

Ron Gilster (MBA, A+, Network+, i-Net+, CCNA, CCSE, AAGG) is a best-selling author of over 30 books on computing, certification, and business, including *PC Hardware: A Beginner's Guide*. Ron has been actively involved with networking and enterprise computing for over 25 years as an educator, executive, and consultant.

About the Technical Editor

Jay Ritchie has been working with Microsoft technologies for over 15 years after starting his career building Excel models for the financial industry. Jay currently works as the Information Worker Practice Architect for Berbee Information Networks Corporation.

Microsoft® Office SharePoint® Server 2007: A Beginner's Guide

RON **GILSTER**

New York   Chicago   San Francisco
Lisbon   London   Madrid   Mexico City   Milan
New Delhi   San Juan   Seoul   Singapore   Sydney   Toronto

The **McGraw·Hill** Companies

Cataloging-in-Publication Data is on file with the Library of Congress

McGraw-Hill books are available at special quantity discounts to use as premiums and sales promotions, or for use in corporate training programs. For more information, please write to the Director of Special Sales, Professional Publishing, McGraw-Hill, Two Penn Plaza, New York, NY 10121-2298. Or contact your local bookstore.

Microsoft® Office SharePoint® Server 2007: A Beginner's Guide

1234567890 DOC DOC 01987

ISBN: 978-0-07-149327-7
MHID: 0-07-149327-1

Sponsoring Editor Jane Brownlow	**Technical Editor** Jay Ritchie	**Composition** International Typesetting and Composition
Editorial Supervisor Jody McKenzie	**Copy Editor** Mike McGee	**Illustration** International Typesetting and Composition
Project Manager Vastavikta Sharma, International Typesetting and Composition	**Proofreader** Ragini Pandey **Indexer** Steve Ingle	**Art Director, Cover** Jeff Weeks
Acquisitions Coordinator Carly Stapleton	**Production Supervisor** Jim Kussow	

To Connie, who keeps me real.

AT A GLANCE

Part III   MOSS and Office 2007

CONTENTS

Part II

MOSS Administration

ACKNOWLEDGMENTS

'd like to thank and acknowledge the contributions made to this book by William S. Hutton.

I'd also like to acknowledge the invaluable contributions made by the McGraw-Hill Technical team of professionals, especially Jay Ritchie, whose technical expertise kept the focus of this book on what a beginner truly needs to know.

INTRODUCTION

nstalling, configuring, and creating a Microsoft Office 2007 SharePoint Server (MOSS) environment can be a somewhat daunting challenge for even the most experienced software or network administrator. However, if you take things one step at a time with a well thought-out plan and a top-down approach, you can create a basic system you can build upon as both you and your users become more accustomed to MOSS's capabilities and how it can best serve your organization.

I have written this book from the viewpoint of the network and applications administrator who has some experience with a Microsoft environment but is new to Microsoft Office 2007 and MOSS. The chapters in this book each focus on one specific area of MOSS and its SharePoint features so you are able to configure each area and feature to create baseline functionality. I've avoided going too deeply into the more advanced features and functions so the beginner, for whom this guide is written, is able to get his or her MOSS environment up and running in quick order.

Part I of this book discusses the activities that precede and immediately follow the actual installation of MOSS. This discussion includes an overview of MOSS, how to plan for your installation, the pre-installation actions you need to take, installing MOSS, and the post-installation actions the MOSS administration should perform to ensure its functionality.

Part II covers the specific features and functions that can be used in an MOSS environment, including the purpose and use of SharePoint sites, lists, libraries, workflows, document management, Web Parts, search, and views. In addition, this part of the book also includes the functions performed by the MOSS administrator to maintain and monitor the MOSS environment and to configure and manage its security. This part of the book, while helpful as a startup guide, should also serve you later as a general reference on the day-to-day operations of your MOSS installation.

Part III of the book covers the integration of Microsoft Office 2007 applications with MOSS. One of the very best features of MOSS is that it works hand in glove with the Office applications to facilitate its use for all levels of user abilities, knowledge, and training. Part III includes information on how the Word, Excel, Access, and Outlook applications are integrated into MOSS to create a two-way interaction for users. Also included in Part III is an overview of the Business Intelligence functions of MOSS and how it can be integrated with line-of-business application software to further advance its usefulness and value to your users.

To assist you in your understanding and to provide you with checkpoints as you work through the step-by-step procedures included in the book, you will find ample figures that show the screen captures and illustrations of the dialog boxes, windows, and displays you encounter as you install, configure, and employ MOSS and its features. In addition, sidebars are used to introduce, explain, or comment on some of the lesser-known terminology, protocols, and services described in each chapter.

Using this book, regardless of how much of a beginner you may be, you will be able to install, configure, and make available the most commonly used features of an MOSS environment. I truly hope you find this experience rewarding and feel I've been able to help you in some small way.

Ron Gilster

PART I

Getting Started

CHAPTER 1

Microsoft Office SharePoint Server 2007: Overview

This chapter provides a fairly high-level look at Microsoft Office SharePoint Server 2007 (MOSS) and Microsoft Office 2007 and its applications and services. Before we get into MOSS too deeply in later chapters, you should first have a general understanding of the capabilities and functions of the various Office 2007 applications and services, and the role in an MOSS environment each plays.

However, first things first. Since we're focusing on MOSS, let's start with a general overview of MOSS and then discuss Office 2007 and its applications.

THE BENEFITS OF MOSS

The overall benefit of implementing a Microsoft Office SharePoint Server 2007 (MOSS) environment is that it provides an enterprise with the means to solve a variety of information and data sharing collaboration requirements with a variety of new and upgraded features that give it the functionality to do so. A fully implemented MOSS environment provides benefits to a company and its employees, and perhaps its customers, agents, and vendors, in the following areas:

▼ Familiarity
■ Productivity
■ Information management
■ Information retrieval
■ Data accessibility and audit
■ Business application interface
■ Sharing information
▲ Single platform solution

Each of these general feature categories is discussed in the following sections.

Familiarity

Unless a company is completely new to the Microsoft Office suite of applications, the amount of training required for its employees to be functional with the MOSS world will be minimal. Beyond its revamped user interface, which may take some getting used to for some users, the basic functionality of the Office suite of applications remains essentially the same. However, because the Office applications and a web browser provide the primary user interface in the MOSS environment, users are more likely to accept the "new" system readily and without the typical new system resistance.

The MOSS system integrates the desktop applications and e-mail, along with their web browser, that users are accustomed to using. In addition, since all users access, store, and share data, information, and documents through the same interfaces and out-of-the-box features, the user experience, not to mention the resulting information, remains consistent for all users.

Productivity

MOSS defines a variety of workflows that simplify the users' ability to create, track, and retrieve frequently used data to enable their most common business information-based functions. Users are able to easily perform a number of document-based activities, including review, tracking, approval, and even signature tracking. The good news for systems administrators is that nearly all of this functionality is already defined within MOSS and can be implemented without the need for creating new macro-functions or programming. However, if new workflow processes are needed, the Microsoft Office SharePoint Designer 2007 (formally Microsoft Office FrontPage) can be used to easily create the function needed.

Information Management

For most of us, storing documents and other types of organized data has been largely a process involving which media to write to, setting permissions to control who can and can't access documents, and, when necessary, reviewing the company's policies regarding how to retain, safeguard, and possibly dispose of the document. One of the better features of MOSS is that much of the process of managing documents can be done through the definition and application of document management policies.

Document and Content Use, and Their Application

One of the driving forces behind MOSS is the support of collaboration among users. A key feature and benefit of MOSS is its ability to facilitate the presentation of collaborative work to team members using web portal inclusion. In fact, a user's web browser provides his or her entry point and working window to the data, documents, and information managed and controlled by the system. MOSS even has features that allow an original document, in any language, to be referenced and linked to translated versions of that document.

Another nice feature, especially for salespeople and teachers, is that MOSS will manage PowerPoint slides as a library that can be accessed to reuse slides from a number of presentations to make up a new presentation.

Document Policies

Like a written guideline or policy, MOSS document policies can be defined to include who can and can't access a document, how long a document is to be retained, what to do with the document when its retention period expires, and whether or not an audit trail should be kept to track who accesses a document and when. The details of document and information management policies are discussed in more detail in Chapter 9.

Information Retrieval

In the past (meaning anytime before Microsoft Office 2007's release), a company's documents and other electronic content were stored in one of two primary locations: on a network server or on an end-user's desktop or portable PC. Sharing documents in this arrangement involved—beyond the administration of sharing, folder, and file permissions—the user knowing the name of the document's folder and share name or filename, and which mapped network drive the document was on. This system worked very well, as long as any users wishing to share data, documents, or other content formats had the information needed and the permissions required for accessing it. (Let's totally discount and leave sneaker-net file sharing completely out of the discussion, okay?) However, a user trying to access a document over the company's intranet and virtual private network (VPN) may have had some difficulty locating and retrieving a recently saved document without speaking with its originator.

MOSS includes features that, from the user's point-of-view, revolutionize their ability to access and use data and documents stored on both local and remote servers throughout the company.

Data Accessibility and Audit

Working with MOSS, a company can store all of its electronic documents and supporting data in one central repository and provide its users with the ability to easily locate, access, and retrieve whole documents or important bits of information. MOSS provides users with the ability to concentrate on their work, accessing the data they need without having to know just exactly where and in which document the data they want is stored or named. If they have been granted access under the document storage policies in effect, they can get the data they need and in a format most useful to them.

The document policies described earlier are used to define the access rights and security, as well as the storage and retention, and even create an audit trail as required by regulatory or accounting guidelines. The result of these policies is that MOSS, working in conjunction with WSS, can track, efficiently and in the background, who requested or accessed a document and when. Since the policies are defined centrally for the entire system, and specifically to an individual document by its creator, the managed control of information is largely transparent to the end user.

Business Application Interface

MOSS provides a number of "configurable back-end connections" or established interfaces that allow users to access the data managed by a variety of common business and enterprise systems, such as SAP and Siebel, to create individual views of the data. Users can also work through back-end connectors to set up data management interactions with these third-party systems using the Office 2007 applications on their desktops.

MOSS also allows users to create electronic forms that can be used to enter, collect, and distribute data to and from external sources—such as customers, business partners, and vendors—through a web page interface on the company's extranet or from the Internet and Web. The MOSS electronic forms feature allows for the definition of data integrity and validation rules, ensuring that data flowing into back-end systems is correct, thus eliminating the chance for data-entry errors or data duplication that could occur if the data had to be reentered manually.

Sharing Information

The Enterprise Search capability in MOSS uses information about documents, users, and web pages that can be applied to provide users with meaningful search results. A key feature of the Search function is that users can set alerts to be notified when new information is available on a particular subject, content, or from a particular user.

A good example of how MOSS facilitates information sharing is the Excel Services feature it includes. Users can have access to up-to-date, real-time spreadsheet data using a web browser from a central source to enable their productivity. Of course, sensitive or proprietary information in the documents is protected and shared only with those meeting the document and security policies established.

MOSS uses Business Intelligence (BI) portals to retrieve and display information from a variety of document sources. The BI portal feature includes a number of functions,

---

XML and SOAP

The Extensible Markup Language (XML) is a standard defined by the World Wide Web Consortium (W3C) that is used to define related data as a hierarchy of data objects or entities. The following is an example of XML-encoded data:

```
<?xml version="1.0" encoding="ISO-8859-1" ?>
- <!--

  An example of an XML document

  -->
- <message>
  <to>Ron</to>
  <from>Editor</from>
  <heading>Reminder</heading>
  <body>Meet your deadlines!</body>
  </message>
```

In this example, note that after the version of XML has been declared, the data in this document has been structured into the hierarchy of to, from, heading, and body within the overall container or message. Many examples of XML data and documents are available on the Web, but start your research at this link: www .w3schools.com/xml/xml_examples.asp.

The Simple Object Access Protocol (SOAP) allows software running on one operating system, say Windows Server 2003, to interact with software running on a different operating system, such as Fedora Linux. SOAP uses Hypertext Transfer Protocol (HTTP) and XML to make data transfers between the two systems. The beauty of the SOAP is that using HTTP, most data transfers across the Internet will get through firewalls.

such as user dashboards and defined information pieces that can be incorporated into a user-defined web page, scorecards, and visual presentation tools called key performance indicators (KPIs). The tools available to create BI portals are discussed in Chapters 17 and 22.

Single Platform Solution

Because MOSS incorporates the functions of the Office 2007 applications and is based on a scalable, open architecture, it provides a broad-based single platform solution. In larger installations, MOSS, installed on Microsoft Windows Server 2003, provides a single-source interoperable system solution by extending the capabilities of Microsoft SQL Server and WSS.

MOSS extends its interoperability through its support of Extensible Markup Language (XML) and Simple Object Access Protocol (SOAP) (see the sidebar entitled "XML and SOAP" in this chapter), which allows it to communicate with other systems and networks seamlessly. This is an important feature in that it allows the MOSS system to interface with any existing or future non-Microsoft systems the company may have or add.

THE MOSS ARCHITECTURE

Microsoft Office SharePoint Server 2007 can, working with other components of the Microsoft Office 2007 suite of applications, provide the functionality and benefits described previously. However, the amount of functionality derived from an MOSS installation depends on the features implemented and activated, as well as whether or not the MOSS environment is used to extend other building blocks, such as WSS and SQL Server. Figure 1-1 illustrates the structure of a complete MOSS environment. MOSS provides much of the functionality, but that functionality can be enhanced by the inclusion of other extended capability systems.

The MOSS Common Framework

MOSS 2007 supports other server-based applications and services with a set of common administrative services, as shown in Figure 1-2. The primary elements in the common group of services are (as shown in Figure 1-2, left to right):

▼ **Collaboration** This service supports discussions and shared task lists on server-based portals and determines the status of each member of a collaborative team, which could be online, offline, away, in a meeting, on the phone, and so on.

■ **Enterprise Content Management (ECM)** Using this service, users can create data validation and workflow procedures for Office 2007 documents through the Windows Workflow Foundation (WWF). MOSS includes a variety of predefined workflows, but users can create custom workflows using MOSS Designer 2007 or Visual Studio 2005.

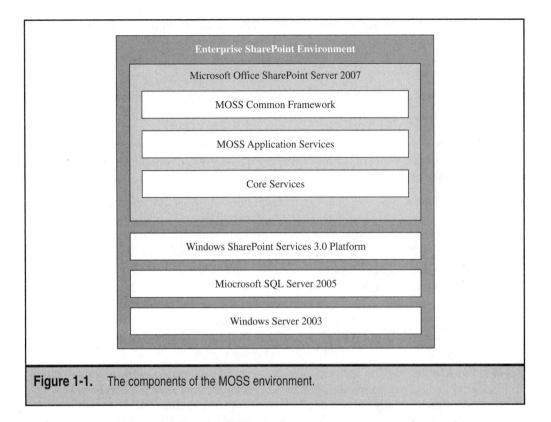

Figure 1-1. The components of the MOSS environment.

- ■ **Excel Services**   This service provides the ability for users to display all or selected portions of server-based Excel workbooks using a web browser. An Excel web services application programming interface (API) is available to support server-based calculations and complex graphics renderings.

- ■ **Portal**   At the core of MOSS is the portal manager, which has been brought forward and upgraded from the previous version, Microsoft Office SharePoint Portal Server 2003. The portal services provide the user experience and content display functions used by all other SharePoint functions.

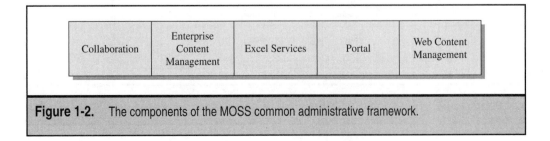

Figure 1-2. The components of the MOSS common administrative framework.

▲ **Web Content Management (WCM)** The capabilities enabled by the WCM service include support for Office SharePoint Designer 2007 for web template development, and web authoring using a template, site navigation services, security and access control, and site publishing.

MOSS Application Services

MOSS includes or supports a wide range of application- and activity-related services to facilitate information sharing, collaboration, and document management. As shown in Figure 1-3, these services include:

▼ **Document Libraries** A series of document libraries that allow a company to manage, organize, and categorize its information in a consistent form. There are three primary levels in the document libraries: the Managed Document Library, the Divisional Library, and the Translation Library.

■ **Web Parts** MOSS contains a number of predefined ASP.NET web page segments that can be included in user- or information-based portal pages or used as standalone web pages. A few of the Web Parts available out-of-the-box are document roll-up Web Parts, Members and Colleagues Web Parts, and Social Networking Web Parts. Custom Web Parts can be created using Visual Studio 2005.

■ **Workflows** MOSS includes a wide range of predefined workflows, which are in effect work unit scripts that define the step-by-step processes to be performed in order to accomplish a given work product. MOSS workflows are built on the Windows Workflow Foundation, which is a part of the .NET Framework.

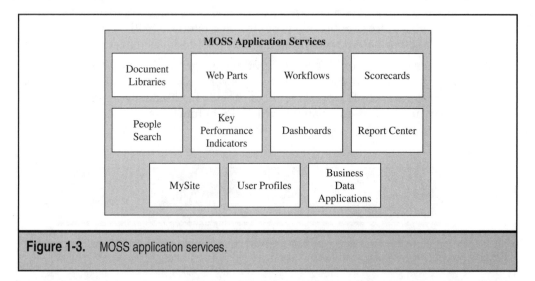

Figure 1-3. MOSS application services.

■ **Scorecards**   MOSS 2007 supports the business information report units created under the Microsoft Business Scorecard Manager 2005, although this particular feature has been upgraded to the Microsoft PerformancePoint Server 2007. Scorecards are custom business performance tracking reports.

■ **People Search**   This feature allows users to search for people and information defining what or who they know. This feature supports indexing, Lightweight Directory Access Protocol (LDAP) directories, and Active Directory distribution lists.

■ **Key Performance Indicators (KPIs)**   A KPI presents business intelligence information in a visual way to signal how a certain product, function, or any other business activity is doing. For example, a KPI might display a green light if customer returns are below a preset level, a yellow light if they approach the accepted level, and a red light if they exceed it. MOSS includes a variety of KPIs out-of-the-box that work with Excel 2007 and WSS.

■ **Dashboards**   A dashboard is essentially a web page that contains a number of elements that can be automatically updated independently, as well as lists, links, and other commonly accessed elements. The analogy is to an automobile dashboard. MOSS supports the creation of custom dashboards that can include KPIs, Excel workbooks, and information from SQL Server Reporting Services.

■ **Report Center**   The Report Center hosts predefined and custom web pages and sites that display, manage, and maintain links to reports and spreadsheets.

■ **MySite**   Perhaps one of the user-friendlier features of MOSS, MySite allows a user to customize a personalized view (using the Personalization Sites feature) of existing portal web pages, such as MyFinanceWeb or MyBenefits, based on their user profile and access permissions information.

■ **User Profiles**   User profile information from Active Directory is used by the Notification Service to target alerts to appropriate users, Social Networking to define common interests, and the Memberships Web Part for group and distribution list memberships.

▲ **Business Data Applications**   MOSS provides a number of services that support the cataloging, storage, and access to business information and links related to each defined line-of-business (LOB) area using the Business Data Catalog, Business Data SharePoint Lists and Web Parts, and Business Data Actions services.

Understand that the services and applications in the preceding list are only the proverbial tip of the iceberg. MOSS includes a wide range of administrative services that can be employed to create a customized environment suited to any particular company. As we discuss the whys and hows of implementing these features in later chapters, we will also discuss the specific MOSS services used in each area.

MOSS Core Services

As shown in Figure 1-4, MOSS includes a number of core services that enable a company to get up and running quickly and provide users with ease of use and a variety of tools to help increase their productivity. The major services supported by MOSS out-of-the-box are:

▼ **Templates**   Like the document templates included with each of the Office 2007 applications, MOSS includes templates for a variety of web pages (sites), lists, and documents that can be deployed to enable collaboration, reporting, and timed or triggered events.

■ **Personalization**   Users can be defined by their name, position, location, job, department, work responsibilities, and other characteristics. This information, along with other identification information entered in other Office 2007 applications, such as Outlook 2007, is used by additional MOSS services, like MySite, to create views and information feeds that meet the needs of the user.

■ **Targeting**   This feature, brought forward from Office SharePoint Portal Server 2003, develops target audiences for certain documents, reports, and functions using a rule-based criteria, groups defined in WSS 3.0, and Outlook 2007 and Exchange distribution lists.

■ **Single Sign-on**   This service is one that most users really appreciate. MOSS provides a Single Sign-on (SSO) capability that stores and maps user credentials for use in signing into back-end applications and third-party systems that are included in the user's portal. However, in cases where a company already has an SSO system in use, MOSS supports pluggable SSO that allows non-MOSS SSOs to be used.

■ **Site Directory**   This service is basically what its name suggests, a directory of web sites and network locations referenced by the system. It also includes

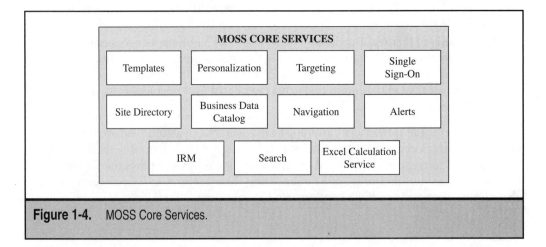

Figure 1-4.   MOSS Core Services.

a mechanism that can be used to scan for broken links, changed site Uniform Resource Locators (URLs), or missing sites.

- **Business Data Catalog**   This service enables MOSS to merge data from external applications and back-end systems into its lists, Web Parts, and search results, as well as in custom applications developed under the .NET environment.

- **Navigation**   This service manages the navigation links included on personal web pages and other web-browser supported displays provided through Office 2007 and MOSS.

- **Alerts**   This feature enables users to identify and tag events and data elements that are then continuously monitored for changes that fall within the parameters set by users defining specific conditions. The Notification service then sends an alert to the user indicating the condition that has occurred.

- **Information Rights Management (IRM)**   This feature is present throughout the Office 2007 applications suite to enable a company to protect its data from unauthorized access and use. IRM is integrated with the Rights Management Services (RMS) of Windows Server 2003, which allows system administrators to specify exactly who can access data, what they can do with the data, and how they can access the data.

- **Search**   MOSS includes extensive data and document search capabilities that support search functions across an enterprise-level network, intranet, and even the Internet.

NOTE   For those organizations that don't wish to take advantage of other MOSS features, Microsoft has a separate product, Microsoft Office 2007 SharePoint Server for Search (MOSS4S), that can be implemented to provide search capabilities like those incorporated in MOSS across enterprise networks and intranets.

NOTE   The search and indexing services in the Microsoft Office 2007 SharePoint Server for Search are performed by the Enterprise Search service that also incorporates relevance rules, alerts, customizable user views, and a web API.

- ▲ **Excel Services**   This general service includes three specific services:

  - **Excel Calculation Services (ECS)**   This is the core of the Excel Services. ECS performs real-time calculations on Excel workbooks in conjunction with Office Excel 2007, incorporates external data, and manages active sessions.

  - **Excel Web Access (EWA)**   A predefined Web Part that provides the display and interaction with an Excel 2007 workbook illustrated by a web browser using Dynamic Hierarchical Tag Markup Language (DHTML) and JavaScript as part of a dashboard or embedded into another Web Part page.

■ **Excel Web Services (EWS)** This is an MOSS web service that provides an API to support the development of custom applications that incorporate an Excel 2007 workbook.

It is the combination and synergy of the MOSS services and functions that provide the wide range of capability, productivity, and collaborative environment through which a company can better manage, control, share, and report its business functions and information resources.

MOSS AND OFFICE 2007

To determine the software and operating system's architecture of your particular MOSS installation, we must start not at the server end (don't worry, we'll get to that later), but at the user end of the system. Microsoft Office 2007 comes in a variety of versions and levels, which provide varying levels of interface and capability within the SharePoint environment. So, let's begin by looking at the various Office 2007 versions.

Microsoft Office 2007

Different versions of MS Office 2007 are available to support the needs of the end user. The versions range from Basic, the most limited version, to the Ultimate version, which includes everything the user might need or use in MS Office, except a coffee pot. Of course, there is always the caveat that when you are upgrading from one version of a Microsoft product to a newer version, you should be sure that your hardware meets the minimum requirements of the newer version and that your operating system is up-to-date as well.

NOTE MS Office 2007 is designed to be a companion system for Windows Vista, but will function on Windows XP. MS Office 2007 is a 32-bit system, but will run on Windows 64-bit systems, such as those available for Windows XP and Windows Server 2003, through the Windows-on-Windows 64-bit (WOW64) operating subsystem included on the 64-bit systems.

Hardware Requirements

For the most part, the different versions of Office 2007 have the same general hardware requirements. Table 1-1 summarizes the hardware and operating system requirements for each Office 2007 version.

In addition to the hardware requirements listed in Table 1-1, there are a few system requirements as well:

▼ To gain the full functionality of the collaboration services in Office 2007 (any version), a user's computer must have connectivity to a server running Windows Server 2003 with SP1 (or later) with MOSS or Windows SharePoint Services (WSS) 3.0. Most of the out-of-the-box (OOB) features, such as the PowerPoint Slide Library feature, in Office 2007 need only MOSS, but, because MOSS extends the features of WSS to the Office 2007 applications, many of its advanced services require WSS as well.

▲ A connection to MOSS is needed to enable full use of Microsoft Office InfoPath 2007 services (more on InfoPath in the following section).

Office 2007 Applications

Obviously, each of the Office 2007 versions must be a unique bundle of Office applications, otherwise why would there be so many of them, right? Depending on the functionality you wish the users in your MOSS environment to have, you need to choose and implement

Version	Processor	Memory	Hard Disk Space	Drives	Display Resolution	OS
Basic	500 Megahertz (MHz)	256 Megabytes (MB)	1.5 Gigabytes (GB)	CD or DVD	1024×768	XP-SP2 or Server 2003-SP1
Standard	500MHz	256MB	1.5GB	CD or DVD	1024×768	XP-SP2 or Server 2003-SP1
Home and Student	500MHz	256MB	1.5GB	CD or DVD	1024×768	XP-SP2 or Server 2003-SP1
Professional	500MHz	256MB	2GB	CD or DVD	1024×768	XP-SP2 or Server 2003-SP1
Small Business	500MHz	256MB	2GB	CD or DVD	1024×768	XP-SP2 or Server 2003-SP1
Professional Plus	500MHz	256MB	2GB	CD or DVD	1024×768	XP-SP2 or Server 2003-SP1
Enterprise	500MHz	256MB	2GB	CD or DVD	1024×768	XP-SP2 or Server 2003-SP1
Ultimate	500MHz	256MB	3GB	CD or DVD	1024×768	XP-SP2 or Server 2003-SP1
Accounting Professional	1 Gigahertz (GHz)	512MB	2GB	CD or DVD	1024×768	XP-SP2 or Server 2003-SP1

Table 1-1. Minimum Hardware Requirements for Microsoft Office 2007 Versions

the appropriate version of Office 2007. Table 1-2 shows the applications included in each version, which Microsoft refers to as "suites," of Office 2007.

Assuming you are at least somewhat familiar with the most common of the Office applications (Word, Excel, Outlook, Access, Publisher, and PowerPoint), let's look briefly at each of the other applications listed in Table 1-2 and what they would add to your system.

Microsoft Office InfoPath Microsoft Office InfoPath 2007 enables users to create and use data entry forms based on raw XML. Once created, an InfoPath form can be passed across a network (either internal or external) using Microsoft XML Core Services (MSXML) and SOAP. InfoPath forms can also interface with other application systems using SOAP, Universal Description, Discover, and Integration (UDDI), and the Web Services Description Language (WSDL).

InfoPath helps users fill out forms, checking the validity of the data on their desktop or portable computer even when they are offline. The user can also attach a digital signature should they wish, or should your rules require it. When the user next connects to a network, the form is submitted (as an XML document). If desired or required, the form can be distributed for approval to other network users.

Application	Office 2007 Suites							
	Basic	Home & Student	Standard	Small Business	Professional	Ultimate	Professional Plus	Enterprise
Word 2007	X	X	X	X	X	X	X	X
Excel 2007	X	X	X	X	X	X	X	X
PowerPoint		X	X	X	X	X	X	X
Access					X	X	X	X
Outlook	X		X			X	X	X
Publisher				X	X	X	X	X
OneNote		X						X
Outlook with Business Contact Manager				X	X			
InfoPath						X	X	X
Communicator						X	X	X
Groove								X

Table 1-2. Applications Included in the Different Office 2007 Suites

UDDI and WSDL

The Universal Description, Discovery, and Integration (UDDI) Registry is an XML-based directory supported by the Organization for the Advancement of Structured Information Standards (OASIS) on which businesses working across the Internet can be listed. UDDI is supported on Microsoft Windows Server 2003 as Enterprise UDDI.

The Web Services Description Language (WSDL) is supported in the Microsoft world in the .NET environment and is used to generate code that describes the protocols and message formats used to interact on a network or the Internet.

Office Communicator 2007   Office Communicator provides a means for a company's system users to, well, communicate in real time. A system user can find, through integration with the company directory, another user with whom he or she needs to coordinate and establish a communications link, regardless of the remote user's location, time zone, using Outlook and Microsoft Exchange Server capabilities.

The need to keep continually checking if someone is available is eliminated by Communicator in that a user can tag another user and be notified when he or she becomes available. Communicator then supports text, voice, and/or video instant messaging communication between the two parties. Phone calls can be initiated from Outlook or other Office applications and uses your Outlook contacts information to pop up information about incoming callers. You can also manage your desk phone through Communicator's features that provide you with the ability to answer, transfer, or forward your calls to a mobile phone from your computer. Communicator will also set up and manage audio conferencing.

Office Groove 2007 and Office Groove Server 2007   Office Groove 2007 interfaces with other components of the Office 2007 suite of applications to provide a Windows Desktop application for users to create and manage collaborations with other networked users, regardless of their locations. Groove works with MOSS, InfoPath, Communicator, and WSS 3.0 to provide a wide range of collaboration means.

Office Groove Server 2007 facilitates the deployment of Groove across an enterprise. Groove Server includes the system software used to implement, manage, and integrate Groove throughout a company and its networks. Although Groove users can work off-line, Groove Server provides synchronizing services that keep all members of a team up-to-date on documents on which a team is collaborating.

Office Live   Although not technically an application in an official Office 2007 suite, Office Live can play a role in establishing a company's MOSS environment. Office Live is primarily designed to work for small companies through a set of online services that help a company create a domain name and a web site, and establish the company's user e-mail accounts.

A small company looking to ease into online collaboration and commerce may want to check out the services available in the subscription-based (no advertising) version of Office Live. There is also a subscription-based version of Groove (Office Live Groove) available as well.

THE MOSS INFRASTRUCTURE

While most end users typically interface with only the results of the integration of this environment, the basic building blocks of the SharePoint infrastructure (that is, the components that must exist for the "magic" to work) are the Microsoft products and services working together.

Underneath all of the software applications and services discussed in the preceding sections at least two layers of foundation systems are required: an operating system and the Microsoft Office SharePoint Server 2007 (MOSS). MOSS can be installed on a single computer, in which case, the operating system must be Windows Server 2003. However, if MOSS is to support an enterprise network and a large volume of related documents with complex document management policies, it may be better to install MOSS on a Windows Server 2003-based server farm with Microsoft SQL Server support. To fully integrate MOSS in an enterprise implementation, these four pieces (see Figure 1-5) must be integrated to provide full functionality. In fact, even without MOSS, many Office 2007 functions require services from Windows Server 2003 and WSS.

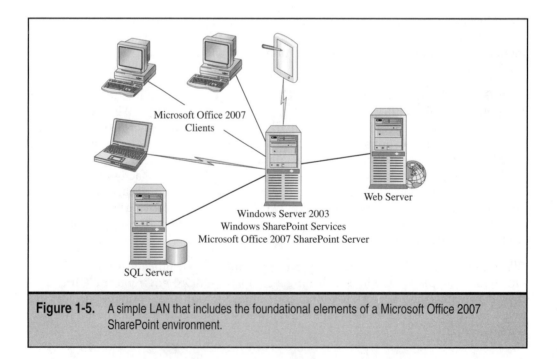

Figure 1-5.   A simple LAN that includes the foundational elements of a Microsoft Office 2007 SharePoint environment.

SUMMARY

Yes, that was a fairly high-level overview of MOSS and Office 2007, but in the following chapters we will continue to gain an understanding of the functions performed by each system element needed to implement a small to medium-sized MOSS system.

MOSS, working with the applications in the Office 2007 Suite, can provide a company with many benefits, including increased worker productivity, better data, records, and documents management and security, team collaboration on documents and projects, and increased communications capabilities. MOSS can't take all of the credit; the Office 2007 applications also contribute a significant part of the overall functionality of the shared system.

CHAPTER 2

Plan and Configure an MOSS Installation

Okay, so you've decided to take the plunge and install Microsoft Office 2007 SharePoint Server (MOSS) for your company. Good decision! However, before you actually insert the DVD and run Setup, some planning must be done and some significant decisions and choices must be made by you and your company before actually getting started. Like virtually every project in the Information Technology (IT) world and beyond, developing a plan helps ensure you achieve the result you wish.

The potential of a SharePoint system, if fully implemented, can change the way your company does business, internally and possibly externally as well. So, just diving into SharePoint isn't something you should do without first analyzing the impact it may have on your business and understanding where the impacts will be felt and the changes that may be necessary to the processes and procedures currently in use. Microsoft Office 2007 and MOSS together just aren't the type of system you should launch into without a plan.

Many of the decisions and choices that must be made before and during the MOSS installation directly impact how well the system will run, the features available to your users, and the ease with which you can later activate additional features and services. This chapter takes you through the planning and preinstallation steps you and your company should perform to ensure a successful implementation. Since you've decided to install SharePoint in your company, some plans, decisions, and preliminary actions must be put into motion to get ready, all of which depends both on your installation and your company's needs.

THE PLAN FOR AN MOSS ENVIRONMENT

Although it's not always at the forefront of systems planning, new enterprise systems are more about the company, its employees, and the business processes needed to better serve the company's customers and fulfill its mission. In the past, application systems like Microsoft Office were easily integrated into existing workflows and procedures, providing a modicum of efficiency to the tasks performed by individual workers. What Office 2007 and SharePoint bring is perhaps a whole new way of doing business, at least on the worker and interaction levels.

The Planning Team

Because MOSS isn't just a desktop end-user system, but rather a companywide initiative, the planning for its implementation far exceeds the authority and decision-making abilities of just the IT department. All of the key decision-makers and stakeholders need to be involved in the planning for an MOSS installation. Just who these people (or their functions or titles) are in your company may vary, but in general the planning team should include at least someone to represent each of the following areas:

▼ Key decision-makers who understand and can drive the vision of what MOSS brings to the company and its IT systems.

■ Key knowledge workers who know the processes and procedures and who can help with the improvements that better knowledge, collaboration, and document management can provide. In many cases, these team members may also have the responsibility of acceptance testing the system.

■ Any key external entities that may be integrated into the workflows or information sharing provided by the system.

■ IT professionals from the company's central IT authority, as well as the IT technicians from each of the company's divisions or departments.

▲ Key members of the design team who will be tasked with creating the visual look and feel of the system by developing the company's templates, forms, Web Parts, workflows, and other custom features, which, to the end user, represent the "new system" and the "face of the change."

PLAN FOR SYSTEM SUCCESS

To make informed decisions regarding how your particular SharePoint environment will be integrated into the company's IT solutions and which of its features are to be implemented when, it's recommended that each of the planning team members be educated and trained to the level that best supports their responsibilities. This could mean that, if you haven't already done so, the planning process, as well as the installation itself, may need to be delayed until the company and its planning team are better informed.

The planning process for the implementation of a system with the potential impact of SharePoint on a company should take a top-down approach, such as the one depicted in Figure 2-1. Since the basic purpose of any networked client/server environment is to support the business needs of the company, the system objectives for the MOSS implementation should directly support the fulfillment of the enterprise mission. The overall system objectives can then be digested into the specific functionality the company needs to meet those objectives.

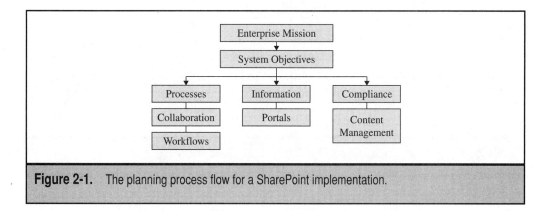

Figure 2-1.   The planning process flow for a SharePoint implementation.

Define the Objectives

When you begin identifying the objectives for the system, you may want to use a matrix that allows you to tie those MOSS features and services that need to be activated to the specific needs of the company and its networked users. Table 2-1 is an example of a planning matrix you could use.

Link Objectives to System Features

The matrix shown in Table 2-1 represents the type of planning that would be done at the highest level. From the information shown in this example, the planning would move to the next stage, which develops each of the columns and each of the cells within each column into the specific features each function requires from the MOSS system. Table 2-2 shows a brief example of the detail developed in the next level of planning.

Objective: Information Retrieval/ Analysis to Support Increased Market Penetration

Function/Purpose

Function/ Activity	Security & Management	Data Collection	Information Retrieval	Collaboration
Senior Management	Government & industry compliance		Business intelligence & analysis	Low
Financial	Government & industry compliance	Accounting & sales projections	Financial analysis & projections	Medium
Operations	Proprietary information & documents	Production & plan performance	Operational analysis & projections	Medium
Sales/ Marketing	Sales plans	Sales performance	Sales analysis & projections	High
Research & Development	Design documentation	Testing & quality information	Design performance analysis	High

Table 2-1. A Planning Matrix Used to Map Objectives to MOSS Features

Function: Document/Information Security & Management

Function/ Activity	Information Records Management (IRM)	Search Scope	Forms	Workflow
Senior Management	Access and retention policies	Open	Interface to third-party application	None
Financial	Access and retention policies	Limited by function and authority	Data entry and interface to third-party application and Excel	Approval routings
Operations	Access and retention policies	Limited by function and authority	Data entry and interface to third-party application and Excel	Coordination and approval routings
Sales/ Marketing	Access policies	Limited by function and authority	Data entry and interface to Excel	Order processing and customer relations management (CRM)
Research & Development	Access and retention policies	Limited to authorized only	Testing results and project management	Project management

The header row above is labeled with the span **Function/Purpose** over the Information Records Management (IRM), Search Scope, Forms, and Workflow columns.

Table 2-2.   Second-Level Planning for MOSS Features by Organizational Unit

Link Generic Features to System Components

The third-level of the MOSS planning process is one that the IT function should be able to perform, with inputs from the appropriate stakeholders, of course. At this level of planning, the features, functions, and applications required by each of the major functional areas of the company are tied to specific system services. Essentially, this is the phase in the planning process where the activities being performed are more design than planning.

Remember that end users tend to be visual. By focusing on what the user wishes to see, the specific MOSS components required to produce what the user wishes to see should, more or less, become obvious. To paraphrase an old IT saying: What the User Wishes to See Is What the User Gets or WUWSIWUG or "Whoozey-Whug." Okay, I made that up, but I think you get the point. If the user wishes to include daily performance information from a segment of a centrally managed Excel worksheet, then the Excel Services function of MOSS must be linked to the Web Part incorporated into the user's portal.

However, since you are in the preliminary stage of design, the focus can shift away from specific users to specific web sites or portals. Typically, users with similar information needs, access privileges, and other common requirements—very much like a user group in the Windows Server world—can share the basic structure of a web site or portal. If you are able to determine which user or set of users a site or portal is to serve, the remaining characteristics, such as security and access settings, can be easily defined.

Once you have identified the site and portals required, you should begin defining the following characteristics and capabilities for each:

▼ The users, or groups of users, who will access, update, or participate through the site or portal

■ Any search capabilities needed

■ Any custom programming needed

■ The degree to which the users require personalization of the site or the information displayed

▲ The MOSS services to be incorporated, such as business intelligence, document management and control, forms, workflows, and so on

Design MOSS Sites and Portals

Once you've decided on and defined the application and services needed to satisfy the functional needs of the organization, the next step in planning your MOSS implementation is to begin planning the specific portals, Web sites (for use by people outside the organization, such as a prospective customer visiting your company's web site), and customized sites required to display the information and processes to the end users. At this level of your planning and design, the focus is placed on the function, content, and arrangement of the displays needed to fulfill user needs.

One important planning and design objective for MOSS should be to concentrate the focus of MOSS sites. MOSS sites should be focused, as much as possible, on a single function or team because when a large number of too specific or too complex sites are deployed, it can become very difficult to maintain them and keep them up-to-date, and they go unused. Trying to make a few complex sites serve the needs of all users, overly complicates the implementation, and increases the need for additional staff resources to maintain these sites.

As a part of determining the number of sites and site groupings an MOSS implementation should include requires that you and the planning team gain an understanding of how sites will be used and who will be using them. This can be accomplished by getting the answers to the following questions:

▼ What is the purpose of the site? Meaning, what is/are the business questions the site should answer?

■ Who, meaning what departments or functions, will use the site and how many users will access it regularly?

■ What data or information is needed to support the site's content?

■ How does the site service the common relationship that "ties" the site users together?

■ Is all of the information presented on a site consistent with the relationship of the site users?

▲ Is the information to be included on the site too complex to include with other, even related, information?

NOTE   As you've probably noticed, I make a distinction between data and information. Data is a collection of facts, numbers, and measurements, while information presents an analysis, summarization, or calculation made on data.

With these questions in mind, you should begin determining the sites needed to fulfill the users' needs. In doing so, the following portals and sites should be considered and designed:

▼ Organizational portal sites

■ Function specific sites

▲ Internet sites

Organizational Portal Sites

Each level of your company likely has different information needs, depending on where a user (or group of users) is in the company's hierarchy. Each portal designed into the MOSS environment should be constructed specifically for the information and functional needs of a particular department, division, or project. Using the hierarchy of the organization or the membership of project teams as your guide, you should be able to define the information, collaboration, and security levels relevant to a portal for each specific group or user. The organizational hierarchy also allows you to see which portal sites will be a part of information rollup as the need moves from detail information to summary information in the hierarchy.

As appropriate to your organization's structure and needs, you should look to portal site planning and design at the following levels:

▼ **Division or department portal sites**   A good place to begin the planning for the portal sites needed within one specific organizational unit is to set up one portal site for the entire unit. In larger companies, you may need to work with the hierarchy of the organizational unit, but in a small or medium-sized company, one portal should serve the general information needs of the entire unit.

■ **Collaboration portal sites**   Under the perhaps false assumption that not everyone in your organization needs to routinely collaborate with other internal or external users, collaboration portals should be linked to the portals from which users are likely to launch their collaboration activities. The content on a collaboration portal site depends on the function and information needs of the collaborative team.

▲ **Information rollup portal sites**   Not everyone in the organization wishes to, needs to, or should see all of the detail data that is available in the content database. A rollup portal site typically contains a series of subsites that provide summarizations of information specific to a function, team, or organizational unit. In effect, an information rollup portal site provides a summarized view of a group of related portal sites.

TIP   Microsoft has prepared a series of planning forms for use in planning and designing portal, Internet, and other sites. Forms are available for both MOSS and Windows SharePoint Services 3.0 (WSS) that can be helpful for planning a MOSS implementation. You can access these forms at http://technet2.microsoft.com/Office.

Function-Specific Portal Sites

In contrast to the organizational portal sites discussed in the preceding section, some portal sites may be needed to support a particular process or information application, such as completing company forms, accessing generalized information, or perhaps operate a digital dashboard used to view and update project or employee performance information.

Other examples of function-specific portal sites include:

▼ **Help desk portal sites**   With access to a customer's history or a knowledge base on related incidents

■ **Order desk portal sites**   With product information, customer profiles, and order status

■ **Employee information portal sites**   With salary, benefits, and other employment-related information.

▲ **Document or record center portal sites**   With the ability to search, manage, and maintain documents and records management policies.

Internet Sites

Internet sites, or what Microsoft refers to as "Internet presence sites," are the web sites companies make available on the Internet for public viewing. While most companies now have a web site on the Internet, MOSS can provide additional functionality and information support to the web site. An Internet site can be the portal of entrance for customers and suppliers into a company's extranet, the virtual private network (VPN) entrance for employees, or any other type of limited access as well. While the "home page" of the site, in terms of its look and feel, may be somewhat static, its content and its supported functions can be very dynamic by including MOSS functions and services.

The point of including any Internet sites your company supports in the planning and design of a MOSS implementation is to determine whether or not certain MOSS services are to be included.

Internet, Intranet, and Extranet

Not everyone is up to speed on just what an Internet, intranet, and extranet are and how they relate. If you aren't sure what each is and how they are integrated into your network, planning for it could be confusing and result in no effective planning in the end.

The Internet is the Big WAN—the big client/server network that spans the globe interconnecting many public and private networks into one big wide area network (WAN). In fact, the name *Internet* is a short form of the term internetwork, meaning communications among connected networks. The prefix *inter* means "among or between," just like interscholastic sports is between colleges and schools.

An intranet is an internal network that operates like an Internet wannabee, only it's limited to the network within a single company or enterprise. Many companies do allow their remote employees to access their intranet either through a direct-dial connection or using a VPN, a secure and private "tunnel" through the Internet, provided the employee has the proper username and password and can be authenticated. The prefix *intra* means "within," such as intramural sports are between students of the same college or school.

An extranet is actually a kind of hybrid between the Internet and an intranet. A company can allow its customers, suppliers, stockholders, and other trusted people to gain access to nonproprietary or public information portions of its intranet. The external access is gained via the open Internet, as opposed to a VPN, and access is granted through an authentication process similar to that used by a remote employee accessing the intranet. The prefix *extra* means "in addition," such as clubs and the like are extracurricular activities at colleges and schools.

PLAN MOSS FUNCTIONAL REQUIREMENTS

There are a number of areas that must also be included in your planning for an MOSS implementation to define how many of MOSS's foundation and core services will function. The primary areas you should plan are:

▼ Security and authentication methods

■ Search capabilities

■ Document and record management

■ Forms

■ Workflows

▲ Maintenance procedures

Security and Authentication

Actually, authentication is a large part of security in browser-based information access systems, such as MOSS. Authentication is the process used by a system to verify that a user is who they are portraying themselves to be through the username and password used to log in to the system. Your plan for the security of the system should address, at minimum:

▼ The authentication method(s) to be used

■ The types and groups into which users are to be classified

■ The permissions and access privileges users are to be assigned

▲ Which system elements, such as lists, libraries, sites, portals, and so on, are to be secured and who will have access

NOTE MOSS security and each of the preceding planning areas is discussed in more detail in Chapter 7.

Search

The depth and scope that users and user groups are permitted to search can vary quite a bit. The search scope a user site is allowed will vary with the nature of the data itself, how the data relates to the site from which the search is launched, and who is requesting the data. An internal user will typically be allowed to search in more detail and depth than an external user visiting the company's web site.

When developing your search plan, you must examine each planned site and portal to determine, based on the security planning, who has what rights, not only to access specific data, but how much data can be retrieved.

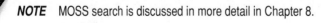

NOTE MOSS search is discussed in more detail in Chapter 8.

Document and Records Management

This is an extremely important planning step, especially in companies with large amounts of digitally stored proprietary information. A company doesn't have to be a bank, stock brokerage, pharmacy, hospital, or nuclear power plant to have a need to manage and control its documents. The MOSS document management and control services can be used to create, review, publish, archive, and destroy documents, data records, and even sites. Within the MOSS environment, nearly every function involves at least one of these document activities, so it is very important that some thought be given to how documents and records are to be managed and controlled by the system. Be sure you coordinate with the legal or compliance authority of your company when planning out the document management policies to be used.

NOTE Document and records management is discussed in more detail in Chapter 9.

Forms and Workflows

A preset form can ease both data entry and the format display of information on portals and especially collaborative sites. Forms can be used to gather status information, sampling data, as well as such routine data groups as timecards, status reports, and even calendar events.

If you plan to use forms in your portals or sites, be sure each site is indicated as requiring a form in its planning. (We discuss using InfoPath forms in Chapter 10.)

A workflow is a set sequence of events that are routinely used to accomplish a task, such as routing a document for review or approval. MOSS includes several preestablished workflows that can be used to route a document, track and issue to its resolution, and others. If a workflow is to be invoked from a collaborative portal, its inclusion should be indicated on the portal or site on which it will be included. If your company requires customized workflow procedures, they must be created with new programming through Visual Studio 2005 or SharePoint Designer 2007.

Maintenance

The primary maintenance activity that should be planned for from the beginning is site maintenance. If your company's MOSS environment will have multiple sites or site collections, you need to determine just who will have the responsibility for maintaining the sites, including removing them when they become obsolete or inactive.

As the MOSS administrator, you will have plenty to worry about without the added burden of site maintenance. So, you should decide early on, whether or not you want to tightly control the creation and status of sites, or wish to delegate this responsibility to the users.

NOTE Site maintenance is discussed in more detail in Chapter 15.

SUMMARY

Planning for your MOSS environment, especially in an organization to which many of the features and services it provides may alter the way in which users accomplish their tasks, can be the difference between a successful implementation and a reversion back to old practices. The planning team should include the appropriate decision-makers and each of the MOSS features should be discussed for its applicability and possible usage.

Knowing the vision for the system before you begin its installation will help you, the MOSS administrator, deliver on the promises that lead you to consider the MOSS installation in the first place. We discuss the actual installation processes in many of the chapters that follow, but in each case, as you activate a feature or service, it should be done in compliance with your planning.

CHAPTER 3

MOSS
Preinstallation

After you've completed your planning for your Microsoft Office 2007 SharePoint Server (MOSS) implementation (see Chapter 2), you are ready to begin the installation of the MOSS environment. However, depending on the type of installation you're creating, some preliminary actions are necessary to ensure MOSS has the supporting system and application software it needs to support your requirements.

In this chapter, we look at the preliminary steps needed in each of the two basic types of MOSS installations. MOSS can be installed on a single standalone (nonclustered) server or into a clustered server farm. In each case, Windows Server 2003 must be installed along with different levels of SQL Server and other services and applications, which are listed as applicable.

SERVER FARM VS. STANDALONE

An enterprise typically installs network-wide servers and common services in a cluster of computers, commonly referred to as a server farm. A server farm is two or more networked computers in a single location that host server software or shared network services. Server farms distribute the processing of client requests and server workload between the clustered computers in the farm using load-balancing techniques to more efficiently provide services across a client/server environment.

At the enterprise level, MOSS is installed on a server farm to better process user client requests to and from other servers, which could also be clustered into the server farm (more on this in the next section). However, MOSS can also be installed on a single, standalone computer—meaning, a single server application. It can be installed on a single desktop computer, too, but much of its benefits would be lost. However, as we discuss a bit later in the chapter, SharePoint can provide some benefits on a peer-to-peer network. Overall though, MOSS and the collaborative features built into Microsoft Office 2007 would be best in an enterprise installation.

NOTE   Chapter 4 details the installation processes used for Microsoft Office 2007 SharePoint Server (MOSS) in either a server farm or a standalone server.

Regardless of the type of installation you wish to make, the computer must meet the requirements listed in Chapter 1, but it must also be configured as a web server (see the "Standalone Server Pre-installation" section later in this chapter).

SERVER-FARM PRE-INSTALLATION

Typically, an enterprise MOSS environment is installed on at least a simple server farm, one with at least two—but often more—computer servers clustered behind a load-balancer appliance or server. This section covers the processes used to prepare and install an MOSS environment in a server farm configuration.

Server Farms

A server farm is a group or cluster of interconnected computers (servers) created to provide processing capabilities beyond the capabilities of a single computer server. The primary configurations of a server farm are commonly of three types: a high-availability (HAC) cluster, a high-performance cluster (HPC), a load-balancing cluster (LBC), or some combination of all three.

An HAC server farm is configured so each primary computer server, dedicated to a single task, application, or activity, has a backup computer server also dedicated to the same functions. This arrangement allows the server support to continue without interruption should the primary server fail while the backup server is being activated in place of the primary (an action called failover). This is commonly used in situations where system availability is of extreme importance.

An HPC server farm divides a computational workload across several processor nodes in the cluster. This type of cluster is most commonly used in scientific and complex engineering situations.

An LBC server farm is what is most commonly referred to as a server farm. Each of the computer servers in the cluster has one or more specific functions it fulfills to support client requests to the server farm. The workload in this arrangement is distributed using a front-end load-balancer appliance or specialized server software. This is the type of server farm and clustering best suited to an MOSS installation.

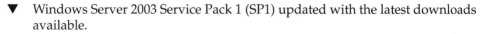

NOTE Before you consider creating a standalone (single server) installation, you should know there is no direct migration path to upgrade a standalone installation to a server farm installation for MOSS.

Pre-installation Steps

A series of steps must be taken before you can actually begin installing an MOSS environment. The following sections detail the tools—meaning the systems and services—that must be installed or configured before Microsoft Office 2007 and the Microsoft Office 2007 SharePoint Server can also be installed and configured.

Before you start the process to install MOSS, the following systems must either exist or be installed and a few configurations must be verified or completed:

▼ Windows Server 2003 Service Pack 1 (SP1) updated with the latest downloads available.

TIP   Updates for Windows Server 2003 and other Microsoft products can be found on the Windows Update web site at www.microsoft.com/technet/downloads/default.mspx.

■   The server's hard drive(s) must include an NTFS partition large enough to support the version of Office 2007 and MOSS you are installing (see Chapter 1).

TIP   MOSS will not work with an FAT partition.

■   If you've decided you need the optional support of Microsoft SQL Server 2005, you should install it. However, MOSS will work with SQL Server 2000 SP4, should you already have that installed and don't wish to update it.

■   Microsoft Internet Information Services (IIS) 6.0 must be installed and available.

■   The ASP.NET 2.0 Component must be installed and enabled.

▲   Windows Workflow Foundation (WWF) must be installed. However, there are a few configuration steps you must perform first (see the "Install the .NET Framework" section later in the chapter).

TIP   You can find the latest upgrades and downloads for Windows products and services, including WWF, on the Microsoft download web site at www.microsoft.com/downloads.

Once the systems and services listed in the previous section are installed, configured, and running, you must perform the following get-ready configurations:

▼   A domain account you plan to use when installing MOSS must be created.

■   Create a local administrator domain account. This account should be later used as your administrator account for any administrative functions for MOSS and its supported services, such as SharePoint Administrator, Index Crawler, and the application pool.

■   Assign the domain account to SQL Server with rights as a DB Creator, the system administrator (sysadmin), and security administration privileges.

▲   Now you can install WWF.

The steps listed in the preceding bulleted lists are explained in more detail in the following sections.

Install and Verify Windows Server 2003

If you are new to Windows Server 2003 or have not worked with any of the other tools listed here, follow the steps detailed in this section. Even if you are a seasoned veteran of Windows Server 2003, you may want to review this information to ensure the operating system is appropriately configured.

Windows Server 2003 Configuration

Windows Server 2003 SP1 is an absolute must as the foundation operating system for a server farm installation. Like all other Microsoft operating systems, and those of its competitors, you must plan ahead for a Windows Server 2003 installation in terms of minimum hardware requirements and the network to which the server is to be connected. Table 3-1 shows the minimum hardware requirements for Windows Server 2003.

While the requirements listed in Table 3-1 are sufficient for Windows Server 2003, a server on which you are installing MOSS and SQL Server 2005 has additional system requirements. A front-end web server or an application server computer must be a dual-processor computer with processor clock speeds of 2.5 gigahertz (GHz) or higher and at least 2 gigabytes (GB) of RAM. A back-end database server must also be a dual-processor computer with processor clock speeds of 2.0 GHz or higher and a minimum of 2 GB of RAM.

Remember that the more you are able to exceed the minimum requirements for Windows Server 2003, the better the system will function. You should also take care to ensure that the hardware system on which you are installing Windows Server 2003 is compatible with the network operating system.

> **TIP** To verify that your hardware system and its components are compatible with Windows Server 2003, check the Windows Server Catalog of Tested Products at www.windowsservercatalog.com.

Your primary partition on a Windows Server 2003 system must be at least 1.5 GB, but, depending on your system and the amount and type of hard disk space available, you may want to give it more. Windows Server 2003 supports file partitions up to 16 terabytes (TB), but a partition that size may be a bit overkill. A partition between 1.5 GB and 5 GB is typically adequate in nearly all situations.

Windows Server 2003 gives you the following four file system choices during its install process:

▼ Format the partition using the NTFS file system (Quick)

■ Format the partition using the FAT32 file system (Quick)

Hardware Feature	Minimum Requirement	Recommended Requirement
CPU speed	133 megahertz (MHz)	550 MHz
Memory	128 megabytes (MB)	256 MB
Hard disk space	1.5 gigabytes	
CD-ROM drive	At least 12X	
Monitor resolution	Super VGA (SVGA) 800 × 600	SVGA 1024 × 768

Table 3-1. Minimum/Recommended Hardware Requirements for Windows Server 2003

- Format the partition using the NTFS file system
- ▲ Format the partition using the FAT32 file system

The third choice in the list (format the partition using the NTFS file system) is the default and should be highlighted. This is the choice you want.

> **TIP** The Quick formatting option doesn't actually format the partition and uses whatever formatting is already present in the partition.

NTFS is the recommended file system for Windows Server 2003 and the file system required for MOSS. This file system is less likely to be corrupted and is able to recognize and overcome disk errors and bad sectors on the hard disk drive.

MOSS SERVER FARM CONFIGURATION

Depending on the size and scope of the MOSS environment you are creating, the components that make up your server farm will vary somewhat. While there are no hard and fast rules or metrics to gauge the size of the server farm needed, recommended configurations exist for MOSS server farms in small, medium, and large environments:

- ▼ A small MOSS server farm commonly includes the following:
  - Front-end web and application servers to provide web content and MOSS services, such as search and indexing
  - A database server running Microsoft SQL Server (optional)
  - A server supporting IIS and MOSS
- A medium MOSS server farm consists of the following:
  - An MOSS application server
  - One or more front-end servers to provide IIS and MOSS services, such as indexing and Excel calculation
  - A front-end web server
  - A database server running Microsoft SQL Server (optional)
- A large MOSS server farm consists of the following:
  - Multiple load-balanced front-end web servers providing IIS and MOSS services
  - Multiple applications servers supporting specific MOSS applications or services
  - At least two clustered database servers running Microsoft SQL Server

MOSS requires that each of the web servers in the server farm have the same MOSS services and applications installed, regardless of the primary purpose of the server.

This means that a standalone server cannot be added to the server farm to support a single Microsoft Office 2007 application. For example, a Microsoft Office Project Server 2007 server cannot be added to the server cluster and hope to integrate the Project 2007 data into the MOSS environment. The new server must also have MOSS installed—to the same level as any other web or application servers in the server farm—to function properly. However, on a particular application or web server, specific functions and services can be disabled as a security measure.

Configure a Server as a Web Server

Whether you are installing MOSS in a server farm configuration or as a standalone server, a few preinstallation steps must be taken before installing MOSS. The environment needs to be established by installing and configuring the following systems or services:

▼ **Internet Information Services 6.0**   This allows your server to perform as a web server, something essential to MOSS operations.

▲ **Microsoft .NET Framework 3.0 and ASP.NET 2.0**   These services are required to support Web Parts and Web Parts pages.

NOTE   See Chapter 15 for more information on Web Parts and Web Parts pages.

Install and Configure IIS

When Windows Server 2003 is installed, IIS is not installed nor enabled automatically. Therefore, you must install and activate IIS yourself prior to installing MOSS so your standalone server is enabled to function as a web server.

To install and configure IIS on a Windows Server 2003 server, perform the following steps:

1. Open the Administrative Tools menu on the Start Menu and choose the Configure Your Web Server option.

2. Click Next on the Welcome To The Configure Your Server Wizard page, shown in Figure 3-1.

3. The Preliminary Steps page displays (see Figure 3-2). Read the information on this page and if all is well—meaning your network is set up appropriately—click Next to continue.

4. The Server Role page displays (see Figure 3-3). If the Application server (IIS, ASP.NET) option is set to No, select this option and click the Next button. If the Configured column indicates Yes, you can exit this process because IIS is already enabled. Otherwise, continue with the configuration.

5. The Application Server Options page displays (see Figure 3-4). Click the checkbox for Enable ASP.NET and then click Next.

6. The Summary Of Selections page displays (see Figure 3-5). Read through the items included in the list in the Summary box. If anything is missing from the list, use the Back button to return to a previous page to make the correct selections. The list should include, at a minimum:

   ■ Install IIS

   ■ Enable COM+ for remote transactions

   ■ Enable Microsoft Distributed Transaction Coordinator (DTC) for remote access

   ■ Enable ASP.NET

7. Click the Next button on the Summary Of Selections page.

8. The system then begins the installation and configuration of the IIS and ASP.NET services. If these services were not included in the initial installation of Windows Server 2003, you will need your installation CD for Windows Server 2003 (see Figure 3-6) in order to complete the installation and configuration process.

9. When the installation and configuration of IIS and ASP.NET completes, the completion page, shown in Figure 3-7, displays. Click Finish to complete this action and display the Manage Your Server page, which you can close.

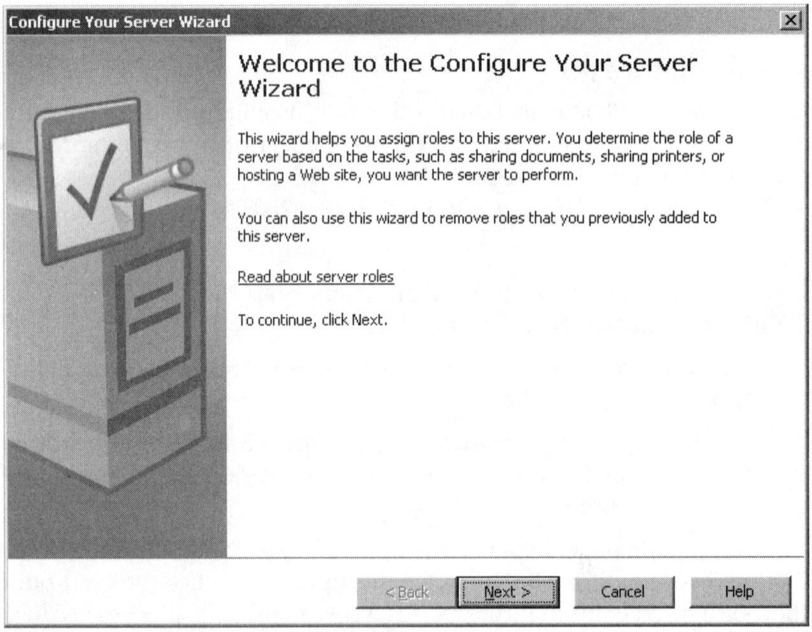

Figure 3-1. The Welcome To The Configure Your Server Wizard page.

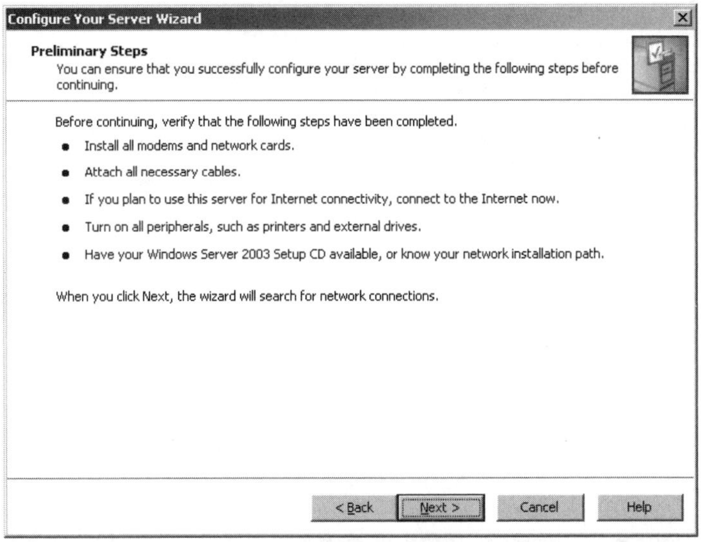

Figure 3-2. The Preliminary Steps page in the Configure Your Server Wizard.

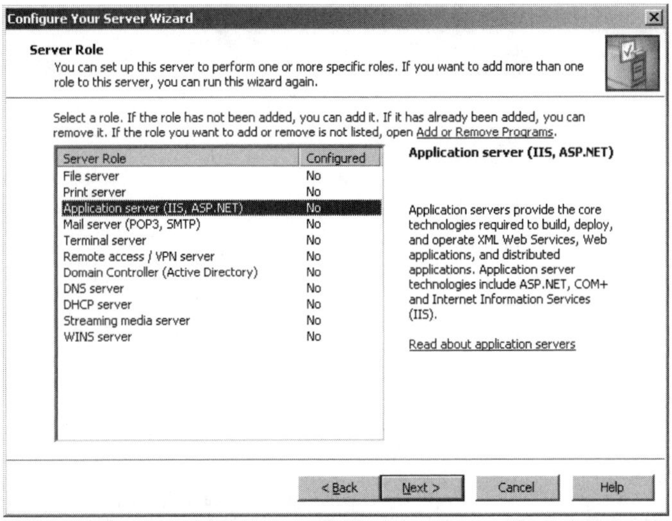

Figure 3-3. The Server Role page.

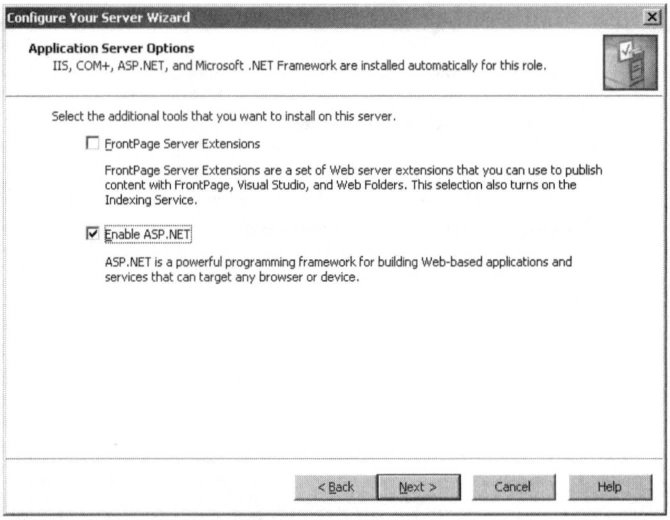

Figure 3-4. The Application Server Options page.

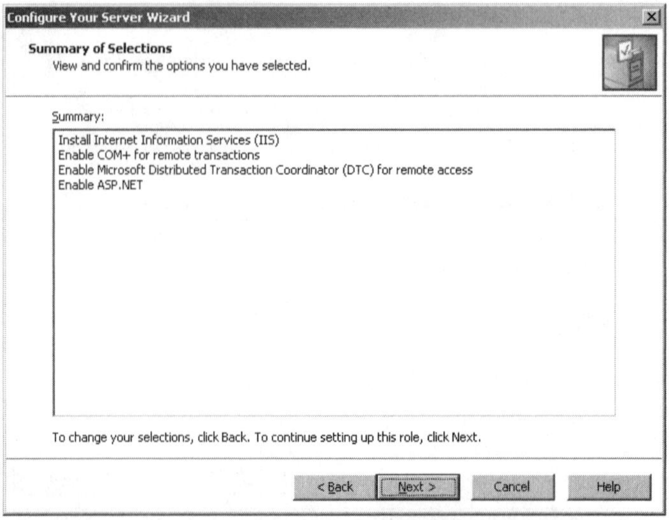

Figure 3-5. The Summary Of Selections page.

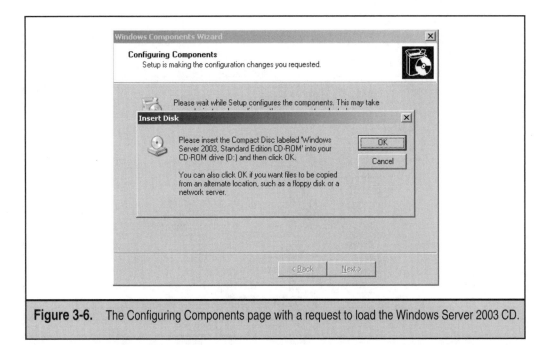

Figure 3-6.   The Configuring Components page with a request to load the Windows Server 2003 CD.

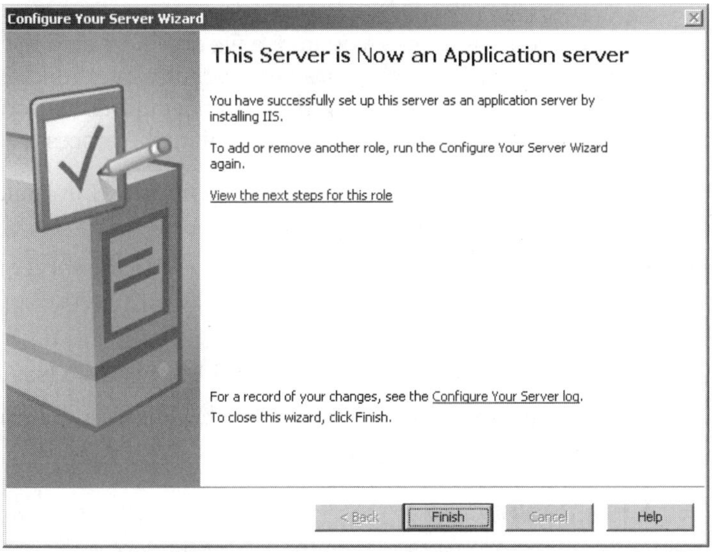

Figure 3-7.   The Configure Your Server Wizard completion page.

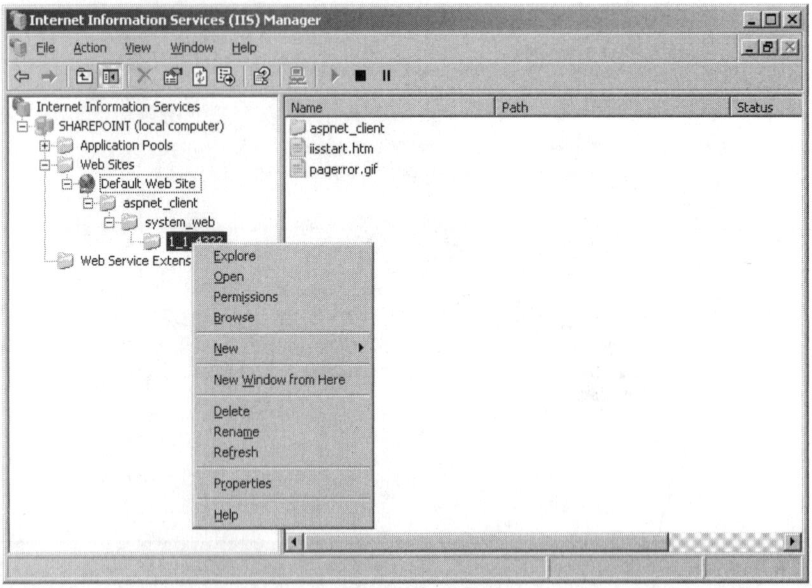

Figure 3-8.   The pop-up menu for the server's Web Sites folder on the IIS Manager page.

Once the preceding process completes, you may have one more step to perform. If the server on which you will be installing MOSS has been recently upgraded from Windows Server 2000 and was running IIS 5.0, you must perform one additional series of steps. If you need to do this, perform the following steps to complete the process:

1. From the Administrative Tools menu, choose the Internet Information Services Manager selection.

2. On the IIS Manager page, click the plus sign (+) next to the server name and then right-click the Web Sites folder. Lastly, select the Properties option (see Figure 3-8).

3. In the Web Sites Properties dialog box, choose the Service tab (see Figure 3-9).

4. In the Isolation mode area, unselect (clear) the checkbox for the Run WWW Service In IIS 5.0 Isolation Mode option, if needed, and click OK.

Install the .NET Framework

The Microsoft .NET Framework provides a significant portion of the common programming solutions and also controls programs written for the .NET framework while they are running. Like virtually all new applications created for the Windows and Vista platforms, the .NET Framework is one of the foundation software components for MOSS.

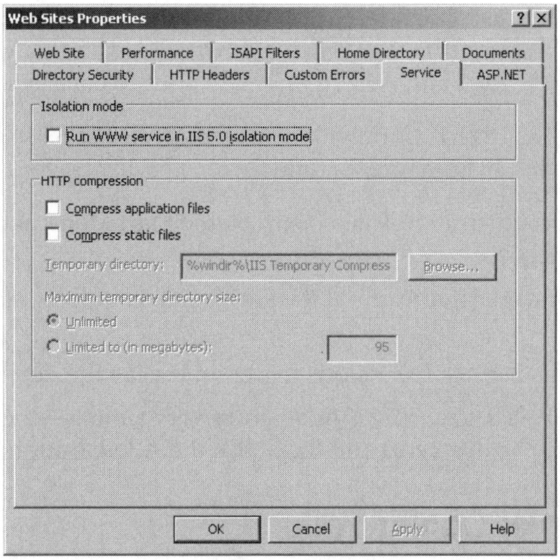

Figure 3-9.   The Web Site Properties dialog box's Service tab.

As a part of the pre-installation process of a new MOSS environment, both the .NET Framework 2.0 (also known as DotNetFX) and the .NET Framework 3.0 (also known as WinFX) should be installed. The .NET Framework 2.0 is needed by Microsoft SQL Server 2005 and Visual Student .NET 2005. Although .NET 2.0 is included on the Server 2003 release 2 media, it is not installed by default and must be installed separately.

The .NET Framework 3.0 includes a number of application programming interfaces (APIs) that extend its effectiveness into both the Vista and the future Windows Server 2008 releases. However, it also contains software components that support SharePoint Web Parts and an update to the Windows Workflow Foundation (WWF).

TIP   Separate versions of each of the .NET Framework releases for x86 and x64 processor-based computers are available.

Install .NET 2.0 Framework   The first step in installing the .NET 2.0 Framework is to download the .NET 2.0 Framework Redistributable Package installation file (dotnetfx.exe) from the Microsoft download center (www.microsoft.com/downloads). Once you have downloaded this file and saved it to your system, you can launch the installation by double-clicking the file to start it. From that point, the Microsoft Setup Wizard takes you through the installation step-by-step. You may need to close some running applications during the installation, but you will be advised which applications should be stopped, such as Outlook and IIS.

Install .NET 3.0 Framework   To install the .NET 3.0 Framework, first download the Microsoft .NET Framework 3.0 Redistributable Package file (dotnetfx3setup.exe) from the Microsoft Download Center. Once you have saved the downloaded file on your system, double-click the file and follow the Setup Wizard's instructions to complete the installation.

Activate ASP.NET 2.0   ASP.NET 2.0 must be enabled on all MOSS servers. This process is performed through the IIS Manager, as follows:

1. Open the Administrative Tools menu on the Start Menu and click the IIS Manager selection.

2. In the IIS Manager tree, expand the server name node by clicking the plus sign (+).

3. Click the Web Service Extensions folder to display the detail pane.

4. Find the ASP.NET v2.0.50727 (or an entry very similar—the version and build numbers may be different) and then click the Allow button.

Microsoft SQL Server Configuration

If your server farm and MOSS environment will include a database server running SQL Server, SQL Server should be installed and configured prior to configuring MOSS. Assuming you have Microsoft SQL Server 2005 installed on a server farm database server, you should perform of the following steps to ensure the database server is properly configured:

▼   Set the surface area configuration in SQL Server 2005.

■   Configure the database owner accounts and their collation.

■   Configure the SQL Server login accounts to be used by MOSS.

▲   Create any databases required for the MOSS environment.

It is not absolutely necessary you have a database server in your MOSS environment or install SQL Server on your standalone system. For this reason, we have chosen to not go into detail in this area. Should you decide you need to install a database server, or one already exists in your server farm, you should follow the configuration guidelines for SQL Server in an MOSS environment, which can be found on the following web site: http://technet2.microsoft.com/Office.

STANDALONE SERVER PREINSTALLATION

In situations where you wish to only evaluate MOSS 2007 or where you wish to publish only a small number of MOSS-based web sites, it may be more useful and certainly more administratively efficient to install MOSS on a standalone (meaning, not in a server farm) server. The complexity of the preinstallation process, along with that of the actual installation of MOSS, is greatly reduced. In fact, installing MOSS on a single server using the default configuration settings—assuming that Windows 2003 Server is the installed operating system on that server—is largely taken care of by MOSS itself.

As a part of the standalone MOSS installation process, several system elements are installed automatically.

▼ **Microsoft SQL Server 2005 Express Edition** Used during installation to create the configuration and content databases.

■ **Shared Service Provider (SSP)** Created during installation by the Setup utility.

▲ **SharePoint site collection and default site** These elements are created during installation along with the SharePoint Central Administration web site.

TIP Remember that while some processes can be used to migrate a standalone server into a server farm using backup and restore processes, the MOSS portion of the migration cannot be directly upgraded from a single-server installation to a server farm installation. So for at least the MOSS portion of the installation, if you decide to move the installation into a server farm, you'll essentially need to reinstall the MOSS environment.

Configure Server as a Web Server

A few preinstallation steps must be carried out before installing MOSS on a standalone server. As shown in the server farm preinstallation steps covered in the preceding sections, the environment must be established through the installation and configuration of the following systems or services:

▼ **Internet Information Services 6.0** This allows your server to perform as a web server, something essential to MOSS operations.

▲ **Microsoft .NET Framework 3.0 and ASP.NET 2.0** These services are required to support Web Parts and Web Parts pages.

Install and Configure IIS

When Windows Server 2003 is installed, IIS is not installed nor enabled automatically. Therefore, you must install and activate IIS yourself prior to installing MOSS so your standalone server is enabled to function as a web server. Use the same steps detailed earlier in the "Install and Configure IIS" section. This part of the process is the same for a standalone server or a server farm server.

Install and Configure the .NET Framework and ASP.NET

Just as the MOSS servers in a server farm should be configured with the .NET 3.0 Framework and ASP.NET 2.0, so should a standalone MOSS server. Follow the steps detailed in the section entitled "Install the .NET Framework" earlier in the chapter to complete this process on your standalone server.

TO BE CONTINUED... AND SUMMARY

The steps remaining to complete your installation of the MOSS environment are detailed in Chapter 4 for both a server farm and a standalone server.

In a server farm installation, the preinstallation steps needed to prepare for an MOSS 2007 environment must be performed on every server on which MOSS and other related services will run. However, in a single standalone server environment, obviously the sole server must be configured to act in the capacity of a web server, application server, and database server, all at the same time.

It would be foolhardy to try to operate an enterprise MOSS environment from a single server and it would be just as silly to create a server farm installation for a small company with a limited number of web sites and shared documents.

If you were unable to complete any of the steps outlined in this chapter for any reason, remember that Microsoft has a vast array of help, technical notes, and knowledge base information for you to research your particular situation.

CHAPTER 4

MOSS Installation

Once you have your server farm or standalone server configured with Windows Server 2003, SQL Server 2005, .NET Framework 3.0, Internet Information Services (IIS) 6.0, and ASP.NET 2.0 (see Chapter 3), you are ready to begin the installation of Microsoft Office 2007 SharePoint Server (MOSS) and its associated applications and services.

This chapter takes you through the process of installing MOSS in both a server farm and a standalone server configuration. If you are in the process of learning or trying out MOSS, you would be well advised to first install it on a standalone server. After you are fully impressed with its capabilities and are ready to install MOSS for your entire organization and its network users, you can take on a server farm installation. When that time comes, follow the step-by-step instructions included here and the task should go smoothly.

Please understand that the information in this chapter and the steps recommended presume you are performing a "clean" installation and not an upgrade. If you do decide to start with a standalone server installation, keep in mind that there is no migration path from a single server to a server farm for MOSS.

STANDALONE SERVER INSTALLATION

Installing MOSS 2007 on a single standalone server is a fairly uncomplicated process. Like all other software system installations though, you do have a few decisions to make and, during the installation, one or two actions you may need to take.

Before You Begin

If you have previously installed either of the MOSS Beta or Trial versions, you'll need to do the following before you begin your installation process (which is called a *deployment* by Microsoft, by the way):

▼ Delete any existing MOSS databases, including the configuration database, that may be on the server (see the "Configuration and Content Databases" section later in the chapter).

■ If there is a version of SQL Server installed on the server earlier than SQL Server 2005, remove it using the Add or Remove Programs utility found on the Control Panel.

NOTE The standalone server installation for MOSS also installs SQL Server 2005 Express Edition.

▲ Uninstall any existing MOSS Beta or Trial versions on the server using the Add or Remove Programs utility found on the Control Panel.

Configuration and Content Databases

Just in case you need to locate and remove any existing SharePoint configuration and content databases, you also need to be able to find them. SharePoint's databases are stored in one of the following directories, depending on the type or version of the MOSS system previously installed:

▼ C:\Program Files\Microsoft SQL Server\MSSQL$SHAREPOINT\Data

▲ C:\Program Files\Microsoft SQL Server\MSSQL.1\MSSQL\Data

In most cases, you should find two or possibly three types of files in this directory (see Figure 4-1): database files (with an extension of .mdf), transaction log files (with an extension of .ldf), and possibly a security certificate (with an extension of .cer). The file names you find should be one of the following:

▼ **%computername%_DB.mdf**   Such as Sharepoint_DB.mdf

■ **%computername%_DB_log.ldf**   Such as Sharepoint_DB_log.ldf

■ **%sitename%_content.mdf**   Such as portalsite_content.mdf

▲ **%sitename%_content_log.ldf**   Such as portalsite_content_log.ldf

Another method you can use to locate any MOSS or SharePoint databases is to use the Microsoft SQL Server Management Studio (see Figure 4-2), which is available for both SQL Server 2005 standard and express versions. This tool can be especially helpful when you are trying to delete a database file that SQL has locked for some reason.

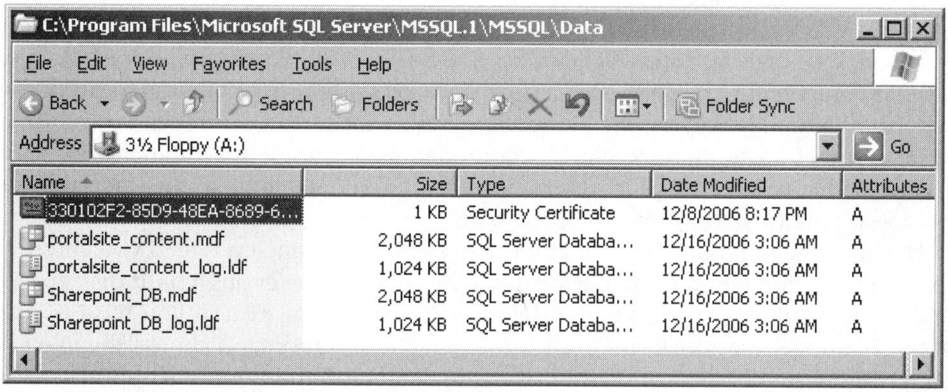

Figure 4-1.   The contents in a SharePoint databases directory.

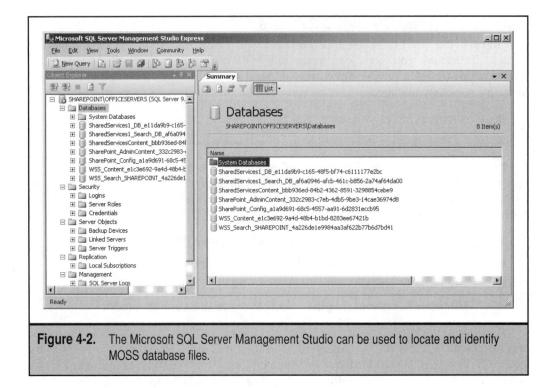

Figure 4-2.   The Microsoft SQL Server Management Studio can be used to locate and identify MOSS database files.

Install MOSS on a Standalone Server

In the installation process, when the AutoRun starts from the CD or DVD deployment disc, a dialog box (see Figure 4-3) displays. After you enter the product key and it is validated and you've accepted the End User License Agreement (EULA), it will ask you to choose the type of server on which MOSS is to be installed. Since you are installing on a standalone server, the choice should be fairly obvious: Choose the Standalone option and click Install Now. Notice that the Standalone option includes the information (shown in Figure 4-3) that this option installs all components on a single machine, including SQL Server 2005 Express. You should also make note of the statement that the standalone version doesn't allow for servers to be added to create a server farm.

The next page that displays (of any importance) is the one on which you choose the type of installation you wish to perform. Provided you have enough hard disk space on the C: drive, you can proceed with a Basic installation. However, if you wish to install MOSS on another hard disk drive, click the Advanced button and choose the File Location tab. Enter the drive location for installation and click the Continue button.

If during the installation process, setup determines that certain services are either unavailable or disabled, you may see a message box similar to the one shown in Figure 4-4. Should an error message box appear, you must interrupt the setup and take the corrective action prescribed.

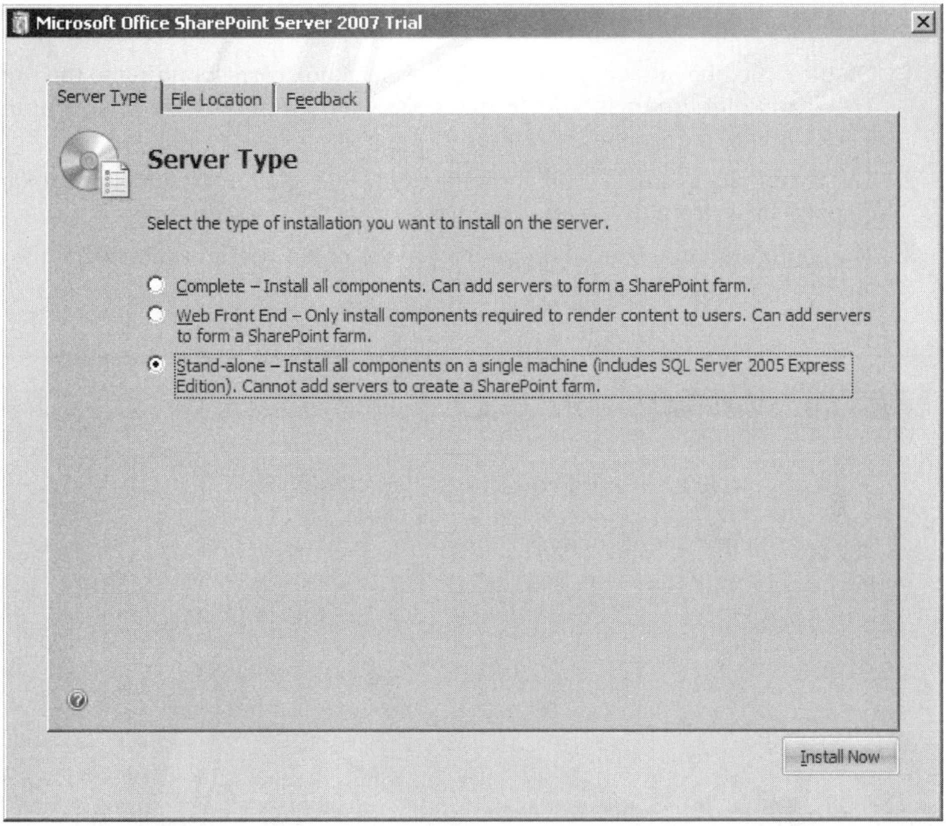

Figure 4-3.   The MOSS Installation Server Type dialog box.

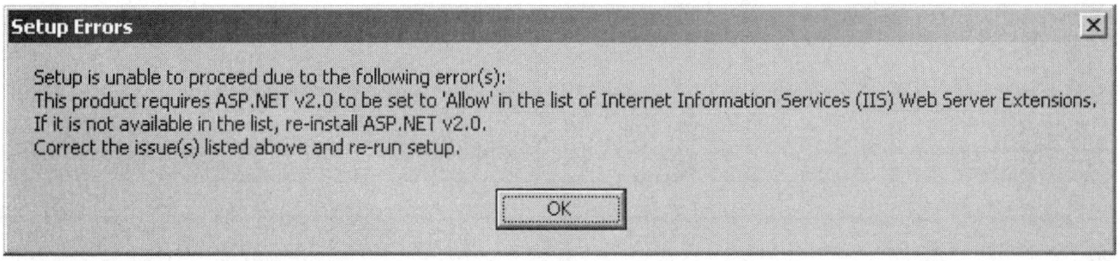

Figure 4-4.   A SharePoint setup error message box.

When setup completes, you are prompted to complete the configuration of the MOSS server. To complete the configuration, follow these steps:

1. On the dialog box that appears, select the checkbox corresponding to the Run The SharePoint Products And Technologies Configuration Wizard Now option. Click Close to launch the configuration process.

2. The SharePoint Products And Technologies Configuration Wizard starts up and displays its welcome page (see Figure 4-5). Click Next to continue.

3. The configuration wizard then begins a series of ten configuration steps automatically (see Figure 4-6).

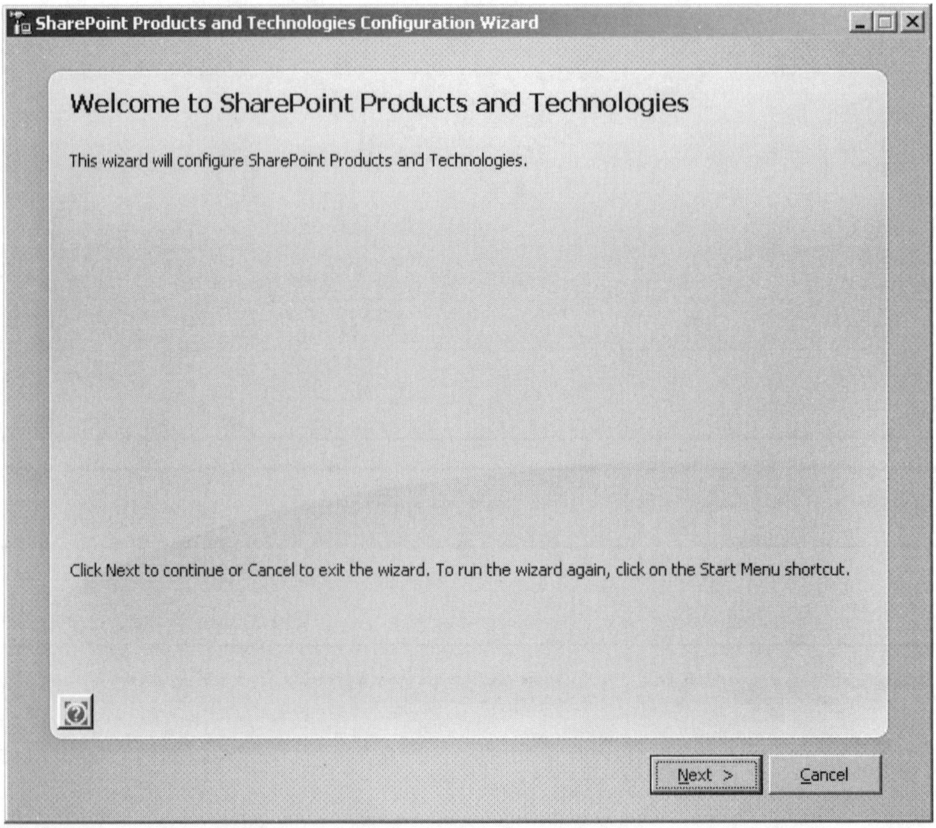

Figure 4-5. The SharePoint Products And Technologies Configuration Wizard Welcome page.

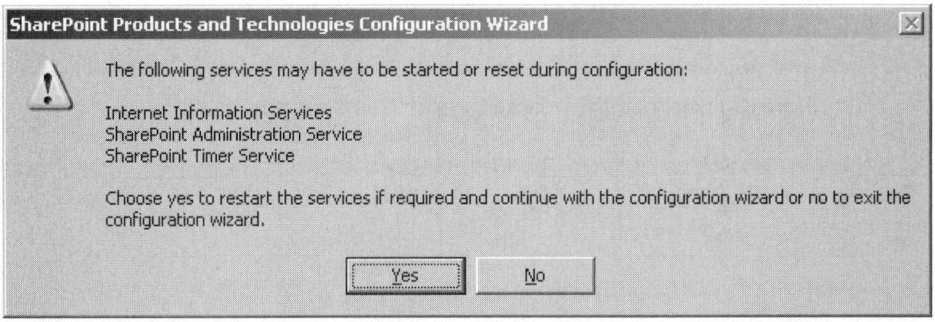

Figure 4-6.   The SharePoint Products And Technologies Configuration Wizard advisory
message box.

4. If during the configuration process an error or a condition advice situation
occurs, you may see a message box similar to the one shown in Figure 4-7.
Typically, a message box that displays during the configuration process concerns
the need to restart certain services needed to complete the configuration. In the
instance shown in Figure 4-7, which is the message you are most likely to see,
click the OK button to allow the Configuration Wizard to correct the issue.

   If you wish to learn more about what the SharePoint Products And Technologies
Configuration Wizard is doing or if you need help to deal with an error
message box, click the Help button located at the lower left-hand corner of the
configuration wizard page (see Figure 4-8) to display the SharePoint Products
And Technologies Configuration Wizard Help pages (see Figure 4-9).

5. When the configuration wizard completes the configuration, a Configuration
Successful page displays. Click the Finish button to open the SharePoint site
you've just created.

Installation Exceptions

After completing the installation and configuration of MOSS, you may need to perform
one or two additional configuration steps so your SharePoint site functions without exceptions. If you are asked to enter a username and password when your SharePoint site
displays or if you are using a proxy server, use the steps in the next two sections to get
around these exceptions.

Trusted Sites

When the newly installed and configured SharePoint system starts, you may be prompted
for your username and password. If this happens, it means your SharePoint site must be

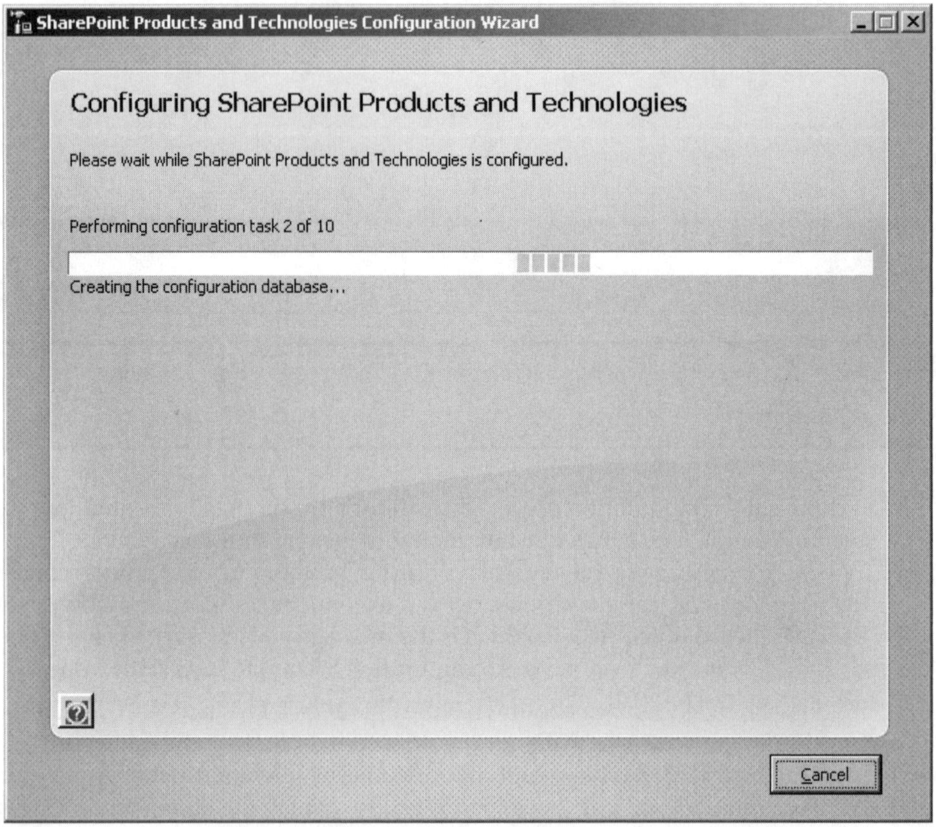

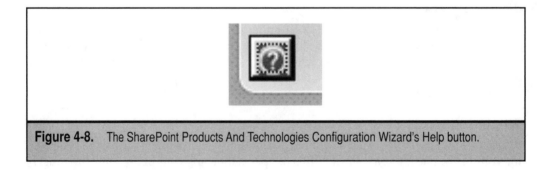

Figure 4-7. The SharePoint Products And Technologies Configuration Wizard status page.

Figure 4-8. The SharePoint Products And Technologies Configuration Wizard's Help button.

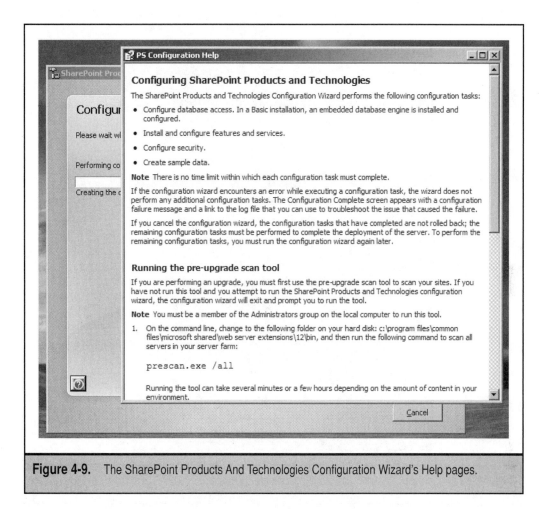

Figure 4-9.   The SharePoint Products And Technologies Configuration Wizard's Help pages.

added to the list of trusted sites and Internet Explorer's authentication settings must be adjusted. Make a note of the site's location address for later use.

To add the SharePoint site to the trusted sites list, do the following:

1. Open Internet Explorer.

2. Select the Tools menu option and click Internet Options.

3. Select the Security tab. In the Select A Web Content Zone to specify its security settings pane at the top of the dialog box, click the Trusted Site icon (see Figure 4-10) and then click the Sites button.

4. On the dialog box that appears (see Figure 4-11), make sure the Require Server Verification (https:) For All Sites In This Zone checkbox, located beneath the Websites box, is not selected (unchecked).

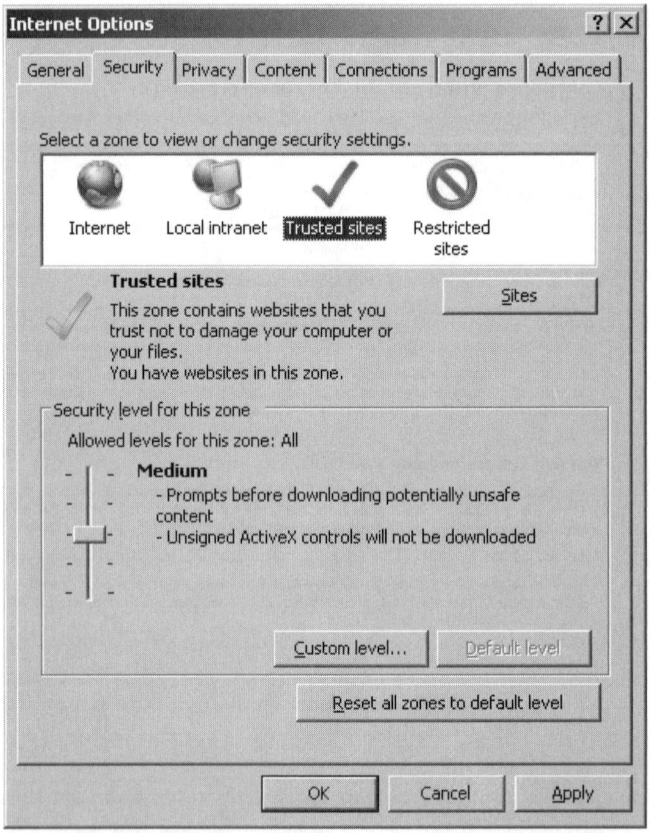

Figure 4-10. Internet Explorer's Internet Options dialog box.

5. Enter the location address of your SharePoint site in the Add This Website To The Zone text box (as shown in Figure 4-11) and click the Add button to add your SharePoint as a trusted site.

6. Click the Close button to close the Trusted Sites dialog box and then click OK to close the Internet Options dialog box.

Proxy Server

You should set Internet Explorer to bypass a proxy server for all local addresses if your network includes a proxy server. To configure the proxy server to bypass all local addresses, such as your SharePoint site, do the following:

1. Open Internet Explorer and click the Internet Options selection on the Tools menu (see Figure 4-10 earlier in the chapter).

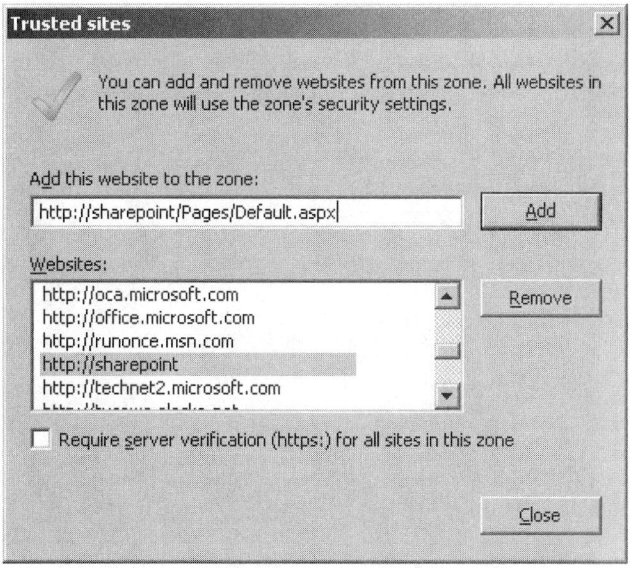

Figure 4-11.   Internet Explorer's Internet Options Trusted SiteS dialog box.

2. Select the Connections tab and click the LAN Settings button in the Local Area Network (LAN) area of the Connections dialog box. The Local Area Network (LAN) Settings dialog box (see Figure 4-12) displays.

3. In the top area, Automatic Configuration, make sure the Automatically Detect Settings checkbox is not selected (unchecked).

4. In the lower area, Proxy Server, check the box corresponding to Use A Proxy Server For Your LAN and enter the network address and port number (typically port 80) for the proxy server in the Address box. Check the box corresponding to the Bypass proxy server for local addresses. Your completed LAN settings box should look very similar to the one shown in Figure 4-12.

5. Click OK on the LAN settings box and the Internet Options box to close them.

After Installation Steps

After the SharePoint installation (Setup.exe) completes as it should, the home page of your SharePoint site will display in your default Internet browser. While the temptation will be to start customizing the site collection and adding content immediately, you should review at least two groups of settings for possible changes: antivirus settings and diagnostic logging settings. While it is true that you don't actually have to configure these settings before you go on to other actions, it is recommended you at least review these two settings areas before you do.

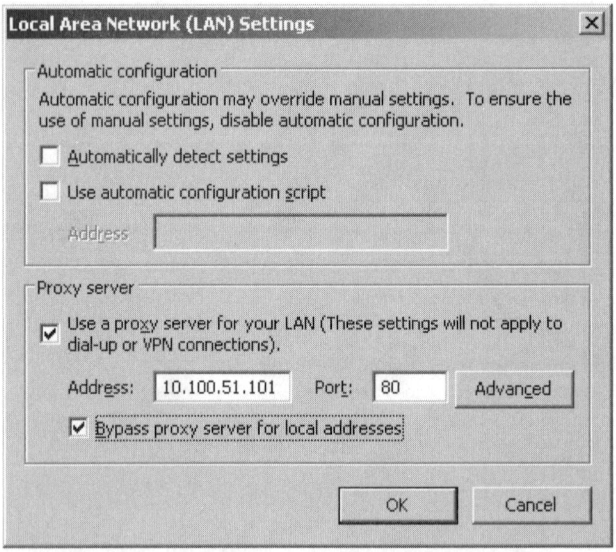

Figure 4-12.   Internet Explorer's Internet Options Local Area Network (LAN) Settings box.

As illustrated in Figure 4-13, when the SharePoint Central Administration page displays immediately after you complete the installation and configuration processes, it lists a number of administration tasks already assigned to you. Depending on your particular environment, you can put some of these tasks off for a while, but you really should address the antivirus and diagnostic logging areas so they are in effect from the beginning.

Each of the configuration tasks listed and described in the following sections are optional or can be put off until you are ready to add the features discussed to your SharePoint system.

To configure each of these settings groups, use the SharePoint Central Administration page, shown in Figure 4-13. To access this page from the desktop, select Start | All Programs | Microsoft Office Server | SharePoint 3.0 Central Administration, and then make your selections (see Figure 4-14).

NOTE   The other configuration tasks in the Administrator Tasks list on the SharePoint Central Administration page are covered in other chapters of this book. For example, e-mail and workflow settings are covered in Chapter 6 and search settings are covered in Chapter 8.

TIP   If you prefer, you can set or alter the configuration of MOSS using the administrative utility stsadm.exe at a command line. Figure 4-15 shows only a portion of the information for this command.

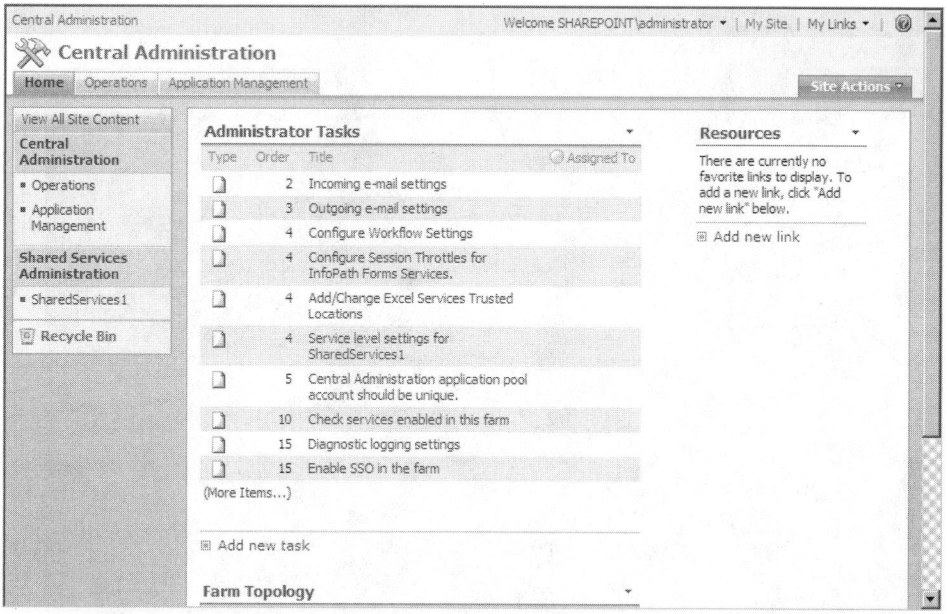

Figure 4-13.   The SharePoint Central Administration page.

Antivirus Settings

While every computer should have antivirus protection, not every antivirus system is designed to work with MOSS. If the antivirus protection system is installed on the server running MOSS, you can configure SharePoint's antivirus protection settings to define whether or not, and when, uploaded or downloaded documents are virus scanned. This can also include options as to whether users are permitted to download an infected document knowingly, as well as the timeout period for the antivirus scan and how many instances of the antivirus program can run on the server.

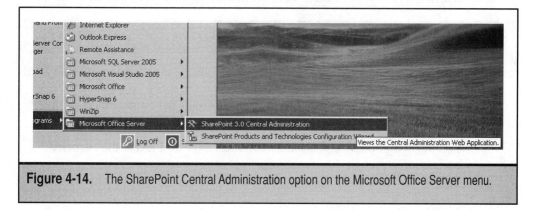

Figure 4-14.   The SharePoint Central Administration option on the Microsoft Office Server menu.

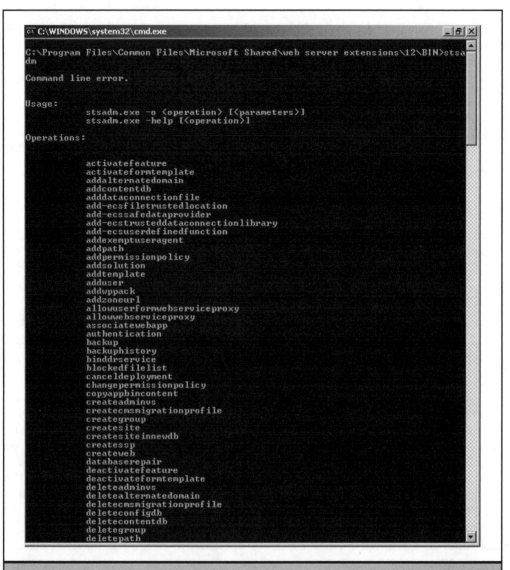

```
C:\WINDOWS\system32\cmd.exe                                                    _ 8 X

C:\Program Files\Common Files\Microsoft Shared\web server extensions\12\BIN>stsa
dm

Command line error.

Usage:
        stsadm.exe -o <operation> [<parameters>]
        stsadm.exe -help [<operation>]

Operations:

        activatefeature
        activateformtemplate
        addalternatedomain
        addcontentdb
        adddataconnectionfile
        add-ecsfiletrustedlocation
        add-ecssafedataprovider
        add-ecstrusteddataconnectionlibrary
        add-ecsuserdefinedfunction
        addexemptuseragent
        addpath
        addpermissionpolicy
        addsolution
        addtemplate
        adduser
        addwppack
        addzoneurl
        allowuserformwebserviceproxy
        allowwebserviceproxy
        associatewebapp
        authentication
        backup
        backuphistory
        binddrservice
        blockedfilelist
        canceldeployment
        changepermissionpolicy
        copyappbincontent
        createadminvs
        createcmsmigrationprofile
        creategroup
        createsite
        createsiteinnewdb
        createssp
        createweb
        databaserepair
        deactivatefeature
        deactivateformtemplate
        deleteadminvs
        deletealternatedomain
        deletecmsmigrationprofile
        deleteconfigdb
        deletecontentdb
        deletegroup
        deletepath
```

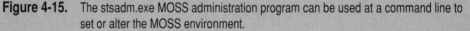

Figure 4-15. The stsadm.exe MOSS administration program can be used at a command line to set or alter the MOSS environment.

To configure the antivirus settings for MOSS, assuming your antivirus is compatible with MOSS (check with your antivirus vendor), perform the following tasks:

1. Open the SharePoint Central Administration page and locate the Security Configuration section.

2. Click the Configure Antivirus Settings option to open the Antivirus page, shown in Figure 4-16.

3. If you wish to scan all downloaded documents for viruses, check the Scan Documents On Download box.

4. If you wish to scan all uploaded documents for viruses, check the Scan Documents On Upload box.

5. If you wish to allow users to save a file that is infected with a virus on their local hard disk, check the Allow Users To Download Infected Documents box. This option is not selected by default and must be overridden to allow an infected file to be downloaded.

6. By default, MOSS allows an antivirus program 5 minutes (300 seconds) to scan a document. However, if you wish to allow more (or less) time for the scan, change the number of seconds in the Time Out Scanning After _____ Seconds box. Five minutes should be enough time for any antivirus program to complete its task, but if antivirus scanning is affecting system performance, you may want to alter this field.

Figure 4-16.   The SharePoint Central Administration Antivirus page.

7. If your antivirus software is server-based, it is likely that multiple instances of it may be active at any one time. The default number of threads allowed by MOSS for antivirus scanning is five, but should you wish to allow more or fewer antivirus scanning threads, you can change the value in the Allow Scanner To Use Up To _____ Threads box.

8. Click OK to complete the antivirus settings and enable this function.

Diagnostic Log Settings

MOSS logs its administrative and event messages to a variety of log files, as shown in Figure 4-17. Through the Central Administration page, you can enable the specific diagnostic logs you may need for troubleshooting an MOSS issue, including log files for event messages, user error messages, trace logs, and, if you wish to participate, events related to the Customer Experience Improvement Program.

To configure the diagnostic logging settings for MOSS, perform the following steps:

1. Open the Central Administration page.

2. Choose Diagnostics logging settings from the Administrator Tasks list or choose Diagnostic logging from the Logging and Reporting area of the Operations page. Either choice displays the Diagnostic Logging page, shown in Figure 4-18.

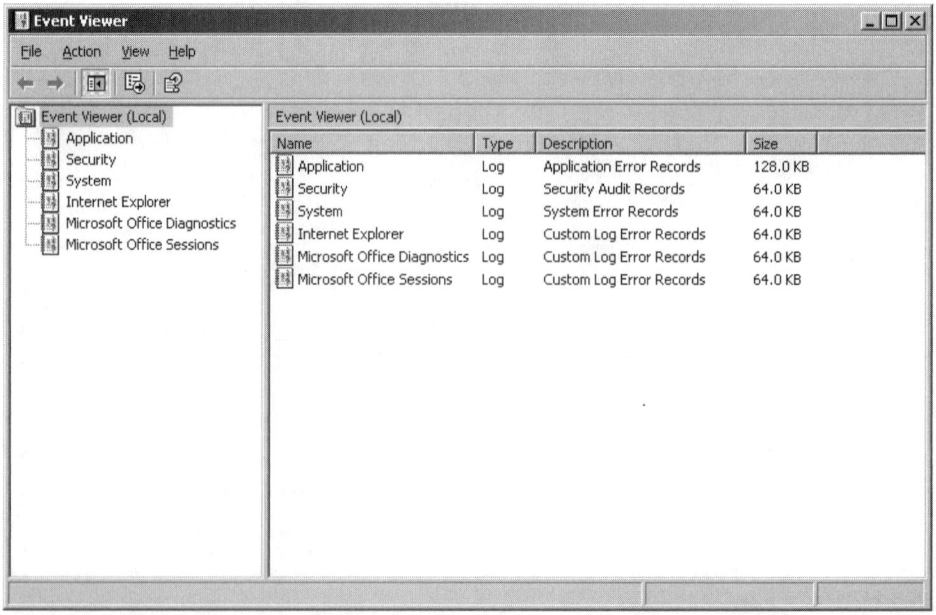

Figure 4-17. The Event Viewer showing the log files of an MOSS system.

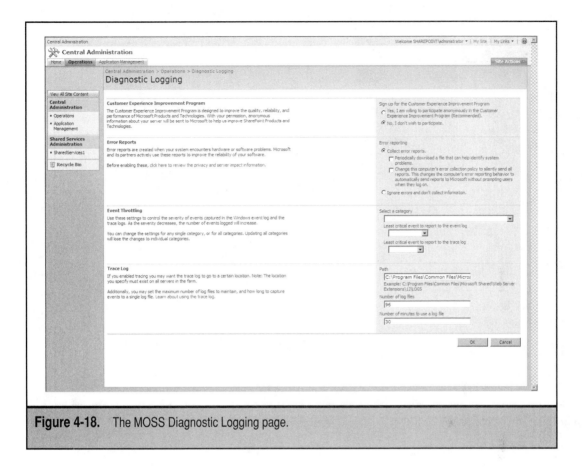

Figure 4-18.   The MOSS Diagnostic Logging page.

The Diagnostic Logging page has four configuration areas:

▼ **Customer Experience Improvement Program**   If you are willing to work with Microsoft by providing anonymous information on your experiences regarding the reliability and performance of their products, you should select the Yes, I Am Willing … radio button. Otherwise, leave the default No, I Don't Wish To Participate option selected.

■ **Error Reports**   Whenever MOSS experiences a hardware or software issue, a report is generated for use by Microsoft (and its partners) to improve system quality and reliability. If you wish to allow error reports to be collected, select the Collect Error Reports radio button option and check the box for the method you wish to use. Otherwise, choose the Ignore Errors And Don't Collect Information option.

■ **Event Throttling**   You are able to set the event severity for each of the different service types for which you can capture event notices. Figure 4-19 illustrates

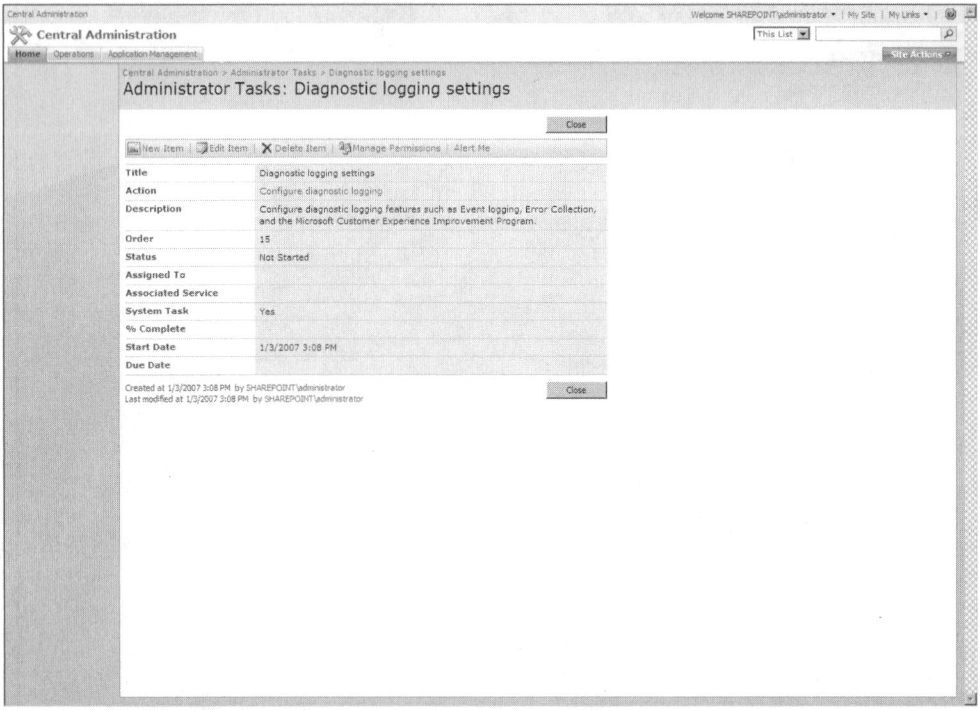

Figure 4-19. The Administrator Tasks on the MOSS Diagnostic Logging Settings page.

sample settings for MOSS general events logging. You can also set a threshold for the severity of the events to be captured using the Least Critical Event To Report To The Event Logs and the Least Critical Event To Report To The Trace Logs pull-down lists. These lists are preordered with the most critical event types listed first.

▲ **Trace Log**   Should you wish to enable event tracing, you can designate where you wish the trace logs to be located, how many logs to keep, and the trace duration each log records.

SERVER FARM INSTALLATION

MOSS is designed to be installed fairly easily into a server farm environment for those larger organizations that have their applications and network services deployed across multiple, integrated computer servers or any organization that plans to support a large number of web sites that draw on a large database or data store. However, you should understand that a server farm installation of MOSS assumes its SharePoint services are implemented across two or more servers dedicated to MOSS support.

NOTE   A server farm deployment for any system, and especially an MOSS deployment, requires some planning and server preparation. Before you begin your server farm installation of MOSS, you should review the material and processes discussed in Chapters 1, 2, and 3.

Server Farm Types and Sizes

Microsoft defines three server farm types, designated by size:

▼   **Small server farm**   This type of server farm consists of at least two servers: a database server and an application server. The application server supports web services and MOSS content and web site services.

■   **Medium server farm**   A medium MOSS server farm adds additional front-end servers to the topology of a small server farm. The front-end servers assume the role of web services and MOSS basic services, relegating the application server to supporting indexing, web crawling, processing search queries, and such features as Excel Calculation Services.

▲   **Large server farm**   A large MOSS server farm involves multiple clustered database servers, multiple front-end servers that are load-balanced to support web services and MOSS, and multiple applications servers, each supporting a specific MOSS function.

Regardless of the size and topology of your server farm, each server on which all or part of the MOSS environment is to be installed must be configured essentially the same. The following sections outline this common configuration.

NOTE   It is not a good idea to install MOSS on a domain controller for a variety of reasons, the primary one being that additional, and somewhat complex, configuration is required. If this is something you are considering, visit the Microsoft TechNet site (http://technet2.microsoft.com/Office/en-us/library) for additional information.

Topology Considerations

Let's review a brief checklist of the services, technologies, and configuration you must have in place before starting a server farm installation of MOSS. The following must have been installed, configured, or completed before you begin to install MOSS in a server farm environment:

▼   All server hardware meets or exceeds (highly recommended) the minimum system requirements of the operating system, the database system, and MOSS.

■   The network operating system must be Windows Server 2003 with at least Service Pack 1 (SP1) installed.

■   The database server must be running either SQL Server 2005 (with all updates applied) or SQL Server 2000 with SP3a or later installed.

- Internet Information Services (IIS) must be installed and enabled on each of the servers on which MOSS is to be installed.

- Each MOSS server must have .NET Framework 3.0 and ASP.NET 2.0 installed and enabled.

- MOSS must be installed on the same disk drive (for example, each of the disk drives must be designated as C:) in every server that will be a part of a load-balancing scheme.

▲ Each indexing server included in the server farm must have a different Shared Services Provider designated for it.

MOSS Installation

As outlined in Chapter 3, you should configure your database server and, if possible, install your database content, before starting the installation of MOSS. If you have all of the preinstallation tasks completed and your computer servers are ready to go, install MOSS and run the SharePoint Products and Technologies Configuration Wizard on each server (as outlined in the "Install MOSS on a Standalone Server" section earlier in the chapter.

The next major step in the MOSS installation process for a server farm deployment is to run the Setup program for MOSS on each of the appropriate servers in the server farm. You should install MOSS on each server before you configure the server farm itself.

The MOSS setup program prompts you to indicate the type of installation you wish to perform. As shown earlier in the chapter in Figure 4-3, the choices are:

▼ **Complete**   Indicating you wish to install all MOSS components and configure a server farm after installation.

- **Web front-end**   Indicating you wish to install only the MOSS components required on this type of server.

▲ **Standalone**   This is not the choice you want for a server farm installation. There is no upgrade path available to move from a standalone installation to a server farm installation.

Once the MOSS installation completes, you should run the SharePoint Products and Technologies Configuration Wizard, at the end of which the Central Administration page should open. If this page fails to open, open the SharePoint 3.0 Central Administration page from the Start menu (Start | All Programs | Microsoft Office Server | SharePoint 3.0 Central Administration).

Configure the Shared Services Provider

MOSS uses a three-layer topology for providing content to users. The top layer (or the layer closest to the end user) is the web server (such as IIS), the middle layer is the application server (such as MySites), and the bottom layer is the database server (SQL Server). Because of this arrangement, MOSS requires that you create and configure a Shared Services Provider (SSP) for the MOSS environment.

An SSP consists of a group of related services, even if the relationship is that they are frequently used together without having any other common bond. The SSP allows these services to be configured once and then shared across any number of MOSS portals and sites and even Windows SharePoint Services (WSS) sites. An MOSS shared service is any of the application services included in a particular MOSS environment, such as Search, Index, audience management, My Sites, Excel Services, Single Sign-on, and usage reporting. Within the SSP, these MOSS services, which are likely to be shared among a variety of sites, can be implemented on one or more servers as the MOSS environment grows, without any limitations as to which application server they reside on or the number of servers involved.

One important distinction about an SSP is that the SSP isn't affiliated with a specific portal or site, but rather each SSP is connected to one or more web applications. Each MOSS web application, which can have more than one portal or web site, has access to any of the services configured within its SSP. Because of this one-to-one relationship, you should first create a web application, then its SSP (which requires the inclusion of a web application when its created), and finally the web application's site collection. The end result is a web application and a site collection that is automatically associated to the web application's SSP.

Create and Configure SSP   The recommended first phase of this process is to create and configure the SSP. To create and configure a new SSP, perform the following steps:

1. From the Central Administration page, select Shared Services Administration from the Quick Launch menu on the left-hand side of the page. This displays the Manage This Farm's Shared Services page, shown in Figure 4-20.

2. Click the New SSP selection to display the New Shared Services Provider page, shown in Figure 4-21.

3. To create a new SSP, enter the appropriate values in the blue area on the right-hand side of the page. The values you need to enter are

   a. **SSP Name**   Enter a unique and descriptive name for the new SSP. The name should be somehow related to the web application to which the SSP is to be associated. Select the web application to be associated with the SSP from

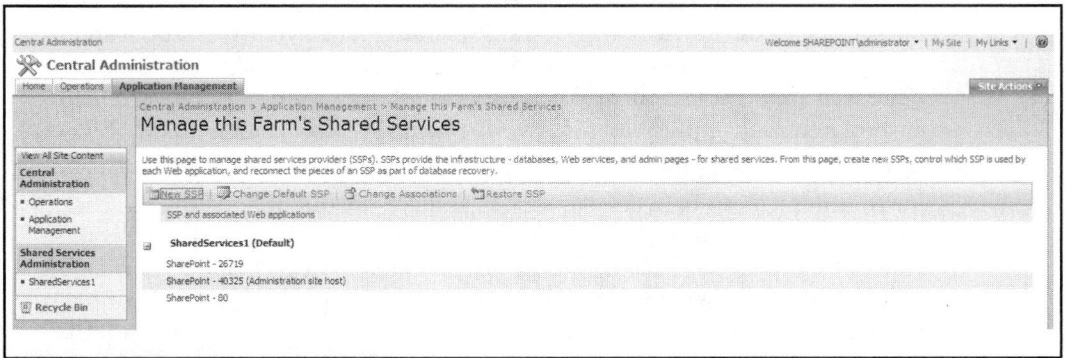

Figure 4-20.   The Manage This Farm's Shared Services page.

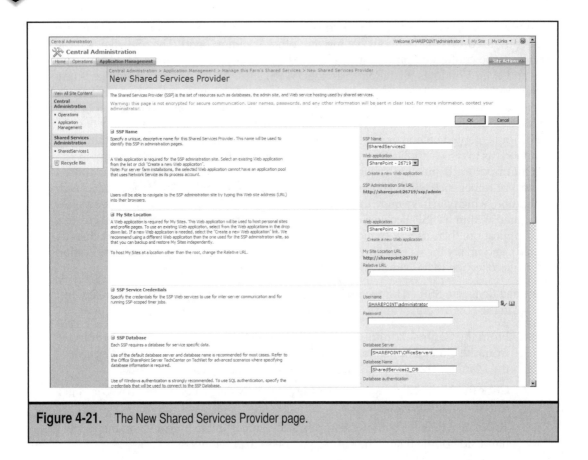

Figure 4-21. The New Shared Services Provider page.

the pull-down list, and choose the web application to which the new SSP is to be associated.

b. **My Site Location**   My Site pages require an associated web application. You should designate a different web application for any My Site pages that will interface with the services within the SSP. Using a different web application allows My Site content to be backed up separately and independently from other web application content. Click the Create A New Web Application link to create a new web application for any My Site pages associated with the SSP.

c. **SSP Service Credentials**   Enter the username and password (credentials) for communication between servers. If you are unsure of a username, click the browse icon (the address book icon) to search for it. The Select People And Groups web page dialog box displays. Enter all or part of the username you wish to identify in the Find box and click the spyglass icon. For example, if you wish to identify the administrators of the SharePoint sites, enter **admin** in the Find box and click the spyglass. The results of this search are shown in Figure 4-22. Highlight the username you wish to use for intercomputer communications and click OK.

d. SSP Database An SSP requires a link to a database for specific information about its service bundle. MOSS will provide the name of the default database, which is the recommended option. This configuration area also requests the type of database authentication to be used. It is highly recommended you use Windows authentication.

e. Search Database You should allow the default values for this configuration as well.

f. Index Server This entry specifies the index server to be used to crawl web application content within this SSP. Allow the default value, unless you have existing index servers you wish to designate.

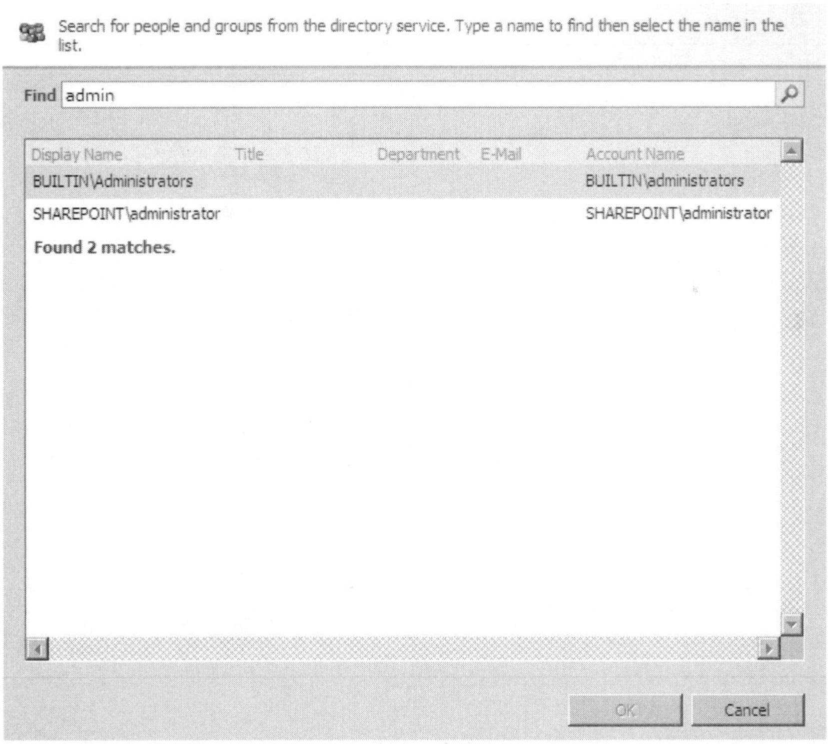

Search for people and groups from the directory service. Type a name to find then select the name in the list.

Find	admin				

Display Name	Title	Department	E-Mail	Account Name
BUILTIN\Administrators				BUILTIN\administrators
SHAREPOINT\administrator				SHAREPOINT\administrator

Found 2 matches.

OK   Cancel

Figure 4-22. The Search For People And Groups... dialog box.

g. **SSL for Web Services**   If your Web applications require the use of Secure Sockets Layer (SSL) for secure communications between computers, choose the Yes option.

Create New Web Application   As a part of your installation processes, you should create an initial web application and SSP. To do this, perform the following steps:

1. From the Central Administration page, choose Application Management. The Application Management page displays (see Figure 4-23).

2. To begin creating an initial Web application, click the Create Or Extend Web Application link under the SharePoint Web Application Management heading.

3. On the Create Or Extend Web Application page (see Figure 4-24), click the Create A New Web Application link located in the right-hand panel of the page.

4. Click the Create A New Web Application link to open the Create New Web Application page, shown in Figure 4-25.

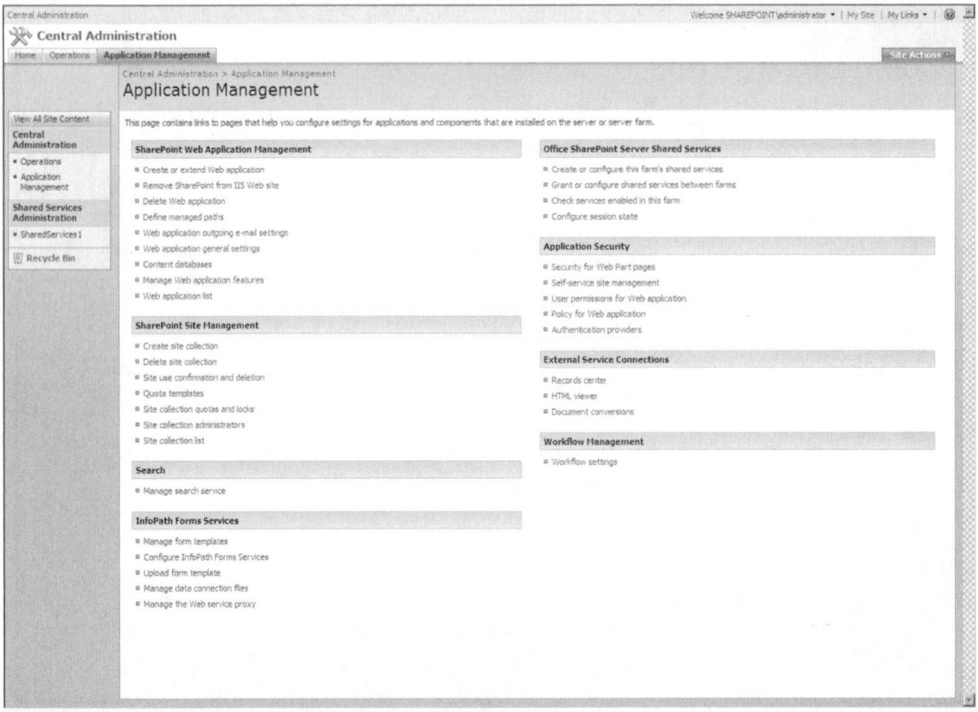

Figure 4-23.   The SharePoint Application Management page.

Figure 4-24. The Create Or Extend Web Application page.

5. For the purposes of creating a Web application only to demonstrate the creation of an SSP, choose the Use An Existing IIS Web Site option and Default Web Site in the list box for this option, as illustrated in Figure 4-25.

6. Choose the Use An Existing Application Pool option and DefaultAppPool (Network Service). Leave all other settings as-is.

7. Click OK.

8. If any error condition messages are generated from the creation of the web application, they will appear in red text at the top of the page and the web application will not be created. Otherwise, an Operation In Progress page displays, followed by the Application Created notice page, shown in Figure 4-26.

9. Open the Internet Information Services (IIS) Manager from the Start menu (Start | All Programs | Administrative Tools | Internet Information Services (IIS) Manager) and restart IIS, as shown in Figure 4-27.

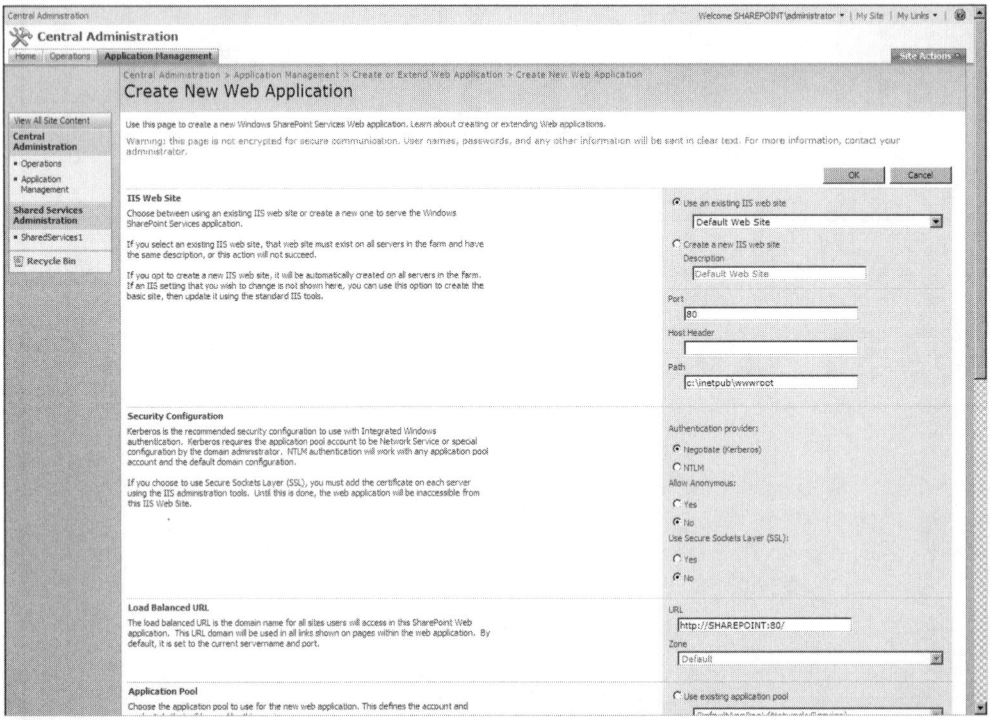

Figure 4-25.   The Create New Web Application page.

Install Additional Application Servers

The completion of the MOSS installation on the first farm server involves the creation of the site collections and sites that make up your MOSS environment. These tasks should be completed as early as possible, but they can be delayed until after you have completed the installation and configuration of the remaining application servers in the server farm.

> **NOTE**   Part 2 of this book covers the steps used to create site collections and content sites for an MOSS environment.

The process used to install MOSS on each of the application servers in your server farm is essentially the same as that used to install the first server in the farm. However, MOSS will accommodate some differences automatically. After the MOSS Setup program completes, the SharePoint Products and Technologies Configuration Wizard starts,

Figure 4-26.   The Application Created page.

but it doesn't create a Central Administration site on the additional servers or any additional databases on the server farm's database server.

You should install and configure MOSS on all application servers in the server farm before you configure services and create sites on any of the application servers. When you install MOSS in a farm environment and run the Config Wizard, you'll need to indicate for each server that the server is joining an existing farm. Only then will all of the servers in the server farm be shown on the Central Administration page, as explained in the following section.

Configure Server Services

After you've completed the creation and configuration of an initial SSP, you should then configure the services you wish the server to run. To view or modify the configuration of the services on a server, do the following:

1. Click the Operations selection on the Central Administration page.

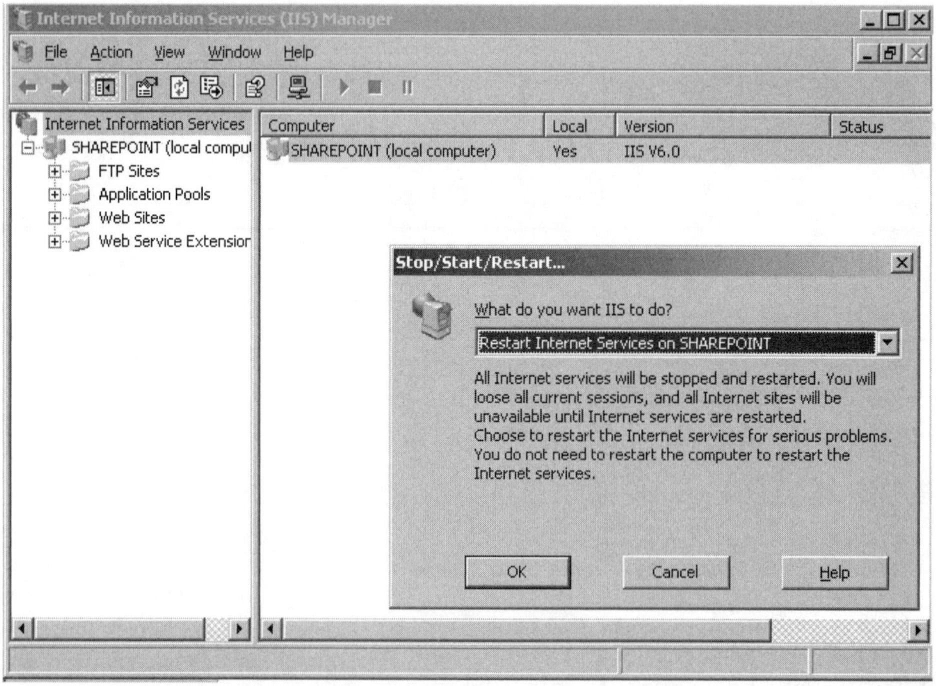

Figure 4-27. The Internet Information Services (IIS) Manager dialog box.

2. Under the Topology and Services heading, click the Services On Server item to display the Services On Server page (see Figure 4-28). The name of this page is followed by the name of the current server, but you can change it to a different server in the server farm by choosing the server from the Server pull-down menu at the top of the server status area.

3. The top portion of the Services On Server page shows the current configuration of the server selected. If you wish to add or remove services from the server, use the lower portion of the page. On the left-hand end of the blue bar in the center of the page is a toggle you can use to list either the configurable services or all services available to the server. Under the action heading, you can stop running services, or start services not currently running on the server.

If you wish to allow the MOSS environment's users to search across the server farm for Help content, you must start the Windows SharePoint Services (WSS) Search service. If you don't wish to allow this feature to users, you can skip this step. To configure the WSS Search service:

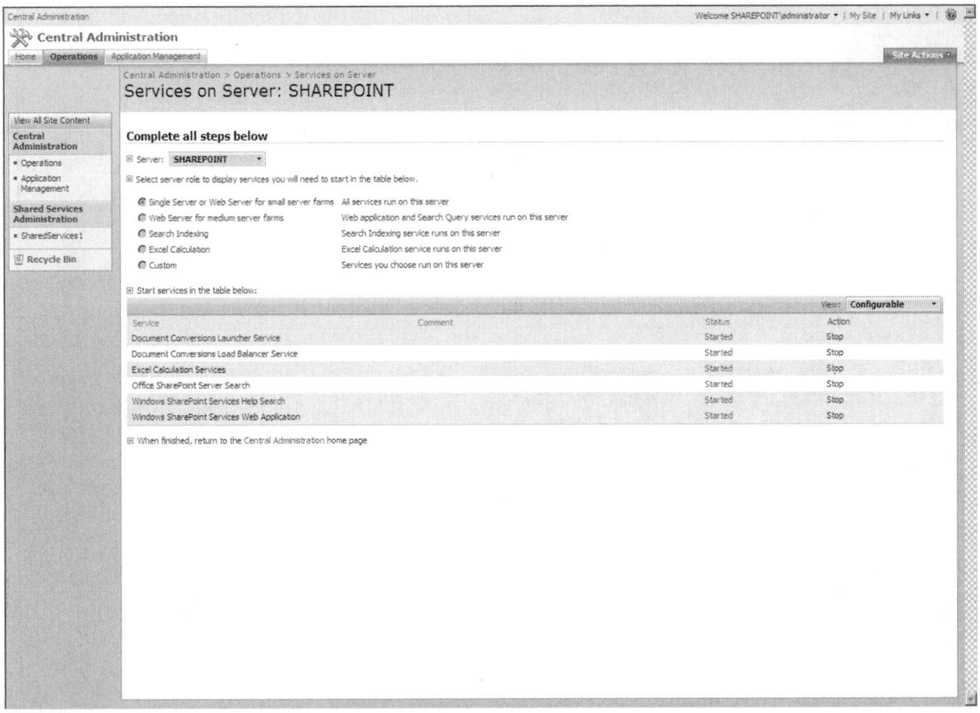

Figure 4-28. The Services On Server administration page.

1. Open the Services On Server page.

2. In the lower portion of the page, double-click Windows SharePoint Services Help Search in the Service column to open the Configure Windows SharePoint Services Search Service Settings page, shown in Figure 4-29.

3. In the Service Account area, enter the username and password of the user account under which the WSS Search service is to run.

4. In the Content Access Account area, enter the username and password of the user account the search service is to use when searching content. Ensure that the username and password used here has read access to all the content to be searched. If you leave this entry blank, the username and password entered for the Service Account is used.

5. In the Indexing Schedule area, you may want to accept the default values initially and then later adjust the schedule to define when the search service should perform its searching to minimize any impact on performance.

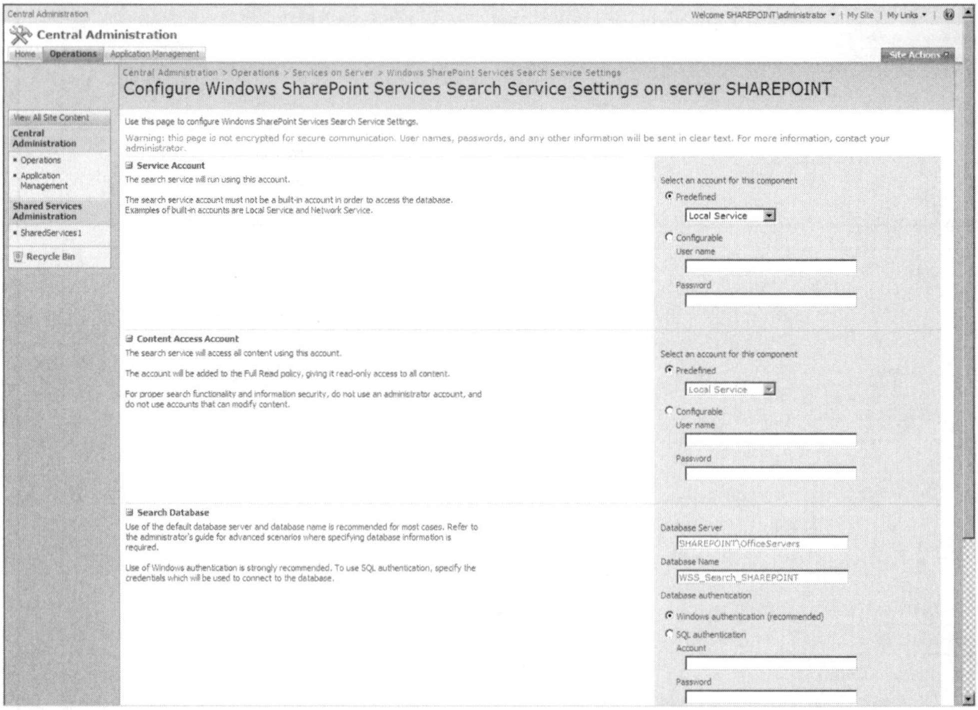

Figure 4-29. The Configure Windows SharePoint Services Search Service Settings page.

6. Click OK to return to the Services On Server page.

7. Start the Windows SharePoint Services Help Search service.

NOTE The WSS Search service must be started on every computer server you wish to include in the search.

Configure Internet Explorer to Bypass Proxy Server

If your local area network (LAN) includes a proxy server, you should configure MOSS to bypass the proxy server for its local addressing. This phase of the server installation is performed outside of MOSS as a configuration step in Internet Explorer (IE).

To configure IE to bypass the proxy server for local network addresses, do the following:

1. Start Internet Explorer, open the Tools menu, and click Internet Options (as shown in Figure 4-30) to open the Internet Options dialog box (see Figure 4-31).

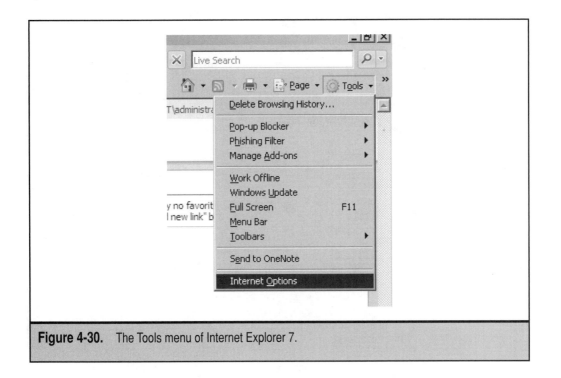

Figure 4-30.   The Tools menu of Internet Explorer 7.

2. Choose the Connections tab. In the Local Area Network (LAN) settings area (in the lower portion of the box), click the LAN Settings button to open the Local Area Network (LAN) Settings dialog box, shown in Figure 4-32.

3. Clear the Automatically Detect Settings checkbox in the Automatic Configuration area.

4. Check the Use A Proxy Server For Your LAN box in the Proxy Server area and enter the address and port number (if applicable) of the proxy server in the Address and Port boxes, respectively.

5. Check the Bypass proxy server for local addresses box and click OK on the LAN Settings box and the Internet Options box to store these settings.

Clean Up Servers

Okay, you're in the home stretch of the MOSS installation. You have only two relatively small tasks remaining and then you can move on to the construction of your SharePoint sites, site collections, and other user-related displays. The two remaining tasks are to disable the SharePoint Administration service on all but the one server you wish to use to access the SharePoint 3.0 Central Administration web site and the SharePoint Web Application service on any server that won't be providing application or content support.

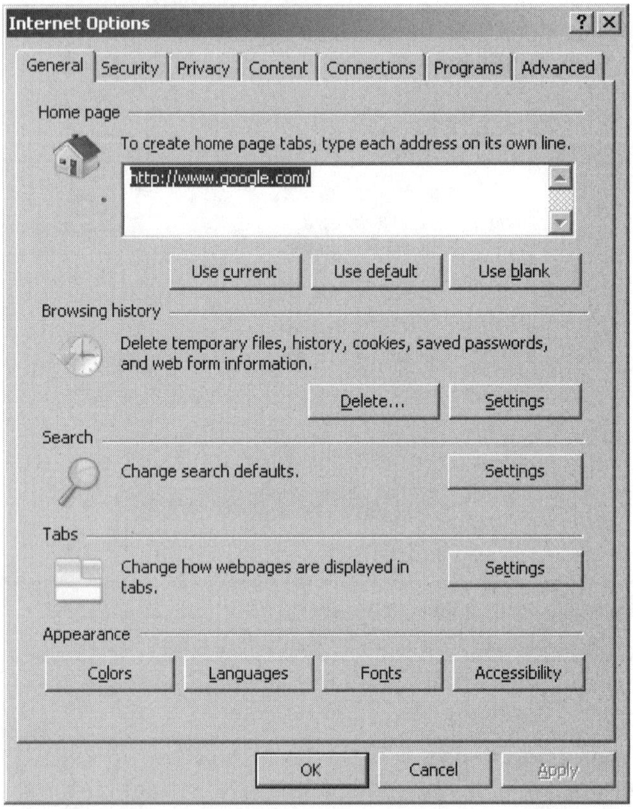

Figure 4-31. The Internet Explorer Internet Options dialog box.

To disable the WSS Administration service on any server not hosting the Central Administration site), do the following:

1. Open the Windows Server 2003 Computer Management dialog box (see Figure 4-33) from the Administrative Tools menu (Start | All Programs | Administrative Tools | Computer Management).

2. Expand the Services and Applications item in the left-hand pane.

3. Right-click the Windows SharePoint Service Administration service in the list and choose Properties from the pop-up menu.

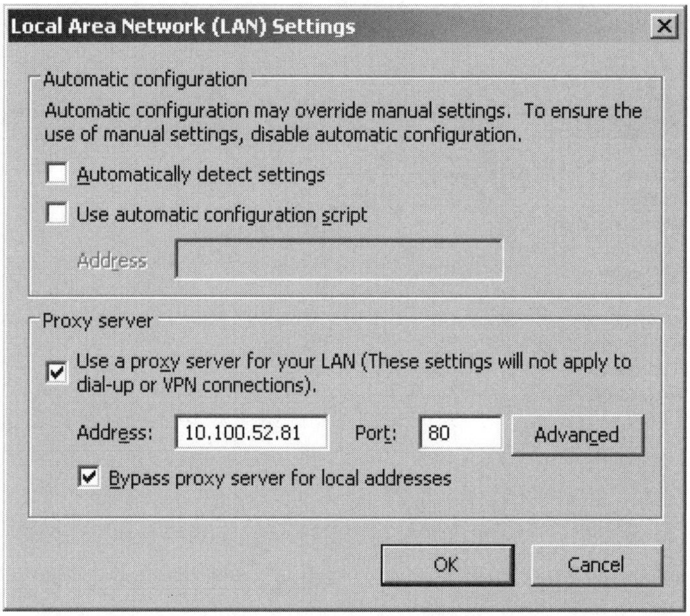

Figure 4-32. The Local Area Network (LAN) Settings dialog box.

4. On the General tab of the Properties dialog box, select Disabled from the Startup type list and click the Apply button.

5. Click the Stop option (to stop the service) and click OK.

To disable the WSS Web Application service on any server that won't be providing content, such as an administrative server or an indexing server, do the following:

1. Open the SharePoint Central Administration page and choose the Operations tab.

2. In the Topology and Services area, click Services On Server.

3. Find the Windows SharePoint Services Web Application in the lower portion of the page and choose Stop under the Action column.

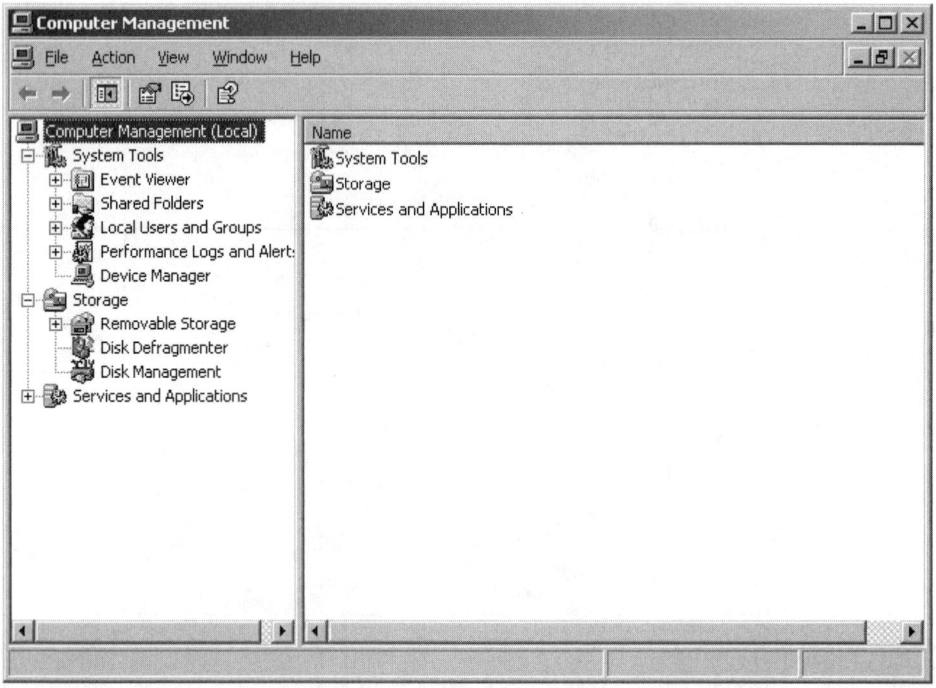

Figure 4-33. The Computer Management dialog box.

SUMMARY

To complete the installation of a full-blown MOSS environment, you still have a ways to go, but the information and installation steps outlined in this chapter will get your standalone server or server farm servers up and running. As you have seen, MOSS has streamlined the installation and configuration processes and provided you with the administrative tools needed to manage and monitor your MOSS environment. In the chapters that follow, and especially the chapters in Part 2 of this book, the steps used to create your sites, site collections, and other user content delivery vehicles are explained.

CHAPTER 5

Post-Installation Configuration

After the Setup program has completed and your MOSS system is installed, you must now configure your MOSS environment. Actually, you will likely be modifying the settings and configuration of your MOSS environment for some time to come, as you, your users, the data content, views, lists, libraries, and supporting services all mature together.

This chapter, along with Chapter 6 and the other chapters in Part 2 of this book, guide you through the processes used to complete the configuration steps that must be done before you release your MOSS system to your users. Not all of these tasks and activities discussed are needed in every installation, but you should at least consider whether or not each should be completed. As you consider each configuration area, give serious thought to the benefits and ramifications of completing a task or not.

THE ADMINISTRATOR TASKS LIST

When you first access the Central Administration page after installing MOSS on a server, the Administrator Tasks List is displayed (see Figure 5-1). The Tasks list contains the administrative tasks you should consider and perform as appropriate to complete the configuration of MOSS on each server. These important tasks complete the configuration and settings required for MOSS to completely function. As you complete each task, it is automatically removed from the task list. You can also remove any unnecessary or unwanted tasks, but you should review what each is asking you to do before doing so.

The Administrator Tasks list commonly includes most, if not all, of the following, depending on your particular installation:

▼ Read the Quick Start Guide

■ Configure Incoming E-mail Settings

■ Configure Outgoing E-mail Settings

■ Create New Web Application

■ Configure Workflow Settings

■ Configure InfoPath Forms Services

■ Add/Change Excel Services Trusted Locations

■ Service Level Settings for SharePointServices1

■ Change Service Accounts

■ Check Services Enabled in this Farm

■ Configure Diagnostic Logging

■ Enable SSO in the Farm

▲ Add Antivirus Protection

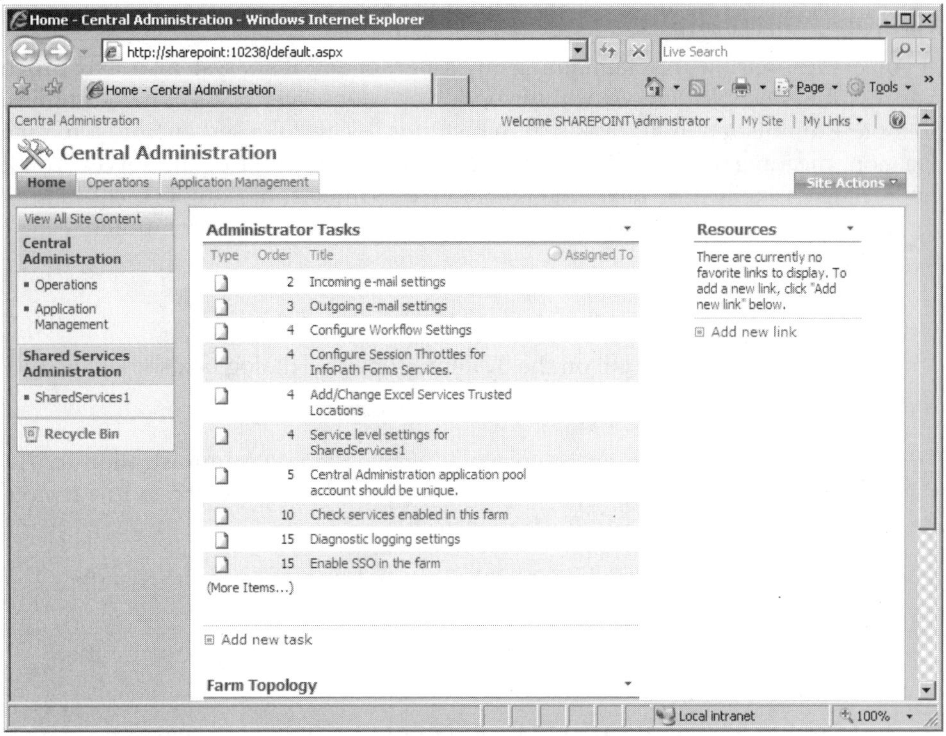

Figure 5-1.   The Central Administration Administrator Tasks list.

In the following sections, each of the tasks typically included in the Tasks list are discussed and the steps used to complete each task are listed. As you will see, not all tasks are appropriate for every installation, so you may or may not need to complete each task. Some tasks can be deferred until later or deleted as unnecessary.

NOTE   You should first, before starting any of the Administrator Tasks, read the Quick Start Guide. The Quick Start Guide describes the administrative tasks required to complete your MOSS installation. The guide contains links to various help topics that explain how to perform each of the administrative tasks listed in the Administrative Tasks list.

SMTP for IIS

SharePoint sites can be configured to perform a number of actions on incoming e-mail, including archiving incoming e-mail, saving e-mail attachments, or adding meeting

Remote Administration

If you are responsible for maintaining any aspect of an MOSS system, it may prove very helpful to enable Remote Administration on your server(s). As its name implies, Remote Administration allows an administrator to control a server from a remote location, meaning somewhere other than physically in front of the server. You'll appreciate this ability the next time you receive an after-hours support request.

To set up Remote Administration on a Windows Server 2003 computer:

1. On the Windows Desktop, right-click My Computer.
2. Select Properties from the pop-up menu.
3. Choose the Remote tab on the System Properties dialog box shown below.
4. Check the Enable Remote Desktop on this computer box

By default, domain administrators already have Remote Administration access. All other user accounts or groups must be individually granted access to a remote desktop. To grant Remote Administration access:

5. On the Remote tab, click the Select Remote Users to open the Remote Desktop Users dialog box.
6. Click the Add button and enter a username or security group and then click Check Names to verify the user or group name.
7. Click OK to grant the user or security group access.
8. Click OK to close the Remote Users window.
9. Click OK to close the Remote tab.

invites to site calendars. Incoming e-mail settings may be configured automatically if the Simple Mail Transfer Protocol (SMTP) is installed with Internet Information Services (IIS). If you prefer not to use SMTP, you can use the advanced setting option (explained in the "Enable Incoming E-mail" section later in the chapter) to specify incoming e-mail settings such as an e-mail drop folder, which MOSS will then check periodically for new e-mail messages.

To install and enable SMTP for IIS, perform these steps:

TIP   To install SMTP for IIS, you may be prompted for your Windows Server 2003 installation CD, so have it available.

1. Log in to your MOSS standalone server or each of your MOSS Web front-end servers.
2. Open the Control Panel and click the Add or Remove Programs icon.

3. In the left-hand side panel, click the Add/Remove Windows Components icon.

4. Select Application Server and click Details.

5. Select Internet Information Services (IIS) and click Details.

6. Check the SMTP Services checkbox (as shown in Figure 5-2) and click OK.

7. Click OK on the Application Server components dialog box and Next on the Windows Components dialog box to start the Windows Components Wizard.

8. If you are asked to insert the Windows Server 2003 CD, do so, and then click OK to continue the installation of the SMTP service.

Incoming E-mail Settings

To enable your MOSS server to accept and process incoming e-mail, perform the following steps:

1. Log in to your MOSS standalone server or each of your MOSS web front-end servers.

2. Open the SharePoint 3.0 Central Administration page.

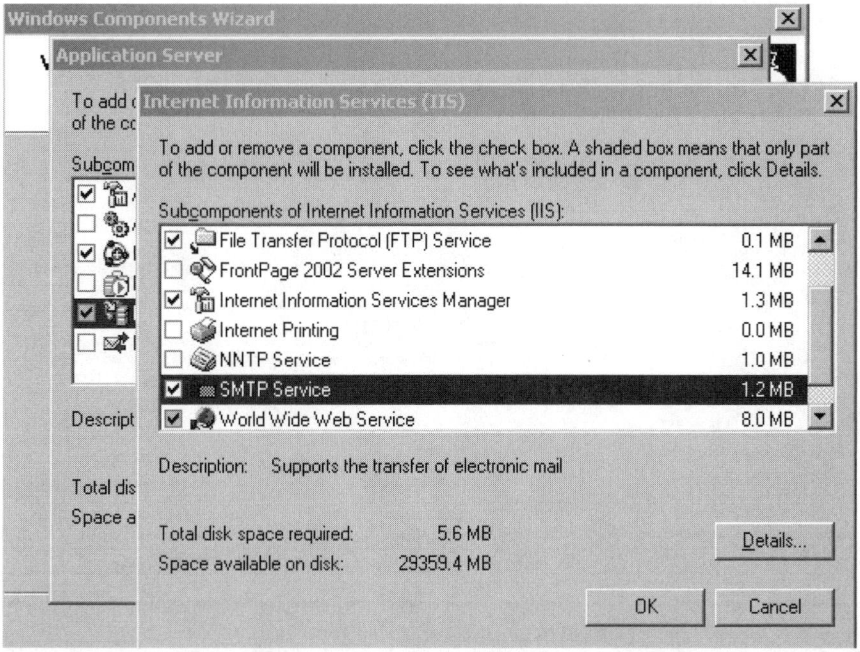

Figure 5-2. The Internet Information Services (IIS) components dialog box within the Add Windows Components function.

3. Click the Operations tab.

4. Click Incoming E-mail Settings under the Topology and Services heading to open the Incoming E-mail Settings page, shown in Figure 5-3.

   If your network environment includes a Microsoft Exchange Server, or if you choose not to run SMTP on your MOSS web front-end server(s), you must use the advanced settings mode to configure incoming e-mail settings. Additional server configuration may also be required and is outlined on the configuration page. Be sure you read the text associated with each configuration setting.

5. Set the Enable Sites On This Server To Receive E-Mail option to Yes.

6. Set the Settings mode to Automatic.

7. Click OK to save the settings and return to the Operations page.

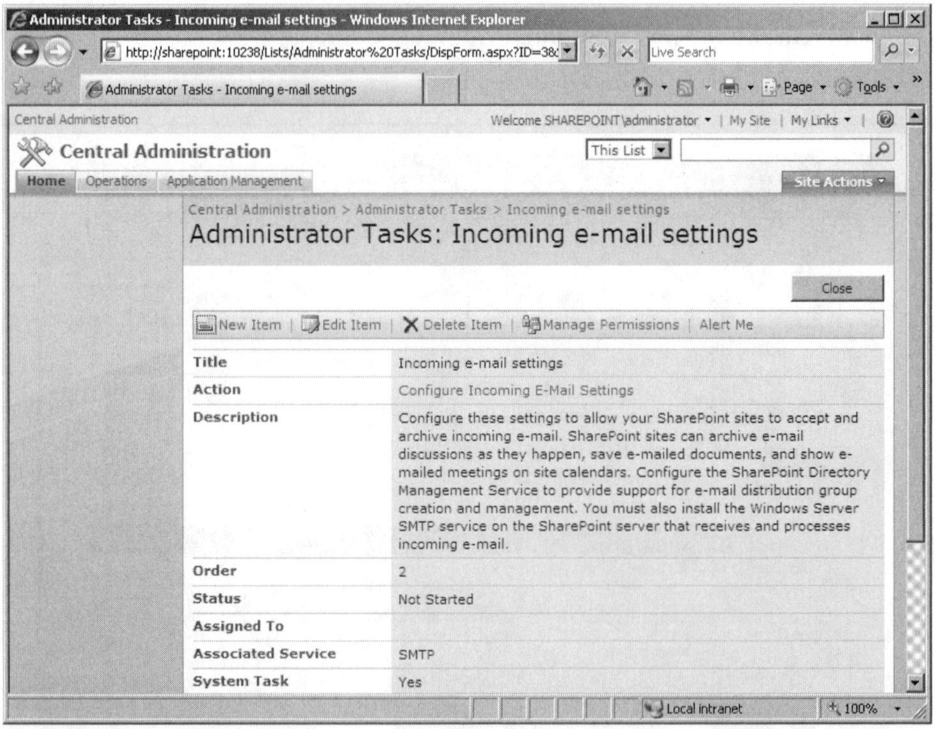

Figure 5-3.   The Incoming E-mail Settings page.

Outgoing E-mail Settings

To enable your MOSS server to use SMTP to send content alerts to users and administrative notifications to administrators, you must configure the outgoing e-mail settings as follows:

1. Open the Operations page of the SharePoint 3.0 Central Administration web site.

2. Click the Outgoing E-mail Settings option under the Topology and Services heading to open the Outgoing E-Mail Settings page, shown in Figure 5-4.

3. Set the Outbound SMTP server to SHAREPOINT.

   If you have previously installed SMTP for IIS to configure incoming e-mail settings, you may use the same SMTP server for outgoing mail or, alternatively, specify a different SMTP server. In this example, SMTP has been installed on the local MOSS server SHAREPOINT.

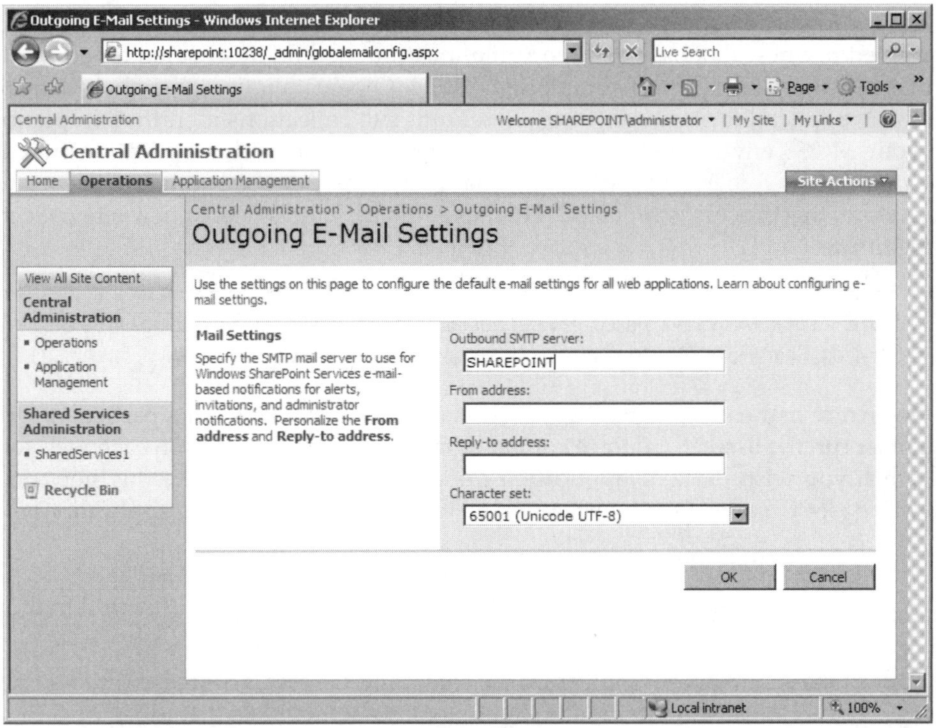

Figure 5-4. The Outgoing E-mail Settings page.

4. Set the From address to something like sharepoint@yourdomain.com. You may specify any e-mail address you wish in this field, but it is helpful to indicate that the e-mail was automatically sent from SharePoint.

5. Set the Reply-to address to something like support@yourdomain.com. Like the From address, you may specify any e-mail address in this field. Although the recipients of the e-mails sent out from MOSS wouldn't typically need to reply to these messages, they may, and if so, it's likely they need assistance. For this reason, the reply-to e-mail address should be a valid address that is monitored by the administrator.

6. Click OK to save the settings and return to the Operations page.

Create Web Applications

IIS is able to isolate multiple web sites and web applications running on the same server to create a unique application pool for each web site or web application. An application pool consists of one or more worker processes. If a worker process fails for any reason, only its application pool and the associated web site or web application is affected because of the isolation. Isolating a web site or web application greatly improves its reliability.

As outlined in Chapter 4, when you create a new web application, it is automatically connected to a new database and the authentication method designated for connecting to that database. As a part of completing your MOSS installation, you should create a new Web application for each of the SharePoint site collections identified in planning for your MOSS environment using the Create or Extend Web Application function, shown in Figure 5-5. As your MOSS environment and your users gain experience with the system, this process is repeated when user requirements need a new site collection in the future.

NOTE When MOSS is installed, several web applications are created, including Office Server Web Services, SharePoint:80, and SharePoint Central Administration v3.

To ensure that each new web application created is available on a particular server, you must run the iisreset /noforce command at a command prompt on each web server on which you wish the web application to be available. To complete this step, do the following (see Chapter 4 for information on how to create a new web application):

1. Log in to each IIS server.

2. Open a command prompt by clicking Start | Run, and then type **cmd** in the Open: box.

3. At the command prompt, enter the command **iisreset /noforce** and press Enter. The command and its results should look something like that in Figure 5-6.

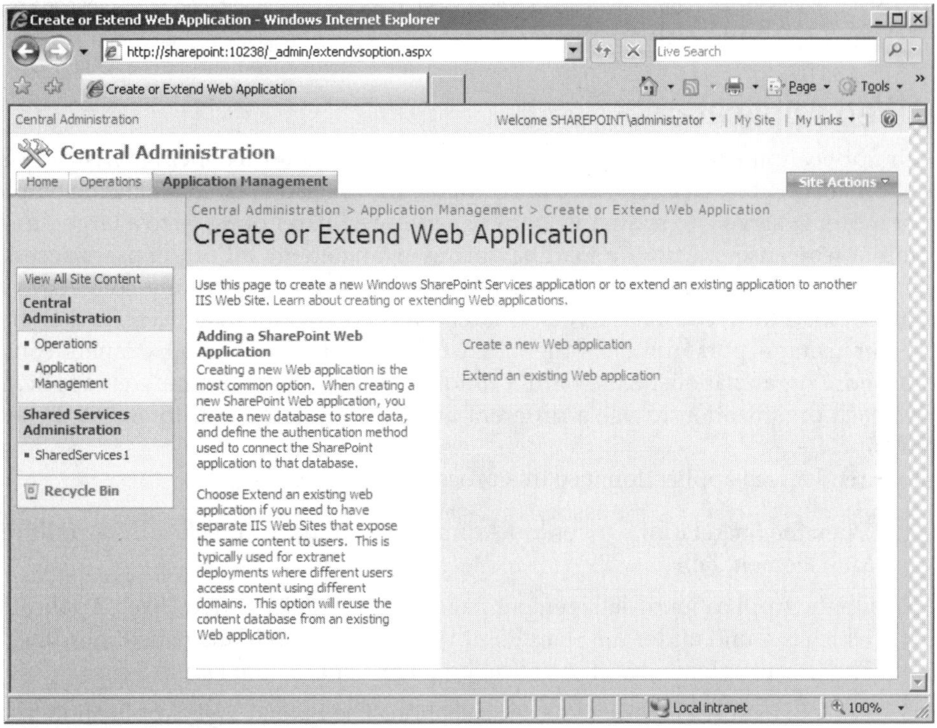

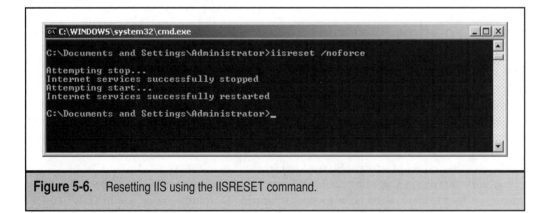

Figure 5-5.   The Create or Extend Web Application page.

Figure 5-6.   Resetting IIS using the IISRESET command.

TIP   If the IISRESET command fails to stop or restart IIS (as indicated by an error message to that effect), simply run the command again.

Extend Web Applications

A web application needs to be extended if you enable load balancing, wish to serve SharePoint content on an alternative port, or create an extranet. Load balancing employs two or more IIS servers to share the work of serving a SharePoint site to a large number of simultaneous users. Under a load balancing arrangement, all of the users accessing a SharePoint site use the same URL for the web site, but may actually connect to any one of the load-balanced IIS servers. SharePoint content can also be served from an IIS server using a port number other than the default of port 80. Extranets connect two or more organizations, each with a unique domain. Extending a web application allows each organization to use a different authentication method to access the same SharePoint site.

To extend a web application, use this process:

1. Open the SharePoint 3.0 Central Administration page and click the Application Management tab.

2. On the Applications Management page, click Create Or Extend Web Application, which is found under the SharePoint Web Application Management heading. The Create or Extend Web Application page displays (see Figure 5-5).

3. Click Extend An Existing Web Application. The Extend Web Application to Another IIS Web Site page (see Figure 5-7) displays.

4. Complete the information on the Extend Web Application to Another Web Site page as required to extend the web application to another IIS server, or to set a URL for the site for use in load balancing.

5. Click OK to save your settings.

Configure Workflow Settings

In conjunction with Windows SharePoint Services 3.0 (WSS), MOSS supports workflows. Workflows allow users to create, coordinate, and otherwise share documents and other business information to facilitate the flow of a work process or document creation, coordination, or approval. A workflow process can be used to create or control any SharePoint document or content item throughout the entire life cycle of that element, including both the human functions and the automated system functions. A SharePoint workflow can be initiated either by a user or by MOSS itself, based on some event or action that has taken place on a SharePoint item.

A very simple example of an MOSS workflow is the routing of a document to a group or team of users for comments or approval. In this case, a workflow can be created that automatically sends an e-mail message to a targeted group of users when a document is available and ready for viewing. The users included in the target group

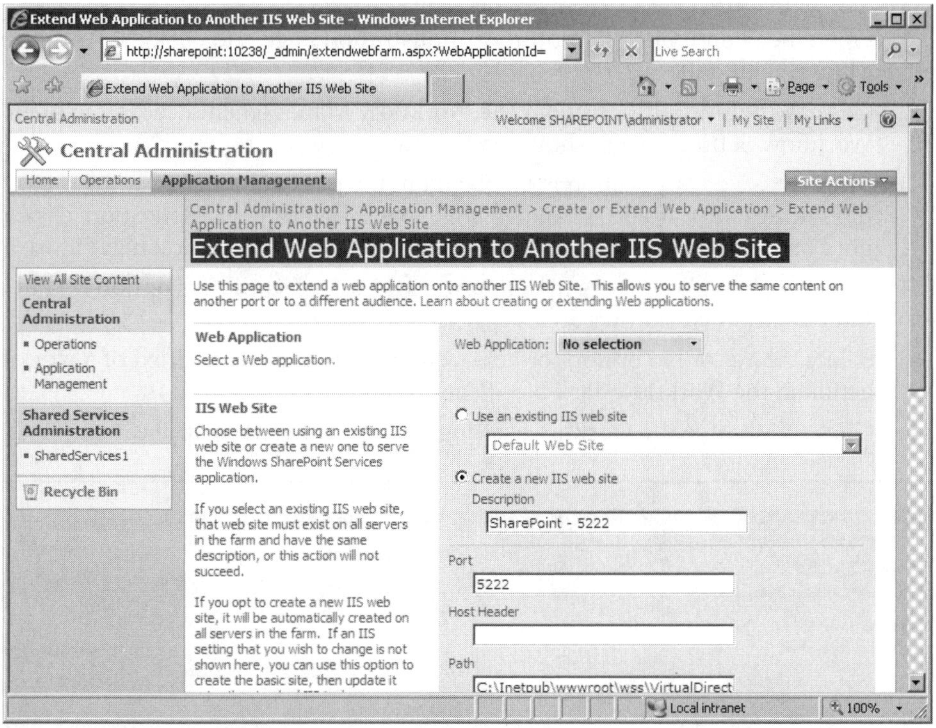

Figure 5-7.   The Extend Web Application To Another IIS Web Site page.

would perform their review, add their comments or approvals, and notify MOSS when they have completed their tasks.

TIP   MOSS workflow settings are configured for each web application.

By default, MOSS users are allowed to assemble new workflows, and users without site access cannot participate in workflows. However, external users may participate in workflows by receiving copies of documents via e-mail.

NOTE   See Chapter 11 for more information on the design and use of workflows in a MOSS environment.

To configure workflow settings, follow these steps:

1. Open the SharePoint 3.0 Central Administration page and click the Application Management tab.

2. Click Workflow Settings under the Workflow Management heading to open the Workflow Settings page (shown in Figure 5-8).

3. The active web application is displayed in the gold-colored bar at the top of the settings area. If you wish to change to a different web application, click the gold bar to open the Change Web Application dialog box, shown in Figure 5-9.

4. If you wish to allow users to define workflows, select the Yes option in the User-Defined Workflows area.

5. Select the Yes or No option for how you wish users to be notified of a workflow action in the Workflow Task Notifications area.

6. Click OK to save the workflow settings for the active Web application.

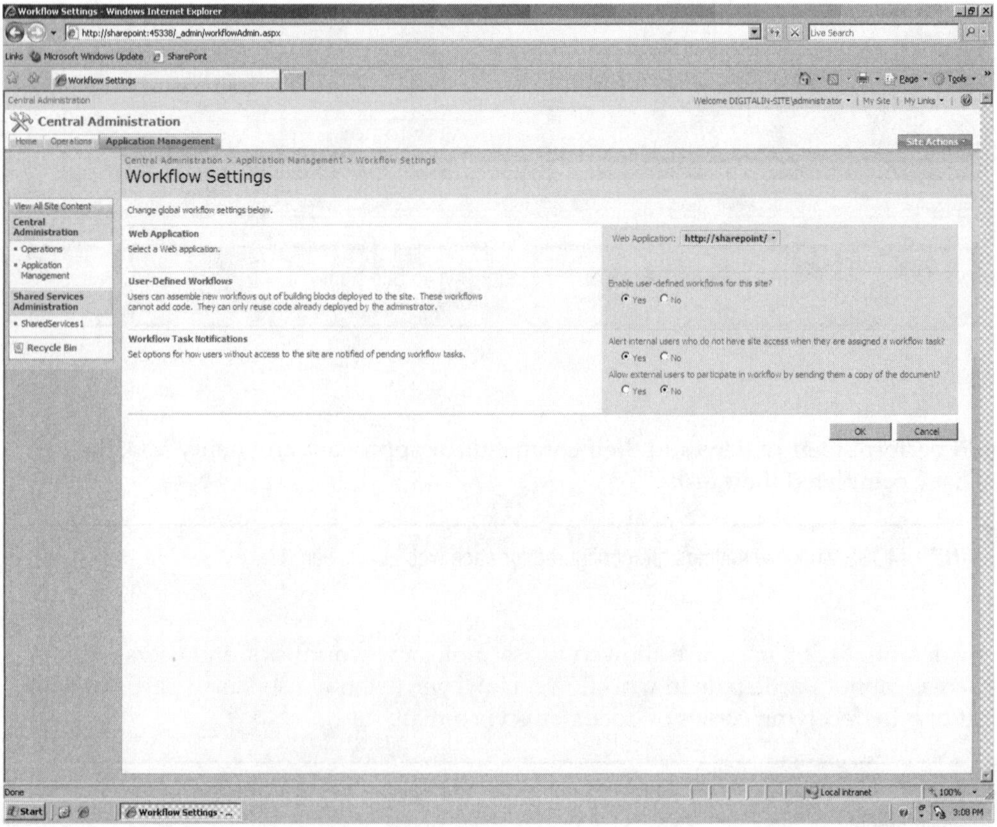

Figure 5-8. The Workflow Settings page.

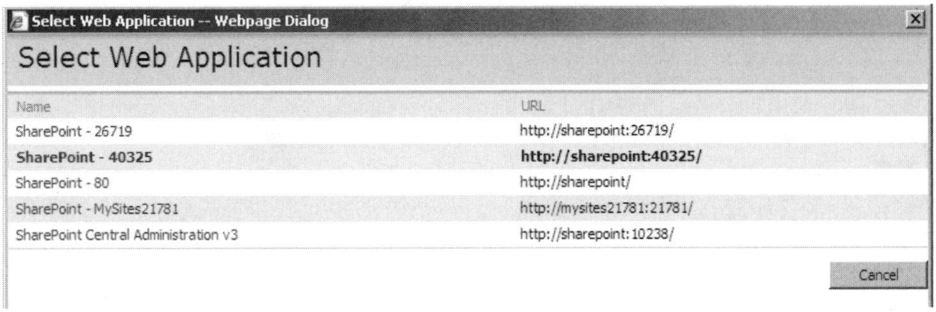

Figure 5-9.   Change the web application on which a workflow is to be created.

Configure InfoPath Forms Services

Unless you are well-versed on the application of InfoPath Forms, you should probably skip this administrative task altogether or until such time as you configure the InfoPath Forms service in your MOSS environment. If you wish to not perform this task, you may delete it from your task list.

> **NOTE**   For more information on the InfoPath Forms service, see Chapter 10.

Add/Change Excel Services Trusted Locations

If the location(s) of all Excel workbooks are to be loaded, you can ensure that only those locations are permitted. As a part of its security functions, MOSS Excel Services only loads Excel workbooks from predefined, designated locations, which can be specified as a document library, a file share with a Universal Naming Convention (UNC) path, or a web site URL.

If you wish to designate the trusted locations for the Excel workbooks to be accessed by MOSS Excel Services, use the following steps:

1. On the SharePoint 3.0 Central Administration page, select the Application Management tab and click Create Or Configure This Farm's Shared Services under the Office SharePoint Server Shared Services heading.

2. Click SharedServices1 (the default SSP) to launch the Shared Services Administration: SharedServices1 home page, shown in Figure 5-10.

3. Under the Excel Services Settings heading, click the Trusted File Locations option to display the Excel Services: Trusted File Locations page (see Figure 5-11).

4. If you wish to add a trusted location, click the Add Trusted File Location link to open the Excel Services: Add Trusted Location page.

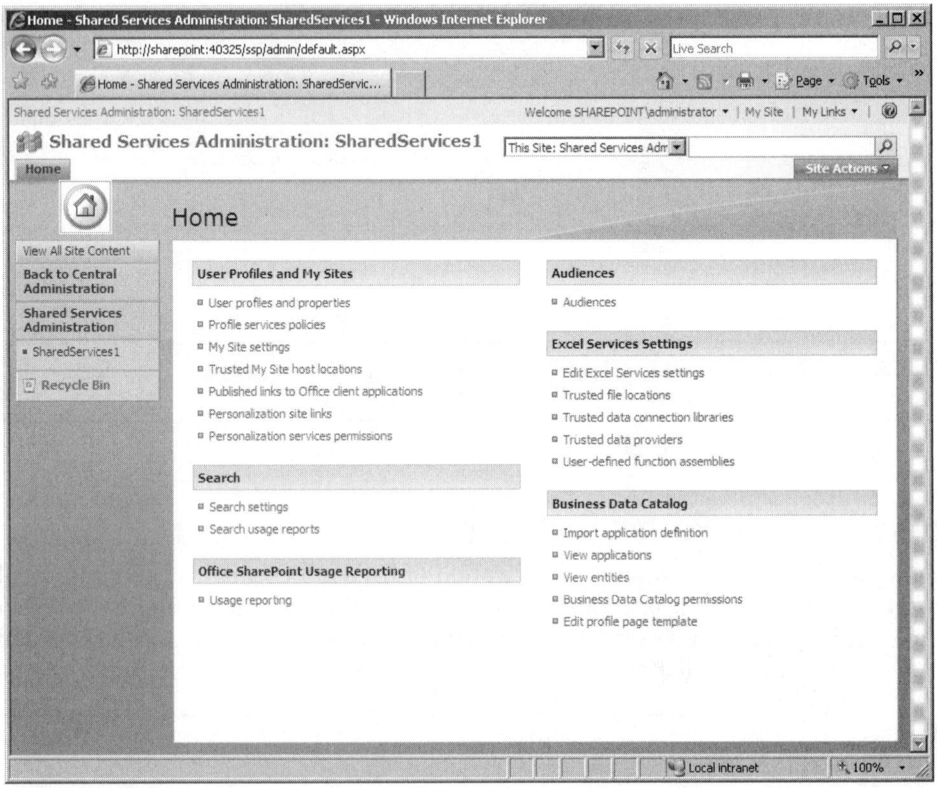

Figure 5-10. The Shared Services Administration: SharedServices1 page.

5. On the Add Trusted Location page, enter the following information, as applicable:

   a. The document library name, file share path, or web site URL.

   b. Select a location type appropriate to the address entered.

   c. Review the remaining settings, which are mostly security and performance-based settings. In most cases, the default values are acceptable and, unless you have good reason to change them, accept these settings.

   Click OK to save the trusted location.

Service Level Settings for SharePointServices1

MOSS installs all shared services with default settings. For many situations, the defaults settings may not provide the best performance or security. However, in the initial phases

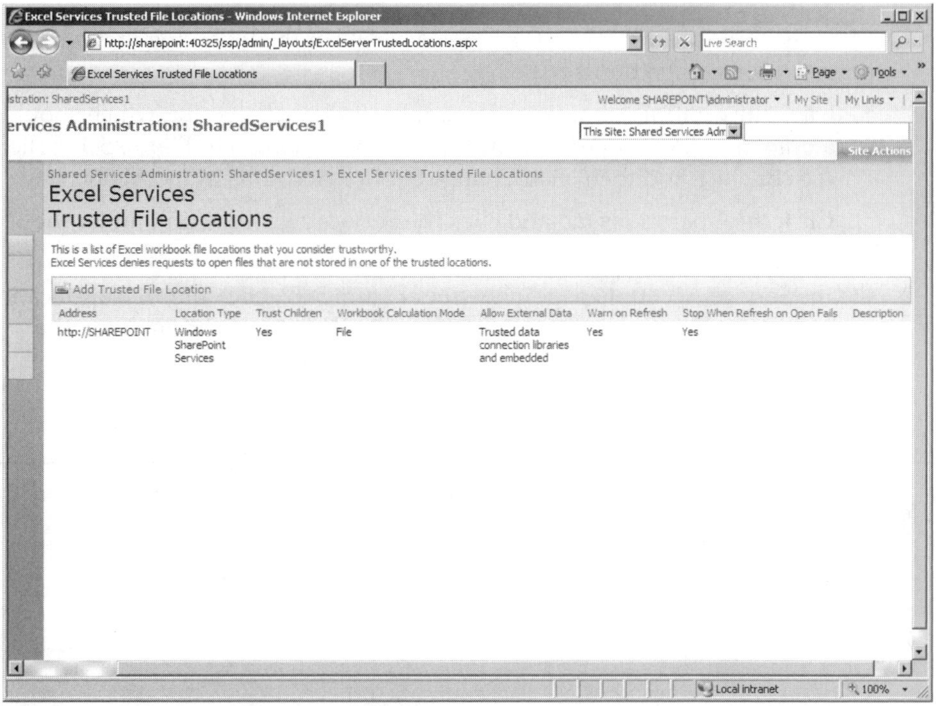

Figure 5-11.   Excel Services Trusted File Locations page.

of creating your MOSS environment, you can consider this task to be optional. As you gain experience with the performance and security of your shared services and SSP, you can begin to alter these settings to fine-tune your MOSS environment's performance and security. It is generally recommended that you defer making changes to the default values on your shared services until you have gained some experience with your system.

The Central Administration Application Pool Account

When you are setting up the application pool accounts used for the web applications on your server farm servers, the account used to access Central Administration should be a unique account not used for other purposes. If the account for accessing Central Administration is being used by some other web application, you must reassign the Central Administration access to a unique account.

To change the Central Administration account, do the following:

1. From the Central Administration page, use one of the following methods to open the Service Accounts page.

    a. Click the Central Administration application pool account, which should be a unique task in the Administrator Tasks List (shown in Figure 5-1 earlier in the chapter), and then click Change Service Accounts in the Action row.

    b. Click the Operations tab and click the Service Accounts link under the Security Configuration heading.

2. On the Service Accounts page, shown in Figure 5-12, click the web applications and select the Windows SharePoint Services Web Application. Now the application pool on your Central Administration service is enabled.

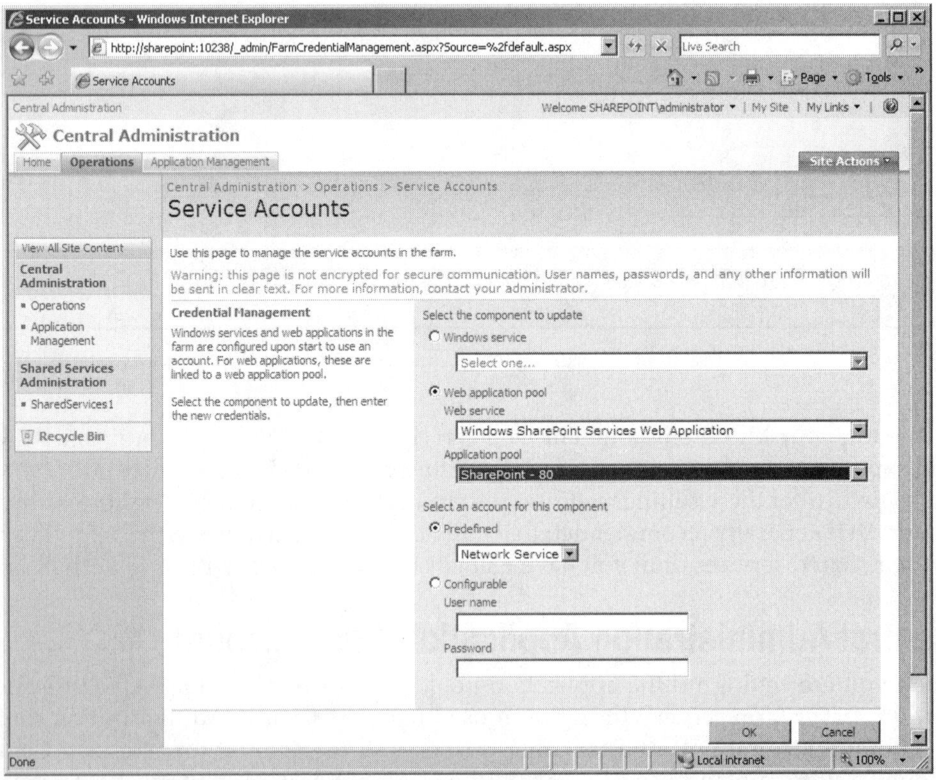

Figure 5-12. The Service Accounts page.

3. Enter the credentials (username and password) for the account to be used to access the Central Administration functions.

4. Click OK to save these settings.

Change Services Enabled in this Farm

You should verify that the services appropriate to the role of each server farm are enabled. If any of the required services are not enabled, use this task and its Action link to configure and start each service needed.

To verify or change the services enabled on a server farm server (or a standalone server, as the case may be), follow these steps:

1. From the SharePoint 3.0 Central Administration page, open the Check Services Enabled In This Farm page using one of the following methods:

   a. Choose the Application Management tab and click the Check Services Enabled In This Farm Link under the Office SharePoint Server Shared Services heading.

   b. Click the Check Services Enabled In This Farm Task in the Administrator Tasks List and then the Action link on the task page.

2. Any issues for a particular server are listed on the Check Services Enabled in this Farm page, as shown on Figure 5-13. Use the items listed on this page much the same as the Administrator Tasks list to complete the configuration of the server.

3. Use the link included in the Action column for each service to access the administrative page for each service issue.

TIP This check can be done at any point in the future by clicking the Check Services Enabled In This Farm option under the Office SharePoint Server Shared Services heading on the Application Management page.

Configure Diagnostic Logging

As discussed in Chapter 4, MOSS logs its administrative and event messages to a variety of log files. You can enable the specific diagnostic logs you may need for troubleshooting an MOSS issue, including log files for event messages, user error messages, trace logs, and, if you wish to participate, events related to the Customer Experience Improvement Program. See Chapter 4 for the process used to configure and enable the various diagnostic logging features.

Enable SSO in the Farm

SharePoint Excel Services requires either the Single Sign-On (SSO) service or Kerberos to be enabled on a server in order to access external data, meaning data stored on other

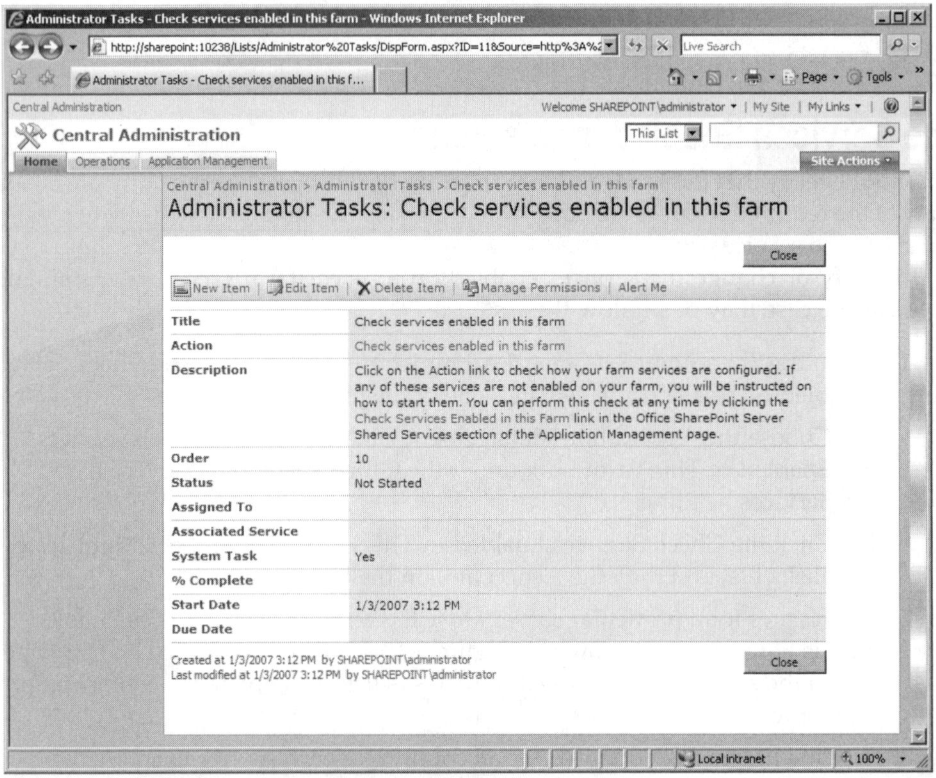

Figure 5-13. The Check Services Enabled In This Farm page.

server farm servers or outside the MOSS environment. The SSO service must first be started on all web front-end servers and any servers running Excel Services before it can be enabled.

Three steps are involved in configuring the SSO service on a server:

▼ Start the SSO service

■ Enable the SSO service

▲ Manage the encryption key

Start the SSO Service

To start the SSO service on a web front-end server, do the following:

1. Log in to your SharePoint front-end web server.

2. From the Start menu, navigate to the Services option on the Administrative Tools menu (Start | All Programs | Administrative Tools | Services).

3. On the Services dialog box (see Figure 5-14), right-click the Microsoft Single Sign-on Service and choose Properties from the pop-up menu.

4. Select the Log On tab of the Single Sign-on Service Properties dialog box (see Figure 5-15).

5. Select the This account option for the log on as entry and enter the SSO service account credentials (username and password).

6. On the General tab of the Single Sign-on Service Properties dialog box (see Figure 5-16), set the Startup type to Automatic.

7. Click the Start button and then click OK to start this service.

You may receive a message that the changes won't take effect until the service has been restarted. Select the Microsoft Single Sign-on Service and use the Stop and Play buttons in the toolbar to stop and start the service.

Enable SSO Service in MOSS

To enable the SSO service in your MOSS environment, do the following:

1. Open the SharePoint 3.0 Central Administration page and click the Operations tab.

2. Click the Manage Settings For Single Sign-On link listed under the Security Configuration heading to display the Manage Server Settings for Single Sign-On page, shown in Figure 5-17.

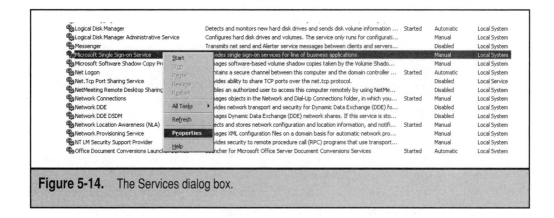

Figure 5-14.   The Services dialog box.

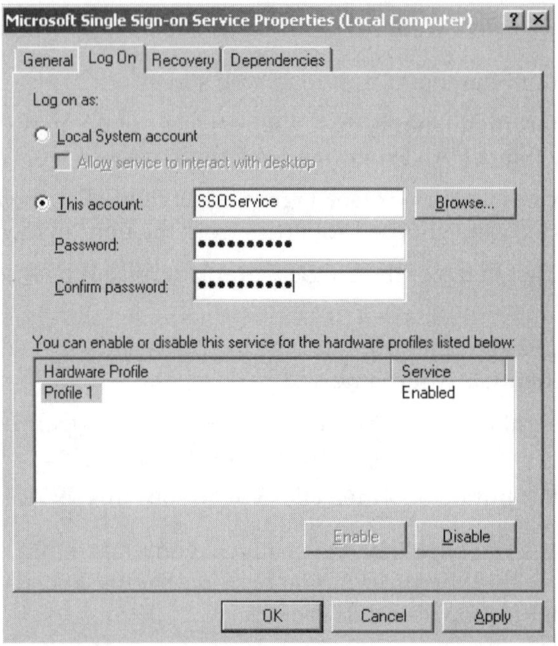

Figure 5-15.   The Log On tab of the Single Sign-on Service Properties dialog box.

3 Enter the SSO service account credentials in the Single Sign-On Administrator Account section.

4. Enter the SSO service account credentials in the Enterprise Application Definition Administrator Account section.

5. Click OK to save the SSO service settings.

Manage SSO Encryption Key

Once SSO has been configured, you must create an encryption key, which is used to encrypt all the credentials stored in the SSO database. To do this, use the following steps:

1. Open the SharePoint 3.0 Central Administration page and select the Operations tab.

2. On the Operations tab, click the Manage settings for single sign-on under the Security Configuration heading.

3. Click the Manage Encryption Key link and then the Create Encryption Key button to encrypt the SSO database using the new generated key.

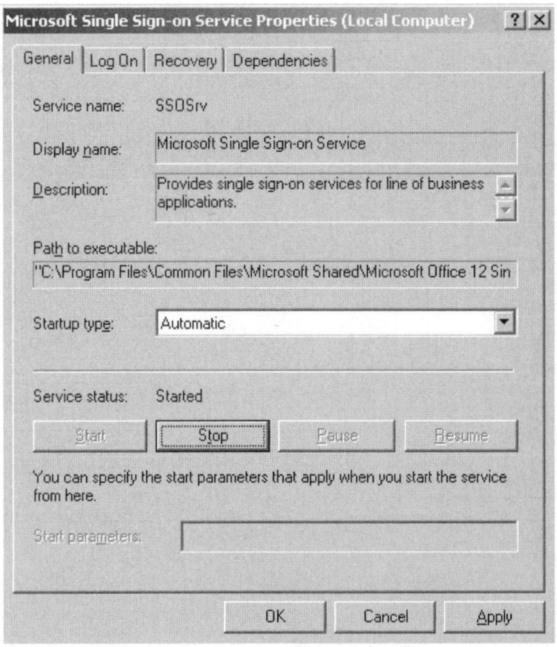

Microsoft Single Sign-on Service Properties (Local Computer)   ? X

General | Log On | Recovery | Dependencies |

Service name: SSOSrv

Display name: Microsoft Single Sign-on Service

Description: Provides single sign-on services for line of business
                 applications.

Path to executable:
"C:\Program Files\Common Files\Microsoft Shared\Microsoft Office 12 Sin

Startup type: Automatic

Service status: Started

[Start]   [Stop]   [Pause]   [Resume]

You can specify the start parameters that apply when you start the service
from here.

Start parameters:

[OK]   [Cancel]   [Apply]

Figure 5-16.   The Log On tab of the Single Sign-on Service Properties dialog box.

Click OK to save these settings.

TIP   Ensure that the account you create for single sign-on is a member of the Power Users group for all SharePoint servers.

NOTE · It is highly recommended you make a backup of the encryption key to a removable media and store that media in a secure location, just in case.

Add Antivirus Protection

If you have installed a MOSS-compatible antivirus program on your MOSS web front-end servers, you should enable the antivirus scanning of documents during upload or download from document libraries. See Chapter 4 for more information on enabling MOSS-compatible antivirus scanning on your servers.

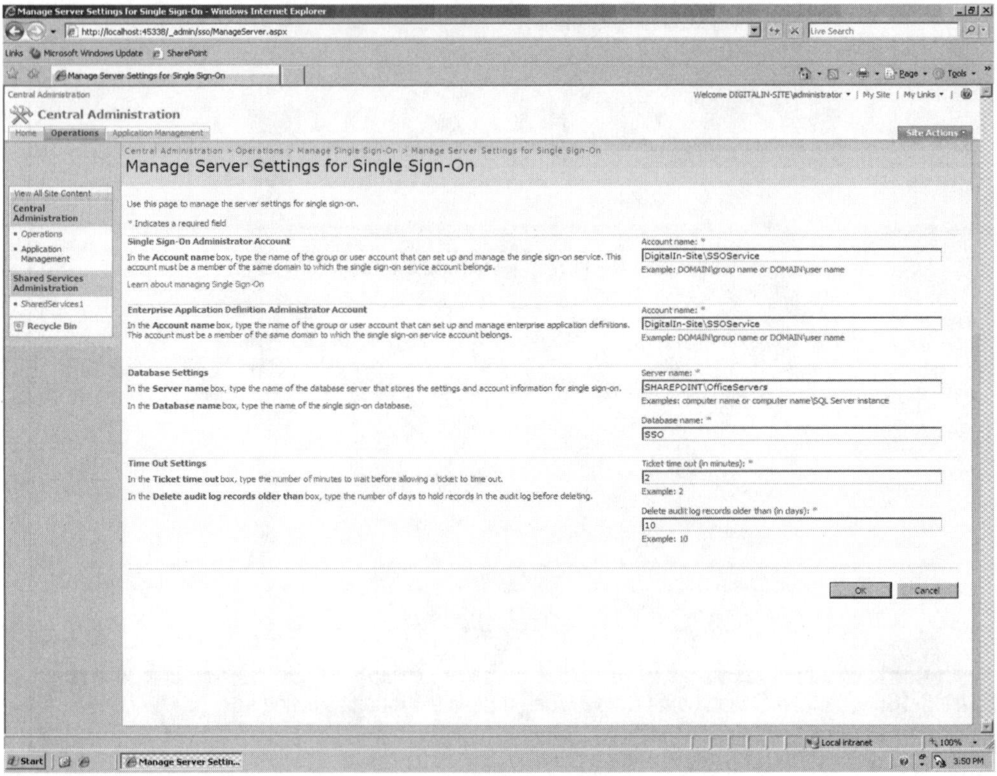

Figure 5-17. The Manage Server Settings For Single Sign-On page.

SUMMARY

The process of installing and configuring an MOSS environment extends beyond merely running the Setup program. In addition to the decisions that must be made during installation about the services, technologies, and programs to be installed on a particular server, once the installation completes, you have additional decisions, regarding services, settings, and configurations to make.

Using the information in this chapter, you have a guide to making the decisions needed to complete your MOSS environment, making it ready for users, and the organization, to begin reaping its benefits. Of course, not every environment requires all of the tasks listed here. Larger organizations and enterprises may install all of MOSS' functions, while smaller organizations, and especially those on a standalone MOSS server, may install only its basic functionality. In either case though, ensuring that the services you need are enabled and properly configured goes a long way toward creating an environment that serves the information needs of the organization and its users.

PART II

MOSS Administration

CHAPTER 6

MOSS Administration

The responsibilities of an MOSS administrator, especially in a large organization, can be a daunting task for a single administrator, and because of this, these duties are often shared among several administrators. However, if you have been awarded complete responsibility for an MOSS environment, you should understand that the job may not be as tough as you think.

As the administrator of an MOSS environment, you are likely responsible for server administration, SQL Server administration, and all of the products and technologies that make up the MOSS environment itself. Within the MOSS environment, your responsibilities include managing the site structure, site content, security permissions, and perhaps, in an enterprise setting, an MOSS server farm, as well as importing user profiles from Windows Server 2003's Active Directory and the ever-popular backup and restore operations.

The administrative tasks of an MOSS environment fall into two separate categories, based upon when these tasks are performed. Some administrative tasks are performed only once since they are configured during setup and function automatically for the most part thereafter. But, yes, many tasks must be done by you every day. You'll find if you take the time to perform the setup tasks carefully during the implementation or startup stage, these tasks will be essentially completed. It's kind of like a set-it-and-forget-it-thing. Your daily administrative tasks, involving such actions as managing security permissions on content and users, should quickly become routine.

This chapter provides you with an overview of the administrative tasks included in the general responsibilities of an MOSS system administrator. While you may not be responsible for all of the areas discussed, it's always a good idea to know how to support an administrative area, should it become necessary. In addition to the information in this chapter, you should also look at Chapters 4, 5, 13, and 14 for more information on the duties and responsibilities of an MOSS administrator.

GENERAL ADMINISTRATION

In addition to the general configuration tasks described in Part 1 of this book (especially those in Chapters 4 and 5), there are some configuration tasks you may need to complete, depending on how you've set up your MOSS environment and whether you have included certain services in the deployment. In the next few sections, these additional tasks are discussed.

User and Group Permissions

Modifying security permissions is a common SharePoint task typically reserved for the administrator, primarily because the security schemes in MOSS are somewhat complex and generally confusing to end-users. It is more efficient for the administrator to respond to user requests for permissions and security setting modifications than it is to train users to perform these tasks on an infrequent basis.

MOSS has two main areas of security permissions: site settings and Web Parts settings. Site permissions are usually set at a top-level site and inherited by subsites and the Web Parts on the site and its subsites. Unique permissions may be assigned to each site or subsite, but doing so typically requires that the permissions on these sites be manually and individually managed each time the permissions on any related sites are changed.

In actual practice, it is much less of an administrative headache to only assign unique permissions at the Web Part level. This approach allows a site to continue to inherit its permissions settings from its top-level site and any specific restrictions, and then apply only a specific Web Part that contains sensitive content. Using the same approach, if a specific user or user group requires a special set of permissions to update certain content, he, she, or they can be granted this special permission at the Web Part level—a security best practice called least privilege. Granting permission at the Web Part level protects other Web Parts, and the site in general, from unauthorized modifications.

This section is included to introduce you to the process used to set user permissions and security. It discusses only the steps used to configure user settings for the Central Administration site collection. Understand that the process discussed here won't modify the settings of the sites a typical user would access. In addition to the process described in the next few sections, additional administrative tasks must be performed (see Chapter 7) to affect user access to other site collections.

> **NOTE**   For more information on MOSS security and permissions settings, see Chapter 7.

The Users and Permissions section of the Modify All Site Settings menu allows the administrator to manage the level of access a specific user and group has to a site. Users and security groups defined in the Windows Server 2003 Active Directory along with the permissions assigned to MOSS site groups define the role assigned to a user or group, such as viewer, contributor, designer, or Administrator.

To access the People and Groups settings, use these steps:

1. On the Central Administration page, click the Site Actions button to open its drop-down menu and select Site Settings.

2. On the Site Settings page, click the People and Groups option under the Users and Permissions heading to open the People and Groups: Farm Administrators page, shown in Figure 6-1.

On the People and Groups: Farm Administrators page, you can use the New, Actions, and Settings options to perform a wide range of user and group actions. The following options are available on the pull-down menus for these three options:

▼   **New**   As shown in Figure 6-2, the options on the New menu are Add Users and New Group, which are used to add users to a group or site, or to create a new SharePoint group.

Figure 6-1.   The People and Groups: Farm Administrators page.

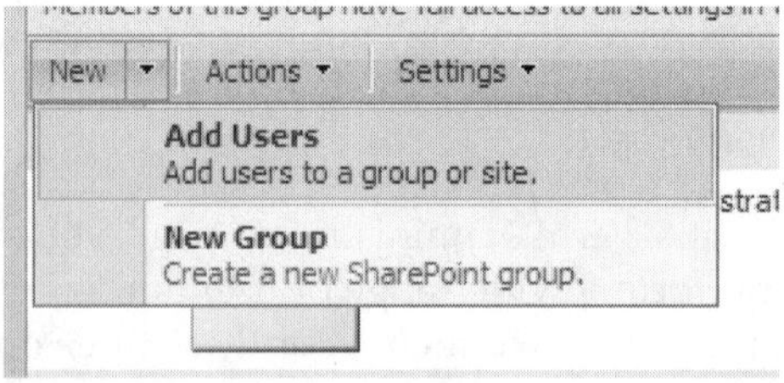

Figure 6-2.   The drop-down menu for the New option on the People and Groups page.

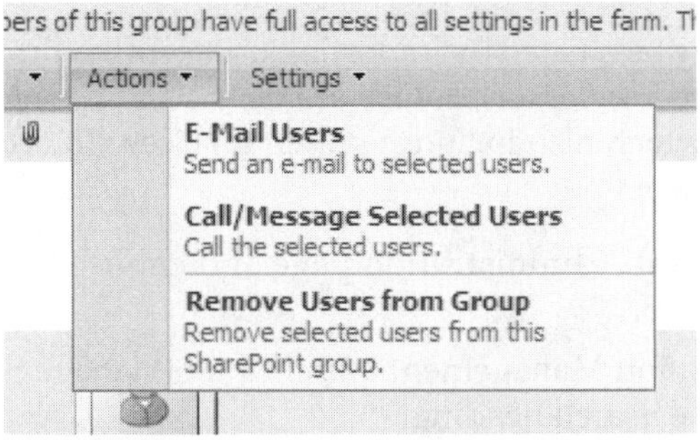

Figure 6-3.   The drop-down menu for the Actions option on the People and Groups page.

- ■ **Actions**   As shown in Figure 6-3, the options on the Actions menu are E-Mail Users, Call/Message Selected Users, and Remove Users from Group, each of which does essentially what its name describes.

- ▲ **Settings**   As illustrated in Figure 6-4, the options on the Settings menu are Group Settings, View Group Permissions, Edit Group Quick Launch, Set Up Groups, and List Settings. Perhaps the Settings menu options used most often are the Group Settings and List Settings options, which are used to manage group and list settings and permissions.

Figure 6-4.   The drop-down menu for the Settings option on the People and Groups page.

User Profiles

MOSS user profiles may be created by importing user profiles directly from the Windows Server 2003 Active Directory. User profiles are defined as a part of the Shared Services server configuration, which also includes search services. To access and configure user profiles, follow these steps:

1. Open the Central Administration page and choose the Application Management tab.

2. On the Application Management tab, click the Manage Search Service link listed under the Search heading.

3. Click the SharedServices1 link in the Shared Service Providers With Search Enabled section to display the Shared Services Administration: SharedServices1 home page, shown in Figure 6-5.

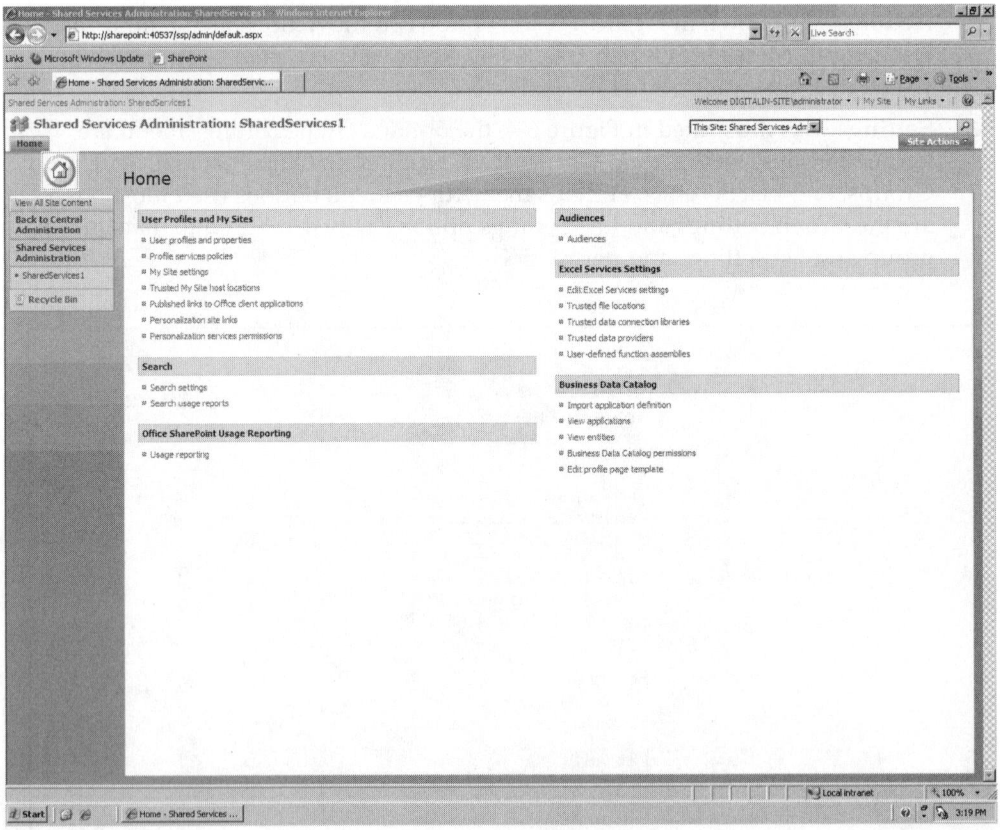

Figure 6-5. The Shared Services Administration: SharedServices1 home page.

113

4. Click the User profiles and properties link in the User Profiles and My Sites section to display the User Profiles and Properties page.

5. On the User Profiles and Properties page, scroll down to the Profile And Import Settings section and click the Start Full Import link (see Figure 6-6).

   Depending on the number of user accounts in your Active Directory, the import process could take a while. If you wish to check the progress of the import action, click the Refresh link (see Figure 6-6). When the import action has completed, the start and end times for the import are displayed on the Import time line.

6. To verify that the profiles have been imported successfully, click the View user profiles link.

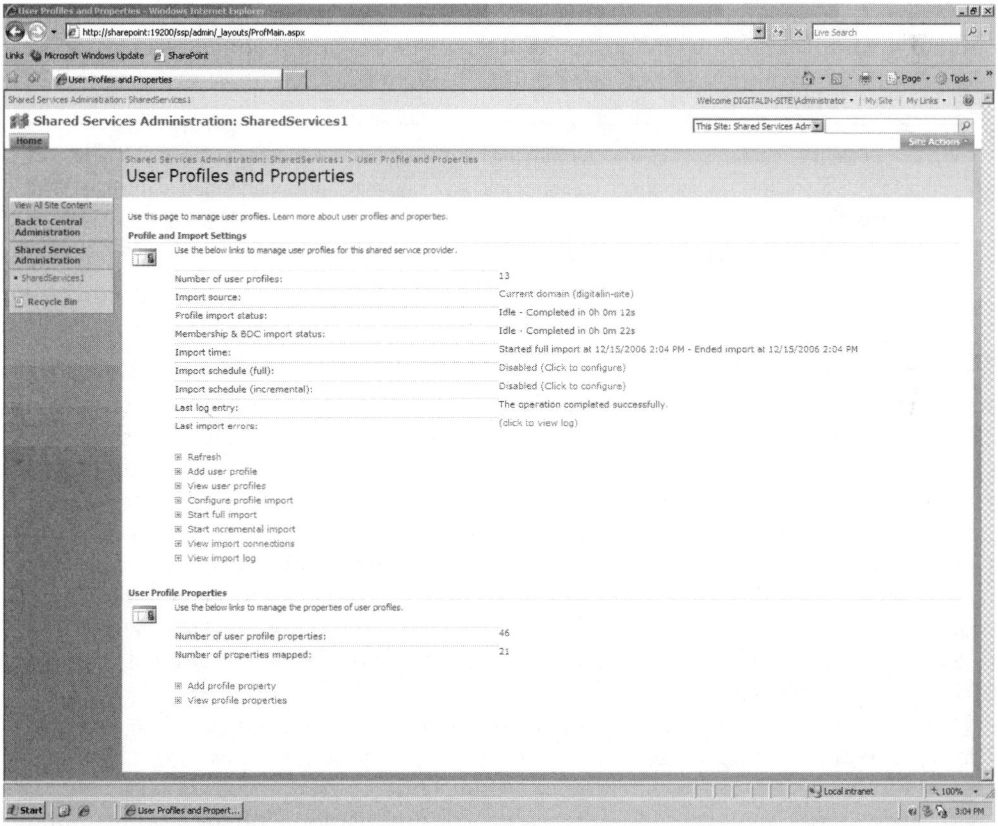

Figure 6-6. The User Profiles and Properties page.

ENVIRONMENT ADMINISTRATION

On an ongoing basis, most of the duties of a MOSS administrator involve web application, site, page, and document library and list maintenance. This is especially true in a new MOSS installation, where the visual displays, document content, and user needs tend to mature through usage. However, in the initial stages of your MOSS environment, you are likely to be called upon to create and maintain the following foundation elements:

- ▼ Web applications
- ■ Site structures
- ■ Team and user sites
- ■ Site content
- ▲ Backup and restore

In the sections that follow, the tasks involved to create and maintain each of these elements, with the exception of web applications (covered in Chapter 4), is discussed.

NOTE While the preceding section dealt with user permissions and security settings at the system administration level, this section brings you back into administrative tasks performed at the user level for site collections and sites. Some of the processes used to administer your MOSS environment are performed at the Central Administration level. However, as you'll learn, certain specific administrative processes are performed within each MOSS element.

Site Creation

In the SharePoint world, you may be confused at first about the difference between a site and a site collection. A site collection is a logical grouping of individual sites that are grouped for administrative purposes. While some administrative tasks and settings can be performed on an individual site, other settings and functions can only be done at the site collection level. To further confuse the issue, the top-level site in a site collection can create settings and functions that are inherited by subsites associated with it. For the most part, a user doesn't actually see a site collection, but rather its top-level site, which appears as just a regular SharePoint site. A site collection has a top-level site, which can have many subsites added to it. However, taken on the whole, a site at any level is, in the eyes of the user, just a site.

When it comes to deciding who has permission to create sites, you can keep control of site creation, preventing users from creating sites, or you can allow users to create their own top-level sites and subsites, or, of course, both.

Several good reasons exist for keeping control of site creation with the administrator, such as enforcing site structure rules, avoiding redundant sites, and limiting the number of sites created. The downside to restricting site creation to only an administrator is that the administrator could quickly become a bottleneck trying to keep up with user requests for new sites, especially in the early stages of an MOSS installation.

Unless you have the capability to process new site requests in a timely manner, you may want to consider allowing users to create their own sites and use your time reviewing the new sites users produce for standards and functionality. If you do decide to allow users to create their own sites, you must change the Self-Service Site Creation settings.

TIP   You also have the option of requiring a new site to pass through two review or contact points before the site is made available for general viewing. This allows you to keep yourself, or another user you trust with standards monitoring, in the loop for a new site.

Self-Service Site Creation

To enable the Self-Service Site Creation setting, which allows users to create their own site collections, do the following:

1. Open the SharePoint 3.0 Central Administration page and select the Application Management tab.

2. On the Application Management tab, click the Self-Service site management link under the Application Security heading to open the Self-Service Site Management page (shown in Figure 6-7).

3. Click the Web application button to open its drop-down list and then select the web application for which you are enabling users to create sites.

4. Select On for the Enable Self-Service Site Creation option.

5. If you wish to have a second contact for a new site, check the Require secondary contact checkbox and enter the secondary contact's information when prompted.

NOTE   If you later decide to disable the Self-Service Site Management option, select the Off option for Enable Self-Service Site Creation instead.

6. Click OK to save this setting.

Create a Top-Level Site

To create the first site page (top-level page) for a new site collection within a web application, perform the following steps:

1. On any Central Administration page, select the Application Management tab and click the Create Site Collection link under the SharePoint Site Management heading (see Figure 6-8).

2. On the top portion of the Create Site page (see Figure 6-9), enter the appropriate information in each of the following fields:

    a. Enter a unique and descriptive Title for the new site. Remember that the Site Title is used to identify the site in search results, so carefully give each site a unique and descriptive title.

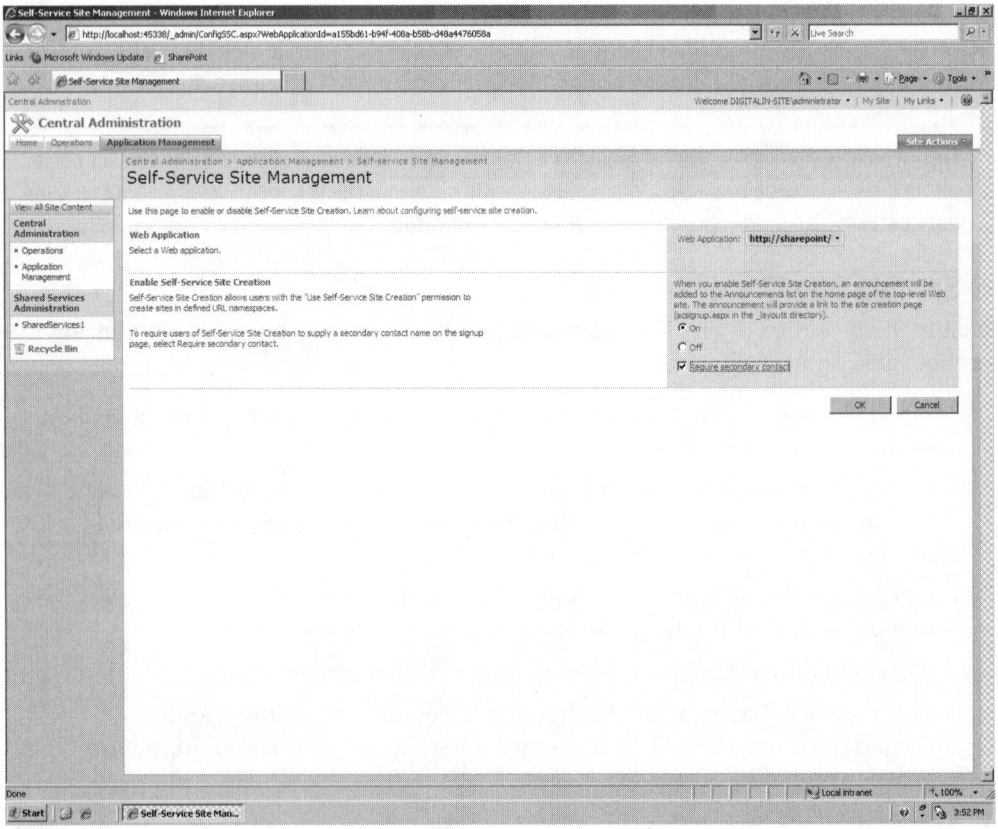

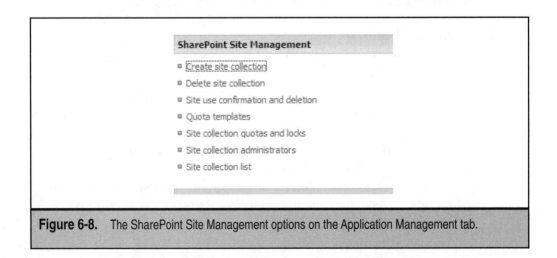

Figure 6-7. The Self-Service Site Management page.

SharePoint Site Management

- Create site collection
- Delete site collection
- Site use confirmation and deletion
- Quota templates
- Site collection quotas and locks
- Site collection administrators
- Site collection list

Figure 6-8. The SharePoint Site Management options on the Application Management tab.

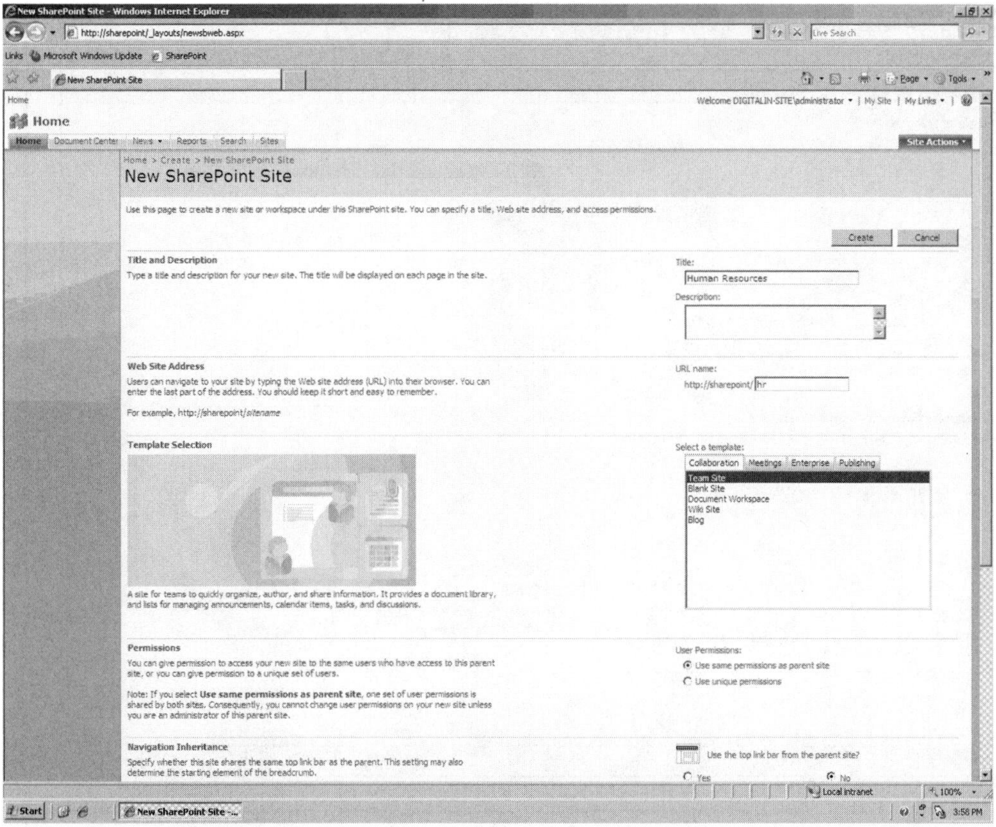

Figure 6-9. The upper portion of the Create Site page.

b. Enter a statement that summarizes the site's purpose in the Description field. The description is displayed in the top panel of each site.

c. Enter a simple page (URL) name for the new site. The URL name doesn't need to be as descriptive as the site title, but it should be easy for users to remember and type.

3. Scroll down the page to the Template Selection section (see Figure 6-10). Most new sites are created from a template. Notice that the Select A Template box is tabbed with each tab listing the templates available in each grouping. Choose the tab of the group that best fits the purpose of the new site and then choose a template from its list. See the "Site Templates" section later in this chapter for more information.

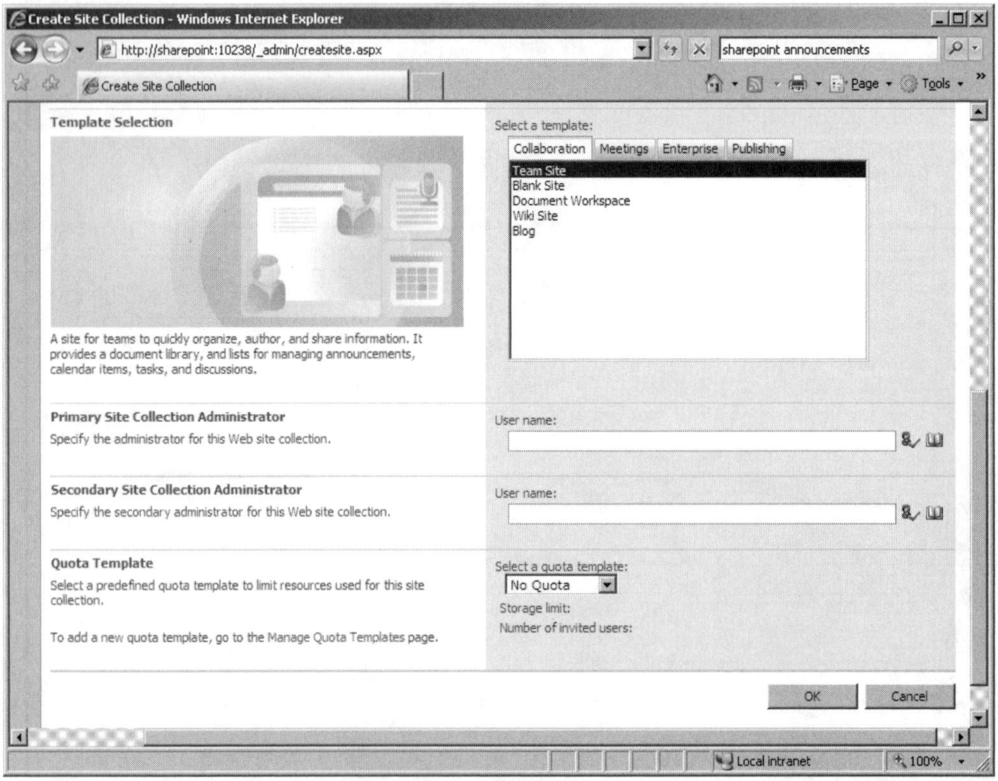

Figure 6-10. The lower portion of the Create Site page.

4. In the Primary Site Collection Administrator section, enter the username for the person who is the Administrator for this site collection. You can use the browse and address book icons to the left of the textbox for this entry to search for a username.

5. If you wish to enter a secondary level Administrator, which is optional, enter that person's username in the Secondary Site Collection Administrator section.

6. If you wish to limit the amount of disk space a site can take up, assign (or create) a quota template to the site. To assign a quota template to the site, select an existing quota template from the pull-down list. If you wish to create a new quota template, click the Manage Quota Templates link to open the Quota Templates page (discussed in the next section).

7. Click the OK button to create the top-level page for the site. When the site page has been created and added to the SharePoint content database, a page displays letting you know the site was successfully created.

When you create a new site (site collection), the first page you create is designated as the top-level page of the site. So, before you create a site's first page, plan out its hierarchy and what type of page (meaning which template) should be created at each level of the site collection. When a site collection is created, a tab is added to the top of the navigation bar on all of the site's pages.

Quota Templates

You can limit the amount of disk storage space available to a site collection by assigning a quota template to the site. In a quota template, you define the maximum amount of storage space you wish to allow a site to occupy, as well as a trigger level (of storage space usage) at which an e-mail is to be sent to the site collection administrator warning that the site is approaching its limit.

You can open the Quota Templates page, shown in Figure 6-11, from the Application Management tab on the SharePoint Central Administration page using the Quota

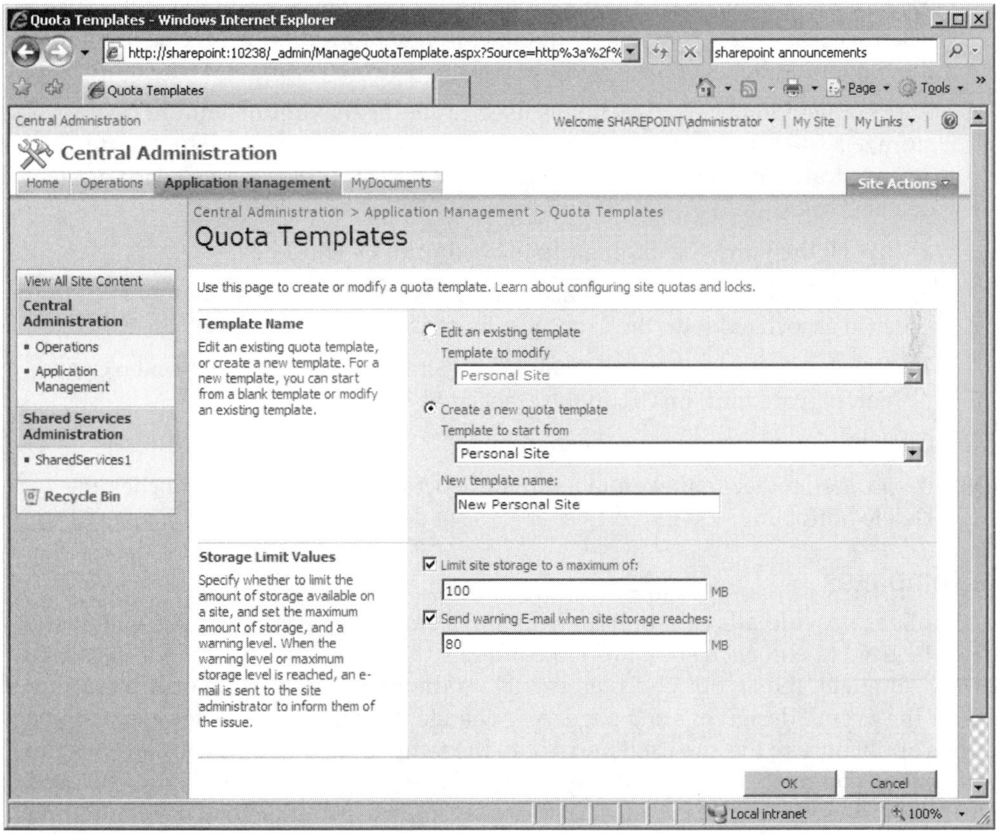

Figure 6-11. The Quota Template page.

templates link under the SharePoint Site Management heading or from the Create Site Collections page (see Figures 6-9 and 6-10).

1. To edit an existing quota template:

   a. In the Template Name section, select the Edit An Existing Template option and choose the template name from the Template To Modify pull-down list.

   b. Modify any of the settings on the page and then click OK to save the template.

2. To create a new quota template:

   a. In the Template Name section, select the Create A New Quota Template option.

   b. In the Template To Start From pull-down list, choose either the new blank template selection or the name of an existing template you wish to use as a template.

   c. Enter a name for the new quota template in the New Template name field.

   Whether you are creating a new quota template or modifying an existing one, the remaining fields on the Quota Template page are configured the same.

3. The Storage Limit Values section is used to set the maximum amount of storage a site can occupy, and, optionally, to send an alert e-mail to the site administrator. Remember that you don't have to limit the storage space usage of a site, but should you wish to do so:

   a. Check the Limit Site Storage To A Maximum Of checkbox.

   b. Enter the total amount of space in megabytes (MB) a site can grow to in the field associated with the Limit Site Storage To A Maximum Of checkbox.

   c. Check the Send Warning E-mail When Site Storage Reaches checkbox and enter an amount, in MB, in the associated field.

4. Click the OK button to save the template.

5. If you wish to delete the quota template, skip steps 2 through 4 and click the Delete button.

Site Templates

Site templates provide a layout and an initial placement for Web Parts for a new site and can be used to enforce a standard look and feel to sites added to a web application. Like any template, the layout and placements on the template provide only a starting point for the overall design of a site page. Any changes you make to the new site using a template apply only to the site itself and not to the template. However, you can save the modifications you make to a new site layout as a custom template that can then be used to create new sites. Saving a new site's layout as a template can save time by eliminating the need to completely re-create a unique site layout that will be frequently used.

The site templates included with MOSS are categorized by function, including:

▼ Collaboration

- ■ **Team Site** For teams to quickly organize, author, and share information. Initial Web Parts include a document library, announcement, calendar, and task lists, and discussion Web Parts.

- ■ **Blank Site** A blank team site, customizable to your requirements.

- ■ **Document Workspace** Allow colleagues to work together on a document. Initial Web Parts include a document library, task, to-do, and link lists (see Figure 6-12).

- ■ **Wiki Site** A community-based site to brainstorm and share ideas. Provides web pages that can be quickly edited and linked together via keywords.

- ■ **Blog** Post individual or team ideas, observations, and expertise. Visitors may comment on posts.

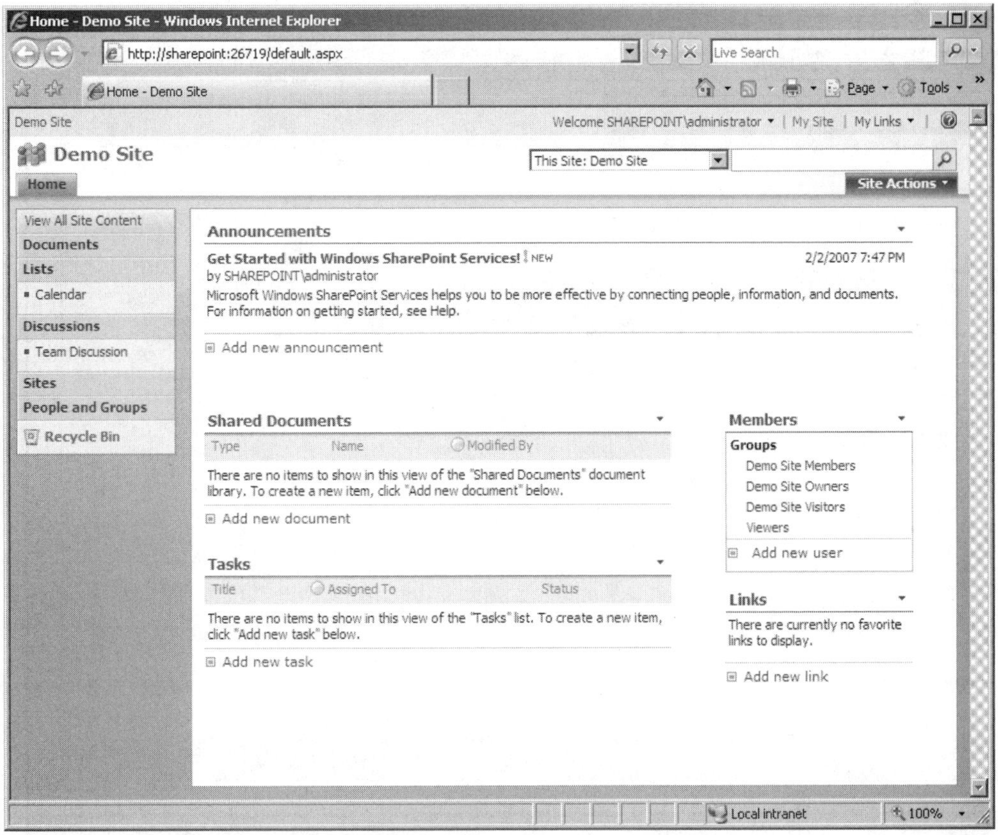

Figure 6-12. A site page created using the Document Workspace template.

- Meetings
  - **Basic Meeting Workspace**   Plan, organize, and capture meeting results. Initial Web Parts include agenda and meeting attendee lists, and a document library (see Figure 6-13).
  - **Blank Meeting Workspace**   A blank meeting site, customizable to your requirements.
  - **Social Meeting Workspace**   Plan social gatherings. Initial Web Parts include attendee lists, directions, and picture library.
  - **Multiple Meeting Workspace**   Similar to a basic meeting workspace. Includes two tabbed pages that can be customized to your requirements.
- Enterprise
  - **Records Center**   Configure routing to direct documents to specific storage locations. Once stored, documents cannot be modified.

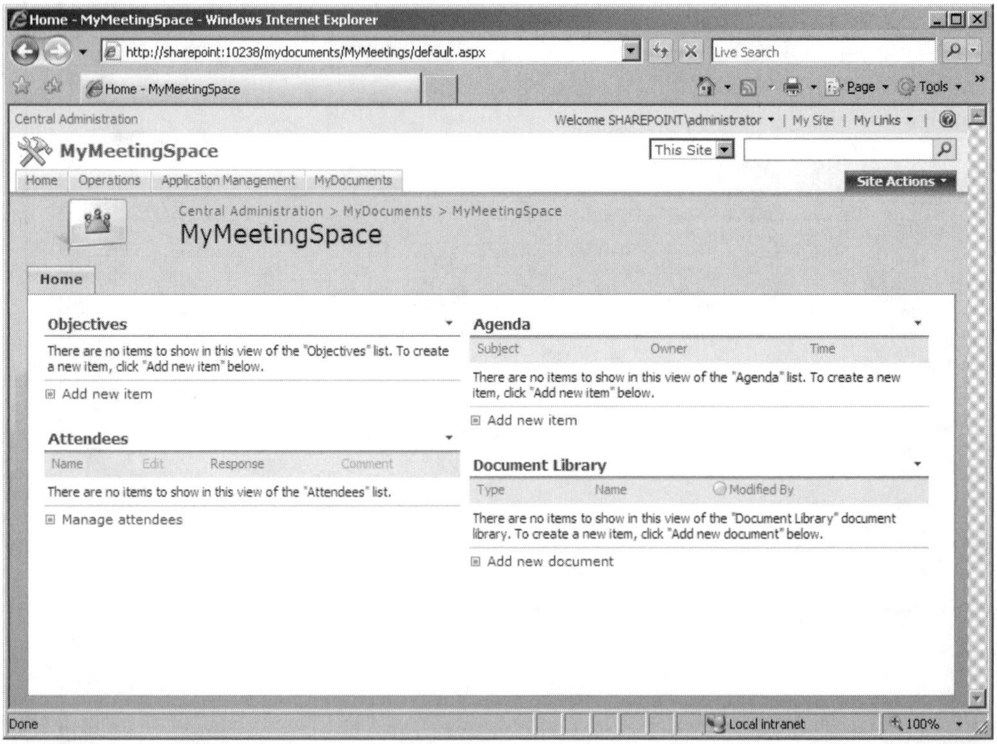

Figure 6-13.   A site page created using the Basic Meeting Workspace template.

- **Report Center**   Create, manage, and deliver web pages, dashboard, and key performance indicators. Communicate goals and business data.

- **Search Center**   Delivers search experience. Includes pages for advanced searches and search results (see Figure 6-14).

NOTE   The templates included in the remainder of this bulleted list are available only for a top-level site.

- **Document Center**   Centrally manage enterprise documents.

- **Site Directory**   List and categorize important sites in your organization. Includes categorized sites, top sites, and site map views (see Figure 6-10).

- **Personalization Site**   Deliver personalized views, data, and navigation optimized for My Site sites.

- **Search Center with Tabs**   Similar to the Search Center site. Includes search boxes for general and people searches. Custom tabs allow for additional search scopes or modified search results.

▲ Publishing

- **Publishing Site**   A blank site for publishing web pages.

- **Publishing Site with Workflow**   Similar to a publishing site, but requires pages to be scheduled and approved via workflow.

- **News Site**   Publish news articles and links to news articles. Includes archival capability.

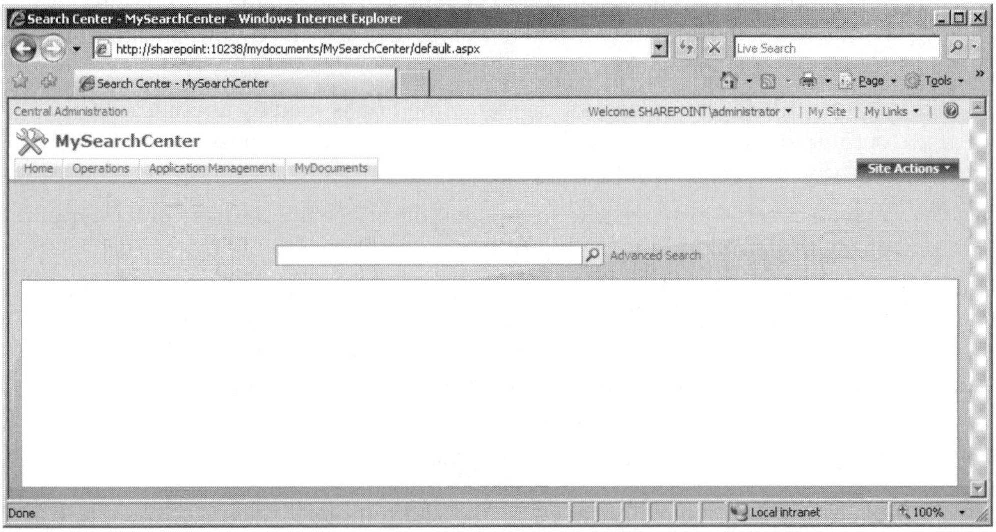

Figure 6-14.   A site page created using the Search Center template.

TIP   A variety of specialized site templates may be downloaded from Microsoft and third-party vendors as well. Once downloaded, a site template (*.stp file) is uploaded to the site template gallery and available for use when creating new sites.

Create a Site Template

It is common for an administrator or the users in an MOSS environment to create sites that have a common or very similar layout, include the same Web Parts, and perhaps even have the same content. For these sites, it can be more efficient for everyone to create the layout of the site once and then save it as a template, allowing the administrator or users to quickly and easily create new sites using the template.

To save a site as a site template, do the following:

1. Navigate in SharePoint to the site you wish to save as a template.

2. Click the Site Actions button to open its drop-down menu and choose the Site Settings option to open the Site Settings page.

3. Under the Look and Feel heading on the Site Settings page, click the Save Site As Template link to display the Save Site As Template page (see Figure 6-15).

NOTE   Not every site can be saved as a site template—for example, a site created as a variation of a site template—because the Save Site As Template link is hidden for these sites.

4. On the Save Site As Template page (shown in Figure 6-15), enter values for the following items:

   a. Enter a filename for the template. The template's filename is seen only by the MOSS administrator. Site template files are saved with an .stp file extension.

   b. Enter a title for the template. The template title is seen by anyone with permission to create a new site and should, as much as possible, accurately describe the site template.

   c. Enter a description for the template that describes the purpose of the type of site the template is used to produce.

5. If you wish to include library and list content in the template, check the Include Content checkbox. This optional setting is the only way you can save certain site customizations, such as a workflow. However, because security permissions for this type of content are not brought forward to the template, be careful if a site may eventually include any sensitive information.

6. Click the OK button to save the site template.

Site templates are automatically saved to the site template gallery of the site collection in which the site template was created. To save a site template to another site

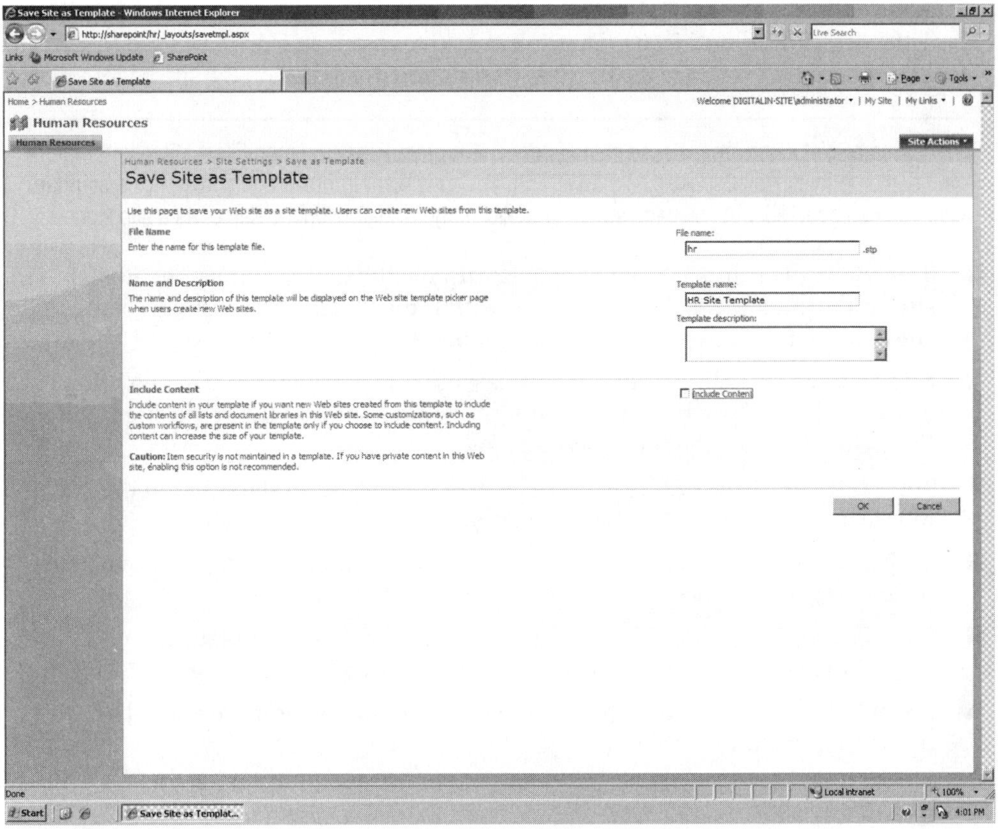

Figure 6-15. The Save Site As Template page.

collection, you must first export the site template to an external (outside of MOSS) storage location and then upload it into the site template gallery of the new site collection (see the "Upload Site Templates" section later in this chapter).

Site Look and Feel

The links in the Look and Feel column on the Site Settings page are used to configure the visual appearance and function of a site. *Look* refers to the visual appearance of a site, while *feel* refers to how the site functions. Each of the links in the Look and Feel column can be used to affect a particular visual quality to the site title, description, icon, navigation, and the site's overall visual theme.

The following is a brief description of how and why each of these links is used:

▼ **Title, description, and icon**   This link is used to assign an icon to be used to select a site page and to change the title and description displayed on the site page.

TIP   SharePoint icons are installed in the folder C:\Program Files\Common Files\ Microsoft Shared\ web server extensions\12\TEMPLATE\IMAGES\. You may want to browse this folder for a standard icon that can be used, but you can use any graphic image available on the server as a site icon.

■ **Tree view**   This link is used to enable/disable the Quick Launch menu on a site and to enable/disable a tree view within the Quick Launch menu of the site collection, as illustrated in Figure 6-16.

■ **Site theme**   This link allows you to assign a prescribed color scheme to a site, making it consistent with any other site(s) using the same site theme. Figure 6-17 shows the Site Theme page.

■ **Top Link Bar**   This link opens a page that allows you to start or stop the inheritance of the top-level page's link bar to all pages in the site.

■ **Quick Launch**   This link opens a page on which you can add or remove items from the Quick Launch menu and order the items in the menu.

■ **Save Site as Template**   This link opens the Save Site as Template page (see Figure 6-15) used to create a template of an existing site page.

▲ **Reset to Site Definition**   This link is used to reset one or more pages back to the version included in the site definition.

Site Galleries

Site galleries are collections of various SharePoint elements, including site and list templates, Web Parts, and workflows, that may be reused within a site collection and throughout its top-level site and subsites.

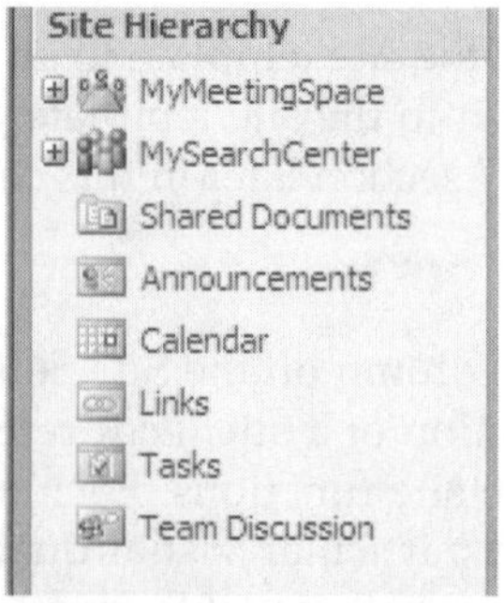

Figure 6-16.   A tree view applied to a site's Quick Launch menu.

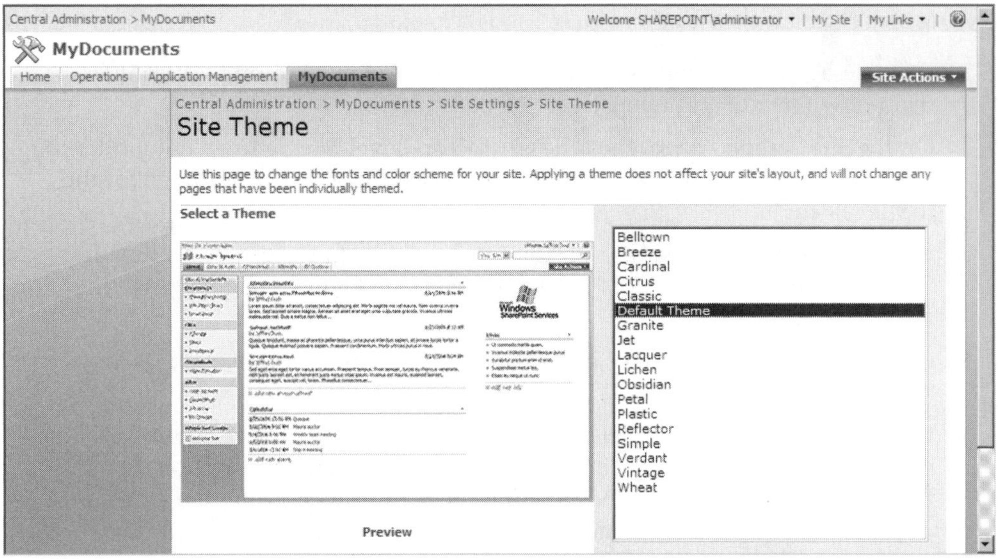

Figure 6-17. The Site Theme page.

The following is a brief description of how and why each of the links listed under the Galleries heading is used:

▼ **Master page gallery** This link opens the Master Page Gallery page that lists all of the master pages available for use in this site and all subsites.

■ **Site content types** This link opens the Site Content Type Gallery page that is used to create and manage the content types defined for the current site and any parent sites. The content types listed in the gallery can be used on the site and any subsites.

▲ **Site columns** This link opens the Site Column Gallery page, which can be used to create and manage the column types defined by the current site and any parent sites. The column types listed in the gallery can be used on the site and any subsites.

Upload Site Templates

Once a site template is created, it is available only in the site collection in which it was created. If you wish to include a site template in other site collections, it must be uploaded to the site gallery of each site collection where you want it available.

To upload one or more site templates into the SharePoint site gallery, perform the following steps:

1. From a page in a SharePoint site, click the Site Actions button to display its drop-down menu, and then select Site Settings.

2. On the Site Settings page, click the Go To Top Level Site Settings link under the Site Collection Administration heading to open the Site Settings page for the top-level site.

3. Under the Galleries heading on the top-level Site Settings page, click the Site Templates link to display the Site Template Gallery page, shown in Figure 6-18.

4. On the Site Template Gallery page, click the Upload option to open its drop-down menu (see Figure 6-19).

5. Click either Upload Document or Upload Multiple Documents to upload either one or multiple templates. Choosing the multiple documents option displays the Upload Template page shown in Figure 6-20, and choosing the Upload document displays the Upload template page shown in Figure 6-21.

Figure 6-18.   The Site Template Gallery page.

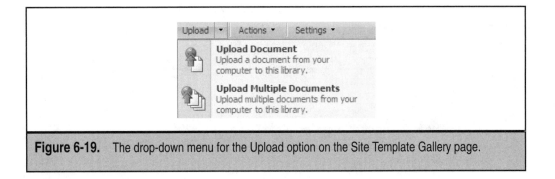

Figure 6-19.   The drop-down menu for the Upload option on the Site Template Gallery page.

6. On the multiple documents upload page (see Figure 6-20), browse to the location of the site template files and check each template (.stp) file to be included in the upload. On the single template upload page (see Figure 6-21), enter the file path and filename of the file you wish to upload.

7. Click OK to upload the template document(s).

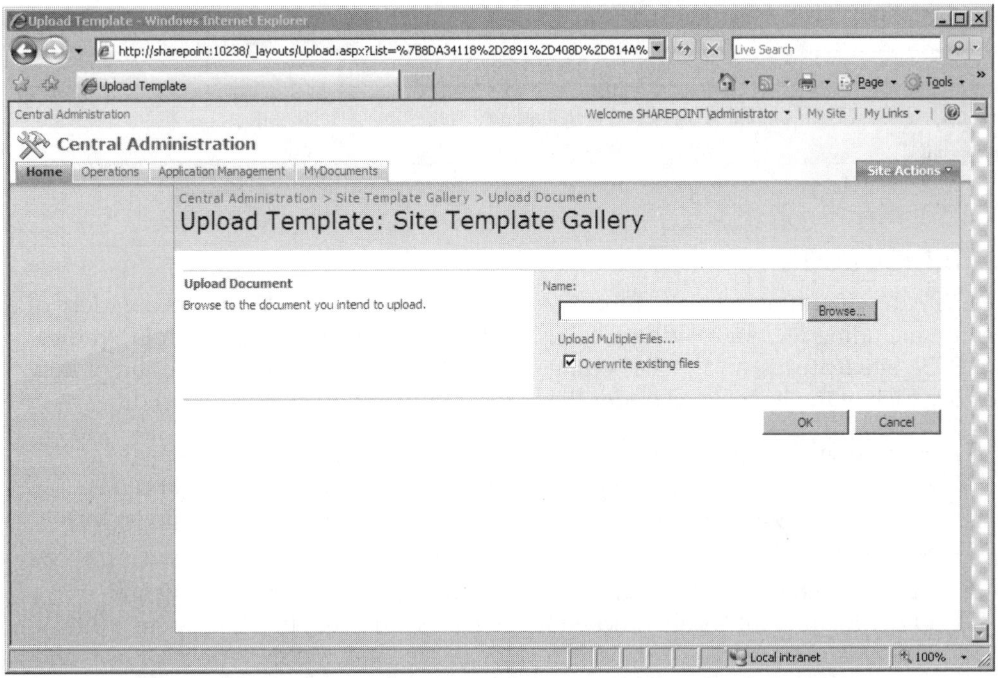

Figure 6-20.   The Upload Templates page used to upload multiple template documents.

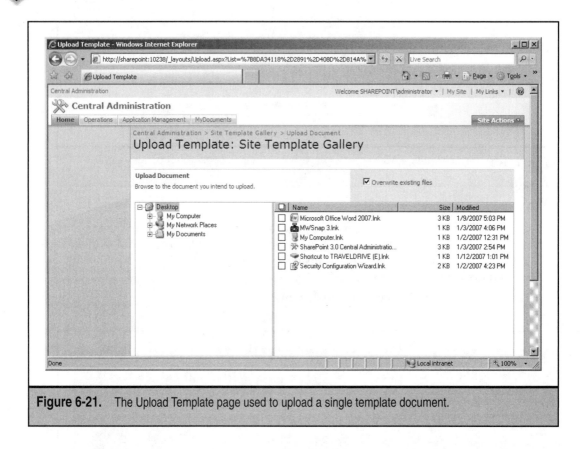

Figure 6-21. The Upload Template page used to upload a single template document.

Site Administration

The Site Administration section of the Site Settings (see Figure 6-22) covers a variety of features, including regional settings, site usage reports, user alerts, Real Simple Syndication (RSS), site features, and cache settings. The following is a brief description of how and why each of the links listed under the Site Administration heading is used:

▼ **Site libraries and lists:** This link opens the Site Libraries and Lists page on which the current libraries and lists of the site are listed as links that can be used to access each element for customization. For more information on this selection, see Chapter 12.

■ **Site usage reports**   If Windows SharePoint Services Usage Logging and Office SharePoint Usage Processing have been enabled, this link opens a Site Usage Summary page from which you can access summary reports of user and resource usage. For more information on this selection, see Chapter 15.

■ **User alerts**   Each user can be configured with certain alert triggers. This link is used to access the User Alerts page through which user alerts can be assigned.

Figure 6-22.   The Site Administrations heading and options on the Site Settings page.

■   **RSS**   This link opens the RSS page through which you can enable/disable the RSS capability in the site. For more information on this selection, see Chapter 17.

■   **Search visibility**   This link opens the Search Visibility page on which you can indicate whether a site and its contents should be included in displayed search results. For more information on this selection, see Chapter 8.

■   **Sites and workspaces**   This link opens the Sites and Workspaces page (see Figure 6-23) on which you can see the sites, document workspaces, and meeting workspaces that exist within a site collection. You can also create new sites. For more information on sites and workspaces, see Chapters 12 and 13.

▲   **Site features**   This link opens the Site Features page on which you can activate or deactivate several of the features available in MOSS. As shown in Figure 6-24, you can activate or deactivate MOSS publishing, MOSS standard site features, team collaboration lists, and the translation management functions.

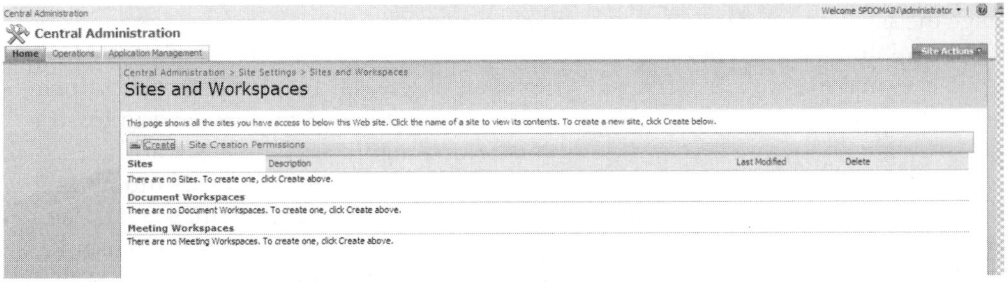

Figure 6-23.   The Sites and Workspaces page.

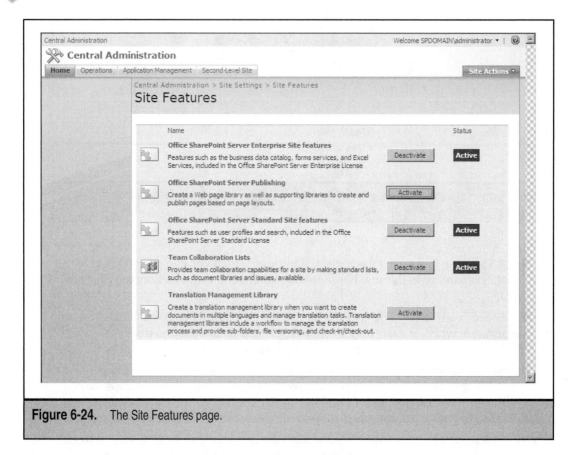

Figure 6-24. The Site Features page.

Site Structure

To set the structure of a site, or the way in which a site displays its content, you basically have two options: you can list sites alphabetically, or you can sort them in some other list sequence manually. Unless you have a very good reason for choosing to manually arrange the site list, you should use the alphabetical sort option. The reason is simple: no matter how intuitive you think your scheme for manually ordering the site list may be, it isn't likely to make sense to every one of your users. Users can adapt to a standard alphabetical listing, but anything else, especially in a new environment, may lead to frustration, lost productivity, and even—the administrator's nightmare—bad user attitudes.

A site structure should also be as shallow as possible. A good rule of thumb is to limit sites to no more than three levels to help users locate the elements they need. Users commonly use what is called "read and click" to find a link on a web page. If a user has to navigate through more than three levels of menus and lists to find the content they are looking for, they may just give up in frustration, leading to those bad attitudes about the system mentioned earlier. In these cases, seize the opportunity to train these users on how to use the search feature.

The Content and Structure interface is patterned after Windows Explorer. While the tasks you perform with it are new, the interface itself should feel familiar. All site content and structure may be reorganized, moved, copied, or deleted using the Site and Content interface. List and site properties may be quickly modified using a drop-down list that appears when your mouse is hovered over an item.

1. Click the Site Actions button to open its drop-down menu and select Site Settings.

2. On Site Settings menu, click Modify All Site Settings

3. On the Site Settings page, click the Content And Structure link under the Site Administration heading to open the Site Content And Structure page, shown in Figure 6-25.

Use the Site Content and Structure page (see Figure 6-25) to move individual list items from one list to another list of the same kind, anywhere in the site. You can also remove list items, lists, and entire sites on this page.

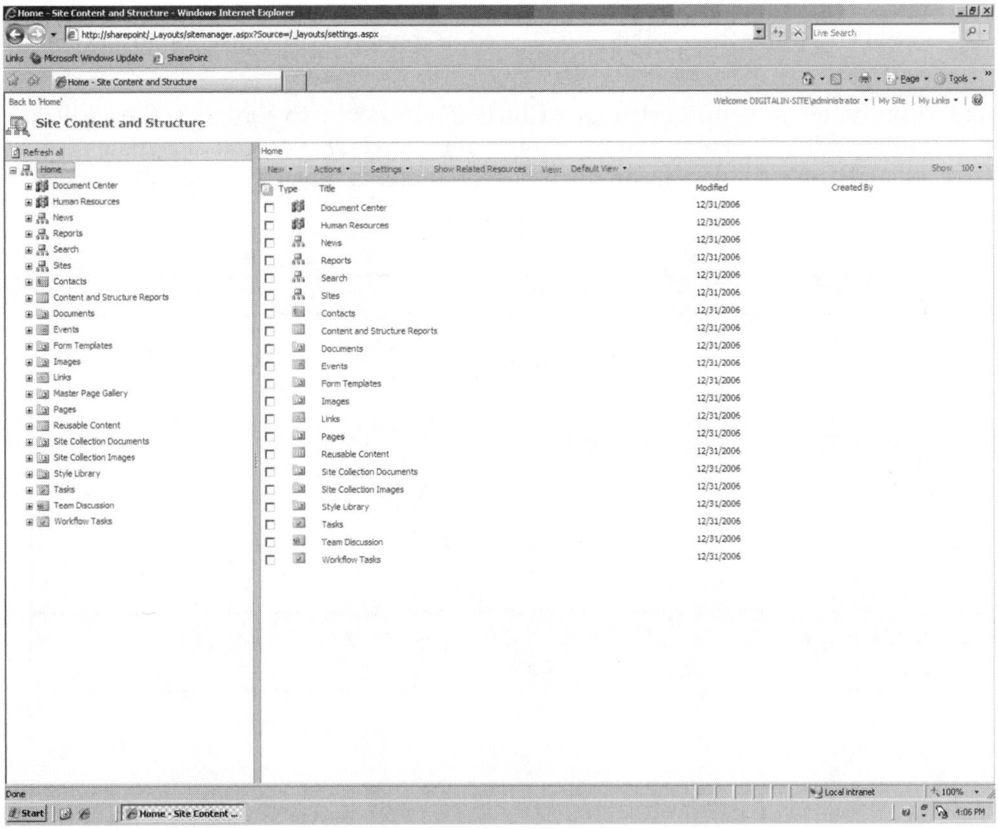

Figure 6-25. The Site Content and Structure page.

Site Collection Administration

The Site Collection Administration section of the Site Settings (see Figure 6-26) includes links that can be used to access pages that support a variety of site collection administrative functions, including:

▼ **Recycle bin** This link allows you to view and manage the contents of the recycle bin for a site collection, including the capabilities to restore a document or site from the recycle bin, delete an item from the recycle bin, or empty the recycle bin of its contents.

■ **Site collection features** Like the Site Features selection under the Site Administration heading, the Site Collection Features page (see Figure 6-27) is used to activate and deactivate several MOSS features a site collection may require, depending on its purpose and function, including workflow options.

■ **Site hierarchy** This page shows the current hierarchical relationships of the sites and pages within the active site collection.

■ **Portal site connection** This link is used to connect a site collection to a portal web site.

■ **Site connection audit settings** This link allows you to configure the audit settings for a site collection. As shown in Figure 6-28, you can designate a variety of audit actions on documents and items, as well as lists, libraries, and sites.

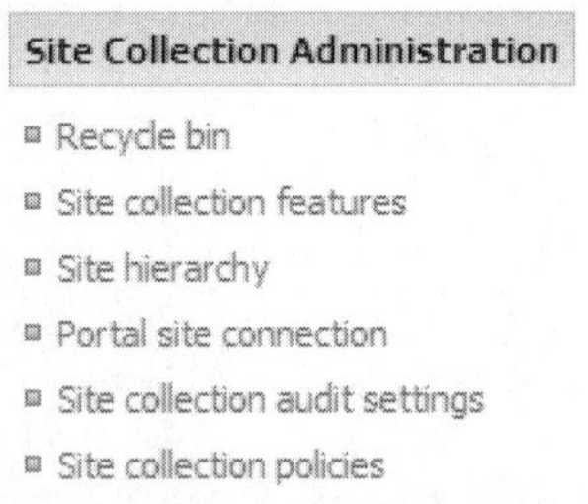

Site Collection Administration

▫ Recycle bin
▫ Site collection features
▫ Site hierarchy
▫ Portal site connection
▫ Site collection audit settings
▫ Site collection policies

Figure 6-26. The Site Collection Administration column on the Site Administration page.

Central Administration > Site Settings > Site Features

Site Collection Features

	Name		Status
	Collect Signatures Workflow Gathers signatures needed to complete a Microsoft Office document.	Deactivate	**Active**
	Disposition Approval Workflow Manages document expiration and retention by allowing participants to decide whether to retain or delete expired documents.	Deactivate	**Active**
	Office SharePoint Server Enterprise Site Collection features Features such as the business data catalog, forms services, and Excel Services, included in the Office SharePoint Server Enterprise License	Activate	
	Office SharePoint Server Publishing Infrastructure Provides centralized libraries, content types, master pages and page layouts and enables page scheduling and other publishing functionality for a site collection.	Activate	
	Office SharePoint Server Search Web Parts This feature uploads all web parts required for Search Center	Deactivate	**Active**
	Office SharePoint Server Standard Site Collection features Features such as user profiles and search, included in the Office SharePoint Server Standard License	Activate	
	Reporting Creates reports about information in Windows SharePoint Services.	Activate	
	Routing Workflows Workflows that send a document for feedback or approval.	Activate	
	Three-state workflow Use this workflow to track items in a list.	Activate	
	Translation Management Workflow Manages document translation by creating copies of the document to be translated and assigning translation tasks to translators.	Activate	

Figure 6-27.   The Site Collection Features page.

▲ **Site collection policies**   This link is used to define the records management policies for a site collection. A policy establishes the compliance issues for information retention and retirement that apply to a site from organizational, legal, and governmental regulations and guidelines. Policies define who has access to which documents, how documents are accessed, how long documents are retained, and the process used to dispose them. For more information on records management policies, see Chapter 9.

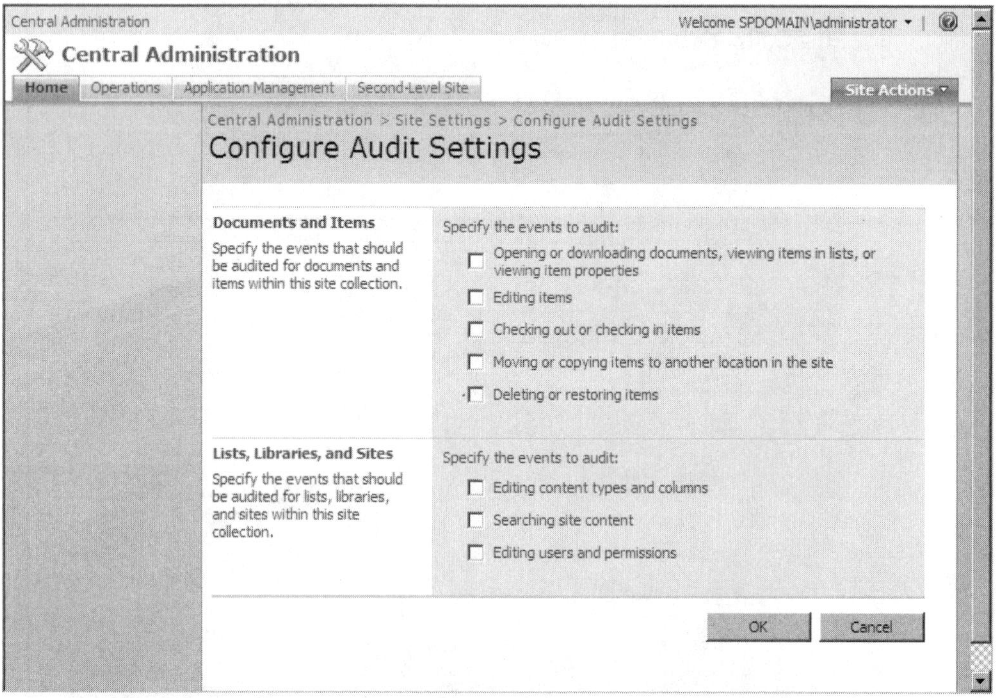

Figure 6-28.   The Configure Audit Settings page.

TIP   The Site Collection Administration section of the Site Settings page is only available on the top-level site of a site collection. Subsites have only a link to Site Collection Administration.

Create Additional Pages in a Site

In many MOSS environments, you seldom have the need to add an additional page to a site. However, should you need to create a dashboard or need to extend a site to include more Web parts or list data, you may need to add a page to a site. Should that situation arise, perform the following steps to add a page:

1.   After you have created the site collection and its top-level page, the Site Settings menu's Create option opens a slightly different Create page (see Figure 6-29). This page is slightly different than the one used to create the site collection and its top-level page.

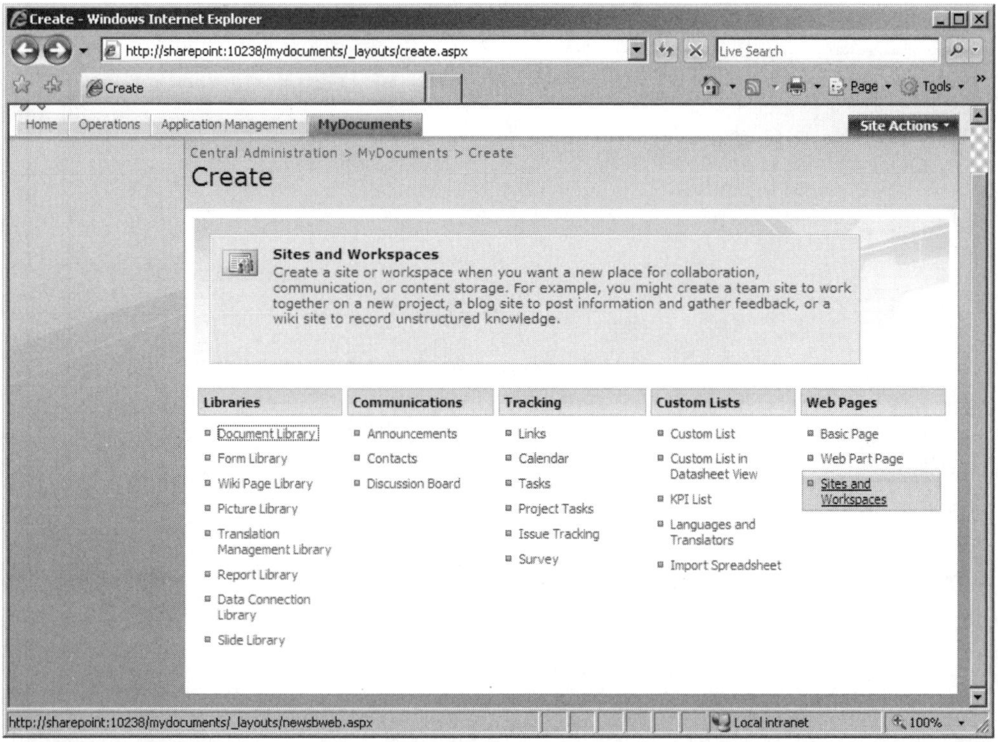

Figure 6-29.   The Create page is used for adding site pages to a site collection.

2. On the Create page, click the Sites And Workspaces link under the Web Pages heading to open the New SharePoint Site page, shown in Figure 6-30.

3. On the top portion of the New SharePoint Site page (see Figure 6-30), enter the appropriate information in each of the following fields:

   a. Enter a unique and descriptive title for the new site. Remember that the Site Title is used to identify the site in search results.

   b. Enter a statement that summarizes the site's purpose in the Description field. The description is displayed in the top panel of each site.

   c. Enter a simple page (URL) name for the new site. The URL name doesn't need to be as descriptive as the site title, but it should be easy for users to remember and type.

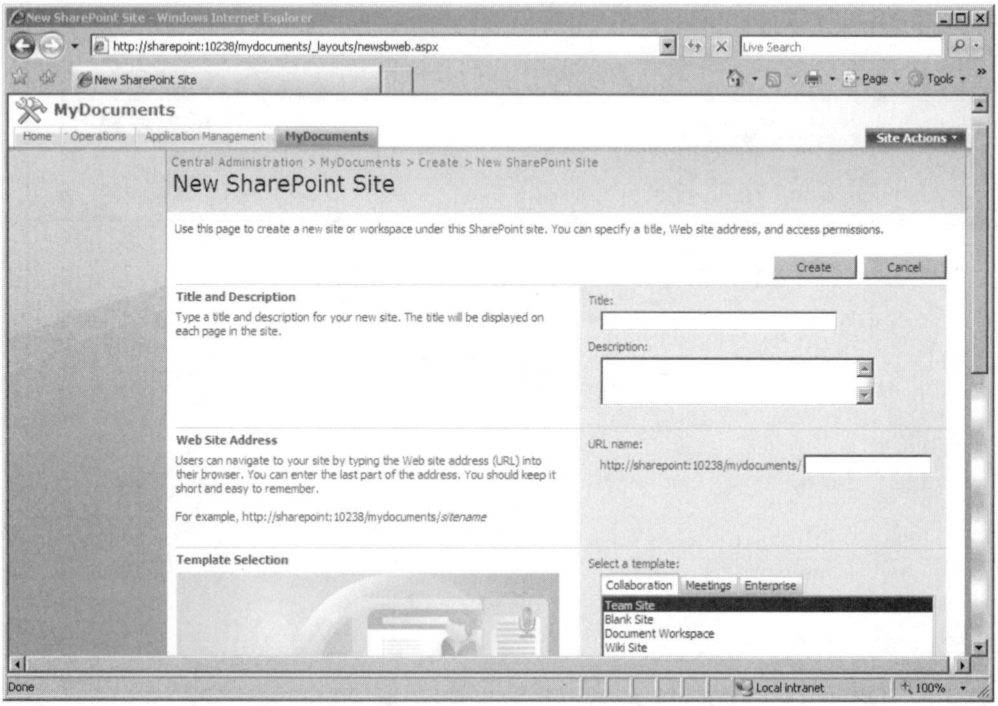

Figure 6-30. The New SharePoint Site page is used to add new pages to a site collection.

4. Scroll down the page to the Template Selection section (see Figure 6-31). Most new sites are created from a template. Notice that the Select A Template box is tabbed, with each tab listing the templates available in each grouping. Choose the tab of the group that best fits the purpose of the new site and then choose a template from its list. See the "Site Templates" section earlier in this chapter for more information.

5. In the Permissions section, choose either the Use Same Permissions As Parent Site (meaning the top-level page) option or the Use Unique Permissions option to either inherit or assign permissions to the page.

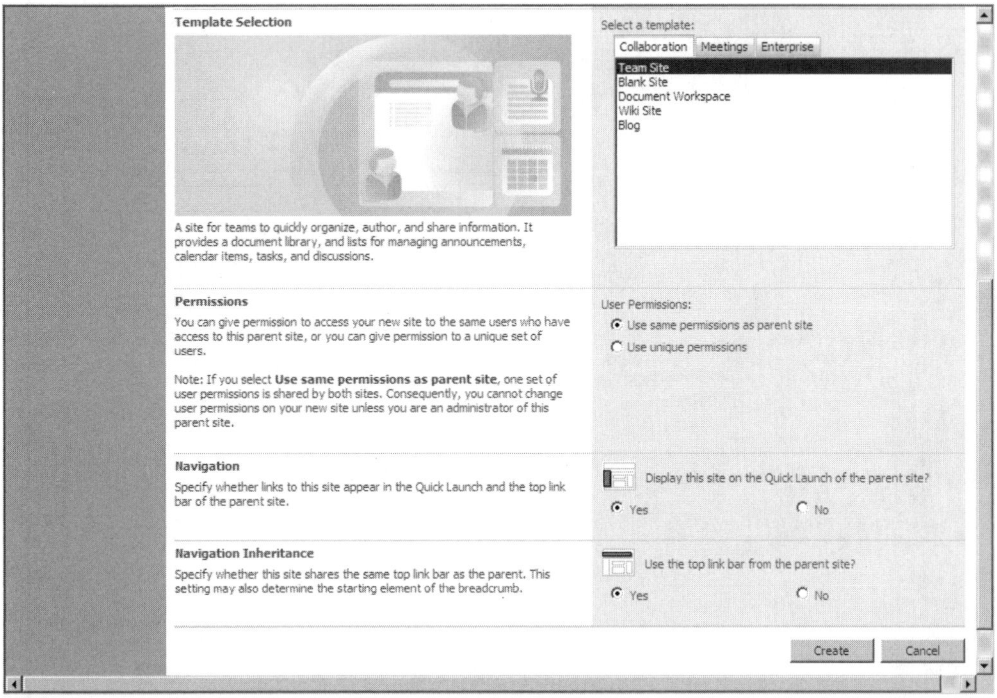

Figure 6-31. The lower portion of the New SharePoint Site page.

6. In the Navigation and Navigation Inheritance sections, indicate your preference for including the page in the Quick Launch menu and to use the top link bar from the parent page or not in either case.

7. Click the Create button to create the page.

8. If you have elected to assign unique permissions, the Set Up Groups for this site page displays (see Figure 6-32). Enter the appropriate user and group names to assign the access permissions for the page and click the OK button to continue the page creation process.

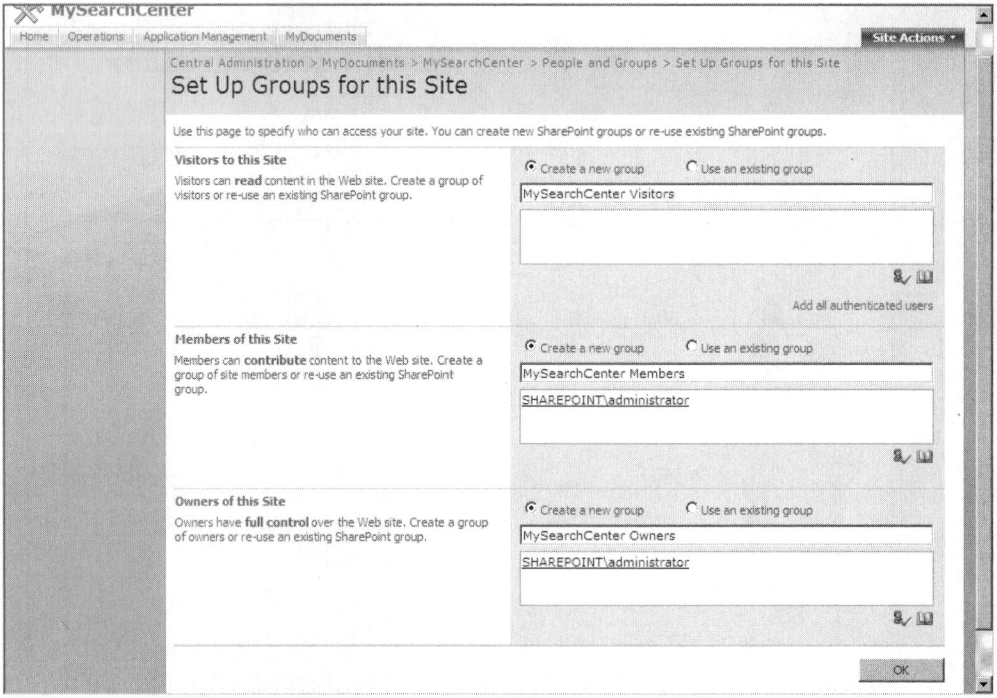

Figure 6-32. The Set Up Groups for this Site page.

SUMMARY

MOSS 2007 is a stable, mature application that runs smoothly when the administrator takes the time and care to properly configure it and monitor it closely. Because MOSS is a complex, tightly interwoven set of applications, not every single task facing an MOSS administrator is included in this chapter. However, this chapter has touched upon some of the more common administrator tasks performed in an MOSS environment. In each of the chapters that follow, additional administrator duties and responsibilities are spelled out, each focused on a specific area or functionality of MOSS.

A wide variety of administrative tools are available, including Windows Server 2003 administrative tools, such as the Services console and Active Directory. The MOSS server or server farm is administered through the Central Administration page and its tabs and menus. Individual sites are managed through a web browser by accessing the Site Settings option on the Site Actions drop-down menu available on all site pages. The administrative tasks of MOSS may be shared at any level, including MOSS users who may be identified as site-level administrators.

CHAPTER 7

MOSS Security

A MOSS administrator has two primary security concerns: securing your MOSS servers and protecting your MOSS data. A MOSS environment and especially its servers must be protected against both internal and external threats. A production MOSS environment must be protected against accidental or intentional data or document access and loss, as well as the unintended disclosure of information.

This chapter discusses how you should go about setting up the security and protective systems to guard against authorized access into your MOSS environment from both internal and external threats.

SECURITY IN A SERVER ENVIRONMENT

After MOSS has been installed (see Chapter 4), your next task should be to harden your MOSS servers before deploying them. If your servers are not hardened before they are deployed, the system could be compromised before you are able to put suitable defenses in place, which is definitely not a good thing.

Server Hardening

I'm not exactly sure where this term came from, but when you *harden* a server, you take the steps necessary to make the server as difficult as possible to break into, as in "harden your defenses." In general, the steps involved in hardening a server, or a server farm, is to perform the following six general steps:

▼ Purchase your operating system software from a known, reliable source.

■ Apply all operating system vendor-supplied software patches, service packs, and updates.

■ Identify and remove all unnecessary user accounts, software, system services, and device drivers.

■ Enable and regularly monitor access and process event logging.

■ Configure security parameters and file protections to the highest reasonable level.

▲ Disable unused usernames and passwords and frequently (yet irregularly) change all passwords, including those on default accounts.

When hardening a server environment, research to find the recommended hardening procedures for each element in the environment. For an MOSS environment, this would include Windows Server 2003, SQL Server, Internet Information Services (IIS), and MOSS itself.

And don't fall into the trap of looking only to the outside. Too often, administrators, just like people in slasher movies, focus their efforts on outside threats, when the threat may actually be from within. A security policy and plan should avoid protecting a server only against attacks from outside a network (outside its router). The reality is that the majority of security threats actually exist inside a network in the form of disgruntled users and, unfortunately, from well-meaning, yet way too curious users who simply have too much access to too many parts of a network.

You could just stop all access and have a totally secure system, but that would kind of defeat the point of the network altogether. Properly managing security is a balancing act between restriction and usability. While it's important to protect and defend a server from attack, it is equally important to set security measures that are appropriate to the level of risk. Remember that the server and its network exist to serve the needs of the users.

SECURITY IN AN MOSS ENVIRONMENT

The level of security required for your MOSS environment depends in part on the type of environment in which you deploy. An MOSS environment can be integrated into three general types of deployment:

▼ **Intranet environment**   This type of MOSS deployment typically requires the least amount of external security because the servers are typically secured behind an external firewall on a private network. In an intranet environment, the risk of external threats is generally low and the primary focus is on internal threats.

■ **Extranet environment**   This type of MOSS environment typically requires the most security because the extranet consists of two or more private networks that are interconnected via a public network (meaning the Internet). In this type of deployment, the MOSS environment must be protected from both internal and external attacks. You must ensure that the MOSS environment doesn't become an attack vector entry point or an open door for authorized intruders. As much as possible, it is very important that both of the private networks be secured to prevent unauthorized access to the MOSS environment coming from the external private network.

▲ **Internet environment**   A deployment of MOSS that connects to an external network exists to facilitate access to public data. However, inherent in this purpose is the need for very robust security measures to prevent external threats. Fortunately, the elements for this level of security are both fairly straightforward to implement and readily available.

Attack Vector

A path, port, or other means through which a hacker or a cracker can gain unauthorized access to a server or any networked node to mount an attack on the server or network is an attack vector. An attack vector can be a common, everyday network-related object, such as e-mail attachments, web pages, pop-up windows, chat rooms, and even instant messaging. The purpose of an attack vector is to take advantage of a user's trust in its delivery form to deposit a malicious payload. Common payloads in an attack vector are viruses, worms, spyware, and malware. Because they trust the delivery mechanism (the attack vector), users or administrators drop their guard and permit the attack vector to enter, allowing its payload to carry out its evil from inside a system.

Generally, safeguards like antivirus software and firewalls are effective tools against an attack vector. However, malicious users continue to evolve attack vectors to defeat these safeguards, which, unfortunately, occur sometimes at a faster rate than the safeguards themselves can evolve.

The various safeguards, technologies, systems, and other means you can use to secure your MOSS environment are discussed in the sections that follow. Not every one of these tools must be implemented in every security situation, but you should consider both its security benefits and its impact on the MOSS users when deciding on whether to use it or not.

Regardless of the level of security your deployment planning and security policies require, all MOSS environments have the following security elements in common:

▼ Physical security

■ Authorization and authentication

■ Encryption

■ Software updates (security vulnerability patches)

■ Antivirus protection

▲ Microsoft Baseline Security Analyzer (MBSA)

Each of these security elements and a discussion of some security best practices are discussed in the sections that follow.

Physical Security

You've applied the latest software updates, disabled unused services, installed the latest antivirus software, and you require your users to log in using fingerprint authentication. Is your server secure? As far as an attack from a network source, yes. However, none of these electronic or software defenses can protect your server from outright theft or vandalism. In just about every case, the first line of security is a locked door. Don't overlook the importance of physical security.

At a minimum, your MOSS servers should be protected in a room with a door that can be locked. The fewer keys the better. A locked room with a keycard reader that can be audited for who has gained access is even more secure. Auditing physical access to your servers can help enforce nonrepudiation, which means you know who has gained access to the server area and those who did cannot deny the fact, a crucial aspect of any security plan.

Authentication

Authentication determines that users are who they claim to be using some form of identification, such as a username and a password, which only the user is supposed to know. Windows Server 2003 implements a variety of authentication methods that add to the security level of an internal network and support the authentication schemes that can be configured in your MOSS environment. Without writing a book-in-a-book on Windows Server 2003 and Active Directory, the best choice for your foundation authentication method is Integrated Windows.

MOSS adds another layer of authentication methods to those of the network operating system (NOS), primarily to ensure the authentication of web browser clients and their users. MOSS can be configured to support one or more of the following authentication methods:

▼ **Anonymous authentication**   Perhaps the least secure of the available authentication methods. An anonymous user can be granted access to a web site by Internet Information Services (IIS) and given a temporary identify. The security burden for allowing anonymous authentication then falls on the authorization methods in place (authorization is discussed in the next section).

■ **Basic authentication**   Basic authentication is included in the Hypertext Transfer Protocol (HTTP) specification and is supported by most web servers and web browsers. Authentication information is exchanged unencrypted or "in the clear" and must not be considered secure. Anyone between the client and server could intercept the authentication data and replay it to gain access.

■ **Digest authentication**   This type of authentication is essentially the same as basic authentication, except that the exchange of authentication information is encrypted using an MD5 algorithm. Digest authentication is a popular authentication method for Web Distributed Authoring and Versioning (WebDAV), an extension to HTTP that supports remote collaboration of files.

■ **.NET Passport authentication**   The Microsoft .NET Passport service provides secure single sign-on for users. .NET Passport, which is implemented through the Internet Explorer browser and IIS, uses standard technologies and methods, including Secure Sockets Layer (SSL), symmetric key encryption, and the authentication features of HTTP to authenticate and then track the user.

▲ **Client certificate mapping**   This is an optional authentication scheme and can be enabled on a system where SSL is in use to provide a two-layer authentication process. The client requesting access must have a public key (X.509) certificate. With a valid certificate, the user is permitted to move to the second-level by entering a username and password. This type of authentication is common to extranets.

More secure implementations of MOSS may require additional authentication methods such as multifactor and biometric authorization. Multifactor authentication and authorization, which is also called strong authentication, involves the use of several forms of user identification, including something that identifies who the user is (like a fingerprint or retinal scan), something the user has (like a security token or even a cell phone), and something the user knows (like a password or personal identification number [PIN]). Biometric authentication uses some physical aspect of the user's body, such as fingerprints, retinal scan, or voice print) to identify and authorize the user.

Authorization

Once a user has been authenticated, he or she then must be authorized. Authorization is used to determine if an authenticated user should be granted or denied access to a specific resource. Now that you know who they are, just what should they be able to access? The key to understanding the role played by user/group authorization in MOSS security is to understand first that authorization is based on permission.

In the MOSS environment, the foundation for authorizing an authenticated user is to determine the site group(s) in which the user is a member. Access to any SharePoint site for a user is based on which site groups the user is included in. Thus, what the user can do with the information to which he or she has access is then controlled by the permissions associated, either directly or indirectly, with those groups. Site groups are role-based, which means the users included as members of a site group perform essentially the same tasks and require access to, and authorized actions on, the same types of content.

The hierarchy of user and site group permissions in MOSS exists in four levels:

1. **Individual users**   Permissions for individual users can be directly added, edited, or deleted from a site collection or subsite, granting, modifying, or removing their authorization to the site.

2. **Active Directory groups**   On a Windows Server 2003 server, users are assigned to one or more security groups within the Active Directory services. Like individual users, Active Directory groups can be directly added, edited, or deleted from a site collection or subsite, granting, modifying, or removing their authorization to the site.

3. **Cross-site groups**   A cross-site group is an easy way to group those users who collaborate frequently on several sites within a site collection. Permissions are assigned to a cross-site group the same way they are to single users in a site collection.

4. **Anonymous access** While not typically used in an MOSS environment looking to secure its site collections, permission to access a site collection or one or more of its subsites can be universally granted to all users.

Authorization in an MOSS environment is controlled through the definition of site groups and the permission levels assigned to them. See the section entitled "Site Collection and Site Security" later in this chapter for more information on this topic.

Encryption

Encryption is the process of encoding information for the purpose of making it unusable and unreadable to anyone but the sender and receiver. Encryption is particularly valuable to an MOSS environment's security. Encryption can be a useful tool in an MOSS intranet environment, but it is an essential part of your security scheme for MOSS in an extranet or Internet deployment.

While encryption can be a very complex topic, it is something you must consider as a part of the security for an MOSS environment. Several types of encryption can be applied at all levels of MOSS data and documents. You should investigate each of the encryption technologies MOSS supports and consider whether each or all are appropriate for protecting your MOSS content.

The encryption technologies with which MOSS is compatible are as follows:

▼ **Transport-Level Security (TLS)** Encrypts data at the network transport level

■ **Virtual Private Networks (VPN)** A secured connection methodology that allows remote users to connect to an intranet using public network facilities

■ **Point-to-Point Tunneling Protocol (PPTP)** A VPN protocol that creates an encrypted "tunnel" network between two points across a public network

■ **Layer 2 Tunneling Protocol (L2TP)** An arguably more advanced (over PPTP) VPN protocol

■ **Public Key Infrastructure (PKI)** A certificate-based encryption method that applies non-reversible keys

■ **Secure Socket Layer (SSL)** An encrypted instance of Hypertext Transfer Protocol (HTTP)

■ **Encrypted File System (EFS)** The Microsoft Windows method for encrypting a computer's file system that can provide the last line of defense

▲ **IP Security (IPSec)** A Transmission Control Protocol/Internet Protocol (TCP/IP) protocol that employs encryption to move data between a server and a client

Your MOSS environment may require any number of these encryption methods if the possibility exists that sensitive data may be intercepted by hackers anywhere between the MOSS server and the intended user's client. This can include unauthorized disclosure of data on an intranet.

Security Updates

Your first concern with any new software installation should be to check for security updates and service packs for each of the system software components running on your servers, including Windows Server 2003, Microsoft Office 2007, SQL Server, and MOSS.

Microsoft Windows Server 2003 can be configured to receive Automatic Updates from Microsoft. You can choose from four options to receive automatic updates:

▼ Automatic (recommended).

■ Download updates for me, but let me choose when to install them.

■ Notify me but don't automatically download or install them.

▲ Turn off Automatic Updates.

If you select automatic (see Figure 7-1), you can choose to download updates at a specific time every day, or once a week on a specific day, such as Sunday. Automatic Update will

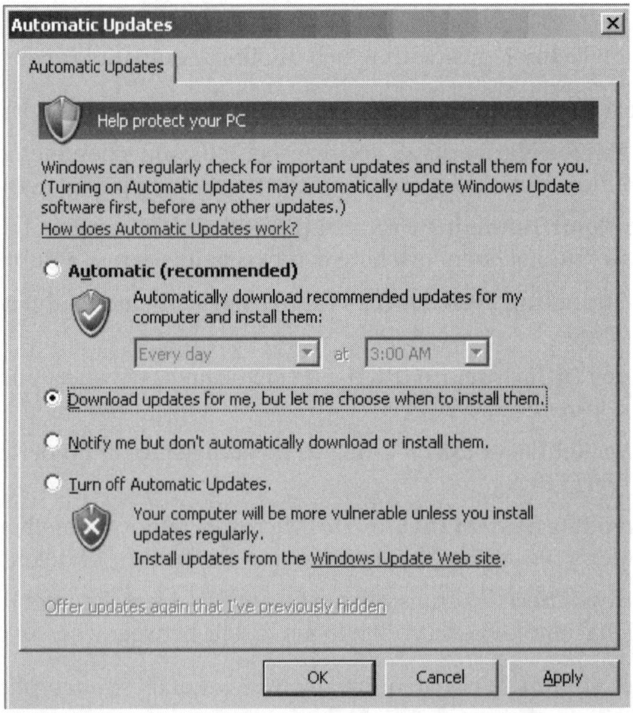

Figure 7-1. Configuring Automatic Updates.

download and install any available updates and you will be automatically protected, unless a reboot is required to complete the installation. Keep in mind that the automatic setting still requires some administrative oversight.

Some administrators prefer to review updates before installing them, in which case the second and third options allow you more control over which updates are installed and when they are installed. This is a good compromise if you require additional testing or approval before installing updates. You may choose to turn off automatic updates if you have another process for installing updates or wish to manually manage updates.

Antivirus

No server environment is complete without some form of antivirus protection. Antivirus software protects the server at the file level, but some antivirus programs can be configured to work directly with MOSS at the library Web Part level.

When MOSS is configured to work with a compatible antivirus program, any files that are added to, or viewed from, a library will be scanned for viruses, and an appropriate action will be taken if a virus is found. These actions include attempting to remove the virus from the file or blocking the file from being accessed.

More on this topic later in the chapter in the section entitled "Applying Antivirus."

Microsoft Baseline Security Analyzer

The Microsoft Baseline Security Analyzer (MBSA) is a free downloadable tool that can be used to scan your MOSS environment for common security vulnerabilities, incorrectly configured security options, and missing security updates and operating system service packs.

1. Download and install the latest version of MBSA at http://www.microsoft .com/mbsa.

2. Launch the MBSA. The installation should create a desktop icon, as well as add MBSA to the Start menu under All Programs.

3. On the MBSA start page (see Figure 7-2), click the Scan A Computer link and specify the computer to be scanned by its computer name or IP address.

4. Click the Start Scan link. MBSA connects to Microsoft to download updated security information and then begin scanning your computer. The scan can be resource intensive at times, but doesn't take very long to run. When the scan is complete, a comprehensive report is generated. The report (see Figure 7-3) can be copied or printed for future reference as you resolve your existing security issues.

5. Correct any deficiencies the report identifies promptly.

It is a good habit to periodically run MBSA to analyze your MOSS servers and ensure your security environment has not changed.

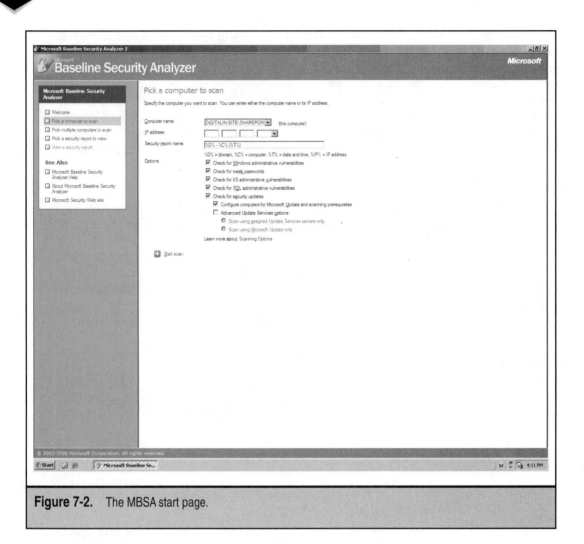

Figure 7-2. The MBSA start page.

Security Best Practices

In addition to the technologies and services discussed in this section, there are additional security best practices you should consider implementing to protect your MOSS servers:

▼ Restrict console logon to administrators only.

■ Consider eliminating hardware that uses removable media.

■ Use complex passwords. A complex password consists of eight or more characters and is a mix of upper- and lowercase letters, numbers, and symbols.

■ Don't allow existing passwords to be reused.

■ Consider implementing an account lockout policy to limit the effectiveness of a hacker guessing passwords through brute force.

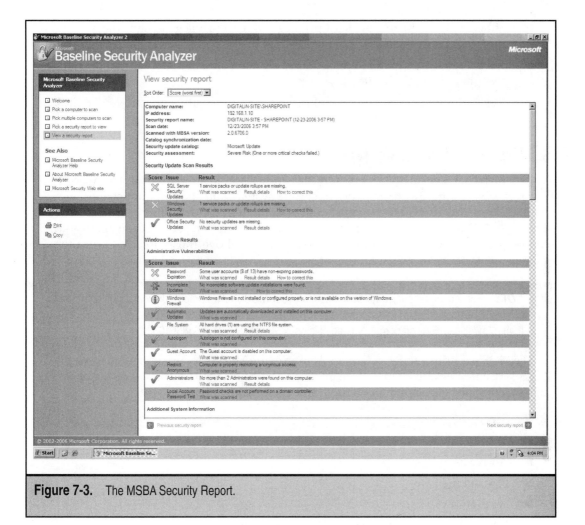

Figure 7-3. The MSBA Security Report.

- Restrict BIOS access with a password.
- Disable unused services. By default, all MOSS web front-end and applications servers run the following services:
    - Office MOSS Server Search
    - Windows MOSS Services Administrator
    - Windows MOSS Services Search
    - Windows MOSS Services Timer
    - Windows MOSS Services Tracing
    - Windows MOSS Services VSS Writer

- Adhere to the principle of "least privilege." (Least privilege assigns the minimum permissions to a user to accomplish their job duties.)

- Use the *run as* command to temporarily elevate your standard account to perform administrative tasks.

- ▲ Use auditing to log successful and failed access to sensitive or confidential files.

MOSS SECURITY SETTINGS

Even if you have taken all of the necessary steps described so far in this chapter to secure your server, server hardware, network operating system, and support applications, you should also secure MOSS itself against attacks, data loss, and unauthorized disclosure of content. MOSS includes a number of security configuration settings you can use to enforce your security planning and policies over and above those used to secure the other elements of the MOSS environment.

NOTE For a comprehensive guide to securing your MOSS environment, download the document "Plan and Design for Security (Windows SharePoint Services and Office SharePoint Server combined)" from http://office.microsoft.com/download/afile.aspx?AssetID=AM101638561033.

The MOSS security settings, which apply to an entire MOSS site, are configured using the MOSS 3.0 Central Administration page interface. On the MOSS 3.0 Central Administration page's Operations tab, shown in Figure 7-4, the following options are listed:

- ▼ Service accounts
- Information Rights Management (IRM)
- Antivirus
- Blocked file types
- Farm administrators
- Information management policy configuration
- Single sign-on
- ▲ Web Parts security

Each of these settings options is discussed in the following sections, along with two other areas you should use and understand to further secure your MOSS environment: MOSS site collection and site security, and the non-native content sources.

Service Accounts

MOSS services can be configured to run under the context of two predefined services accounts: Local Service or Network Service. However, many security-conscious organizations have a policy that disallows the use of local service accounts. In this case, each service can be configured to use whichever username and password you desire.

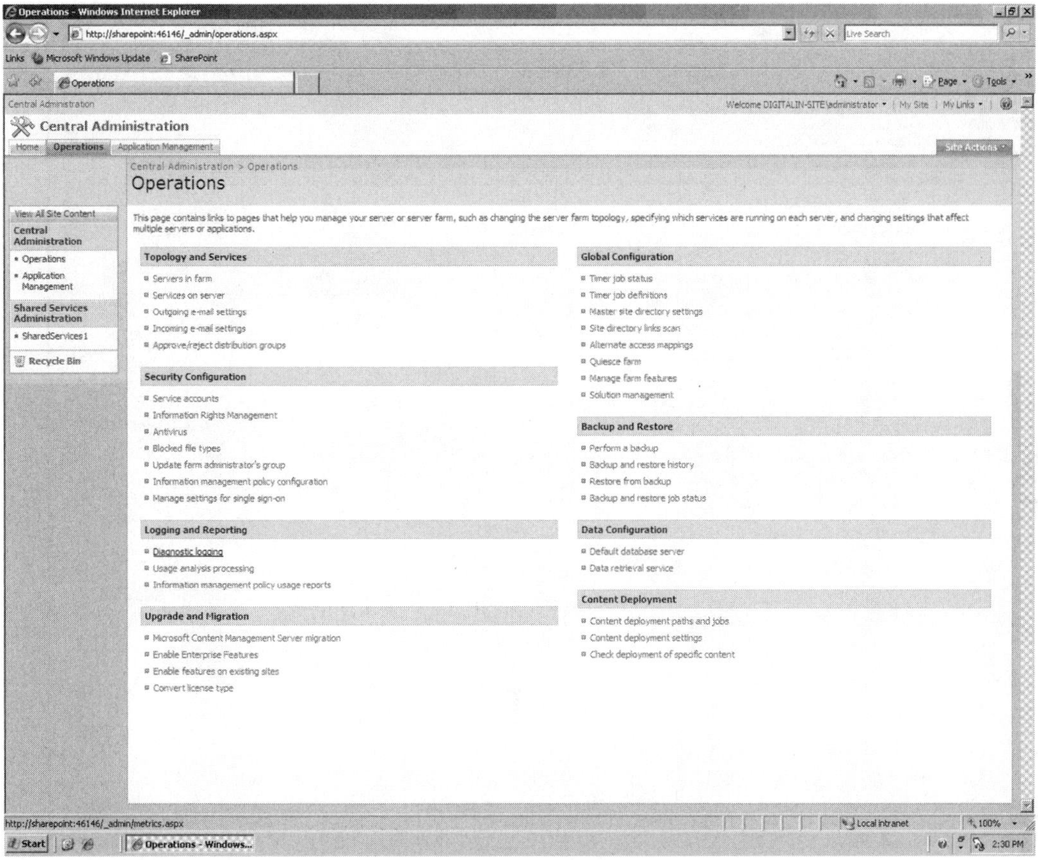

Figure 7-4.   The MOSS Central Administration page's Operations tab.

The following MOSS services can be configured on the Service Accounts settings page (see Figure 7-5):

▼   Document Conversions Launcher Service

■   Document Conversions Load Balancer Service

▲   Single Sign-on Services

Likewise, you can configure which application pool each service will run under. Each application pool, for all effective purposes is a separate and distinct instance of the IIS web server.

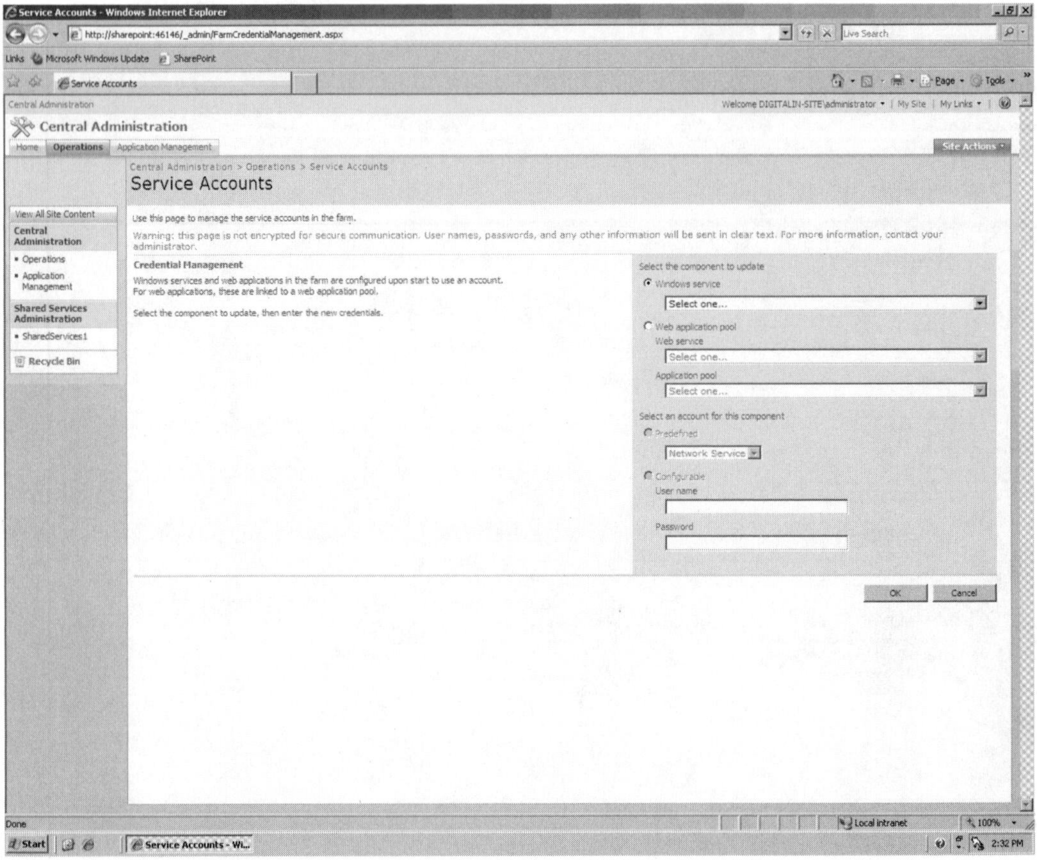

Figure 7-5. The Service Accounts settings page.

Information Rights Management

Information Rights Management is a Microsoft Office technology that restricts what can be done to a file once it has been downloaded. The creator of a document or an administrator can assign file-level permissions that control who can access a document or an e-mail message and specifically what each allowed user can do with it. The permissions assigned to a document through IRM are stored as a part of the document and control printing, copying, and even forwarding.

Traditionally, once a file was downloaded, there was no limit to what a user could do with that file. For example, you draft a confidential memo using Microsoft Word. You send that memo as an e-mail attachment to a co-worker for review. Before the application of IRM, when that Word document arrives in your co-worker's inbox, he or she could print it, make copies of it, modify the file, or forward it to another person. However, IRM allows you to place restrictions on what a user can do with a particular file. IRM encrypts the file, which makes it useless outside of applications not supporting IRM, making it impossible to defeat the restrictions placed on the file.

TIP IRM is a separate Microsoft Office product to which MOSS is able to integrate. For more information on IRM, visit this web site:
http://office.microsoft.com/en-us/ork2003/CH011480781033.aspx.

Applying Antivirus

Once you have installed MOSS-compatible antivirus software, you can configure MOSS to scan documents when they are uploaded to a document library. You also have the option to scan documents downloaded from a document library. If a document is determined to have a virus, you can attempt to clean the infected document. Strangely enough, you also have the option to allow users to download infected files.

Additional antivirus settings include how long the antivirus scanner should run when scanning documents. If MOSS becomes unresponsive during antivirus scanning, you can also decrease the number of threads dedicated to virus scanning to improve MOSS performance.

NOTE You must install a compatible antivirus program on every web front-end server in your MOSS environment before configuring antivirus settings in MOSS.

To access the security configuration area to set up antivirus protection, perform the following steps:

1. Open MOSS 3.0 Central Administration.

2. Click the Operations tab.

3. Click the Antivirus link under Security Configuration (shown in Figure 7-6).

Blocked File Types

As an MOSS administrator, you are ultimately responsible for the content uploaded to your MOSS servers. A good number of file types that could be cause for concern are blocked by default. Blocked file types are listed by file extension.

You should review this list, both for additional files to block and for file types blocked by default but that you wish to allow. To do so, perform the following steps:

1. Open MOSS 3.0 Central Administration.

2. Click the Operations tab.

3. Click the Blocked File Types link under Security Configuration to display the Blocked File Types page (see Figure 7-7).

4. Modify the list by adding or deleting the file type extensions listed.

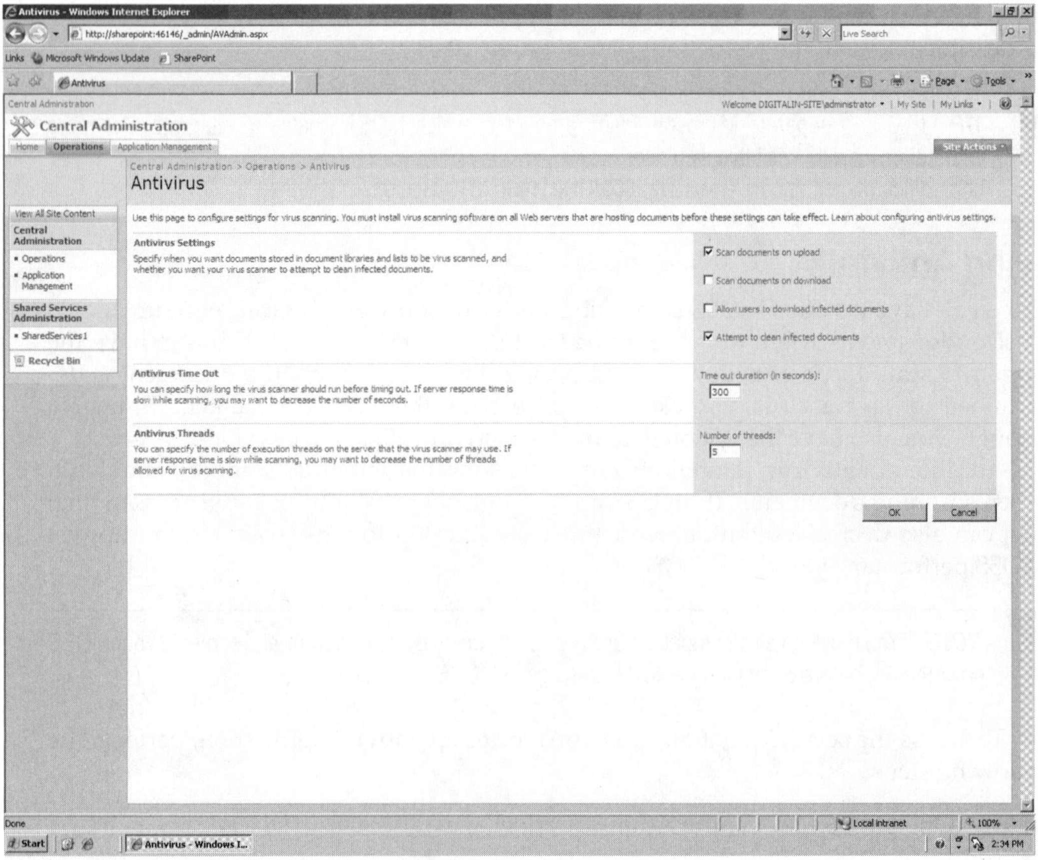

Figure 7-6.   The Antivirus settings page.

Farm Administrators Group Membership

If your MOSS environment is installed on a server farm, it is important to limit the membership to the Farm Administrators group. Users granted membership in the Farm Administrators group have full access to MOSS, its sites, and its contents, which means that Farm Administrators can modify or change any MOSS configuration setting and view and take ownership of all SharePoint content. The members of the administration security groups on both the local server and the domain controller are automatically assigned to the Farm Administrators group.

Due to the power inherent for members of the Farm Administrators group, this group should contain the least number of users as possible to adequately support your MOSS environment. You should review this group membership to ensure an unintended membership didn't occur as a result.

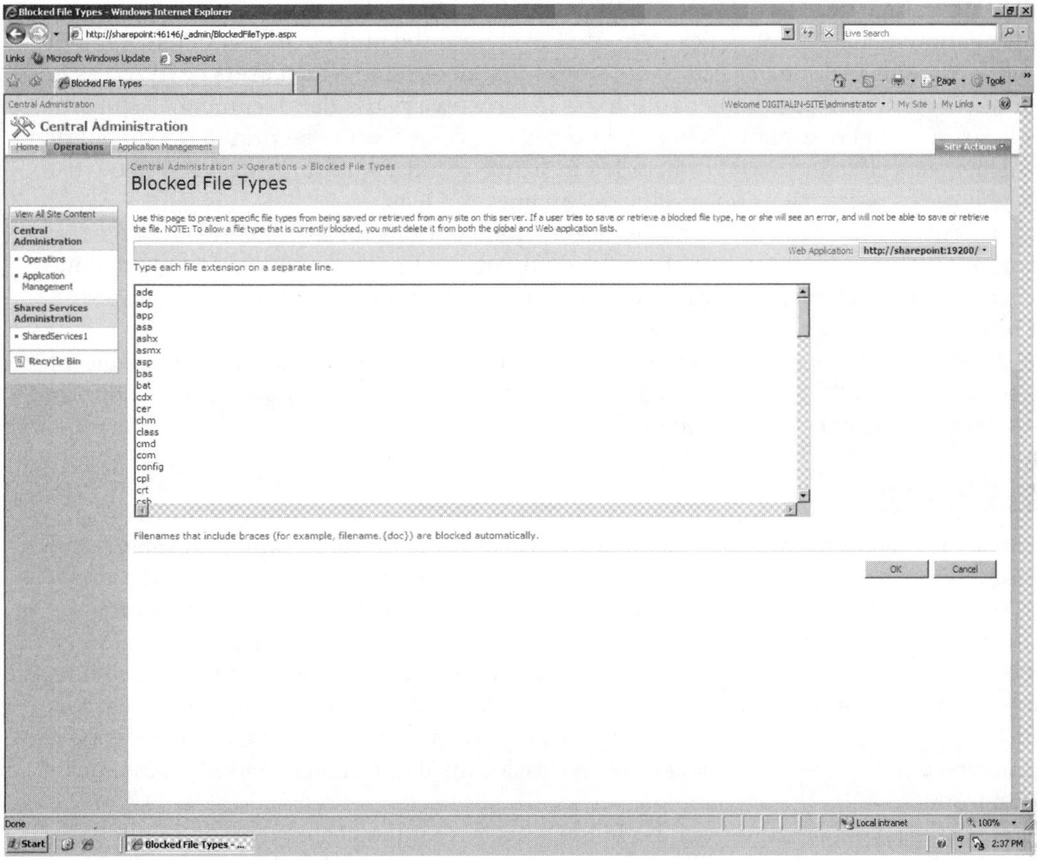

Figure 7-7. The Blocked File Types page.

The Update Farm Administrator's Group options on the SharePoint Central Administration page include adding and removing users and site groups, notifying selected users by e-mail, or even calling selected users if you have a Session Initiation Protocol (SIP)-enabled telephony device.

Session Initiation Protocol (SIP)

The Session Initiation Protocol (SIP) is an Internet Protocol (IP) text-based telephony protocol based on Hypertext Transfer Protocol (HTTP) and Multipurpose Internet Mail Extensions (MIME). SIP is primarily employed for real-time Voice over IP (VoIP) calls using human readable Uniform Resource Locators (URLs), such as sip:admin@mysharepoint.com.

Information Management Policy Configuration

Information management policies are used to control the policies of SharePoint content and documents included in lists and libraries that determine which users have access to certain documents and whether auditing is in force on a particular document. Document policies in SharePoint play a key role in whether or not a user can print a document or whether a specific document is included in search results. Auditing policies set how the system tracks user actions on specific documents and lists.

Information management policies also include options for expiration and barcodes. Expiration allows for the automatic deletion or archiving of a document at a given date. Barcodes can be inserted into Microsoft Office documents and specific business processes. A nice feature of MOSS is that these barcodes are searchable.

MOSS information management policy features can be set to either available or decommissioned. When a feature is decommissioned, it may not be applied to new policies, but it remains in effect for existing policies.

Single Sign-On

In many business environments, complex passwords are in use on multiple systems and applications, resulting in multiple passwords (and possibly usernames) for the users. A common complaint of users in such an environment is that complex passwords are difficult to remember. This situation often leads to users writing their passwords down and effectively undermining the security the password was attempting to provide. To minimize the impact of multiple complex passwords on the user's ability to access information quickly and efficiently, MOSS supports a single sign-on feature. However, as is typically the case, what makes access easier for the user, also makes access easier for intruders.

The concept of single sign-on is simple: a user is authenticated once and only once, commonly on a portal. From that point forward, any additional authentication required by other systems is performed on behalf of the user through the single sign-on service. Single sign-on capitalizes on the strength of computers to store, recall, and protect complex passwords, and attempts to overcome the inherent weakness of users who are reluctant to use them.

As additional applications and systems are added to the user environment, adding additional complex passwords, they can be added to the MOSS single sign-on service and added to the users' portals.

Web Parts Security

By default, SharePoint users are allowed to create connections between separate Web Parts to allow one Web Part to export some or all of its data to another Web Part. Share-Point users are also able, by default, to browse the Online Web Part Gallery to search, browse, and add Web Parts to Web Part Pages. If you determine that either of these capabilities is a security risk, either or both features can be disabled using Application Management.

To access MOSS Application Management:

1. On the SharePoint Central Administration page, open the Application Management tab.

2. Click the Application Security option and choose Security for Web Part pages (see Figure 7-8).

3. Choose the appropriate Web security area to enable and disable these functions.

Aside from granting permissions at the site-level in MOSS, you can specify unique permissions to a list or library that are more restrictive than the permissions assigned to the entire web site, which is the common action taken.

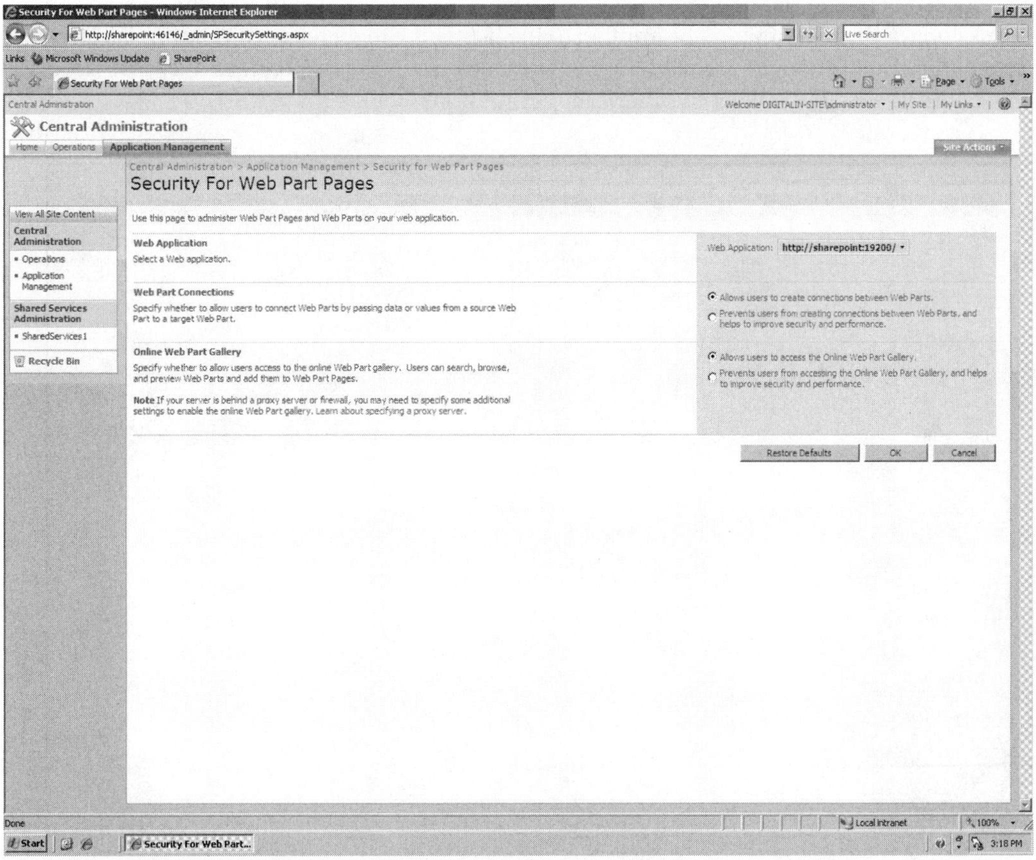

Figure 7-8. The Security For Web Part pages administrative page.

To change the permissions assigned to a list:

1. From the site containing the list, choose the list you wish to manage from the List portion of the Quick Launch menu. (You might want to provide an alternate description to get to a list's settings through Site Settings in case the list is not in the QLM.)

2. Click the Settings option to display its drop-down list.

3. Select List Settings.

4. Click the Permissions For This List link under Permissions and Management on the List Settings page.

At this point, if you wish to assign unique permissions to the list, it must stop inheriting its permissions from the site or its parent list. The result of breaking the inheritance relationship between the list and the site or parent list is that any future changes to the permissions of the parent won't be applied to the list. This can increase your administrative burden if frequent changes are made to the site, because the same changes may also need to be made to each list not set to inherit its permissions.

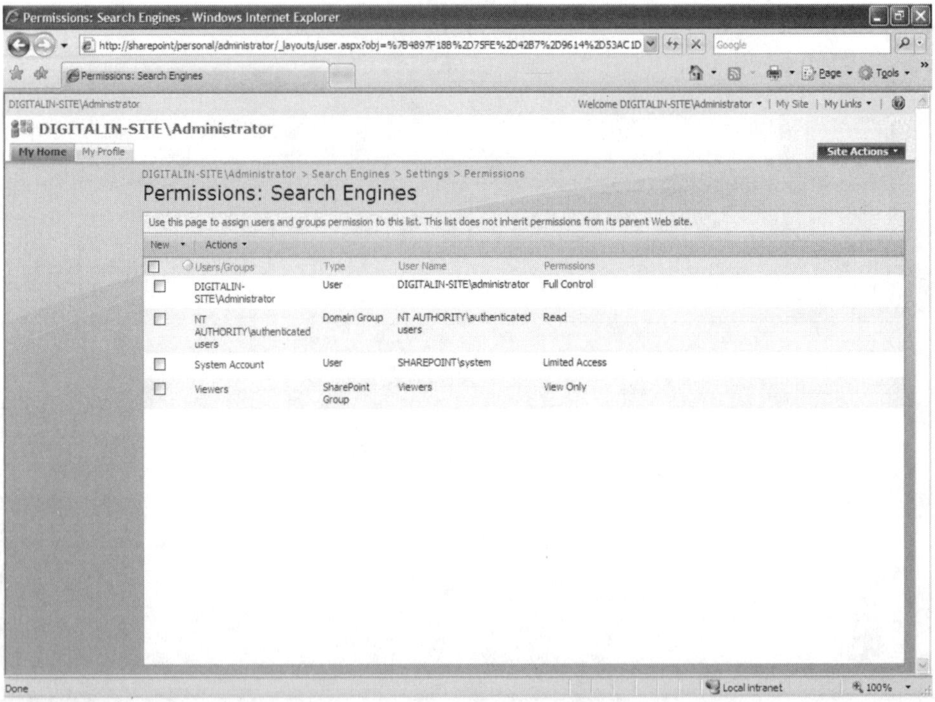

Figure 7-9.   The Search Engines List with unique list permissions.

If you wish to proceed:

5. Open the Actions drop-down menu and select Edit Permissions. You will receive a warning about creating unique permissions, as discussed earlier.

6. Click OK.

The parent permissions are copied and applied to the active list as its unique permissions, which can then be removed, changed, or added to without affecting the parent site, as illustrated in Figure 7-9.

SITE COLLECTION AND SITE SECURITY

While MOSS integrates with Windows Server 2003 Active Directory, allowing administrators to assign MOSS permissions to domain users and security groups, MOSS also defines its own security groups. MOSS security groups are role-based and allow MOSS administrators to quickly assign MOSS permissions to groups of users or individual users based on the role of the group or user in relation to the content in MOSS.

Site Groups

A site group is essentially a collection of user permissions that, depending on the site template used to create a site, authorizes site users to access site elements and content and perform a certain set of actions. For example, when a new top-level site is created, three default site groups are created, depending on the site template used: Visitors, Members, and Owners. The name of the site group reflects the site to which the site group is created and will be something like Shared Documents Visitors, Shared Documents Members, and Shared Documents Owners. Obviously, each of the site groups has a different level of permissions to permit or deny their actions on the site.

NOTE Another level of site group permissions exists within the Shared Services Provider (SSP). However, only the domain administrator has any default permissions in the SSP.

Site groups are created specifically to a particular site. A user can belong to multiple site groups by inclusion in a cross-site group. MOSS doesn't define any cross-site groups by default, and in a fairly small MOSS environment, it isn't likely you would need to create any. However, in larger environments, you may have the need to use cross-site groups to organize group memberships.

Site Permission Levels

Depending on the template used to create a site, MOSS can define up to nine default site permission levels that control what actions or access an owner or member of a site group can do. These site permission levels include the following:

▼ Approvers

■ Designers

■ Hierarchy Managers

- Quick Deploy Users
- Restricted Readers
- \<Site\> Members
- \<Site\> Owners
- \<Site\> Visitors
- ▲ Authenticated Users

The name of each of these site permission levels is fairly self-descriptive of just what the users assigned one or more of the permission levels can do. The permission level assigned to a site group or user also depends on the type or level of the site in question. Table 7-1 lists the default user rights for each of these site groups for the two primary SharePoint site levels: regular web site and Central Administration.

The hierarchy of user permissions and group membership in an MOSS environment starts with the permissions granted to the user at login by Windows Server 2003 (see Figure 7-10), based on the Windows security group to which the user belongs. If the user has been added to a cross-site group, the user is assigned the user rights from the sites to which he or she has been granted access. If the user is not included in a cross-site group, the user is then assigned the permissions of the site at the level the user has been granted for working with the site contents.

Group Permissions

You are certainly not limited to using only the default groups defined by MOSS and their preset permissions. You can modify the permissions of the default groups and create additional groups as needed in your particular MOSS environment.

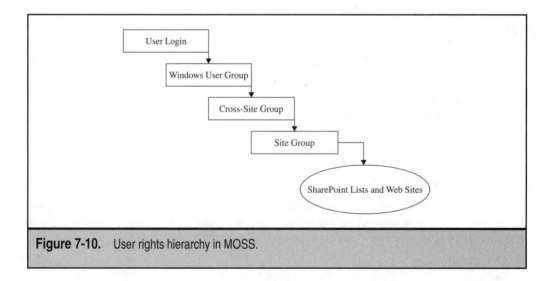

Figure 7-10.   User rights hierarchy in MOSS.

Permission Level	Site Group(s)	Default User Permissions
Full Control	\<site\> Owner Farm Administrators BUILTIN\ Administrators	All web designer site group rights Manage site groups Manage permissions Monitor usage data
Design	Designers	All contributor site group rights Create and customize site pages Manage lists
Contribute	\<site\> Members	All reader site group rights Add, edit, and delete content items Manage private Web Parts and personal views Browse directories Create cross-site groups
Read	\<site\> Visitors	Create sites for personal use View pages View items
Limited Access	Approvers Designers Hierarchy Managers Quick Deploy Users Restricted Readers Authenticated Users	All reader site group rights View specific lists, document libraries, list items, folders, or documents as permitted
Approve	Approvers	Edit and approve pages, lists, and documents
Manage Hierarchy	Hierarchy Managers	Create and customize site pages Edit pages, list items, and documents
Restricted Read	Restricted Readers	View specific lists, document libraries, list items, folders, or documents as permitted Cannot view historical versions of elements

Table 7-1.   MOSS Default Site Group Permission Levels

To view or manage the permissions assigned to an MOSS group, do the following:

1. On the Site Collection's top-level site page, click Site Actions.

2. From the drop-down menu, select Site Settings and then select People and Groups to display a list of the existing groups in the Quick Launch menu in the left-hand panel of the page.

3. To view the permissions assigned to a particular group, click the name of the site group you wish to view. The People and Groups administration page for the group chosen displays (see Figure 7-11).

4. To add a user to an existing group, click New and then select Add Users to display the Add Users administrative page (shown in Figure 7-12).

5. Enter the data required to create the user, including User/Group name, the group you wish to add the user to, and assign the permissions of that group to the user or the permissions you wish to directly assign to the user.

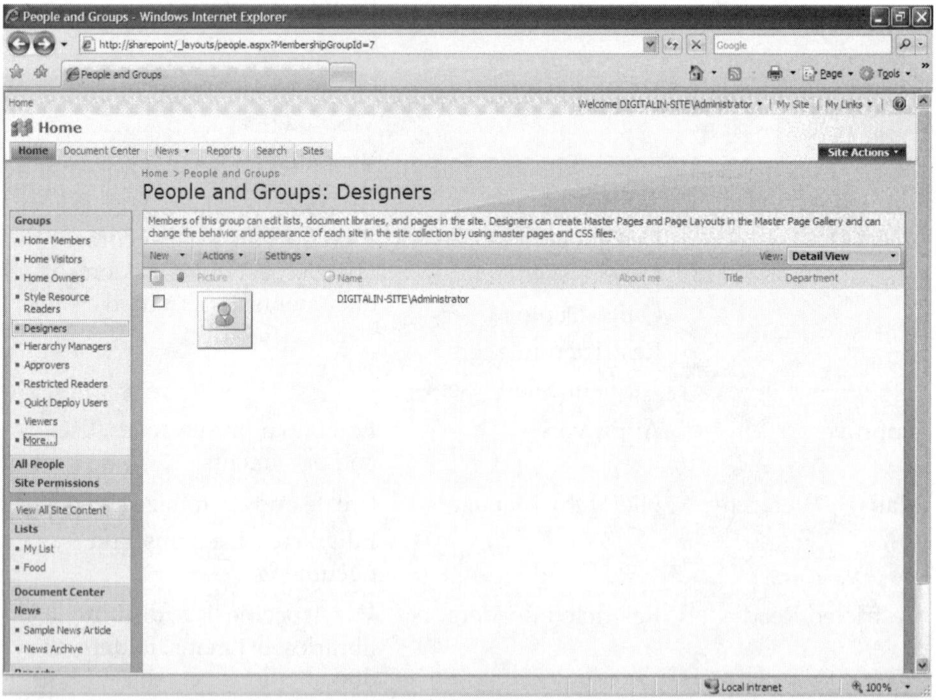

Figure 7-11. The People and Groups page.

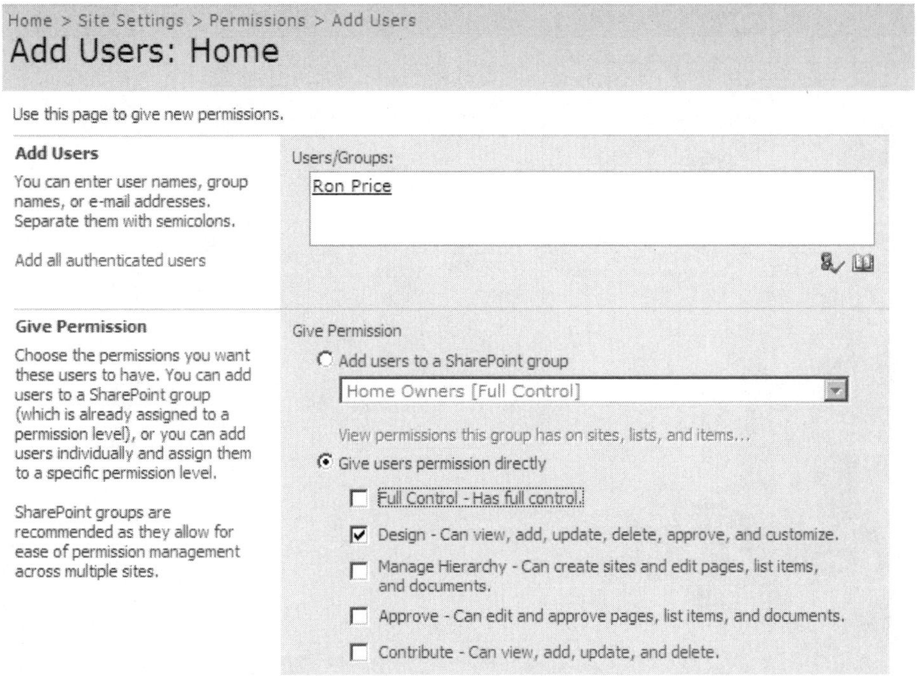

Home > Site Settings > Permissions > Add Users

Add Users: Home

Use this page to give new permissions.

Add Users

You can enter user names, group names, or e-mail addresses. Separate them with semicolons.

Add all authenticated users

Users/Groups:

Ron Price

Give Permission

Choose the permissions you want these users to have. You can add users to a SharePoint group (which is already assigned to a permission level), or you can add users individually and assign them to a specific permission level.

SharePoint groups are recommended as they allow for ease of permission management across multiple sites.

Give Permission

○ Add users to a SharePoint group

Home Owners [Full Control]

View permissions this group has on sites, lists, and items...

● Give users permission directly

☐ Full Control - Has full control.

☑ Design - Can view, add, update, delete, approve, and customize.

☐ Manage Hierarchy - Can create sites and edit pages, list items, and documents.

☐ Approve - Can edit and approve pages, list items, and documents.

☐ Contribute - Can view, add, update, and delete.

Figure 7-12.   The Add Users administrative page.

You can also create a new MOSS group and directly assign MOSS permissions to it. Creating a new MOSS group allows you to create advanced security roles that can be used to quickly assign complex permission sets to users and security groups.

To create a new user group:

1. On the SharePoint Central Administration page, click Site Actions.

2. From the drop-down menu, select Site Settings and then select People and Groups.

3. Click New and choose New Group from the drop-down menu to display the New Group page (see Figure 7-13).

4. Enter a name for the group, assign the group an owner (group owners can change group settings, and add, remove, and manage the group's users), and assign the group settings (see Figure 7-16).

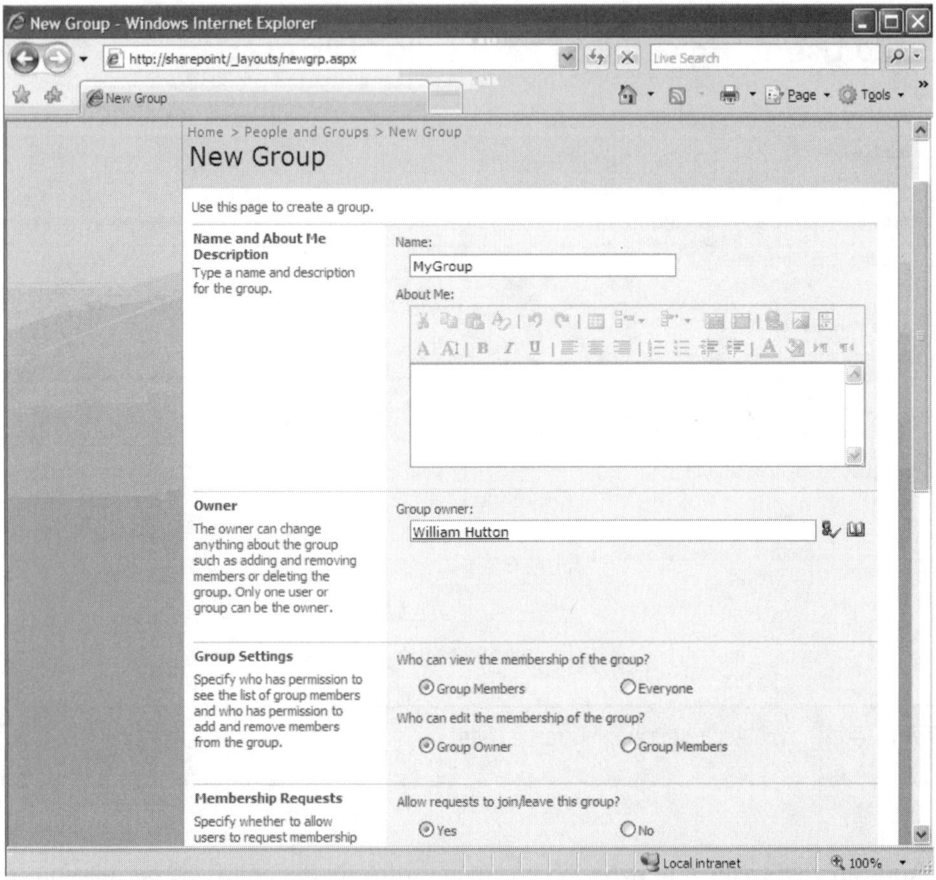

Figure 7-13. The New Group administration page.

5. Assign membership request settings and indicate whether users are to be auto-accepted into the group (see Figure 7-17).

   By default, users cannot request to join or leave a group, but if you choose to allow users to request to join a group, you need to enter an e-mail address where such requests are to be sent.

6. Assign specific permissions to the group by checking the appropriate checkboxes.

7. Click Create.

It can be useful to allow users to request to join a group. When users encounter a site they wish to access but can't, they can request to join a group that does have such permissions. MOSS then sends an e-mail to the group owner with the request. The group owner can then automatically add the user simply by clicking a link included in the e-mail. If the group owner doesn't wish to add the user, no further action need be taken. The request to join a group feature can ease some of the administrative burden of the SharePoint administrator by allowing users and group owners to manage their own group requests.

NOTE Newly created groups don't immediately or automatically have access to any sites. The group must first be added to the site (see Chapter 6 and the "Site Groups" section earlier in this chapter for information on adding a group to a site).

User Permissions

MOSS provides 21 user permissions that can be granted to a site group to enable the access, functionality, and privileges of the group. Table 7-2 lists the 21 MOSS user rights.

Each of the user permissions included in Table 7-2 are connected to one or more of the default site groups listed in Table 7-1. However, provided you have the appropriate permissions, you can assign or remove user rights from a site group to create a custom site group as needed.

Change Permissions for an Individual User

Once permission inheritance has been broken for a particular site or page, you can change the permission level of an individual group or user by clicking the link for the group or user you wish to change. To access the permission level of a group or user, perform the following steps:

1. On the Edit Permission page of the site, or the page on which you wish to change permissions, click the user or group link to be changed. This opens an Edit Permissions page for that user or group (as shown in Figure 7-14).

2. Check or uncheck the permissions you wish the group or user to have for the affected site or page.

3. Click OK.

Permission Inheritance

By default, MOSS is configured for permission inheritance. This means that within your MOSS environment, group and user permissions flow down from a site collection from its top-level site to any subsites in the collection. Depending on the site template used to create the top-level site and the administrator or user that creates it, the permission set that is inherited by lower-level sites, lists, libraries, Web Parts, and so on is set at the site collection level. However, permission inheritance can be turned off, which means you can allow MOSS to automatically assign user permissions to elements associated with top-level sites or you can take on the responsibility to assign user permissions for each element added to a site collection.

User Right	Function/Access Allowed
Add and customize pages	Create pages for a web site
Add items	Add items to a list or documents to a library
Add/remove private Web Parts	Add and remove Web Parts from a Web Part page
Apply style sheets	Apply a style sheet to a web site
Apply themes and borders	Apply a theme or border to a web site
Browse directories	Browse a web site's directory structure
Cancel check-out	Cancel another user's check-out action
Create cross-site groups	Create, modify, or delete cross-site groups
Create subsites	Create subsites and workspace sites
Delete items	Delete list items and web site documents
Edit items	Edit list items and web site documents
Manage lists	Add, edit, and delete lists and their settings
Manage list permissions	Modify the permissions of a list from a document library
Manage personal views	Add, edit, or remove personal list views
Manage site groups	Add, edit, or remove site groups and their memberships
Manage web site	Gain administrative control of a web site
Update personal Web Parts	Personalize a Web Part
Use self-service site creation	Create a top-level web site using the self-service site creation tool
View items	View list items, library documents, and discussion comments
View pages	View web site pages
View usage data	View web site usage reports

Table 7-2.   MOSS User Rights

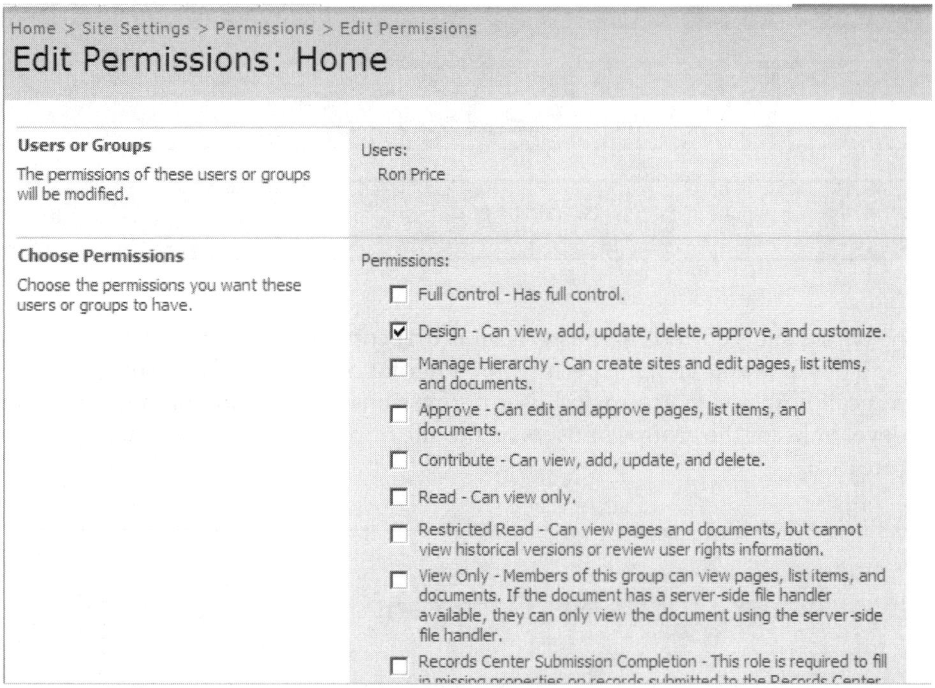

Home > Site Settings > Permissions > Edit Permissions

Edit Permissions: Home

Users or Groups

The permissions of these users or groups will be modified.

Users:
Ron Price

Choose Permissions

Choose the permissions you want these users or groups to have.

Permissions:

☐ Full Control - Has full control.

☑ Design - Can view, add, update, delete, approve, and customize.

☐ Manage Hierarchy - Can create sites and edit pages, list items, and documents.

☐ Approve - Can edit and approve pages, list items, and documents.

☐ Contribute - Can view, add, update, and delete.

☐ Read - Can view only.

☐ Restricted Read - Can view pages and documents, but cannot view historical versions or review user rights information.

☐ View Only - Members of this group can view pages, list items, and documents. If the document has a server-side file handler available, they can only view the document using the server-side file handler.

☐ Records Center Submission Completion - This role is required to fill in missing properties on records submitted to the Records Center

Figure 7-14. The Edit Permission page of a single group or user.

Break Permission Inheritance

You can break permission inheritance for a particular SharePoint element. Should you really want to do so, perform the following steps:

1. On the SharePoint element for which you wish to break permission inheritance, click the Actions button and choose Edit Permissions.

2. A warning box appears (see Figure 7-15) letting you know you are about to break permission inheritance for the element and that any changes made on the parent site within the site collection will no longer affect this particular element.

3. Click OK, if this is really what you want to do.

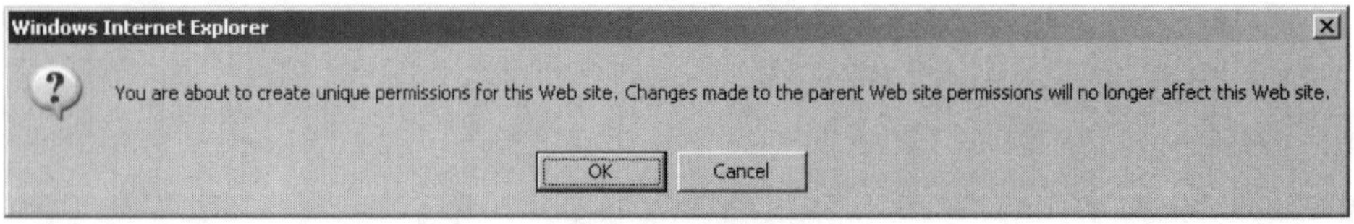

Figure 7-15. Permission inheritance warning box.

The parent site's current permission set is first copied to the affected SharePoint element as a baseline and then the permission inheritance link is broken. The good news is that you can now assign group and user permissions individually because the permissions level links for the groups or users on the site or page become active links, as shown in Figure 7-16.

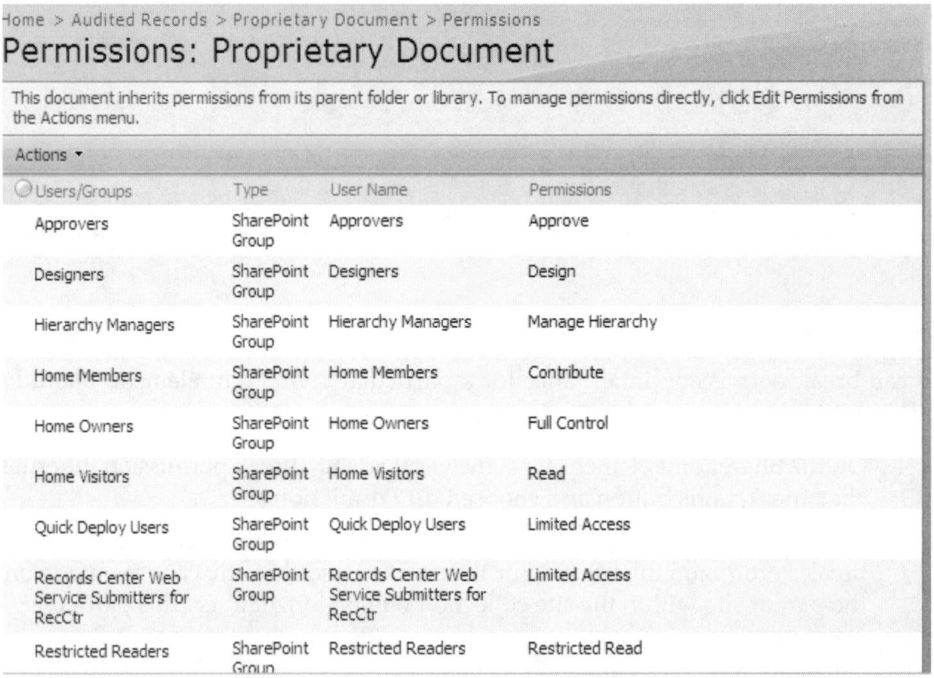

Home > Audited Records > Proprietary Document > Permissions

Permissions: Proprietary Document

This document inherits permissions from its parent folder or library. To manage permissions directly, click Edit Permissions from the Actions menu.

Actions ▾

Users/Groups	Type	User Name	Permissions
Approvers	SharePoint Group	Approvers	Approve
Designers	SharePoint Group	Designers	Design
Hierarchy Managers	SharePoint Group	Hierarchy Managers	Manage Hierarchy
Home Members	SharePoint Group	Home Members	Contribute
Home Owners	SharePoint Group	Home Owners	Full Control
Home Visitors	SharePoint Group	Home Visitors	Read
Quick Deploy Users	SharePoint Group	Quick Deploy Users	Limited Access
Records Center Web Service Submitters for RecCtr	SharePoint Group	Records Center Web Service Submitters for RecCtr	Limited Access
Restricted Readers	SharePoint Group	Restricted Readers	Restricted Read

Figure 7-16. The Edit Permissions page of a document library.

NON-NATIVE CONTENT SOURCES

Perhaps the largest role MOSS plays in an organization is to centralize the access to shared content and information. For the most part, this information is stored within the MOSS environment. MOSS-controlled content and information is said to be native. However, MOSS also supports the capability of accessing and sharing externally stored information (external to the MOSS environment) as well, providing access to information and content stored on a non-native source. Non-native content sources are stores of information that are external to MOSS' mechanisms for storing and accessing content. Two examples of non-native content sources are public folders of Microsoft Exchange Server and foreign file server shares.

After a non-native content source has been identified to it, MOSS will crawl and index that content source. When these operations are complete, the information stored in the non-native content source appears in MOSS' search results.

> **NOTE** For more information on an MOSS search, web crawls, and non-native content sources, see Chapter 8.

As a part of its security makeup, MOSS honors the Access Control Lists and security settings of the non-native content source. For example, let's say you identify the location \\FileServer\HR\ConfidentialFiles as a non-native content source, which is limited to only the members of the Human Resources security group. On its host server, only the members of the Human Resources group have been assigned permission to view the files in the ConfidentialFiles share. MOSS respects the security settings of the foreign server (FileServer) and won't allow access to the files in the ConfidentialFiles share

---

Web Crawling

You will come across the term *crawl* in much of the MOSS documentation. A web crawler is a piece of software that browses a web site, a group of web sites, or even the entire World Wide Web. A web crawler, in the context of a search engine, uses crawling (or as it is also called, spidering) to seek out new or updated content. The crawler either creates a list of, or copies, visited pages so they can be indexed by the search engine for retrieval. A prime example of a web crawl program is the Web Crawler software from InfoSpace, Inc. (www.webcrawler.com).

However, in the context of MOSS, the crawl function is generally limited to a single enterprise SharePoint web site and is even further limited by a specific content type. Users can schedule crawls for a particular content type to take place at times when they are less likely to access the information. MOSS even provides for four levels of web crawls: full crawl, incremental crawl, incremental-inclusive crawl, and adaptive crawl. See Chapter 8 for more information on MOSS' web crawl functions.

unless the requesting user is a member of the Human Resources security group. In fact, MOSS won't even list the files that would be listed in a search result to anyone who doesn't have the permission to view them.

Non-native content source security settings consist of two parts: share permissions and NTFS permissions. Because MOSS honors the security settings of all non-native content sources, it is important to understand how these security settings work.

Two good reasons to understand share-level and NTFS permissions are 1) ensuring that non-native content sources are secure, and 2) troubleshooting any access to non-native content sources. The effective permissions of a file or folder are a result of combining the most restrictive permissions assigned from both the share model and the NTFS model. For example, a user would need to be assigned read permission from both the share and NTFS to read a file.

Share permissions, which can only be assigned to folders, limit what a sharing (remote) user is allowed to do with a folder and its contents, subject to the NTFS permissions assigned to the folder or its files. In contrast, NTFS security creates an Access Control List for each file or folder stored on an NTFS partition. The Access Control List identifies the file actions that a particular security group or individual user may perform on a specific file or folder.

Unlike share-level permissions, the NTFS security settings of a file or folder can be inherited from its parent folder(s). This ability to inherit security settings "from above" simplifies the task of managing security settings by eliminating the need to repeat identical security settings on a folder's subfolders and files. However, the inheritance of security settings can be disabled, which can make troubleshooting permission issues fairly complicated. For instance, if the security settings of a file or folder are unique to those of its parent folder, it can be difficult to track down why a file or folder is seemingly violating its presumed security settings.

> **TIP**   When creating a share for a folder, assign all three permission levels to the Everyone group, then restrict access using the NTFS permission settings on the folder.

To view the permissions of a network share, do the following:

1. Right-click the name of the folder and click Properties on the pop-up menu that appears.
2. Choose the Sharing tab on the File Properties dialog box (see Figure 7-17).
3. On the Share Properties dialog box, click the Permissions button to display the Permissions For Share dialog box (shown in Figure 7-18).

To view the security settings for an NTFS folder or file:

1. Right-click the name of the folder and click Properties on the pop-up menu that appears.
2. Choose the Security tab on the Properties dialog box (see Figure 7-17).

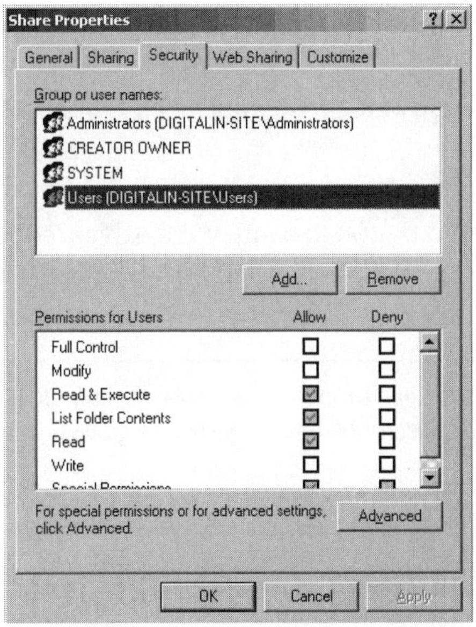

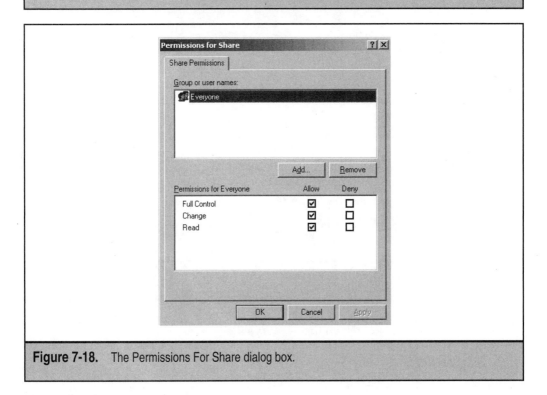

Figure 7-17. The Properties dialog box for a file or folder.

Figure 7-18. The Permissions For Share dialog box.

As stated earlier, the effective permissions for a file or folder are created as a combination of any share-level permissions it may have, as well as its NTFS permissions. To view the effective permissions for a file or folder:

1. Right-click the name of the folder and click Properties on the pop-up menu that appears.

2. Choose the Security tab on the Properties dialog box that displays.

3. Click the Advanced button to display the Advanced Security Settings For Share dialog box.

4. Choose the Effective Permissions tab (see Figure 7-19).

TIP   To view the effective permissions for a particular security group or user, click the Select button to the right of the Group or username box and select the group or user from the pull-down list.

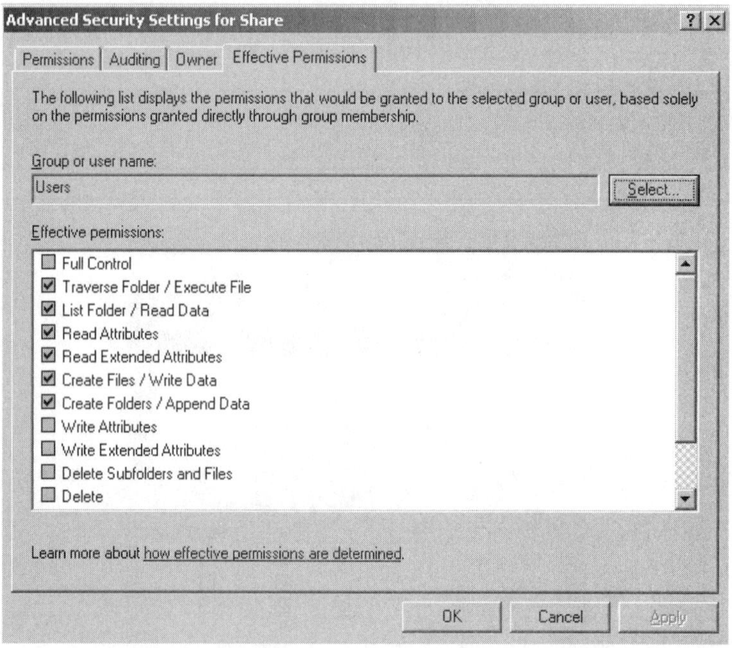

Figure 7-19.   The Advanced Security Settings For Share dialog box.

SUMMARY

MOSS security, like the security for all systems, is a complex and often confusing area. Often large organizations assign the responsibility for each piece of the network puzzle to a specific software or network analyst. However, if you find yourself responsible for all of the security in an MOSS environment, take some comfort from the fact that you won't have to reinvent the wheel. There is a massive amount of best practice information available to help you through the complex process of securing your MOSS environment.

The network operating system and the various technologies and applications each contain have a variety of security settings and tools that can be used either directly or indirectly to secure your MOSS environment. You should carefully study each of these elements and how they interact with MOSS to secure your site from hackers and the unauthorized disclosure of content.

Because MOSS is designed to share information, you must use every tool at your disposal to protect that information from inappropriate use by 1) securing your network infrastructure; 2) securing your operating system; 3) securing your applications; and 4) securing your MOSS content. If you take a layered approach to securing MOSS, you should be successful.

CHAPTER 8

MOSS Search

S earch is perhaps one of MOSS's most useful (and most used) features. In most new MOSS installations, the first set of sites and portals are typically lists of links to important documents. However, as is often the problem with any list, because everyone wanted to include their documents, the list becomes unmanageable. Lists can be organized into folders, but eventually even folders themselves can become unmanageable. The solution is to use the MOSS Search feature to find folders and documents as needed and forego the maintenance of an all inclusive list.

This chapter introduces the three components that make up MOSS Search (content sources, content indexes, and search scopes) and how to configure each component to best support your users' requirements. However, you should also look at Chapters 12 and 18 to completely understand how MOSS Search can be used in an effective site design that incorporates the use of metadata and libraries.

MOSS SEARCH SETTINGS

MOSS content can be classified into two groups: native content and non-native content. Native content refers to any content created and stored directly in the MOSS environment, such as lists and libraries. Non-native content includes such items as network shares, web sites, and Microsoft Exchange public folders. MOSS has the capability to crawl, index, and search both native and non-native content, which allows an organization to immediately leverage a new MOSS installation without the need to migrate existing content, something that can be a lengthy process.

MOSS Search is comprised of three components:

▼ Content sources

■ Content indexes

▲ Search scopes

The MOSS Search components work in a series. MOSS Search crawls content sources, producing content indexes. A search scope includes one or more rules preset by the MOSS administrator. Search scopes are used to limit the search results returned from an MOSS Search operation. With all three of the MOSS Search components in place, users are able to quickly identify and find native and non-native content accessible to their web site or portal.

Search settings are unique to any given Shared Services Provider (SSP), which provides support to the web applications associated with it (see Chapter 4). To access the search settings for an SSP, do the following:

1. Open the SharePoint 3.0 Central Administration page (Start | All Programs | Microsoft Office Servers | SharePoint 3.0 Central Administration).

2. On the Central Administration page, choose the Application Management tab.

3. Click the Create or configure this farm's shared services link under the Office SharePoint Server Shared Services heading to open the Manage this Farm's Shared Services page (shown in Figure 8-1).

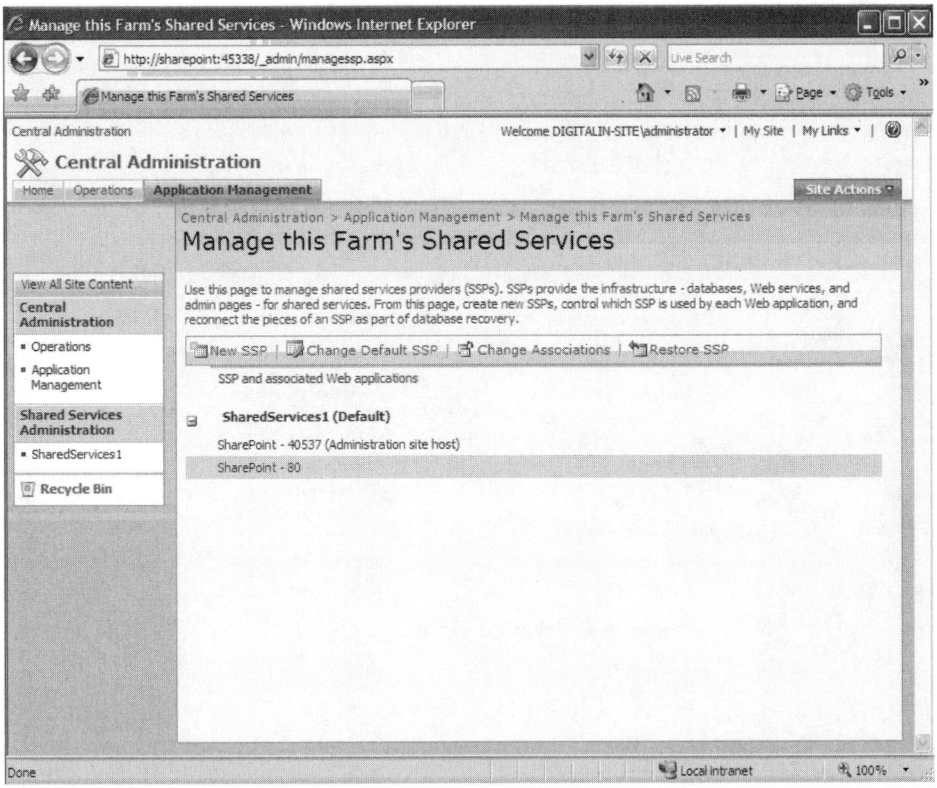

Figure 8-1. The Manage This Farm's Shared Services page.

4. Click SharedServices1 (Default) link to open the Home administration page for the Shared Services Provider (SSP) (see Figure 8-2).

5. Click the Search settings link under the Search heading to open the Configure Search Settings page (shown in Figure 8-3).

The configuration and settings for the majority of search-related functions are accomplished using the Search Settings page within each SSP. As each of the three search components are discussed in the following sections, the settings for each are also discussed.

Content Sources

Content sources are collections of documents and files stored natively to MOSS. Content sources stored externally to MOSS are known as non-native content sources. Each designated content source has an associated content index, which is created when the

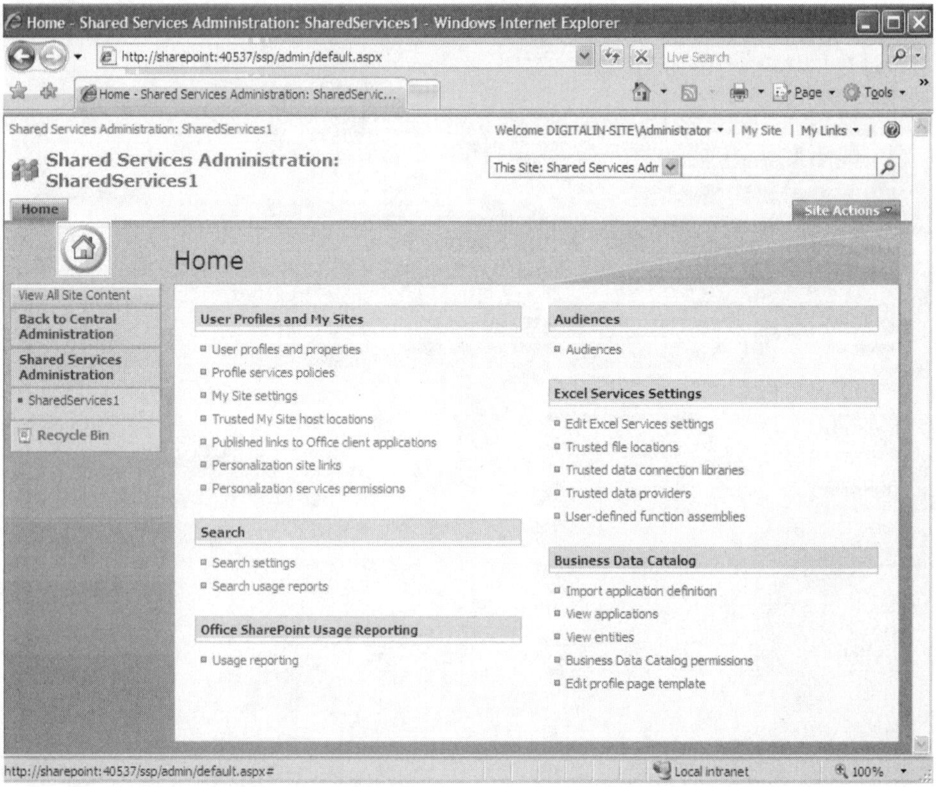

Figure 8-2. The home page for the Shared Services Administration: SharedServices1 web site.

content source is crawled by MOSS. New content sources are not automatically included in a content index. You must configure each content source to be crawled by MOSS at regularly scheduled intervals to ensure that any files added, changed, or deleted from the content source are also added to a content index.

Create and Configure a Content Source

To configure content sources and their inclusion in content indexes, perform the following steps:

1. Open the Search Settings page, shown in Figure 8-3 (see the preceding section "MOSS Search Settings" for the steps used to navigate to this page).

2. Click the Content Sources And Crawl Schedules link under the Crawl Settings heading.

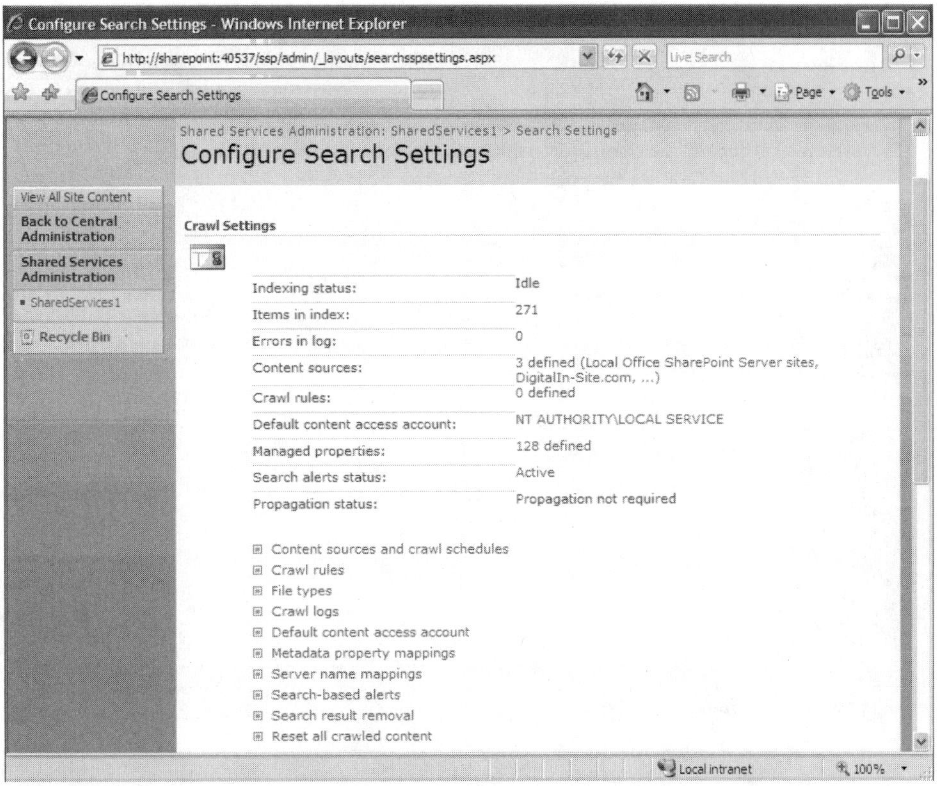

Configure Search Settings - Windows Internet Explorer

http://sharepoint:40537/ssp/admin/_layouts/searchsspsettings.aspx | Live Search

Configure Search Settings | Page ▾ Tools ▾

Shared Services Administration: SharedServices1 > Search Settings

Configure Search Settings

View All Site Content

Back to Central Administration

Shared Services Administration

• SharedServices1

Recycle Bin

Crawl Settings

Indexing status:	Idle
Items in index:	271
Errors in log:	0
Content sources:	3 defined (Local Office SharePoint Server sites, DigitalIn-Site.com, ...)
Crawl rules:	0 defined
Default content access account:	NT AUTHORITY\LOCAL SERVICE
Managed properties:	128 defined
Search alerts status:	Active
Propagation status:	Propagation not required

⊞ Content sources and crawl schedules
⊞ Crawl rules
⊞ File types
⊞ Crawl logs
⊞ Default content access account
⊞ Metadata property mappings
⊞ Server name mappings
⊞ Search-based alerts
⊞ Search result removal
⊞ Reset all crawled content

Local intranet | 100%

Figure 8-3.   The Configure Search Settings page.

3. On the Manage Content Sources page that displays (see Figure 8-4), click the New Content Source button.

4. On the Add Content Source page (shown in Figure 8-5), enter a descriptive name for the content source in the Name field.

TIP   Remember that this is the name your users will use to reference this source, so make it as descriptive as possible.

5. Select the Content Source Type. The choices you have are:

■ **SharePoint Sites**   Crawl all native content associated with another top-level SharePoint site, including libraries and lists—for example, http://sharepoint/sites/HR.

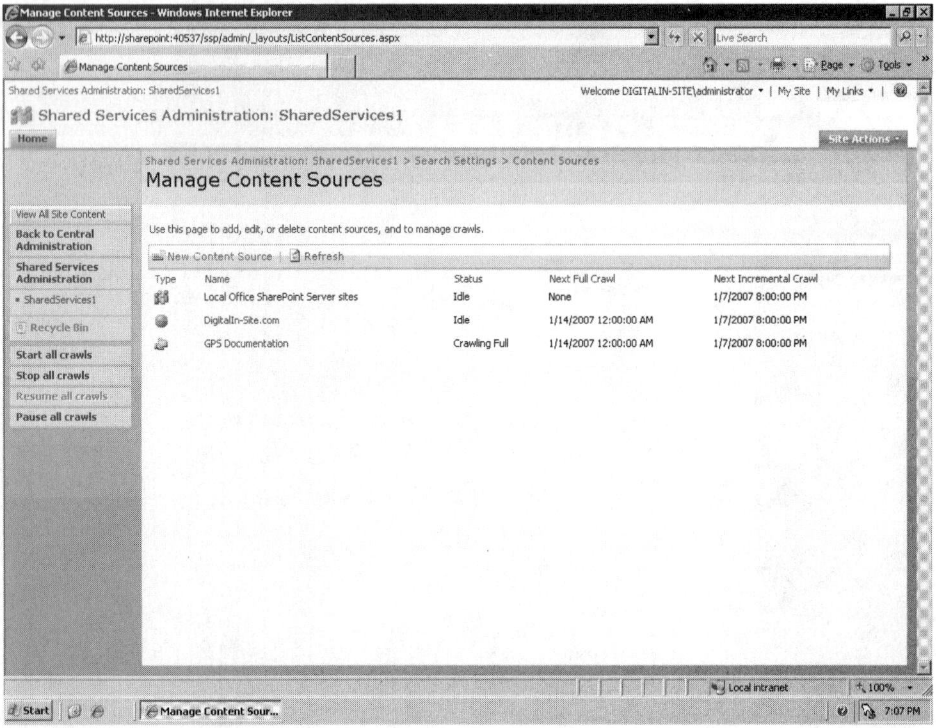

Figure 8-4. The Manage Content Sources page.

- **Web Sites** Crawl any content that can be identified by a URL. For example, http://www.digitalin-site.com.

- **File Shares** Crawl content in network file shares. Network file shares often contain a wealth of collaborative files, files intended for sharing with other departments, and archived files—for example, \\FileServer\Finance\ Reports.

- **Exchange Public Folders** Crawl content in Microsoft Exchange Public Folders. Microsoft Exchange is a messaging application that includes support for hierarchical information stores (public folders). For example, http://email/exchange/public/HR/vacation.

- **Business Data** Crawl application content that has been associated with the MOSS Business Data Catalog. The Business Data Catalog allows for the creation of data warehouses within SharePoint. The entire catalog can be crawled, or just a specific application.

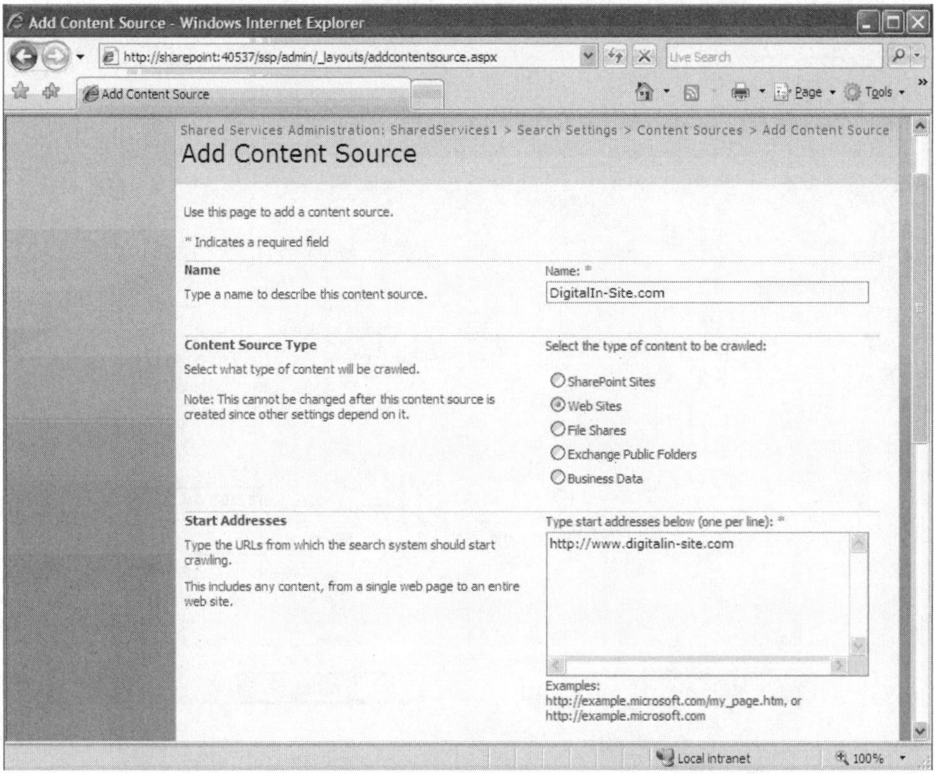

Figure 8-5. The Add Content Source page.

It is likely that an organization already stores business-critical information in one or more content sources. Company web sites, file shares, and Exchange public folders are all potential content sources that should be examined for value prior to your initial SharePoint implementation. Adding these content sources allows an organization to immediately leverage SharePoint without going through the tedious process of migrating existing data to SharePoint.

6. Enter Start Addresses in the form of URLs if you are adding a SharePoint Sites or Web Sites content source. You can also specify whether the crawler should follow links across domain names. Link depth, how many links to follow when crawling, is also configurable.

7. Specify if the crawler should index everything at the site with the Crawl Settings radio buttons.

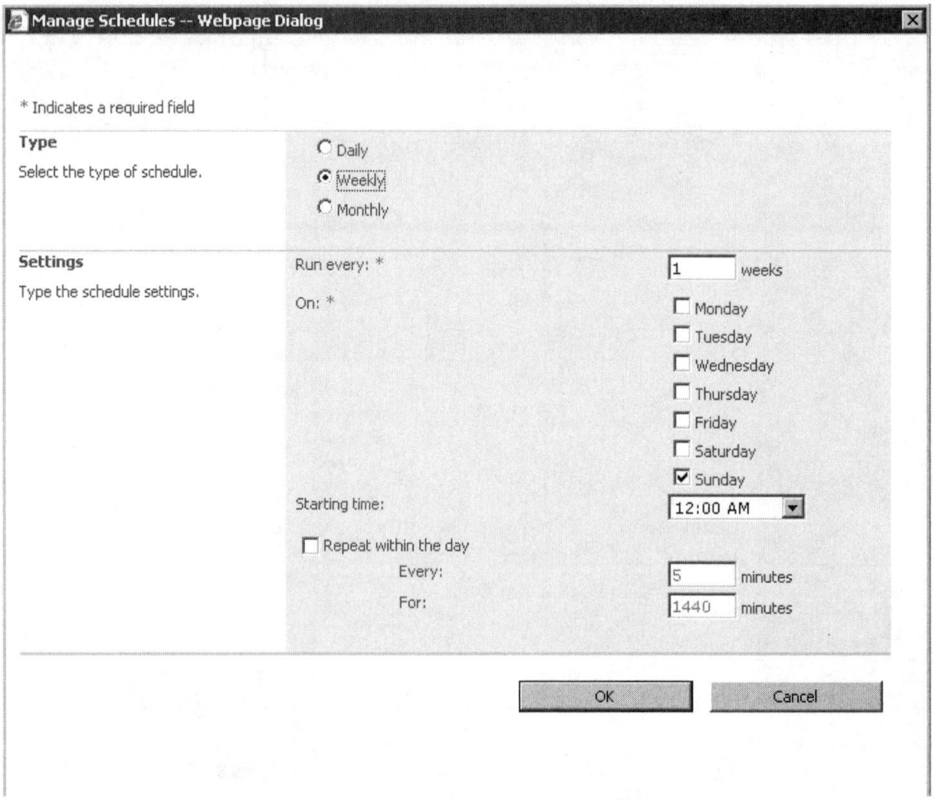

Manage Schedules -- Webpage Dialog

* Indicates a required field

Type
Select the type of schedule.

- ○ Daily
- ◉ Weekly
- ○ Monthly

Settings
Type the schedule settings.

Run every: * `1` weeks

On: *

- ☐ Monday
- ☐ Tuesday
- ☐ Wednesday
- ☐ Thursday
- ☐ Friday
- ☐ Saturday
- ☑ Sunday

Starting time: `12:00 AM` ▼

☐ Repeat within the day

Every: `5` minutes

For: `1440` minutes

[OK]   [Cancel]

Figure 8-6. The Full Crawl Schedule update dialog box.

8. Specify full and incremental Crawl Schedules for the content source using the drop-down menus. Figures 8-6 and 8-7, respectively, show the pop-up dialog boxes used to schedule a full update and an incremental update.

TIP Crawl schedules must be specified in order to ensure accurate search results. Content sources that change frequently should be incrementally crawled frequently to ensure timely content index updates.

9. Check the Start Full Crawl Of This Content Source option if you want MOSS to immediately begin crawling and indexing the content source.
10. Click OK.

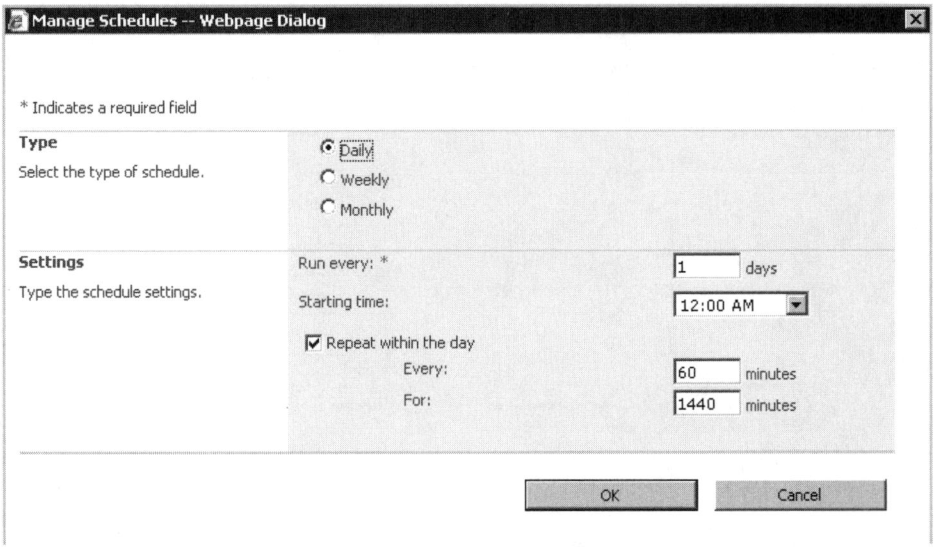

Figure 8-7.   The Incremental Crawl Schedule update dialog box.

When defining a web site–based content source, you have complete control over how MOSS crawls the web site. If a web site is particularly large, you may wish to limit the crawl to a certain page depth. You can also restrict the crawl to the assigned domain name and not "server hop," or follow links from the assigned domain to other web sites.

In the example shown in Figure 8-8, the content source (www.digitalin-site.com) has been configured to crawl only the digitalin-site.com domain to a depth of the Web pages.

Another common non-native content source is the file share, like the one shown in Figure 8-9. Many organizations already make use of an extensive collection of file shares to share documents among network users. (See Figure 8-10.)

You can enable MOSS to crawl and index file share content by creating content sources for each file share, as shown in Figures 8-11 (which shows the top portion of the Add Content Source page) and 8-12 (which shows the bottom portion of the Add Content page). This can be an effective way to immediately leverage MOSS with very little effort.

Manage Existing Content Sources

You may edit or delete existing content sources, view the associated crawl log, start an incremental or full crawl, as well as pause, resume, or stop a crawl already in progress on the Manage Content Sources page, shown earlier in Figure 8-4. The Manage Content Sources page lists all the SharePoint content sources, their current status, and when the next full and incremental crawls for each content source type are scheduled.

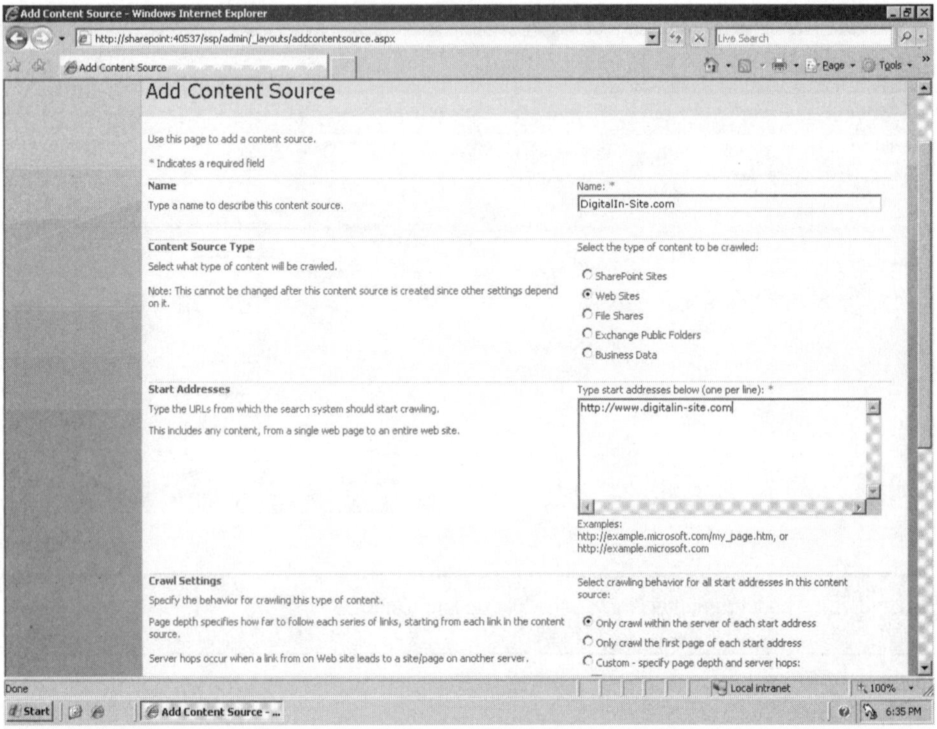

Figure 8-8. Configuring the crawl type.

To manage an existing content source, use the following process:

1. On the Search Settings page (see the "MOSS Search Settings" section earlier in the chapter to open this page) and click the Content Sources And Crawl Schedules link.

2. Place your mouse pointer over the content source you wish to manage and choose a maintenance action from the pop-up menu that appears (see Figure 8-13). The actions on the menu are as follows:

   a. **Edit**   Identical to the Add Content Source interface. Use to make changes to an existing content source.

   b. **View Crawl Log**   View and filter crawl logs by date or status type (all, success, warning, or error).

   c. **Start Full Crawl**   Immediately begin a full crawl and index operation of the content source. This does not affect the next scheduled full crawl.

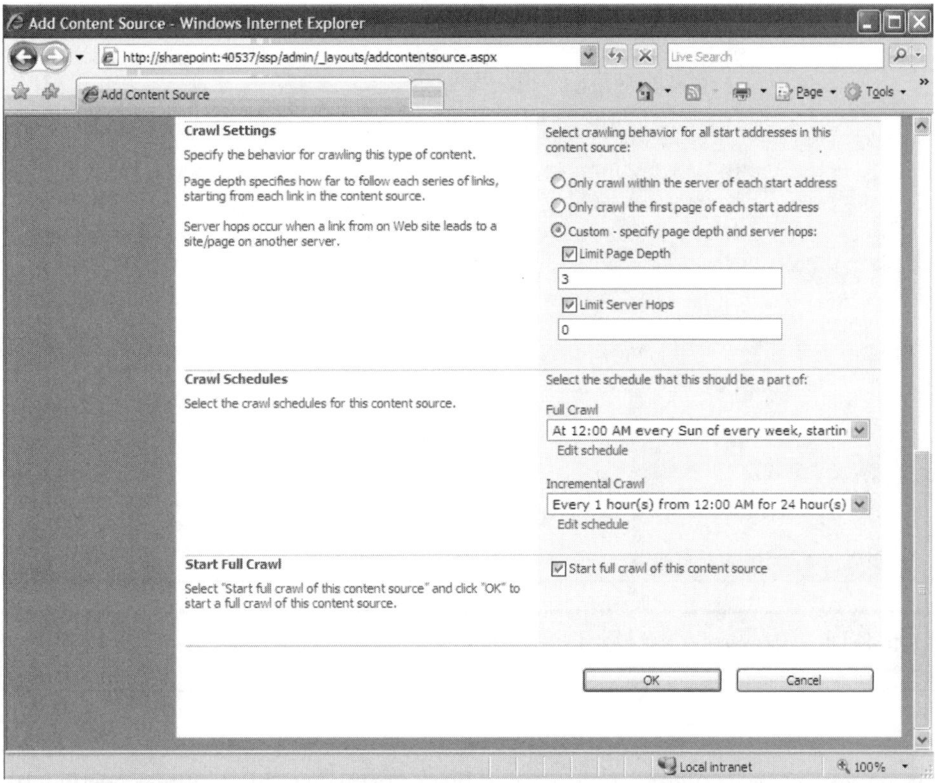

Figure 8-9. Setting the crawl schedule.

d. **Start Incremental Crawl**   Immediately begin an incremental crawl and index operation of the content source. This does not affect the next scheduled incremental crawl.

e. **Resume Crawl**   Resume a currently paused crawl.

f. **Pause Crawl**   Pause a currently running crawl.

g. **Stop Crawl**   Stop a currently running crawl. The current crawl is abandoned until the next scheduled crawl.

h. **Delete**   Delete a content source.

Typically, a full crawl, which crawls the entire content source, is performed when the content source is first created. A full crawl may be scheduled weekly or monthly to ensure an accurate, complete index. An incremental crawl, which only crawls files that

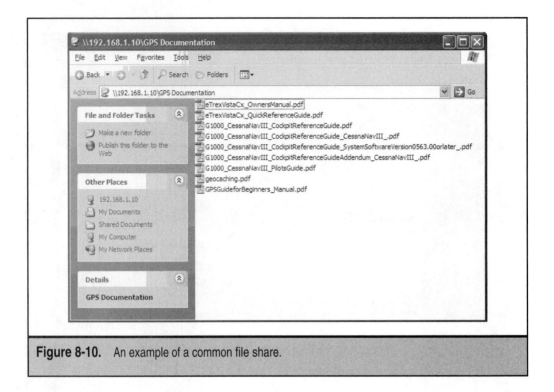

Figure 8-10. An example of a common file share.

have changed in the content source, should be performed as frequently as needed, based on the usage and sensitivity of the content source.

When planning the crawl schedule for your content sources, you should assess how frequently the data, documents, or files in a content source change, and then schedule your crawls accordingly. If the content is relatively static, and seldom changes, you may perform a full crawl monthly, with a daily incremental crawl. Likewise, if the content source files are constantly changing, your incremental crawl may need to be scheduled to run every 5 minutes.

TIP If you have the hardware resources, you may choose to schedule each content source's crawl to take place at the same time. However, by staggering the crawl schedules, you can make more efficient use of your index server's hardware resources.

Content Indexes

MOSS creates a content index for each content source it crawls and indexes. Content indexes are maintained indirectly based on the content source settings and the crawl schedule of the content sources being crawled. By default, content indexes are not automatically updated. A crawl schedule must be configured for each content source.

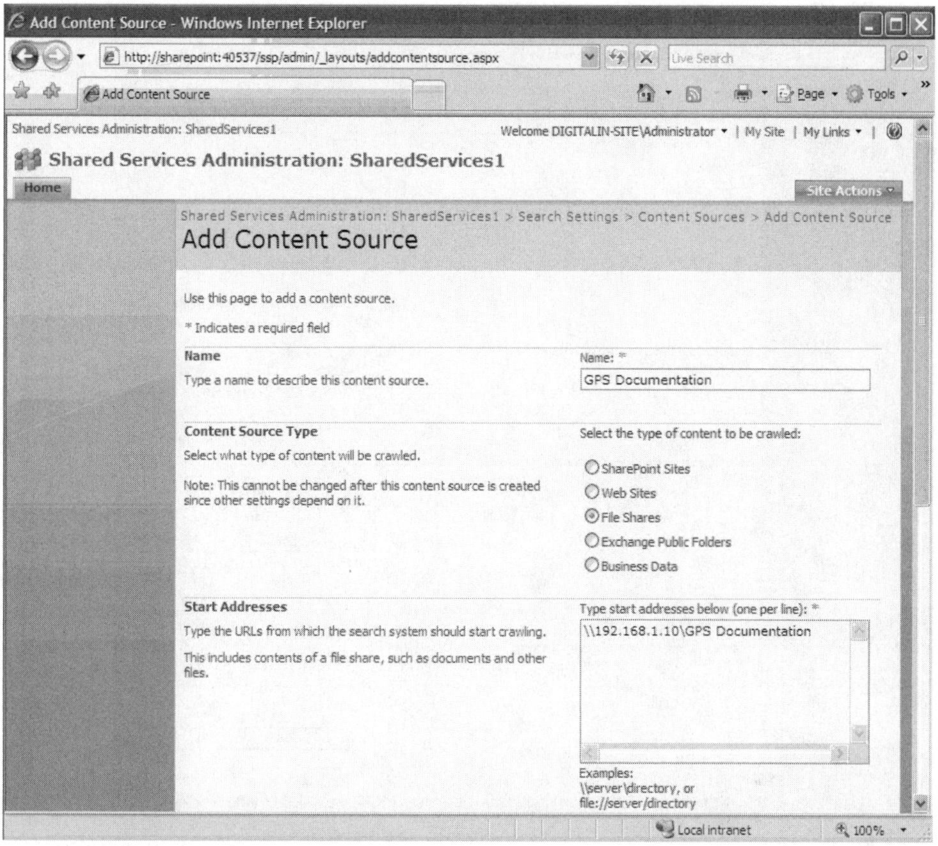

Figure 8-11.   Adding a file share content source.

Plan for Content Index Resources

You should plan for each content index to be approximately 10 percent of the size of the original content source. After the MOSS index server has crawled the content source and created an index, the index is placed on each MOSS search server. If a non-native content source, such as a file share, is 1 Gigabyte (GB) in size, plan for the associated content index to be approximately 100 Megabytes (MB) in size, which means you would need to allocate at least 100 MB of space on both the Index server and the MOSS Search server.

NOTE   If your MOSS environment is installed on a standalone server, both the Index and Search services reside on that one server. Using the previous example, you only need to ensure that 100 MB of disk space is available for the content index.

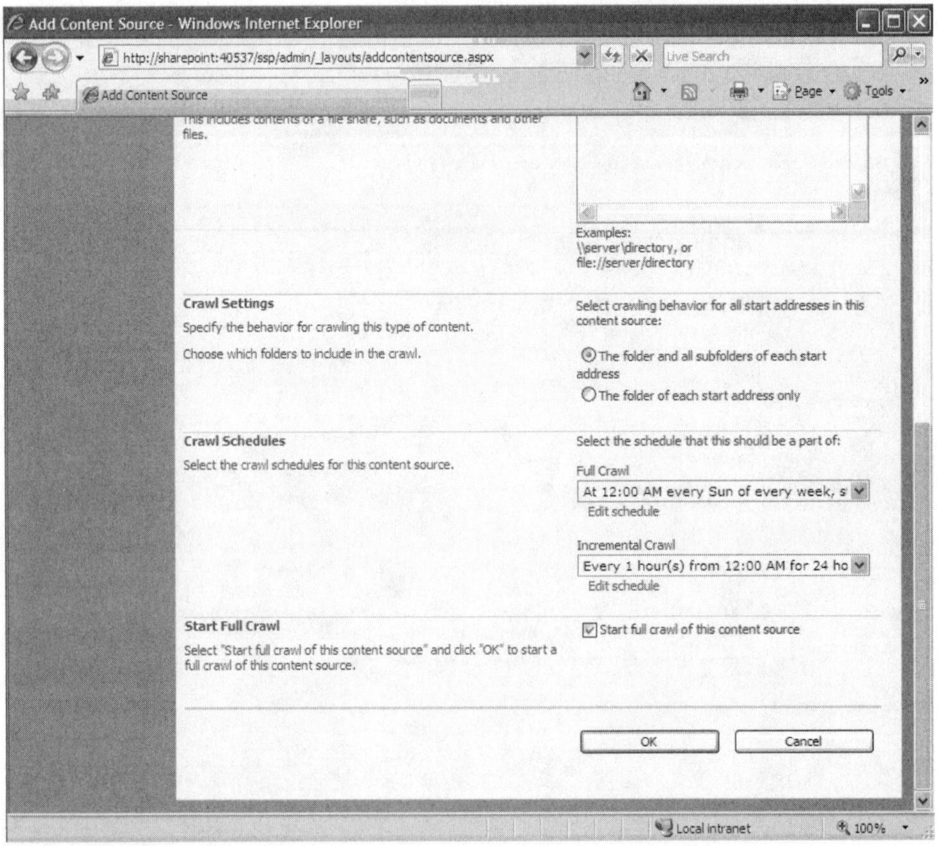

Figure 8-12. Adding a file share content source (continued).

Default Content Access Account

It is important to understand that a default content access account is used to crawl all the content sources. This account must have at least read permission for all files in the content source that are to be indexed. Security permissions are taken into account when a user runs a MOSS search. If the user does not have permission to view a file in a content source, the file will not be returned in the search results.

To manage the default content access account, use the following steps:

1. Open the Search Settings page (see the "MOSS Search Settings" section earlier in the chapter for the steps used to navigate to this page).

2. Click the Default Content Access Account link to display its settings.

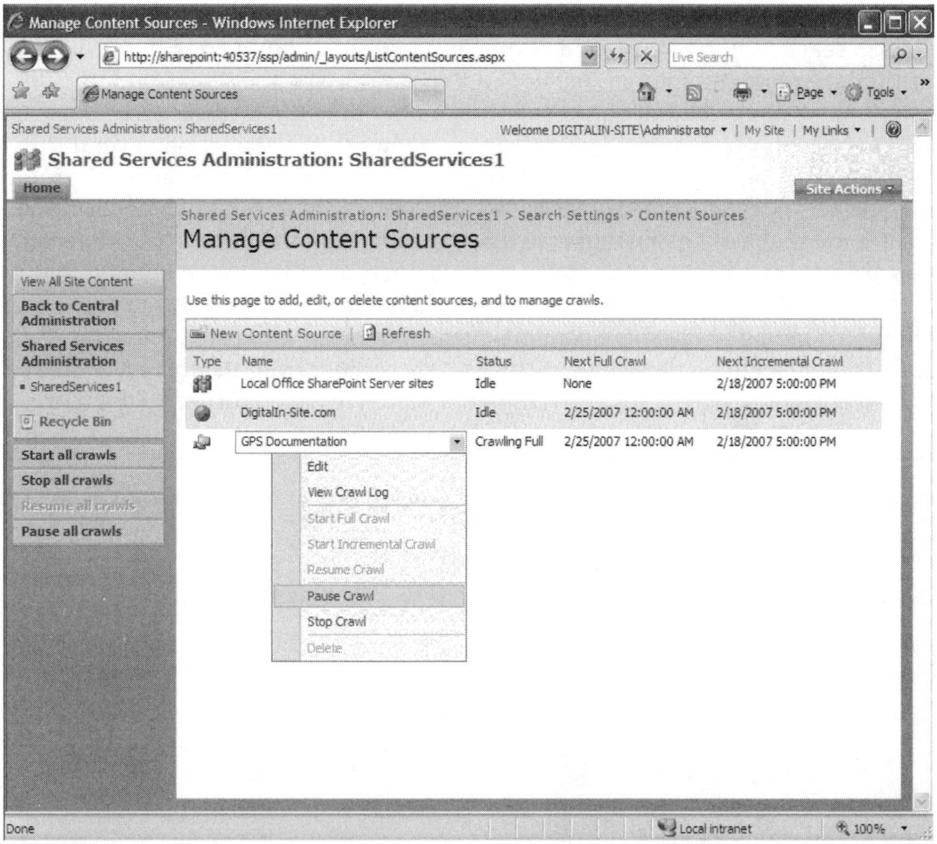

Figure 8-13. The pop-up menu used to manage a content source.

3. Enter the account credentials (username and password) of the account that has been granted—at a minimum, read access to the content source.

TIP Typically, the default content access account is granted read permission to a content source before the content source is created in MOSS. See Chapter 7 for more information.

Search Scopes

Search scopes are used to control the search results returned by MOSS. A search scope is made up of one or more search scope rules, which have been set by the MOSS administrator. Search scopes are available to all MOSS users and listed to the immediate left of the search box (see Figure 8-14). Search scopes are used to limit the search results returned by a MOSS search.

MOSS search scopes are created at one of two levels: within an SSP, or within a site collection, the more common of the two. In either case, a search scope, and its rules, applies to one or more content sources. For example, the Human Resources department of an organization may store data in various network file shares on several different file servers, such as \\FileServer1\HR\Benefits, \\FileServer2\Finance\Payroll, and \\FileServer3\HR\401k. Each of these three file shares are added to MOSS as individual content sources. A new search scope, perhaps named "Human Resources" is created and three search scope rules, one for each content source, is added to the Human Resources search scope. Any search performed using the Human Resources search scope searches all three non-native file share content sources. Because the search scope targets only specific content sources, the search includes only content from the three non-native file share content sources, reducing the number of search results returned to the user.

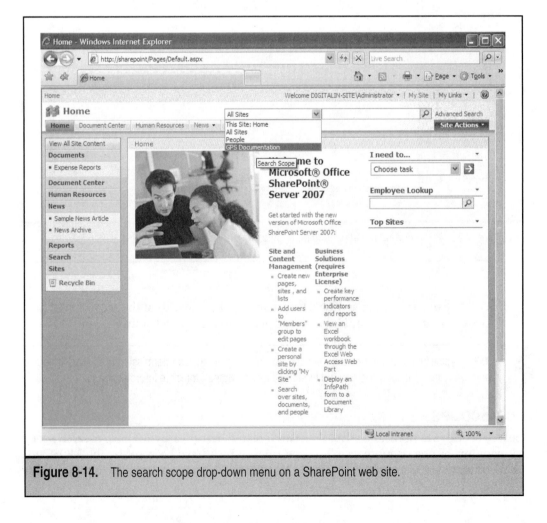

Figure 8-14. The search scope drop-down menu on a SharePoint web site.

A search scope rule and its related content sources may be assigned to multiple search scopes. For example, you may create a Corporate Services search scope, which contains a search scope rule for each department beneath Corporate Services. Additionally, you may create individual search scopes for each department, such as Human Resources, Finance, and Information Services. The number of search scopes defined is dependent on the number of content sources included in the MOSS environment.

Adding a Search Scope

The first step in creating a search scope is to create one or more content sources that are the targets of your search scope rules. You may want to experiment with different content sources, such as creating a content source based on a web site URL (http://...) and another content source based on a local network share (\\server\share).

NOTE For more information on creating content sources, see the "Create and Configure a Content Source" section earlier in the chapter.

To create a search scope, do the following:

1. Open the Search Settings page and click the View Scopes link under the Scopes heading to display the View Scopes page (shown in Figure 8-15).
2. Click the New Scope button and enter a Title for the new search scope.
3. Click OK.

At this point, you need to open the Search Properties and Rules page to configure the settings for the search scope you've just created. A search scope is useless and exists in name only until you configure its rules.

Set Search Scope Rules

To configure a search scope's rules, perform the following steps:

1. On the Search Settings page, click the View Scopes link.
2. From the list of existing search scopes, click the title of your newly created search scope.
3. On the Scope Properties and Rules page that displays (see Figure 8-16), click the New Rule link under the Rules heading.
4. On the Add Scope Rule page (shown in Figure 8-17), select the Content Source radio button and then select the content source to which the scope rule will apply from the Content Source drop-down menu.
5. Choose the behavior property for this search scope rule.
6. Each rule can include, require, or exclude content from the search scope. Include is the default behavior. More complex search scopes can be created by requiring or excluding content from a search scope.
7. Click OK.

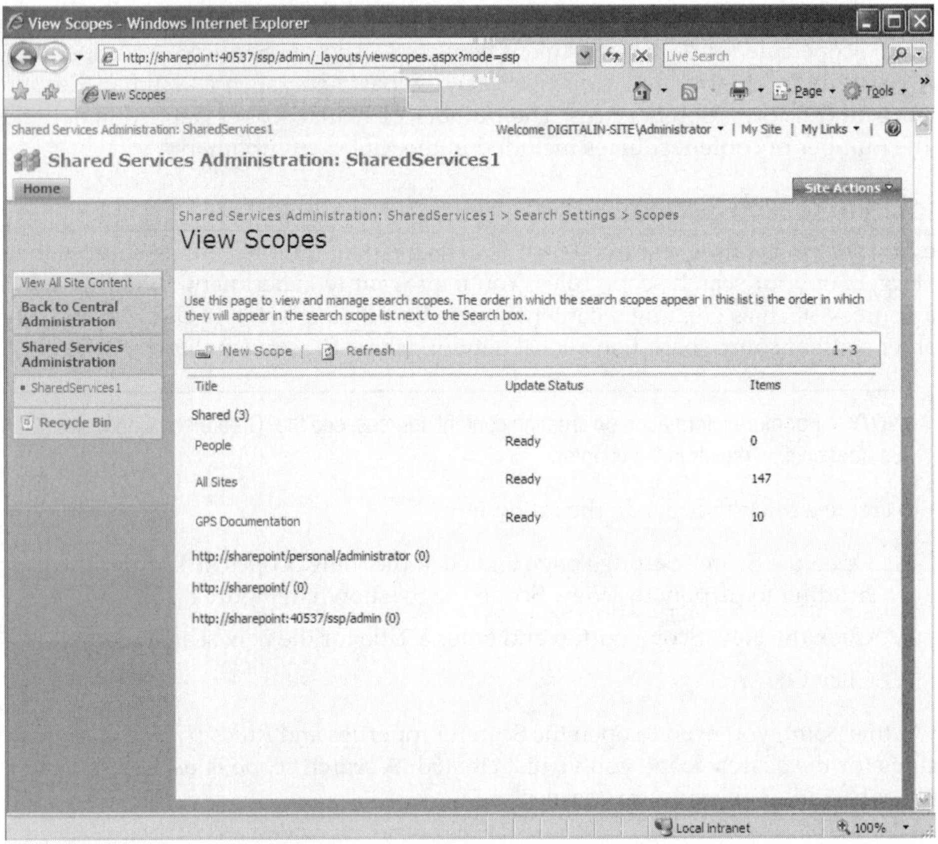

Figure 8-15.   The View Scopes page is used to create a new search scope.

Display Groups

Before a search scope can be accessible by MOSS users, it must be added to one or more display groups. A display group is essentially a drop-down list that users can access to quickly search for content. Each top-level site has its own display group.

To create a new display group and add a search scope to it, use the following process:

1. Navigate to a top-level site on which you wish to include a search scope.

2. Open the Site Actions drop-down list and select Site Settings.

3. Click the Modify All Site Settings option.

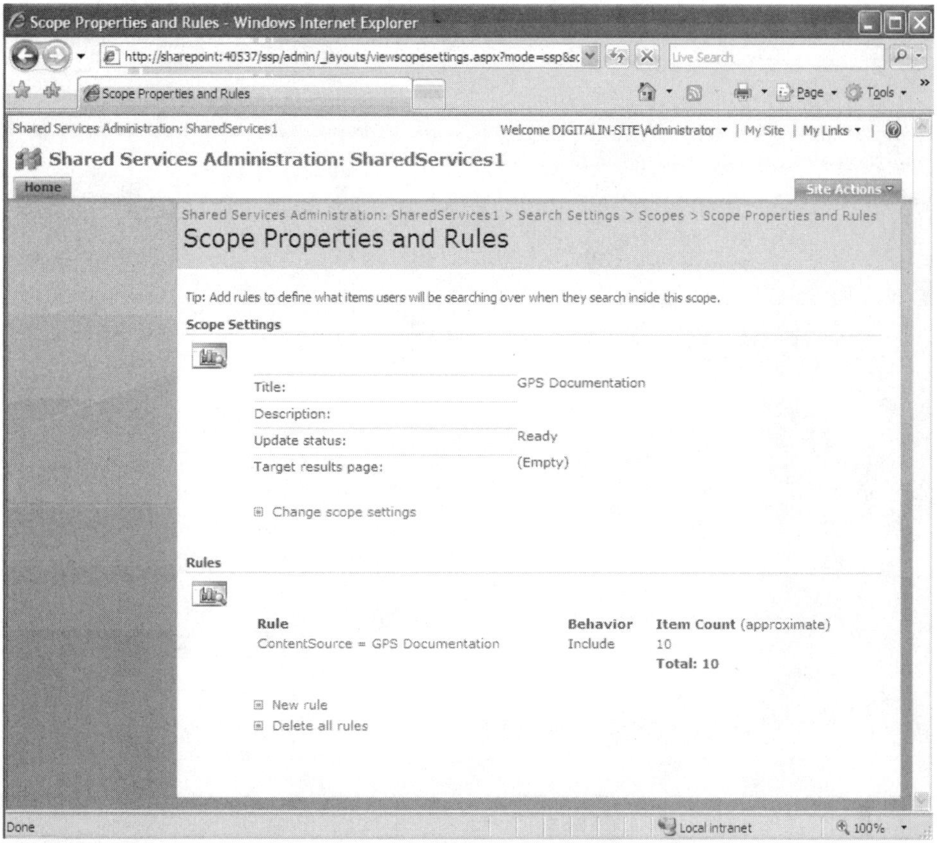

Figure 8-16. The Scope Properties and Rules page.

4. Click the Search Scopes link under the Site Collection Administration heading to display the View Scopes page (see Figure 8-18).

5. Click the title of the display group, under the heading Title, to which you wish to add the search scope. This is Display Group: Search Dropdown (2) in the example shown in Figure 8-17.

6. On the Edit Scope Display Group page that appears (see Figure 8-19), check the Display checkbox to display (or uncheck this box to hide) any of the search scopes listed in the display group.

7. The Position From Top setting controls the order (top to bottom) in which the search scopes selected for display will appear in the display group.

8. Click OK.

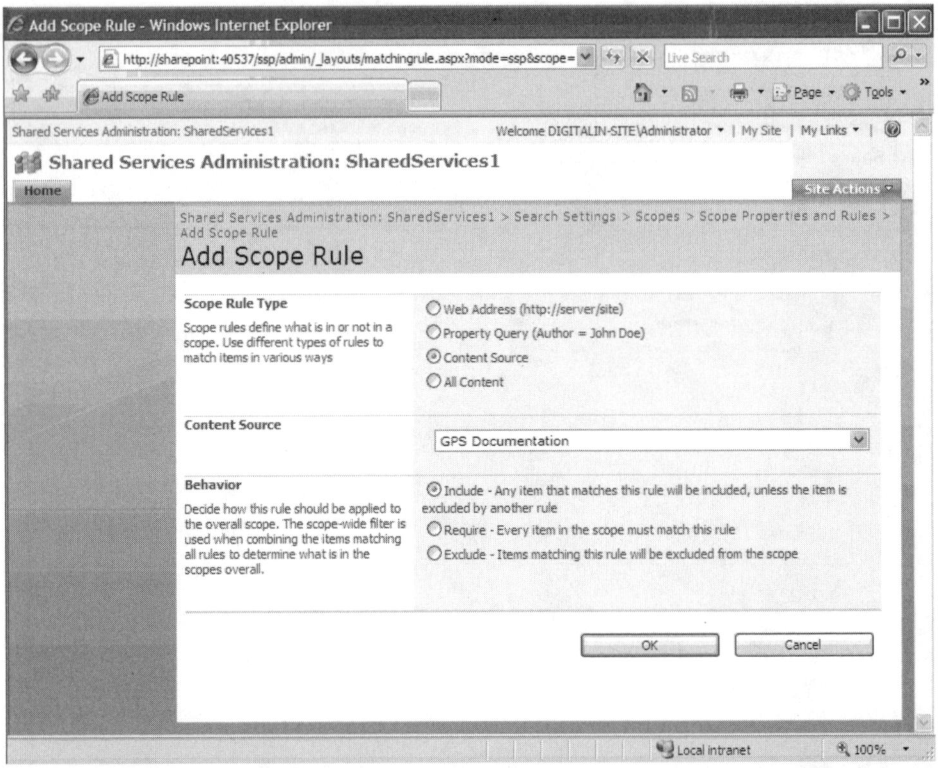

Figure 8-17. The Add Scope Rule page.

Update a Search Scope

By default, search scopes are periodically and automatically updated by MOSS. If you've recently made a change to a search scope and you'd like your changes to take effect immediately, you need to force a search scope update. To do this, use these steps:

1. Open the Search Settings page using the procedure outlined in the "MOSS Search Settings" section earlier in this chapter.

2. Under the Scopes heading, click the Start Update Now link.

When the search scope update is complete, any scope changes you have made are available to all MOSS users.

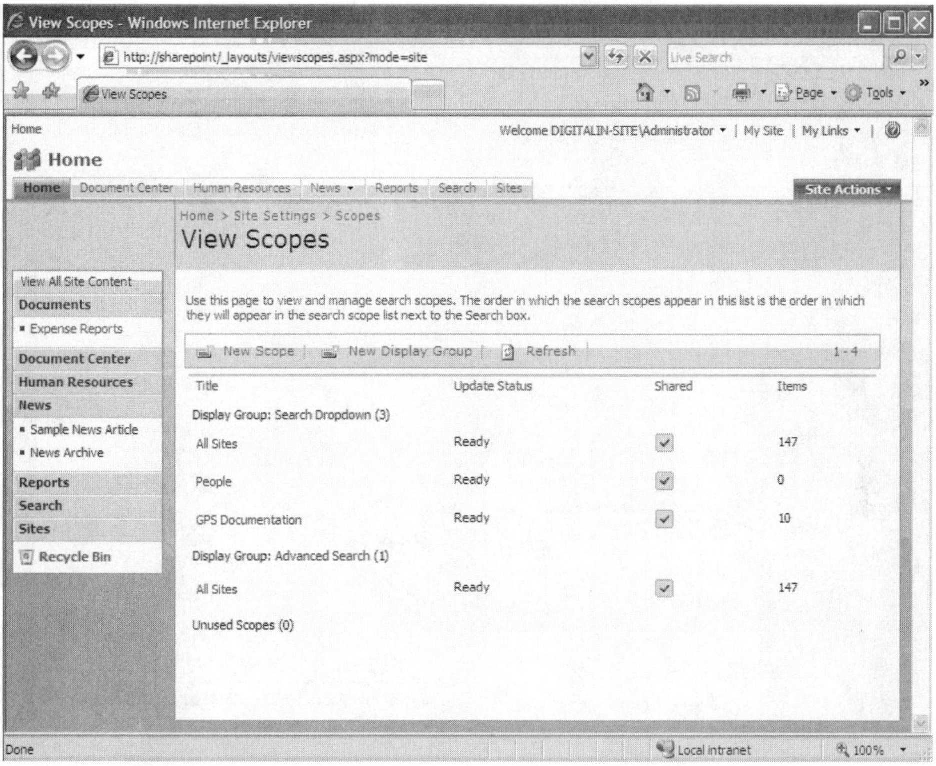

Figure 8-18.   The View Scopes page.

FILE TYPES AND IFILTERS

The MOSS Search feature can crawl and index a variety of file types, but you may be surprised by a few of the file types that MOSS, by default, doesn't crawl and index by default. For example, for all of the file formats that MOSS does include by default, listed in Table 8-1, perhaps the most commonly used file not included is the Adobe Portable Document Format (PDF) file format. In fact, in your particular environment, there may be other file types that are just as glaringly omitted from the default file types list.

> **NOTE**   The Portable Document Format (PDF) file format is a very common file type for intranet and extranet use because of the document security (although somewhat limited) it provides and the fact it is application-, operating system-, and platform-independent, allowing for easy information sharing.

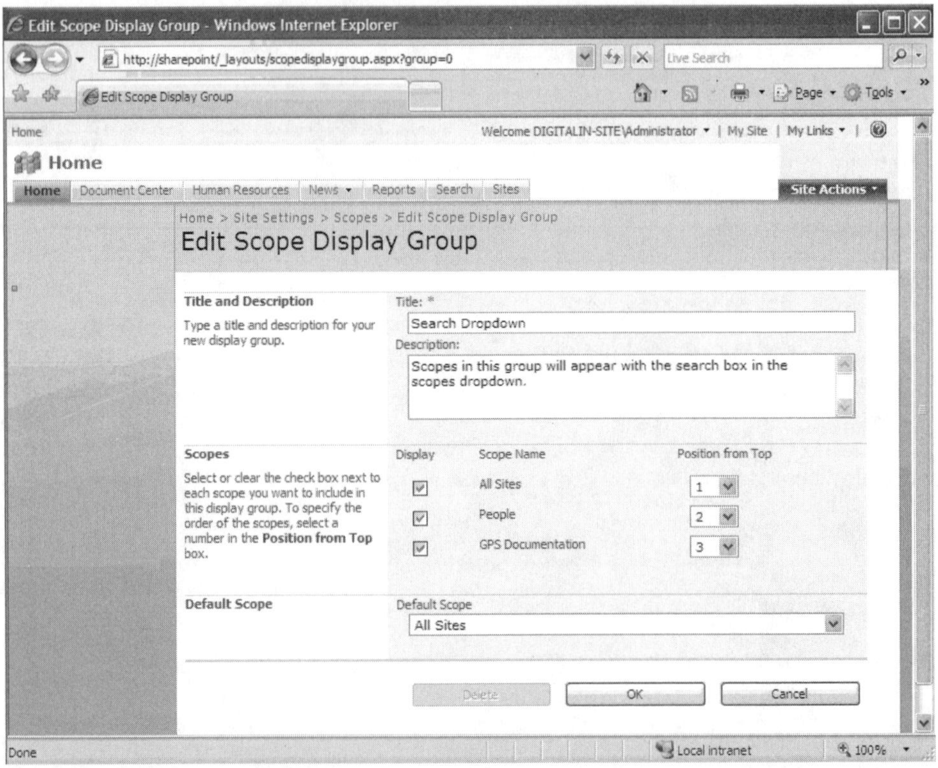

Figure 8-19. Adding a Search Scope to a Display Group.

File Extension	File Format
ASCX	Web User Control
ASP	Active Server Page
ASPX	ASP.NET Source File
DOC	Microsoft Word Document
DOCM	Microsoft Word Open Extensible Markup Language (XML) Format Document with Macros Enabled

Table 8-1. MOSS Default Indexed File Types

File Extension	File Format
DOCX	Microsoft Word Open XML Format Document
DOT	Microsoft Word Template
EML	Microsoft Outlook Express E-Mail
HTM/HTML	Hypertext Markup Language (HTML) File
JHTML	Dynamo Server Page
JSP	JAVA Server Page
MHT	Microsoft Home Publishing Project
MHTML	Multipurpose Internet Mail Extensions (MIME) HTML File
MSG	Exchange Mail Message
MSPX	Microsoft XML-based Web Page
NSF	Nintendo Entertainment System Sound File
ODC	OpenOffice OpenDocument
PHP	Hypertext Preprocessor (PHP) Script
PPT	Microsoft PowerPoint Presentation
PPTM	Microsoft PowerPoint Open XML Format Presentation with Macros Enabled
PPTX	Microsoft PowerPoint Open XML Format Presentation
PUB	Microsoft Publisher Document
TIF/TIFF	Tagged Image Format File
TXT	Text File
URL	Uniform Resource Location (Internet) File
VDX	Microsoft Visio XML
VSD	Microsoft Vision Drawing File
VSS	Microsoft Visio Smartshapes File
VST	Microsoft Visio Template File
XLS	Microsoft Excel Worksheet File
XLSX	Microsoft Excel Open XML Format Spreadsheet
XML	Extensible Markup Language File

Table 8-1. MOSS Default Indexed File Types. (*Continued*)

In order to add search and index capability to MOSS for a non-standard file type, you must locate, download, and install a tool called an IFilter, which is the acronym for indexing filter. There is a growing number of free and commercial IFilters available for a wide variety of file types. Table 8-2 shows only a small sampling of sources where you can find free IFilters for certain file types.

TIP To find an IFilter for a particular file type, search the Internet using the file type's filename extension (such as .ZIP) and the word "IFilter." IFilters are commonly available from the web site of the vendor for a specific file type.

The process used to add search and indexing support for a particular file type is to obtain the appropriate IFilter and install it to the MOSS environment. Fortunately, the process used for adding search and indexing support for any file type is the same.

The steps used to add an IFilter to MOSS are

1. Download and install the IFilter following the vendor or supplier's instructions.

2. Add a file icon to MOSS. This helps identify the file type and indicates that it is supported.

File Format	Source
CAB (Cabinet)	Citeknet (www.citeknet.com)
CHM (Microsoft Compressed HTML Help)	Citeknet (www.citeknet.com)
HLP (Windows Help)	Citeknet (www.citeknet.com)
JPEG/JPG (Joint Photographers Experts Group)	AimingTech (www.aimingtech.com)
MHT (MHTML)	Citeknet (www.citeknet.com)
MP3 (MPEG Audio Stream, Layer III)	AimingTech (www.aimingtech.com)
PDF (Portable Document Format)	Adobe (www.adobe.com)
RTF (Rich Text Format)	Microsoft (www.microsoft.com)
VDX/VSD/VSS/VST (Microsoft Visio)	Microsoft (www.microsoft.com)
WP (WordPerfect)	Corel (www.corel.com)
XML	Microsoft (www.microsoft.com)
ZIP (Compressed File Archive)	Citeknet (www.citeknet.com)

Table 8-2. Sources for Free File Type IFilter Downloads

3. Add the file type to MOSS.

4. Perform a full crawl of all content sources that contain the file type for which you are adding support.

To help you understand this process in more detail, perform the following steps to add an Adobe PDF IFilter to MOSS:

1. Download the Adobe PDF IFilter.

TIP At the time of this writing, v7.0 is the most current. You can download it from www.adobe .com/support/downloads.

2. Stop the Internet Information Service (IIS) Manager service:

   a. From the Administrative Tools menu (Start | All Programs | Administrative Tools) menu, click Services.

   b. Right-click the IIS Admin service and click Stop, as shown in Figure 8-20.

3. Following the vendor or supplier's instructions, run the IFilter installation program on each MOSS Index server in the server farm.

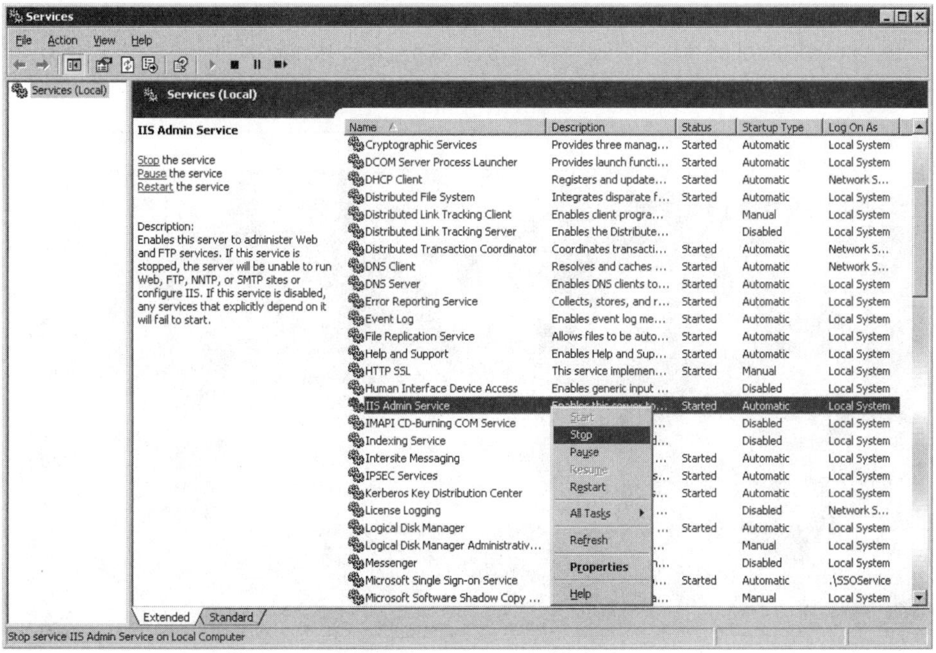

Figure 8-20. Stopping the IIS Admin Service.

4. Register the IFilter by doing the following:

   a. Open a command prompt by either clicking Command Prompt on the Start menu or opening the Run box (Start | Run) and entering **cmd** in the Open box.

   b. At the command prompt, change directories to the IFilter installation directory using the command **cd C:\Program Files\Adobe\PDF Ifilter 7.0**

   c. At the command prompt, enter the command **regsvr32.exe pdffilt.dll** and press the Enter key (see Figure 8-21).

   d. At the command prompt, enter the command **exit** and press the Enter key to close the Command Prompt window.

5. Create an icon for the IFilter by copying a 16 × 16 (pixels) .GIF file for use as the icon of the file type to this location: C:\Program Files\Common Files\ Microsoft Shared\web server extensions\12\TEMPLATE\IMAGES.

NOTE Icon files can typically be found at the file vendor's web site. Alternatively, you could make your own GIF using a screen capture and image editing program.

TIP For consistency, you may want to adopt a naming convention for these files. One suggestion is to use the graphic file extension as a part of the filename. For example, the icon for a PDF file might be named iconpdf.gif or a JPG file may have an icon named iconjpg.gif.

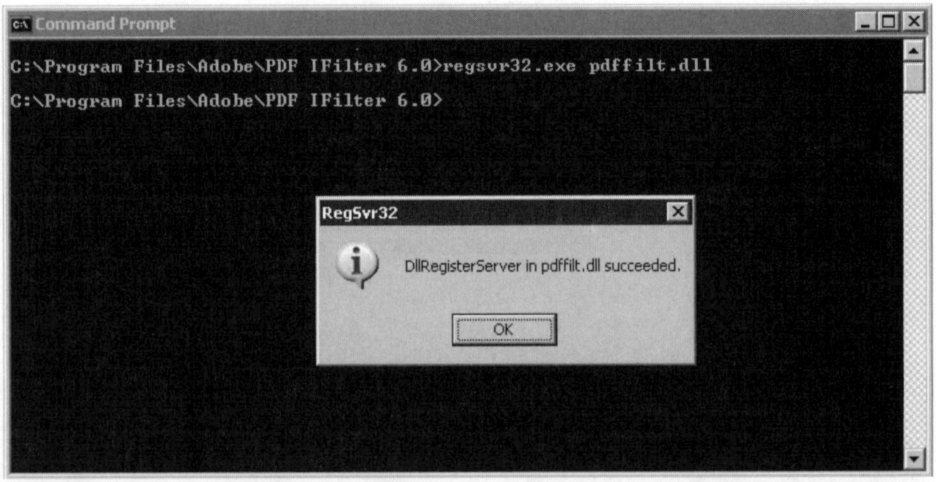

Figure 8-21.   Registering the pdffilt.dll file.

6. Edit the DOCICON.XML file located at:C:\Program Files\Common Files\ Microsoft Shared\web server extensions\12\TEMPLATE\XML\ to include the PDF file type using these steps:

   a. Open the DOCICON.XML file with Notepad.

   b. Locate and copy the PNG entry for use as a template for the PDF. The file is organized alphabetically by the mapping tag key attribute.

   c. Paste the copied entry in the file where the tag key would fall alphabetically.

   d. Change the mapping key entry to **pdf**.

   e. Change the value entry to the name of the icon file—for example, pdffilt.dll.

      Your completed entry for the pdf file type should look like the example in Figure 8-22.

   f. Save and exit the file.

7. Restart the IIS Admin Service

   a. Open the Services utility from the Administrative Tools menu (see step 2a).

   b. Right-click the IIS Admin Service and click Start.

8. Add the PDF file type to the Search Settings by doing the following:

   a. Open the Search Settings page using the steps outlined in the "MOSS Search Settings" section earlier in the chapter.

   b. Click the File Types link.

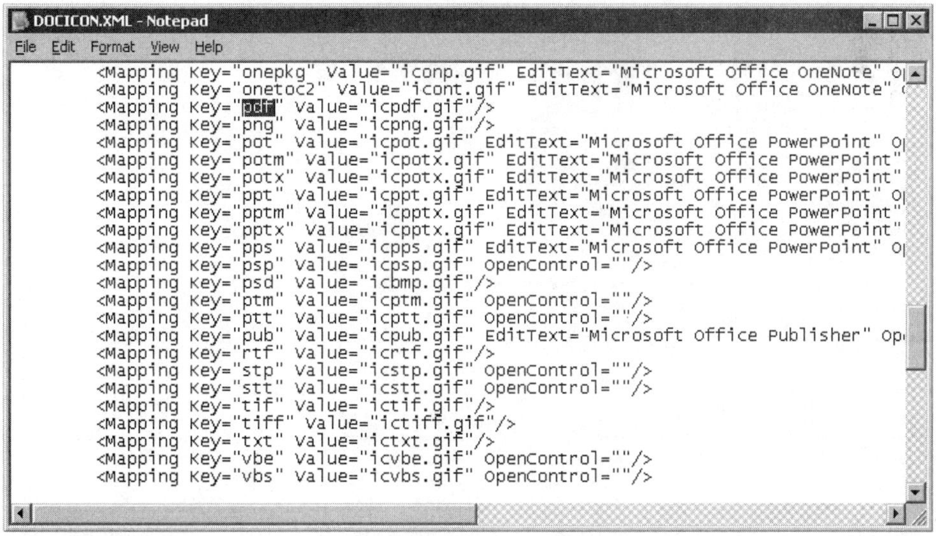

Figure 8-22.   The edited DOCICON.XML file.

    c. Click the New File Type button.

    d. Type **pdf** in the File Extension field.

    e. Click OK.

9. Perform a full crawl on each content source that contains PDF files, or, alternatively, allow scheduled crawls to update content indexes during non-peak hours if performance is a concern.

You should always test any configuration changes to ensure they have the desired effect. To test if PDF files are not being crawled and indexed, publish a PDF file to an MOSS content server. You may have to wait for the next crawl to complete, or you may want to force a crawl update. In either case, until the newly published PDF file is crawled and indexed, it won't appear in your search results. Once the crawl has completed, search for a word you know is contained in the PDF file. If everything is working properly, you will see the PDF file returned in the search results, as illustrated in Figure 8-23.

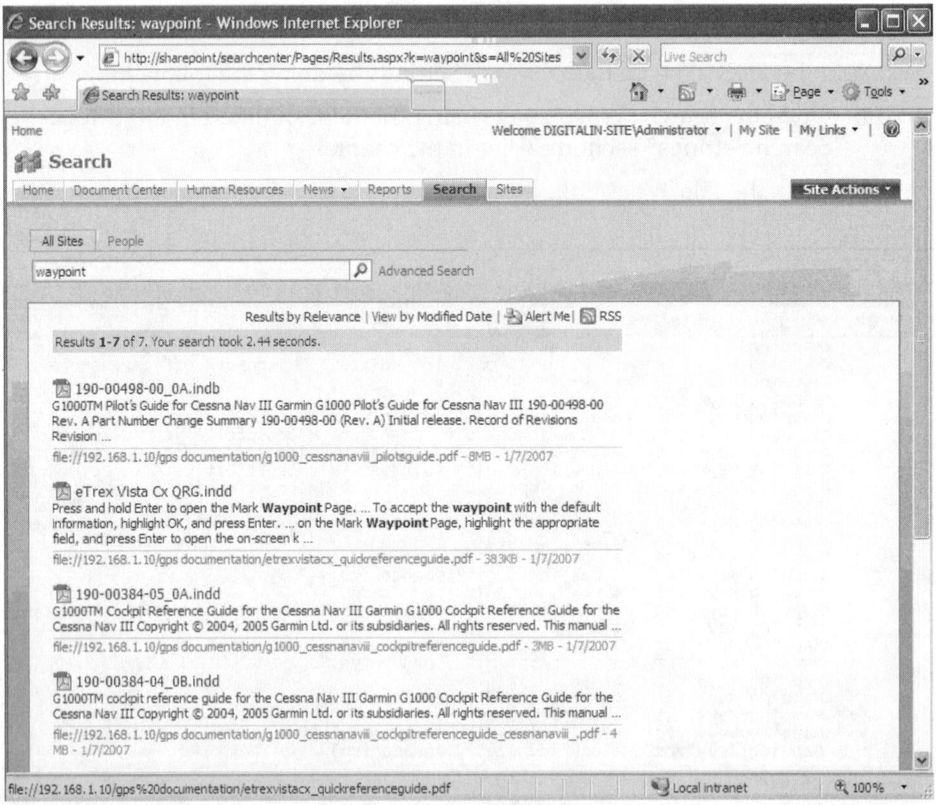

Figure 8-23. PDF search results, including the PDF file icon.

TIP   If your search results don't display PDF files, you may need to restart the applicable server(s) and run another full crawl to completely enable support for the new file type.

SUMMARY

At its core, the MOSS search feature is all about users efficiently finding the information they need. You've looked at two types of search data: native and non-native content sources. Each content source has an associated content index, which must be scheduled for update through the content source properties. Search scopes are collections of search scope rules, which can point to one or more content sources to control the MOSS search results. You've also learned how to add support for additional file types using IFilters.

Take the time to train your users on how to perform a simple search, explaining that it empowers them to find the information they need when they don't know where to look. Often, users know more than they think. They may know the file type, approximately when it was authored, and by whom. These details can be used to perform an advanced search to pinpoint the document in what may otherwise be a sea of search results.

CHAPTER 9

MOSS Document and Record Management

Microsoft's vision of Enterprise Content Management (ECM), as implemented in Microsoft Office SharePoint Server 2007 (MOSS) provides the enterprise with document management control and management capabilities able to track the life cycle of the enterprise's digital content, from creation to disposal or archival. As more and more of a company's information is created, reviewed, signed, and stored as digital media, the ability to effectively and efficiently manage and control its electronic media has become extremely vital to meeting the company's information needs, conformance to regulatory and legal requirements, and, not least of all, conducting its day-to-day business activities.

This chapter provides a brief look into the MOSS functions and features used to implement a document and records management system in a company, as a part of the company's overall ECM. While the discussion focuses on only the basic actions used in configuring MOSS for this purpose, it should give you an understanding of the hierarchy, administration, and document storage and retrieval tools available in MOSS.

DOCUMENTS VS. RECORDS

Information management is implemented in MOSS on two levels: document management and record management. Document management involves the control and maintenance of documents as they move through their life cycle, which includes their creation, review, distribution and storage, access, and disposal or archival. Ultimately, the purpose of a document management system is to facilitate the easy access and sharing of stored information. This is best accomplished by organizing information in a way that is logical to users and applies the same standards across the network for the creation, access, and viewing of documents.

Within the context of MOSS, essentially all stored items created using an Office application, and some other applications as well, are documents (also known as items). On the other hand, a record is a document that carries some significance to business operations, transactions, and legal or regulatory requirements. Once a company is able to define which of its stored documents are records, a record management system then details the how, where, when, and why of storing and accessing individual records. While it may seem that perhaps not all of a company's documents are, in fact, records, most stored documents carry some importance to the operations, welfare, and stability of the company. However, it is common that a company's record management policies may also include physical records as well, with essentially the same management and retention policies applying equally to both the electronic and physical records.

INFORMATION MANAGEMENT POLICIES

A policy, as defined by MOSS, is a set of rules or guidelines that govern the creation, use, and disposition of a particular item, site, collection, list, library, page, and so on. An information management policy then is the rules applied to a particular content type, such as a document. An information management policy defines who can access documents of a certain content type, what users can do with these documents, and, where applicable, how long the document is retained.

MOSS Policy Features

Within MOSS an information management policy is defined through a series of policy features. MOSS has predefined policy features that can be used to define the information management policy applied to a particular site or the content types included on the site. The policy features defined by MOSS are:

▼   **Auditing**   This policy feature supports the analysis of how documents and records are used and what is being done to them by maintaining a log file of the related activities, including such events as checking a document in or out, editing, viewing, deleting, or changing its settings or permissions.

■   **Barcodes**   This policy feature enables a company to keep track of physical documents, records, or items that have been printed from an electronically stored document. The use of the barcode policy feature assigns a unique identification number to each document that links the electronic and physical copies.

■   **Expiration**   This policy feature tracks the lifespan of a document stored on a SharePoint element against a retention period that can be specified in days, months, or years. The retention period can be measured from the date the document was created or the date of its last modification. At the end of the retention period, the document is flagged for deletion or archival and, if enabled, a workflow can be used to obtain consensus on the disposition of the document.

▲   **Labels**   This policy feature works very much like the barcode policy feature, with the exception that in place of a barcode label, a text label is produced to track physical copies of a stored document.

NOTE   MOSS also provides the capability for a company to create and use custom policy features to control or track proprietary documents and records, such as preventing certain documents from being printed on certain printers or restricting access to some documents for only certain hours of the day.

Information management policy features can be configured to a specific content type, a list, or library.

Information Management Policies on a SharePoint Site

A SharePoint information management policy can be created on a site using three different approaches:

▼   Create an information management policy on the site collection.

■   Create an information management policy on a site content type.

▲   Create an information management policy on a list or library.

Where you create an information management policy has a direct impact on where it is applied and to what elements. A site collection policy that is applied to a site content type is inherited by all lists or libraries based on that content type. An information management policy created for a list or library directly applies to only the items included in that element.

Site Collection Policies

Perhaps the best way to ensure an information management policy is applied to all the documents of a certain type is to create the policy at the site collection level and then apply it to the content types to be managed by the policy. There are actually two ways you can accomplish this:

▼   Create a site collection policy and add it to a specific content type, list, or library.

▲   Create a policy for a specific content type and then add it to a list or library.

Create a Site Collection Policy   To create an information management policy at the site collection level, do the following:

1. Navigate to the main page of the site collection to which you wish to add the information management policy.

2. On the site collection page, click the Site Actions button to open its drop-down menu, select the Site Settings option and then click the Modify All Site Settings option on its pop-up menu.

3. On the Site Settings page, click the Site Collection Policies link under the Site Collection Administration heading.

4. On the Site Collection Policies page, shown in Figure 9-1, click the Create button to open the Edit Policy page.

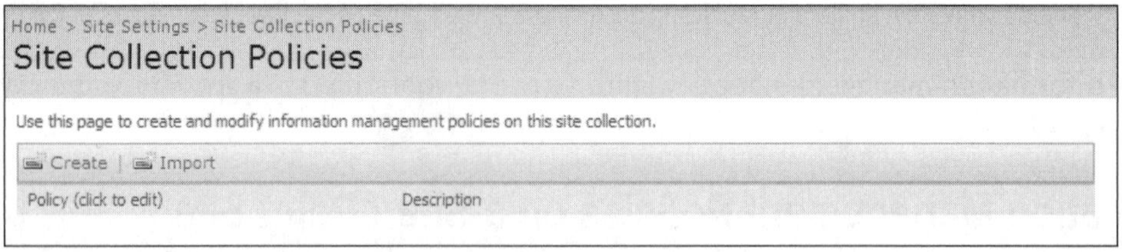

Home > Site Settings > Site Collection Policies
Site Collection Policies

Use this page to create and modify information management policies on this site collection.

Create | Import

Policy (click to edit)	Description

Figure 9-1.   The Site Collection Policies page.

5. On the Edit Policy page (see Figure 9-2), enter the settings information required in each section, as follows:

   a. In the Name and Administrative Description sections, enter a unique name for the policy and a brief description that explains the purpose and application of the policy. The administrative description is displayed when a policy is being added to a SharePoint element by an administrator or site owner. You can enter up to 512 characters, so you don't have to be too brief.

   b. In the Policy Statement section, enter a statement that explains to users the policy features included in the policy and any additional information they need to know about how or what the policy does.

   c. You can either choose to check the checkboxes associated with the policy features included on the Edit Policy page at this point or wait to configure them to specific content types, lists, or libraries. If you configure the policy features at this level, they will be inherited by any elements opened in the site collection, where applicable.

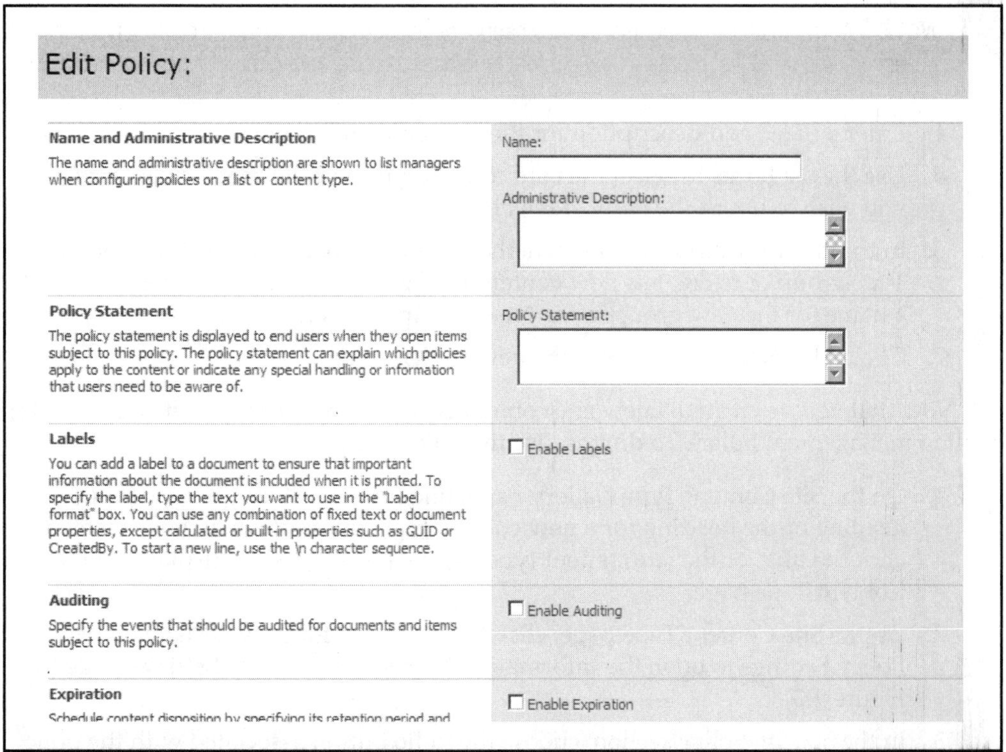

Figure 9-2. The Edit Policy page.

NOTE For more information on configuring the individual policy features see the "Configure Policy Features" section later in this section.

6. Click the OK button to save the policy and return to the Site Collection Policies page.

Add a Policy to a Content Type To add an information management policy to a site content type, do the following:

1. Open the Site Settings page of the site collection on which you wish to configure a policy on a content type.

2. On the Site Settings page, click the Site Content Types link under the Galleries heading.

3. On the Site Content Types Gallery page, click the Create button to open the New Site Content Type page.

NOTE An information management policy cannot be applied directly to a core content type on a site collection. You must first create a new content type based on the core content type you wish to use.

4. Enter a name and description for the new content type.

5. Use the list boxes to select the core content type and the specific content type you wish to use as the basis of the new content type.

6. In the Group section, indicate whether you wish to use the Custom Content Type group or to create a new content type group. If you choose the latter, enter a name for the new group in the New Group text box.

7. Click the OK button to create the new content type.

Now that you've created a new site content type, you can configure it with an information management policy. To do this, use the following steps:

1. On the Site Content Type Gallery page, under the Custom Content Types heading or the heading for a new content type group you may have created, click the link for the site content type you've just created to display its Site Content Type page.

2. On the Site Content Type page, click the link for Information Management Policy Settings to open the Information Management Policy Settings page (see Figure 9-3).

3. In the Specify Policy section, choose the radio button associated with the policy choice you wish to make: None; Define A Policy (create a new policy); or Use A Site Collection Policy. The list box for the Use A Site Collection Policy includes all information management policies defined at the site collection level. If you

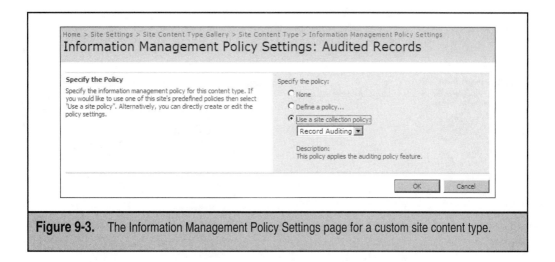

Home > Site Settings > Site Content Type Gallery > Site Content Type > Information Management Policy Settings

Information Management Policy Settings: Audited Records

Specify the Policy

Specify the information management policy for this content type. If you would like to use one of this site's predefined policies then select "Use a site policy". Alternatively, you can directly create or edit the policy settings.

Specify the policy:

○ None

○ Define a policy...

⊙ Use a site collection policy:

Record Auditing ▼

Description:
This policy applies the auditing policy feature.

[OK]   [Cancel]

Figure 9-3.   The Information Management Policy Settings page for a custom site content type.

choose the Define A Policy option, the Edit Policy page displays (see the "Create a Site Collection Policy" section earlier in this chapter).

4. Click the OK button to save the configuration settings for the content type.

Site Collection Auditing

Often, it becomes necessary, or is mandated by company security or auditing policies, that a record be maintained as to who is accessing the information stored in the system, how the information is being accessed, and what actions are being taken. To collect this information, you can enable site collection auditing, which will then log the actions you designate to be tracked.

To enable site collection auditing, do the following:

1. On the site for which you wish to enable auditing, click the Site Actions button, select the Site Settings option, and click Modify All Site Settings.

2. On the Site Settings page, click the link for Site Collection Audit Settings under the Site Collection Administration heading, to open the Configure Audit Settings page (see Figure 9-4).

3. If you wish to have log entries created for the actions taken on SharePoint documents and items, check the checkboxes associated with the events you wish to log in the Documents and Items section. Your choices are:

   ■ Opening or downloading documents, viewing items in lists, or viewing item properties

   ■ Editing items

   ■ Checking out or checking in items

   ■ Moving or copying items to another location in the site

   ■ Deleting or restoring items

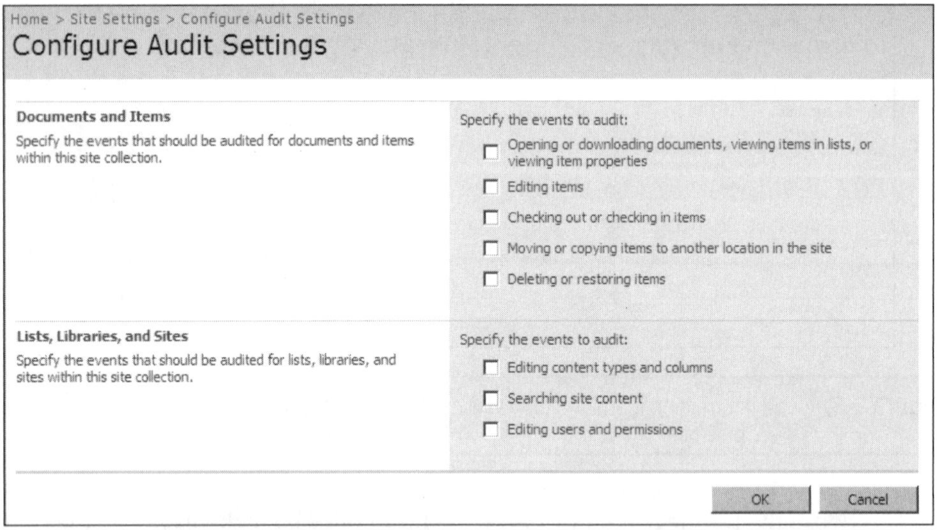

Figure 9-4.   The Configure Audit Settings page.

4. If you wish to have log entries created for the actions taken on SharePoint lists, libraries, and sites, check the checkboxes associated with the events you wish to log in the SharePoint Lists, Libraries, and Sites section. Your choices are:

    ■ Editing content types and columns

    ■ Searching type content

    ■ Editing users and permissions

Remember that you should create log entries for only those events you need to audit. Log files can fill very fast if too much data is being collected and can impact the amount of available disk space on a server if routine events are tracked unnecessarily.

Configure Policy Features

When an information management policy is defined, you can include any or all of the Labels, Auditing, Expiration, or Barcodes policy features available. To enable one or more of these policy features, perform the steps outlined in the following sections.

Label Policy Feature   The Label policy feature allows a site administrator to insert identification labels in printed copies of documents created with Office 2007 applications. The embedded label, which is placed in the document header by default, is used to identify the document's properties on a printed copy of the document. Any of the document's metadata can be included on the label, including its filename, author, creation date, and so on.

To enable the Label policy feature, do the following:

1. Open the Edit Policy page for the policy to which you want to add the Labels policy feature.

2. Check the checkbox associated with Enable Labels option in the Labels section. This causes the page to refresh and display the Labels settings (see Figure 9-5).

3. Check the checkbox associated with the Prompt Users To Insert A Label Before Saving Or Printing option to make sure a label is inserted into the document whenever the document is saved or printed. If you wish users to have the option of inserting a label into the documents, leave this checkbox unchecked.

4. If you wish to lock the label so users aren't able to change it, check the checkbox associated with the Prevent Changes To Labels After They Are Added option.

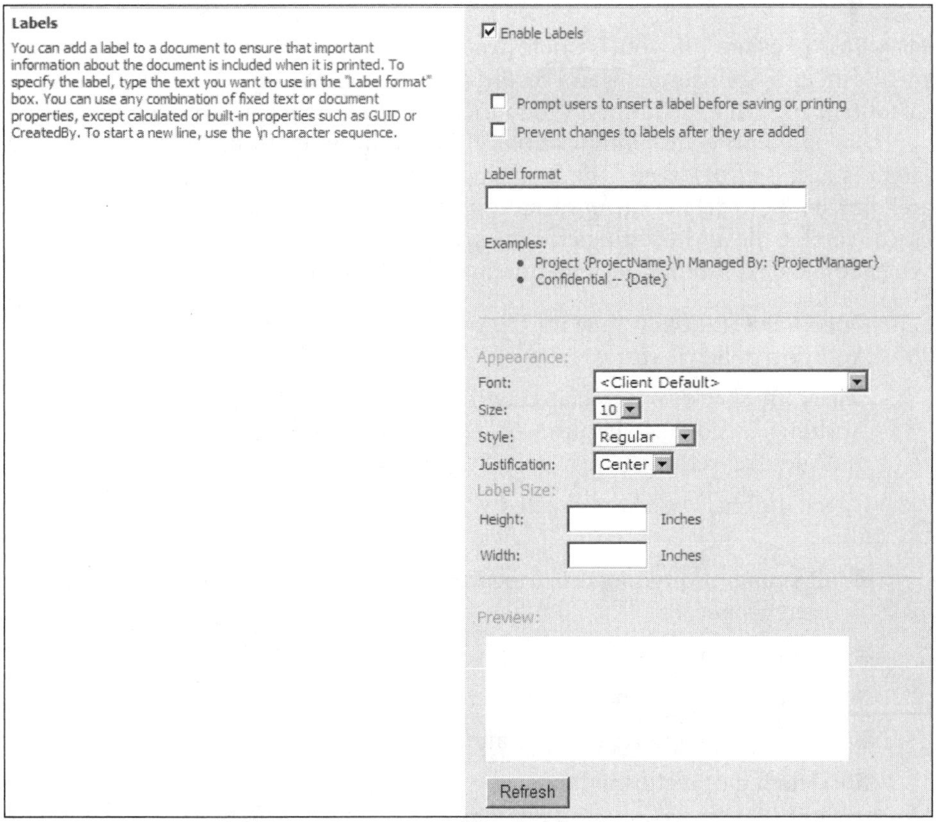

Labels

You can add a label to a document to ensure that important information about the document is included when it is printed. To specify the label, type the text you want to use in the "Label format" box. You can use any combination of fixed text or document properties, except calculated or built-in properties such as GUID or CreatedBy. To start a new line, use the \n character sequence.

☑ Enable Labels

☐ Prompt users to insert a label before saving or printing
☐ Prevent changes to labels after they are added

Label format

Examples:
- Project {ProjectName}\n Managed By: {ProjectManager}
- Confidential -- {Date}

Appearance:
Font: \<Client Default>
Size: 10
Style: Regular
Justification: Center

Label Size:
Height: ____ Inches
Width: ____ Inches

Preview:

Refresh

Figure 9-5. The Labels section of the Edit Policy page.

5. In the Label Format text box, enter the text you wish to appear in the label exactly the way you want it to appear. If you wish to include information from the metadata columns of the document, enclose each column name in braces ({}).

TIP To add a line break in a label, enter **\n**. To add a tab, enter **\t**.

---

6. Select the font size and style you wish to use in the label in the Appearance section.

7. If you wish to set the height and width of the label, enter these dimensions in the Label Size section. The valid size settings for the label size are from 0.25 inches to 20 inches for both the height and the width.

8. If you wish to preview the label's content without any actual metadata values, click the Refresh button.

9. Click the OK button to apply the label policy feature to the policy.

Auditing Policy Feature If you wish to track certain events that occur on SharePoint elements, including documents and records, you can enable the Auditing policy feature for a content type, list, or library. When included in a policy, this policy feature writes log entries, based on your configuration of the Auditing feature, which track each time the item is accessed or saved. The Auditing policy feature applies specifically to those SharePoint items to which an information management policy has been applied and doesn't override the audit settings for the site collection.

To enable the Auditing policy feature, use the following steps:

1. Open the Edit Policy page for the policy to which you want to add the Auditing policy feature.

2. Check the checkbox associated with the Enable Auditing option in the Auditing section (see Figure 9-6). This causes the page to refresh and display the Auditing settings.

3. Check the checkboxes associated with the events you wish to log. Your choices are:

   ■ Opening or downloading documents, viewing items in lists, or viewing item properties

   ■ Editing items

   ■ Checking out or checking in items

   ■ Moving or copying items to another location in the site

   ■ Deleting or restoring items

4. Click the OK button to save the policy with the Auditing policy feature enabled.

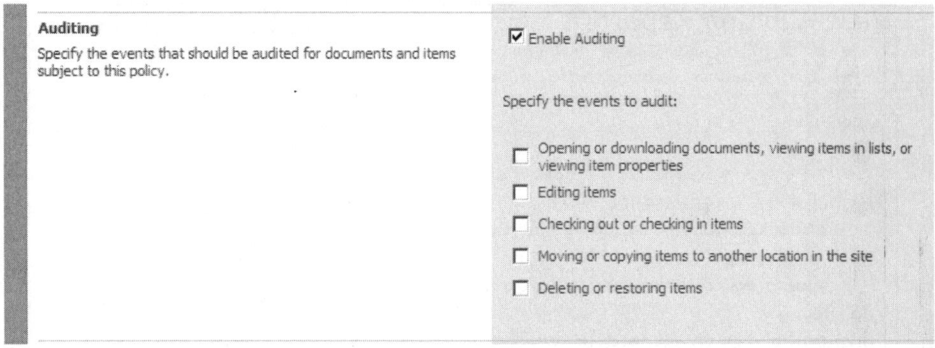

Figure 9-6. The Auditing section of the Edit Policy page.

To view the log entries created by the Auditing policy feature, use the Audit Log Reports. To access the Audit Log Reports, use the following steps:

1. Open the Site Settings page on the site where you wish to review the audit log reports.

2. Under the Site Collection Administration heading, click the Audit Log Reports link to open the Run Reports page.

3. On the View Auditing Reports page, shown in Figure 9-7, choose the report you wish to view. Figure 9-8 shows a sample of the Policy Modifications report. Notice that the report is viewed in an Excel workspace from an XML file produced by the report feature.

Expiration Policy Feature　If the Expiration policy feature is enabled on an information management policy, the site collection is searched for those documents to which the policy is applied, but which have exceeded their retention period. If a document is identified as expired, you have the choice of deleting it (moving it to the Recycle Bin), having a workflow initiated for it, or starting a custom process.

To enable the Expiration policy feature, do the following:

1. Open the Edit Policy page for the policy to which you want to add the Expiration policy feature.

2. Check the checkbox associated with the Enable Expiration option in the Expiration section. This causes the page to refresh and display the Expiration settings (see Figure 9-9).

3. For The Retention Period Is option, choose either to set a retention period as a number of days, months, or years or to have the retention period determined by a custom program or a workflow. If you choose to use a set number of days, months, or years, enter the number in the text box and select the calendar unit from the list box adjacent to it.

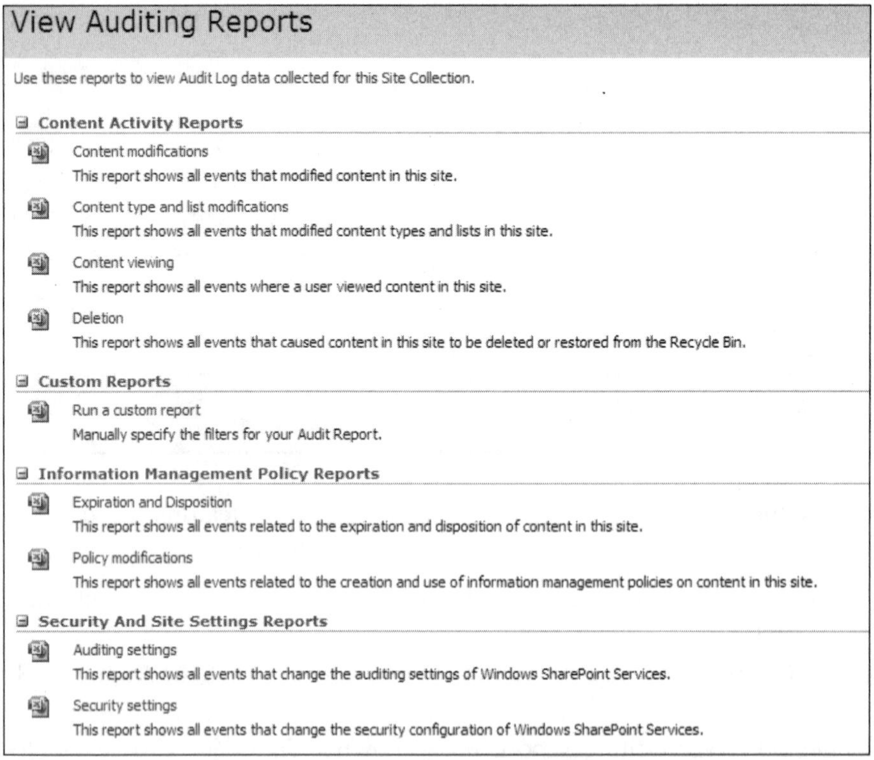

View Auditing Reports

Use these reports to view Audit Log data collected for this Site Collection.

⊟ Content Activity Reports

Content modifications
This report shows all events that modified content in this site.

Content type and list modifications
This report shows all events that modified content types and lists in this site.

Content viewing
This report shows all events where a user viewed content in this site.

Deletion
This report shows all events that caused content in this site to be deleted or restored from the Recycle Bin.

⊟ Custom Reports

Run a custom report
Manually specify the filters for your Audit Report.

⊟ Information Management Policy Reports

Expiration and Disposition
This report shows all events related to the expiration and disposition of content in this site.

Policy modifications
This report shows all events related to the creation and use of information management policies on content in this site.

⊟ Security And Site Settings Reports

Auditing settings
This report shows all events that change the auditing settings of Windows SharePoint Services.

Security settings
This report shows all events that change the security configuration of Windows SharePoint Services.

Figure 9-7. The View Auditing Reports page.

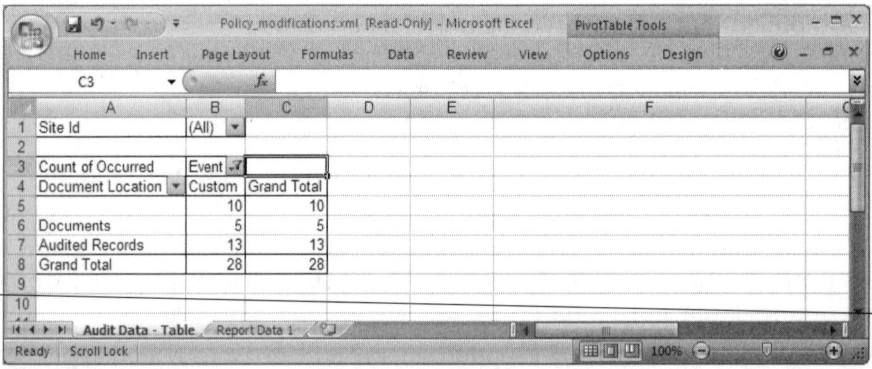

	A	B	C	D	E	F
1	Site Id	(All)				
2						
3	Count of Occurred	Event				
4	Document Location	Custom	Grand Total			
5		10	10			
6	Documents	5	5			
7	Audited Records	13	13			
8	Grand Total	28	28			
9						
10						

Figure 9-8. Audit reports are displayed in an Excel workspace.

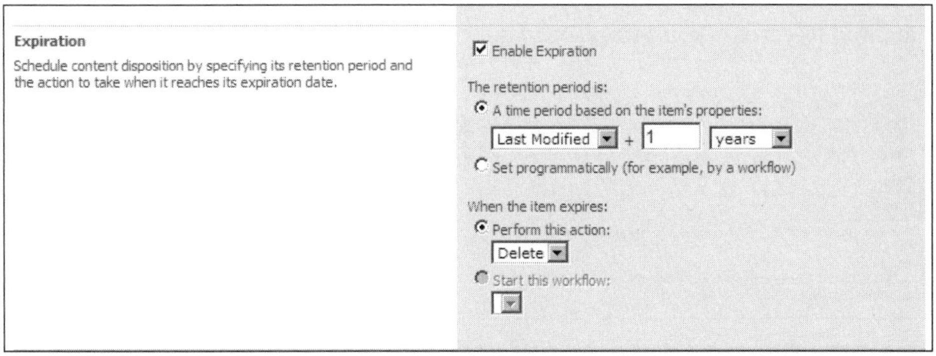

Figure 9-9.   The Expiration section on the Edit Policy page.

4.   If you wish to take a certain action when an item exceeds its retention period, choose the radio button associated with the Perform This Action option and then choose that action from the list box.

5.   If you wish to start a workflow associated with either the SharePoint item or its content type, such as a Disposition Approval workflow, select the Start This Workflow option and choose the workflow from the list box.

6.   Click the OK button to save the settings for the information management policy.

Exempt an Item from an Expiration Policy   If you wish to exempt a document from an expiration policy applied to a list or library, perform the following steps:

1.   Open the main page of the list or library containing the document or item you wish to exempt from the Expiration policy feature.

2.   Select the item or document on the page to open its drop-down menu and then click the View Properties option.

3.   On the document or item properties page, click the Exempt From Policy link (see Figure 9-10). This link doesn't appear if the document is not subject to an information management policy.

4.   On the Set Policy Exemption page (see Figure 9-11) that displays, click the Exempt button to exempt the document or item from the Expiration policy applied to the document library or list.

The Barcodes Policy Feature   The Barcode policy feature can be used for tracking physical copies of stored items, such as original documents that have been scanned into the system and printed copies of stored documents and records. Barcodes can also be used

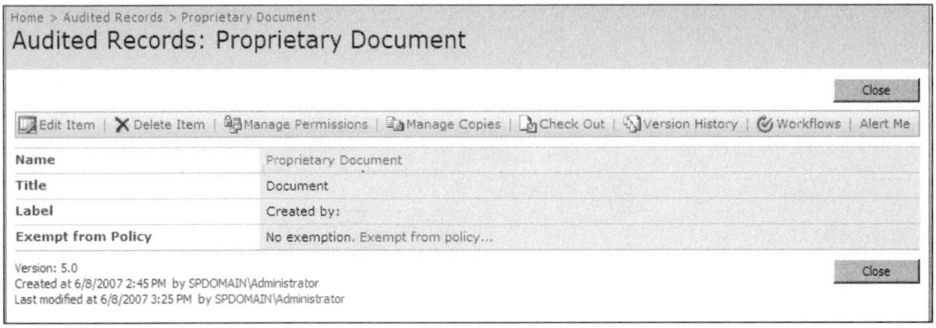

Figure 9-10. The Audited Records: Proprietary Document page.

to track physical assets, tying each asset to an asset record stored in a SharePoint list. Using barcodes in lieu of a label provides less information about the item since a barcode doesn't contain information about the item the way a label does.

Like the label used with the Labels policy feature (see the "Labels Policy Feature" earlier in this chapter), a barcode is added to the header of a document on which the Barcode policy feature is applied. The barcode is in the Code 39 barcode standard and includes a line of text below the barcode symbols so that, if necessary, the barcode identification can be entered manually as well.

To enable the Barcode policy feature for an information management policy, do the following:

1. Open the Edit Policy page for the policy to which you want to add the Auditing policy feature.

2. Check the checkbox associated with the Enable Barcode option in the Barcodes section. This causes the page to refresh and display the Barcodes settings (see Figure 9-12).

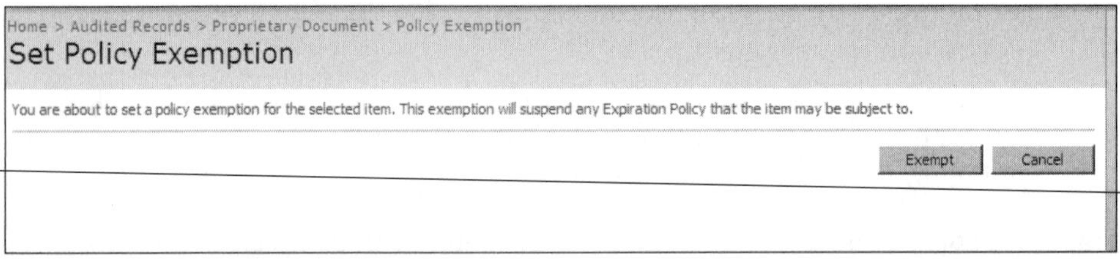

Figure 9-11. The Set Policy Exemption page.

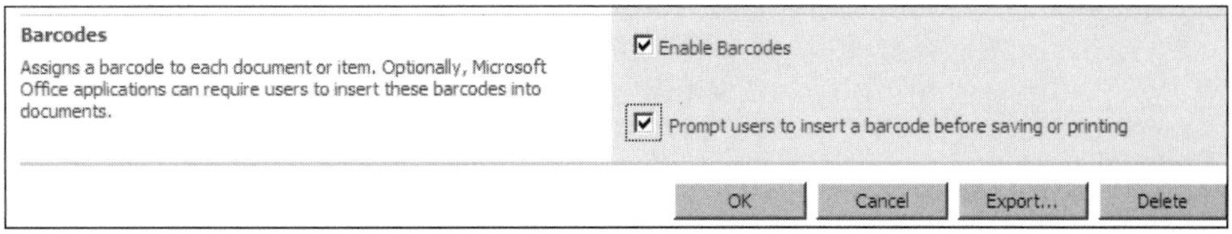

Figure 9-12. The Barcodes section of the Edit Policy page.

3. In the Barcodes section, check the checkbox associated with Enable Barcodes to turn on this feature.

4. If you wish to prompt users to insert the barcode when they save or print a document, check the checkbox associated with this setting.

5. Click the OK button to save the settings for the information management policy.

Information Management Policy Reports

The purpose of configuring an information management policy on a site, list, or library is to force certain management and tracking actions to take place and to track these actions through the event log files. To track the events logged for the policies and policy features configured to a site, list, or library, use the information management policy reports. However, before you can access these reports, they must be configured at the Central Administration level for the MOSS environment.

Configure MOSS for Logging and Reporting

Information management reports are configured for the MOSS environment from the Central Administration function. To set the configuration for these reports, perform the following steps:

1. Open the Central Administration page and open the Operations tab.

2. On the Operations tab, under the Logging and Reporting heading, click the link for Information Management Policy Usage Reports.

3. On the Information Management Policy Usage Reports page (shown in Figure 9-13), verify that the active web application is the one you wish to configure. If it isn't, click the Web Application button and then click the Choose Web Application button to open the Select Web Application dialog box. Double-click the web application you wish to configure.

4. In the Schedule Recurring Reports section of the Information Management Policy Usage Reports page, check the Enable Recurring Policy Usage Reports checkbox if you wish to have these reports produced on a regular schedule.

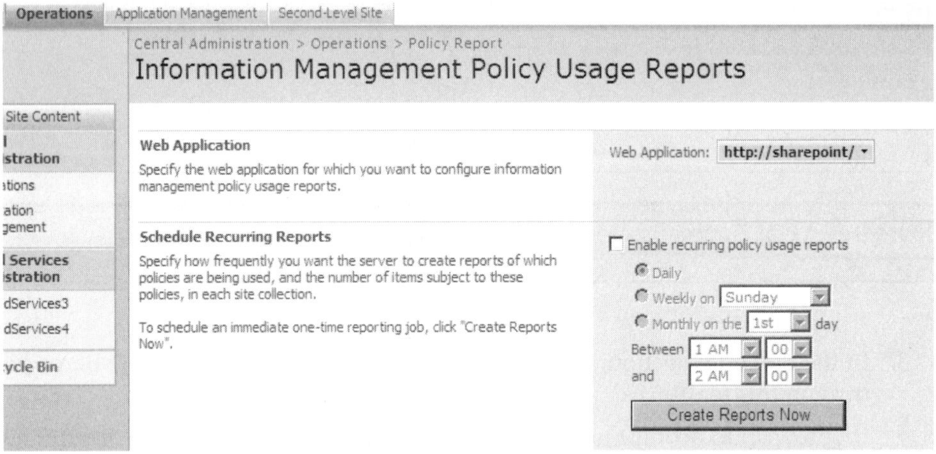

Figure 9-13. The Information Management Policy Usage Reports page.

5. After the display refreshes and activates the options associated with the Enable Recurring Policy Usage Reports checkbox, choose the radio button associated with the frequency with which you wish the reports produced. Your choices are daily, weekly on a certain day of the week, or monthly on a certain date of the month. You can also set the time of day you wish the reports to be produced, or revert to the default setting of between 1 and 2 AM.

6. In the Report File Location section, enter the URL of the network location where the reports are to be stored.

7. In the Report Template section, choose either to use a default report template or a custom template by selecting the radio button corresponding to your choice. If you choose to use a custom report template, you must enter the URL location for the template you wish to use. Use the Test Template button to verify that the template will function.

8. If you wish to run the usage reports on a one-time basis (for example, to produce a sample set of reports), scroll back up to the Schedule Recurring Reports section and click the Create Reports Now button.

9. Click the OK button to save the information policy usage reports configuration.

Audit Log Reports

The MOSS audit reports provide you with the information needed to manage, diagnose, troubleshoot, or analyze the performance, utilization, and effectiveness of the MOSS environment. The audit reports provide information on the SharePoint items that have been added, viewed, modified, removed, restored, or copied. Information on administrative changes (such as permissions changes, property changes, and searches) is also available.

To access the audit reports, use the following steps:

▼ Open the home page of the site collection for which you wish to see the audit reports.

■ Under the Site Collection Administration heading, click the Audit Log Reports link.

■ On the View Auditing Reports page (see Figure 9-7 earlier in the chapter), choose the report you wish to view. The reports available are:

■ Content Activity Reports

  ■ **Content modifications**   This report lists any changes made to stored content, such as modifying, deleting, checking in, and checking out a document.

  ■ **Content type and list modifications**   This report lists any additions, edits, and deletions to the content types on the site.

  ■ **Content viewing**   This report lists those users who viewed content on a site.

  ■ **Deletion**   This report lists items deleted from the site.

■ Custom Reports

  ■ **Run a custom report**   This option allows you to create a custom report using specified filters that can be used to list a particular event(s), the activity on a specific list or library, the activity between two dates, or the activity of a specific user or group.

■ Information Management Policy Reports

  ■ **Expiration and disposition**   This report lists the events occurring from the actions taken to remove an item after its retention period is exceeded.

  ■ **Policy modifications**   This report lists the logged events resulting from changes made to the information management policies on the site collection.

▲ Security and Site Settings Reports

  ■ **Auditing settings**   This report lists the logged events resulting from changes made to the auditing settings of a site.

  ■ **Security settings**   This report lists the events resulting from changes made to the security settings of a site or SharePoint element, such as user or group permissions changes.

The report generated is displayed in an Excel workspace, as shown in Figure 9-14. This lets you use Excel's features to format, reorganize, or extract the data presented.

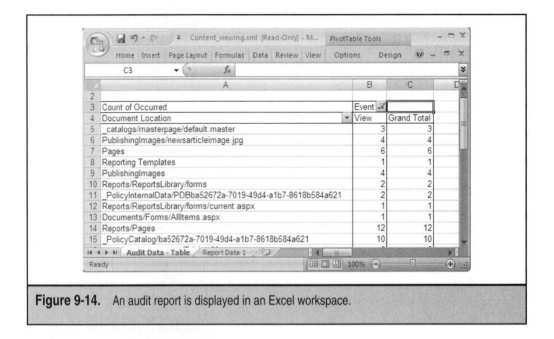

Figure 9-14. An audit report is displayed in an Excel workspace.

THE SHAREPOINT RECORDS CENTER

MOSS includes a site template for creating a Records Center site within a site collection. The Records Center provides a combination of a standard SharePoint site and predefined records management policies. The benefit of creating a Records Center site, which is created by default by MOSS for an initial site in a site collection, is that the records you need to manage, track, and administer are stored in a single site under a standard set of information management policies.

The Record Center site template provides three primary information management benefits:

▼ **Information management policy enforcement** The information management policies and policy features discussed earlier in this chapter are available and can be configured as needed.

■ **Record routing** Records can be sent to the Records Center and automatically placed in the appropriate document library based on the content type of the record and the entries in the record routing table.

▲ **Hold** The Records Center administrator or owner can apply a Hold policy to certain records that suspends the expiration policy feature's actions for a period.

Create Records Center Site

Before you actually create a Records Center site in your MOSS environment, you should review the planning (see Chapter 2) to ensure that the document libraries and lists needed to store each record type have been created. A best practice when using a Records Center site is to have a document library for each of the content types you included in your planning.

To create a Records Center site, perform the following steps:

1. Open the home page of the site collection to which you wish to add a Records Center site.

2. Click the Site Actions button to open its drop-down menu and then click the Create Site option.

3. On the New SharePoint Site page, fill in the Name, Description, and URL fields.

4. In the Template Selection section, choose the Records Center option from the Enterprise tab.

5. Select the settings you wish to apply in the Permissions and Navigation sections.

6. In the Site Categories section, check the checkbox associated with the List This New Site In A Site Directory option if you wish the Records Center to be included in a site category. Choose the site categories in which you wish to include the Records Center.

7. Click the Create button to create the Records Center site, which opens after the site has been created (see Figure 9-15).

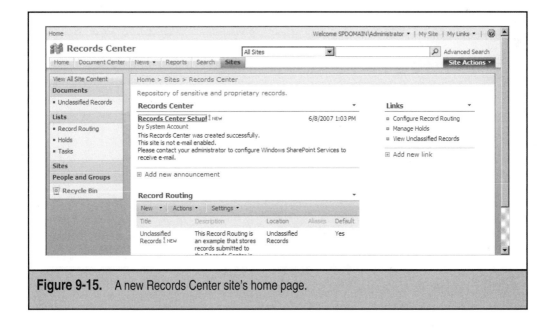

Figure 9-15.   A new Records Center site's home page.

Configure Record Routing

Rather than burden your users with the task of remembering just where each document type is to be stored, the Record Center uses its Record Routing list to store a document into the document library set up for that document type. The Record Routing list creates a cross-reference, using document metadata, to identify the library to which a document is to be stored. Within the Record Routing list, a rule item is created for each document type that links documents to the appropriate library. One such rule should be created for each document type and library within the Records Center.

When a document is submitted to the Records Center, its content type is matched to rule items included in the Record Routing list. If there is a match, the record is routed to the document library indicated by that rule. If there is no match, the record is routed to the library associated with the default rule. One rule in the Record Routing list is designated as the default rule.

To add rules to the Record Routing table, perform the following steps:

1. Navigate to the Records Center's home page. If you don't have the URL of the Records Center, you can find it using these steps:

   a. Open the home page of the site collection on which the Records Center is located.

   b. In the Quick Launch menu, click the Sites link.

   c. On the Site Directory page, click the Site Map tab to open the Site Map page.

   d. On the Site Map page (see Figure 9-16), click the Records Center link, typically found under Sites, to open the Record Center's home page.

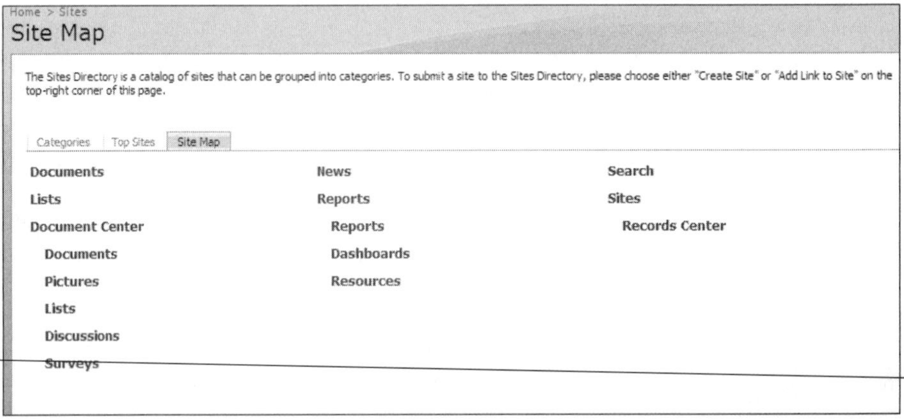

Figure 9-16. A Site Map page for a site collection.

2. On the Record Center's page, locate the Record Routing list.

3. To add an item to the Record Routing list, click the New button and choose New Item from the drop-down menu.

4. On the Record Routing: New Item page (shown in Figure 9-17), enter the following data:

    a. Enter a title for the routing rule. This title should match that of the content type stored in the document library to which this rule is linked.

    b. Enter an optional description that briefly explains the documents covered under this rule.

    c. Enter the name of the document library in which the records falling under this rule are to be stored.

    d. Enter other names used within the MOSS environment for the same document type in the Aliases box.

    e. If you wish this rule to be the default rule for the Record Routing list, check the checkbox associated with this setting.

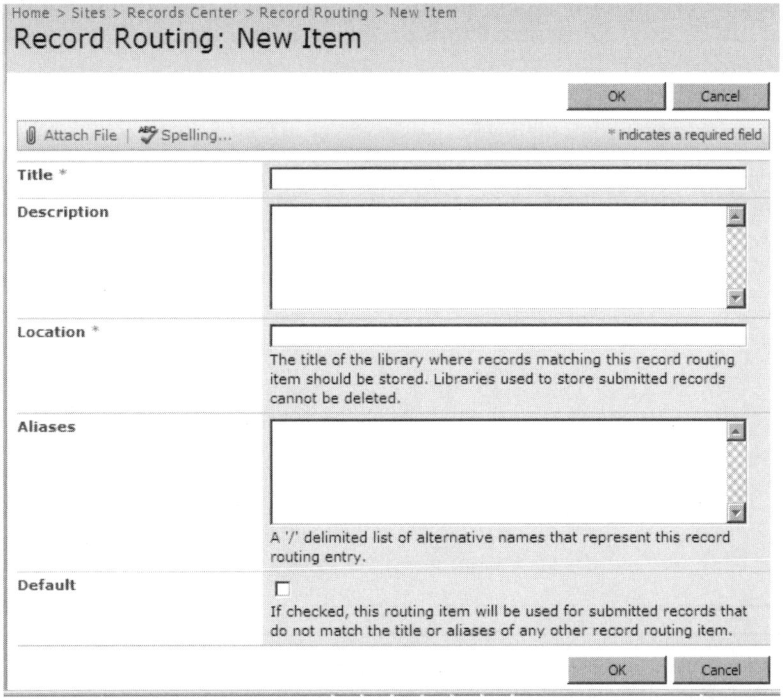

Figure 9-17.   The Record Routing: New Item page.

Send Documents to the Records Center

Documents can be sent to the Records Center for storage using either a menu selection, an e-mail transfer in conjunction with an Exchange server, or through custom programming. To manually send a document to the Records Center, do the following:

1. Navigate to the library or list containing the document you wish to send to the Records Center.

2. Select the document, opening its drop-down menu.

3. On the document's menu, select Send To and choose SharePoint Records Center from the pop-up menu that appears (see Figure 9-18).

4. If any of the data needed to match the document to the Records Routing list is missing from the document, you are prompted for it. Enter the data required and click OK to complete the routing operation.

To use e-mail to move documents to the Records Center, a folder must be configured on an Exchange Server 2007 server into which users can move e-mail messages for transfer to the Records Center. A document library with the appropriate properties must exist in the Records Center as well. MOSS, working with Windows SharePoint Services (WSS) 3.0, provides an application programming interface (API) that includes the WSS object model that can be used to create custom programs or workflows that move documents into the Records Center.

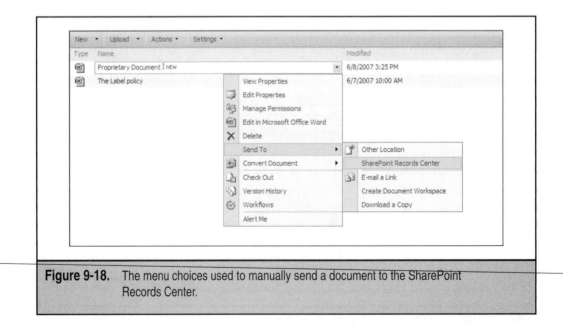

Figure 9-18. The menu choices used to manually send a document to the SharePoint Records Center.

Use Hold to Suspend Records

When you create a Records Center site, a Holds list is created within the site that can be used to apply a hold to a document to override an expiration policy feature that may be in force on the document. Included on the Holds list are some tools to help the Records Center administrator find, view, hold, and release documents.

Create a Hold

To create a Hold item on the Holds lists, perform the following steps:

1. Open the Records Center site, and then click the Holds link under the Lists heading in the Quick Launch menu.

2. On the Holds list, click the New button to open its drop-down menu and choose New Item to open the Holds: New Item page (see Figure 9-19).

3. Enter a title for the hold, such as the name of the event or activity that the documents must be held for.

4. Optionally, enter a description that further explains the purpose of the hold.

5. Enter the name of the person or group responsible for managing the hold and the records affected by it.

6. Click the OK button to create the hold.

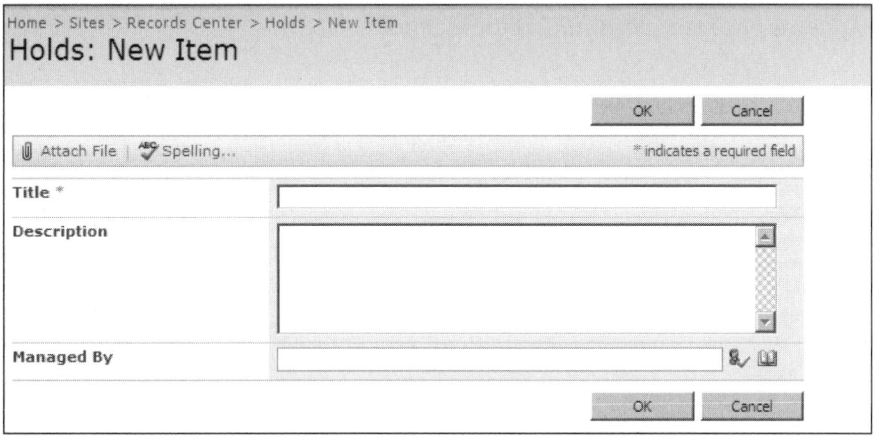

Figure 9-19.   The Holds: New Item page is used to create a new hold.

Add a Record to a Hold

If a particular record requires a hold, that record can be added directly to the hold from its current list or library. To add a record to a Hold list, do the following:

1. Navigate to the list or library containing the record to be added to a Hold list.

2. Select the record to open its drop-down menu and click the Manage Holds option to open the Item Hold Status page (see Figure 9-20).

3. Choose the Add To A Hold option and then select the Hold list to which you want to add the record. A record can be added to multiple Hold lists, but they must be configured one at a time. If you wish to remove the hold at a later date, simply choose the Remove From A Hold option.

4. Enter a comment if needed.

5. Click the Save button to add the record to the Hold.

Add Records to a Hold Using Search

In many situations, you may have multiple documents to which you need to add a hold. Rather than manually finding each individual document, you can use Search to locate the documents and add them to a hold. This can done through the following process:

1. On the Records Center site, open the Holds list using the link in the Quick Launch menu.

2. On the Holds list page, select the hold to which you want to add records to open its drop-down menu, and then click the View Item option to open the Holds page (see Figure 9-21) for that hold.

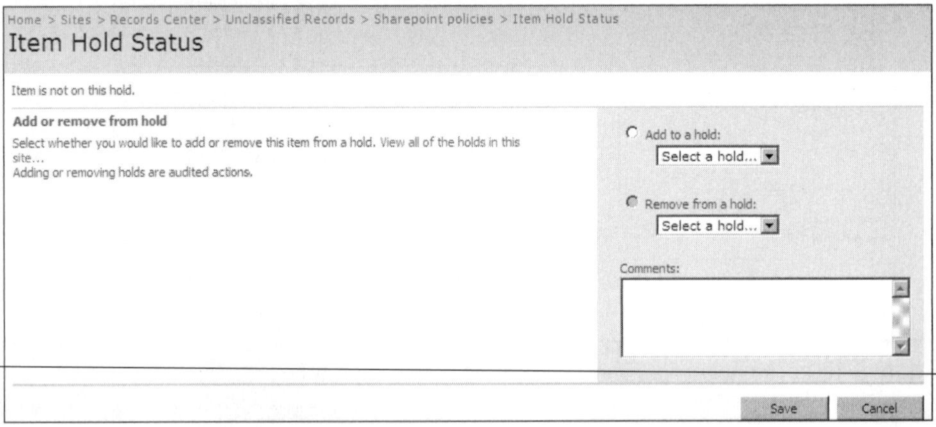

Figure 9-20. The Item Hold Status page is used to add or remove a record from a hold.

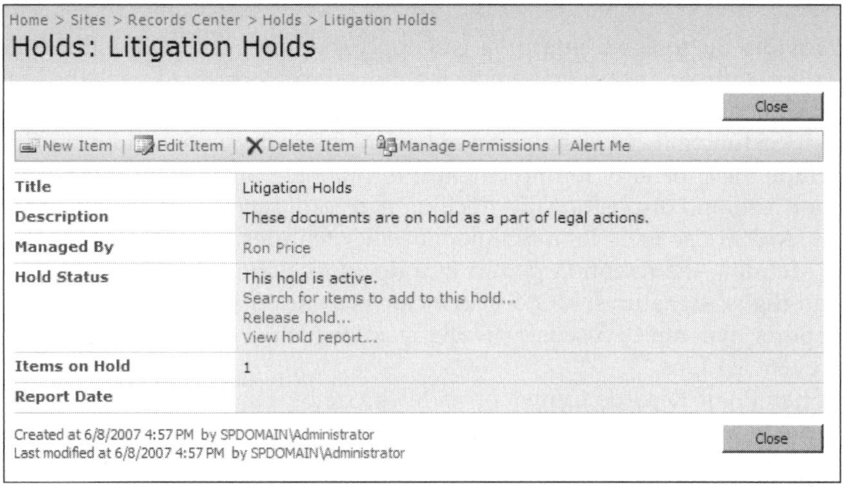

Home > Sites > Records Center > Holds > Litigation Holds

Holds: Litigation Holds

		Close

New Item | Edit Item | ✕ Delete Item | Manage Permissions | Alert Me

Title	Litigation Holds
Description	These documents are on hold as a part of legal actions.
Managed By	Ron Price
Hold Status	This hold is active. Search for items to add to this hold... Release hold... View hold report...
Items on Hold	1
Report Date	

Created at 6/8/2007 4:57 PM by SPDOMAIN\Administrator
Last modified at 6/8/2007 4:57 PM by SPDOMAIN\Administrator   Close

Figure 9-21.   The Holds View Item page.

3. On the Holds page, click the Search For Items To Add To This Hold link in the Hold Status section.

4. On the Search For Items To Hold page (see Figure 9-22), enter a word or phrase to use as the search criteria and click the spyglass symbol to start the search.

5. Select the documents from the results list you wish to add to the hold.

6. Under the heading of Add Search Results from the Records Center to the following hold, use the list box selections to pick the type of hold you want to apply to the selected records.

7. Click the Hold button to add the selected records to the chosen Hold list.

Home > Sites > Records Center > Holds > Litigation Holds > Search for items to hold

Search for items to hold

Search for items to hold

[   ] 🔍

Enter one or more words to search for in the search box.

Add search results from the Records Center to the following hold:

[Litigation Holds ▼] [Hold]

Figure 9-22.   The Search For Items To Hold page.

SUMMARY

MOSS provides the tools an enterprise can apply to implement well-defined document management control policies. These policies allow the enterprise to track the life cycle of its digital content from creation to disposal or archival.

The MOSS functions and features used to implement document and records management include the capability to implement information management policies to control the creation, use, and disposition of a document, record, site, collection, list, library, page, and so on. MOSS also includes a number of policy features that provide capabilities for auditing, defining the retention period of a document and the inclusion of labels, bar codes, and digital signatures. MOSS also includes a variety of information management policy reports that can be used for tracking information management policy actions through event log files.

The SharePoint Records Center provides a combination of a standard SharePoint site and predefined records management policies. The Records Center site is used to store the records you need to manage, track, and administer in a single site using a standard set of information management policies.

CHAPTER 10

Workflows

W e've all been there: The boss asks for a new system proposal that must be reviewed and approved by certain department managers, and all in a week's time. You painstakingly write up the proposal and e-mail it to all of the managers that must review it, asking each to respond with his or her comments and, hopefully, his or her approval. A few managers respond immediately with their approvals. A day or two later you receive responses from another two. A day after that, you receive additional feedback and suggestions from another. Unfortunately, the two managers whose approvals are essential to acceptance by the boss don't respond at all. With a day left before your deadline, you follow up, only to find out one forgot about it and the other claims she never received your message. Frantically, you e-mail it again hoping this time you'll get their responses quickly. The reality of this situation is that every business has several similar formal or informal business processes it depends on every day to conduct its internal and external business affairs. The bottom line is that business processes are really about people getting things done in a particular sequence and in a timely manner.

Microsoft Office SharePoint Server 2007 (MOSS), along with Windows SharePoint Services 3.0 (WSS) and Windows Workflow Foundation (WWF), provides support for a variety of human workflow applications that communicate interactively with the members of a team or work group to complete a sequence of tasks. This capability is implemented in an MOSS environment as workflows. Through the integration of MOSS, WSS, and WWF, as well as the use of Microsoft InfoPath forms and the Microsoft Office 2007 applications, such as Word, Excel, and Outlook, workflows interact with designated users to guide the completion of one or more tasks in sequence to accomplish a work project. Actually, it is WSS and WWF that provide most of the functionality of workflows. However, MOSS and Office 2007 Enterprise edition do add some additional features to facilitate the integration of workflows into the MOSS environment.

Through the use of a human workflow application (the embodiment of a SharePoint workflow), maybe the next time the boss wants a proposal written, coordinated, and approved as quickly as possible, it may actually get done as quickly and completely as desired. This chapter provides an overview of the products and technologies used to create and execute a workflow in an MOSS environment.

INTRODUCTION TO WORKFLOWS

At the risk of over-simplification, a workflow is basically what its name suggests: a series of work steps. This flow of work steps (tasks), like the blocks and symbols in a flowchart, are performed (usually) one at a time, creating a workflow. A workflow helps people collaborate on documents and manage project tasks by implementing a business process based on a document or other item in a SharePoint site. A workflow helps a company consistently apply a defined set of business process steps to a routine series of tasks. Use of a workflow enables those responsible for performing the tasks involved to focus on the work rather than the management of the process.

MOSS 2007 includes three primary workflow features in addition to those provided by WSS and WWF:

▼ The capability to associate Microsoft Office 2007 Enterprise edition documents and clients with a workflow

■ A variety of predefined workflow templates

▲ The capability for a workflow to use an InfoPath form.

The ability to interact with Microsoft Office applications lets an MOSS user view a workflow form directly in an Office application, as well as view workflow tasks in Outlook, associate a task list in a Word document, an Outlook e-mail, and other types of Office documents. MOSS provides predefined workflow templates for use in routing a document for approvals, collecting feedback or (digital) signatures, and document translations.

Workflows can be initiated and managed on documents and items stored in an MOSS site or from within certain Microsoft Office 2007 applications, including:

▼ View workflows available for a document or item

■ Initiate a workflow on a document or item

■ View, modify, or reassign a workflow task

▲ Complete a workflow task

To briefly summarize just what an MOSS workflow is… An MOSS workflow is a software-supported process made up of two primary elements: a form used to interact with users and the logic statements that control its functions. In most cases, the MOSS workflow templates are able to facilitate most common business processes. However, you can create custom workflows specific to a particular or proprietary procedure, but that's beyond the scope of this book.

MOSS Workflow Processes

An MOSS workflow essentially involves only a small number of processes, from start to finish. While it may be easier to imagine a workflow as a process that flows fluidly from one participant to the next, a workflow actually creates a task for each of the users identified as participants by the workflow initiator. Unless defined as parallel tasks, when one task is completed, the next task on the task list is activated.

As illustrated in Figure 10-1, the life cycle of an MOSS workflow has four general phases:

1. **Select workflow and document** The administrator or user (the *initiator*) chooses the workflow template he or she wishes to use. Depending on the type of workflow template selected, the workflow template may include an association to a SharePoint document content type. A workflow must be associated with a list or a content type (it cannot be associated directly to a document). Association can be thought of as "making it available to be used" and often includes default setting properties for the workflow that are applied in each instance. Only a list or site administrator can create this association.

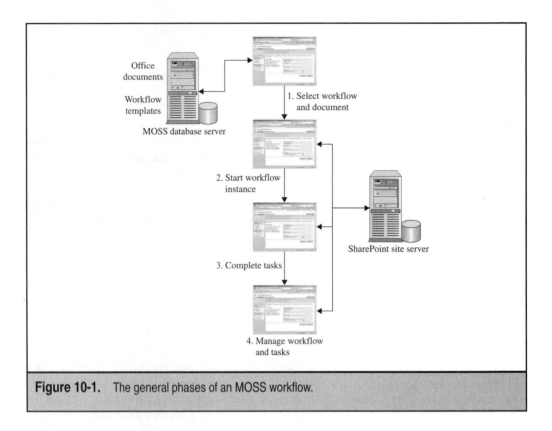

Figure 10-1.   The general phases of an MOSS workflow.

2. **Start the workflow instance**   The initiator creating the workflow instance sets
    the feature options she or he wishes to use in the workflow, such as the list of
    users (*participants*) and how much time each participant has to complete the
    task(s) assigned to her or him. Many MOSS workflows can be defined to start
    automatically based on a document's content type or library.

3. **Complete tasks**   Each of the workflow's participants has access to a workflow
    form through which he or she performs the assigned task, provides any
    required information, and completes the task.

4. **Manage workflow and tasks**   Many workflow templates allow the initiator
    to modify a workflow instance while it is active. For example, the initiator may
    be able to add or remove participants, or change the completion dates of any
    uncompleted tasks.

Workflow Templates

While most of the advanced capabilities in MOSS workflows require some programming
and development, MOSS does include a set of predefined workflows that users can simply
customize for use in a variety of workflow situations. MOSS includes workflow templates

(see the "MOSS Workflows" section later in the chapter) to fit the most common types of workflows a user should need to employ.

MOSS Workflow Actions

Workflows must be configured to a SharePoint library, list, or document content type before they are available for use with the items stored in that element. However, where a workflow is added to a site controls where in the site the workflow is available. Remember that an MOSS environment has a specific hierarchy of elements: a web application contains a site collection (site), a site contains libraries and lists, and these libraries and lists are made up of certain document content types. This hierarchy, which is very important in setting and inheriting user permissions, is also very important to the availability of a workflow within a SharePoint site.

> **NOTE**   For more information on document content types, see Chapter 9.

This hierarchical relationship comes into play like this:

▼ A workflow added to a particular content type at the site level is available to all documents of that content type stored in every list or library on the site.

▲ A workflow added to a specific library or list is available only to the items contained in that specific library or list.

> **NOTE**   To configure a workflow to a SharePoint element, an administrator or user must have Manage Lists permission for the element to which the workflow is to be configured.

The following sections outline the processes used to enable and add workflows to the hierarchical levels within an MOSS environment.

Configure a Web Application for Workflows

To configure a Web application for workflows, do the following:

1. Open the Central Administration page on the MOSS server.

2. Click the Application Management link to open the Application Management page.

3. On the Application Management page, click the Workflow settings link in the Workflow Management section to open the Workflow Settings page.

4. On the Workflow Settings page (see Figure 10-2), click on the gold Web Application name associated with Web Application to select the web application on which you wish to configure workflows.

5. In the User-Defined Workflows section of the Workflow Settings page, select either Yes or No for allowing user-defined workflows within this Web application. A user-defined workflow is a custom workflow template created by SharePoint users as opposed to an MOSS predefined workflow template.

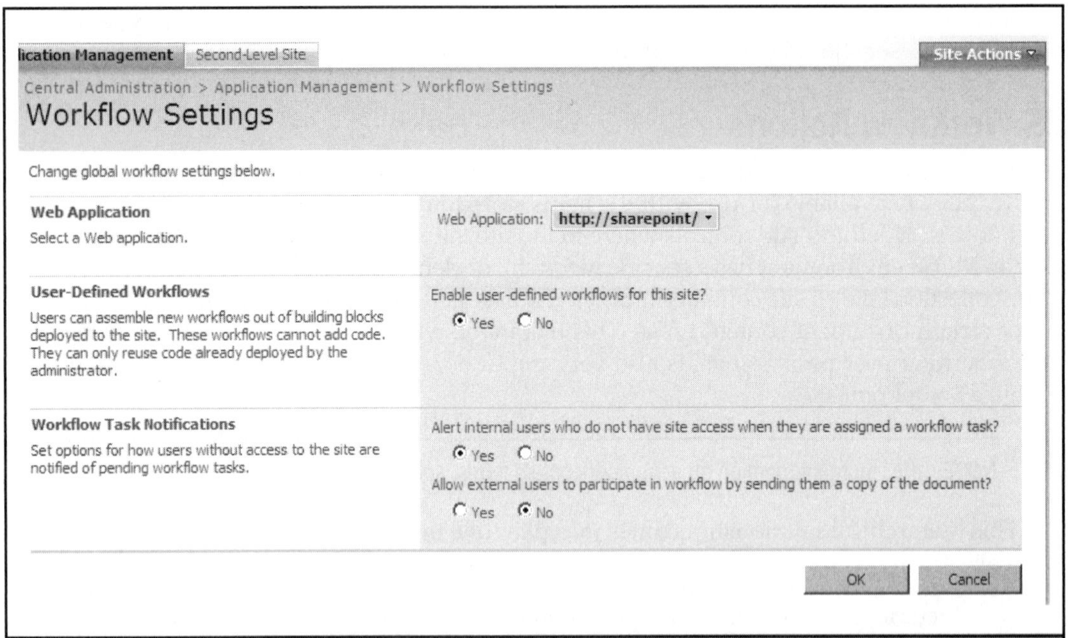

Figure 10-2.   The Workflow Settings page.

6. In the Workflow Task Notifications section, select either Yes or No for the Alert Internal Users Who Do Not Have Site Access When They Are Assigned A Workflow Task option to allow or deny internal users [generally users with a connection to the company's local area network (LAN)], who don't have permission to access a site, so they can be notified by e-mail when a workflow assigns a task to them.

7. Select either Yes or No for the Allow External Users To Participate In Workflow By Sending Them A Copy Of The Document option to allow or deny external users (users external to the company, such as suppliers, customers, and so on) to receive copies of a workflow's document or list item when they are assigned a task in a workflow.

8. Click the OK button to save the workflow settings.

Add a Workflow to a Content Type

To make a workflow generally available across the lists or libraries within a site collection that is made up of items of a particular document content type, the workflow should be added directly to the site's specific content type. This action allows users to start workflows on any instance of that content type within every library or list on the site. In fact, each time a document of that particular content type is added to a list or library, the workflow settings of the content type are copied to the list or library as well. The most commonly used content type is the Document content type, which has three workflows associated with it by default: Approval, Collect Feedback, and Collect Signatures. However, if you wish to add a workflow to another particular content type, use the following steps:

1. Navigate to the main page of the site on which you wish to add a workflow, click the Site Actions button to open its drop-down menu and choose the Site Settings option.

2. On the Site Settings page, click the Site Content Types link under the Galleries heading to open the Site Content Type Gallery page.

3. On the Site Content Gallery page, locate the content type to which you wish to add a workflow and click its link to open its Site Content Type page (see Figure 10-3).

4. Under the Settings heading, click the link for Workflow Settings to open the Change Workflow Settings page (see Figure 10-4).

5. On the Change Workflow Settings page, you can change the settings of the workflows already added to this content type, add a workflow, remove a workflow, or change the inheritance rules for the workflows on this content type.

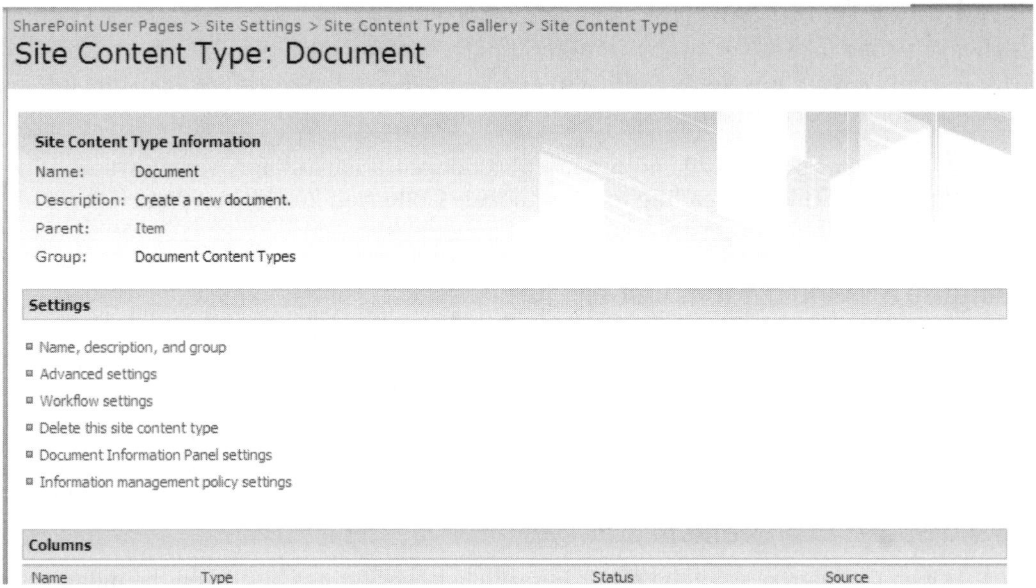

SharePoint User Pages > Site Settings > Site Content Type Gallery > Site Content Type

Site Content Type: Document

Site Content Type Information

Name: Document

Description: Create a new document.

Parent: Item

Group: Document Content Types

Settings

▫ Name, description, and group
▫ Advanced settings
▫ Workflow settings
▫ Delete this site content type
▫ Document Information Panel settings
▫ Information management policy settings

Columns

Name	Type	Status	Source

Figure 10-3. The Site Content Type page.

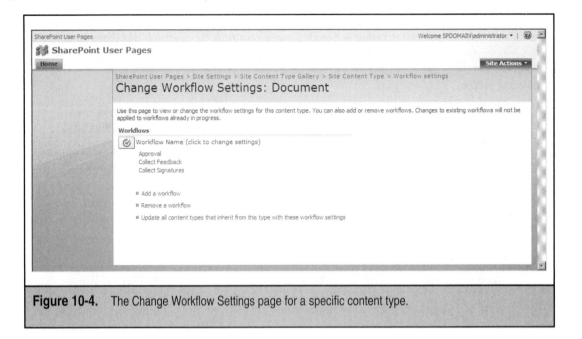

Figure 10-4.   The Change Workflow Settings page for a specific content type.

View a Site's Workflows

It's always a good idea to verify any configuration action you take in an MOSS environment. To verify a workflow you've added to a content type, or the workflows existing for a site collection through inheritance, do the following:

▼   On the Site Settings page of the site collection, click the link for Workflows under the Galleries heading to open the Site Collection Workflows page (see Figure 10-5).

Configure a Workflow to a List or Library

Workflows—actually workflow templates—are associated (scoped) to a site collection, a site, or a content type. When a new site is created, its lists and libraries may have workflows pre-associated with their content types. So, the critical element of this task is to ensure an administrator has scoped a workflow to the content type of the list or library to which you are adding a workflow. The content type of a SharePoint list or library determines which workflows it will have available, but you can add or modify a workflow configured to the list or library. To do so, perform the following steps:

1. Open the main page of the list or library, click the Settings button on the menu bar, and choose the settings option for the list (library).

2. On the Customize page, shown in Figure 10-6, click the link for Workflow Settings under the Permissions and Management heading to open the Add A Workflow page (see Figure 10-7), where you can add a workflow or modify the settings of a workflow.

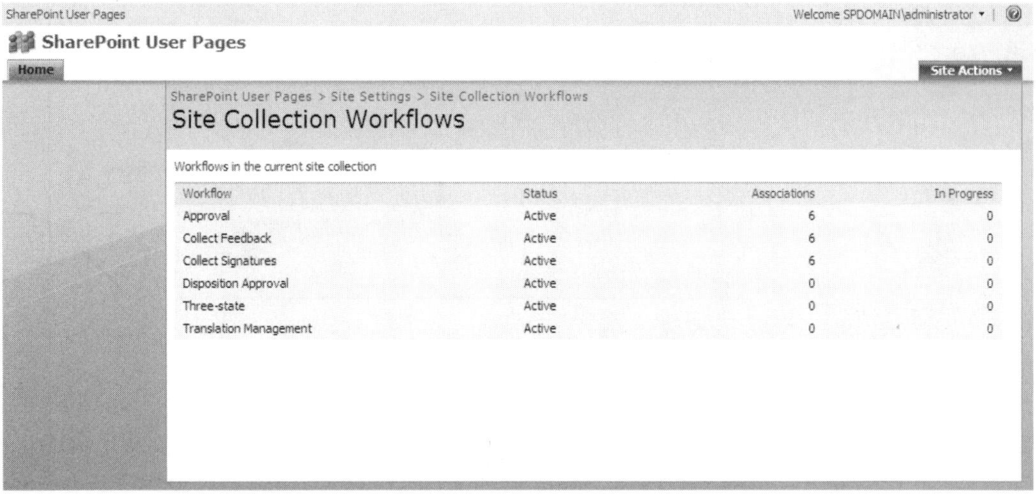

Figure 10-5. The Site Collection Workflows page lists the workflows configured to a site.

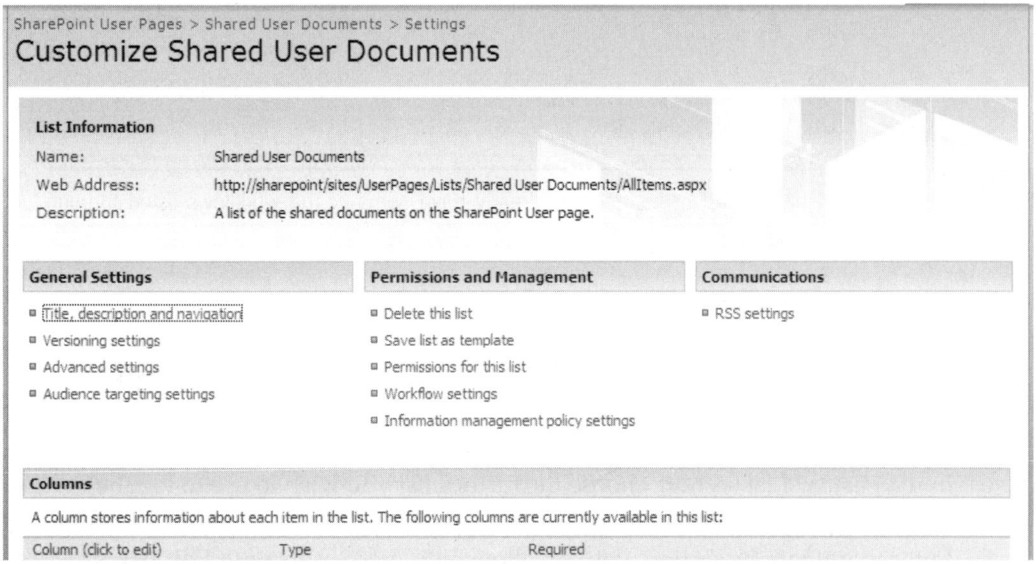

Figure 10-6. The Customize page is used to manage the configuration of a SharePoint list or library.

SharePoint User Pages > Shared User Documents > Settings > Workflow settings > Add or Change a Workflow

Add a Workflow: Shared User Documents

Use this page to set up a workflow for this list.

Workflow

Select a workflow to add to this list. If the workflow template you want does not appear, contact your administrator to get it added to your site collection or workspace.

Select a workflow template:

Approval
Collect Feedback
Collect Signatures
Disposition Approval

Description:

Routes a document for approval. Approvers can approve or reject the document, reassign the approval task, or request changes to the document.

Name

Type a name for this workflow. The name will be used to identify this workflow to users of this list.

Type a unique name for this workflow:

Task List

Select a task list to use with this workflow. You can select an existing task list or request that a new task list be created.

Select a task list:

Tasks

Description:

Use the Tasks list to keep track of work that you or your team needs to complete.

History List

Select a history list to use with this workflow. You can select an existing history list or request that a new history list be created.

Select a history list:

Workflow History (new)

Description:

A new history list will be created for use by this workflow.

Figure 10-7. The Add A Workflow page is used to add a workflow to a SharePoint list.

3. On the Add A Workflow page, choose the workflow you wish to add from the list box in the Workflow section.

TIP Remember that the list or library may already have some of the workflows listed through inheritance.

4. In the Name section, assign a short name to the workflow. This name is used to identify the workflow to users and participants.

5. In the Task List section, indicate whether you wish to use the existing task list (Tasks) or create a new task list by choosing either Tasks or New Task List from the list box.

6. In the History List section, choose the history list you wish to use to log the actions taken on the workflow.

7. In the Start Options section, you can allow only those users with Edit Items permissions to start a workflow or raise this permission level up to those users who have Manage Lists permissions. You can also set the workflow to start any time a new item is created on the list or library, or whenever an existing item is modified (and saved to the list or library).

8. Depending on the workflow type you are adding, you may have a Next button that leads to a customization page. The Next button opens the Customize Workflow page for the Approval, Collect Feedback, and Three-state workflows. Figure 10-8 shows the Customize Workflow page of an Approval workflow on which you can customize this workflow type. The Collect Signatures and Disposition Approval workflow options display an OK button, which is used to complete the add workflow action.

9. If you are adding an Approval, Collect Feedback, or Three-state workflow, the Customize Workflow page appears (see Figure 10-8). On this page, you can alter the default settings of these workflow types as you need. The options available on the Customize Workflow page include whether to assign tasks to all participants at once (parallel) or serially (one at a time, in sequence), provide a list of workflow participants, send a brief message to each participant, set a due date for the workflow, set the criteria for when the workflow should be considered complete or when to cancel the workflow, and what action should be taken at the end of the workflow. These options are explained in more detail later in the chapter for each of the different workflow types.

10. Click OK on either the Change Workflow Settings page or the Customize Workflow page, as applicable, to save the settings you've changed.

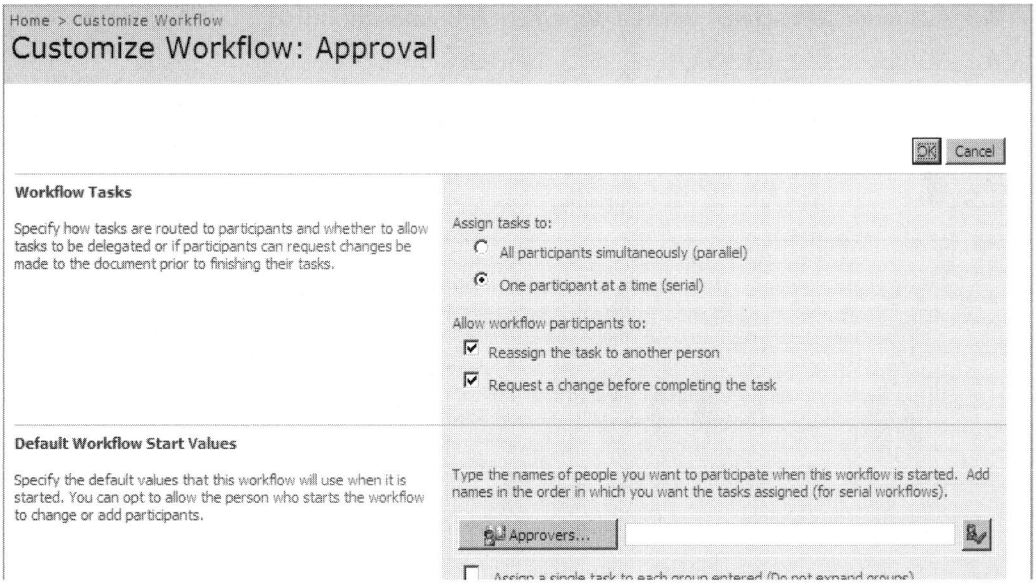

Figure 10-8. The Customize Workflow page for an Approval workflow.

User Tasks

When a workflow is initiated, a task is opened for any of the users associated with the workflow that asks each user to perform the action required by the workflow, such as approve a document, provide feedback on the document, or provide a signature for the document. Each site lists the tasks assigned to the users or groups associated with the site and, if enabled through a Web Part on the site page, lists the tasks pending to those users or groups on its home page (as illustrated in Figure 10-9).

MOSS maintains a task list for every site and a running workflow can add tasks to this list, specifying who each task is for. Each user of that site can see what work is waiting for him either by accessing his task list via a web browser (see Figure 10-10) or by synchronizing this site's task list with his or her Outlook 2007 task list.

If an initiator wishes to launch a workflow for a particular SharePoint document, he or she opens the focus document and chooses to initiate a workflow for it. However, in actual practice, MOSS workflows can be, and are typically, initiated automatically when a particular document type or document is created, modified, or a disposition action is started.

Start a Workflow Instance

MOSS supports three methods that can be used to start a workflow instance:

▼ Manually started by a user

■ Automatically started when a document or item is modified

▲ Automatically started when a document or item is created.

Of course, as explained in the previous section, these options depend upon the settings configured to the workflow by the site administrator and the permissions level set for users.

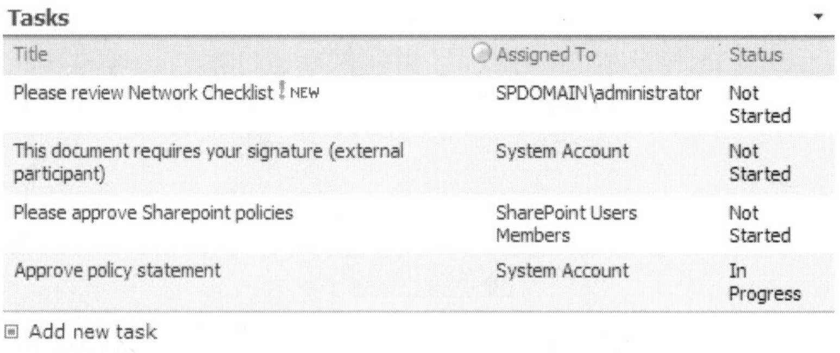

Tasks		
Title	Assigned To	Status
Please review Network Checklist ! NEW	SPDOMAIN\administrator	Not Started
This document requires your signature (external participant)	System Account	Not Started
Please approve Sharepoint policies	SharePoint Users Members	Not Started
Approve policy statement	System Account	In Progress
⊞ Add new task		

Figure 10-9. The tasks list on a SharePoint site page.

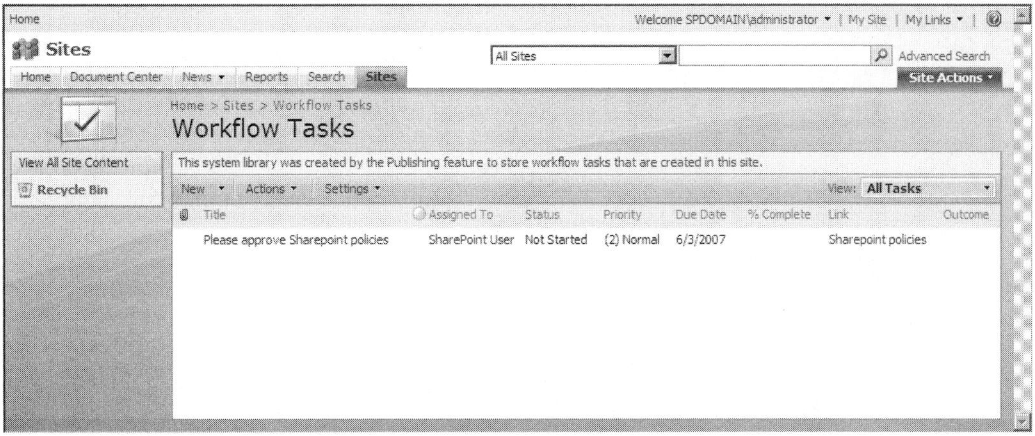

Figure 10-10.   A workflow task assigned to a participant of a workflow.

You should be aware of two important characteristics regarding MOSS workflows:

▼   A workflow runs from the beginning every time

▲   A new instance of a workflow associated with a particular document, site, list, or library can't be started while a workflow on that same element is active.

Start a Workflow Manually

To start an MOSS workflow manually, use the following procedure:

1.   Choose a specific document from a SharePoint library or list and click its name to open its drop-down menu and select the Workflows option.

2.   On the Workflows page that displays, locate the Start A New Workflow section. Any workflows defined for the list, library, or document content type are listed in this section. As illustrated in Figure 10-11, this particular library item has two workflows defined: Approval and Collect Feedback workflows. Click the icon associated with the workflow you wish to start.

3.   The Start Workflow page is displayed (see Figure 10-12). This page contains the default settings configured for the workflow selected. Depending on the type of workflow you're starting, you can alter the default values for the workflow before creating a workflow instance.

4.   After entering any necessary information, click the Start button to execute the workflow.

5.   Each listed participant has a task generated in their task list requesting them to perform the required workflow task.

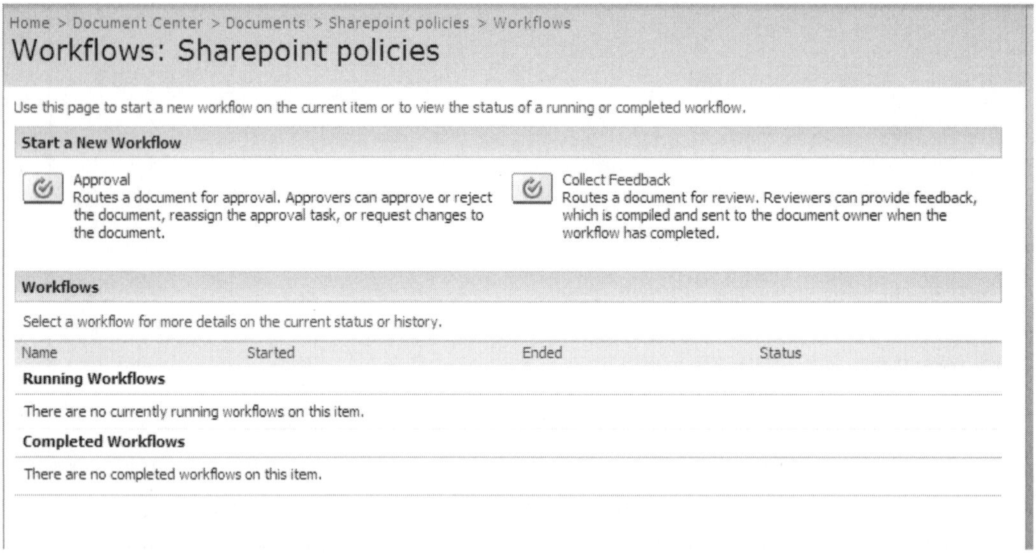

Figure 10-11.   The Workflows page is used to manually start a workflow on a specific library or list item.

Start a Workflow Automatically

A SharePoint workflow can be started automatically from an Office application. Any time a document—for example, a Microsoft Word document—is saved to a site's document library, any workflow associated with that library is automatically executed.

MOSS WORKFLOWS

MOSS includes six standard workflow templates that are fully defined and ready for use in many of the most common situations in which you are likely to initiate a workflow. The predefined workflows available in MOSS are:

▼ **Approval**   This workflow allows a user to add a list of users to whom a document is routed in a set sequence for approval, rejection, or modifications. A user included in the routing list can reassign the approval task to another user, who then can perform the tasks included in the workflow.

■ **Collect feedback**   Like the Approval workflow, a document is routed to a list of users, but in this case, the purpose is to collect input from each user. The feedback comments collected from the users to whom the document is routed is compiled into a single document and sent to the document owner (workflow initiator)

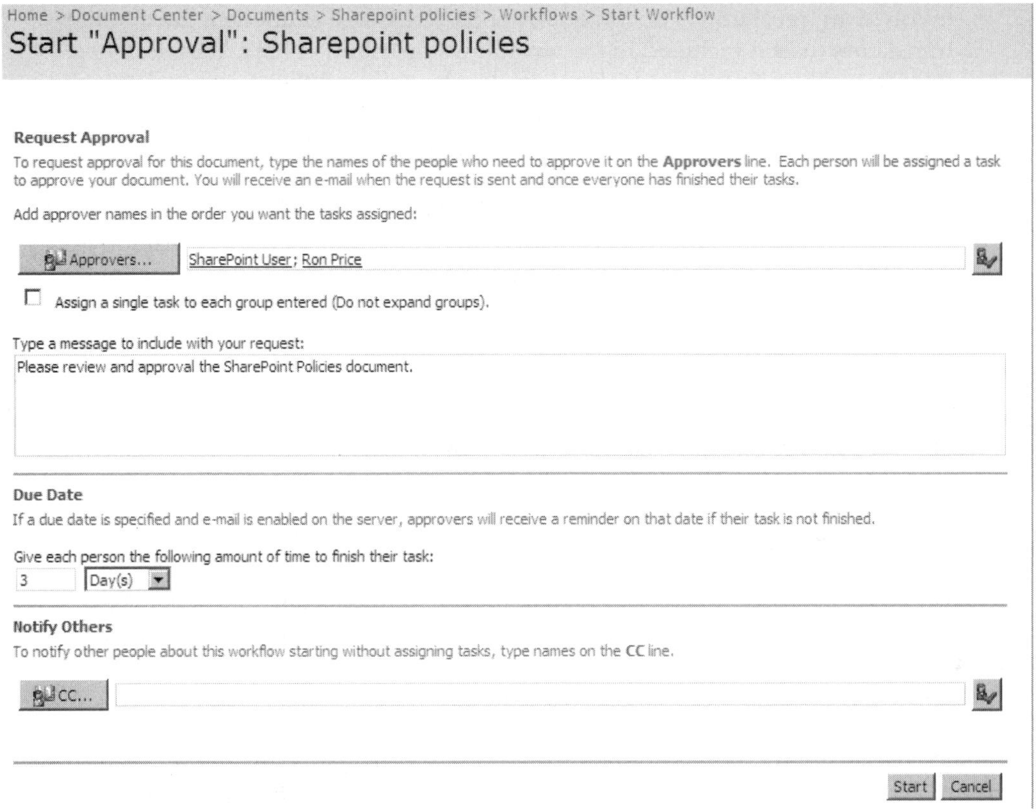

Home > Document Center > Documents > Sharepoint policies > Workflows > Start Workflow

Start "Approval": Sharepoint policies

Request Approval

To request approval for this document, type the names of the people who need to approve it on the **Approvers** line. Each person will be assigned a task to approve your document. You will receive an e-mail when the request is sent and once everyone has finished their tasks.

Add approver names in the order you want the tasks assigned:

| Approvers... | SharePoint User ; Ron Price | |

☐ Assign a single task to each group entered (Do not expand groups).

Type a message to include with your request:

> Please review and approval the SharePoint Policies document.

Due Date

If a due date is specified and e-mail is enabled on the server, approvers will receive a reminder on that date if their task is not finished.

Give each person the following amount of time to finish their task:

| 3 | Day(s) ▾ |

Notify Others

To notify other people about this workflow starting without assigning tasks, type names on the CC line.

| CC... | |

| Start | Cancel |

Figure 10-12. The Start Workflow page is used to finalize and initiate a workflow instance.

when the workflow tasks are completed. Unlike the Approval workflow, the Collect feedback workflow sends out the original document to all users included on the distribution list.

■ **Collect signatures** This workflow is used to route an Office document to a list of users to obtain the required signatures on the document. Because this workflow relates directly to a document specifically, it must be initiated from within an Office application.

■ **Disposition approval** When the time has come or is approaching for a document to be retired or disposed of, this workflow can be used to route a request for approval or disapproval to keep or destroy a document to a list of specified users. The results of this workflow, essentially a tally of the votes, are returned to the user initiating the workflow.

- **Translation management**   This workflow is used to manage the tasks involved in translating a document from one language to another. Each of the translators (users) included in the workflows distribution list can be assigned specific translation tasks, which are tracked by the workflow.

▲ **Group approval**   This workflow is available only in the East Asian version of MOSS and can be used to track a group-based document approval process.

All of these predefined workflows use InfoPath workflow forms and can be accessed directly from Office 2007 applications, provided the Office 2007 Enterprise edition is in use. In addition to the discussion of the Approval workflow in the preceding section, the application and how to create, associate, start, and interact with the Collect Feedback, Collect Signatures, Three-state, and Disposal Approval workflows are outlined in the following sections.

NOTE   For each of the workflows described in the following sections, the same process is used to add and edit each workflow type.

The Collect Feedback Workflow

The Collect Feedback workflow type is used to route a saved document to a list of designated users (participants) for the purpose of letting each person provide some feedback on the document itself. Along with the Approval workflow, the Collect Feedback workflow is a default workflow for the Document content type.

A Collect Feedback workflow can be started directly from a document stored in a SharePoint list or library. When notified of the task, participants are able to open the document for review and then either insert their comments directly into the document itself or modify the document working in the native Office 2007 application. Any comments they wish to pass back to the workflow initiator are entered into the workflow task form (see Figure 10-13).

To complete or update a Collect Feedback task, do the following:

1. Open the main page of the site on which the focus document is stored and click the Task lists on the site.

2. On the Tasks page, click the All Tasks button to open its drop-down menu and then choose the My Tasks option (as illustrated in Figure 10-14) to open the Tasks page for the currently signed-in user (meaning you, of course).

3. On the Tasks page, move your mouse over the task you wish to access, click the down arrow to display the drop-down menu for that task (see Figure 10-15), and choose the Edit Item option.

   a. On the Task page that opens, you can choose to view the contents of the document or item for which you are being asked to provide feedback, you can enter your feedback into the text box provided and send it to the workflow initiator, or you can reassign the task to another user.

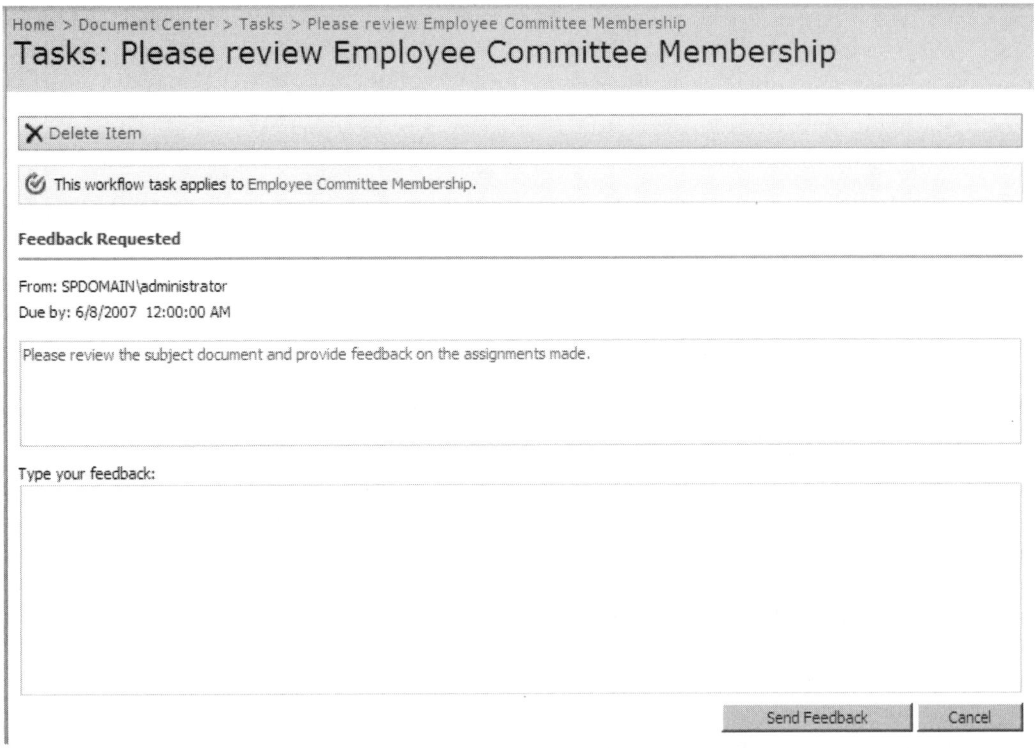

Home > Document Center > Tasks > Please review Employee Committee Membership

Tasks: Please review Employee Committee Membership

✕ Delete Item

🗸 This workflow task applies to Employee Committee Membership.

Feedback Requested

From: SPDOMAIN\administrator

Due by: 6/8/2007 12:00:00 AM

Please review the subject document and provide feedback on the assignments made.

Type your feedback:

Send Feedback   Cancel

Figure 10-13.   A Collect Feedback workflow task form.

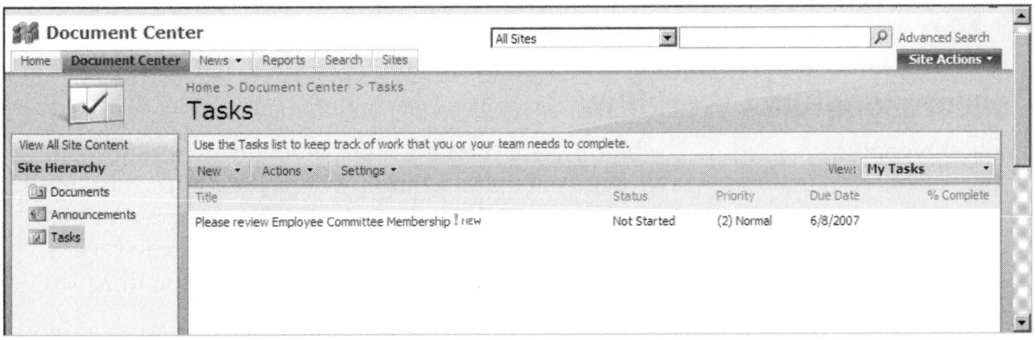

📰 **Document Center**

All Sites   🔍 Advanced Search

Home | **Document Center** | News ▾ | Reports | Search | Sites   Site Actions ▾

🗸   Home > Document Center > Tasks

Tasks

View All Site Content   Use the Tasks list to keep track of work that you or your team needs to complete.

Site Hierarchy   New ▾ | Actions ▾ | Settings ▾   View: **My Tasks** ▾

📄 Documents

📢 Announcements

✅ Tasks

Title	Status	Priority	Due Date	% Complete
Please review Employee Committee Membership ! NEW	Not Started	(2) Normal	6/8/2007	

Figure 10-14.   The Tasks menu includes the My Tasks option.

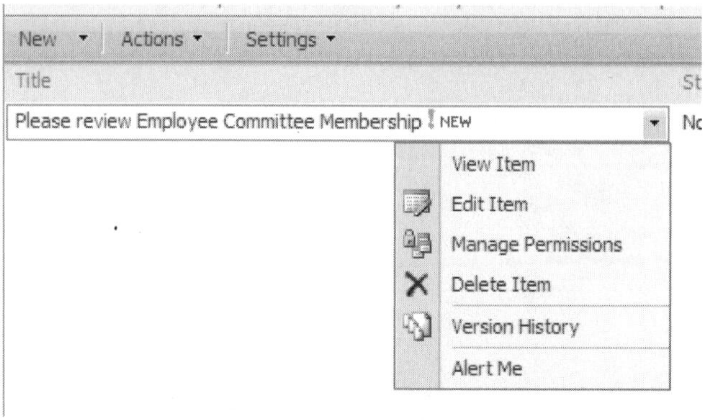

New ▾ | Actions ▾ | Settings ▾

| Title | | St |

Please review Employee Committee Membership ⸗ NEW ▾ | Nc

- View Item
- Edit Item
- Manage Permissions
- ✕ Delete Item
- Version History
- Alert Me

Figure 10-15.   The drop-down menu for a workflow task.

   b. To open the document, click the document link at the top of the task form.

   c. To enter your feedback, type your comments in the Feedback text box and then click the Send Feedback button.

4. To reassign the task to another SharePoint user, click the Reassign Task option on the task menu, enter the user name of the person to whom you wish to reassign the task, and click the Send button.

5. If you wish to request a change in the task, choose the Request A Change option, enter the user name of the person from whom you wish to request the change, enter a description of the change you are requesting, and click the Send button.

TIP   The Reassign Task and Request Change options may not be activated if they were not included in the configuration of the original workflow by its initiator.

The Collect Signatures Workflow

A Collect Signatures workflow is a bit different than the other predefined workflows in MOSS. A Collect Signatures workflow is only started from within the Office 2007 application in which the document or item to be signed was created. The purpose of this workflow is to collect digital signatures from a group of participants who are to review and sign the document to mark its acceptance, all from within the application in which the document was created.

The Collect Signatures workflow creates tasks, like all MOSS workflows, but it can only be used to route a Word or Excel document, which must be created with enough Office Signature Lines to accommodate the signatures of all of the participants listed in the workflow. Figure 10-16 shows a Word document that contains Signature Lines on which the Collect Signature workflow participants can add their digital signatures.

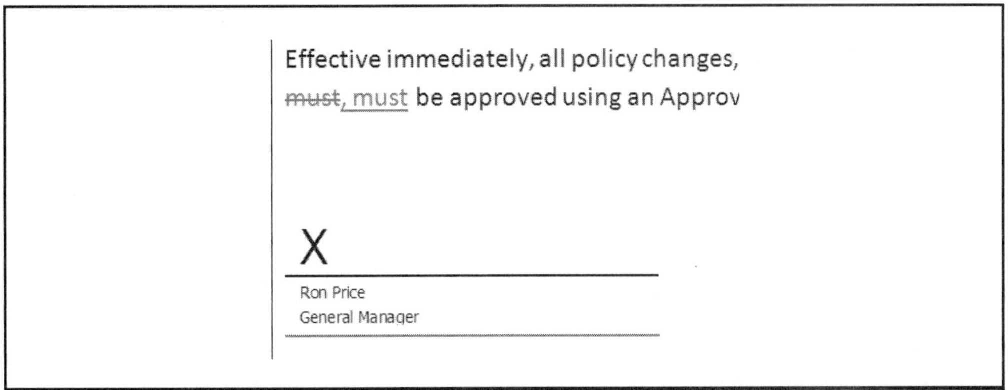

Effective immediately, all policy changes,

~~must~~, must be approved using an Approv

X
_____

Ron Price
General Manager

Figure 10-16.   An Office Word 2007 document with Signature Lines for use with a Collect Signature
workflow.

Before you can start a Collect Signature workflow, you must first create an Office
document and save it to a SharePoint document library configured with the Collect
Signature workflow, as available. After the document has been saved to the document
library, it can be opened and (if they aren't already included in the document) the
Signature Lines added to the document.

To launch a Collect Signatures workflow from within an Office application client,
perform the following steps:

1. Once the document to be routed in the workflow is open in the Office
   application client, click the Office button in the upper left corner of the window
   to open its menu.

2. Click the Start Workflows option and from the dialog box that displays, choose
   the Collect Signatures workflow.

3. On the Workflow initiation form that appears, enter the names of the workflow
   participants (the users you wish to sign the document). You can either have
   the workflow tasks assigned in the sequence indicated by the sequence of the
   Signature Lines or have all of the participants assigned a task in parallel.

Participants in a Collect Signatures workflow complete their assigned task by adding a digital signature to the document. To do this, they must open the document to be
signed in the Office application in which it was created.

To digitally sign a Collect Signatures workflow document, do the following:

1. When you open the document in its application, a Signatures message bar is
   visible at the top of the window with a View Signatures button (see Figure 10-17).

NOTE   If the SharePoint site collection or document library requires the document to be checked out
before you can take action on it, you must check out the document before the Sign button appears
or is made active.

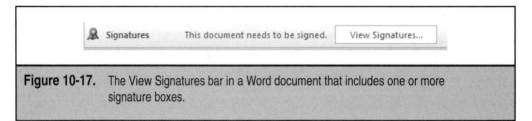

Figure 10-17. The View Signatures bar in a Word document that includes one or more signature boxes.

TIP If for some reason you need to sign a document in more than one place, meaning that multiple Office Signature Lines are embedded in the document for you to sign, a separate task is generated for each separate signature line.

2. Click the View Signatures button to open the signatures pane (shown in Figure 10-18).

3. To add your digital signature, do the following:

   a. Click your name in the list in the Signature pane to activate and open the signature box embedded in the document. At this point, you have following three options:

     i. You can create a printed version of your signature by typing your name in the text box adjacent to the signature "X," entering an optional comment in support of the signature, and clicking the Sign button.

NOTE If the signature box contains a red "Invalid signature" message in the top left corner after the signature is submitted, a certificate needs to be created for the signer. Click the Invalid signature message and validate the signor to eliminate the invalid signature message in the future.

     ii. You can enter an image file of your handwritten signature by clicking Select Image, browsing to the file location of your signature image file in the Select Signature Image dialog box, selecting the image file, and then clicking the Select button.

     iii. If you are using a form of tablet PC, simply sign your name in the signature box adjacent to the "X" using your stylus and your PC's inking features to capture your signature. Afterward, click the Sign button.

The Three-State Workflow

The Three-state workflow does essentially what its name implies: It tracks a list item though three phases (states) or status changes, including up to two changes between each of its states. One or more workflow tasks are generated to track the processes that cause the change in the item's states and when these tasks are completed, the item is moved into its next state. While the Three-state workflow is designed to work with the

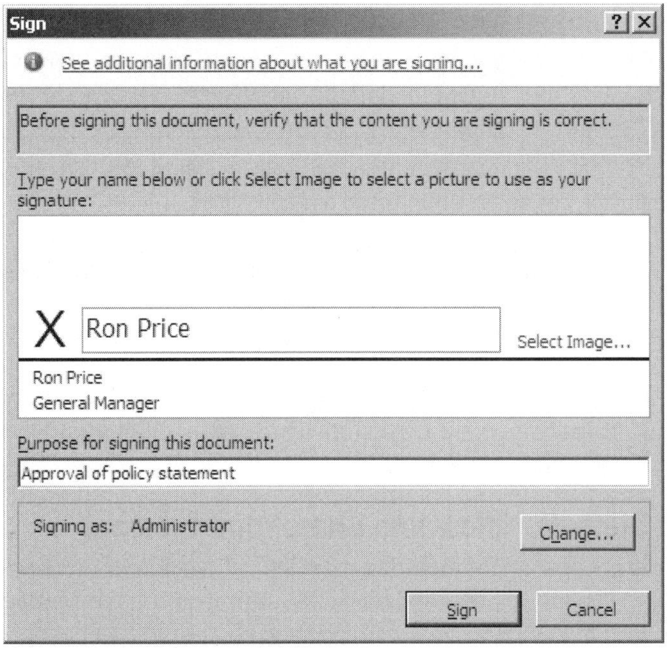

Figure 10-18. The Sign dialog box.

Issue Tracking List template, it will work with other list formats, as long as the list includes a Choice column that contains at least three values (each representing a state).

An example of how a Three-state workflow can be used is in tracking a sales contact from a lead status (state) to a contacted state to a closed state, based on tasks that occur between each state, such as a sales call, interview, placed order, and so on. Or it could be used to track a software testing project through the stages of "ready for review," "in testing," and "approved" or "disapproved," as you like. If a project can be defined with three major milestones, a Three-state workflow can be used to track its progress.

Issue Tracking Lists

The Issue Tracking list template is the default vehicle of a Three-state workflow. Since the purpose of an Issue Tracking list is to, well, track an issue, it is logical then that the workflow used to track an issue through its phases would be associated with it. To create an Issue Tracking list on a SharePoint site, perform the following steps:

1. On the All Site Content page of the site to which you wish to add an Issue Tracking list, click the Create button or use the Site Actions button and choose Create from its drop-down list.

2. On the Create page, under the Tracking heading, click the Issue Tracking link to open the Create page.

3. On the Create page, enter a unique and descriptive name for the new Issue Tracking list in the Name box and, optionally, enter a description.

NOTE Like the names of most SharePoint elements, the name of a list is fairly important since it becomes part of the web address of the page and any menus.

4. If you wish to include a link in the Quick Launch menu for the new list, select the Yes option in the Navigation section.

5. Click the Create button to create the Issue Tracking list.

If you wish to create a custom list for use in a Three-state workflow, remember that you must add a Choice column to the list in which the values used by the workflow to track state changes are to be entered.

Add a Three-State Workflow to a SharePoint Element

The Three-state workflow is not included as a default workflow on most site collections, but is available to be added when needed. Assuming you have Manage Lists permissions, use the following steps to add a Three-state workflow to a list or library:

1. Navigate to the list to which you wish to add a Three-state workflow.

2. Click the Settings button to open its drop-down menu and choose the Settings option for a list or library.

3. On the Settings page, click the Workflow settings link located under the Permissions And Management heading.

4. If workflows are enabled for the list, the Add A Workflow page is displayed. If the Change Workflow Settings page is displayed, click the Add A Workflow link to open the Add A Workflow page.

5. On the Add A Workflow page, choose the Three-state option from the Select A Workflow Template list box in the Workflow section and provide the following information:

   a. In the Name section, provide a unique and descriptive name for the workflow. This is the name participants will see on their Tasks list.

   b. In the Task List section, select the Task list where you wish to include workflow tasks. You should accept use of the default Tasks list, which allows the workflow participants to view the tasks they are assigned on the My Tasks view of the Tasks list. However, if you wish to create a new tasks list or use another tasks list already in use, choose the New task list option and enter the name of the task list.

TIP   Two reasons to use a task list other than the default are sensitive, confidential, or private information in the tasks or workflows that generate a large number of tasks.

   c. In the History list section, select either the Workflow History list or choose to create a new history list.

   d. In the Start Options section, choose the settings that implement your policies concerning which user permissions levels are needed to start the workflow manually, if at all, and when, if ever, the workflow should be started automatically.

6. Click the Next button to move to the Customize The Three-State Workflow page.

7. In the Workflow States section of the Customize The Three-State Workflow page (see Figure 10-19), select the column to be used for the Choice field in the workflow. The Choice field indicates the column that contains the values to be used for the workflow states. For each column value, indicate whether the value represents the Initial state, the Middle state, or the Final state of the workflow.

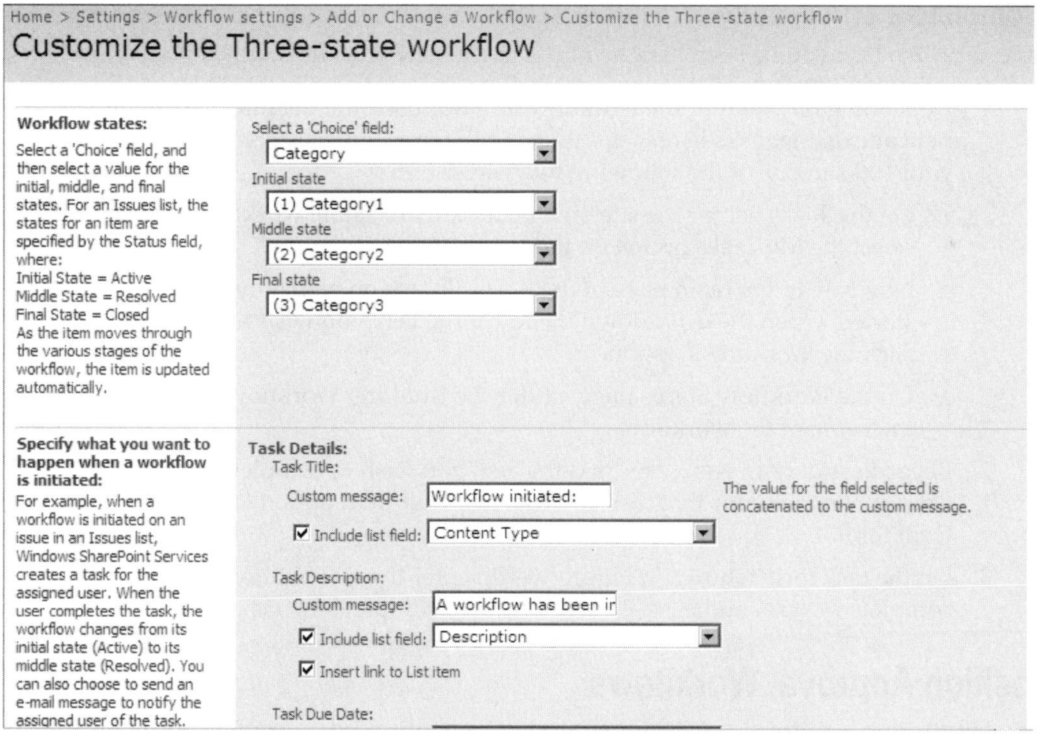

Home > Settings > Workflow settings > Add or Change a Workflow > Customize the Three-state workflow

Customize the Three-state workflow

Workflow states:

Select a 'Choice' field, and then select a value for the initial, middle, and final states. For an Issues list, the states for an item are specified by the Status field, where:

Initial State = Active
Middle State = Resolved
Final State = Closed

As the item moves through the various stages of the workflow, the item is updated automatically.

Select a 'Choice' field:

    Category   ▼
Initial state
    (1) Category1   ▼
Middle state
    (2) Category2   ▼
Final state
    (3) Category3   ▼

Specify what you want to happen when a workflow is initiated:

For example, when a workflow is initiated on an issue in an Issues list, Windows SharePoint Services creates a task for the assigned user. When the user completes the task, the workflow changes from its initial state (Active) to its middle state (Resolved). You can also choose to send an e-mail message to notify the assigned user of the task.

Task Details:
  Task Title:

    Custom message: Workflow initiated:

    ☑ Include list field: Content Type   ▼

The value for the field selected is concatenated to the custom message.

  Task Description:

    Custom message: A workflow has been in

    ☑ Include list field: Description   ▼

    ☑ Insert link to List item

  Task Due Date:

Figure 10-19.   The Customize Workflow page for a Three-state workflow.

8. In the Specify What You Want To Happen When A Workflow Is Initiated and the Specify What You Want To Happen When A Workflow Changes To Its Middle State sections, enter the task details for the task generated when the workflow is started and when it moves to its middle state, respectively. For each task, provide a title, description, due date, and the user(s) to whom the task is to be assigned.

9. If you wish to have workflow participants receive e-mail messages with information about the tasks they have been assigned, check the Send E-mail Messages checkbox. For each participant or person you wish to receive e-mail alerts concerning workflow status changes, enter their e-mail address, a subject line for the e-mail message, and the text to be included in the e-mail. Check the Include Task Assigned To checkbox to send an e-mail alert to the task owner, and check the Use Task Title checkbox to include the task title on the subject line of the e-mail message. This option requires that the e-mail capability be configured to the site collection.

10. Click the OK button to save the configuration settings for the Three-state workflow.

Complete a Three-State Workflow Task

To complete a task you've been assigned by a Three-state workflow, do the following:

1. Depending on whether the workflow initiator used the default Tasks list or a new or existing tasks list (as discussed in the preceding section), you can access your tasks in one of the following two ways:

   a. On the Tasks list for the site on which the Three-state workflow was started, select the My Tasks option on the View menu.

   b. Navigate to the main page of the list or library on which the workflow was started. Open the drop-down menu for the task you wish to complete and click the Workflows option.

   c. On the Workflow Status page, under the Running Workflows heading, click the name of the workflow.

2. Regardless of how you've located the task you wish to complete, open the drop-down menu for that task and click the Edit Item option to open the task form for it.

3. On the task form (shown in Figure 10-20), enter the information needed to complete the task and click the OK button to complete the task.

Disposition Approval Workflows

The Disposition Approval workflow is most commonly used in conjunction with the information management policies implemented in the MOSS environment. The tasks generated by this workflow provide participants with the ability to vote on whether an

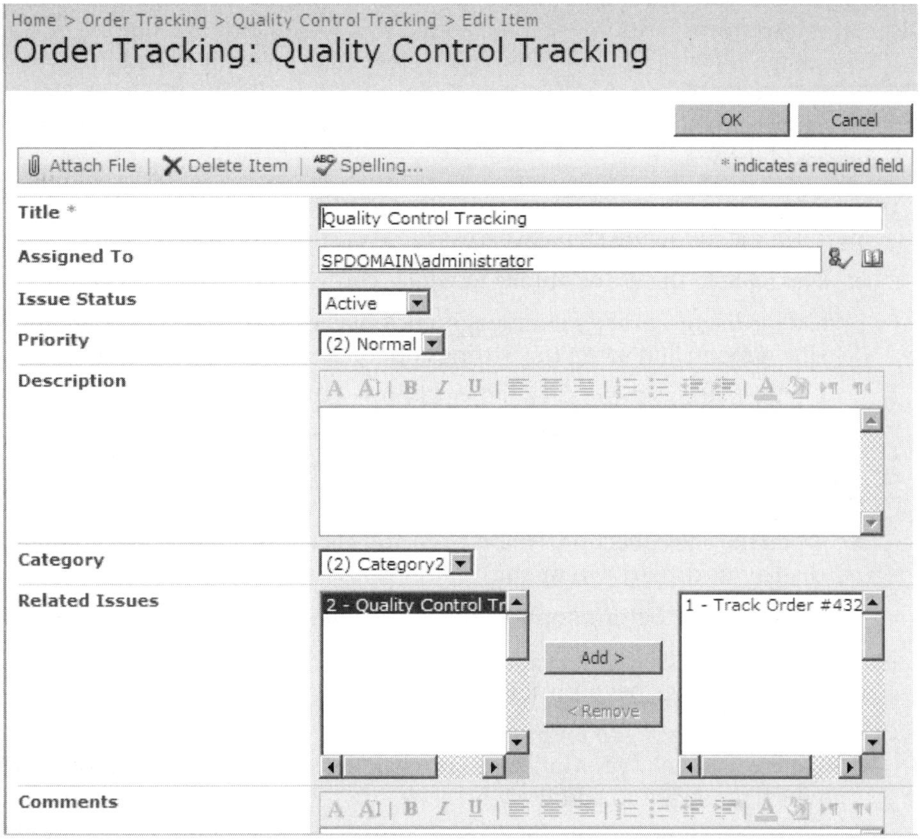

Figure 10-20.   A Three-state Workflow task.

expired document, according to the retention policy in use, should be retained or deleted. A Disposition Approval workflow can be started either manually by a user wishing to gain consensus on the disposal of a document, or automatically as the result of a document reaching its expiration date as computed by the Expiration policy feature of MOSS.

The Disposition Approval workflow is not limited to only documents stored on lists or libraries, but can also be used for SharePoint sites, pages, lists, and libraries as well. However, it is specifically designed to work with the Records Center site as a part of a company's information management functions.

NOTE   See Chapter 9 for more information on MOSS information management policies and the Records Center site.

Add a Disposition Approval Workflow to a SharePoint Element

A Disposition Approval workflow can be added to a SharePoint list, library, or content type. Depending on which of these SharePoint elements you want to add this workflow to, the process used to access the Workflow Settings page is slightly different. Use one of the following three methods to open the Workflow Settings page, depending on where you want to add the workflow:

1. To add a Disposition Approval workflow to a SharePoint list or library, perform the following steps to access the Workflow Settings page:

   a. Navigate to the list or library to which you wish to add the workflow.

   b. On the list or library's main page, click the Settings button to open its drop-down menu and select the Settings option for the list or library.

   c. On the Settings page, click the Workflow settings link under the Permissions And Management heading.

2. To add a Disposition Approval workflow to a specific content type at a site collection level, do the following:

   a. Open the site collection's main page and click the Site Actions button to display its drop-down menu.

   b. Select the Site Settings option and choose Modify All Site Settings from its pop-up menu.

   c. On the Settings page, click the Site Content Types link under the Galleries heading.

   d. On the Content Type Gallery page, click the link for the content type to which you want to add the workflow.

   e. On the Customize page, click the Workflow settings link.

3. To add a Disposition Approval workflow to a specific content type on a list or library, follow these steps:

   a. Navigate to the list or library to which you wish to add the workflow.

   b. On the list or library's main page, click the Settings button to open its drop-down menu and select the Settings option for the list or library.

   c. Under the Content Types heading, click the link of the content type to which you wish to add the workflow.

   d. On the Customize page, click the Settings button and choose the Workflow Settings option.

4. On the Change Workflow Settings page, click the Add A Workflow link to open the Add A Workflow page.

5. On the Add A Workflow page, click the link for the Disposition Approval workflow template, which is listed in the Workflow section.

6. On the Customize Workflow page, enter values or choose the appropriate settings for the Name, Task List, and History sections.

7. In the Start Options section, indicate and enter any required data to set the who, when, and how settings for the workflow.

8. If versioning is enabled on the site collection, the Start This Workflow To Approve A Major Version Of An Item option is displayed. When this option is used, the approval of a new major version equates to the approval for the disposition of the previous major version.

9. If you are adding the Disposition Approval workflow to a site content type, indicate whether or not you wish this workflow to apply to all content types within the site that inherit their configuration from the content site to which the workflow is being added in the Update List and Content Types section.

10. Click the OK button to add the workflow to the SharePoint element.

Disposition Approval Workflow and Expiration Policy

To add a Disposition Approval workflow to a list, library, or content type that is automatically started by the Expiration policy of the list, library, or content type when its retention period expires, do the following:

1. The first step in this process is to configure the Expiration policy of the list, library, or content type. Each of these SharePoint elements uses a slightly different process to accomplish this. However, it is only the first few steps of this process that are unique. Once you have opened the Information Management Policy settings page, the rest of the process is the same. Depending on which element you are configuring, do one of the following:

    a. To configure an Expiration policy on a list or library:

        i. Navigate to the list or library for which you wish to configure an Expiration policy.

        ii. On the list or library's main page, click the Settings button to display its drop-down menu and click the Settings (List Settings or Document Library Settings) option.

        iii. On the Settings page, click the Information management policy settings link under the Permissions and Management heading.

    b. To configure an Expiration policy on a list content type:

        i. Navigate to the list or library for which you wish to configure an Expiration policy.

        ii. On the list or library's main page, click the Settings button to display its drop-down menu and click the Settings (List Settings or Document Library Settings) option.

        iii. On the Settings page, under the Content Types heading, click the name of the content type you wish to configure.

        iv. On the Customize page, under the Settings heading, click the Information management policy settings link.

c. To configure an Expiration policy on a site content type:

   i. Navigate to the site collection's home page, click the Site Actions button to display its drop-down menu, select Site Settings and click Modify All Site Settings on its pop-up menu.

   ii. On the Settings page, click the Site Content Types link under the Galleries heading.

   iii. On the Site Content Types page, click the link for the site content type you wish to configure and on the Customize page that displays, click the Information Management Policy Settings link.

2. On the Information Management Policy Settings page (see Figure 10-21), click the Define A Policy option in the Specify The Policy section and then click the OK button to open the Edit Policy page.

3. On the Edit Policy page, shown in Figure 10-22, enter a description of the Expiration policy in the Name and Administrative Description section.

4. The Name of the policy defaults to the library content type for which you are creating the policy.

5. Enter an explanation of the policy in the Policy Statement section. This is the text displayed to users when they open any document or other SharePoint item that is subject to the policy.

6. In the Expiration section, shown in Figure 10-23, you can set the length of a retention period for the items to which the policy is applied. Check the Enable Expiration checkbox and then enter the retention period in days, months, or

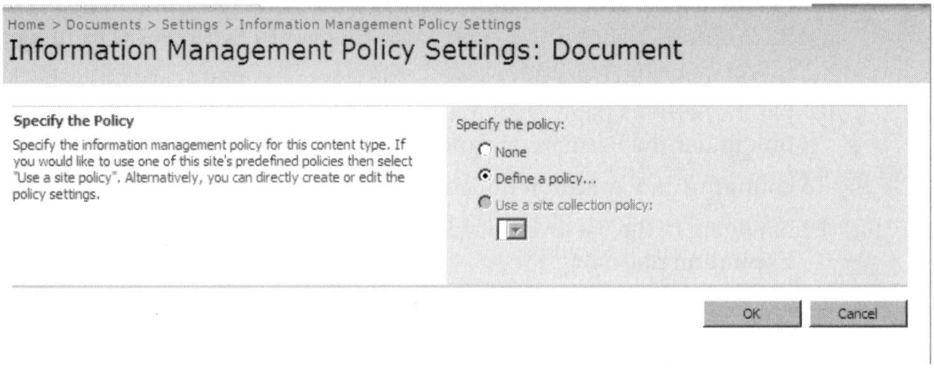

Figure 10-21. The Information Management Policy Settings page.

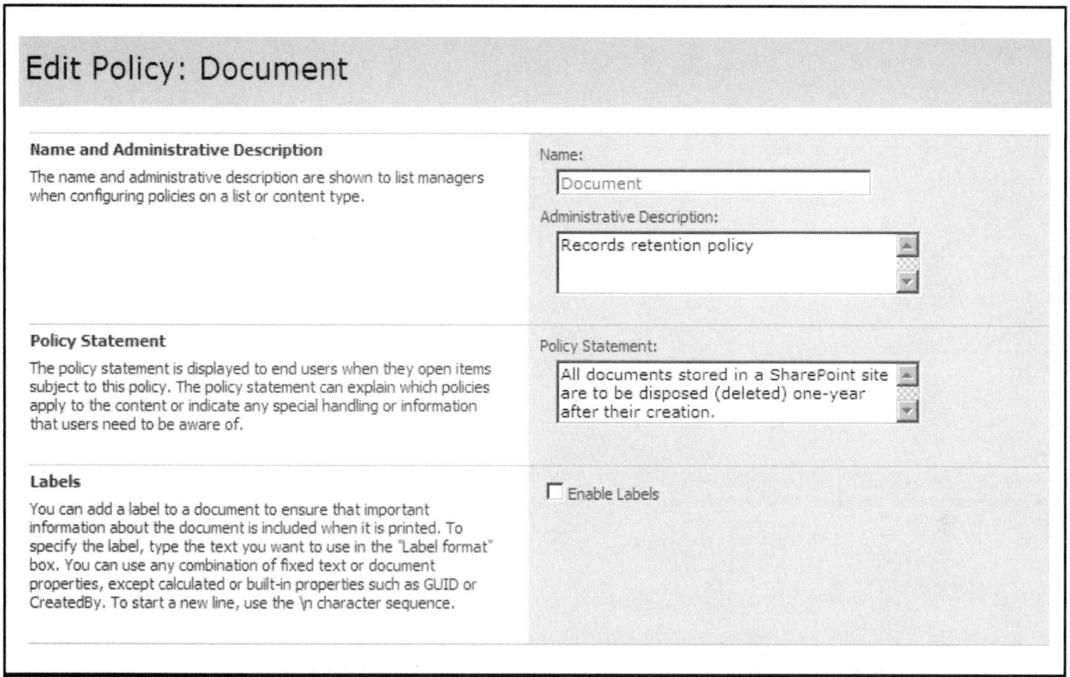

Edit Policy: Document

Name and Administrative Description

The name and administrative description are shown to list managers when configuring policies on a list or content type.

Name:

> Document

Administrative Description:

> Records retention policy

Policy Statement

The policy statement is displayed to end users when they open items subject to this policy. The policy statement can explain which policies apply to the content or indicate any special handling or information that users need to be aware of.

Policy Statement:

> All documents stored in a SharePoint site are to be disposed (deleted) one-year after their creation.

Labels

You can add a label to a document to ensure that important information about the document is included when it is printed. To specify the label, type the text you want to use in the "Label format" box. You can use any combination of fixed text or document properties, except calculated or built-in properties such as GUID or CreatedBy. To start a new line, use the \n character sequence.

☐ Enable Labels

Figure 10-22. The Edit Policy page.

years and the action you want initiated at the end of the retention period. You can specify when a retention period expires in three major ways:

a. **Use a date property**   If you wish the expiration date to be based on one of the date properties of the SharePoint element, such as its Created date or its Modified date, click the A time period based on the item's properties, choose the property you want to use as the basis for expiration, and specify the retention period in days, months, or years.

b. **Use a workflow**   You specify a workflow that is to start when the retention period expires (this is the one we are configuring in this section).

c. **Use a customized retention formula**   You can invoke a custom program to determine if the document has expired.

7. Under the When The Item Expires option, click the Start This Workflow option and select the specific Disposition Approval workflow you wish to start.

8. Click the OK button to save your Expiration policy settings.

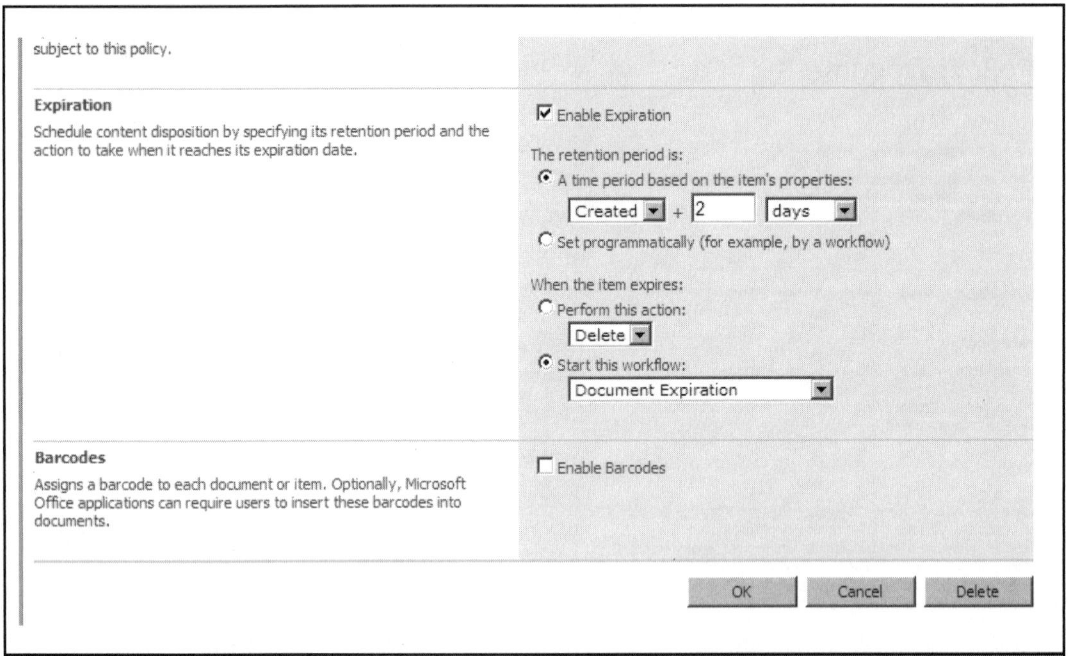

subject to this policy.

Expiration

Schedule content disposition by specifying its retention period and the action to take when it reaches its expiration date.

☑ Enable Expiration

The retention period is:
⦿ A time period based on the item's properties:
    [Created ▼] + [2] [days ▼]
○ Set programmatically (for example, by a workflow)

When the item expires:
○ Perform this action:
    [Delete ▼]
⦿ Start this workflow:
    [Document Expiration ▼]

Barcodes

Assigns a barcode to each document or item. Optionally, Microsoft Office applications can require users to insert these barcodes into documents.

☐ Enable Barcodes

[OK] [Cancel] [Delete]

Figure 10-23. The Expiration section of the Edit Policy page.

Complete a Disposition Approval Workflow Task

To complete a Disposal Approval workflow task you have been assigned, do the following:

1. Open the Tasks list on the site where the Disposal Approval workflow was initiated.

2. Open the drop-down menu for the Disposal Approval task you wish to complete and click the Edit Item option.

3. To review the SharePoint item that the task applies to, click the link associated with This Workflow Task Applies To.

4. After reviewing the SharePoint items, choose one of the actions listed under Disposition, as illustrated in Figure 10-24:

   a. **Delete this item**   Click this link to indicate that you wish to delete the item and specify whether a copy of the item's metadata should be written to the audit log.

   b. **Do not delete this item**   Click this link to indicate that you oppose deleting the SharePoint item.

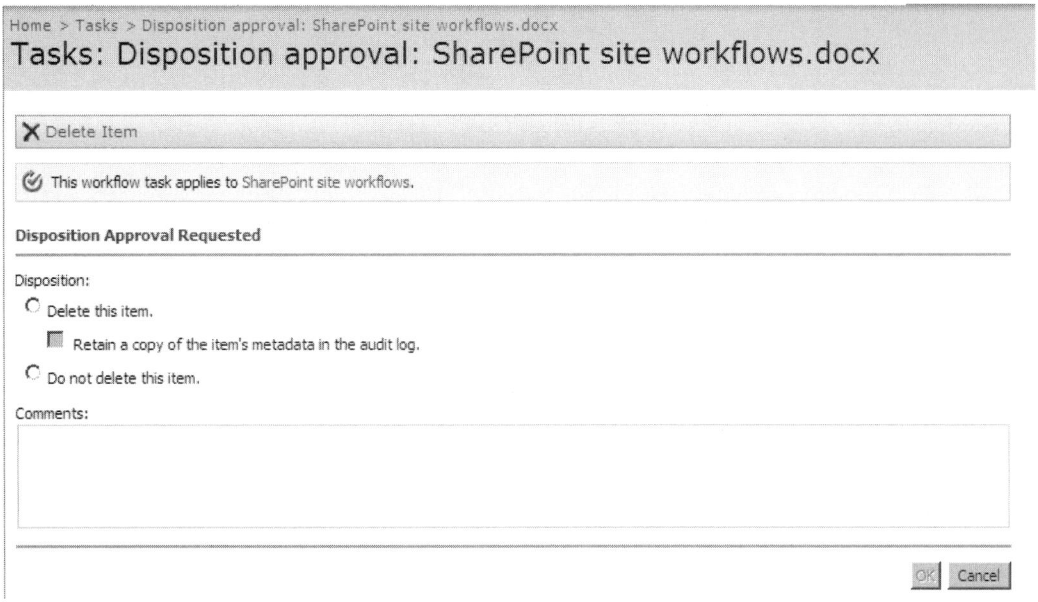

Home > Tasks > Disposition approval: SharePoint site workflows.docx

Tasks: Disposition approval: SharePoint site workflows.docx

✖ Delete Item

✔ This workflow task applies to SharePoint site workflows.

Disposition Approval Requested

Disposition:
- ○ Delete this item.
  - ☐ Retain a copy of the item's metadata in the audit log.
- ○ Do not delete this item.

Comments:

[   ]

OK Cancel

Figure 10-24.   A Disposition Approval workflow task form.

5. Enter any comments you wish to provide to the workflow initiator in the Comments section.

6. Click the OK button to complete the task.

SUMMARY

MOSS includes a variety of prebuilt workflows that can be initiated to organize the actions needed to complete an activity. Each user who is designated as a participant in the workflow is assigned a task either serially or in parallel to other users.

MOSS workflows can be associated with SharePoint lists, libraries, and specific content types, and started either manually or automatically when an item is edited or created. Workflow can be used to gather feedback, gain approvals, coordinate on the disposition of an item, collect signatures, and track a three-phase project through tasks issued to project participants.

CHAPTER 11

SharePoint Libraries

L ibraries are a cornerstone of Microsoft Office SharePoint Server 2007 (MOSS) functionality. They are one of two native storage content methods; the other being lists. While lists store individual pieces of information, libraries store collections of documents, graphic images, and other user-based files. Actually, a library is a specialized type of SharePoint list. Anything you can do to a list, including adding extra columns and views, you can also do to a library.

While you'll find libraries mentioned in several chapters of this book as a part of an MOSS function or in support of an MOSS feature, this chapter focuses specifically on libraries. In this chapter, you learn about the role of the library in the MOSS environment and how a library is created, managed, and secured.

NOTE The discussion on MOSS libraries touches on security, lists, and Web Parts. For more detailed information on these areas, see Chapters 7, 13, and 17, respectively.

MOSS LIBRARIES

An MOSS library works much like a super-folder. Just like permissions set on a Windows folder are passed down (inherited) by the files and subfolders beneath the folder, a library inherits its security permissions from the SharePoint site on which it is created. Likewise, the content of a library, meaning the documents and files included in the library, inherit their security permissions from the library. Permissions are typically not set at the individual file or folder level, but at the library level and then inherited by each file and folder in that library. For example, if a document needs to be available at several different security permissions levels, the document must be included in multiple libraries, each with the permissions levels needed to provide access to different users or groups.

MOSS is essentially made up of two products with two distinct purposes: MOSS and Windows SharePoint Services (WSS). The primary purpose of MOSS is to facilitate shared access to information, while the purpose of WSS is to facilitate the creation of new information while supporting collaboration. However, both of these products use the same content types and delivery method to provide their services: the site.

Shared and Personal Libraries

Throughout MOSS are various types of shared libraries. For example, most My Site pages include content from one or more Shared Documents and Shared Pictures libraries, both of which have the designed purpose to share files between MOSS users.

On the other hand, personal libraries are a more restrictive type of MOSS library in that they aren't shared libraries. Personal libraries don't inherit permissions from a parent page and don't include any explicit permission settings. Documents published to a personal library aren't visible to anyone other than the owner/creator, and of course, MOSS administrators.

Library Types

An MOSS library is actually a specialized type of list that exists to store files for retrieval by users. However, because content can vary in its data, format, and size, MOSS includes many different types of libraries, each suited to the storage and retrieval of a specific type of content. Within the MOSS environment, the following library types may be created:

▼ **Document library** This type of library supports collections of documents or other file types to be shared among users. The primary features of a document library include the ability to organize documents and files into folders, the capability of tracking the version of a document or file, and the capability to monitor the check-in or check-out of a document or file by specific users.

■ **Forms library** Form libraries support XML-based business forms and reports, such as project status or purchase orders, and integrate with MOSS-compatible XML editors like Microsoft Office InfoPath.

■ **Picture library** This type of library provides special features for managing and displaying pictures, including a slide show feature that displays pictures and graphics in a series.

■ **Data Connection library** This type of library is used to share files that contain external data connection information.

■ **Slide library** This library is used to store Microsoft Office PowerPoint slides and to provide features that allow users to find, manage, and reuse or repurpose presentation slides.

NOTE Don't confuse the Slide library with the Picture library and its slide show capability. The Slide library acts essentially like a slide file, much like that used to store 35 millimeter (mm) slides.

■ **Report library** The purpose of this library type is to facilitate the sharing of business intelligence information and to simplify the creation, management, and delivery of Web pages, documents, and key performance indicators (KPIs).

■ **Translation Management library** This MOSS feature can be very valuable to large enterprises that operate in a number of countries, each with a different native language. A translation management library is used to create documents in multiple languages and to manage the translation tasks. The features available with this library type include the creation and use of workflow processes to manage the translation of a document, as well as the features of a Document library.

▲ **Wiki Page library** Wiki (pronounced "WICK-ee") page libraries support interlinked collections of Wiki pages. Wiki pages allow visitors to easily add, edit, or remove page content in a collaborative environment. Wiki page libraries support pictures, tables, and hyperlinks, including Wiki links.

Wiki

In 1995, Ward Cunningham completed and launched software, named WikiWiki-Web after the name of a Hawaiian bus route over his second choice QuickWeb. In fact, wiki is Hawaiian for fast, but its initials have also come to stand for "what I know is" among frequent Wiki users and collaborators.

A Wiki Web site facilitates visitors to use a simple text markup language to share and collaborate on virtually any topic. Unlike a Web log (blog), where content is merely contributed statically, a Wiki is designed for collaboration using a user-centric database for storing and categorizing its content.

For more information on wikis, visit the Widipedia.org Web site at http://en.wikipedia.org/wiki/Wiki.

LIBRARY MANAGEMENT

Managing an MOSS library is simple and straightforward. An MOSS library is essentially a catalog, something like the card catalogs found in public libraries. The library consists of a list of document titles along with each document's location. However, the bottom line is that within your MOSS environment, libraries are the storage mechanism for files.

Like a list, a library can be customized by adding columns to hold relevant data, such as metadata. Metadata means "data about data" and is used to describe the files in the library, making it easier for users to find what they're looking for in the library. Additional library configuration may include creating custom views, modifying security permissions, enabling document versioning, and, of course, uploading documents to populate the library.

NOTE   For more information on metadata, see Chapter 16.

Depending on the library and the type and quantity of documents or files placed into it, you may devote considerable effort into creating a customized library. However, because you can create customized libraries and save them as templates, the creation of future libraries that are close in form and function to an existing library takes much less effort. The next few sections discuss the processes used to create, customize, and secure an MOSS library.

NOTE   See Chapters 12 and 16 for more information on SharePoint Lists and Web Parts, respectively.

Create a Library

By default, only MOSS administrators can create a library. However, this task can be delegated to other users through the use of SharePoint groups, permissions lists, and the use of library templates (see the "Library Templates" section later in the chapter). To get to the Create page in MOSS, do the following:

1. Open the SharePoint site on which you wish to create the library.

2. Either click the Site Actions button to open its drop-down menu and choose View All Site Content or click the View All Site Content link in the Quick Launch navigation pane.

3. On the Site Content page that appears, click the Create button in the upper-left corner of the page to open the Create page (see Figure 11-1).

On the Create page, each of the columns in the lower part of the page contains a list of the different SharePoint elements available.

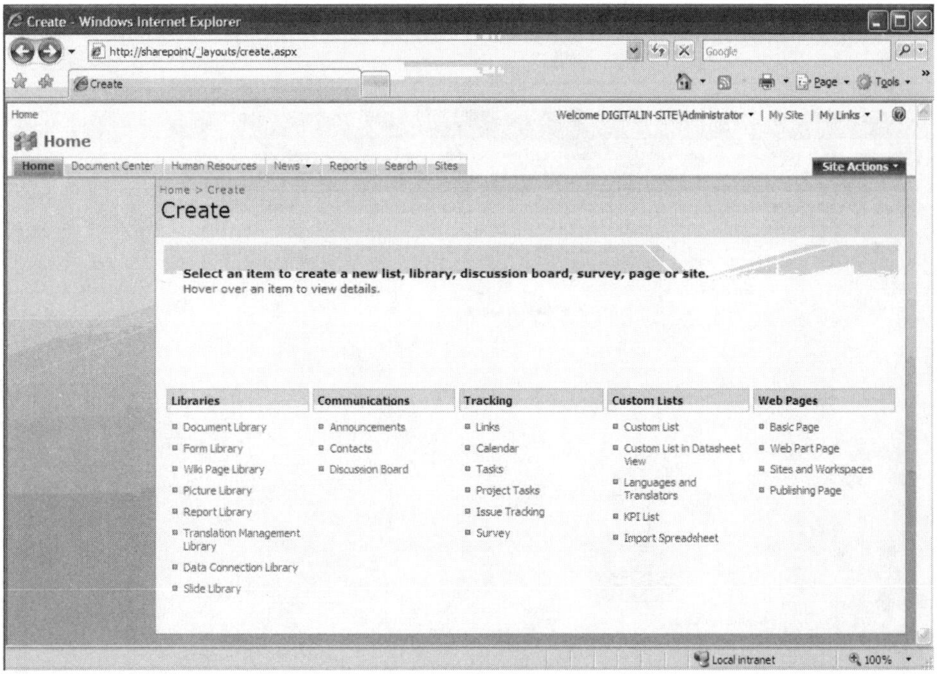

Figure 11-1.   The Create page is used to create a new library.

In the Libraries column, the templates available are:

▼ Document Library

■ Form Library

■ Wiki Page Library

■ Picture Library

■ Report Library

■ Translation Management Library

■ Data Connection Library

▲ Slide Library

See the comments earlier in this chapter regarding which lists are available.

Each library template listed on the Create page launches a slightly different configuration page. However, all library configuration pages have common elements, such as a library name, description, navigation, and versioning settings.

Perform the following steps to create a new Document Library:

1. On the Create page, click the Document Library link to open its New page, shown in Figure 11-2.

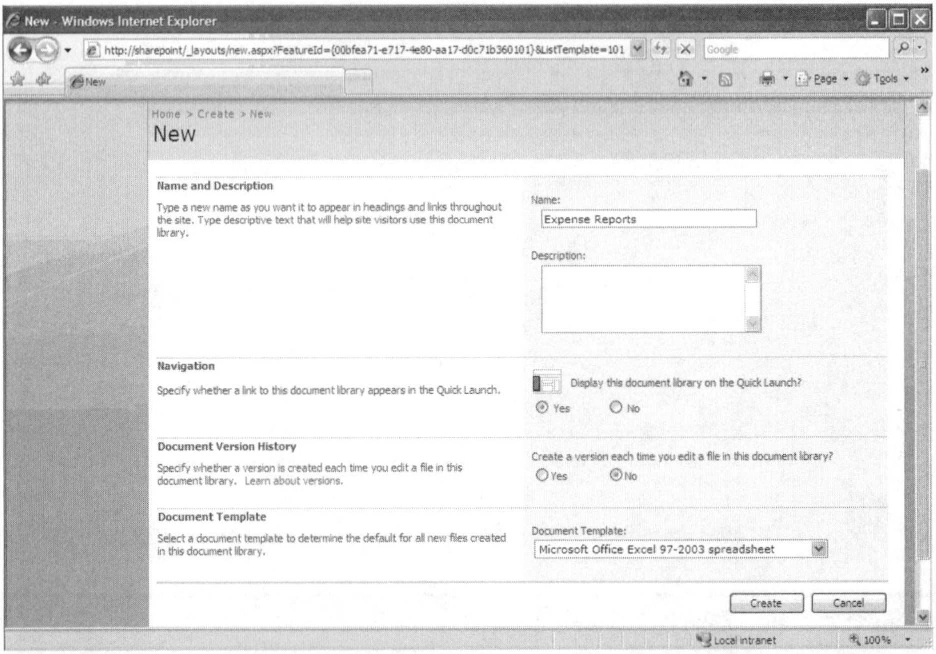

Figure 11-2. The New Document Library configuration page.

2. Enter a Name and a description for the new document library.

3. If you wish to include the new library in the Quick Launch menu, choose the Yes option in the Navigation section.

> **TIP**   The Quick Launch menu is located in the left navigation pane on each SharePoint page and contains the links that the site owner has designated for inclusion. Typically, the Quick Launch menu contains links to those sites or pages used most often.

4. If you want to enable document versioning, choose Yes for the Document Version History option.

5. Use the pull-down list in the Document Template area to select the document template on which you want to base the new library. The template should be appropriate to the type of documents to be included in the library.

6. Click the Create button to create the new library.

Customize a Library

Once a library has been created, it may be customized. Before you begin changing the look, feel, and function of a library (or for that matter just about any SharePoint element), you should ask yourself the following questions about how the library is to be used and accessed by users:

▼   Will the library be accessed through the Quick Launch menu only?

■   Will the library be included on a page using the Library Web Part?

▲   Can it be accessed through both?

You can use two methods to organize a library: folders and metadata columns. While there can be valid reasons to organize a library into a hierarchy of folders and subfolders, in many cases adding additional columns of metadata to the library can be an efficient way to search and locate library contents for users. A metadata column allows users to sort and filter a library to quickly locate files, avoiding a tedious manual search in library folders and subfolders for a file.

> **TIP**   Configure the security settings of a library before you begin uploading documents to it to prevent unauthorized access to sensitive documents, should you forget this step later.

The last step in creating a library is the "put the books on the shelf" task, or in other words, populate the library by uploading its initial files. If you plan for users to populate the library, it's a very good idea to prove them with some training beforehand. The library interface is intuitive enough for most users to use in order to upload a single document or even multiple documents. However, the best way to upload a large number of files to a library is to use the Explorer View, discussed later in the chapter (see the "Explorer

View" section). The Explorer View is very similar to the Windows Explorer or the My Computer functions that most users have experience using.

A library is customized through its settings, which are quite similar to the settings for many other SharePoint elements, such as a SharePoint list. To customize the settings of a document library, perform the following steps:

1. Navigate to the site containing the library you wish to configure.

2. Click the View All Site Content link at the top of the Quick Launch menu.

3. On the All Site Content page, shown in Figure 11-3, choose the type of library you wish to configure. For example, the Documents link.

4. On the Documents page that appears (see Figure 11-4), click the Settings option to open its drop-down menu.

5. On the Settings menu, choose Document Library Settings (as shown in Figure 11-4) to open the Customize Documents page (shown in Figures 11-5 and 11-6).

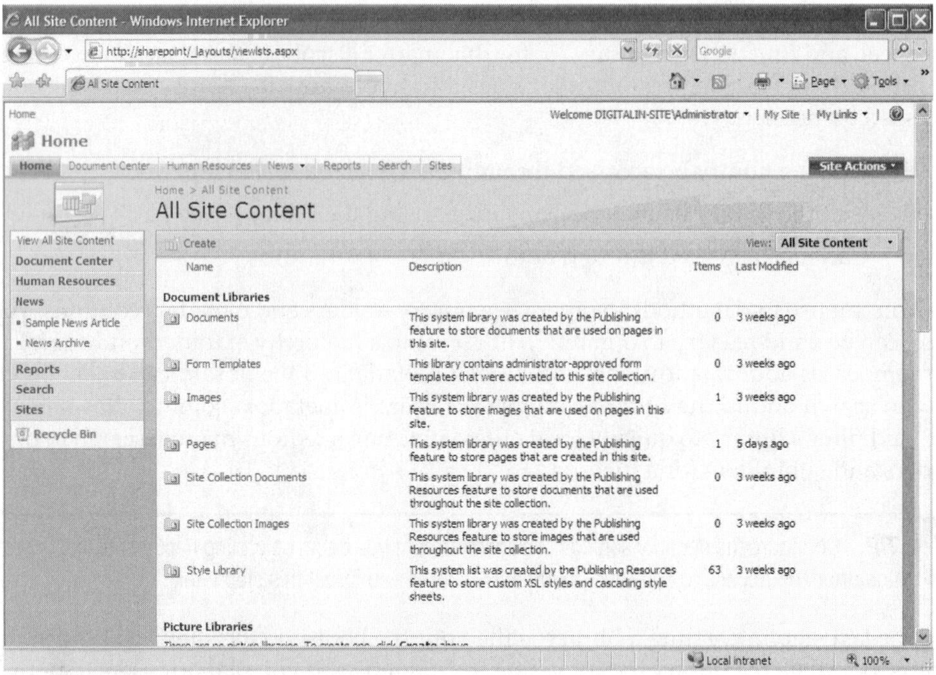

Figure 11-3. The View All Site Content page.

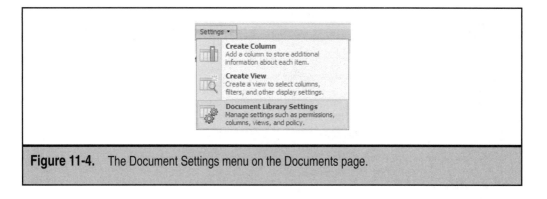

Figure 11-4. The Document Settings menu on the Documents page.

6. On the Customize Documents page (see Figures 11-5 and 11-6), you may customize the settings and properties of a document library, as well as some management actions, including:

▼ General Settings

■ Title, description, and navigation—Change a library title, description, or navigation (Quick Launch) properties

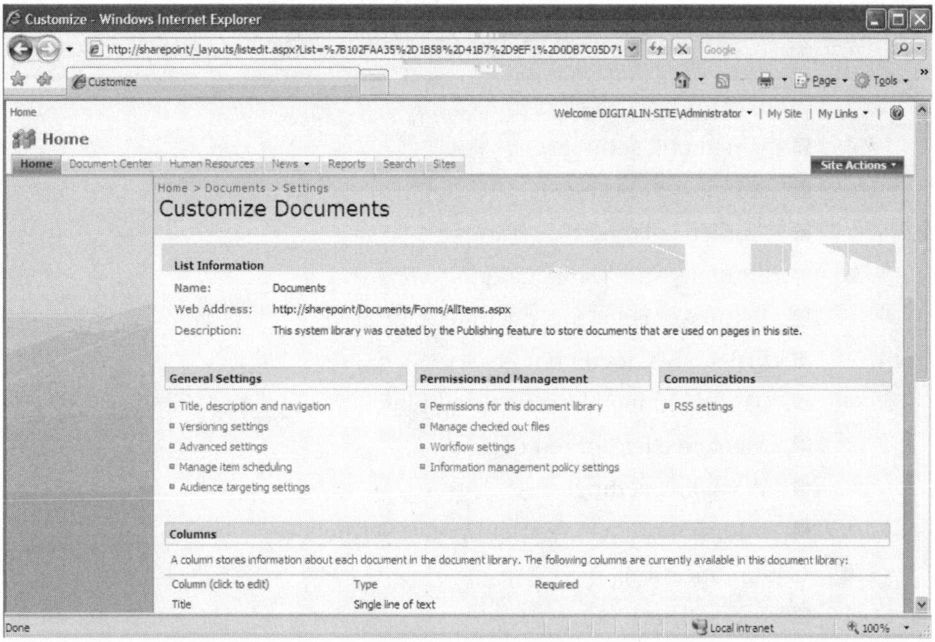

Figure 11-5. The top portion of the Customize Documents page.

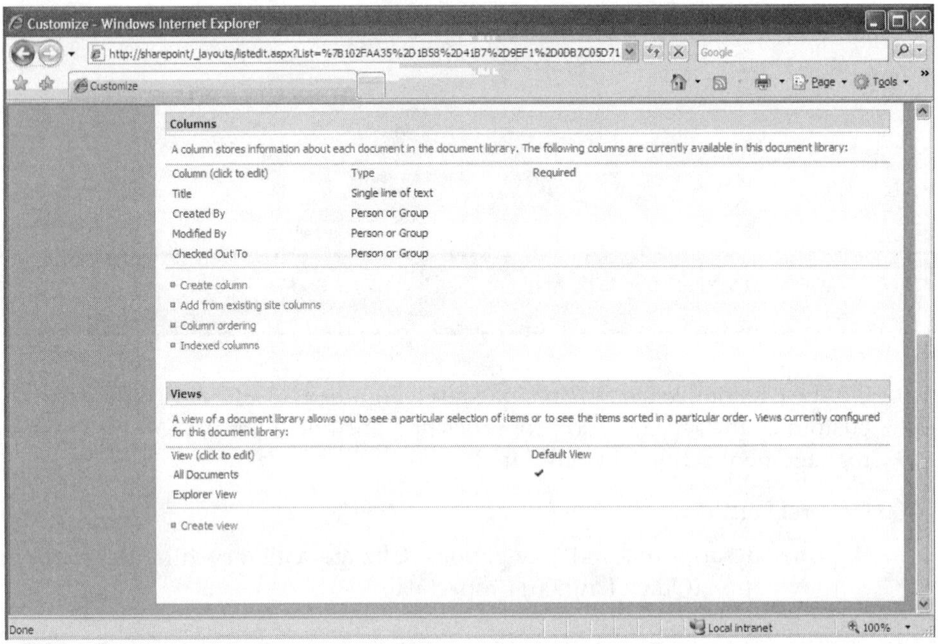

Figure 11-6. The bottom portion of the Customize Documents page.

- ■ Versioning settings
- ■ Advanced settings
- ■ Audience targeting settings
- ■ Permissions and Management
  - ■ Permissions for this document library
  - ■ Delete this document library
  - ■ Save document library as template
  - ■ Manage checked out files
  - ■ Workflow settings
  - ■ Information management policy settings
- ■ Communications
  - ■ RSS settings
- ■ Columns
  - ■ Create column

■ Add from existing site columns

■ Column ordering

■ Indexed columns

▲ Views

■ Create view

The more commonly used of these settings and actions are discussed in the following sections.

Display a Library in the Quick Launch Menu

The Quick Launch menu is the vertical list of links located on the left side of all SharePoint pages. The SharePoint elements that are most frequently accessed should be located in the Quick Launch menu for the convenience of both the administrators and users.

To add a library or any other SharePoint element to the Quick Launch menu, do the following:

1. Navigate to the SharePoint page containing the content you wish to add to the Quick Launch menu and click the View All Site Content link at the top of the Quick Launch menu.

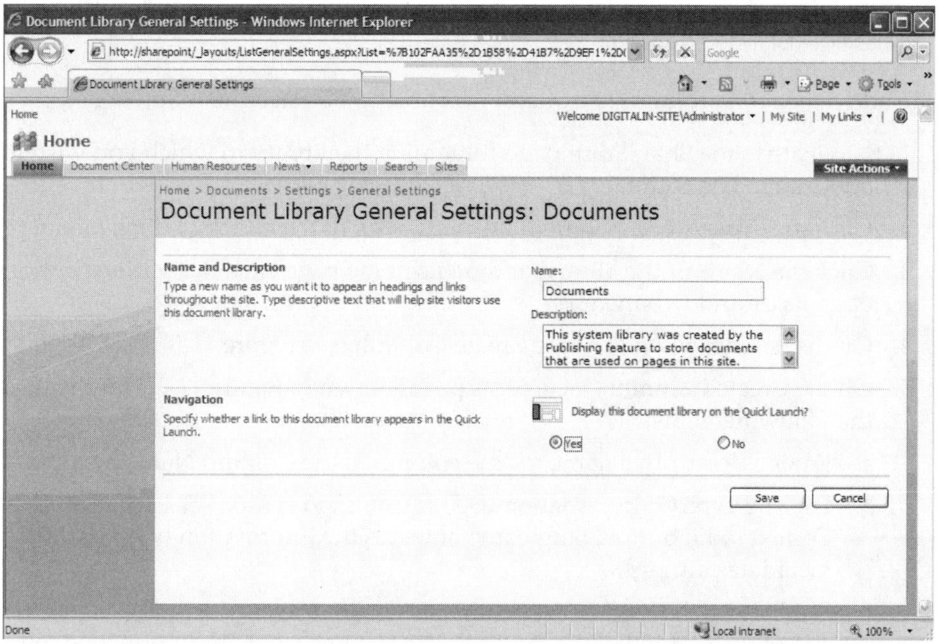

Figure 11-7. The General Settings page of a SharePoint document library.

2. On the View All Site Content (see Figure 11-3), click the name of the Site content element you wish to customize. For example, click the Documents link to access a document library.

3. On the Library Element page, click the Settings option to open its drop-down menu and then click the Library Settings option. In the example shown in Figure 11-4, the selection is Document Library Settings.

4. On the General Settings page of the library element, you may set the title, description, and whether or not you want to include this library in the Quick Launch menu (see Figure 11-7).

5. Click Save to store any changes you've made, or choose Cancel to return to the previous page.

Library Metadata Columns

Adding a metadata column to a library can greatly increase the usability of the library and improve the efficiency of users trying to locate one or more specific files. A metadata column allows a user to quickly locate the files in a library that she or he wishes to access. Using a library's metadata columns, MOSS users can filter and sort a library's files to create a list of only the files they wish to see.

NOTE The use of views and metadata has an entire chapter dedicated to it in this book. See Chapter 17 for more information.

To add a metadata column to a SharePoint library, perform the following steps:

1. Navigate to the SharePoint page containing the library to which you wish to add a metadata column.

2. Click the View All Site Content link at the top of the Quick Launch menu.

3. Click the Name of the library, and on its home page click the Settings option to open its drop-down menu.

4. On the Settings menu, choose Create Column (see Figure 11-8).

5. On the Create Column: Documents page, shown in Figure 11-9, enter values for the following fields:

    a. Enter a descriptive name for the column in the Column Name box.

    b. For The Type Of Information In This Column Is entry, select the Single Line Of Text radio button. Single line of text is the information type used for metadata columns.

    c. Scroll down the page to the Additional Column Settings area (see Figure 11-10), and select Yes for the Require That This Column Contains Information setting to ensure that when users add new files to a library, information is added to the metadata column.

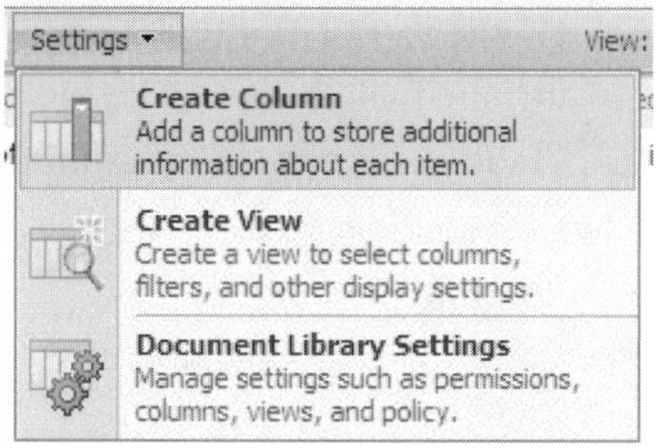

Figure 11-8. The Create Column option on the Settings menu is used to add a metadata column to a SharePoint library.

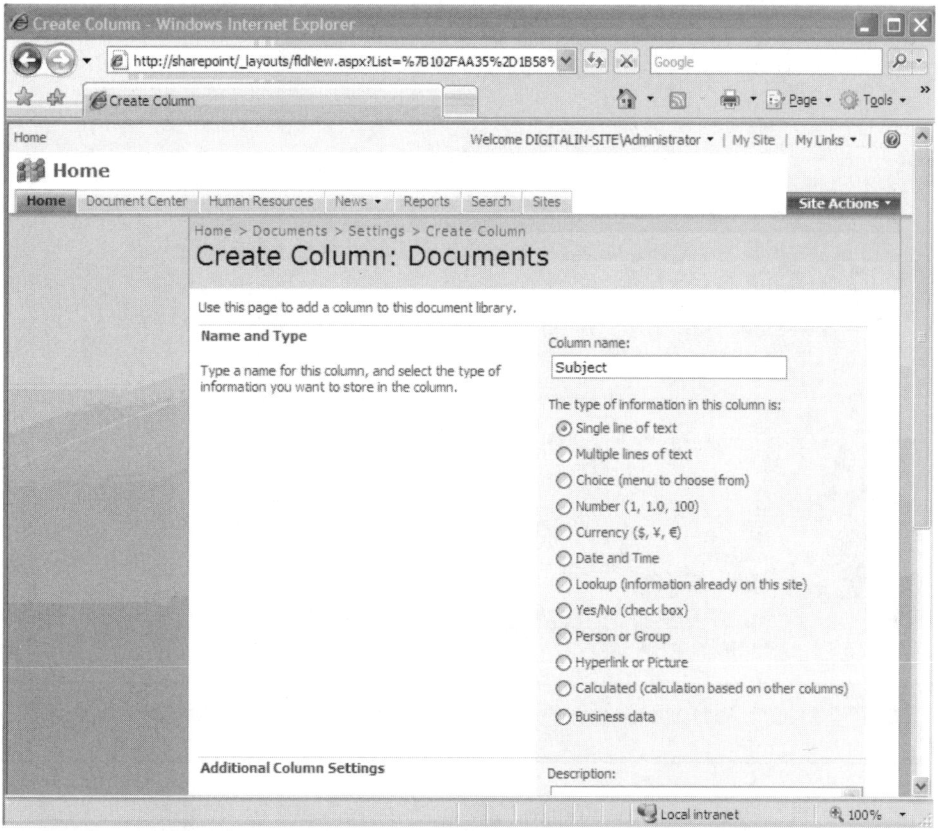

Figure 11-9. The Create Column: Documents page.

    d. Enter a description of the column's purpose, if desired.

    e. Enter a maximum length for the text in the column. The default value of 255 characters is typically adequate.

    f. Select Text as the default value type of the column.

    g. Check the Add To Default view box.

6. Click OK to add the column to the library.

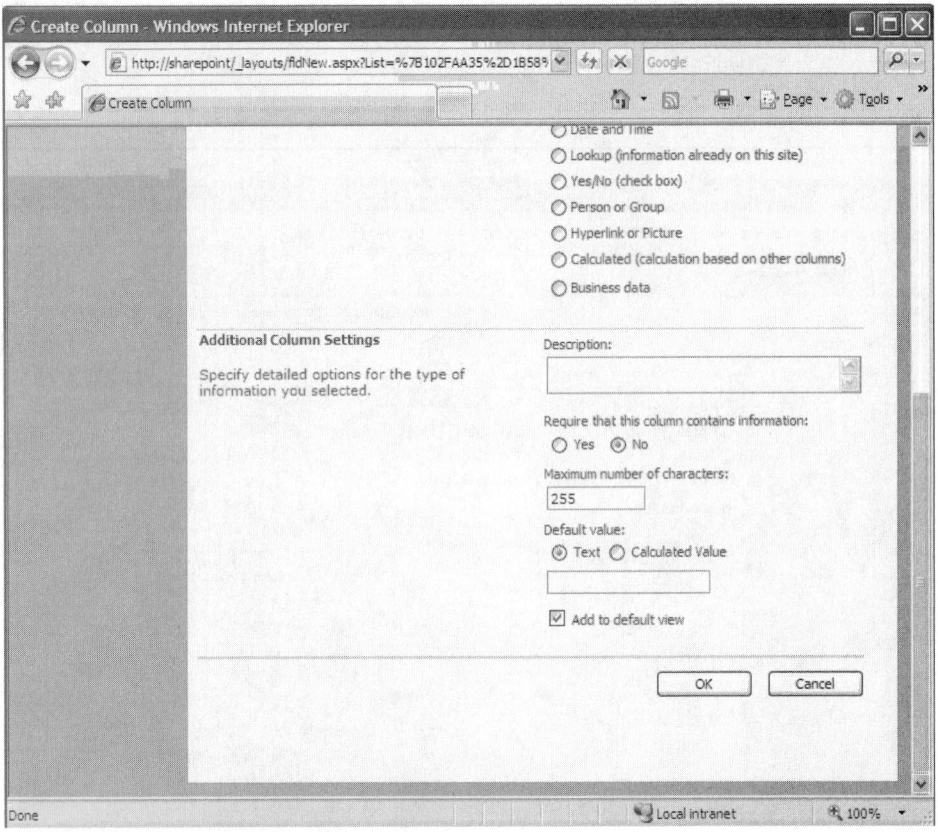

Figure 11-10. The Additional Column Settings area on the Create Column: Documents page.

Use Metadata to Find Library Files

As discussed earlier in the preceding section, a library configured with a metadata column can make a user's file search more efficient. This is especially true when a library contains a large number of files. Without the use of a metadata column, the user would have to visually scan the list of documents on a library's home page.

While the number of files in the following example would enable a user to perhaps just find a file visually, this example demonstrates how filtering library columns can be used to locate specific files:

OBJECTIVE   Locate the "Garmin eTrex Vista CX GPS Quick Reference Guide" using metadata columns in a SharePoint library. Figure 11-11 shows the documents in the example library.

1. Click the Topic column heading to display its options and defined metadata values. Choose GPS to display only those documents that have GPS in their metadata column, as illustrated in Figure 11-12.

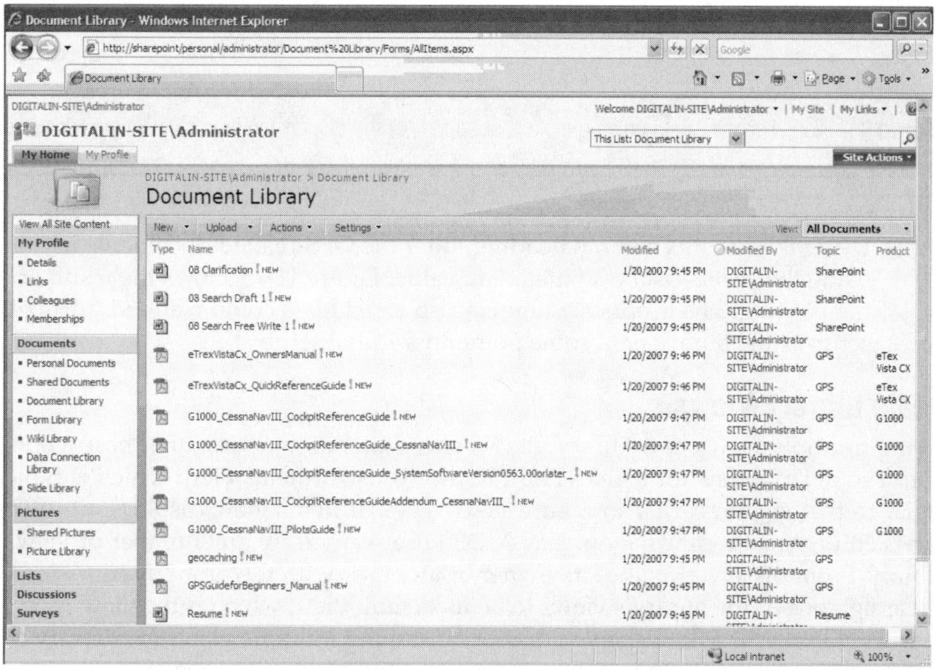

Figure 11-11.   The document contents of a SharePoint library.

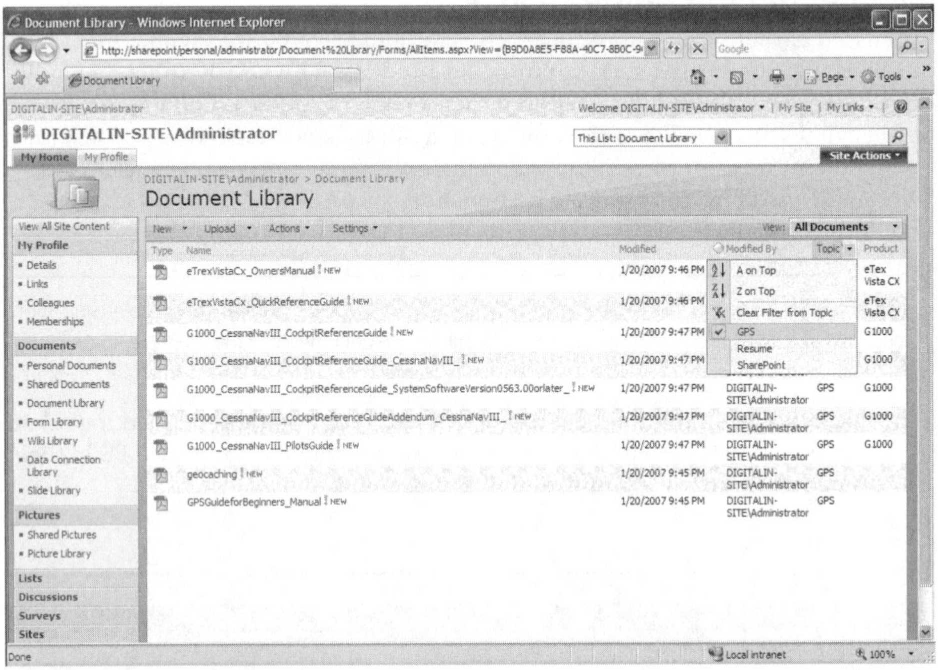

Figure 11-12. The metadata column topic is used to filter the display to show only specific documents.

2. Using the Product column heading, filter the GPS-related documents list using the "eTex Vista CX" metadata value. Figure 11-13 shows the result of the filtering. The Product column is also a metadata column added during the setup of the library or at some point after initial setup.

Create Library Views

Having multiple views of a library allows users to choose a view that best works for them. The default view for a SharePoint library is its All Items view, which is typically similar to that shown earlier in Figure 11-11. The All Items view displays all of the library's columns and information. Any MOSS user can create any number of views for a library. From these views, the site owner or any user with the proper permissions can then assign one of the library's views to be its default view, which is the view users will see when a library is first displayed. However, having multiple views of a library available provides a user with the ability to select an alternate view as needed.

To create a view for a SharePoint library, do the following:

1. Navigate to the page that contains the library and click the View All Site Content link at the top of the Quick Launch menu.

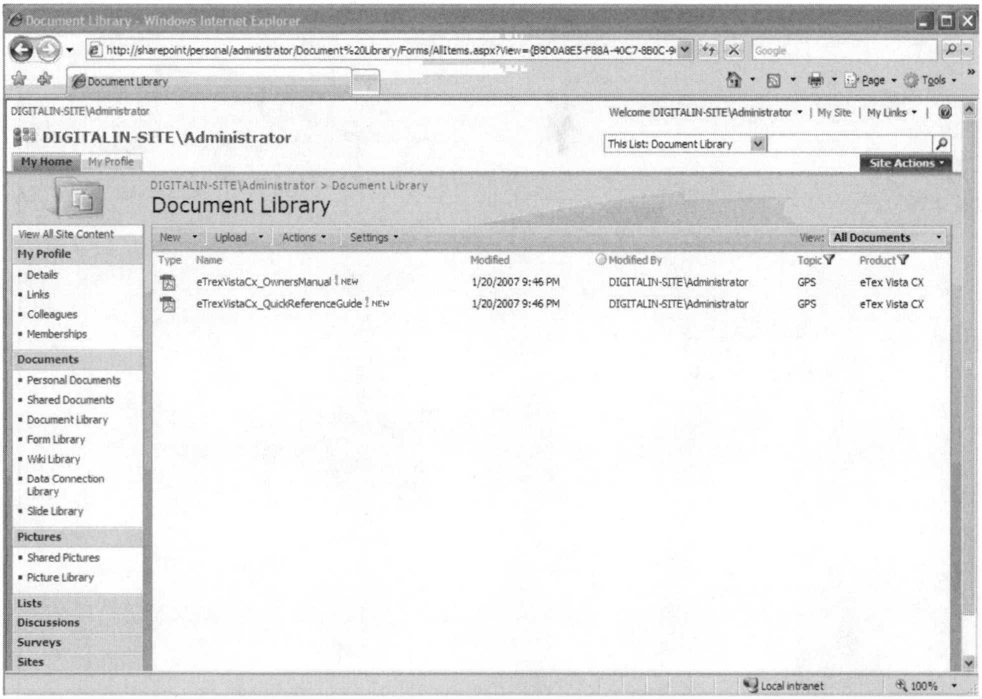

Figure 11-13. The GPS-related list filtered by a Product value.

2. On the View All Site Content page, locate and click the Name of the library for which you wish to create a view.

3. On the selected library's Documents page, click the Settings option to open its drop-down menu and choose Create View, as shown in Figure 11-14.

4. On the Create View page (see Figure 11-15), choose the view format you wish to use from the options listed:

   a. **Standard view**   Choose from a list of display styles to view data.

   b. **Calendar view**   View data as a daily, weekly, or monthly calendar.

   c. **Datasheet view**   View data in an editable spreadsheet format for bulk editing and quick customization.

   d. **Gantt view**   View list items in a graphical representation of how tasks relate to each other over time.

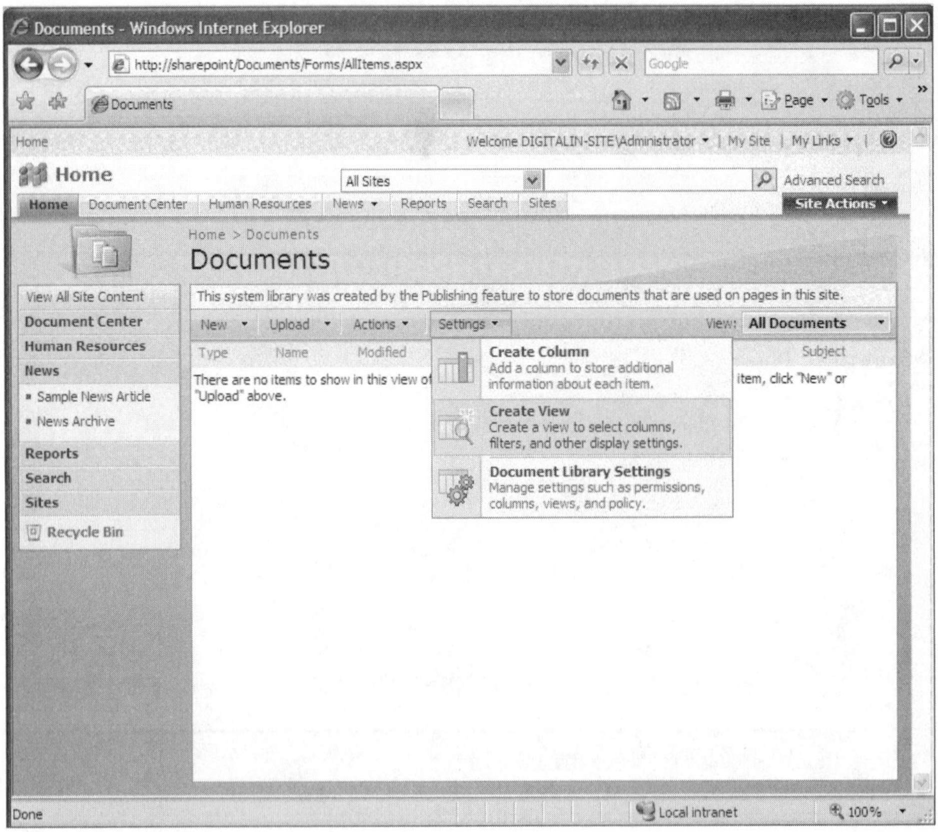

Figure 11-14. The Create View option on the Settings menu.

NOTE The procedure described here is for a Standard view, but since all view formats have a number of similar properties, these instructions also apply to the other view types, in general.

5. On the Create View page for the view format you've chosen (see Figure 11-16 for the Standard View page), enter values in the following settings:

a. Enter a View Name. The View Name should be unique and descriptive at the same time since this is the name that appears in the views menu.

b. If you wish to make your new view the default view, check the Make This The Default View checkbox.

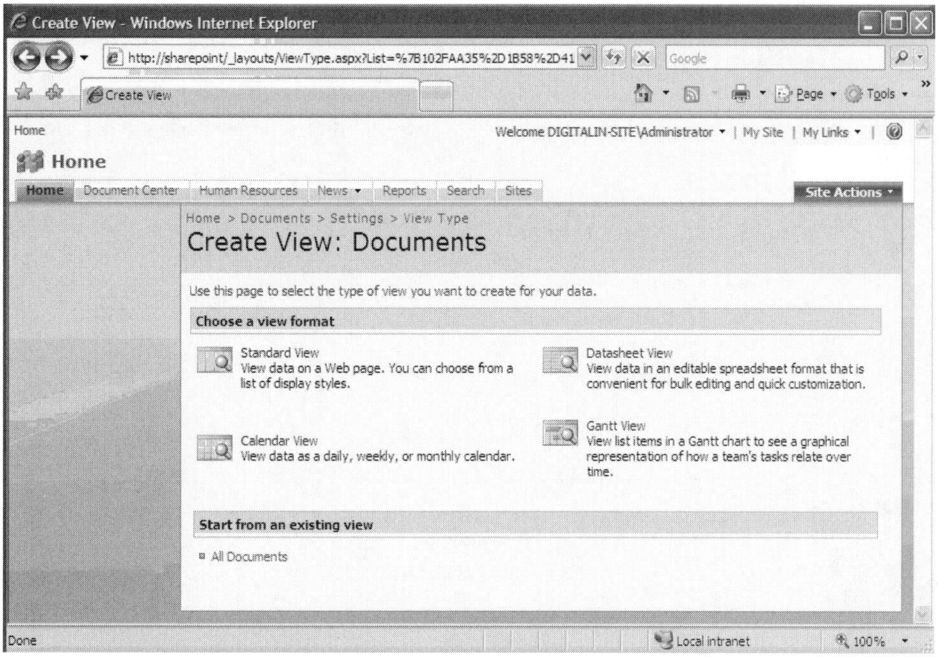

Figure 11-15.   The standard options available for a view's format.

c. All new views are public views that can be accessed by all users. If you wish to designate the view as private, meaning that the view is only available to its creator, select the Create A Personal View option.

d. In the Columns section (see Figure 11-17), check the Display checkbox associated with each column you wish to display in the new view.

e. For each column you've selected for display, use the Position From Left values to order the columns in the view left-to-right.

f. In the Sort section (see Figure 11-18), you can cause the view's information to be sorted before it's displayed. Each of up to two columns of the view can be sorted in either ascending or descending order.

g. If you wish to limit the number of library files displayed by the view, use the Filter section to set simple or complex filtering options. A view's filters are automatically applied to the library's content when the view is opened.

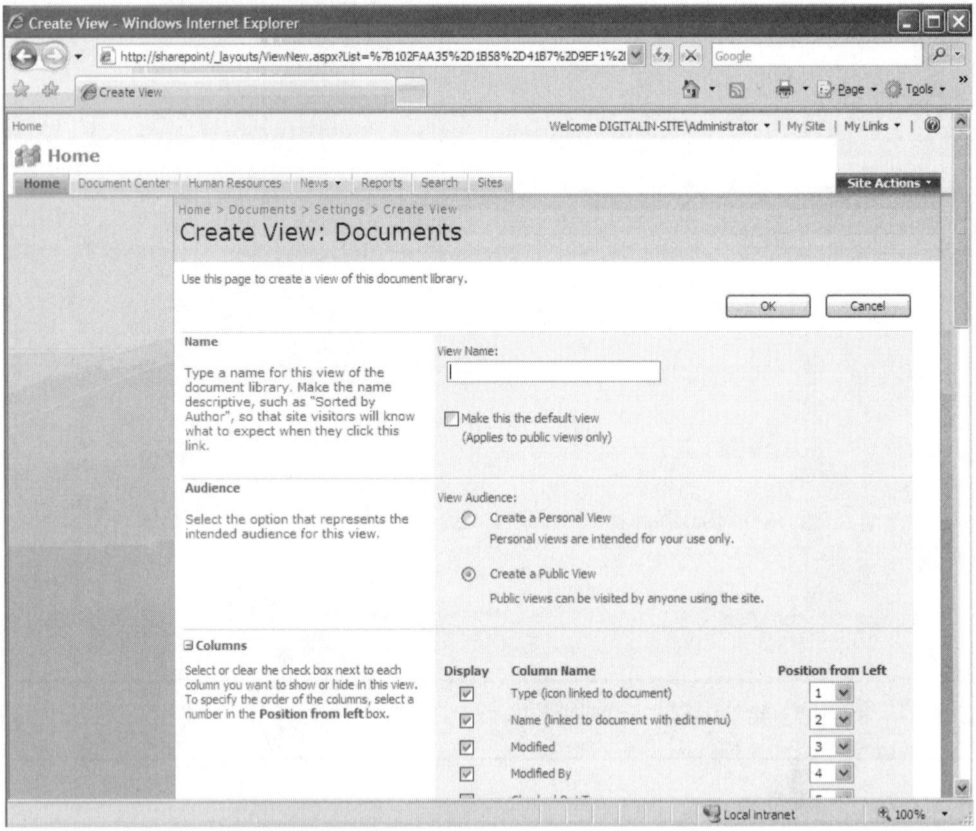

Figure 11-16.   The Create View page for creating a standard view for a library.

6. If you wish to configure additional view properties, use the Group by, Totals, Styles, Folders, Item Limit, and Mobile sections of the Create View page (see Figure 11-19). The following offers a brief description of each:

- **Group by**   Library items may be grouped by up to two columns to simplify the view.

- **Totals**   Library columns may be totaled by count, average, maximum, and minimum.

- **Style**   A view style may be applied to quickly format a view.

- **Folders**   Allows you to ignore a library's folder structure to show all of the items in a library.

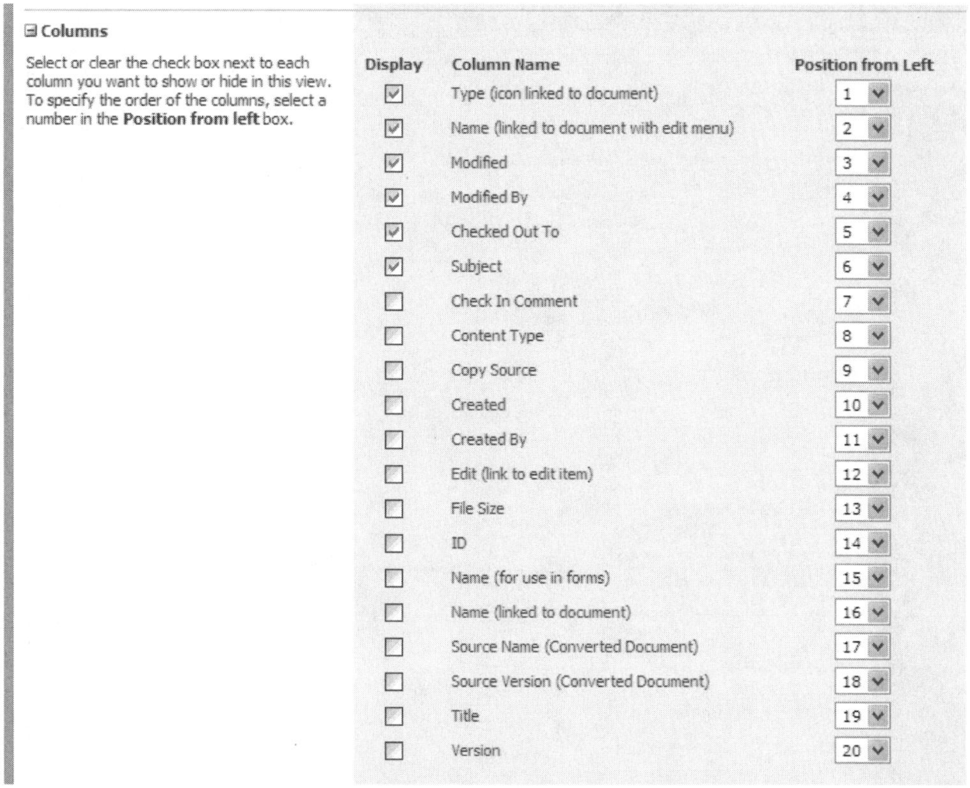

Figure 11-17.   The Columns section of the Create View page.

TIP   Some users may be resistant to the concept of a library without folders. Using two views for a library, a folder view and a flat view, you can create a comfort zone for all users and their needs.

- **Item Limit**   Used to determine the specific or maximum number of library items displayed on a page.
- **Mobile**   Used to designate the view as a mobile view, which is customized to smaller screen resolutions and limited user input.

NOTE   For more information on Views, see Chapter 16.

7. Click OK to create the view.

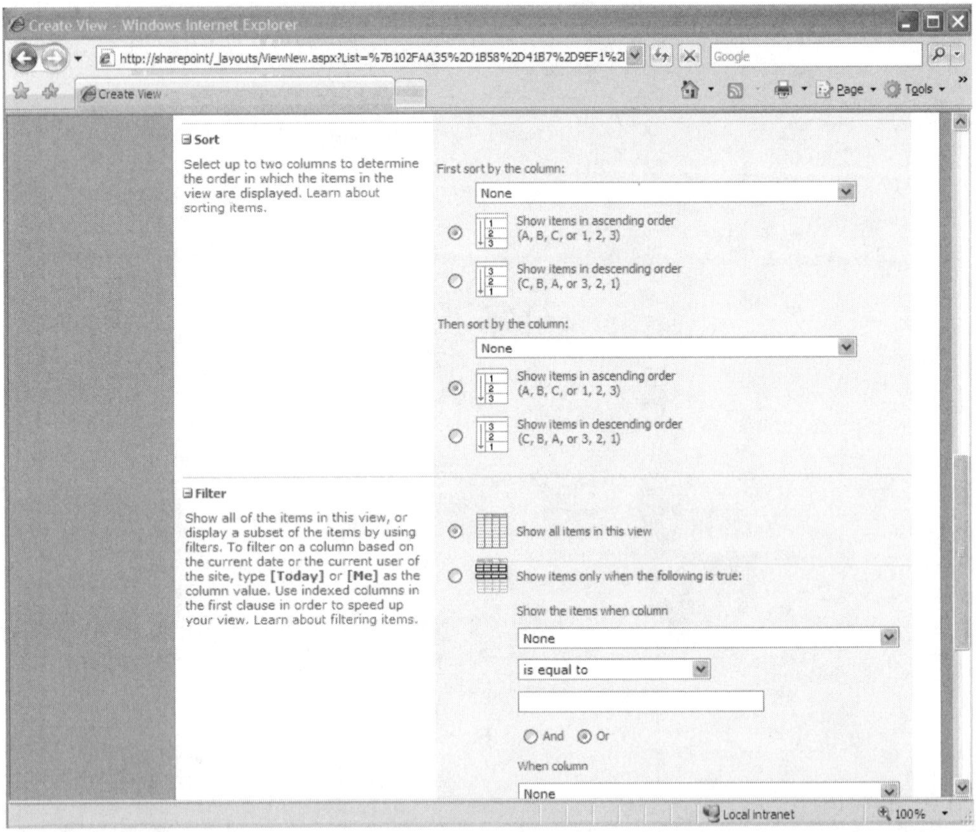

Figure 11-18.   The Sort and Filter sections of the Create View page.

Library Security

SharePoint libraries inherit security permissions from their parent site. However, the site owner or an administrator can assign unique security permissions to a library or a specific file or folder in a library. Because of the security capabilities in MOSS, Windows 2003 Server, and the other applications included in your MOSS environment, you can use a combination or user, group, and top-level or parent site permissions to allow or restrict access to a library and even to documents or files within the library.

It is also possible to avoid the administration of special and exception permission sets within a library. In some cases, it may be easier to create a new library, assign it the special permission set required, and then include the special-case documents or files in

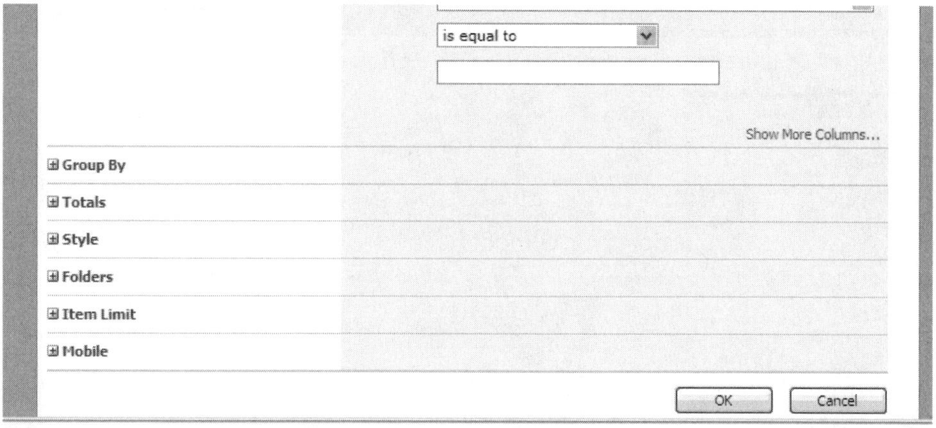

Figure 11-19. Additional Settings that can be applied to a SharePoint view.

the new library, where they inherit its unique security permissions. However, managing special permissions sets, regardless of their levels, will in the long run prove more trouble than it's worth.

To configure the security permission settings on a SharePoint library, do the following:

1. Navigate to the page which contains the library and click the View All Site Content link at the top of the Quick Launch menu.

2. On the All Site Content page, choose the name of the library for which you wish to set security permissions.

3. On the library's Document page, click the Settings option to open its drop-down menu and click Document Library Settings.

4. On the Settings page, click the Permissions For This Document Library link under the Permissions And Management heading.

5. On the Permissions page (see Figure 11-20), click the Actions button to open its drop-down menu and select Edit Permissions. This action copies the permission set of the library's parent (its site) and stops permission inheritance. This allows you to make security permission setting changes that apply only to this library.

6. Click the New option to open its drop-down menu and then select Add Users to open the Select People And Groups dialog box, shown in Figure 11-21.

7. You may browse for Active Directory users and security groups by using the browse function, entering all or part of a user or group name in the Find box, and pressing the spyglass icon on its right.

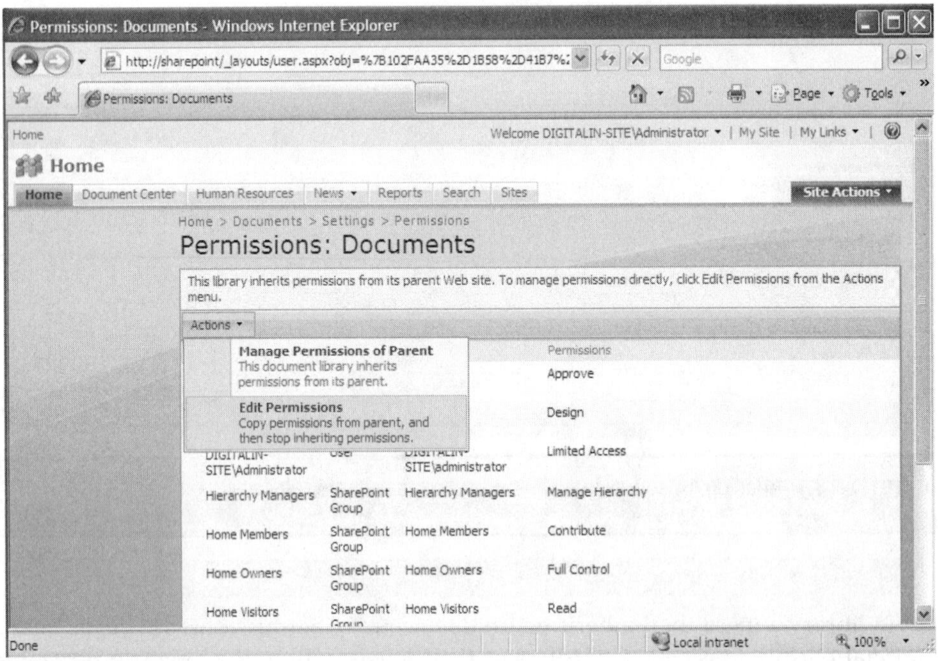

Figure 11-20. The Permissions: Documents page is used to edit a library's security permissions.

8. If you wish to add any of the users or groups returned, double-click its value in the Display Name column to move it to the Add field.

9. Click OK.

10. On the Add Users page, shown in Figure 11-22, use the Give Permission option to add the user to a SharePoint group or assign permissions directly. The new user can be granted the following permissions:

a. **Full Control**   Grants the user all access and control of a library.

b. **Design**   Grants the user the ability to view, add, update, delete, approve, and customize a library.

c. **Manage hierarchy**   Grants the user the ability to create and edit sites, list items, and documents within a site collection.

d. **Approve**   Grants the user the ability to edit and approve documents, list items, and pages within the site collection.

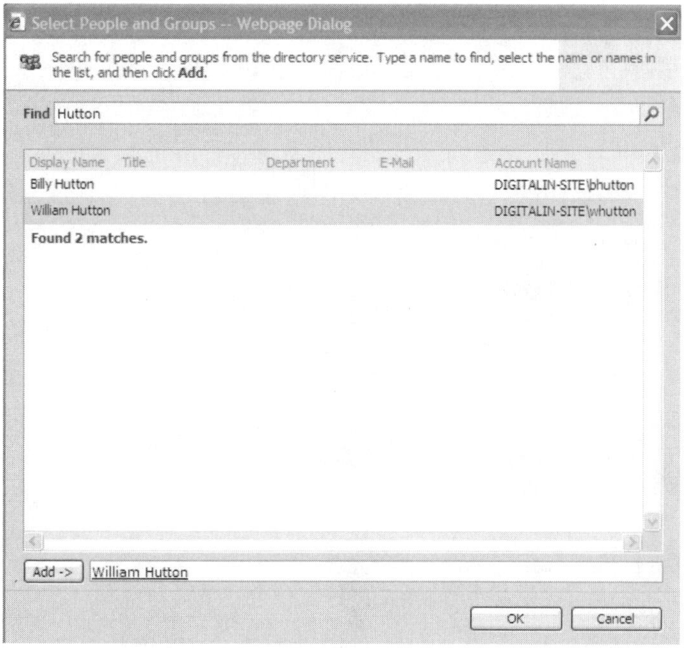

Figure 11-21.   The Select People And Groups dialog box is used to grant access to a library.

    e. **Contribute**   Grants the user the ability to view, add, update, and delete a library.

    f. **Read**   Grants the user only the ability to view the library.

11. If you wish to send an e-mail to the affected user informing them of their new permissions, use the Send Email section on the lower portion of the Add Users page (see Figure 11-23).

12. Click OK to save the security permissions for the user.

Library Templates

It is a common practice in MOSS environments to create multiple instances of a document library for use by many sites and areas. For example, if each department in your organization is assigned to a separate area in which a document library with the same folder structure, Office templates, and default views is to be included. The most efficient way to satisfy this requirement is to create the initial library, load its files, and then after creating and customizing its columns and views, save the library as a template. You can then use the library template to create multiple instances of the library, as needed.

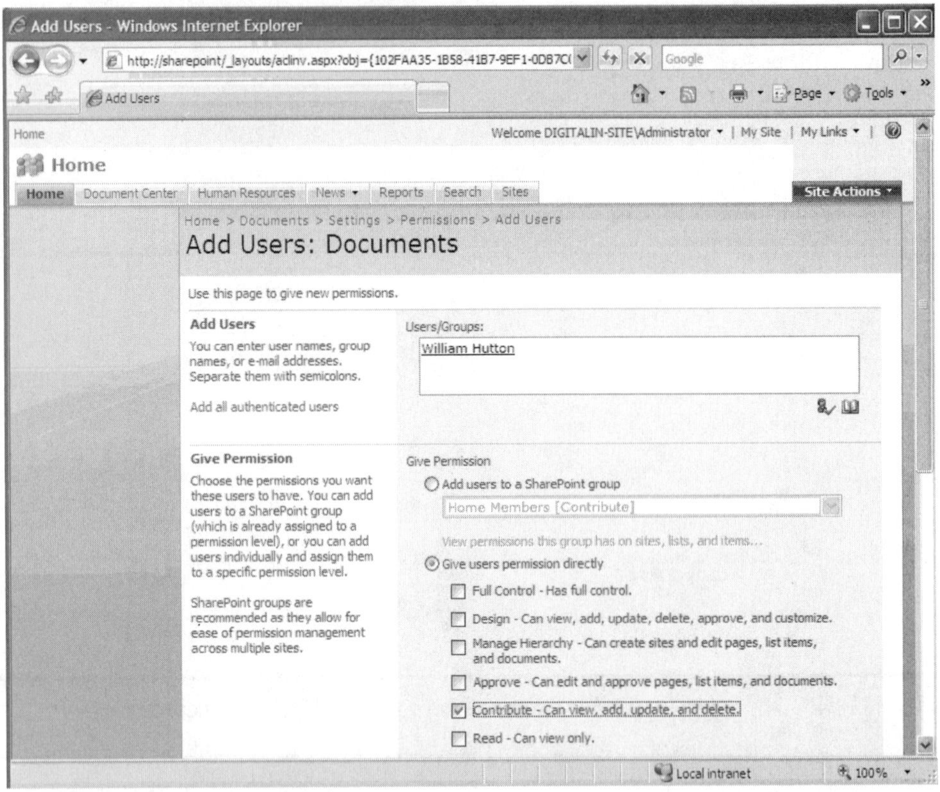

Figure 11-22. The Add Users page is used to grant security permissions to a user.

TIP Library content can be included in a template. However, library security permissions are not saved with the template.

To create a library template from an existing library, perform the following steps:

1. Navigate to the page that contains the library and click the View All Site Content link at the top of the Quick Launch menu.

2. On the All Site Content page, choose the name of the library for which you wish to create a template.

3. On the library's Document page, click the Settings option to open its drop-down menu and then click Document Library Settings.

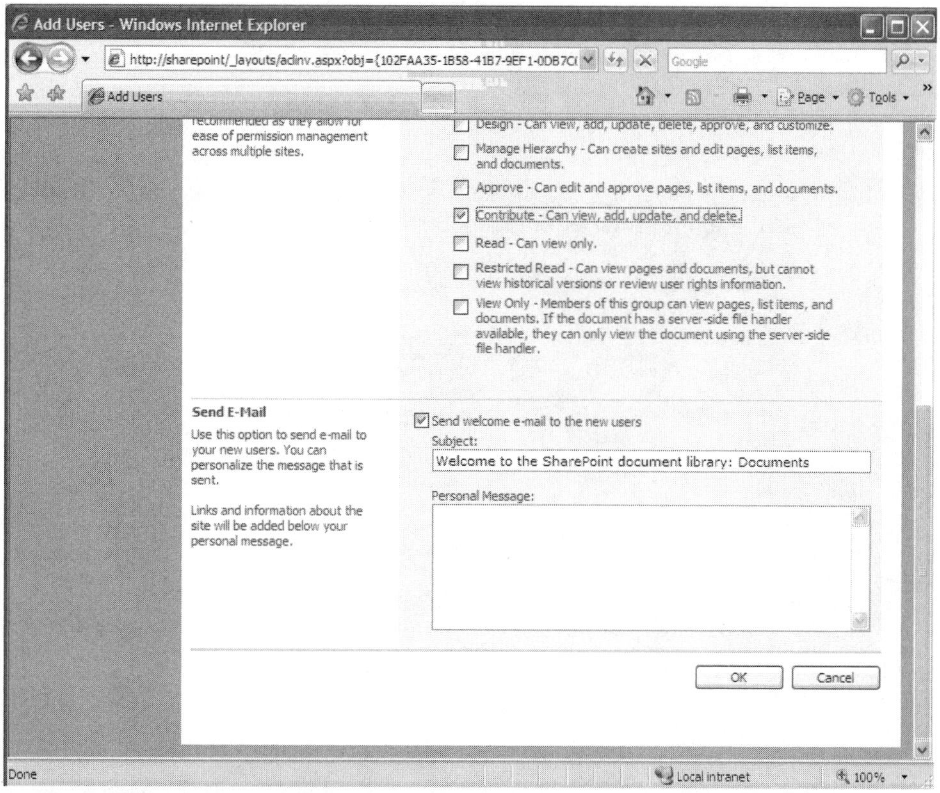

Figure 11-23. The Send Email section of the Add Users page.

4. On the Customize Shared Documents page (see Figure 11-24), click the Save Document Library As Template link under the Permissions And Management heading.

5. On the Save As Template page (shown in Figure 11-25), enter an appropriate value in each of the following settings:

   a. Enter a File name. Although this file name won't be seen or used by SharePoint users, as the administrator, you will still need it to be unique and descriptive.

   b. Enter a unique, descriptive Template name. This is the name users will see, so the more descriptive, the better.

   c. Enter a brief Template description that describes the purpose and features of the library here.

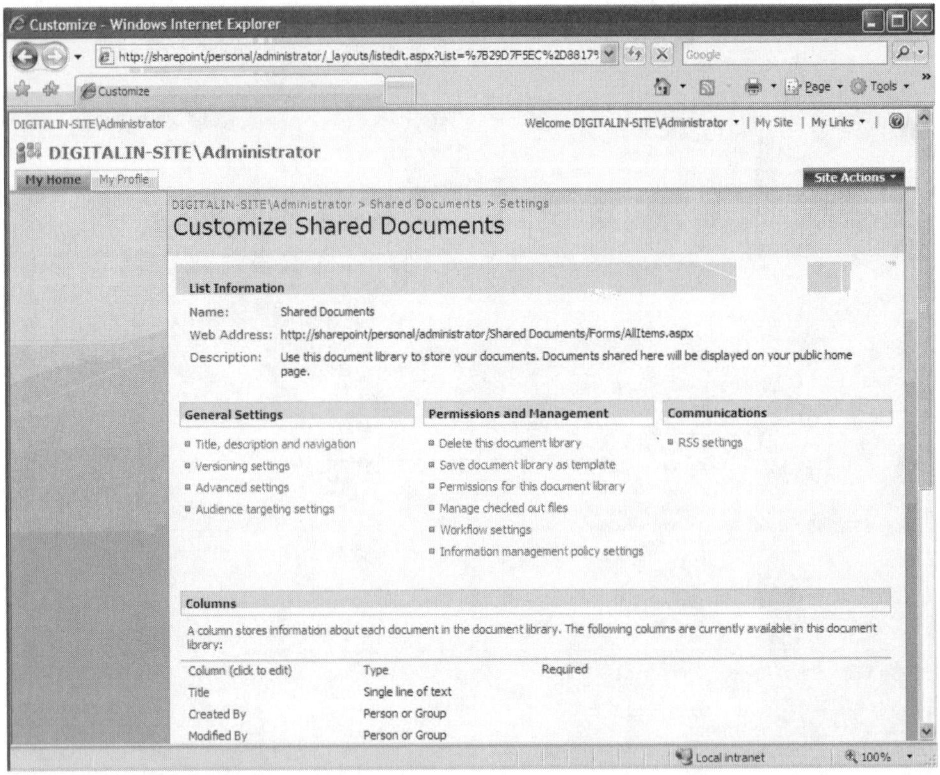

Figure 11-24. The Customize Shared Documents page.

    d. If you want to include a library's content with the template, check the Include Content checkbox.

NOTE Use the Include Content option carefully. Including a library's content with a template has the potential to consume large amounts of hard drive space, duplicate files, and create multiple versions of documents.

  6. Click OK to save the library template.

Delete a Library

If a library and its associated files are no longer needed by the MOSS environment's users or it no longer serves a valid business purpose, the library and its files should be

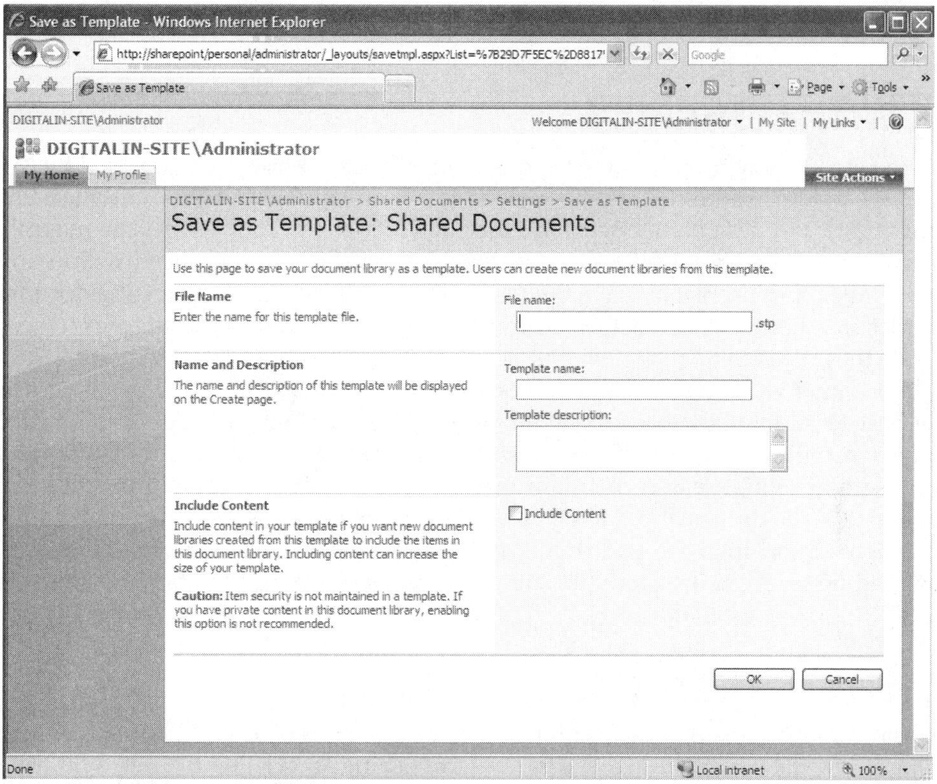

Figure 11-25.   The Save As Template page.

removed from the environment. Deleting a library reclaims hard drive space and simplifies search results by removing its files from the content indexes.

To delete a SharePoint library, after you've satisfied yourself that it is absolutely not needed, do the following:

1. Navigate to the page that contains the library and click the View All Site Content link at the top of the Quick Launch menu.

2. On the All Site Content page, choose the name of the library you wish to delete.

3. On the library's Document page, click the Settings option to open its drop-down menu and click Document Library Settings.

4. On the Customize Shared Documents page (see Figure 11-24), click the Delete This Document Library link under the Permissions And Management heading.

5. Click OK to move the library to the MOSS Recycle Bin.

TIP   Items in the MOSS Recycle Bin are permanently deleted after 30 days automatically.

WORK WITH LIBRARIES

This section deals with library operations in the context of how they are used by MOSS users. As an MOSS administrator, you need to understand how to efficiently use Share-Point libraries to design effective and efficient libraries for your users. The majority of users are concerned primarily with locating the specific files they need within any library, while other users may have the task and responsibility to manage the documents and files in a library. As an MOSS administrator, you must provide support to accommodate these actions.

In working with SharePoint libraries, one of your first responsibilities is to decide how best to support the organization's needs. Should library configuration be solely the responsibility of the MOSS administrator as a service to the users? Or should you train users to configure and maintain their own libraries? In common practice, based on the size of the organization, library maintenance is implemented as a combination of both approaches. However, you should make this decision early in your MOSS deployment and be sure you are ready for either of these approaches to library maintenance, or both.

Publish Files to a Library

You can publish files to a SharePoint library in one of two central ways: creating and saving a new file directly into a library, and publishing an existing file into a library.

New Files

When you create a new SharePoint document library, you have the option of specifying a document template to be used when new documents are created and added to that library. If a document template is specified for a library in its Advanced Settings, whenever the New button is selected, a Microsoft Word (default), Excel, InfoPath, or similar document template is used to create the new library document.

To create a new document in a SharePoint library, use the following steps:

1. Navigate to the page that contains the library and click the title of the library to display its All Items page.

2. Click the New option (see Figure 11-26) to display its drop-down menu and select New Document.

3. Using the document template type indicated in the library's settings, the MOSS- compatible application for that document type is launched.

4. After completing the document, click Save from the application to add the document to the SharePoint library.

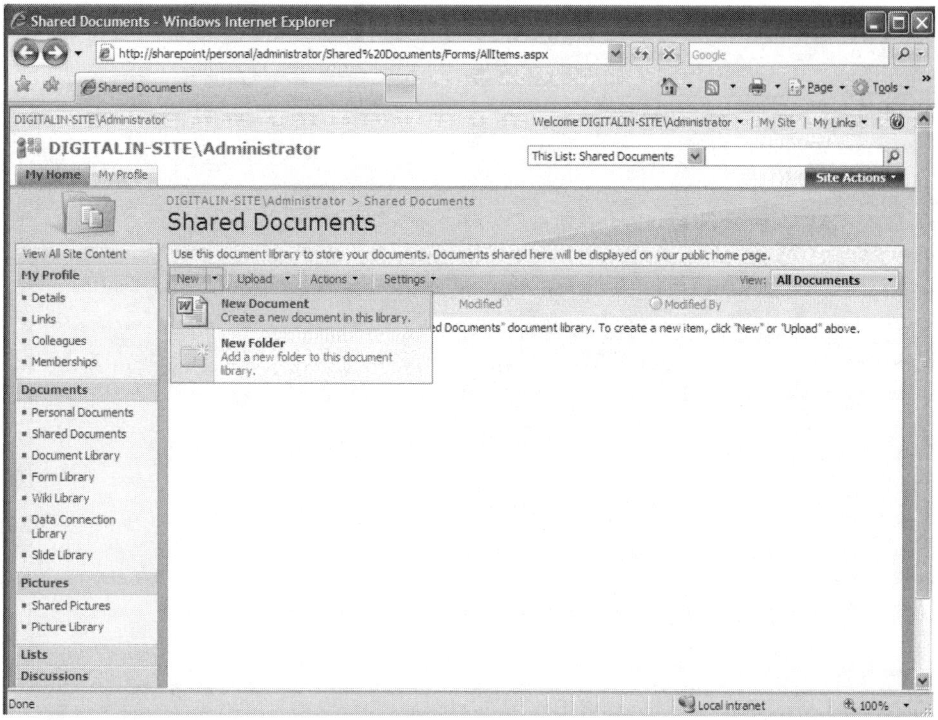

Figure 11-26. The New Document option on a SharePoint library's All Items page is used to create a new library document.

Upload Files

The Upload option on the Documents page (see Figure 11-27) provides two ways to upload existing documents to a SharePoint library:

▼ **Upload Document**   Used to quickly upload a single document

▲ **Upload Multiple Documents**   Used to upload more than one file

Upload Document   To upload a single existing document to a SharePoint library, do the following:

1. Navigate to the page that contains the library and click the title of the library to display its All Items page.

2. Click the Upload option to display its drop-down menu and choose Upload Document.

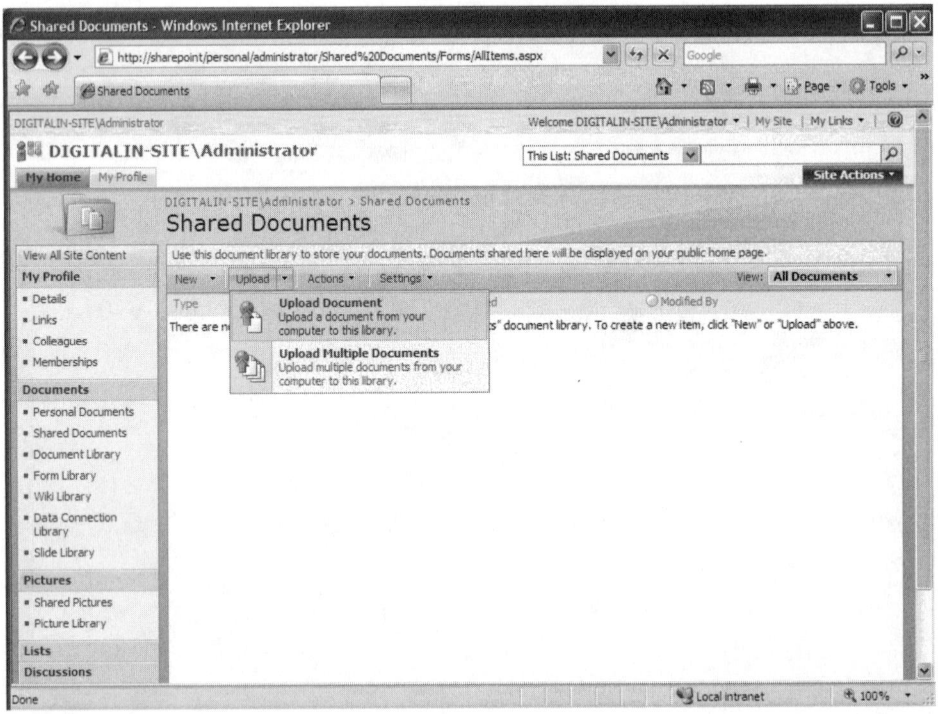

Figure 11-27. The Upload option is used to add existing documents to a SharePoint library.

3. Use the Browse button to navigate to the file you wish to upload (see Figure 11-28).

4. Double-click the file to enter its file path into the Name field.

5. Click OK to upload the document.

Upload Multiple Documents   The Upload Document menu provides an interface very similar to Windows Explorer for uploading multiple files and folders. Figure 11-29 shows an example of this interface.

To upload more than one document to a SharePoint library, perform the following steps:

1. Navigate to the page that contains the library and click the title of the library to display its All Items page.

2. Open the Upload option and choose Upload Multiple Documents.

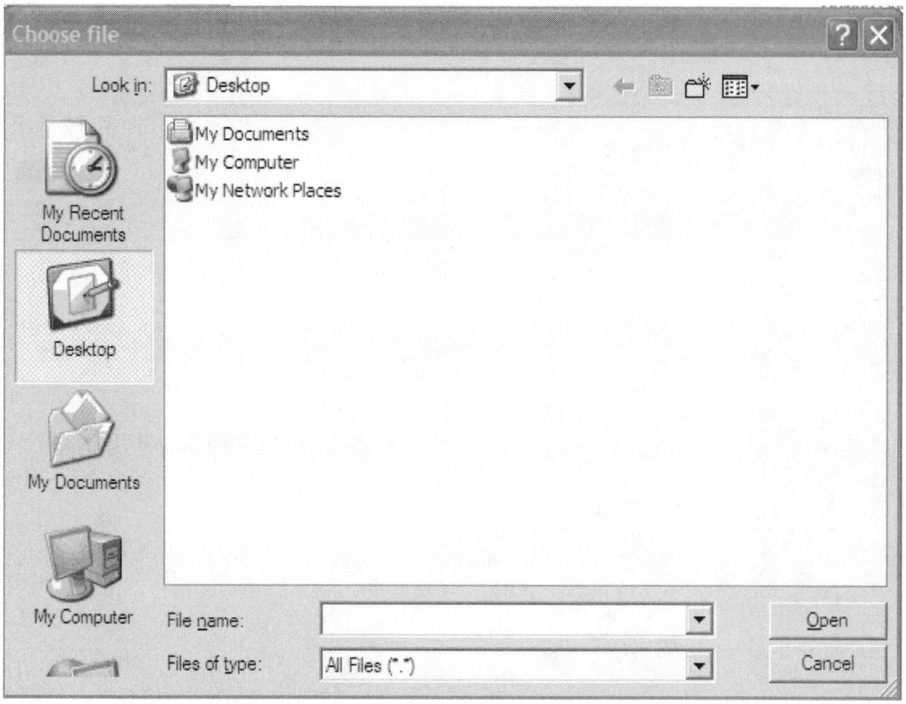

Figure 11-28. The familiar Microsoft Office browse function is used to locate a file you wish to upload.

3. Use the file tree displayed in the left pane to navigate to the location(s) of the files and check the checkbox corresponding to the files you wish to upload.

4. Click OK to upload the selected files to the library.

Explorer View MOSS provides another means to upload files to a library, the Explorer View and drag-and-drop. To use this method to add files into a SharePoint library, do the following:

1. Navigate to the page containing the library list and click the library's title to display its All Items page.

2. Click the View: All Documents option to open its drop-down menu and select Explorer View (as illustrated in Figure 11-30).

3. Using My Computer or Windows Explorer from the computer's Desktop, navigate to the files or folders you wish to upload (see Figure 11-31).

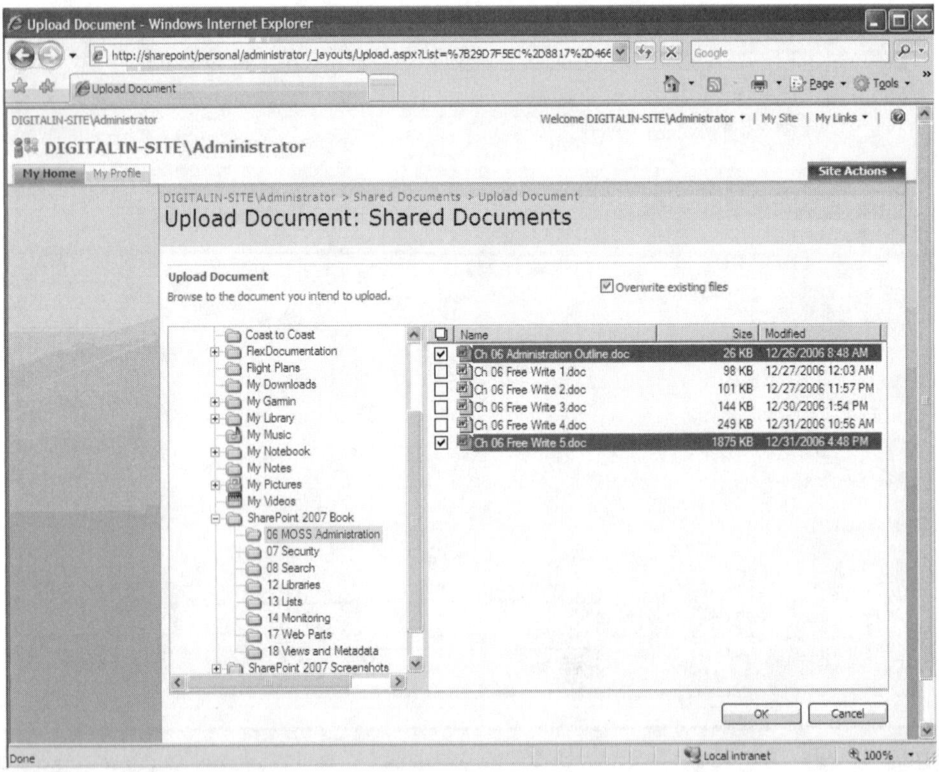

Figure 11-29. The interface used to upload multiple documents is similar to Windows Explorer.

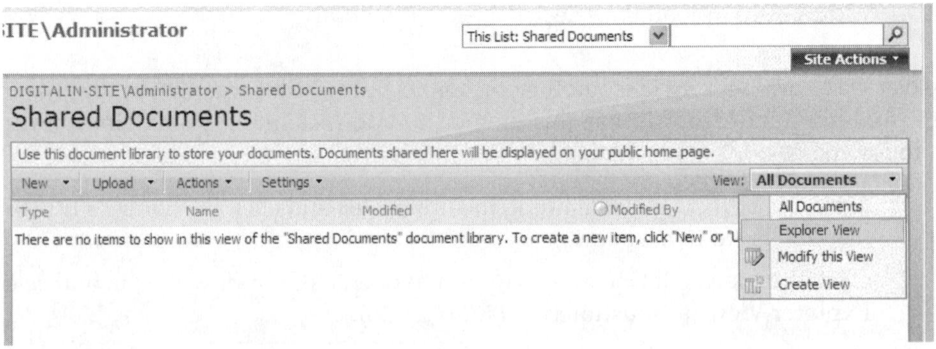

Figure 11-30. Accessing the Explorer View on the View menu.

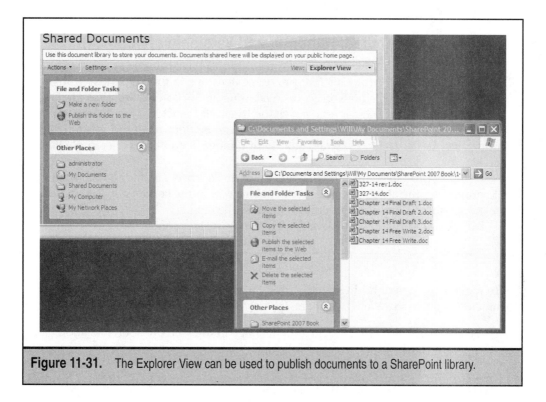

Figure 11-31.   The Explorer View can be used to publish documents to a SharePoint library.

4. Once you have located the files or folders you wish to publish to the library, highlight them and then drag and drop the files and folders onto the library's Explorer View.

TIP   Because of its familiarity and ease of use, you may find you prefer to use the Explorer View and its drag-and-drop publishing for uploading multiple documents to a library.

WebDAV Support

MOSS provides support for the WebDAV protocols, which were developed to make working with files located on remote Web servers as simple as if the files were located on a local computer. WebDAV can be useful for programmatically writing files to a Share-Point library from remote servers running a WebDAV-compatible application, such as Crystal Reports.

NOTE   MOSS uses WebDAV protocols to connect to its own Explorer View.

Web-Based Distributed Authoring and Versioning (WebDAV)

WebDAV, which is also referred to as World Wide Web Distributed Authoring and Versioning, is a set of protocols that provide extensions to the Hypertext Transfer Protocol (HTTP) that facilitate users to collaborate on documents and thus manage those documents on Web servers across the Internet. WebDAV was developed to turn the World Wide Web into a medium that can be both read and written, but supporting the capability to create, modify, and move documents on a remote Web server.

WebDAV provides a number of features for this purpose, including file locking, file properties, the ability to move a document within the server's space, and the creation, removal, and listing of files within a collection.

For more information on WebDAV, visit www.webdav.org.

To make a document addressable with a WebDAV path (in other words, to make a document available as a WebDAV share), perform the following steps:

1. On a SharePoint library's Documents page in the Web browser's location bar, alter the URL of the library as follows:

   a. Replace "http://" with "\\".

   b. Replace all forward slashes (/) with backslashes (\).

   c. Replace all occurrences of "%20" with a space.

   d. Delete any characters after the Forms folder name.

2. Copy the converted WebDAV path from the Web browser and paste it into the library's settings as its location.

   An example of a before-and-after address conversion is:

   - Before – SharePoint library's URL:

     http://sharepoint/personal/administrator/Shared%20Documents/Forms/WebFldr.aspx

   - After – Converted WebDAV path:

     \\sharepoint\personal\administrator\Shared Documents\Forms

SUMMARY

SharePoint libraries provide many features for document management and collaboration. Libraries can be created at any level of MOSS sites. Shared libraries take the guesswork out of security permissions by making any file stored in a shared library readable by all domain users. Likewise, personal libraries allow only the file owner and MOSS administrators to access the files stored within them. All libraries include capabilities such as workflow, approval, versioning, and check-in/check-out.

MOSS includes several specialized libraries designed for specific file types or purposes, including document libraries for Microsoft Office files, form libraries for Microsoft InfoPath XML-based forms, slide libraries for Microsoft PowerPoint slide presentations, picture libraries for sharing digital images of all types, and Wiki libraries designed for user-authored Web pages of pictures, tables, and hyperlinks.

CHAPTER 12

SharePoint Lists

harePoint Lists are one of the easiest and most flexible ways to share information with SharePoint users. Lists are the Swiss army knife of the SharePoint administrator. When you or your users have information to share, chances are a prebuilt list already exists for it, just waiting to be used. If not, a prebuilt list may be modified to suit your needs, and if that still doesn't work for you, you can build your own custom list, and once you've done so, it can be saved as a template for others.

Put simply, a list is just a collection of associated data or content arranged in columns and rows. Each column has a specific name and column type that describes the type of data intended to be stored in that column. Remember that a list is also a Web Part and can be easily included in a site page or portal to provide users with easy access to a list's content or links.

This chapter reviews the prebuilt lists in SharePoint and how they can be modified to suit the needs of your organization and users. We also look at custom lists and how they are created.

PREBUILT LISTS

SharePoint contains several prebuilt lists. Each list is organized by function, based on the type of information the lists are designed to share. It's likely there's some prebuilt list to fit almost any situation, but not necessarily all situations (see the "Custom Lists" section later in the chapter).

SharePoint's prebuilt lists can be categorized into two general groups: communication and tracking. Within each of the categories are lists that can be included on site pages and portals to provide users with quick access to a list's content.

> **NOTE** Lists are actually Web Parts. For more information on working with Web Parts, see Chapter 17.

Communication Lists

Communication lists come in two general types: announcements and contacts. An announcement list includes such things as news, status information, and other information of general interest. A contact list provides people-based information, including contact names, addresses, telephone numbers, and e-mail addresses. However, in either case, these, and all other prebuilt lists, can be modified to include other data, if needed or desired.

Tracking Lists

SharePoint's tracking lists provide a means for users to keep tabs on tasks, calendar events, projects, issues, links, and other areas where users need to be kept up-to-speed. In SharePoint's collection of prebuilt lists, you will find the following:

  ▼ **Calendar** This list is used to share event-related information such as meetings, deadlines, or other important dates in a calendar-based view.

■ **Issue tracking**   This list is used to manage, track the progress of, or review the status of an issue or problem from start to finish.

■ **Links**   This list is used to share a dynamic list of URL links that provides users with access to Web-based resources.

■ **Tasks**   This list is used to identify and track tasks an individual or team has been assigned to complete.

▲ **Project tasks**   This list is used to view the status, in Gantt form, of tasks an individual or team has been assigned to perform.

NOTE   The contacts lists, calendar lists, and project tasks lists are designed to be integrated with the Microsoft Office 2007 applications, including Outlook, Access, Word, Microsoft Project, and so on.

TIP   SharePoint libraries are also a type of list, but because their functionality is highly specialized, they are categorized separately as libraries.

CREATE A SHAREPOINT LIST

Most SharePoint lists are created by users—or at least those users who have been granted the permissions to do so anyway. A list can be added (created) to any SharePoint site from either a site's main page or from a library within the site. The steps listed in this section illustrate the process used to create a new Search Engines List using a Links list, which is one of the Tracking lists available in SharePoint.

To create a SharePoint Links List, use the following steps:

1. Navigate to the SharePoint site where you'd like to add a List and then click the View All Site Content link in the Quick Launch menu, or click the Site Actions button and choose the View All Site Content from its drop-down menu, as shown in Figure 12-1.

2. On the All Site Content page (see Figure 12-2), click the Create button located just above the content area on the page.

3. On the Create page (shown earlier in Figure 12-3), select the Links option— found under the Tracking heading—to display the New page used to define and configure the new list.

4. On the New page (see Figure 12-4), enter a name for the list that is unique and descriptive of the contents the list will display, as well as a short description of what the list will contain. For example, you could enter "Search Engines" in the Name box.

TIP   The name you enter for new content is optionally displayed in the title bar and is searchable. So, try to choose a name that is not only descriptive, but unique. Doing so helps users easily locate your list using the SharePoint search feature.

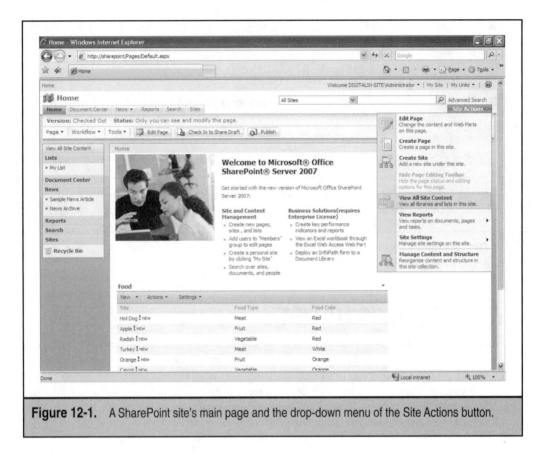

Figure 12-1. A SharePoint site's main page and the drop-down menu of the Site Actions button.

5. If you'd like the new list to be displayed in the Quick Launch navigation bar on the left-hand side of any page on which it's included, select Yes for Display This List On The Quick Launch option.

6. SharePoint creates the Search Engines list and opens an edit page for the new list (see Figure 12-5). The edit page is used to add content of the list.

Enter Contents into a SharePoint List

You can manually add content to a list in two ways:

▼ **Single entry mode** As its name suggests, this mode is used to add items to a list one at a time. Typically, this mode is used to add a list's initial items, or for lists with only a few entries.

▲ **Datasheet mode** This mode is much easier to use, especially for lists with more than just a few entries. The datasheet mode uses a worksheet format that can be used to edit, sort, and arrange the contents of a list.

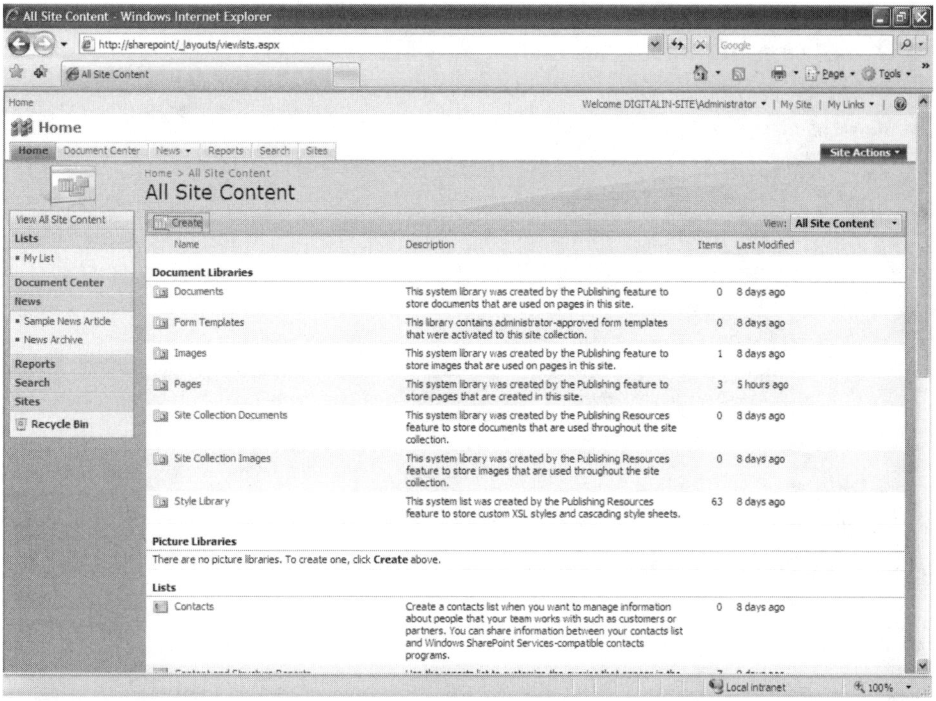

Figure 12-2. The All Site Content page of a SharePoint site.

A SharePoint list can contain URL links, location addresses, or paths to content items that allow users to quickly navigate to web sites, network resources, or content they wish to access. To illustrate not only how a SharePoint list is created, but also how a list is used, the entries in the list being constructed in this example are the URLs for several of the more popular search engines. How to use both the single entry and the datasheet modes to add items to a SharePoint list is discussed in the next two sections.

Single Entry Mode

The single entry mode for adding items to a SharePoint list is best used only when you need to add one or just a few items to a list. To use the single entry mode to add items or entries to a list, do the following:

1. On the New List edit page (see Figure 12-5), click the New button to open its drop-down menu and then select New Item (as illustrated in Figure 12-6) to open the New Item entry page.

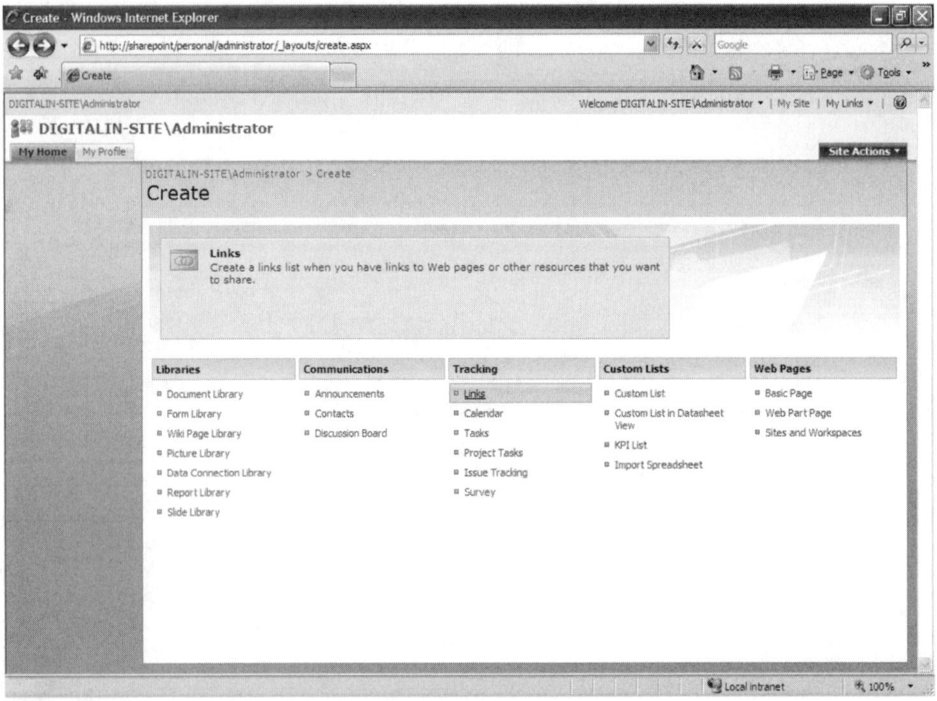

Figure 12-3. The Create page is used to add a list to a page.

2. Because the list being created is a Links list, the New Item page is different that it would be for a Calendar or a Tasks list. In this instance, the first entry on the page is for a URL. Enter the URL and a brief description for the list entry being added. For example, the URL (http://www.google.com) and the name for Google.com are entered, as illustrated in Figure 12-6.

NOTE The asterisk after the URL indicates that the URL is a required entry. However, the description is optional. If entered, the description is displayed in the list. Otherwise, the URL is displayed in the list.

TIP It is generally safer to open the URL in a separate browser window or tab and then copy and paste the URL into the URL box on the New Item page. Before saving the New Item, always use the Click Here To Test link to verify that the URL entered is valid.

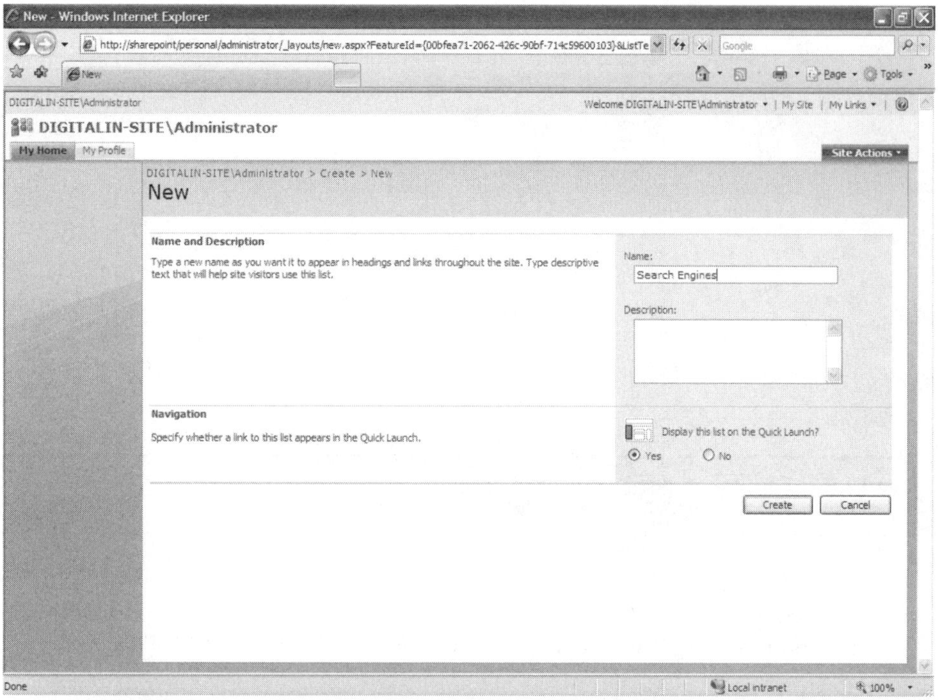

Figure 12-4. The New page is used to configure a new list page.

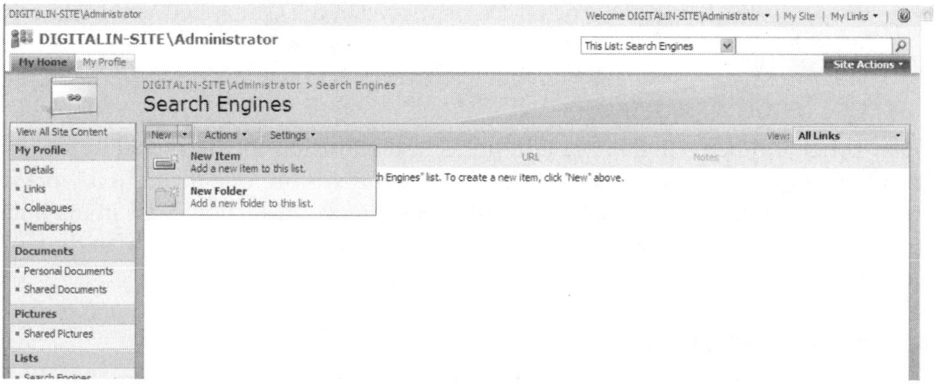

Figure 12-5. The edit page for a new SharePoint list.

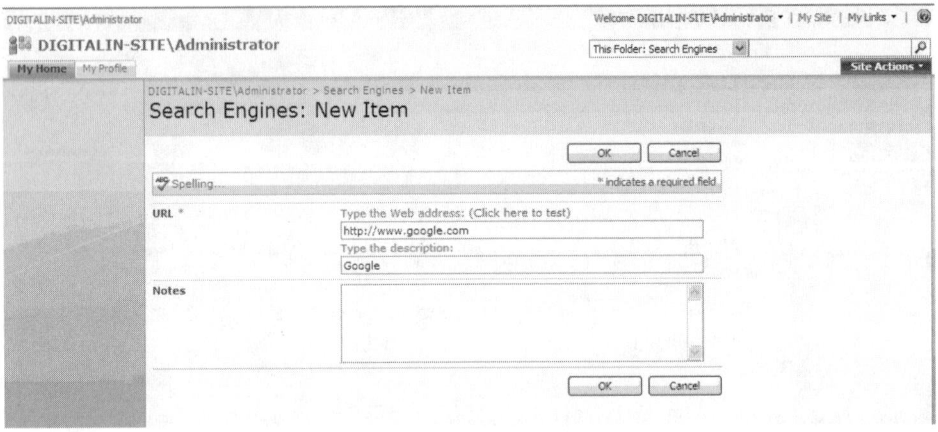

Figure 12-6. The New Item page is used to add items to a SharePoint list.

3. The Notes field is used optionally to provide special instructions or additional information about the URL, where needed.

4. Click OK

   If you wish to enter additional items to the list, repeat steps 1 thru 4 for each additional item. Should you wish to continue the Search Engines list example, enter the URL and a description for other search engines commonly used by your organization.

5. Once you have completed entering the list items and have clicked OK for the last entry, the Search Engines list will appear in the Quick Launch menu on the left side of the SharePoint page, as shown in Figure 12-7.

Datasheet Mode

You can either add items to a list or edit items in them using the datasheet mode. In the datasheet mode, illustrated in Figure 12-8, the data fields are displayed in a worksheet format that is similar to a spreadsheet. Although Figure 12-8 shows list items already entered, you can add additional items by entering the URL and description in the respective columns of the next available row of the list.

Edit a Single List Entry

The process of editing a list entry is very similar to adding a new list entry. To edit a list entry, do the following:

1. Click the Search Engines link under the List heading on the Quick Launch menu.

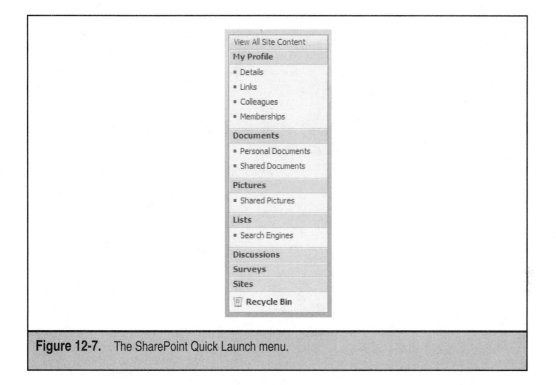

Figure 12-7.   The SharePoint Quick Launch menu.

2. Hold your mouse pointer over a list entry (URL) column to display its drop-down menu, as shown in Figure 12-9.

3. Select Edit Item from the drop-down menu to open the Edit Item page, on which you can make any needed changes.

TIP   If a list contains a large number of entries that require editing, you should use the Datasheet mode.

Edit a List in Datasheet Mode

As is the case with the Single Entry mode, editing the contents of a SharePoint list using the datasheet mode is very similar to adding items to the list using this mode. To edit the contents of a SharePoint list in datasheet mode, do the following:

1. Open the list by clicking its link under the List heading on the Quick Launch menu.

2. Click the Actions button to open its drop-down menu, as shown in Figure 12-10, and choose the Edit In Datasheet option. This opens the list in datasheet mode (see Figure 12-8).

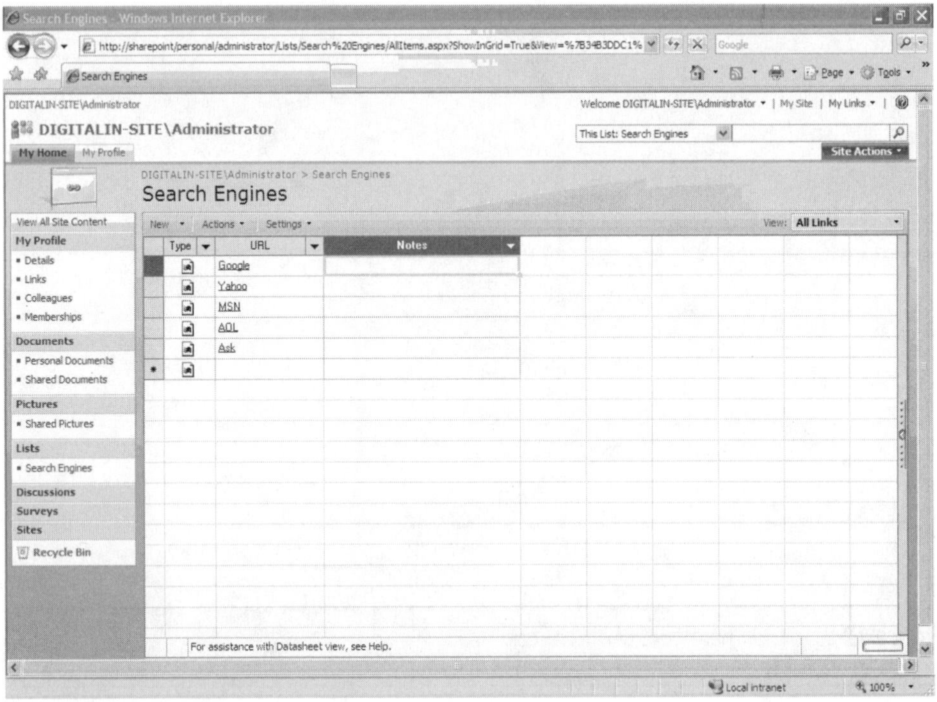

Figure 12-8. The Datasheet edit mode for a SharePoint list.

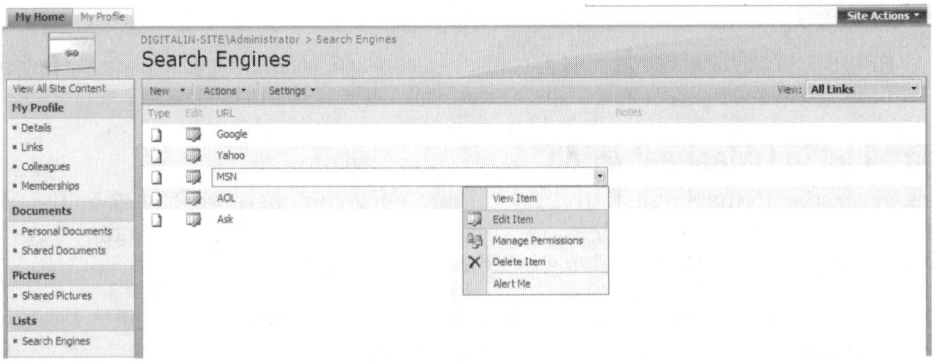

Figure 12-9. Editing a SharePoint list entry.

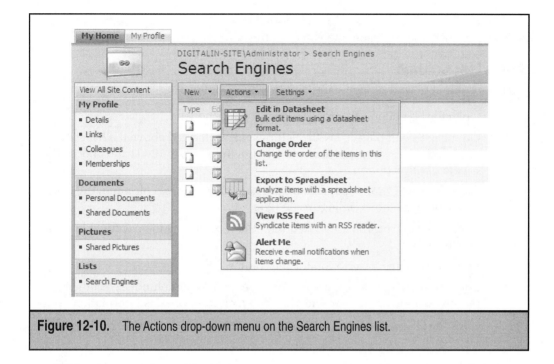

Figure 12-10.   The Actions drop-down menu on the Search Engines list.

3. Make any required changes to the items in the list.

4. When you have finished editing the list, click out of the datasheet mode by clicking the Search Engines link in the Quick Launch menu.

> *TIP*   MOSS automatically saves your list each time you modify the contents of a column.

List Columns

The prebuilt SharePoint lists included in MOSS are very generic and may not completely satisfy every situation. It is possible one or more of the prebuilt SharePoint lists are close to meeting your needs, but you may need to include either more or less information. In these cases, you can modify a list to suit your information needs by adding, changing, or deleting a list column.

Each row of a SharePoint list contains a discrete list entry, and each column identifies a single data field common to all entries, such as the URL, the description, and so on. You are able to adapt one of the prebuilt SharePoint lists to contain the data fields you need by adding, changing, or removing a column in a SharePoint list. You can also arrange a list based on its columns and the data contained in each column so the most frequently used, most highly recommended, or most productive item is displayed first in the list.

In the following sections, a column is added to a list, the column's settings are modified, and the list is sorted using the values in the new column.

Add a List Column

To add a column to an existing SharePoint list, do the following:

1. Open the SharePoint list from the Quick Launch menu.

2. On the list's edit page, click the Settings menu (located above the list content area) to open its drop-down menu (as shown in Figure 12-11) and choose the Create Column option.

3. On the Create Column page, enter the name for the new column in the Column Name field, as shown in Figure 12-12.

4. Select the radio button associated with the type of data to be entered into the new column.

5. Enter an optional description for the column.

6. If you wish to ensure data are always entered into the column, select the radio button associated with Require That This Column Contains Information option.

7. Click the OK button to add the column to the list.

Figure 12-11. The Settings menu on a SharePoint list page.

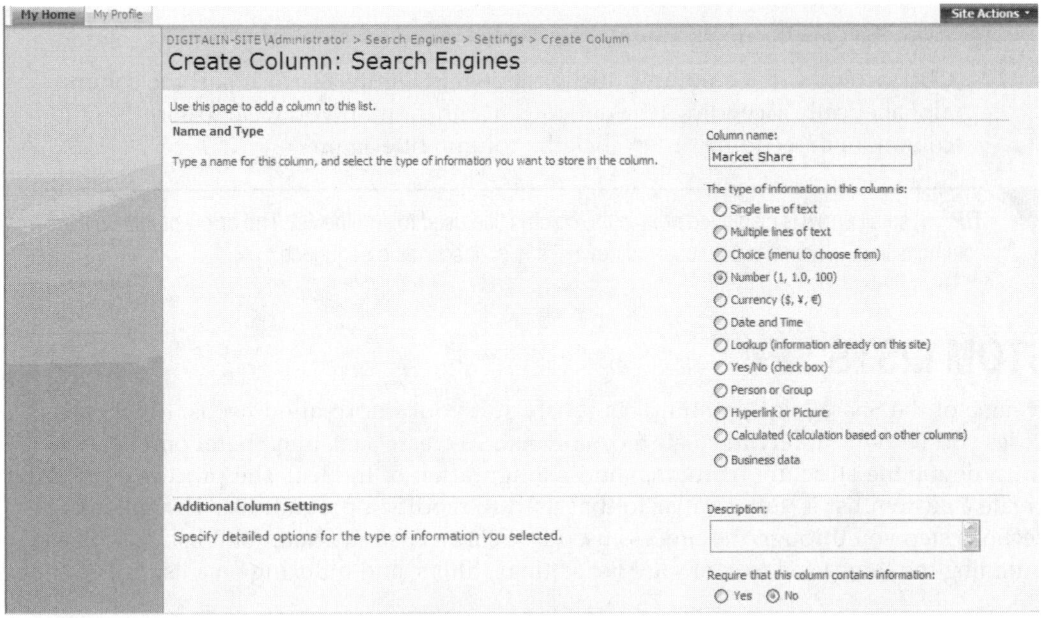

Figure 12-12.   The Create Column page for a SharePoint list.

TIP   You can ensure users enter valid content into a list by assigning additional column settings. SharePoint uses these additional settings to validate list data. Different settings are available based on the column type you select.

If any items were entered into the list before the new column was added to the list, you may need to now edit the list (using datasheet mode) to add data in the new column for each list item.

Sort a List by a Column

A SharePoint list column can be sorted in ascending or descending order by simply clicking the column name when the list is displayed. This feature is particularly useful since it allows users to reorganize the list data in a way that makes sense for them.

Using the Search Engines list as an example, one user may want to sort the URLs or the Names alphabetically in order to find one particular search engine. Another user may only be interested in a search engine's market share so he or she can use either the most used or the least used search engine. The ability to sort a list's contents allows users to answer different questions about the same data.

To sort a column in a SharePoint list, do the following:

1. From the Quick Launch menu, open the list you wish to arrange using a column.

2. Click a Food Color column's title (as shown in Figure 12-15) to sort the column alphabetically ascending (the default sort function). If you wish to sort the column in descending order, click the column title again.

TIP A small arrow is displayed next to the column title used to sort the list. The arrow points up if the column is in ascending sequence, and down if it is in descending sequence.

CUSTOM LISTS

If none of the SharePoint prebuilt lists satisfy suit your information needs, MOSS provides you with the ability to create a custom list. To create a custom SharePoint list, you must define the structure (columns) and configuration of the list. The process used to create a custom list is very similar to that used to modify a prebuilt list. The following sections step you through the process used to create a custom SharePoint list, as well as outlining the steps used to configure list settings, filters, and indexing on a list.

Create a Custom List

The process used to create a custom SharePoint list, other than where you start, involves essentially the same steps used to create and modify a prebuilt SharePoint list. To create a custom SharePoint list, follow these steps:

1. From the main page of a SharePoint site, click the Site Actions button to open its drop-down menu and then choose the Create option to open the Create page (shown in Figure 12-3 earlier in the chapter).

2. On the Create page, click the Custom List link found under the Custom Lists heading (shown in Figure 12-13).

3. On the Create Custom List page, enter a unique and descriptive name for the new list in the Name field and, if you wish, enter a short description for the list in the Description field. Click the Create button to create the list using the default settings.

   a. For each data field you wish to include in the list's data, use the process that was employed to add columns to a prebuilt list described earlier in the chapter (see the "Add a List Column" section).

4. After you have added all the columns for the list, you should be back to the list's main page. On the List page, click the Actions button to open its drop-down menu and click Edit In Datasheet.

5. On the datasheet view of the list, enter the data for each list item in the respective columns. Figure 12-14 shows the display of a newly created custom list.

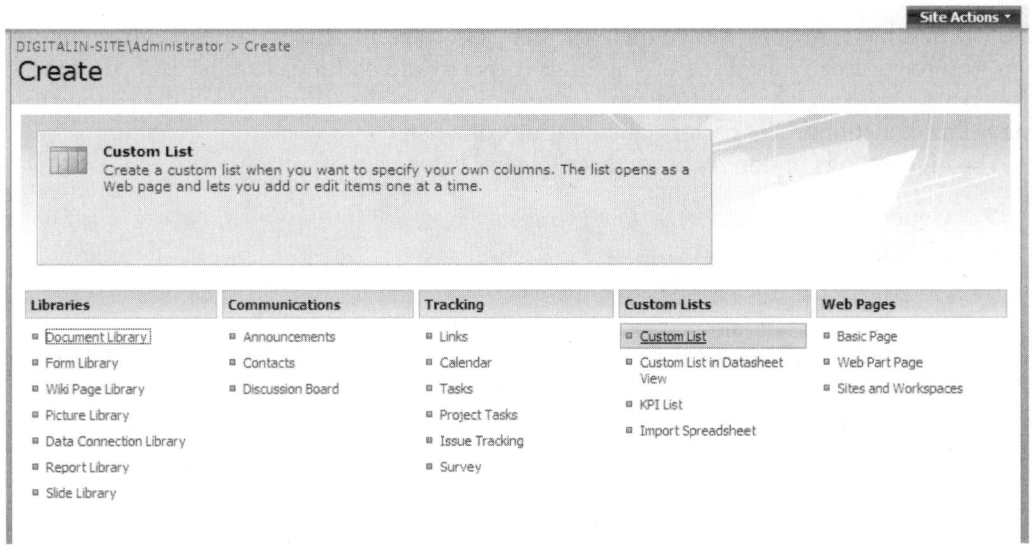

Figure 12-13. Choose Custom List to create a custom SharePoint list.

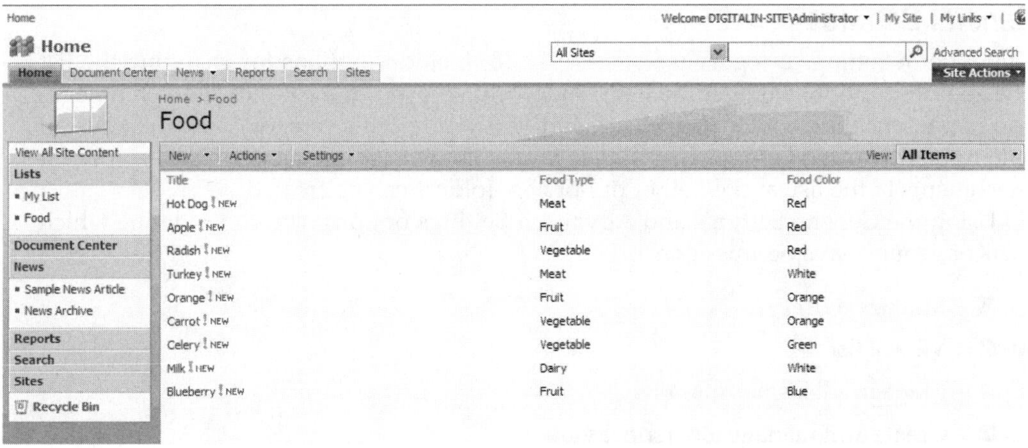

Figure 12-14. A custom SharePoint list.

List Settings

The List Settings functions allow you to further customize a list, whether prebuilt or custom. You have already used the List Settings menu to add columns to a list, but you can also create a custom list view (see the "Create a List View" section later in the chapter) and set the functional and performance settings of a list.

The List Settings option includes three general categories of settings:

▼ General Settings

■ Permissions and Management

▲ Communications

In general, the settings and permissions of a list control, or at least further define, who can access, change, remove, or distribute the list. By default, any user who has access to a site also has access to any of the lists on the site and the ability to change a list's permissions and settings, including:

▼ Viewing lists

■ Inserting, editing, or deleting list items

■ Changing list settings

▲ Changing list security

NOTE For more information on user permissions and site security, see Chapters 6 and 7.

General Settings

The General Settings category (see Figure 12-15) includes options for changing the list title and description, whether the list should be displayed in the Quick Launch navigation menu, enabling content approval, and versioning. This category also includes an option for Advanced Settings that allows you to control item-level permissions, permit attachments to the list, and whether or not new folders can be created.

Using the General Settings and Advanced Settings options, you can redefine which users or groups have permissions to:

▼ Manage a list

■ View a list

■ Manage a list's permissions

■ Create and manage a personal view

▲ Add, change, or delete items in a list

NOTE SharePoint's default settings grant the highest level of permissions for lists (and libraries) to the Administrator site group, which cannot be changed.

Home > Food > Settings

Customize Food

List Information

Name:	Food
Web Address:	http://sharepoint/Lists/Food/AllItems.aspx
Description:	

General Settings	**Permissions and Management**	**Communications**
▫ Title, description and navigation	▫ Delete this list	▫ RSS settings
▫ Versioning settings	▫ Save list as template	
▫ Advanced settings	▫ Permissions for this list	
▫ Audience targeting settings	▫ Workflow settings	
	▫ Information management policy settings	

Columns

A column stores information about each item in the list. The following columns are currently available in this list:

Column (click to edit)	Type	Required
Title	Single line of text	✔
Food Type	Single line of text	
Food Color	Single line of text	
Created By	Person or Group	
Modified By	Person or Group	

Figure 12-15.   The Settings page for the custom SharePoint list Food.

If you enable content approval on a list, any changes to the current list, including additions, modifications, and deletions are initially stored in a pending state. These changes are only visible to the user that made the change, and any users with permission to manage that list. Once an item has been approved, it becomes visible for all users with permission to view the list. If an item is rejected, it stays in its current pending state, and is visible only to users with permission to view drafts.

Versioning, if enabled, stores a numbered copy of the list each time a change is made to the list. This feature is useful, but can require considerable storage space. Therefore, this feature is turned off by default, and must be enabled. When you enable versioning, you have the option to specify the number of versions to keep.

NOTE   For more information on document versioning, see Chapters 9 and 18.

Permissions and Management Settings

The Permissions and Management category's options allow you to remove a list, create a template using a list, and set access and management permissions for the list. Two other settings included under this category are Workflow Settings and Information Management Policy Settings.

> **NOTE**   For more information on workflows and information (document) management policies, see Chapters 9 and 10, respectively.

The actions of the first two options in this category, Delete This List and Save List As A Template, should be fairly obvious. However, it's the third option, Permissions For This List, that you'll likely use most often.

To access the permissions settings for a list, do the following:

1. Open the list from the Quick Launch menu.

2. Click the Settings menu to open its drop-down menu and choose List Settings (as shown in Figure 12-16).

3. On a list's Permissions and Management settings page, you are able to change the list's general settings, manage its permissions, modify the properties of its columns, or modify how it is viewed.

Communications Settings

Under the Communications settings heading, you can manage the Really Simple Syndication (RSS) settings for a SharePoint list. RSS is used on the Web to distribute news, event information, and updates to web logs (blogs), among other content, using an Extensible Markup Language (XML) format.

If RSS support is enabled for a site collection, RSS information can be included in an announcement list or a calendar list, as well as SharePoint libraries, surveys, and discussion forums. The primary reason you would change the Communications settings of an RSS-enabled list is to control the number of items the list includes and how the items are presented to the user.

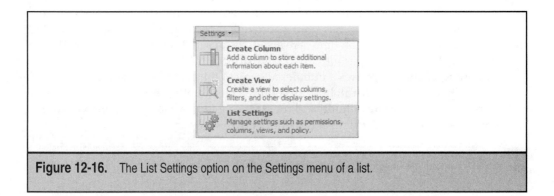

Figure 12-16.   The List Settings option on the Settings menu of a list.

NOTE   Chapter 22 discusses the use of RSS on a SharePoint site.

TIP   If the RSS settings link is not available in a SharePoint list's Communications settings, RSS has not been enabled at the site collection level.

Column Settings

The List Settings page also contains several options for working with the current list's columns, including (see Figure 12-17):

▼   Create column

■   Add from existing site columns

■   Column ordering

▲   Indexed columns

Use of the Create Column option to add a column to a list is outlined earlier in the chapter in the section titled "Add a List Column."

Add from Existing Site Columns   MOSS provides a variety of built-in SharePoint site columns grouped by function. Existing site columns can be included in a SharePoint list to display existing data to which the existing site column is associated.

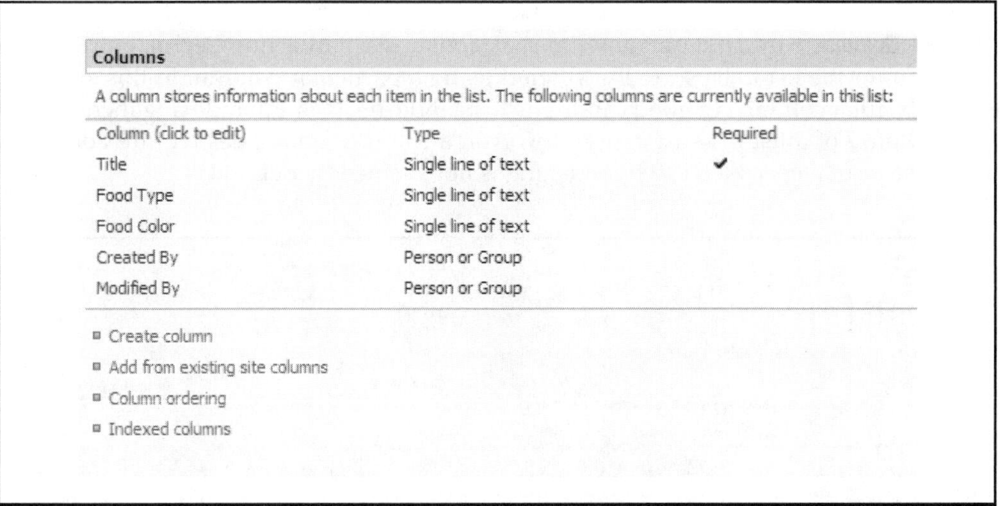

Columns

A column stores information about each item in the list. The following columns are currently available in this list:

Column (click to edit)	Type	Required
Title	Single line of text	✔
Food Type	Single line of text	
Food Color	Single line of text	
Created By	Person or Group	
Modified By	Person or Group	

▫ Create column
▫ Add from existing site columns
▫ Column ordering
▫ Indexed columns

Figure 12-17.   The Columns settings area on the List Settings page.

Site columns are grouped by list type or function, including:

▼ Base Columns

■ Core Contact and Calendar Columns

■ Core Document Columns

■ Core Task and Issue Columns

■ Extended Columns

■ Key Performance Indicators

■ Page Layout Columns

■ Publishing Columns

▲ Reports

To complete the task of adding an existing column to a list, choose the type of column you wish to add. You can then work with the new column's settings, including ordering, sorting, and filtering (see the "List Filters" section later in the chapter) to suit your information needs.

Column Ordering Column ordering is used to alter the physical sequence of a list's columns. When a list is displayed, the columns are displayed using the order number assigned to each column by this setting. Changing the Position from Top number of a particular column changes its relative position to the other columns, which are renumbered automatically. Figure 12-18 illustrates the order numbers assigned to the columns of a SharePoint list.

Indexed Columns In a SharePoint list that contains a large number of entries, it is common for the list to be sorted or filtered using a particular column. In this situation, that particular column is a good candidate to be indexed. Column indexing increases the performance of a list in most cases. However, a column index does require additional database resources, which is why indexing is not enabled by default.

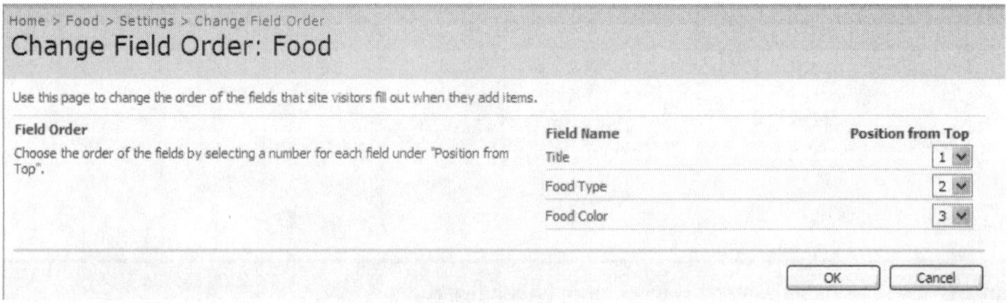

Figure 12-18. The column ordering page of a SharePoint list.

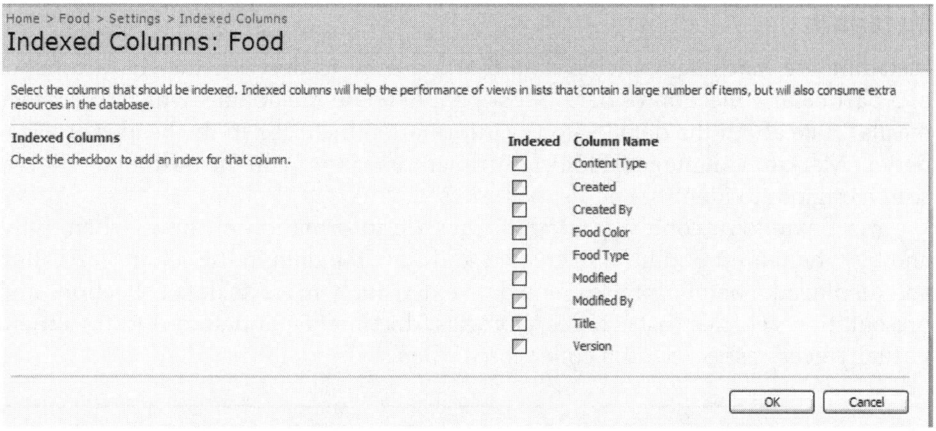

Figure 12-19. The Indexed Columns settings page.

Creating a column index is as simple as checking one or more of the Indexed check-boxes to the left of a Column Name (see Figure 12-19). Understand that as the number of indexes increases, the complexity and the database resources needed to support the list also increases. A list can be indexed by any of its columns, including columns added to a built-in list structure. However, commonly only one of the standard columns included in a SharePoint list is indexed. The standard columns defined for a SharePoint list are:

▼ Content type

■ Created (date)

■ Created by (owner)

■ Column title

■ Modified (date)

■ Modified by (owner/user)

■ Title (list title)

▲ Version

List Filters

A filter is a powerful list feature that helps make finding information in a large list easier. The secret to creating a useful filter is to include a sufficient number of columns and metadata in a list, thereby allowing users to filter and sort a list and find the information they need quickly. A list filter selects only those list entries that meet its criteria, thus reducing the content of a list that's displayed.

Metadata

Metadata are machine-readable data that are used to describe the characteristics of a particular collection of data. Most people relate metadata—which in essence means "data about the data" —to the information included in the header of a Hypertext Markup Language (HTML) document used (more in the past then now) by search engines to identify and list web sites.

In a SharePoint context, metadata provide information on how, when, why, and by whom a set of data was created and how the data in the set are formatted and displayed. SharePoint uses metadata extensively in all its data collections and presentation vehicles (lists, pages, libraries, documents, and so on) to document virtually every aspect of each collection of data.

For example, let's say a SharePoint list contains two columns of metadata on food items—for example, food color and food type. When the entry for hotdog was created, "red" was entered in the food color column, and "meat" was entered in the food type column. Thus, the hotdog entry will be shown in a filtered list for entries with "red" food color, or one for entries with a food type of "meat." A list can have multiple filters, with one or more per column.

A list filter is actually a list column filter. To apply a filter to a list, perform the following steps:

1. Open a SharePoint list and click one of its column headings to open its drop-down menu, which contains the sorting and filtering options for that column (see Figure 12-20).

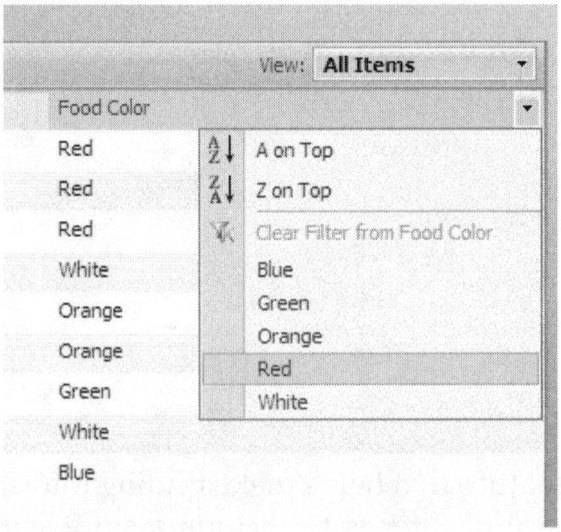

Figure 12-20. The drop-down menu of a list column heading.

2.   Choose one of the metadata values listed to set a filter for that value on the column. A funnel icon is added to the column heading, indicating that a filter is active on that column. The result of this action is that when the list is viewed, only those entries meeting the filter are displayed.

3.   If you wish to apply multiple filters (meaning you wish to add a filter to another column), repeat the process used in step 2 for each column in which you wish to create a filter.

4.   The result of placing filters on two or more columns is that the list now displays only those entries that meet the criteria of all the active filters.

CREATE LIST VIEWS

List Views enable you to display the contents of a list in multiple ways. Some users may only want to see a summary of a list; others may wish all of the details; and still others may constantly apply the same filters or sort operations to a list over and over. To satisfy the needs of all these users, a new view of a SharePoint incorporating your user's filters and sorts can be created, and thus increase their efficiency and productivity. In fact, a view is created each time a user applies a filter to a list.

A list view can be either public or private. A public view can be accessed and seen by all users, while a private view is available only to its creator. When multiple views exist for a SharePoint list, one of the views must be assigned as the default view, with the other views available in a drop-down menu from the upper right corner of the list. When a new list is created, a view is automatically created and designated as its default view.

Create a New List View

A new list view is created from an existing list or view. To create a new list view, perform the following steps:

1.   Open the List for which you want to create a new view.

2.   Click the Settings button to open its drop-down menu and choose the List Settings option.

3.   On the List Settings page, click the Create View option to display the Create View page (shown in Figure 12-21).

As illustrated in Figure 12-21, you can choose from four types of views on the Create View page:

▼   **Standard view**   Displays a columnar list of data

■   **Datasheet view**   Displays data in a format similar to the datasheet entry/edit format mode (see the "Datasheet Mode" section earlier in the chapter)

■   **Calendar view**   Displays event data in a daily, weekly, or monthly calendar format

▲   **Gantt view**   Tracking data are displayed in a Gantt chart format to track a team's progress on a project

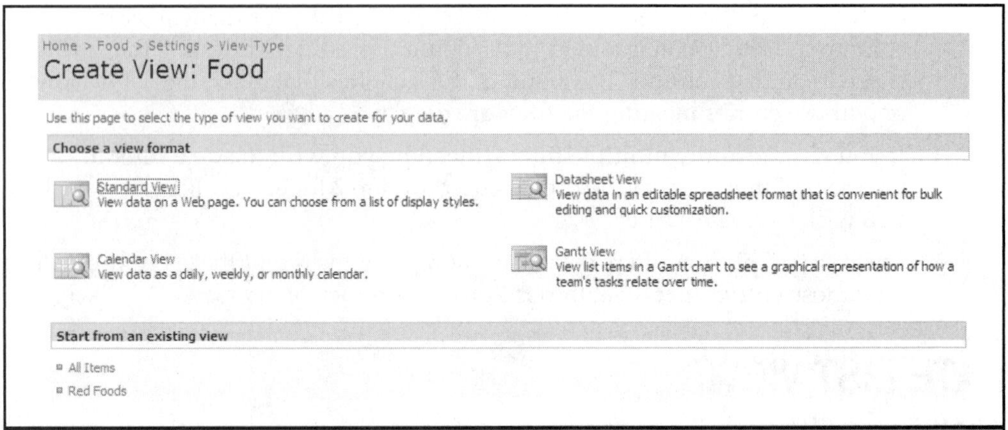

Home > Food > Settings > View Type
Create View: Food

Use this page to select the type of view you want to create for your data.

Choose a view format

Standard View
View data on a Web page. You can choose from a list of display styles.

Datasheet View
View data in an editable spreadsheet format that is convenient for bulk editing and quick customization.

Calendar View
View data as a daily, weekly, or monthly calendar.

Gantt View
View list items in a Gantt chart to see a graphical representation of how a team's tasks relate over time.

Start from an existing view

◘ All Items
◘ Red Foods

Figure 12-21.   The Create View page is used to create a new SharePoint List view.

4. Choose the view type you wish to create. The following steps use the standard view option, which displays the Create View page (shown in Figure 12-22).

5. Enter a unique and descriptive name in the View Name text box.

6. In the Audience section, either accept the default setting of Create A Public View to make this view available to all users, or select the radio button corresponding to the Create A Personal View (private view) option.

7. In the Columns section, select the checkboxes associated with the columns you wish to include in the view. The selection list includes all of the columns defined for the list.

8. In the Sort section (see Figure 12-23), select the column title you wish to sort first from the First Sort By The Column list box. If you wish to sort another column, choose its column title from the Then Sort By The Column list box. For each sort column configured, indicate whether you wish its sort to be ascending or descending.

9. In the Filter section, if you wish to apply a filter, select the Show Items Only When The Following Is True option.

10. If you selected the Show Items Only When The Following Is True option, you must configure the metadata and operator values in the list boxes beneath it. Click the OK button to create a new list view.

TIP   Should a user wish to see the entire contents of a list after viewing its filtered view, he or she can do so by clicking the All Items view in the upper right corner of the list.

Home > Food > Settings > Create View
Create View: Food

Use this page to create a view of this list.

[OK] [Cancel]

Name

Type a name for this view of the list. Make the name descriptive, such as "Sorted by Author", so that site visitors will know what to expect when they click this link.

View Name:

[Red Foods]

☐ Make this the default view
   (Applies to public views only)

Audience

Select the option that represents the intended audience for this view.

View Audience:

○ Create a Personal View
   Personal views are intended for your use only.

◉ Create a Public View
   Public views can be visited by anyone using the site.

⊟ Columns

Select or clear the check box next to each column you want to show or hide in this view. To specify the order of the columns, select a number in the **Position from left** box.

Display	Column Name	Position from Left
☑	Title (linked to item with edit menu)	1 ▼
☑	Food Type	2 ▼
☑	Food Color	3 ▼
☐	Attachments	4 ▼
☐	Content Type	5 ▼

Figure 12-22.   The Create View page with standard view settings and options.

Delete a List

If a list is no longer needed, rarely used, or has been superseded by a new list, you can delete the view. To delete a list view, do the following:

1. Open the list you want to delete.

2. Click the Settings button to open its drop-down menu and choose the List Settings option.

3. On the List Settings page, in the Permissions and Management section, click the Delete this list option.

4. Click the OK button to delete the list.

TEMPLATES

A list template can be a labor-saving tool when you are creating and populating a list. If you or the users create many similar lists, with the same number of columns and essentially the same settings, it can be burdensome to have to replicate the process of creating the list again and again. Instead, after you have created a new list, added and

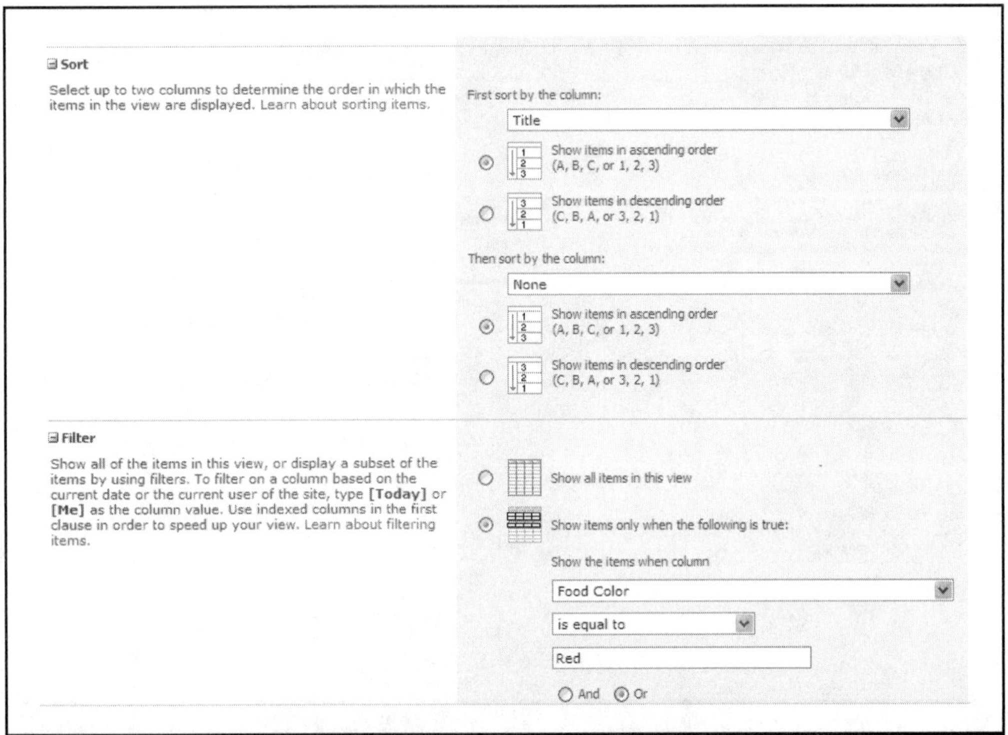

Figure 12-23. The Sort and Filter sections of the Create View page.

modified all the columns you need, entered its data, and created multiple views, you can save the new list as a template. Saving the newly created list as a template allows others to share in some of the hard work that went into creating it, without having to repeat everything.

In a majority of cases, the primary purpose behind creating a template is to share a list's structure, which consists of the column names and types and any custom views created. To create a template from an existing list, do the following:

1. Open the List Settings page for the SharePoint list you wish to save as a template.

2. Under the Permissions And Management heading, click the Save List As A Template option to open the Save As Template page (see Figure 12-24).

3. For administration purposes, each template must be given a short (yet meaningful) file name. This name is only visible to SharePoint administrators. Enter a file name for the template in the File Name text box.

4. In the Template Name box, enter a descriptive name. This is the name used to identify the template to users.

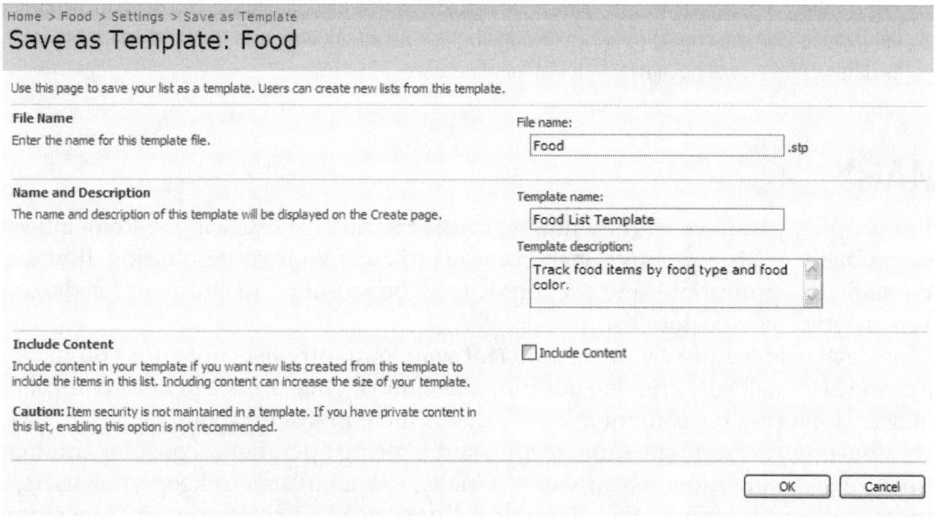

Figure 12-24. The Save As Template page.

5. Optionally, enter a brief description in the Template Description field.

6. Click the OK button to create the List Template, which is now available to users when they create new list content (as illustrated in Figure 12-25).

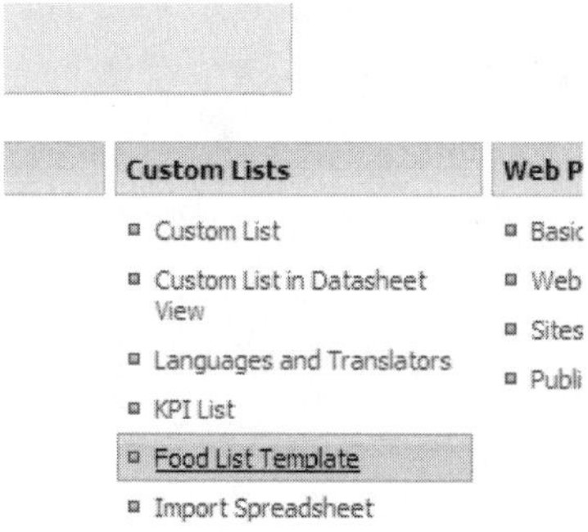

Figure 12-25. The Food List Template as a Create Content choice.

TIP Rarely would you need to include the actual list contents, but should you need to, simply check the Include Content checkbox when saving your list as a template, and then the entire list, including its data contents, will be available for others to reuse.

SUMMARY

In this chapter, you have learned how versatile SharePoint lists can be. Remember that there probably exists a prebuilt SharePoint list to meet your content needs. If you can't find one that's appropriate, any prebuilt list can be modified to suit your needs, or you can create your own custom list.

The datasheet feature can be an efficient way to modify list content if you have several changes to make. By creating additional columns, your users can modify the lists by sorting and filtering the content in a way that is meaningful for them.

If users often perform the same sorting and filtering operations, consider automating these settings through the use of views. Finally, use templates to keep your users, and even yourself, from reinventing the wheel if you need to create multiple instances of similar lists.

CHAPTER 13

Monitor MOSS Performance

As a SharePoint administrator, your job has only just begun once you have installed and configured SharePoint. Monitoring can take up a significant amount of an administrator's time. This chapter will introduce you to the benefits of monitoring, explain which server tools are available to conduct monitoring, and how to use them both for establishing a performance baseline as well as troubleshooting performance issues. Finally, we'll discuss how you can employ monitoring to help determine how effectively your users are using SharePoint.

When done properly, monitoring will allow you to keep SharePoint running smoothly and provide a responsive, dependable experience for your users. Monitoring can alert you to potential performance issues with SharePoint, so you should upgrade hardware resources or performance-tune the application before a minor issue becomes a serious problem. Monitoring can also alert you to potential security issues with SharePoint, or allow you to investigate concerns with the judicious use of auditing.

Finally, monitoring can be an effective way to judge the value SharePoint is providing your users. While your job as an administrator is to keep SharePoint running smoothly, you owe it to your users to ensure SharePoint provides value to them.

INTRODUCTION TO MONITORING TOOLS

Microsoft Windows Server 2003 contains a good group of monitoring tools. For the purpose of this book, we'll assume you are limited to native Windows Server 2003 monitoring tools. These monitoring tools include Task Manager, Performance Console, Event Viewer, and application logs.

The Task Manager

The Task Manager, shown in Figure 13-1, provides a quick overview of the general health of your SharePoint server. Use it to initially monitor CPU usage and memory statistics to quickly identify major problems. Launch the Task Manager by right-clicking the taskbar and choosing Task Manager from the shortcut menu.

The Performance Console

The Performance Console is a collection of Microsoft Management Console (MMC) snap-ins—the System Monitor snap-in and the Performance Logs and Counters snap-in.

The Performance Console (see Figure 13-2) contains a collection of "performance objects," which in turn contain "performance counters" that are used to monitor server resources. The four key hardware resources that require monitoring to maintain a healthy SharePoint environment are CPU, Memory, Disk, and Network.

The System Monitor snap-in (also shown in Figure 13-2) is used to monitor performance counters in real time. By default, the System Monitor launches with three default performance counters.

▼   **Memory**   Pages/Second

■   **Physical Disk (_Total)**   Average Disk Queue Length

▲   **Processor (_Total)**   % Processor Time

These three performance counters taken together form an overview of the health of your SharePoint server in real time. However, a fourth and crucial performance counter is missing from this list. For completeness, you should also monitor your server's network utilization as well. To access this monitoring device, do the following:

1. Launch the Performance Console.

2. Right-click the performance counter list and select Add Counters.

3. Select the Network Interface Performance Object.

4. Select the Bytes Total/sec Performance Counter.

5. Click Add.

6. Click Close.

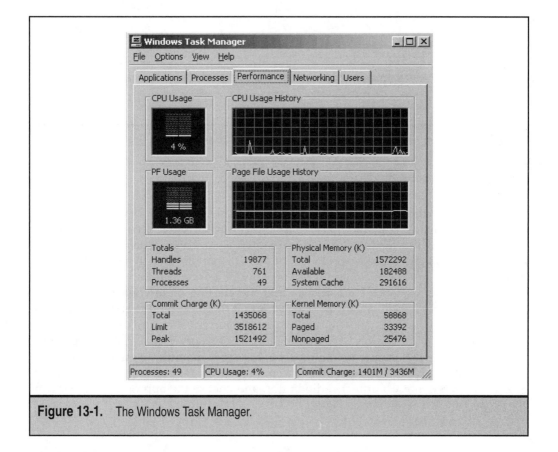

Figure 13-1.   The Windows Task Manager.

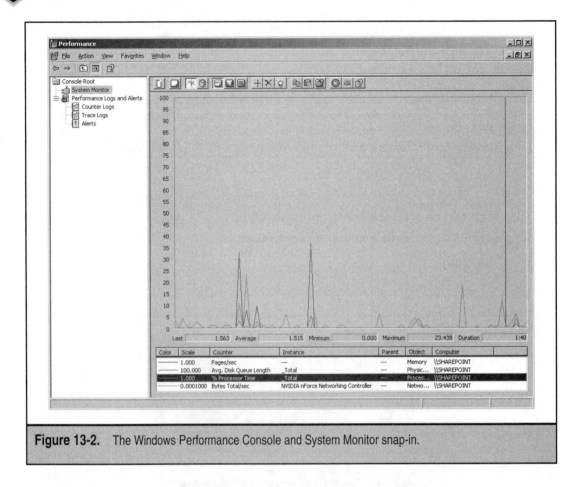

Figure 13-2. The Windows Performance Console and System Monitor snap-in.

In addition to monitoring real-time performance, the Performance Console also contains the Performance Logs and Alerts snap-in that can be used to record various performance counters which can then be used to establish a performance baseline. The snap-in can also be used to monitor performance counters in real time and generate alerts when a performance counter value falls outside of expected normal values.

Capturing performance counter data and the alerting of servers in real time can consume valuable system resources. The Performance Logs and Alerts snap-in lets you monitor performance counters captured from the current server or from several networked servers in one log file. If a separate monitoring server is available, you should take advantage of this feature to minimize the impact of monitoring on SharePoint.

When adding counters from other servers in your SharePoint environment, use the Select Counters From Computer radio button and choose the appropriate server from the drop-down list, as shown in Figure 13-3.

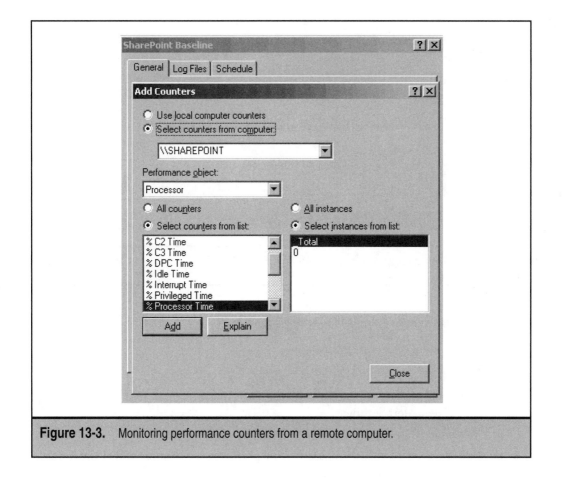

Figure 13-3.   Monitoring performance counters from a remote computer.

To launch the Performance Console, shown in Figure 13-4, click Start, Administrative Tools, and then Performance. Alternatively, you can click Start, Run, and type **perfmon .msc** in the command line box.

Performance counter logs can also be played back for analysis on the local computer or another computer to minimize the impact on hardware resources. Additionally, when you create the performance counter log, you can change the log type to text-delimited. The log can then be imported into Microsoft Excel for additional analysis.

Configure Alerts

The Performance Logs and Alerts snap-in can be configured to alert you when a performance counter exceeds a predefined value. The trigger values do have defaults, but you should set them to create an alert when a monitored condition exceeds the limits of your environment.

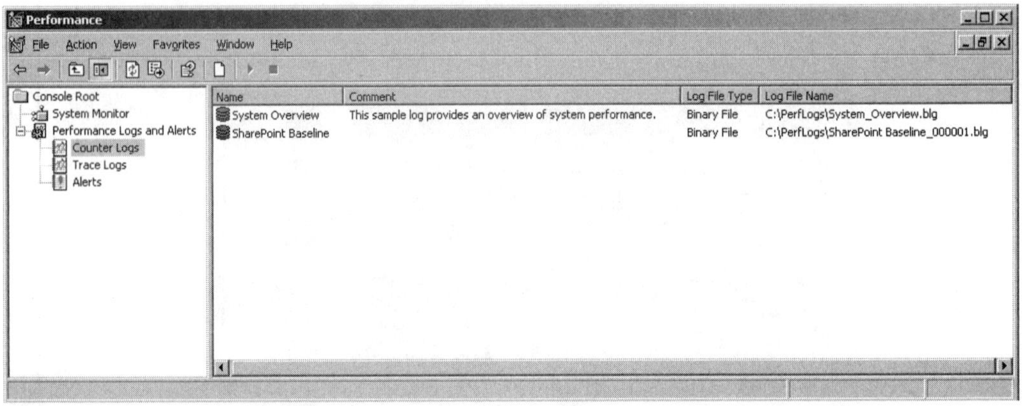

Figure 13-4. Performance Logs and Alerts snap-in.

To set a performance alert, do the following steps:

1. Launch the Performance Console.

2. Expand the Performance Logs and Alerts node.

3. Right-click Alerts.

4. Select New Alert Settings.

5. Name the Alert CPU Utilization (see Figure 13-5).

6. Add the Processor / % Processor Time performance counter and click Close.

7. Alert when the value is Over a Limit of 90 and click Add.

8. Click Close.

9. Click the Action tab.

10. Click the OK button.

You have several options when it comes to choosing an action to take when an alert is triggered. The default action is to log an entry in the application event log. You can also send a network message, perhaps to your workstation. You could start a performance data log, which can be helpful in automatically capturing data when troubleshooting an intermittent performance issue. Lastly, you can also run a program of your choosing to take a specific action based on the alert.

When creating an Alert, you can use the Schedule tab to automatically start and stop the alert process at a specific time or after a certain number of seconds, minutes, hours, or days. You can also run the Alert manually at any time using the Performance Console.

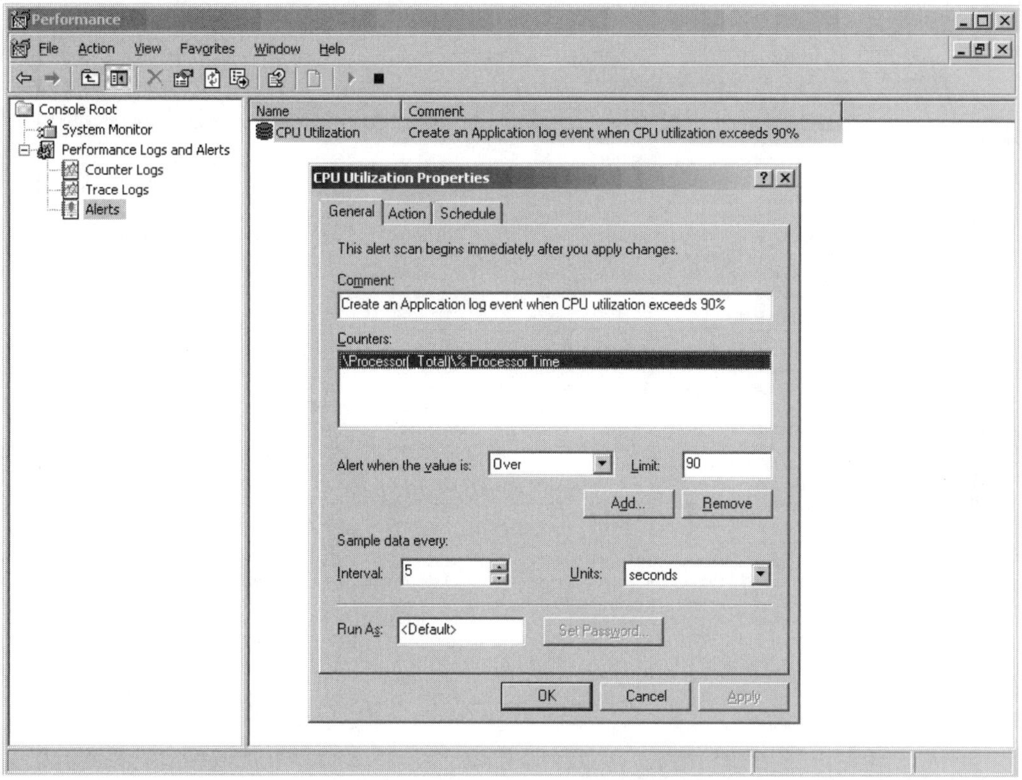

Figure 13-5. Configuring Performance Alerts.

Event Viewer

The Event Viewer can be used to view various server logs. By default, all Windows Server 2003 operating systems contain three logs:

▼ **Application log** A collection of software-related events and errors.

■ **Security log** Contains logon and resource access–related events. This data is collected as the result of audit policies configured manually by an administrator.

▲ **System log** Contains service-related information such as start, stop, and failure events.

You may also see additional logs listed in the Event Viewer's log list (see Figure 13-6), if additional roles have been assigned to the server.

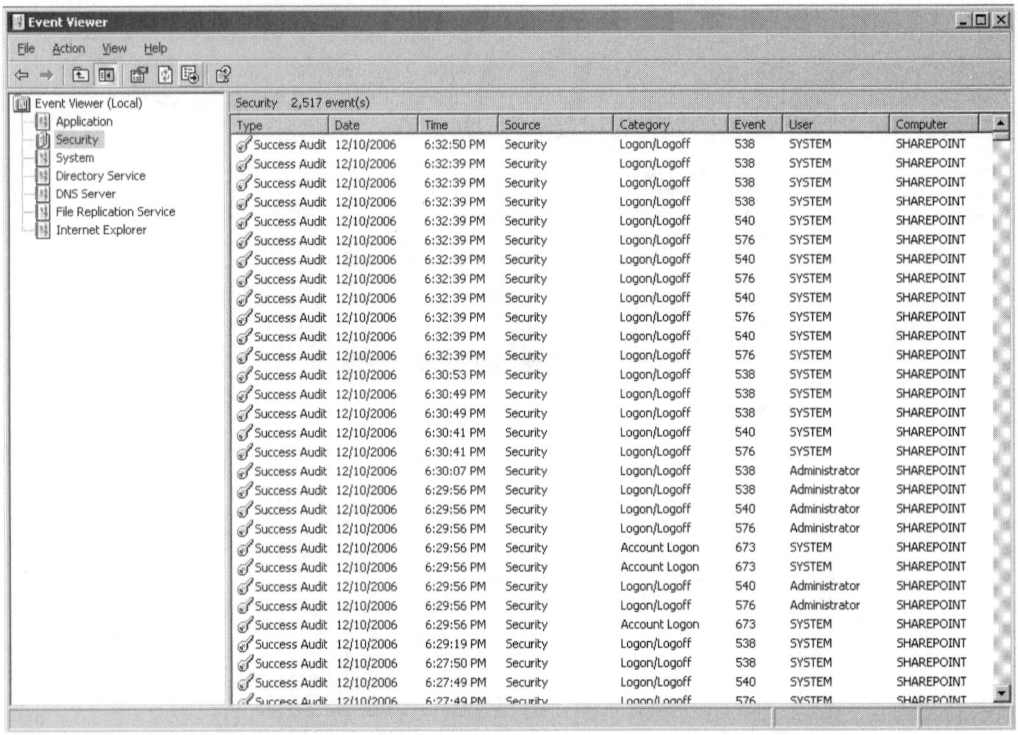

Figure 13-6. Windows Server 2003 Event Viewer.

To launch the Event Viewer, click Start, Administrative Tools, and Event Viewer.

Event Log Filtering

The volume and size of the logs being generated by the server can seem excessive at first, but you can use Event Viewer to filter the logs to focus on the information needed for monitoring MOSS or troubleshooting a specific problem.

Take a close look at the example in Figure 13-7. As you can see from the date and time of each event in the application log, there is an overwhelming amount of information. Over 6,000 events were created in a single afternoon on a nonproduction SharePoint server with no user load! Imagine the volume of entries a production SharePoint server would generate. This is why filtering is critical if you wish to use the Event Viewer as part of your monitoring process.

For example, assume you have set up several performance alerts, and you want to know if any performance-related events have been logged over the weekend while you

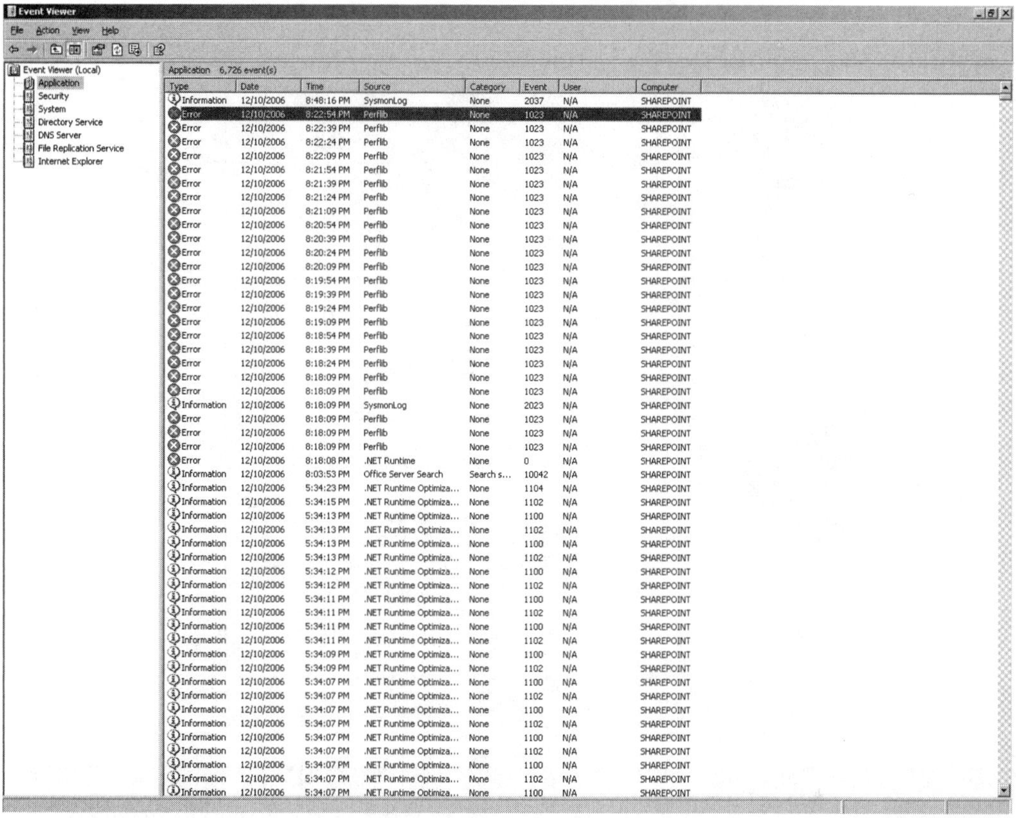

Figure 13-7. Unfiltered Application Event Log.

were away from work. Perform the following steps to extract from an event log only the events and log entries you need (refer to Figure 13-8):

1. Launch the Event Viewer.

2. Select the Application log.

3. Click View, then Filter.

4. Select SysmonLog as the Event Source.

5. Use the From drop-down list to select Events On, and then select the start date (day) and time of the period you wish to review.

6. Use the To drop-down list to select Events On, and then select the end date (day) and time of the period you wish to review.

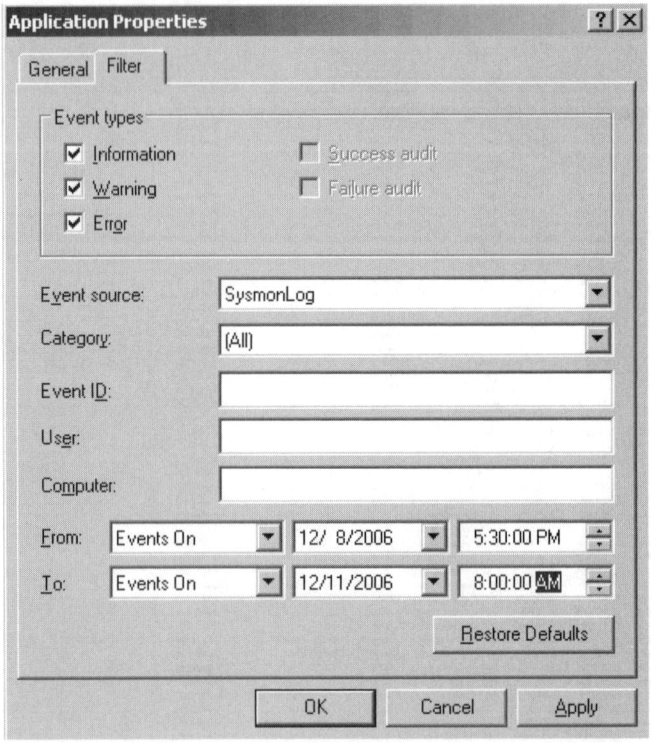

Figure 13-8. Filtering an Event Log.

NOTE The From (start) and To (end) dates and times are inclusive.

7. Click OK to apply the filtering you have just defined.

As you can see in Figure 13-9, the Application log (as shown earlier in Figure 13-7) is now filtered and includes only the events falling within your criteria.

If after filtering, the volume of alerts was still too large, you can repeat the process to further narrow down the time span you wish to view, or you can choose to display only errors.

TIP Warnings and information type events tend to generate a considerable volume of data. You may want to focus on just the error events, which are more serious.

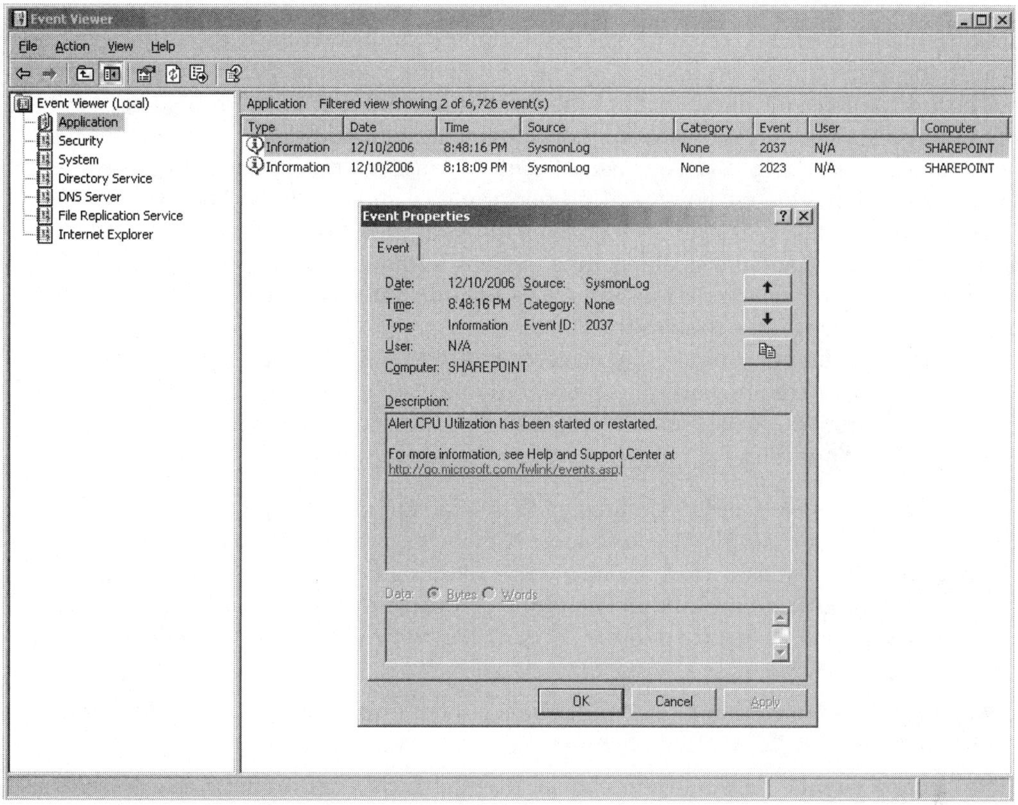

Figure 13-9. Filtered Application Event Log.

Log Files

The log files, which are raw text-based files, used for monitoring an MOSS environment are contained in several locations on a Windows Server 2003 system. However, two primary folders contain the log most often used:

▼ **C:\WINDOWS\system32\LogFiles folder** Primarily contains Internet Information Services (IIS) logs.

▲ **C:\Program Files\Common Files\Microsoft Shared\web server extensions\12\LOGS folder** Contains various MOSS-related logs, including installation and configuration logs.

Performance Auditing

Auditing the performance of an MOSS environment can be a complicated affair, but it is worth the effort to gain an understanding of how the system is performing. In many enterprise situations, it's likely that another system administrator, and probably not the MOSS administrator, is responsible for configuring system auditing. However, because of customer requirements and your need for monitoring the performance of the system to meet those requirements, you may find performance auditing to be a necessity.

By default, Windows Server 2003 enables the auditing of only some default events. Auditing must be manually enabled by a system administrator for most events. The system administrator must select which events to audit, and then enable auditing for the particular computer(s) you wish to track.

Auditing consumes valuable system resources and has the potential to create vast amounts of data. Therefore, auditing should only be used to investigate or monitor specific cases or purposes, such as monitoring a suspected security breach.

You may find auditing the following MOSS events useful:

▼ **Account logon events**   Created each time an attempt to log in to a computer is made. For example, if you suspect someone is attempting to guess the administrative password to one of your MOSS servers, enable account logon events, and audit for failure. Each time an unsuccessful logon attempt is made, an event will be recorded in the Security log, which can be reviewed using the Event Viewer.

■ **Account management**   Account management events can be used to track any changes made to existing accounts.

■ **Logon events**   Logon events can be used to track access to network resources. The majority of SharePoint security-related events will be logon events.

▲ **Object access**   Logs an event when an attempt is made to access resources. Along with logon events, object access is a good candidate for targeted auditing. There may be a legal requirement to audit both failed and successful object access events to information that is confidential or sensitive in nature.

Events can be audited for one of three results. You can audit events for success, failure, or success and failure. For example, if you believe a user is attempting to guess another user's password, you could audit logon events for failure. Each time an unsuccessful logon attempt was made, a failure entry would be created in the Security log.

Baseline Performance Model

The task of monitoring should begin long before your users begin using your new MOSS environment. By establishing a baseline performance model, you can establish what your MOSS environment looks like under no load, average load, and peak load. This knowledge is incredibly useful for preventing performance bottlenecks and allowing you to proactively address them before they impact your users. Knowing what a healthy performance baseline looks like will also help with troubleshooting existing performance issues.

Depending on your server configuration, not all of the performance objects and counters listed in Table 13-1 may be available. The performance counters listed in Table 13-1 represent only one recommended model. As you work with your particular MOSS environment, you may choose to monitor additional performance counters, depending on your server configuration and the quality of service (QoS) requirements of your users.

Server Role	Category	Include in Baseline	Performance Object	Counter
All Servers	Memory	Yes	Memory	Available Mbytes
	Memory	Yes	Memory	% Committed Bytes in Use
	Memory	Yes	Memory	Pages/second
	Processor	Optional	System	Processor Queue Length
	Processor	Yes	Processor	% Processor Time
	Network	Optional	Network	Network Queue Length
Web Front-End Server	Process	Yes	Process	% Processor Time
	Process	Yes	Process	Private Bytes
	Application load	Yes	Web Service	Connection Attempts/Sec
	Application load	Yes	ASP.NET	Worker Process Restarts
	Application load	Yes	Web Service	Current Connections
	Network	Optional	Web Service	Bytes Sent/Sec
	Network	Optional	Web Service	Bytes Received/Sec
	Application load	Optional	.NET Common Language Runtime (CLR) Data	SQL Client: Current # Pooled and Non-Pooled Connections
	Application load	Optional	.NET CLR Data	SQL Client: Failed Pooled Connections
Back-End Database Server	Processor	Yes	SQL Server	% Processor Time
	Memory	Yes	SQL Server	Private Bytes
	Database	Yes	SQL Server	Current Connections
	Database	Yes	SQL Server	Logins/Sec

Table 13-1.   Suggested Performance Counters to Use to Monitor an MOSS Environment

Establish a Baseline Performance Model

It is very important to establish a baseline performance model of a newly installed MOSS environment before users begin to put a load on the system. To create a baseline performance model, perform the following steps:

1. Start the Performance Console by clicking the Start button in the taskbar, choosing Administrative Tasks, and finally Performance.

2. Expand the Performance Logs and Alerts node in the folder pane and then select Counter Logs.

3. Right-click anywhere in the detail pane (right side of the Performance window) and select New Log Settings.

4. Name the log SharePoint Baseline and click OK.

5. Use the Add Counters button, as shown in Figure 13-10, to add the counters indicated in Table 13-1 as recommended for inclusion as a baseline counter.

6. If your SharePoint environment consists of more than one server, repeat this process for each server in your environment, paying attention to the server roles (as illustrated in Figure 13-4).

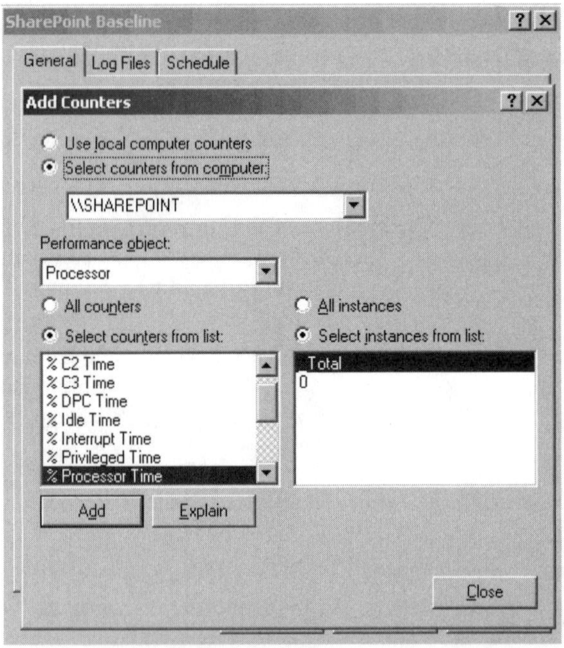

Figure 13-10.   Adding performance counters.

Potential Performance Bottlenecks

As a SharePoint administrator, you definitely need to monitor how MOSS is consuming server resources. On any system, the four major server resources are CPU, memory, disk space, and network bandwidth. These four resources combine to indicate the overall health of your MOSS environment. When analyzed together, they provide you with a fairly good idea of how responsive MOSS is for your users.

Table 13-2 lists the operating limits recommended for an MOSS environment. As indicated, CPU utilization should not exceed 80 percent regularly. At least 50MB of primary memory should be available for the system, available hard disk space should not drop below 10 percent, and the bandwidth for MOSS clients should remain at or above 256 KBps.

Should the MOSS system, or the operating system for that matter, on any of the network's servers begin operating below normal standards, your first investigation should be to determine if one of the limits listed in Table 13-2 has been exceeded and begin using the event logs to determine the cause. Of course, the cause could also be that the available resources needed for the system may need to be enhanced or upgraded.

MOSS LOGGING AND REPORTING

On the Operations page of the MOSS Central Administration site, the section entitled Logging and Reporting (see Figure 13-11) provides you with three general areas in which you can apply logging and reporting functions. The information collected and reported in each of these areas is designed to provide you with the capability to diagnose, analyze, and monitor the performance of your MOSS environment.

The three areas included in the Logging and Reporting section are:

▼ Diagnostic logging

■ Usage analysis processing

▲ Information management policy usage reports

Component Condition	Operating Limit
CPU utilization	80 percent
Memory available	50 Megabytes (MB)
Disk space available	10 percent
Bandwidth available	256 Kilobytes per second (KBps)

Table 13-2.   Minimum Operating Conditions for a MOSS Environment

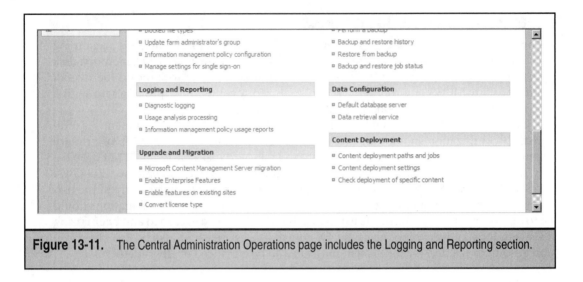

Figure 13-11. The Central Administration Operations page includes the Logging and Reporting section.

Diagnostic Logging

While the diagnostic logging functions of MOSS are valuable in determining a variety of performance issues, there is a downside to configuring logging functions: disk space. The MOSS trace and event logs can eat up disk space fairly quickly. By default, MOSS trace logging is enabled, and without any throttling applied, and because MOSS maintains slightly less than one hundred log files, these files can eat up around 5GB of disk space fairly quickly.

Configuring the diagnostic logging settings for MOSS to provide you with the information you need to troubleshoot system problems requires that you identify the maximum number of log files to be maintained (based on the specific amount of data and how critical it is) and the time span for the data collected.

To configure the diagnostic logging settings, do the following:

1. Log in to the server hosting the SharePoint Central Administration site with an account that has Administrator group permissions.

2. Open the SharePoint Central Administration site.

3. From either the Quick Launch menu or the top navigation bar, click the Operations tab to open the Operations page.

4. Click the Diagnostic Logging link in the Logging and Reporting section (see Figure 13-11).

Within the Diagnostic logging function, you can configure the following data capture and reporting actions:

▼ Participation in the Customer Experience Improvement Program (CEIP)

■ Error Reporting

- ■ Event Throttling
- ▲ Trace Log

The procedure used to configure each of these areas is outlined in the following sections.

Customer Experience Improvement Program

To configure the settings for the Customer Experience Improvement Program (CEIP):

▼ On the Diagnostic Logging page's Customer Experience Improvement Program section (shown in Figure 13-12), select the radio button option corresponding to either the Yes, I Am Willing To Participate… or the No, I Don't Wish To Participate options. The default value is the No option.

NOTE Selecting the Yes option registers you in the CEIP from which you will automatically receive periodic requests from Microsoft for feedback on how you use certain Microsoft products. Your feedback is combined with information about your system configuration (only Microsoft products) to assist Microsoft in resolving issues and improving its products.

Error Reporting

Microsoft does not intentionally collect any personal information. However, error reports could contain data from log files, such as usernames, IP addresses, URLs, file or path names, and e-mail addresses. Although this information, if present, could potentially be used to determine your identity, the information will not be used in this way. The data that Microsoft collects will be used only to fix problems and improve software and services. Error reports will be sent by using encryption technology to a database with limited access, and will not be used for marketing purposes.

Whenever your system encounters a hardware or software problem, a report can be sent to Microsoft to report the error. These reports are used by Microsoft and other companies to improve the reliability and performance of your system. The error reports generated by the system typically include such information as the condition of the server when a problem is detected, the operating system version, the computer hardware model,

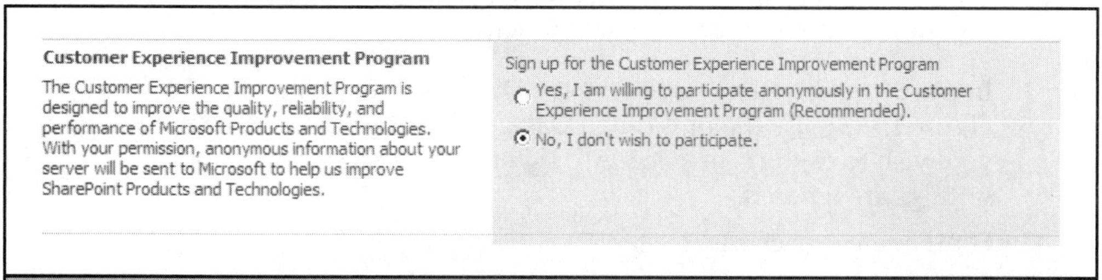

Customer Experience Improvement Program

The Customer Experience Improvement Program is designed to improve the quality, reliability, and performance of Microsoft Products and Technologies. With your permission, anonymous information about your server will be sent to Microsoft to help us improve SharePoint Products and Technologies.

Sign up for the Customer Experience Improvement Program

○ Yes, I am willing to participate anonymously in the Customer Experience Improvement Program (Recommended).

◉ No, I don't wish to participate.

Figure 13-12. The Customer Experience Improvement Program section of the Diagnostics Logging page .

the licensing information of the software involved in the error, and the Internet Protocol (IP) address of your computer.

The default setting for this function is the Collect Error Reports option, but you are not obligated to participate and may choose not to do so.

If you wish to participate in the Error Reporting program:

▼ Select the radio button corresponding to the Collect Error Reports option.

▲ Mark the checkbox corresponding to the method you wish to use to submit error reports. You can choose to periodically download files to identify system problems or change the error policy of the computer to silently (in the background) submit error reports.

If you choose not to participate in the Error Reporting program, select the radio button corresponding to the Ignore Errors And Don't Collect Information option.

Event Throttling

The settings in the Event Throttling section of the Diagnostic Logging page control the amount of data collected to the log files based on how critical the event being logged is determined to be. This section contains three pull-down lists, one that contains over 100 separate event categories, including the All and General categories, and one each for the least critical event level to record to the event log and the trace log.

MOSS has no default settings for event throttling, which means that unless you configure these settings, all events are recorded to the event and trace logs. The settings in the Event throttling section control the minimum level of severity to be captured in the event and trace logs. At a lower severity level, more items are recorded to the logs, and as the severity level rises, fewer events are likely to occur, which means that fewer entries are written to the logs. These settings are made to either an individual category or to all categories, with an all category selection overriding a single category selection.

Events can be logged to the Windows Event log, the Trace log, or both, and event throttling can be used to control the number of events recorded in the logs. The volume of events recorded to the log files is controlled by the category configured in this section. The category choices range from all events to those defined by a single service or a group of related events. For the category selected, you can set the lowest level (least critical) of event to log, with all higher level (more critical) events also being logged.

To configure event throttling, do the following:

1. In the Event throttling section of the Diagnostic Logging page (shown in Figure 13-13), use the pull-down Category list to choose the event category you wish to capture, or select All. If you leave this setting blank, all other settings are ignored.

2. For the category chosen in step 1:

   a. Use the pull-down list for the Least Critical Event To Report To The Event Log to choose the least critical event to be reported, choosing from None, Error, Warning, Audit Failure, Audit Success, and Information.

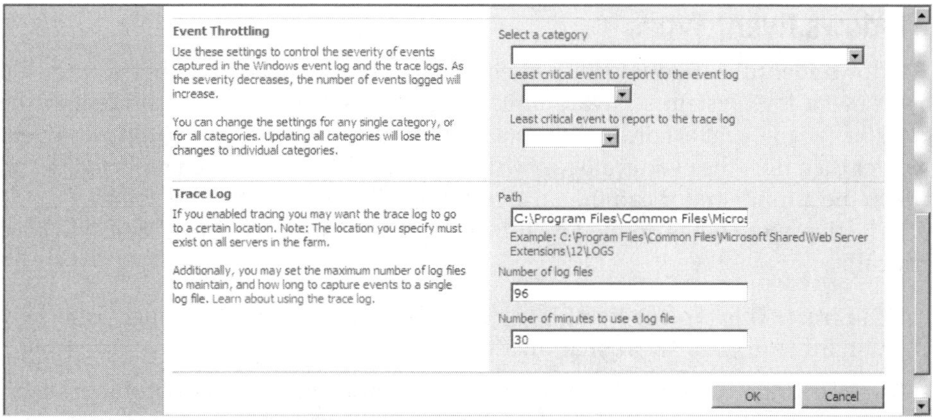

Figure 13-13.   The Event Throttling and Trace Log sections of the Diagnostic Logging page.

b.   Use the pull-down list for the Least Critical Event To Report To The Trace Log to choose the least critical event to be recorded to the trace logs, choosing from None, Unexpected, Monitorable, High, Medium, and Verbose, which are listed in order of least to most critical.

TIP   You should use the Verbose level only when necessary because it can cause the size of the log files to grow quite large. To record only those items when you need them, especially on a production server, select only a specific category. The size of the logs can grow to be quite large. To turn off all logging, select the Empty category, and None for the trace log least critical event. To record relatively few events, select High or Monitorable.

Trace Log

If you have chosen to set a least critical level for recording to a trace log in the Event Throttling section, you should also configure the number of log files to be maintained and the length of time to be recorded to each log file in the Trace Log section of the Diagnostic Logging page, shown in Figure 13-13.

To configure the Trace Log section, do the following:

1.   In the Trace Log section, enter the local path to be used for the trace logs on the local server or within the server farm. In a server farm environment, the path entered must exist on each of the servers in the farm.

2.   Enter the maximum number of log files you wish the system to create and maintain in the Number Of Log Files text box.

Windows Event Types

Windows identifies five levels of events that can be logged to either a trace log or an event log. System software units or application programs each identify the category of an event according to a standardized set of rules. The Windows Event Viewer then uses the event category to assign an event icon to each reported event, which the administrator can then use to sort or filter the log for reporting.

The five event types defined by the Event Viewer are (from most critical to least critical):

▼ **Error**   This type of event is triggered by a serious problem, such as a hardware or software malfunction or loss of data.

■ **Warning**   This type of event typically identifies a potential problem such as low disk space availability or an incident from which an application is able to recover without interruption.

■ **Information**   This type of event is created when a tracked function is successful, such as a device driver loading successfully. Information events are in effect memo notices of events that may or may not be occurring during a normal process.

■ **Success Audit**   This type of event is created when a security-related activity is successful, such as a user login.

▲ **Failure Audit**   This type of event is created when a security-related activity is unsuccessful, such as an unsuccessful attempt to log in to a network.

3. Enter the number of minutes each log file is to be used in the Number Of Minutes To Use A Log File text box. A smaller number means that each log file will be in use for a shorter period of time, but depending on the settings in the Event Throttling section and in the Number Of Log Files, this could mean that a log file may be overwritten before it can be analyzed or reported.

4. Click the OK button to save the Diagnostic Logging settings.

Usage Analysis and Reporting

SharePoint portal usage analysis and reporting is a feature that, once enabled, collects and reports on a multitude of statistics about how users are interacting with MOSS over the past 30 days, including top referring and destination pages, users, requests, and search results. Monitoring these usage reports can provide you with a sense of how well your MOSS implementation is serving your users.

With usage analysis and reporting enabled, the MOSS administrator (or the site collection administrator) can monitor usage data in summary or chart form for the MOSS environment in the last 30-day period, including:

▼   Average requests per day

■   Highest volume referring hosts

■   Highest volume requests and queries

■   Highest volume page requests

■   Highest volume users

▲   Most frequently requested destination pages

To set up Usage Analysis and Reporting, you must first enable usage analysis processing for your MOSS server or, if you have more than one MOSS server, for the entire server farm. Once this is done, reporting services must be activated. With usage analysis processing and reporting services running on the MOSS server(s), usage analysis must be enabled for each site.

To set up the Usage Analysis and Reporting function for an MOSS environment, perform the following steps.

Enable usage analysis:

1. Open the Central Administration web page (see Figure 13-14).

2. Click Usage Analysis Processing in the Logging and Reporting section.

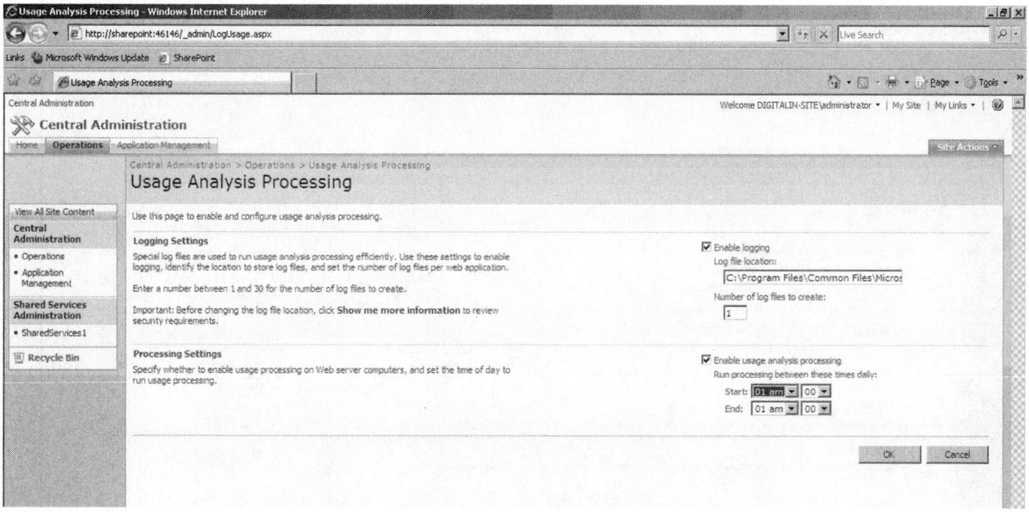

Figure 13-14.   The MOSS Usage Analysis Processing window.

3. Check Enable Logging.

4. Check Enable Usage Analysis Processing.

5. Select a start and end time to run processing.

6. Click OK.

Enable reporting:

1. Open the Central Administration web page if it is not already open.

2. Click Site Actions.

3. Click Site Collection Features (see Figure 13-15).

4. Click the Activate button.

View usage reports:

1. Click Site Actions.

2. Click Site Settings.

3. Click Usage Summary under the Site Collection Administration section.

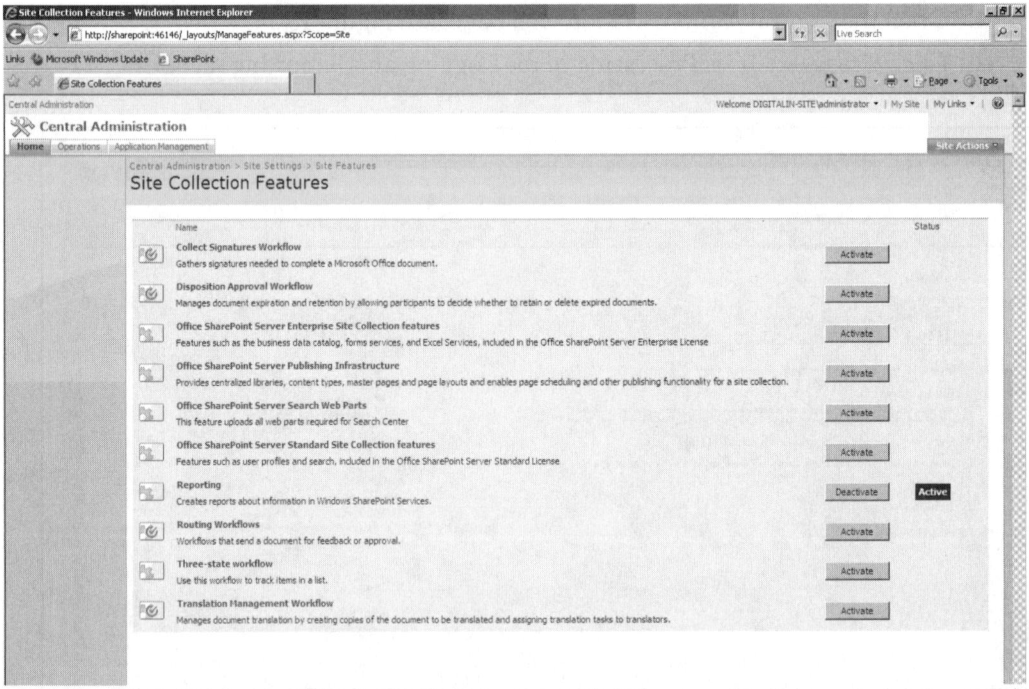

Figure 13-15.   The MOSS Site Collection Features window.

Information Management Policy Usage Reports

To track the effectiveness and utilization of the information management policies for a site, you can configure the information management policy usage reports to provide information on a regular basis in the form of reports written to a specified site location. The configuration and specifications for the reports you wish to see are set on the Information Management Policy Usage Reports page, shown in Figure 13-16.

To configure the generation and frequency of these reports, do the following:

1. In the Web Application section, accept the default web application or use the pull-down list to select a different application.

2. If you wish to generate recurring reports on policy usage, check the checkbox that corresponds to the Enable Recurring Policy Usage Reports and then set the frequency as Daily, Weekly (on a given day), or Monthly (on a designated date), and between a certain time of the day. If you wish, you can create the reports immediately by clicking the Create Reports Now button.

3. Enter a path or URL for the location to which the reports are to be generated. If you are unsure of the path, use the Test URL button to verify the location.

4. Check the radio button corresponding to the Use The Default Report Template. If you have developed a custom report template, check the radio button for that option and enter the URL or the path of the custom report template. You can use the Test Template button to verify the location of the custom template.

5. Click the OK button to save the policy usage report settings.

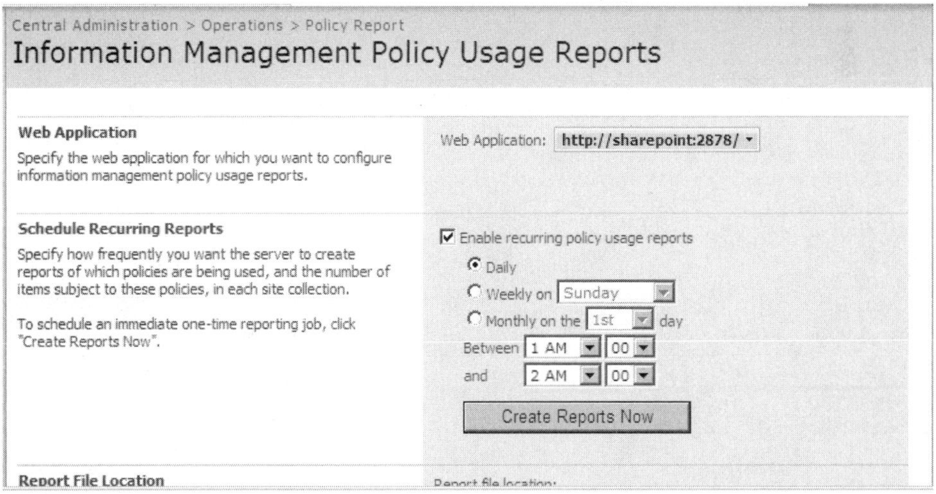

Figure 13-16. The Information Management Policy Usage Reports page.

NOTE For more information on information management policies, see Chapter 9.

SUMMARY

In summary, monitoring is a crucial task of the SharePoint administrator. Monitoring your SharePoint environment ensures that you can provide a responsive, trouble-free experience for your users. Use the Task Manager to assess the overall health of your server. Investigate potential issues with the Performance Console and establish a performance baseline to alert you to any performance counter values that exceed your quality of service agreement. Periodically review the Event Viewer logs, as well as the raw text-based logs. Do so when the system is healthy, and you'll be able to quickly spot and resolve any issues when they arise.

Be sure to enable usage analysis processing and train your subordinate SharePoint administrators and content owners how to review the usage analysis reports. You should also review the high-level usage reports to ensure your SharePoint implementation is meeting your deployment goals.

CHAPTER 14

MOSS Maintenance

You may be wondering what the difference is between configuration, administration, and maintenance. Configuration is any initial actions taken by an MOSS administrator after installation of MOSS or to enable a new MOSS feature. Administration tasks are often performed in response to a user request, such as creating a new site, copying files from one document library to another, assigning permissions, or troubleshooting a performance issue. Maintenance, which is the focus of this chapter, is the repeated tasks associated with keeping your MOSS environment running smoothly, such as site management, reviewing usage data and logs, and performing backups.

Because MOSS is relatively simple to install, you can be easily lead into believing it requires little or no maintenance. However, an administrator's job isn't over once MOSS is installed and configured. In fact, it has just begun. It takes a constant effort on the part of the administrator for MOSS to be an effective resource to an organization. Maintenance is the day-to-day behind-the-scenes activities required to ensure MOSS's value to the organization.

This chapter discusses the various on-going maintenance tasks that commonly fall into the routine and daily activities of the MOSS administrator, including site maintenance, periodic maintenance tasks, and backup and restore actions.

SITE MAINTENANCE

All SharePoint sites can be categorized in one of two ways: sites that are used, and sites that aren't used. With storage space continually at a premium on most servers, an unused site, in addition to taking up disk space, contribute to the overall clutter of an MOSS environment. A site that is no longer in use (meaning it has no activity logged for an extended period of time) takes up disk space on the server and clutters up site lists. Thus, it should be removed from the system.

To properly manage and maintain the sites in your MOSS environment, you should apply a five-step program on a fairly regular basis. A suggested site maintenance process includes the following five steps:

▼   Inventory sites

■   Review site content

■   Analyze site use information

■   Archive inactive or obsolete content

▲   Remove unused or obsolete sites

Each of these steps is outlined in the following sections.

Inventory Sites

As a regular part of your site maintenance activities, you should maintain an inventory of the site collections and pages within your MOSS environment, especially if users are allowed to create new sites. The easiest way to create an inventory list of the sites in your MOSS environment is to generate a complete listing of all SharePoint site collections. To generate this list, do the following:

1. Log in to a web front-end server in a server farm installation.

2. Open a command prompt window. You can do this two ways:

   a. Choose Run from the Start menu, enter **cmd** in the Open box, and press the ENTER key.

   b. Choose Command Prompt from the Start menu.

3. At the command prompt, enter the command

   ```
   cd C:\Program Files\Common Files\Microsoft Shared\web server extensions\12\BIN
   ```

4. Enter the command

   ```
   stsadm.exe -o enumsites -url http://[servername] > C:\sitelist.xml
   ```

   where [servername] is the name of your SharePoint server or the web front-end server (http://sharepoint is the server name used in the example shown in Figure 14-1). The parameter enumsites indicates you are listing site collections. The stsadm command creates an XML file that lists the sites and site collections on the server. This output can be redirected to a file, which was done in this example. The output of the stsadm utility has been redirected to a file named sitelist.xml. You can use any name you like for this file, but be sure to give it an xml extension.

5. If you wish to generate a list of the subsites within each site collection, use the stsadm command again employing the parameter enumsubwebs and providing the name of the site collection:

   ```
   stsadm.exe -o enumsubwebs -url http://[servername][/site] > C:\subsites.xml
   ```

   where [servername] is the name of the SharePoint server or the web front-end server and [/site] is the site collection name. Figure 14-2 shows a command line and the stsadm.exe command used to generate a subsite list.

The XML file(s) generated from the stsadm.exe command can be viewed with an XML editor, such as Altova's XMLSpy (www.altova.com) or CookTop (www.xmlcooktop .com), or a web browser. Figures 14-3 and 14-4 display XML files containing lists of sites and subsites.

Once you have generated your site list and possibly your subsite lists, you should review them looking for anything out of the ordinary, such as a site you didn't know existed or one you thought had been removed earlier. Keep the site lists you've generated since they are used in determining site retention later.

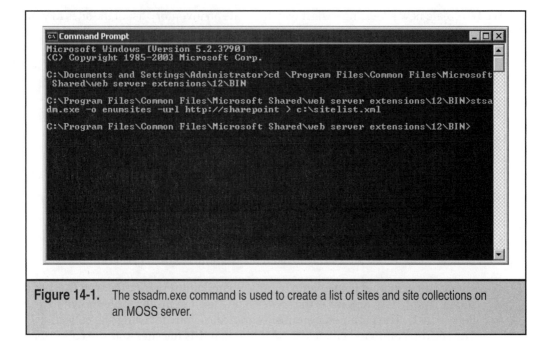

Figure 14-1.   The stsadm.exe command is used to create a list of sites and site collections on an MOSS server.

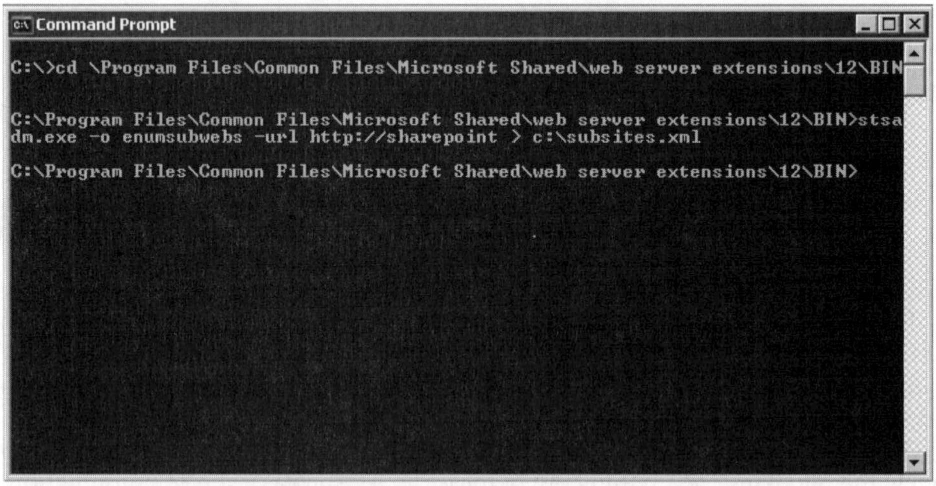

Figure 14-2.   The stsadm.exe command used to create a list of subsites within a site collection.

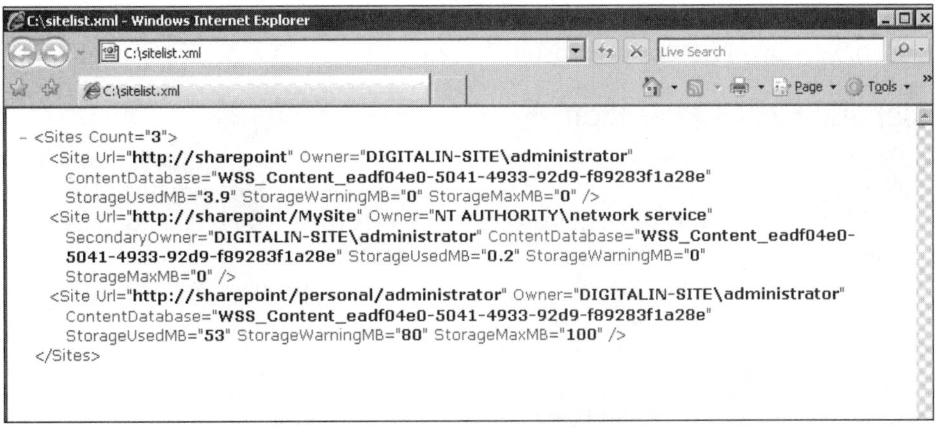

Figure 14-3. A web browser can be used to view the contents of a site list in an XML file.

Review Site Content

It is important for the overall health of your MOSS environment that you review the site content periodically for its relevance and organization. Without a regular review, site content can quickly become disorganized, cluttered, and, worse, inefficient. Your review should look at three important areas of a site's content:

▼ Folder and file organization

■ Version control

▲ Expired content

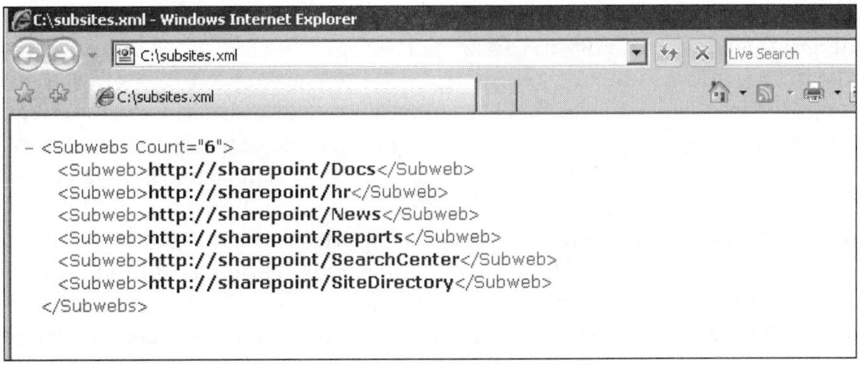

Figure 14-4. A web browser view of the contents of a subsites list in an XML file.

Site reviews should be performed regularly using a planned and published schedule. How frequently you do your site reviews depends on the site content itself as well as the amount of user involvement you wish to have.

Folder and File Organization

SharePoint libraries that use a folder hierarchy to organize their content should be thoroughly reviewed on a regular basis to ensure that files are properly organized into appropriate folders and that any newly created folders are properly named and placed within the folder hierarchy. Libraries that use a flat, or folder-less view, should be checked to ensure proper metadata have been assigned to each file. This review is easily done using a site's All Site Content display.

Version Control

A common problem with SharePoint library files is version control. Users often save multiple versions of the same document to their library using different filenames to indicate a new revision or version of the document.

For example, if a user opens a document named Benefits.doc, makes a few minor changes to its content and saves the revised document as Benefits-rev2.doc, the possibility exists that the original document is now obsolete. This practice can be fairly widespread and can end up consuming valuable storage resources by retaining the original and revised documents, as well as increasing the size of the file indexes.

This practice can also cause issues for users looking for particular content. If an original document file is frequently accessed (and has been for a long period of time), any new version of the document could outrank the original in a search result. In the example of the Benefits.doc and the new Benefits-rev2.doc, nothing in the name of the new file indicates it to be the most recent version. This practice, common in many systems, can create a situation where users don't know if they are working with the most current version of a document.

To counter this problem and to make your life simpler, and that of your users, you should take two actions: develop and publish a standard file naming convention that includes a scheme for indicating document revisions in a file's name; and implement versioning on the document library. To properly apply versioning on a document library, you must first perform some housekeeping, with the help of your users, and then change the settings for the library to enable versioning. First, work with the document author to determine the most recent version of the file. Second, rename the document's current version to identify it as such. Finally, access the library's site settings to enable versioning.

Another problem that can clutter up a library or site is announcement list items. An announcement item includes an expiration property that can be set to automatically delete the item on a certain date. Unfortunately, this feature is seldom employed by users, which means you have two actions to take: delete all obsolete announcements and educate your users on how to set the expiration property on announcements they generate.

Archive Expired Content

Content is deemed to be obsolete because it no longer serves a useful purpose, and (because the content is obsolete) it can be safely removed from the system. In theory, this is a safe assumption to operate under. However, unless you are able to coordinate with every user who may need access to a particular document or its contents, you can never be absolutely sure when removing supposedly obsolete content.

MOSS supports two important features that can help you stay out of the "hey-I-needed-that" trap: data retention policies and the ability to archive data from one MOSS site to another. Your organization should have a defined and formal data retention policy that can be implemented in the MOSS information management functions. You can also move information that has not had activity for some time to a top-level read-only site just in case someone actually does need it, and keep it there for a period of time before actually deleting it. However, if a document is actually obsolete, it should be removed.

Analyze Usage Information

MOSS tracks the usage of each site and you can display these statistics to determine whether a site is still in use or not. SharePoint usage reports, like the one shown in Figure 14-5, displays information about site users, the requests they make, and the pages they access.

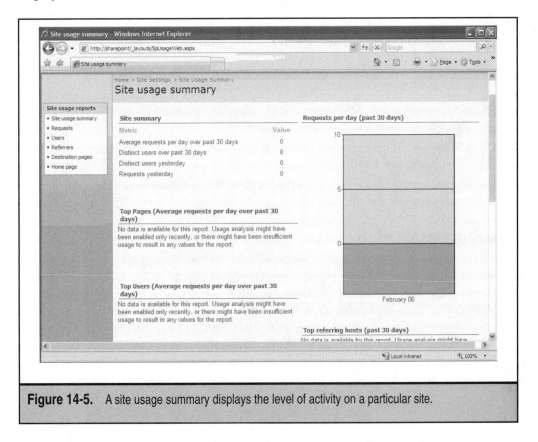

Figure 14-5.   A site usage summary displays the level of activity on a particular site.

With this information, you can coordinate with your users about sites that have had little or no usage and whether users still need these sites.

As a part of this analysis, you can take the opportunity to improve one or more sites to increase its value to your users. Ask users which features they like and which they don't like and use this information to enhance a site or combine two or more low-usage sites together to better serve the needs of the organization.

NOTE   For more information on SharePoint Usage Reports, please refer to Chapter 13.

In situations where Self-Service Site Creation is enabled, users create sites that end up being unused. These unused sites are often the result of the users' learning curve, but could also be the result of user experiments, a project that has gone inactive or has been abandoned, or a creator who has left the company or been transferred. Whatever the reason for a site to be unused, be sure you check with the creator of an unused site to verify it is no longer needed before removing it from the system.

Deleting a site also deletes all of the site content associated with it, including:

▼ Documents and document libraries

■ Lists and list data, such as surveys, discussions, announcements, and calendars

■ All web site settings and configurations

▲ Associated permission levels and security settings

Once you have confirmed that a site is no longer needed, it should be deleted. To do this, perform the following steps:

1. Navigate to the site to be removed, click the Site Actions button to open its drop-down menu, and choose Site Settings.

2. On the Site Settings page, click the Delete This Site link located under the Site Administration heading.

3. On the confirmation page that displays, click the Delete button to confirm you wish to delete the site.

Review Site Permissions

You should periodically, at least quarterly, review the site permissions configuration of each of the active sites in the MOSS environment. The purpose of this review is to identify and remove any users who are no longer associated with a site. In this review, you should apply the practice of least privilege, which says to assign a minimum set of permissions to a minimum number of users, giving them just enough to be able to do their jobs. This review is as much a part of good general housekeeping practices as it is security.

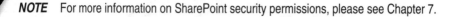

NOTE   For more information on SharePoint security permissions, please see Chapter 7.

SITE PERFORMANCE

Managing a site collection, a top-level site and its content, is a bit different than managing individual sites. With a site collection, you must be concerned with performance issues and user permissions on a more universal level. The settings and configuration of a site collection also apply to the sites and contents created within it.

The three primary areas you should focus your site collection management activities in are the following:

▼   Content database size

■   Site storage space quotas

▲   Use confirmation

Content Database Size

Each site collection, meaning each top-level site, is associated with its own content database. In situations where the Self-Service Site Creation capability has been enabled for a site collection, the size of the content database may grow to the point of becoming inefficient, both in terms of size and performance, as a result of site redundancy.

The best safeguard against this situation occurring, other than disabling the Self-Service Site Creation capability, is to create additional top-level sites. Each top-level site should be limited to not more than 2000 subsites. This same limit should also be applied to libraries and folders. When a site is approaching 2000 libraries or lists, a new library/list site should be created. The good news is that a library can function fairly efficiently with as many as 10,000,000 documents.

If these limits sound large enough that you don't think you'll need to worry about the size of your content databases, remember that each of your users could eventually create five to ten different sites, each with multiple libraries or lists. If you have 500 users, it isn't that far-fetched in a content database for a single top-level site to grow to over 5000 or more sites, libraries, or lists. Over time, as users become more comfortable with the system, they'll create fewer and fewer sites, libraries, and lists, but in the early days of a new MOSS environment, site proliferation can be a problem.

Table 14-1 lists the recommended limits for site collections, sites, libraries, views, and folders in a single content database. Use these limits as a guideline to help ensure the performance of your MOSS environment.

In small to medium-sized organizations, the limits shown in Table 14-1 may never be approached, even with runaway redundancy. In these organizations, the use of site quotas may be a better option.

Site Quotas

The best way to control the amount of space a site uses and the number of items associated with a site is to use site quotas. A site quota can be used to limit the amount of content associated and stored in any one SharePoint site, which also limits the size of its content database.

Content Type	Content Database Limits
Site collection	2000 subsites
Site	2000 libraries or lists
Library	10,000,000 documents
View	2000 items
Folder	2000 items

Table 14-1.   Recommended Content Database Limits

Site quotas are most commonly assigned to a site though the application of a template. An example of how a site quota is used is that, by default, MOSS sets the quota template limits to MySite pages to 100 MB of storage space. The quota template also sets an 80 MB trigger point that causes an e-mail warning message to be sent to the site owner when the site's storage space usage reaches that level. This same approach can also be applied to each top-level site through a quota template in which you can set the total amount of storage space a site can use, the point at which a warning should be issued, and whether or not the site can continue to use additional space beyond the limit or be cut off.

A quota template can be created by accessing the Quota template link on the Application Management tab of the MOSS Central Administration page. Figure 14-6 shows the Quota Templates page that is used to configure the storage space usage limits of a site. Understand that quota templates are created as independent items that can be applied to a site, library, or list.

Create a Quota Template

To create a quota template (see Figure 14-6), perform the following steps:

1. On the Central Administration page, select the Application Management tab and under the Site Management heading, click the Quota templates link.

2. Since you're creating a new quota template, choose the Create A New Quota Template option.

3. Enter a name for the template. The name should describe the type of site on which the quota template is to be applied.

4. If you wish to limit the maximum size of a site, check the Limit The Site Storage To A Maximum Of checkbox and enter the maximum storage size (in MB).

5. If you wish to have a warning e-mail issued when the space used reaches a certain limit, check the Send A Warning E-Mail When The Site Storage Reaches checkbox and enter the space limit (in MB) at which you want the warning to be issued.

6. Click OK to create the quota template.

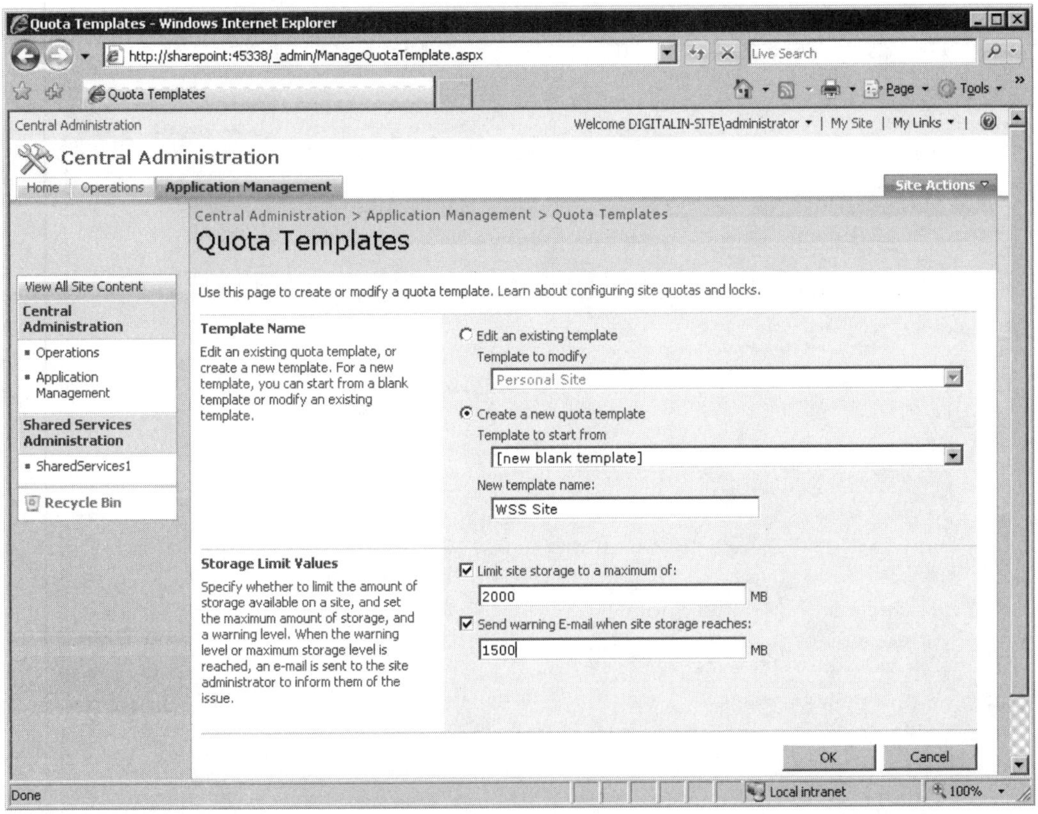

Figure 14-6.   The Quota Templates page.

Apply Quota Template

Once you've created a quota template, it can be applied to a top-level site to limit the storage space usage of all of its subsites. To apply a quota template to a site, do the following:

1. On the Application Management tab of the Central Administration page, click the Site Collection Quotas And Locks link under the Site Management heading.

2. On the Site Collection Quotas And Locks page, shown in Figure 14-7, use the Site Collection pull-down menu to choose the top-level site to which you wish to apply a quota template.

3. In the Site Lock Information section, the current lock status of the site is indicated. Choose an alternative option than the one indicated to change the lock status of the site.

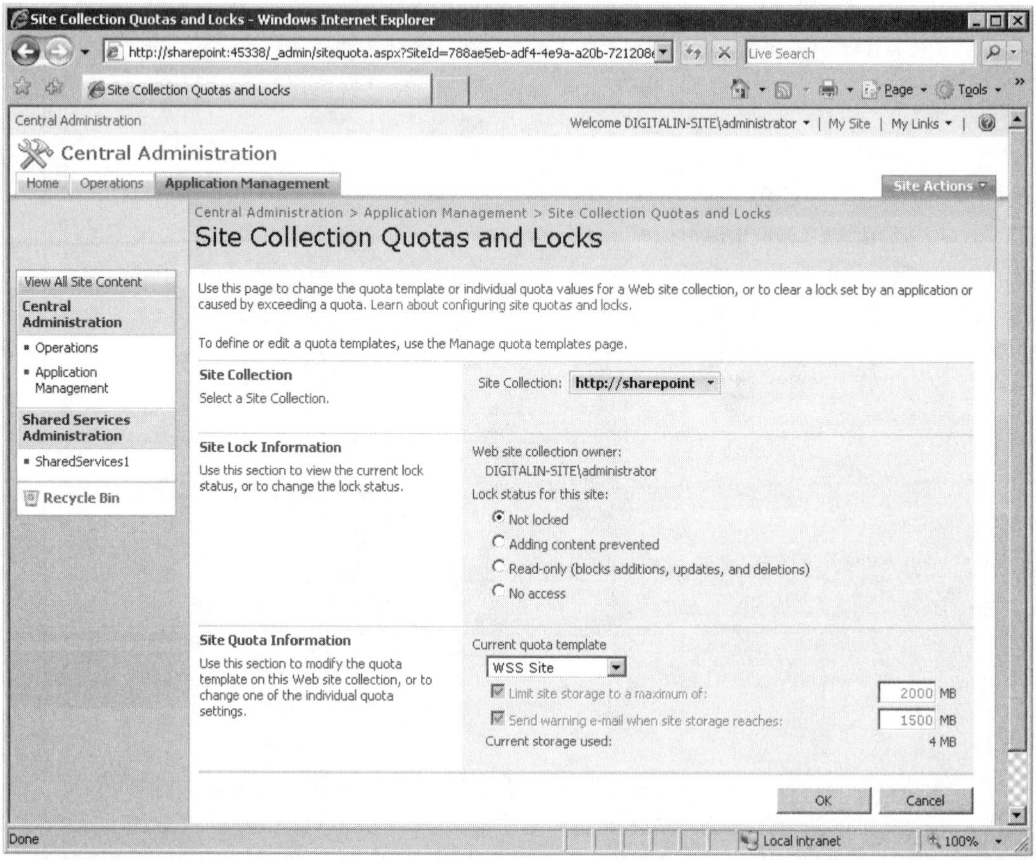

Figure 14-7. The Site Collection Quotas And Locks page.

4. In the Site Quota Information section, choose the quota template you wish to apply from the pull-down list. Notice that the current storage space usage of the site is displayed in this section. Use this as a gauge for which quota template may be the best to apply.

5. Click OK to apply the quota template.

Site Collection Use Confirmation

MOSS includes a feature, the Site Use Confirmation & Deletion, which can be used to confirm the usage of a site collection. Unfortunately, this feature only applies to site collections, and, for the most part, site collections rarely, if ever, go unused. MOSS monitors a web application for any site collections that remain unused for a specified number of days. Should a site collection actually go unused, an e-mail is sent to the site collection owner requesting confirmation that the site collection is indeed being used. MOSS can also be configured to delete any unused site collections after a set number of e-mail notices are sent to the site collection owner.

To configure the Site Use Confirmation and Deletion feature, use the following steps:

1. On the Central Administration page, select the Application Management tab, and click the Site Use Confirmation And Deletion link under the Site Management heading. This opens the Site Use Confirmation And Deletion page, shown in Figure 14-8.

2. Select the web application you wish to monitor from the Web Application drop-down list.

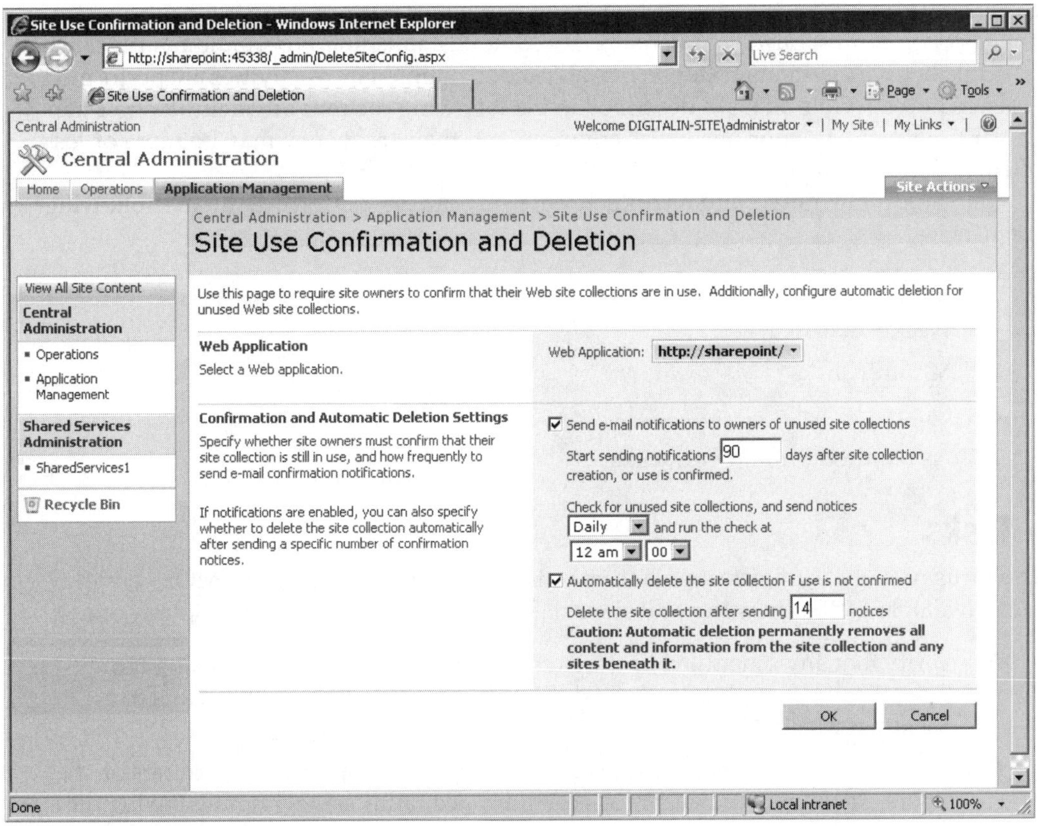

Figure 14-8. The Site Use Confirmation And Deletion page.

3. In the Confirmation And Automatic Deletion Settings section, check the Send E-mail Notifications To Owners Of Unused Site Collections checkbox and select the frequency and time for MOSS to check the web application's site collections and to send the e-mail notification.

4. If you wish any unused site collection to be deleted automatically after a set number of notifications, check the Automatically Delete The Site Collection If Use Is Not Confirmed checkbox and enter the number of notices after which the site collection is to be deleted.

5. Click OK to save these settings.

SCHEDULED MAINTENANCE AND ADMINISTRATION TASKS

Maintaining an MOSS environment effectively involves performing certain administrative tasks on a prescribed maintenance schedule. Establishing a periodic maintenance schedule helps the administrator ensure all needed maintenance activities are performed when required. While all tasks described in the following sections are identified to a particular timeframe, in your particular environment, their frequency may be more or less often, depending on your organization's needs.

MOSS administrative and maintenance tasks can be performed in the following frequencies:

▼ Daily tasks

■ Weekly tasks

■ Monthly tasks

■ Quarterly tasks

▲ As required (infrequent) tasks

Daily Tasks

The focus of daily administration and maintenance tasks is to keep the MOSS environment available and performing as it should. The tasks you should perform daily are:

▼ Verify that any scheduled backups completed without errors by using the Operations tab on the Central Administration page to check the status of a backup (or restore) action.

■ Review all event logs for any security failures and application warnings or errors. Reviewing the event logs each day acquaints you with how the log files normally appear and enable you to pick up on an abnormality quickly. See Chapter 13 for more information on working with event logs.

▲   Respond to any user complaints about overall system, web application, site collection, library, list, or search performance issues. You should treat user complaints as possible red flags about system performance issues.

Weekly Tasks

Each week you should check the available storage space for the MOSS environment and create archives of the event logs from the past week. These tasks are:

▼   Verify that the local hard disk drives on each server have a minimum of 25 percent available storage space. Should a disk drive reach 100 percent of storage capacity, it could lead to very serious problems. Pay particular attention to the partitions on a disk drive that include the operating system, any database files, and all log files.

▲   The event logs on each server should be archived at least weekly. This is important because the event logs fill up quickly, depending on the activity on a server. By keeping the log files relatively small in length, they are much easier to review and filter. You should retain your event log archives for at least three months, so you have the ability to research an issue that may be have been occurring for some time or that has been intermittent.

Monthly Tasks

In addition to any actions prescribed in your disaster plan concerning backups and their retention (see the "Data Integrity Actions" section later in the chapter), you should perform the following tasks, at least once a month:

▼   Review and archive the IIS logs, which, like the event logs, can be a valuable source of information about system use and performance. If you don't review and archive these logs regularly, they can become unwieldy to use in tracking down a problem. If your MOSS environment has a high volume of site and page access activity, you may need to review and archive the IIS logs more frequently than once a month. You can find the IIS logs in the C:\WINDOWS\system32\LogFiles folder.

■   Validate the last full backup of each server. Depending on how much activity is on the server and how often you take a full backup of the servers, you should verify the backup of each server. The worse time to find out your backups are faulty is not when you need them. Should a disaster ever strike your network, users will want you to restore the MOSS environment as quickly as possible. One of the best ways to verify a backup is to restore it to a test server. Your disaster plan or data integrity plan should specify a formal procedure for testing and verifying backups.

■   Verify the integrity of your server's file systems using the Windows CHKDSK utility. CHKDSK can be run in an interactive mode that allows you to address any issues identified. You can start the CHKDSK utility from a command prompt or from the Properties menu of each disk drive listed on the My Computer window. On the Disk Properties window's Tools tab, click the Check Now button to start this utility (see Figure 14-9).

▲ Test your server's uninterruptible power supply (UPS) to ensure its readiness. A power failure is not the time to learn your UPS has failed. Refer to your UPS's documentation for the instructions to its test procedures.

Quarterly Tasks

In addition to the monthly tasks listed in the preceding section, you should also perform the following tasks at least once per quarter:

▼ Change all user passwords on a regular schedule (at least quarterly), following the procedures outlined in your security plan. A complex password should be at least eight characters in length and include a random mix of letters (uppercase and lowercase), numbers, and symbols.

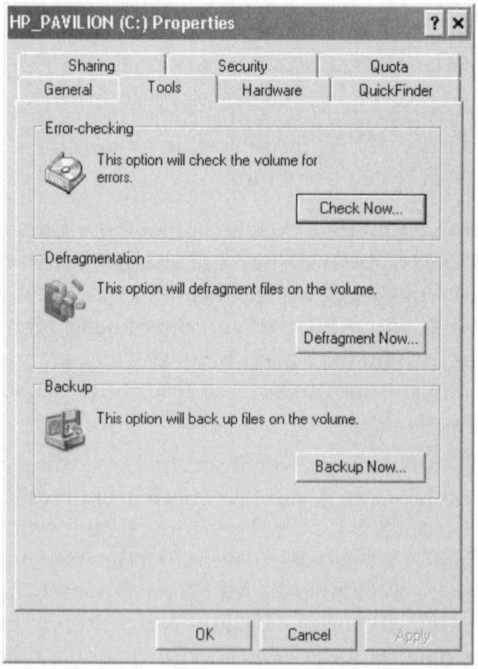

Figure 14-9. Use the Check Now button to start the CHKDSK utility for a disk drive.

▲   Incorporate any procedural notes accumulated during the quarter into your system documentation to ensure the documentation reflects the procedures actually in use. You should also update your server and system maintenance logs to reflect all installation, configuration, maintenance, and customization processes performed during the period. You may want to create a SharePoint site list for these activities in addition to a written record. This documentation can be invaluable in a disaster recovery effort, as well as providing a valuable history that can be used in troubleshooting performance issues.

As Required Tasks

On an infrequent basis, meaning whenever needed, you should test the performance of certain parts of your MOSS environment to ensure it continues to meet system expectations and user requirements. This testing can include processes to answer the following questions, among others:

▼   Is the top-level web site accessible in a timely fashion?

■   Are library and list content accessible?

■   Are e-mail alerts functioning properly?

▲   Does the search feature promptly return appropriate search results?

Another important system maintenance task that should be performed as needed is to conduct MOSS training. This training should teach users how to effectively make use of the system and emphasize the standards and best practices that have been adopted by your organization. You may find you need to conduct this training on a monthly or quarterly basis in a fairly new installation as you add more features to your MOSS environment.

DATA INTEGRITY ACTIONS

Taking a minimalist approach to ensuring the data integrity of your MOSS environment, you and your users can take advantage of the Recycle Bin feature. Like the Recycle Bin available in all Windows-based systems, the MOSS Recycle Bin allows users to restore items that have been accidentally or erroneously deleted from a site.

TIP   The Recycle Bin feature in MOSS 2007 is similar to that in Windows XP and Windows Server 2003. When an item is deleted, it's moved to the Recycle Bin, where it can be retrieved if it was deleted erroneously or by accident. Unless the Recycle Bin is emptied by a user beforehand, the items in the Recycle Bin are permanently removed automatically after 30 days. Each SharePoint site has its own Recycle Bin.

However, to ensure the data integrity of your entire MOSS environment, you must develop and execute a plan that guards against the loss of data on a larger scale as well. This plan should address the actions required to restore the system in the event of a disaster, such as power failure, hardware failure, fire, natural catastrophes (acts of God), and theft. Your plan, which is also referred to as a disaster recovery plan, must address the procedure to be used to restore your MOSS environment to its state in the moment preceding the disaster event.

Most of a disaster plan involves the safety, security, and alternative hardware solutions to disaster-induced situations. However, it must also address the procedures to be used on a regular basis to ensure the integrity of the data resources of your systems. For the most part, data integrity procedures address when and how data backups are taken and verified.

MOSS includes the functions needed to enable you to manage and perform backup and restore. MOSS backup and restore functions are able to back up an entire MOSS server farm, including its content and configuration data. However, in addition to the MOSS backup, you should also back up other essential parts of your systems, such as the operating system's configuration and runtime data, any file-based customizations, and IIS' configuration and content information.

MOSS Backup and Restore

Backup and restore jobs can be initiated from the Operations tab of the Central Administration page. The next two sections detail these actions separately.

MOSS Backups

MOSS backup and restore operations are performed from the MOSS Central Administration page. MOSS supports the creation of both full and differential server and server farm backups. A full backup essentially snapshots the local disk storage devices and copies everything to the backup media. A differential back copies only those files or objects that have been modified since the last full backup was taken.

A robust data integrity plan includes the creation of both types of backups. A full backup should be created, depending on the activity levels of the system, on a weekly basis, perhaps on a Saturday evening. To bridge the gap between the full backups, a differential backup should be created each evening, Sunday through Friday, to capture any changes made to the data resources that day.

Understand that as the week goes along, the differential back requires an increasing amount of media, as the number of data resources that have been modified increases. Using this type of a backup schedule, if the system were to crash on a Wednesday, Saturday's full backup and Tuesday's differential backup are used to restore the system back to the point at which the Tuesday backup was created. If you are in a high-volume environment, you may need to create a differential backup more often than once per day.

Immediately after you complete your MOSS installation and configuration, meaning the point where you are ready to allow users to access the MOSS environment, you should create a full backup of your server farm. This backup provides a benchmark and a disaster recovery backup should you need to completely rebuild the entire server farm. Full backups can be quite large and can take a considerable amount of time to complete. This first full backup should be a comprehensive backup. MOSS allows you to specify the elements you wish to include in your backups. You may want to create a system recovery backup once a month that captures everything on the server farm and then use a full backup that captures only your data content and configuration files in the intervening weeks.

Backup Location   MOSS requires a network path (network share) for the medium to which the backup is to be written. Although you can choose to create the backup on the same server, you can't specify a local path as a backup location—not that you'd want to do this anyway! The best choice for a backup location is to create a secure, hidden network share on which the MOSS administrator, the SQL service accounts, and any service accounts for individual features have full control permissions. Depending on the likelihood that you will need to restore all or part of the backup, you may want to use a local network server as the backup location, to quickly facilitate the restore, and then immediately archive the backup from that location to some form of removable media.

> **TIP**   Always review the log created by a backup job for any failure messages. You may need to assign additional permissions to the backup folder to ensure the backup operation completes successfully.

To assign the backup location to be used for your MOSS backup, perform the following steps:

1. On the server you wish to use as the backup location, create a new folder with a distinctive name, such as MOSSBackups or the like, in a primary partition that is also backed up (in a separate operation, of course).

2. Right-click the folder icon of the new folder and select Sharing And Security from the pop-up menu that appears (see Figure 14-10).

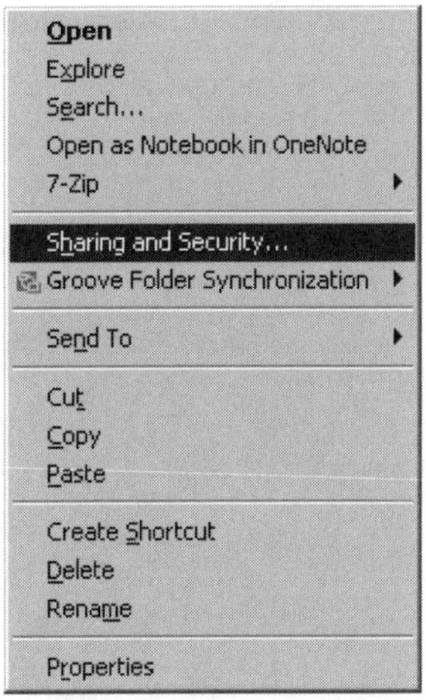

Figure 14-10.   The Sharing And Security option on the pop-up menu of the new backup location folder.

3. On the Sharing tab of the folder's Properties dialog box, select the Share This Folder option and enter a share name for the folder, such as MOSSBackups, as illustrated in Figure 14-11.

4. On the Sharing tab, click the Permissions button, and on its dialog box (see Figure 14-12), applying the principle of least privilege, select only those accounts that need this specific access. If you wish to allow all users this privilege, highlight Everyone in the Group Or User Names pane and check the Full Control checkbox in the Allow column of the Permissions For Everyone pane.

NOTE The principle of least privilege recommends granting permissions to only those accounts that actually require a specific access. This is discussed more fully on the MS TechNet site (http://technet .microsoft.com/en-us/office/bb267362.aspx).

5. Click the Apply button and then the OK button to save these settings and close the dialog box.

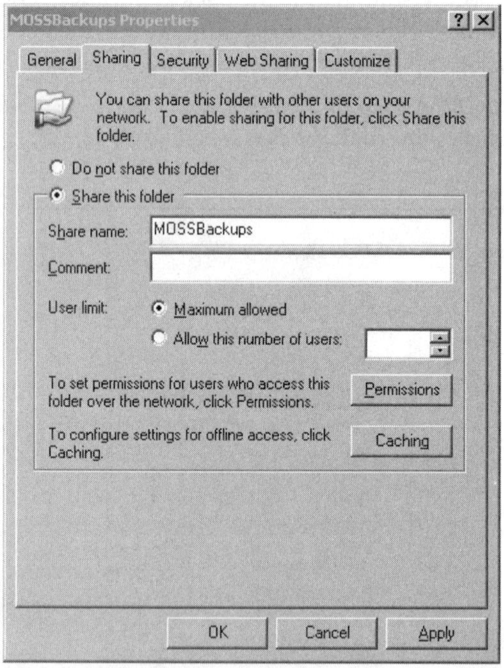

Figure 14-11. The Sharing tab of the backup folder's Properties dialog box.

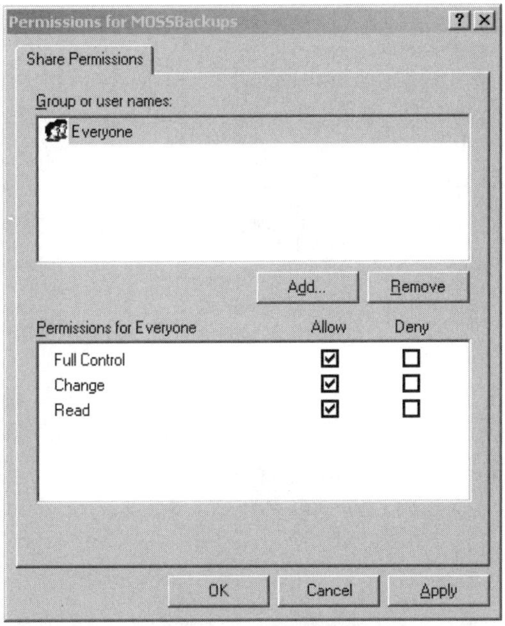

Figure 14-12.   The Permissions dialog box for a backup folder.

6. On the folder Properties dialog box, select the Security tab to open the Security dialog box.

7. Click the Advanced button to display the Advanced Security Settings for your new folder (see Figure 14-13).

8. Unselect (uncheck) the checkbox labeled as Allow Inheritable Permissions From The Parent To Propagate From This Object And All Child Objects. Include These With Entries Explicitly Defined Here.

9. In the Permission Entries pane, highlight any Users groups and click the Remove button.

10. Click the Apply button and then the OK button to save these settings and close the dialog box.

Perform an MOSS Backup   To create an MOSS backup, perform the following steps:

1. Open the Central Administration page, select the Operations tab, and click the Perform A Backup link under the Backup And Restore heading.

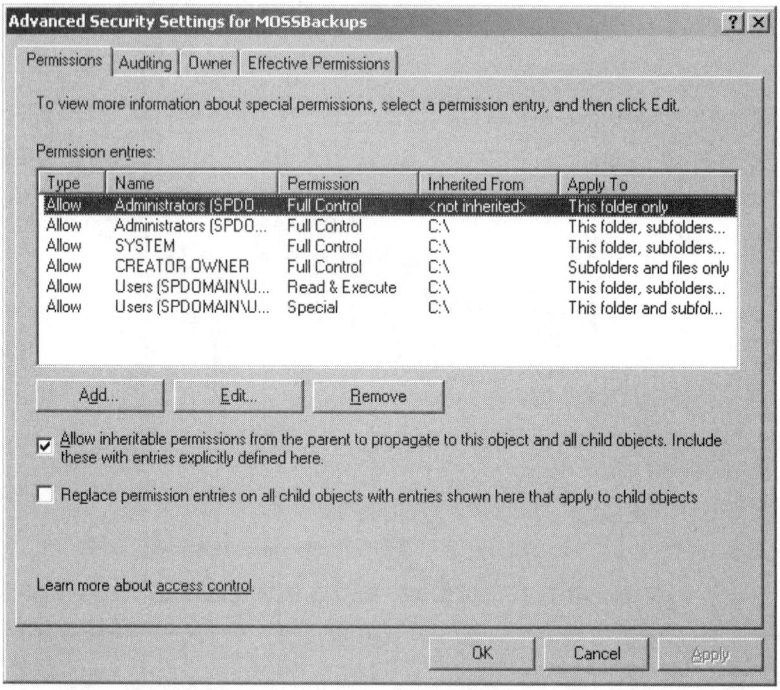

Figure 14-13. The Advanced Security Settings dialog box for a backup folder.

2. On the Perform A Backup – Step 1 Of 2 page (see Figure 14-14), the MOSS components on the server farm (or standalone server) are displayed in a hierarchy. Selecting the higher-level component automatically selects all of the components beneath it. Use the checkboxes to indicate which components should be included in the backup to be created.

3. After indicating the elements to be included in the backup, click the Continue To Backup Options button to move to the Start Backup—Step 2 Of 2 page (see Figure 14-15).

4. In the Type Of Backup section, select the type of backup you wish to perform: either a Full backup or a Differential backup.

5. In the Backup File Location section, enter the location to which you want to write the backup. The location address must be in the form of a network share, such as \\BackupServer\MOSSBackups\.

6. Click the OK button to start the backup operation.

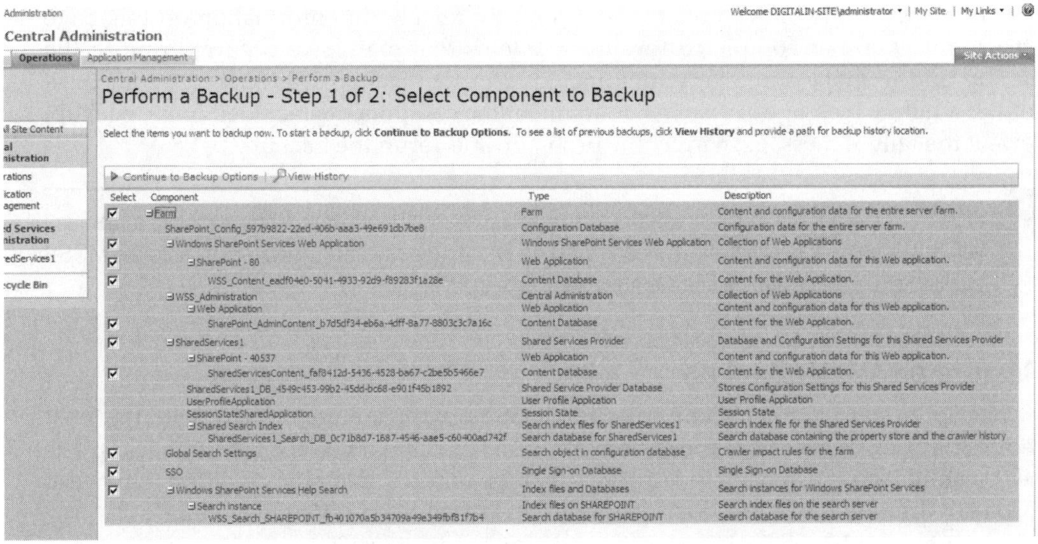

Figure 14-14. The Perform A Backup—Step 1 Of 2: Select Component To Backup page.

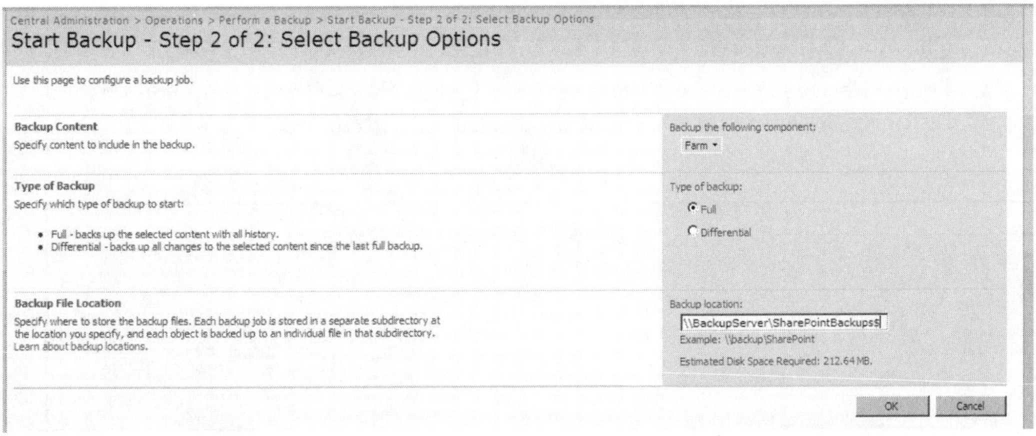

Figure 14-15. The Start Backup—Step 2 Of 2: Select Backup Options page.

After the backup has started, the Backup And Restore Status page should display the current status of the backup operation. Carefully review the information on this page after the backup has completed for any problems that may have occurred during the backup and to make sure everything included in the backup was backed up successfully. If a failure message is displayed for any of the components included in the backup, review the failure message, correct the problem, and rerun the backup.

> **NOTE** If the backup location used in this process was not the location of a removable medium, you may want to use either the Windows Backup or a third-party backup system to write the MOSS backup to a medium that can be stored in an off-site location.

Restore an MOSS Backup

If you ever need to restore all or part of an MOSS backup, be sure you start with the most recent full backup to restore the system to its last benchmark. Once the full backup has been restored, you then need to restore each of the differential backups, oldest to newest, (Monday through Friday, for example) until you reach the point of the failure.

To restore an MOSS backup, perform the following steps:

1. Open the Central Administration page, select the Operations tab, and click the Restore From Backup link under the Backup And Restore heading.

2. The Restore From Backup process includes four steps. On the Restore From Backup—Step 1 Of 4 page (see Figure 14-16), enter the backup location from which you wish to restore, using its network share address, such as \\BackupServer\MOSSBackups.

3. Click the OK button to move to the next restore step (see Figure 14-17).

4. On the Restore From Backup—Step 2 Of 4 page, choose the backup you wish to restore by selecting the radio button associated with it.

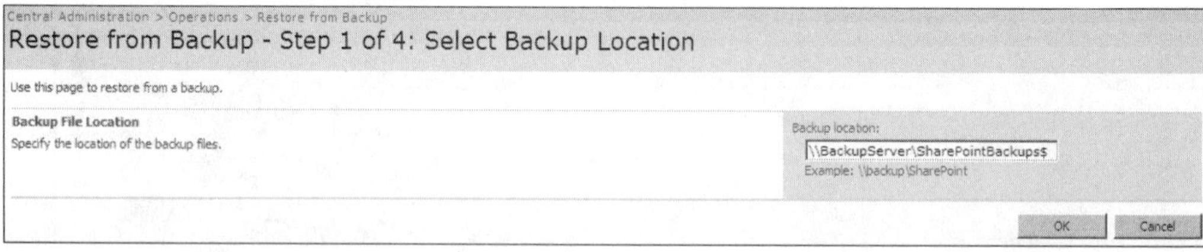

Central Administration > Operations > Restore from Backup
Restore from Backup - Step 1 of 4: Select Backup Location

Use this page to restore from a backup.

Backup File Location
Specify the location of the backup files.

Backup location:
\\BackupServer\SharePointBackups$
Example: \\backup\SharePoint

OK   Cancel

Figure 14-16. The Restore From Backup—Step 1 Of 4: Select Backup Location page.

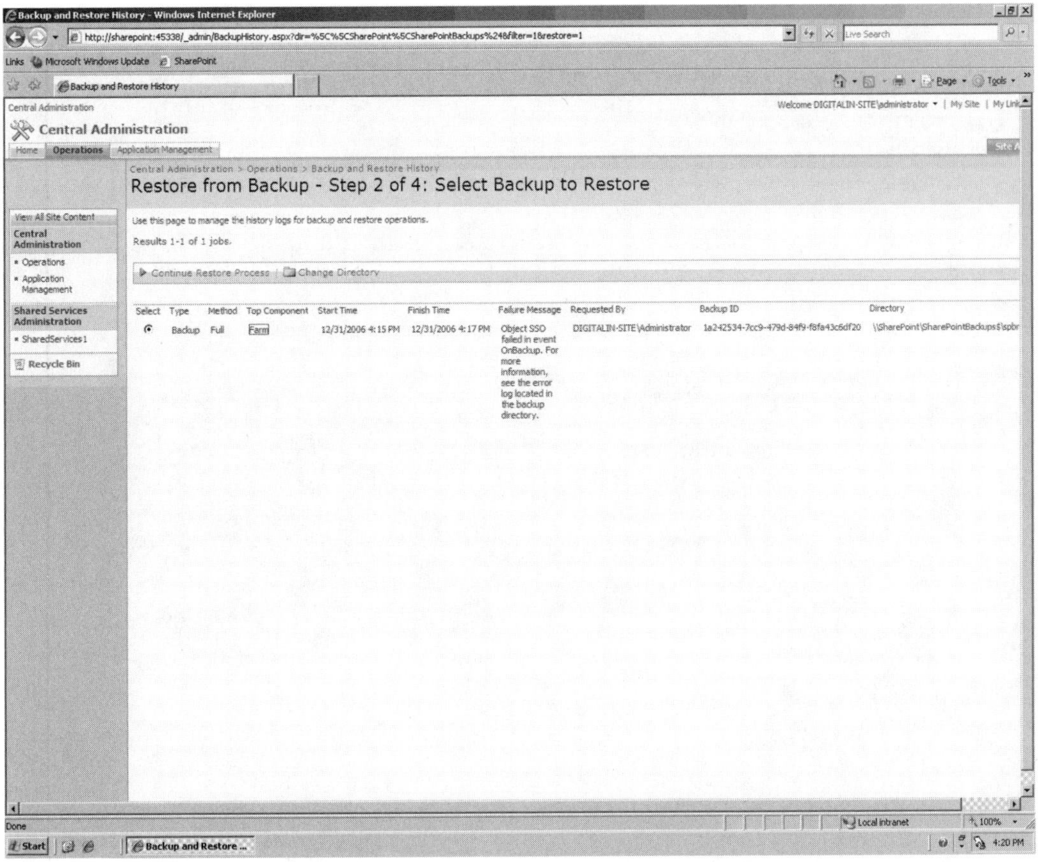

Figure 14-17.   The Restore From Backup—Step 2 Of 4: Select Backup To Restore page.

5. Click the Continue Restore Process button to move to the Restore From Backup—Step 3 Of 4 page (see Figure 14-18).

6. On the Restore From Backup—Step 3 Of 4 page, select the components you wish to restore. The hierarchy displayed duplicates that used to create the backup (see Figure 14-10). Depending on the type of restore you are performing, choose a single component, a component group, or the whole farm to be restored.

7. Click the Continue Restore Process button to move to the Restore From Backup—Step 4 Of 4 page (see Figure 14-19).

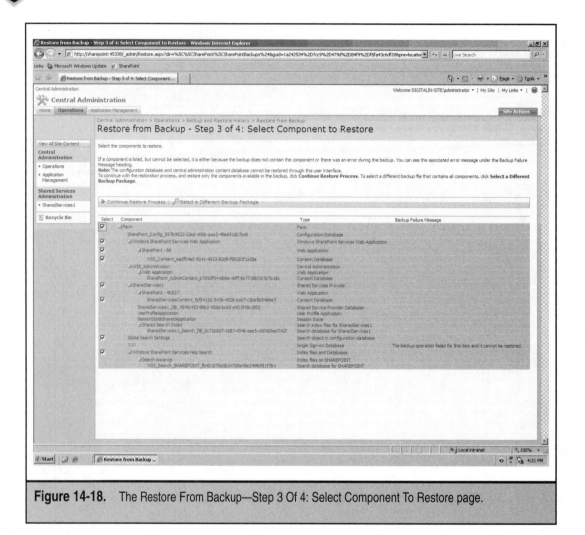

Figure 14-18. The Restore From Backup—Step 3 Of 4: Select Component To Restore page.

8. On the Restore From Backup—Step 4 Of 4 page, select the type of restore you wish to perform. Your choices are:

   a. **New configuration** Choose this option if you are restoring a backup to new hardware or creating a new configuration of all or part of your MOSS environment. If you choose this option, you are prompted to keep or define new web application URLs and database server settings.

   b. **Same configuration** Choose this option if you are restoring a backup to the same MOSS server farm retaining its configuration.

9. Click the OK button to begin the restore operation.

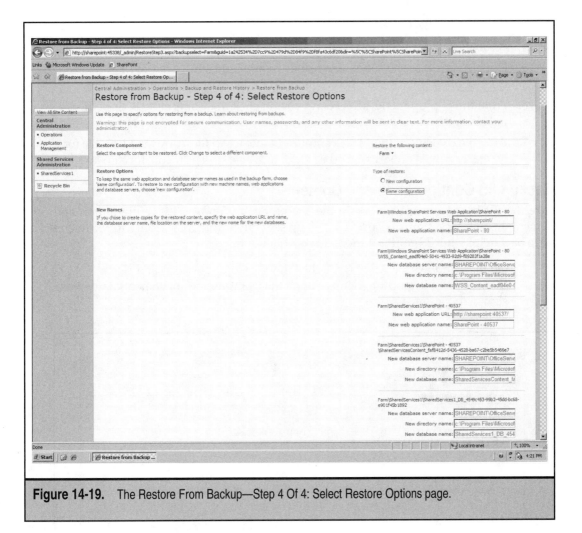

Figure 14-19. The Restore From Backup—Step 4 Of 4: Select Restore Options page.

Backup File-Based Customizations

If you have created any file-based customizations in your MOSS environment, like adding additional file type icons, such as a PDF file icon, these items must be backed up separately from, and outside of, the MOSS backup operation. Any file-based customizations are stored in the files in the C:\Program Files\Common Files\Microsoft Shared\web server extensions\12\ folder. To capture this folder and all of its associated subfolders, which are necessary for disaster recovery purposes, perform the following steps:

1. From the Windows Desktop, open the My Computer window and double-click the C: drive icon.

2. On the C: drive's window, double-click the Program Files folder to display its contents.

3. Double-click the Common Files folder.

4. Double-click the Microsoft Shared folder.

5. Double-click the web server extensions folder and right-click the 12 (representing Microsoft Office version 12) folder to open its pop-up menu.

6. From the pop-up menu, select Send To and click the Compressed (zipped) Folder option.

7. After the contents of the 12 are compressed into a .zip file, copy the 12.zip file (or whatever name you've assigned it) to a removable storage media for safe-keeping.

Backup IIS Configuration and Content

Like the file-based customizations in the preceding section, the IIS configuration and content on each server must also be backed up separately and apart from MOSS. To create a backup of your IIS configuration, do the following:

1. On the Windows Desktop, right-click the My Computer icon and select Manage from its pop-up menu to open the Computer Management dialog box, shown in Figure 14-20.

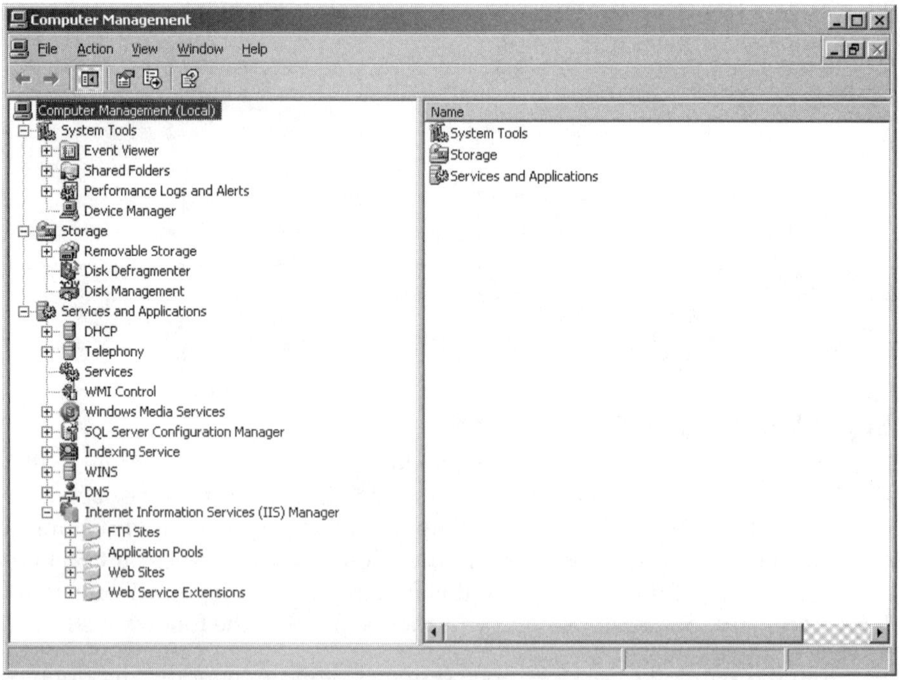

Figure 14-20.   The Computer Management dialog box.

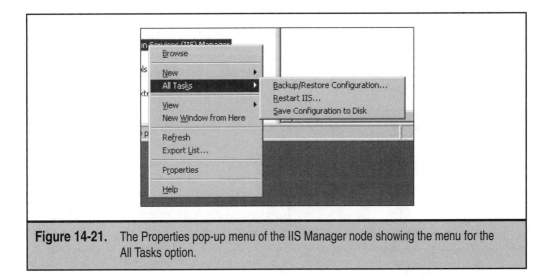

Figure 14-21. The Properties pop-up menu of the IIS Manager node showing the menu for the All Tasks option.

2. In the left-hand pane, find and expand the Services And Applications node.

3. Under Services And Applications, find and expand the IIS Manager node.

4. Right-click the IIS Manager node to display its pop-up menu (see Figure 14-21).

5. Select All Tasks to open its menu and then click the Backup/Restore Configuration... option.

6. In the Configuration Backup/Restore dialog box that displays, click the Create Backup button to display the Configuration Backup dialog box (see Figure 14-22).

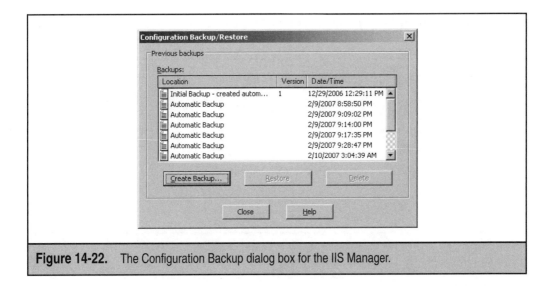

Figure 14-22. The Configuration Backup dialog box for the IIS Manager.

7. In the Configuration Backup Name box, enter a name that clearly identifies the backup to be created, such as "iismetabasemmddyyyy" where mmddyyyy is the current date.

8. Check the Encrypt Backup Using Password checkbox and then enter and confirm a password.

NOTE If you encrypt the IIS Configuration backup file, you are able to restore this configuration to another physical server. However, if you choose not to encrypt this file, the backup can only be restored to the current server.

9. Click the OK button to start the backup operation.

10. When the backup completes, the backup file you've just created is listed in the Backups pane of the Configuration Backup/Restore dialog box. Two files are created using the filename you entered, one with a .MD0 extension and one with a .SC0 extension, in the C:\Windows\system32\inetsrv\MetaBack folder.

11. Copy the new backup files to a removable storage media for safe-keeping.

To create a backup of your IIS content, repeat the steps used to back up the IIS configuration, with the exception that the IIS content should be located in the C:\Inetpub\ folder, by default.

REPAIR MOSS

Should MOSS become corrupt, you can attempt to repair the installation by inserting the MOSS distribution media and selecting the Repair option, shown in Figure 14-23. When the repair operation has completed, you are prompted to reboot the server. After the server reboots, run the SharePoint Technology Configuration Wizard. When the wizard

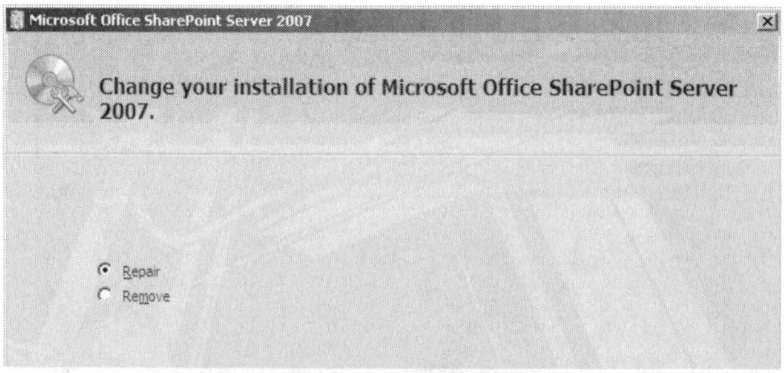

Figure 14-23. The MOSS installation options.

has completed, your MOSS environment should be fully functioning. The repair operation doesn't restore any damaged or deleted content.

> **NOTE**   Should you need to uninstall MOSS for any reason, run the SharePoint Technology Configuration Wizard immediately afterward, even if you plan to reinstall MOSS.

SUMMARY

Careful planning and attention to maintenance will increase SharePoint availability and reliability. Regularly recurring tasks for the administrator to complete—such as backups, reviewing Event Logs, changing passwords, and monitoring hard drive space—are only half of the maintenance puzzle. You should periodically review and monitor the site content in the MOSS environment to ensure it remains current, relevant, logically presented, and adheres to organizational standards.

Backups are an important part of any disaster recovery and data integrity plans. You should perform frequent backups of the MOSS system and its related services, using a regular schedule. Typically, a full backup is created weekly and differential backups are created daily to provide a current restore point for the system.

CHAPTER 15

Web Parts

Across the Web, web sites are commonly crammed with information, some to the point of overwhelming users. The concept of using predefined building blocks of content to construct a portal web site (such as those available from Google, Yahoo, and MSN) allows users to organize and personalize the content to suit their needs. To do this, these web sites are created from independent web page blocks (parts) that a user can include, omit, arrange, and color to fit his or her particular working or viewing needs and save the configuration of the web page so it displays consistently the same when accessed in the future.

On an MOSS system, one of more portal pages are able to satisfy the general information and data access needs for a majority of its users, without the designer trying to satisfy the needs of every single user with one or two static web page designs. In the MOSS environment, the use of Web Parts, Web zones, and Web Parts pages enable the designer to create portal pages that allow the user the flexibility to include, omit, and arrange the content he or she desires on his or her particular customized web page view.

The functionality of the Web Parts framework and its three primary building blocks, Web Parts, Web Parts zones, and Web Parts pages provide a relatively easy means of creating flexible and functional SharePoint web applications. These MOSS elements allow you to easily pull together dynamic web pages with incredible browser-based functionality, using nothing more than a web browser and a mouse.

Understanding Web Parts, Web Parts pages, and Web Parts zones is the key to creating custom web pages and making them available to your network's users. This chapter explains each of the Web Parts elements and how easy it is to get started creating web pages for your MOSS environment's users. The Visual Studio 2005 suite can be used to create customized Web Parts, but let's focus on the basics and how to assemble a Web Parts Page through MOSS functions and services.

WEB PARTS PAGE COMPONENTS

A SharePoint portal is constructed from three basic building blocks: Web Parts, Web Parts zones, and a Web Parts page. Web Parts are inserted into Web Parts zones within the framework of a Web Parts page. A Web Parts page is actually an ASP.NET (.aspx) web page into which one or more Web Parts can be included. A Web Parts zone is a container that applies a particular set of properties to the Web Part(s) placed into it. These building blocks are explained in the following sections.

Web Parts

A Web Part is the basic building block of the SharePoint world. Web Parts are atomic, which means that each is designed to provide an independent web page element typically with a single purpose. Web Parts are also reusable in that multiple instances of a Web Part can be included and published in one or more Web Parts pages.

Web Part Flexibility

To gain a basic understanding of how Web Parts can be used to create a portal or web page, take a moment to look at the customizable portal pages for any of the more frequently used access services, such as Google, Yahoo, or MSN. Figure 15-1 shows a view of one such portal page. On this portal, each of the content blocks (parts) can be moved, omitted, or added to suit the user's desires.

A Web Part is configured using a set of properties that define how it is to perform its particular tasks independently of other instances of similar Web Parts. A Web Part is defined to perform one simple function, such as displaying Outlook calendar information, publishing an RSS feed, or summarizing recent Blog posts.

Web Parts Controls

Each Web Part functions according to how it is defined a control set that is made up of three primary functional controls (see Figure 15-2):

▼ **Personalization** The foundation control of Web Part functionality. This control allows a user to modify a Web Part (and its inclusion, omission, or placement on a Web Parts page) and save the user's personalization data to the ASP.NET application services database for future browser sessions.

TIP The ASP.NET application services database, where personalization data (as well as other Web Part control data) is automatically created the first time a Web Part is customized.

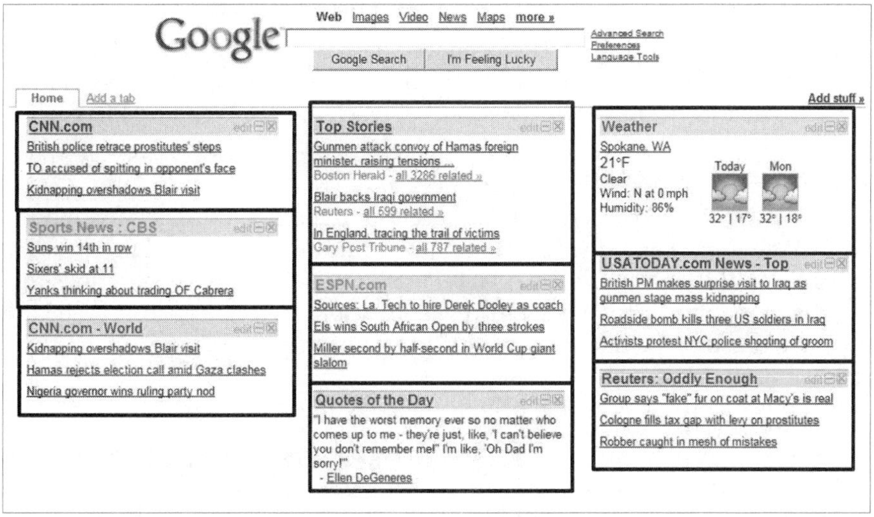

Figure 15-1. An example of how Web Parts are used to construct a portal page.

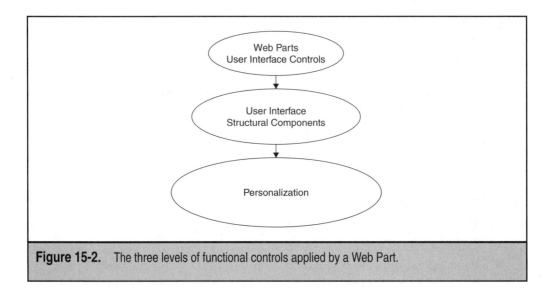

Figure 15-2. The three levels of functional controls applied by a Web Part.

■ **User interface (UI) structural components** Provide the basic structure and services for all Web Parts control sets. Within the UI structural components, perhaps the most important is the Web Part Manager control, which manages the functionality of all of the Web Parts and Web Parts zones on a Web Parts page, including the various display modes available. Another important control component within the UI controls is the Zone Manager that controls the visual presentation of the Web Parts within a Web Parts zone.

▲ **Web Parts UI Controls** The primary UI on a Web Parts Page. This flexible control set supports virtually all of the options and properties used to create the particular set of controls needed when creating a Web Parts Page.

Web Parts Display Modes

A Web Parts Page can be presented in a variety of display modes, as defined in the UI controls. A Web Parts page display mode determines which UI objects are active, disabled, visible, or hidden from view. A Web Parts page's display mode defines the extent to which a user is able to personalize the page view and user interface. A Web Parts page can only have one display mode active at a time, but the user can be allowed to change the display mode, if desired.

A Web Parts control set has five primary display modes:

▼ **Browse** Displays the Web Parts defined in a Web Parts page as prescribed by the browser's settings.

■ **Catalog** Allows users to add, remove, or drag page controls from a catalog of UI objects.

■ **Connect** Allows users to manage connections, including the ability to connect or disconnect to Web Part controls.

- ■ **Design** Allows users to drag Web Parts around on a page to customize the page layout.
- ▲ **Edit** Allows users to edit Web Part controls on a page, including dragging the controls.

Web Parts Zones

A Web Parts zone can be configured on a Web Parts page to contain, control, arrange, and format a Web Part. A Web Part placed in a Web Parts zone can be customized, located, added, or omitted by the user in their browser. However, not all Web Parts must be placed in a Web Parts zone, only those you wish to allow the user to have control over.

When a Web Part is placed into a Web Parts zone, the properties of the Web Part are placed in the content database associated with MOSS and not in the ASPX page itself. By locating a Web Part in a Web Parts zone, users are able to manipulate the Web Part(s) in that zone through their browsers. On the other hand, the properties of a Web Part not placed in a Web Parts zone are placed into the ASPX web page and not into the content database, which, in effect, hard codes the Web Part as a fixed portion of the web page.

Figure 15-3 illustrates how Web Parts zones relate to a Web Parts page and how a Web Part relates to a Web Parts zone. At the top (block "A") of the Web Parts page, a Web Part has been placed into the Web Parts page, but not into a Web Parts zone. The ASP.NET coding and properties for this Web Part are added into the coding of the ASPX Web Parts page definition.

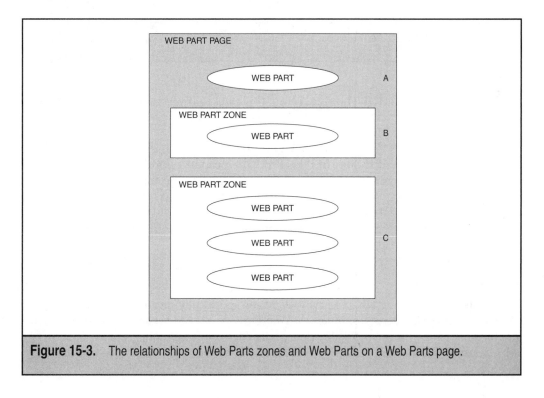

Figure 15-3. The relationships of Web Parts zones and Web Parts on a Web Parts page.

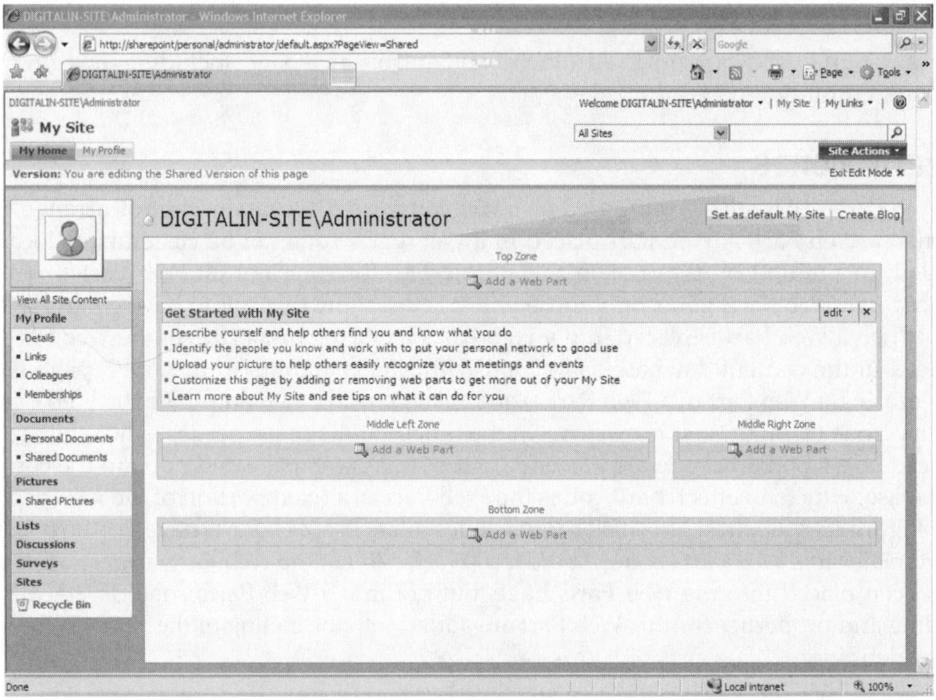

Figure 15-4. An MOSS Web Parts page template showing Web Parts zones.

Block "B" in Figure 15-3 shows a Web Parts zone into which a single Web Part has been inserted. The properties for this Web Part are stored in the MOSS content database, which lets the user modify this Web Part.

Block "C" in Figure 15-3 shows a Web Parts zone into which multiple Web Parts have been inserted. Like the Web Part in Block "B," the properties of the Web Parts in Block "C" are stored in the content database and the Web Parts can be manipulated by the user. The Web Parts in a Web Parts zone can be arranged vertically, as shown, or horizontally to create the initial or default view of the portal page.

Figure 15-4 shows the actual construction shell of a Web Parts page with Web Parts zones and Web Part areas predefined.

Web Parts Pages

Web Parts pages are ASP.NET (.aspx) web pages specifically created for displaying Web Parts zones and Web Parts. Essentially, a Web Parts page is an organized set of Web Parts put together for the purpose of listing data or displaying information, graphics, or both, and which is available to—and possibly customizable by—all or a group of specified users.

The MOSS environment offers a variety of Web Parts page templates that include several different page layouts, one of which is likely to work in most standard situations. Unique or proprietary pages can also be created using Visual Studio 2005.

When you are just getting started with MOSS, the simplest way to create a Web Parts page is to use either the SharePoint Portal Server Area or the My Site feature. In the next two sections, we look at the SharePoint Server Area, followed by how the My Site feature is used to create a Web Parts page.

Create a Web Parts Page Using a SharePoint Portal Server Area

To create a Web Parts page using the SharePoint Portal Server facilities, perform the following steps:

1. With the MOSS 2007 running, open the SharePoint Central Administration service to display the SharePoint Administration Home page, shown in Figure 15-5.

2. Locate the Site Actions pull-down menu on the right-hand side of the page and click it to drop down the menu list (as shown in Figure 15-5).

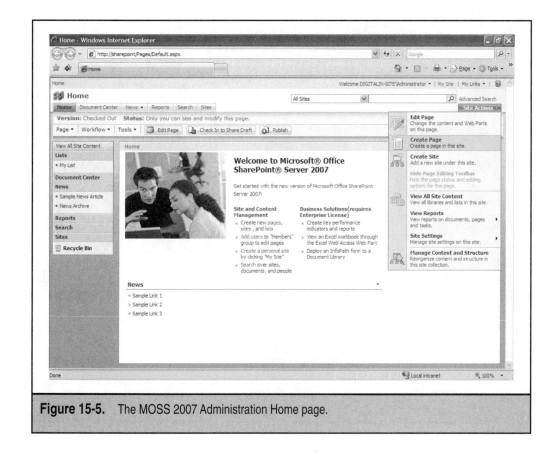

Figure 15-5. The MOSS 2007 Administration Home page.

3. On the Site Actions menu, choose the Create Page option to display the Create page, shown in Figure 15-6.

4. In the lower right-hand side of the Page Layout area, choose a page layout type from the list, such as "(Welcome Page) Welcome Page with Web Part zones."

5. Enter a title and description (optional) for the new Web Parts page. The title is required, but the description, although optional, can be helpful to users when the page is listed in a catalogue.

TIP   By default, MOSS uses the title as the URL name. However, the URL name should be something short, easily remembered, and easily typed by users. So you should feel free to enter a more descriptive URL name.

6. Click Create to have MOSS create your Web Part page and load it as your current page so you can begin customizing it with Web Parts.

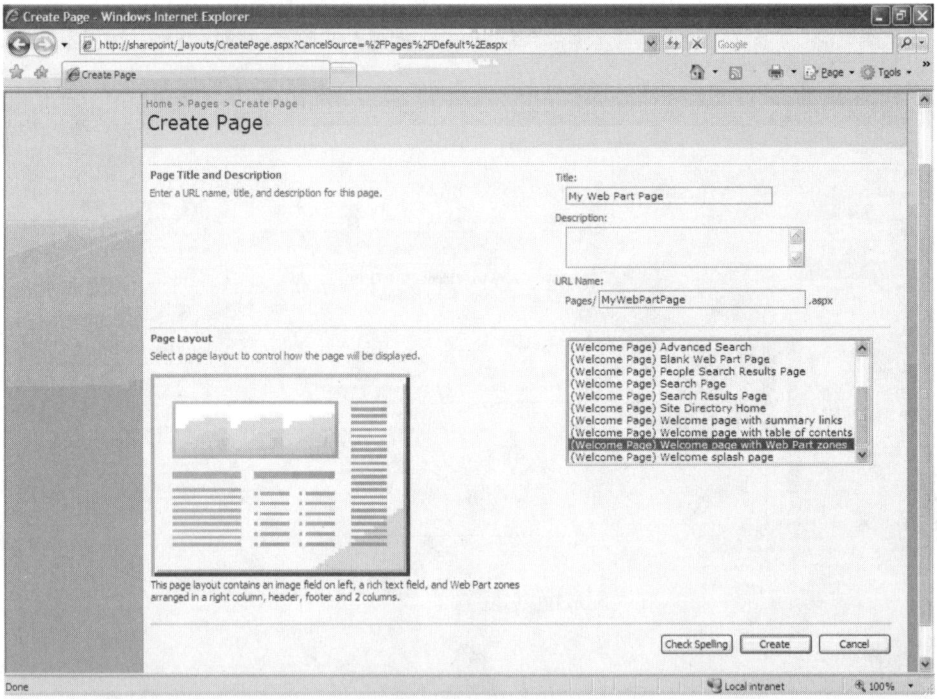

Figure 15-6.   The MOSS 2007 Create page.

Create a Web Parts Page Using My Site

The My Site service was introduced with SharePoint Portal Server 2003 and has been retained as a part of MOSS 2007. My Site facilitates the creation of a personal SharePoint site that includes personalization and customized content. Typically, the site created will contain specific content targeted to a particular group of users. The site provides quick links to a user's documents, colleagues, commonly used web sites, and also supports personal alerts for portal content changes. My Site pages also support both a public view, for access by others, and a private view, for use by the owner.

To create a My Site page, perform the following steps:

1. On the Navigation Bar of the Portal site, choose the My Site option to display the My Site administration page, shown in Figure 15-7.

2. Select the Create Site option on the Site Actions Menu.

3. Click Create to create the site and display the Create page, shown in Figure 15-8.

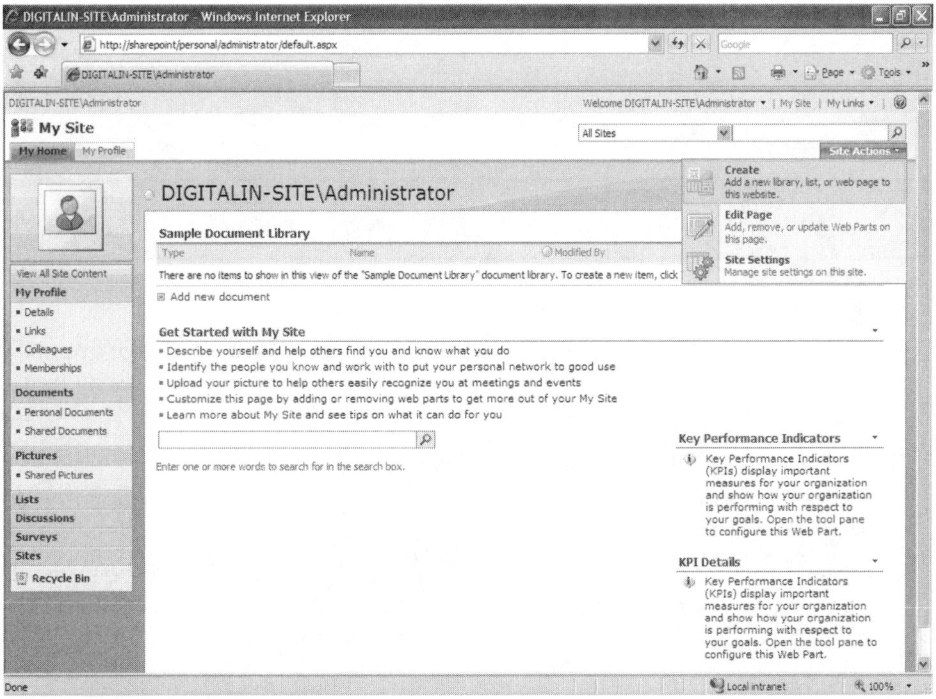

Figure 15-7. The SharePoint My Site administration page.

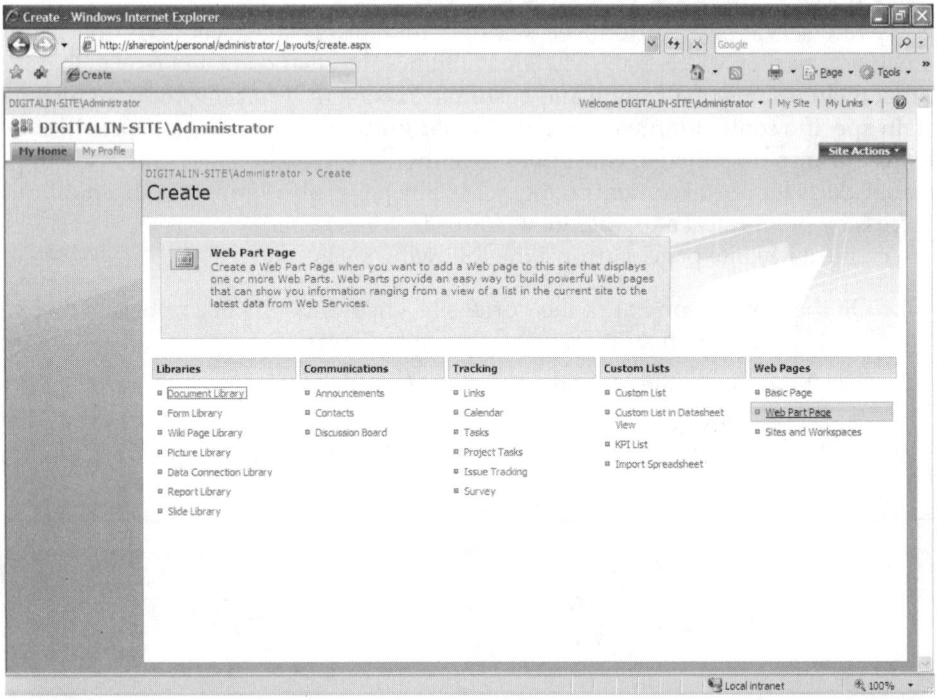

Figure 15-8. The SharePoint My Site Create page.

4. In the far right-hand Web Pages column, choose the Web Part Page option (as shown in Figure 15-8). The New Web Part Page screen will display (see Figure 15-9).

5. Enter a name for the new Web Part page.

6. Choose a layout template (Header, Footer, 3 Column is very functional, unless another template better meets your needs).

7. Select a document library where you'd like the Web Part page to be saved. If you wish to share the page with others, choose Shared Documents. Otherwise, choose the Personal Documents option to make the page unshared and private only to you.

8. Click Create to have SharePoint create your Web Part page, save it to the document library indicated, and then load the Web Part page as your current page so you can begin customizing it with Web Parts.

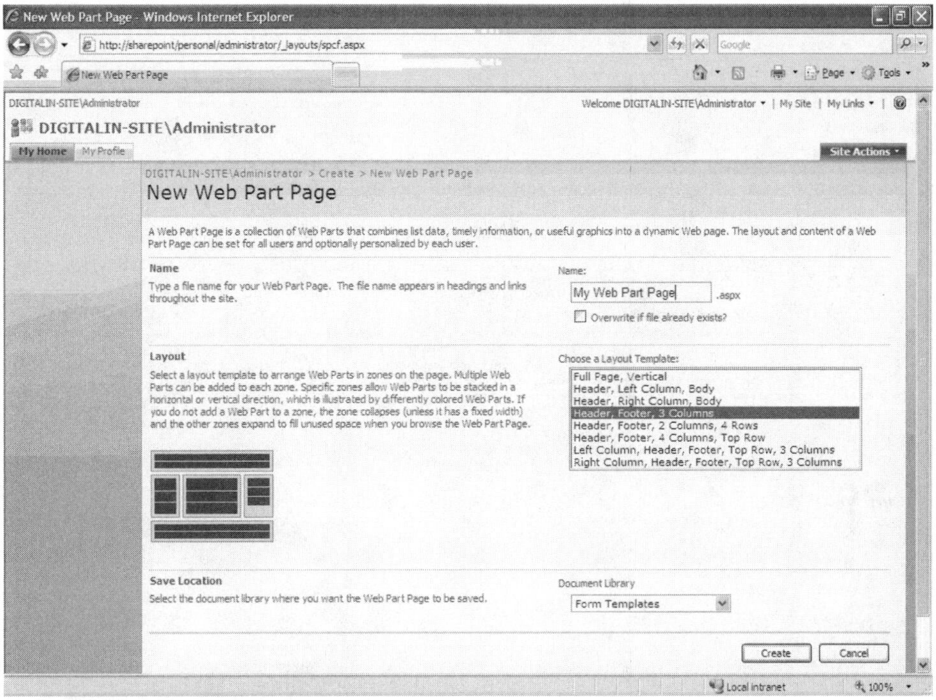

Figure 15-9. The SharePoint My Site New Web Part Page screen.

Adding Web Parts to a Web Parts page

SharePoint displays an Add A Web Part button for each Web Parts zone on a Web Parts page, as shown in Figure 15-10. Clicking the Add A Web Part button launches the Add Web Parts dialogue box (see Figure 15-11) in simple mode. Simple mode suggests Web Parts that are appropriate for that specific Web Parts zone. If the Web Part you want to add is not suggested, you can always expand the All Web Parts node, which categorizes Web Parts by function.

Clicking the Advanced Web Part Gallery And Options link at the bottom of the page opens a design interface (see Figure 15-12) that can be used to quickly drag and drop multiple Web Parts into Web Parts zones.

Keep in mind that not all users' monitors will be set to the same screen resolution. Reserve the upper left corner of your Web Parts page for your most important Web Part, then work your way to the right, and down. This will ensure that no matter what screen resolution your users are running at, your most important data will be visible without the need for users to scroll vertically or horizontally.

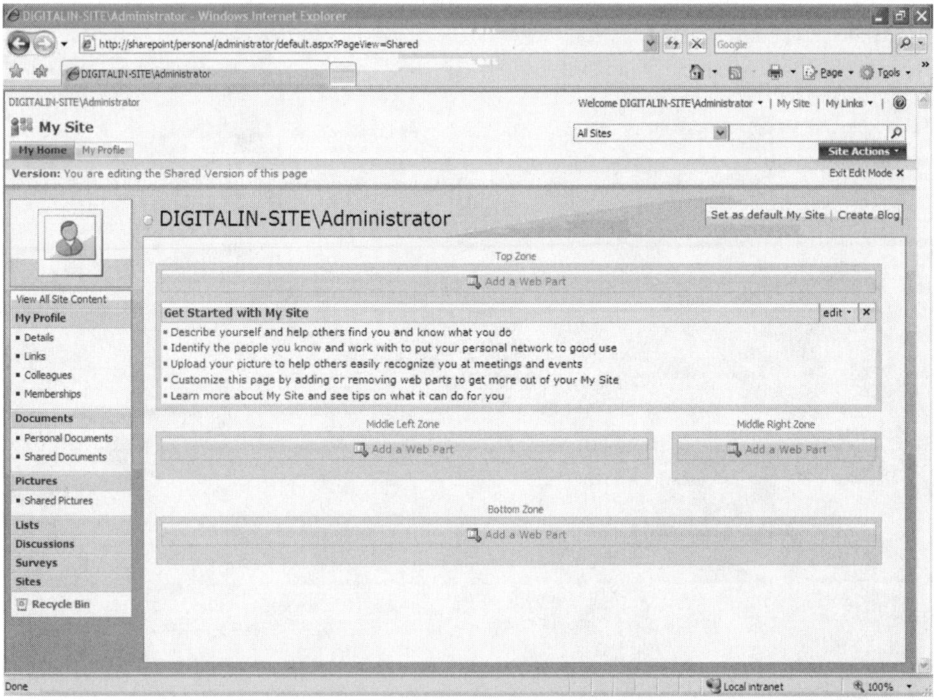

Figure 15-10. The MOSS Add Web Part page.

The Web Part Menu

Each Web Part has a menu that can be accessed by clicking the small black triangle in the right corner of the title bar.

The Web Part menu options include (see Figure 15-13):

▼ **Minimize**   Hides the Web Part content, and displays only the title.

■ **Close**   Closes the Web Part. The Web Part is no longer displayed on the page and is moved to the Closed Web Part Gallery.

■ **Modify Shared Web Part**   Used to change Web Part properties.

■ **Export**   Creates a Web Part Description (DWP) file, which is an XML file containing all of the current Web Part's property settings, as well as a reference to the Web Part's assembly (DLL).

▲ **Help**   Displays an external HTML-based help file, if one has been assigned using the Help URL property.

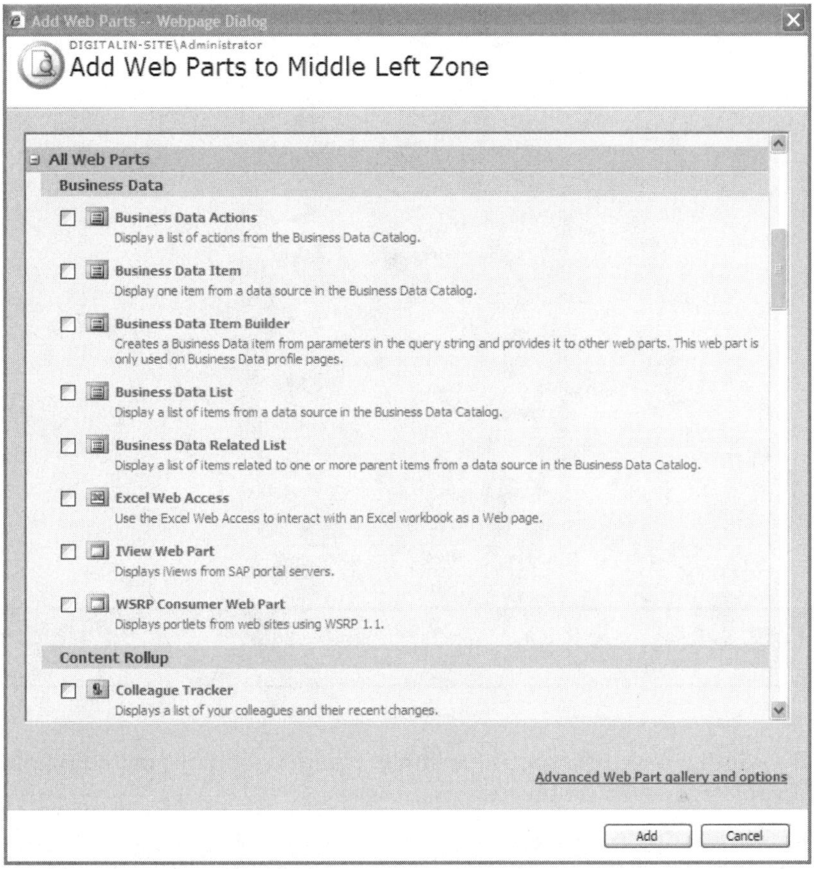

Figure 15-11.   The MOSS Add Web Parts (simple mode) page.

Web Part Properties

All Web Parts share some common properties that control how the Web Part looks and what users can do with it.

These properties include:

▼   **Appearance** (see Figure 15-14)

■   **Title**   Assigns a title to the Web Part, which is searchable.

■   **Height**   Assigns a specific height in a variety of units, including pixels, points, or even centimeters or inches.

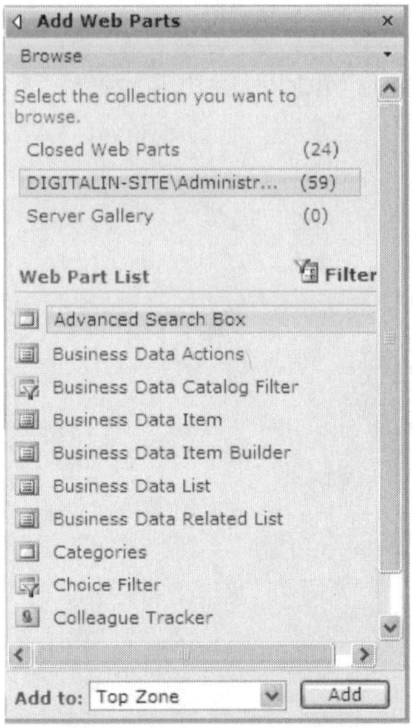

Figure 15-12. Adding a Web Part to a Web Parts zone.

- **Width** Assigns a specific width in a variety of units, including pixels, points, or even centimeters or inches.

- **Chrome State** Minimized or normal. When set to minimize, only the title of the Web Part is displayed. Users can restore the Web Part to view its contents. Useful for saving screen real estate.

- **Chrome Type** Defines how to display the Web Part.

  - **Default** Displays the title, border, and Web Part contents.

  - **None** Displays only Web Part content and hides the title and border.

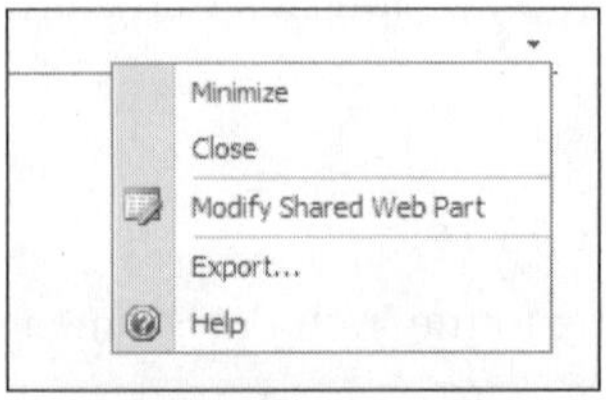

Figure 15-13. The Web Part menu.

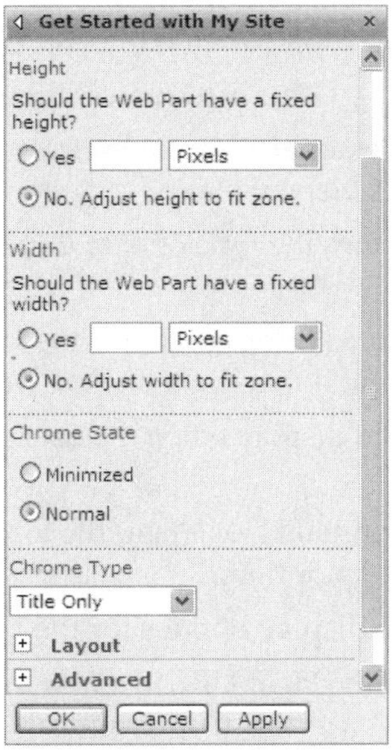

Figure 15-14.   The Appearance Properties dialog box.

- **Title and Border**   Displays only the title and border.
- **Title Only**   Displays only the title.
- **Border Only**   Displays Web Part content with a border.

■ **Layout**

- **Hidden**   Hides Web Parts present on the page to filter, feed data, or otherwise provide additional functionality to other Web Parts. Hidden Web Parts will only be visible when editing the Web Parts page.

- **Direction**   Specifies the text order: left to right or right to left. When set to "None" (the default), the direction is determined by the operating system's language settings.

- **Zone**   Designates the Web Parts zone the Web Part is currently assigned to.

- **Zone Index**   Determines the order in which the Web Part is displayed in the Web Parts zone.

■ **Advanced**   Determines how users interact with the Web Part.

- **Allow Minimize**—Allows users to minimize the browser page.

- **Allow Close**—Allows users to close the browser page.

- **Allow Hide** – Allows users to hide a particular Web Part on a browser page.

- **Allow Zone Change**   Users can move the Web Part to a different zone.

- **Allow Connections**   Users can connect this Web Part to other Web Parts.

- **Allow Editing in Personal View**   Users can modify other Web Part properties for their personal view.

- **Export Mode**   Defines the type of data that can be exported: nonsensitive or all the data.

- **Title URL**   Additional information for the Web Part can be stored in an external HTML file, and then linked to the title of the Web Part.

- **Description**   Text to display when the user hovers their mouse over the Web Part title.

- **Help URL**   The external HTML help file location, which is accessed via the Web Part menu's Help option.

- **Help Mode**   Three display options for the Help URL:

  - *Modal* displays the Help URL in a new browser window. User must close the modal window before control is returned to SharePoint.

  - *Modeless* displays the Help URL in a new browser window. Users may freely switch between both browser windows and continue to use SharePoint with the Help window open.

  - *Navigate* replaces the current web page with the Help URL contents.

- **Catalog Icon Image URL**   Specifies a 16 × 16 pixel image to be used as an icon in the Web Part list.

- **Title Icon Image URL**   Specifies a 16 × 16 icon to display in the Web Part title bar.

- **Import Error Message**   Designates the text to display if an import error occurs.

- **Target Audiences**   Specifies audiences that should be targeted by this Web Part. Audience targeting allows you to "push" content to specific users.

▲ **Custom Properties**   Are unique to each different Web Part and enable their unique functionality such as checking e-mail, displaying RSS data, and so on.

When a Web Part is added to a Web Parts page, it may not be immediately useful. Because Web Parts are generalized so they can be reused multiple times, the properties of a Web Part must be configured for it to function.

For example, if the My Inbox Web Part (see Figure 15-15) is included on a page, it cannot function without additional information and property settings. The My Inbox Web Part interacts with Microsoft Exchange server to read and send e-mail. However, just adding the My Inbox Web Part to a My Site page will not automatically add e-mail functionality to the page. Virtually all Web Parts must have some properties set for them

Figure 15-15.   The My Inbox Web Part properties dialog box.

to function. The My Inbox Web Part must be set to communicate with Microsoft Exchange Server. This means the Mail server address (Mailbox) property of this Web Part must be set to the path location of the Exchange server before the page will receive e-mail from the Exchange server.

Web Part Galleries

A Web Part gallery is a grouping of Web Parts from which specific Web Parts can be selected when you are creating a Web Part page. MOSS organizes four Web Part galleries:

▼   **The Site gallery**   Contains all the default Web Parts available for publishing to the Web Parts page. For example, if your SharePoint site was named Digital In-Site, you would see a Digital In-Site gallery listed (see Figure 15-16). Because the Site Gallery contains a large number of Web Parts, you have the option to filter the list of Web Parts by function.

■   **The Closed gallery**   Contains Web Parts that have been published to a Web Parts zone on the Web Parts page, but that are currently closed and, therefore, not displayed on the Web Parts page.

▲   **The Server gallery**   Holds published common Web Parts that have been made available to all sites to ease Web Part administration.

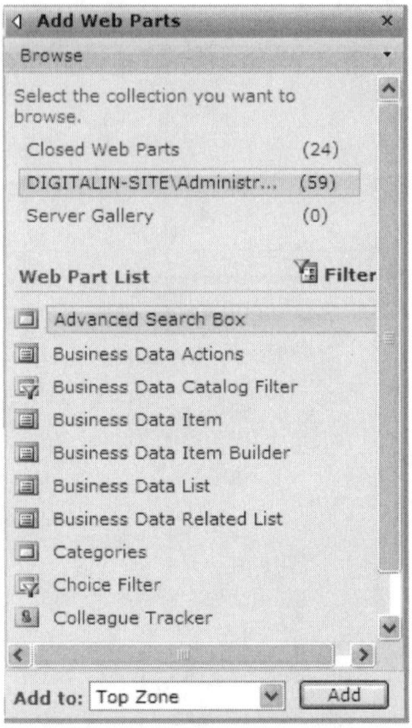

Figure 15-16. Available Web Part galleries are listed in the Add Web Parts dialog box.

TIP You can create custom Web Part galleries and organize your Web Parts as needed.

Built-in Web Parts

MOSS includes over 50 built-in Web Parts, a number that is likely to grow in time. It is easy to feel overwhelmed by the number of Web Parts available, but if you carefully consider the primary purposes for each portal page, the Web Parts needed to fulfill the functions required can then be selected from the various Web Parts groups. Tables 15-1 through 15-7 list the built-in Web Parts available by group that you can include when constructing a Web Parts page as a portal or Dashboard.

An effective way to get comfortable with the function of these Web Parts is to experiment with them. You should filter the Site Gallery by each functional group and drag each Web Part onto a My Site page. You'll find that when you let your mouse hover over the Web Part's name, a tool tip will display, summarizing the function of that Web Part.

Web Part	Used For...
Content Editor	Formatting text, tables, and images
Form	Connecting simple form controls to other Web Parts
Image	Displaying pictures and photos
Members	Listing site members and online status
Page Viewer	Displaying linked content, such as files, folders, or web pages
Relevant Documents	Displaying documents relevant to the current user
User Tasks	Displaying tasks assigned to the current user
XML	XML and XSL Transformation

Table 15-1.   MOSS 2007 Web Parts in Common with Windows SharePoint Server (WSS) 3.0

Library Web Parts

Library Web Parts include individual, content-based Web Parts designed for storing and browsing forms, documents (including a wide range of file types), and graphic images in a specific library. Three primary types of libraries are supported by MOSS:

▼   **Form libraries**   These Web Parts are designed to create and support Microsoft InfoPath forms and to manage them in a form library.

Web Part	Used For...
Business Data Actions	Displaying a list of actions from the Business Data Catalog
Business Data Item	Displaying an item from a Business Data Catalog data source
Business Data Item Builder	Creating a Business Data item and providing it to other web parts
Business Data List	Displaying a list of items from a data source in the Business Data Catalog
Business Data Related List	Displaying data source items in the Business Data Catalog

Table 15-2.   MOSS 2007 Business Data Web Parts

Web Part	Used For...
Colleague Tracker	Displaying a user's list of colleagues and any recent changes
Memberships	Displaying a user's site and distribution list memberships
My Links	Displaying a user's links
My SharePoint Sites	Displaying a user's documents on sites where the user is a member
My Workspaces	Displaying sites created under a user's My Site
Site Aggregator	Displaying sites chosen by a user

Table 15-3.   MOSS 2007 Content Rollup Web Parts

- ■ **Document libraries** This group of Web Parts are the workhorses of MOSS. Document library Web Parts are generically designed to work with all file types, but are specifically oriented to Microsoft Office 2007 (and earlier) Word and Excel documents.
- ▲ **Picture libraries** This group of Web Parts are specifically designed to work with image files. Web Parts to support thumbnail and slideshow views are included.

Two basic types of libraries are offered: shared and personal. Documents or content stored in a shared library are, by default, available to other SharePoint users. A personal library, on the other hand, hides any content published to it from other SharePoint users, by default. A personal library's content is only made available to the content's owner.

> *TIP*   When users create new content such as a document library, it may not be immediately visible on their Web Parts page without some further action.

By default, SharePoint includes new libraries in the Quick Launch area located in the vertical navigation menu on the left-hand side of a Web Parts page. However, this can be overridden, as shown in the following configuration example:

1. Open the Site Actions drop-down menu and choose Create.
2. Under the Libraries category, choose the Document Library option. The page shown in Figure 15-17 displays.
3. Enter a descriptive name in the Name field.
4. In the Navigation section, set the Quick Launch radio button to No.
5. Click Create.

Web Part	Used For...
Authored List Filter	Filtering Web Parts contents using values defined by the page author
Business Data Catalog Filter	Filtering Web Parts contents using values from the Business Data Catalog
Current User Filter	Filtering Web Parts contents using the properties of the currently displayed web page
Date Filter	Filtering Web Parts contents using a date entered or picked by the user
Filter Actions	Allowing users to decide when the content on a page is refreshed
Page Field Filter	Filtering Web Parts contents using information about the current page
Query String (URL) Filter	Filtering Web Parts contents using values entered through a query string
SharePoint List Filter	Filtering Web Parts contents using values from an MOSS list
SQL Server 2005 Analysis Services Filter	Filtering Web Parts contents using a list of values from SQL Server 2005 Analysis Services cubes
Text Filter	Filtering Web Parts contents using text values entered by the user

Table 15-4. MOSS 2007 Filters Web Parts

Using these actions, a user creates and configures a Web Part that will not appear in the Quick Launch list. From these steps, the Web Part is created and placed in the Site Name gallery. However, to this point, it has not been added to the Web Parts page. This requires an additional action: the Web Part must be added to the Web Parts page before it is visible to other users.

1. Open the Site Actions drop-down menu and choose Create (See Figure 15-18).

2. Click the Add A Web Part button in the Top Web Parts zone.

3. Check the check-box associated with the library you wish to reference in the Lists and Libraries node (see Figure 15-19).

4. Click the Add button. The Sample Document Library should be visible on the Web Parts page now.

Web Part	Used For...
Advanced Search Box	Performing an advanced search
People Search Box	Performing a people search
People Search Core Results	Displaying the results of a people search
Search Box	Performing a search
Search Core Results	Displaying the results of a search
Search High Confidence Results	Displaying the results of a special term and high confidence search
Search Paging	Facilitating the paging of search results
Search Statistics	Displaying search statistics
Search Summary	Displaying a summary of search results

Table 15-5. MOSS 2007 Search Web Parts

Content Rollup Web Parts

One of SharePoint's strengths is its ability to aggregate content. By pulling content from various sources and making it all available in one central location, SharePoint can greatly increase efficiency by reducing the amount of time users spend searching for the information they need. Content Rollup Web Parts perform this function and, in some cases, do so by exposing hidden connections between data.

Web Part	Used For...
My Calendar	Displaying the user's calendar from Microsoft Exchange Server
My Contacts	Displaying the user's contacts from Microsoft Exchange Server through Outlook Web Access
My Inbox	Displaying the user's e-mail inbox using from Microsoft Exchange Server through Outlook Web Access
My Mail Folder	Displaying one or more of a user's mail folders from Microsoft Exchange Server through Outlook Web Access
My Tasks	Displaying a user's Task List from Microsoft Exchange Server through Outlook Web Access

Table 15-6. MOSS 2007 Outlook Web Access (OWA) Web Parts

Web Part	Used For...
Key Performance Indicators (KPI)	Displaying a list of important measures for an organization and how the organization is performing
KPI Details	Displaying a single KPI
Site Directory Categories	Displaying Site Directory categories
Sites in Category	Displaying the sites in a category of the Site Directory
Site Directory Top Sites	Displaying the most active sites in the Site Directory
Contact Details	Displaying contact details for a page or site
Excel Web Access	Displaying and interacting with an Excel 2007 workbook
I need to...	Displaying a list of tasks and tools
IView Web Part	Displaying iViews from SAP portal servers
Really Simple Syndication (RSS) Viewer	Displaying the contents of an RSS Feed
This Week in Pictures	Displaying images from the library in the News web
Web Services for Remote Portlets (WSRP) Consumer Web Part	Displaying portlets from WSRP web sites

Table 15-7. The MOSS 2007 Dashboard, Site Directory, and Miscellaneous Web Parts

Examples of Content Rollup Web Parts include:

▼ **Colleagues** Displays user relationships that may not be evident based on an organizational chart. It can even suggest colleagues to add based on your e-mail and instant message usage. For privacy, you can limit who can see this information.

■ **Colleague Tracker** Displays recent changes made by your colleagues, including changes to their profile, blog updates, new documents, and whether they are currently in or out of the office.

■ **Get Started with My Site** Suggests some common tasks to help users get the most out of their My Site, including describing themselves, updating their profile, uploading a picture, and customizing their page.

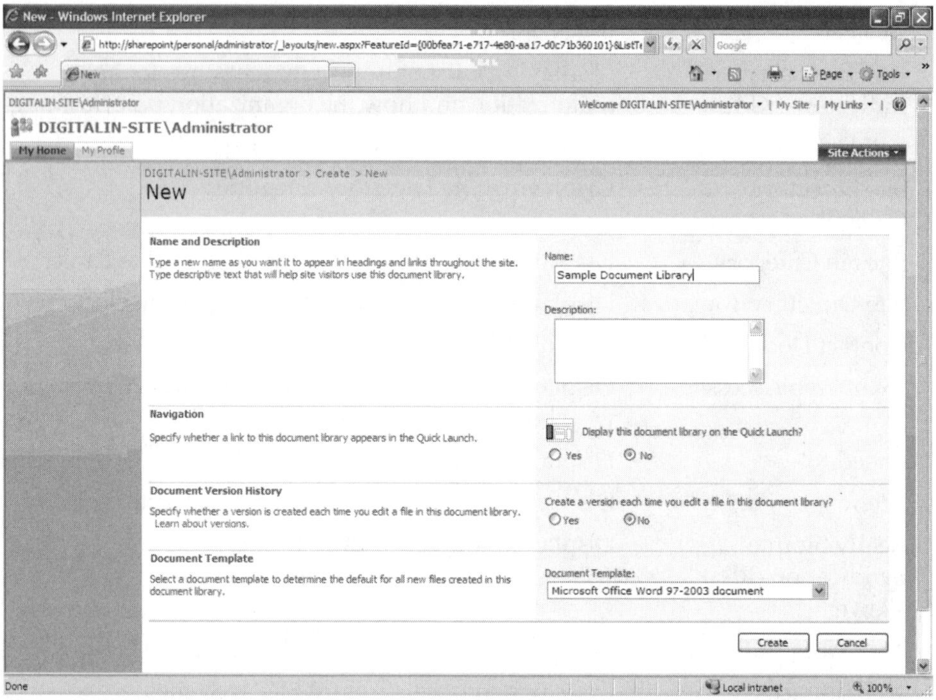

Figure 15-17. The New Document Library page.

■ **In Common Between Us** Displays things you have in common with your page visitor, including managers, colleagues, and memberships.

■ **Memberships** Displays any groups or distribution lists you choose to make available to your users.

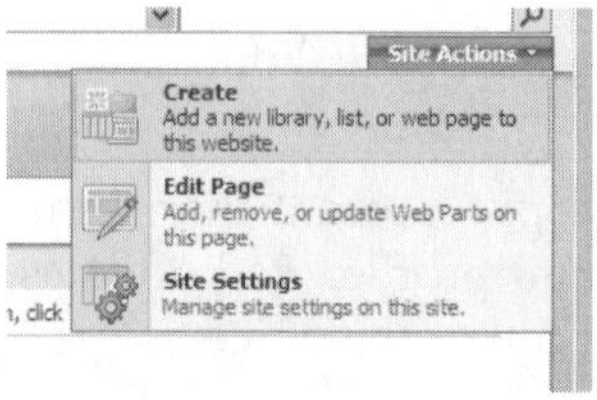

Figure 15-18. The Site Actions menu.

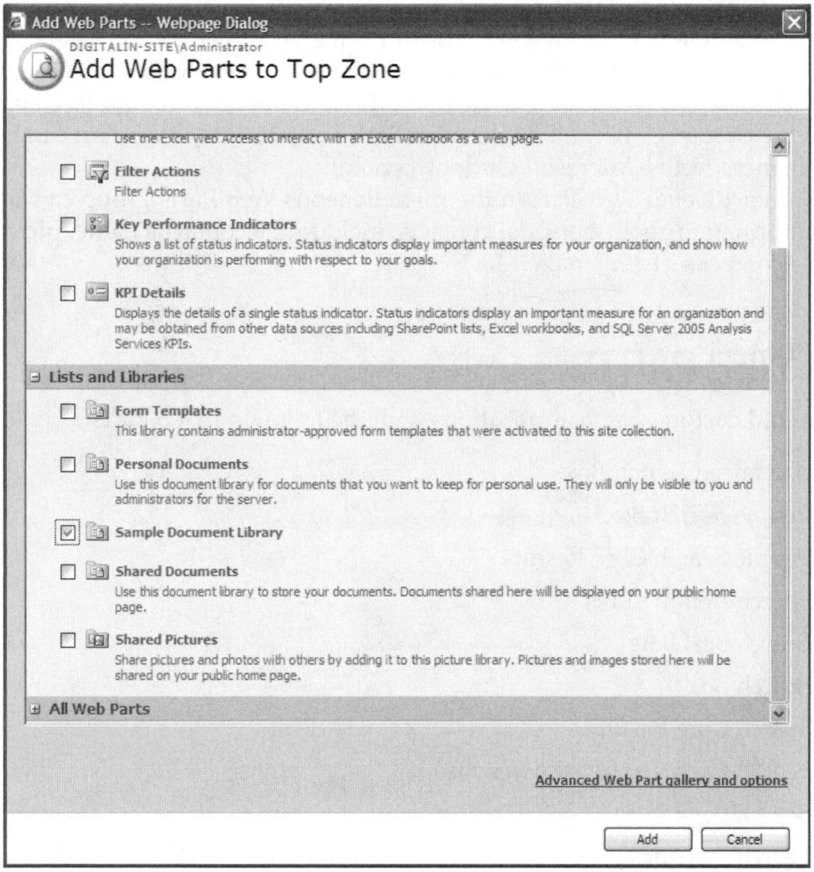

Figure 15-19. A SharePoint Document Library Web Part selected to be added to a Web Parts page.

- **My Links, My Pictures, My SharePoint Sites, and My Workspaces** All of these Web Parts aggregate specific types of like data. For example, the My SharePoint Sites Web Part is a comprehensive list of all the documents you've authored in SharePoint, as well as any SharePoint Sites you choose to share in one location.

- **Recent Blog Posts** May sound self-explanatory, but it is worth mentioning that recent blog posts can be stylized via an XSL (eXtensible Stylesheet Language) Editor, as well as targeted to a specific Audience.

- **SharePoint Documents** Displays any documents you have authored.

- ▲ **Site Aggregator** Allows you to create a list of other SharePoint sites to share with users in a tab-based format.

Outlook Web Access Web Parts

If your organization has deployed Microsoft Exchange Server 2003 or later, a variety of Web Parts can be included to display a number of Microsoft Outlook objects on a page. The My Calendar Web Part, My Contacts Web Part, My Inbox Web Part (see Figure 15-15 earlier in the chapter), My Mail Folder Web Part, and My Tasks Web Part can be used to display their respective Microsoft Outlook content.

The Contact Detail Web Part in the miscellaneous Web Parts group can be used to display information about personal contacts, including a contact's name, picture, and a link to the contact's My Site page.

SEARCH WEB PARTS

You can build custom search applications with the following Web Parts:

▼ Advanced Search Box

■ People Search Box

■ People Search Core Results

■ Search Action Links

■ Search Best Bets

■ Search Box

■ Search Core Results

■ Search High Confidence Results

■ Search Paging

■ Search Statistics

▲ Search Summary

The Advanced Search Box allows users to create highly targeted searches based on logical operators such as "all," "any," and "none," along with properties like author, creation date, or modification date. The search can also be restricted to a specific language.

You'll notice that there is a corresponding Search Result Web Parts for each Search Box Web Part. The primary purpose for including a Search Box Web Part on your page is to override the default properties of the Search Box or Search Result Web Part.

Additional Web Parts

MOSS is built on the Microsoft .NET 3.0 Framework, which contains a vast SharePoint namespace and application programming interface (API). It is relatively easy for software developers to leverage the .NET Framework to create new Web Parts using Visual Studio 2005.

TIP   Additional Web Parts are available at www.microsoft.com.

In addition, many third-party vendors have created Web Parts to perform a wide variety of tasks. To import a Web Part, perform the following steps.

Import Web Parts

1. Open the Site Actions drop-down menu and select the Edit Page option.
2. Click the Add A Web Part option.
3. Click on the Advanced Web Part Gallery And Options link.
4. Click on the Menu icon (the small triangle on the right side) on the Browse title bar.
5. Choose the Import option, as shown in Figure 15-20.
6. Click on the Browse option and navigate to the location of the Web Part file (.DWP) you wish to import.
7. Click on the Open button.
8. Click Upload, then select the Web Parts zone into which you wish to upload the Web Part and click the Add button.

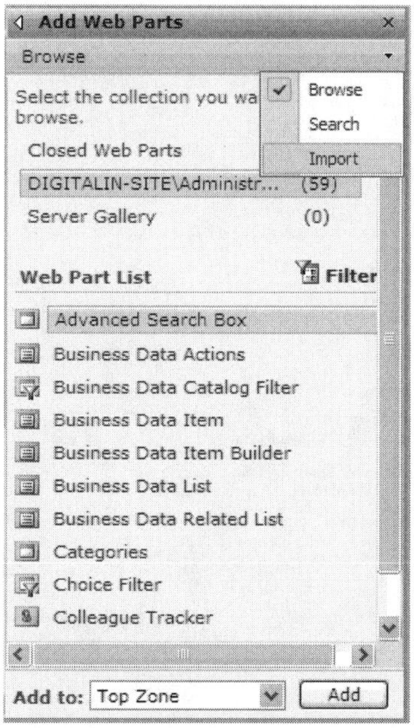

Figure 15-20.   Importing a Web Part.

Add People Search to a Web Parts Page

Search functions are commonly incorporated into many personal Web Parts pages, including the ability to search for other users. To include a people search action on a page, use the steps in the following example. In this example, the People Search functions are simplified by hiding the "Search Options" and displaying the People Search Core Results Web Parts on the same page.

1. Navigate to your My Site page.

2. Click on the Site Actions button to open its drop-down menu and select the Edit Page option.

3. Click on the Add A Web Part button for the Middle Left Zone and then expand the the All Web Parts Node.

4. Scroll down to the Search Web Parts section and check the checkboxes associated with the People Search Box and People Search Core Results Web Parts (see Figure 15-21).

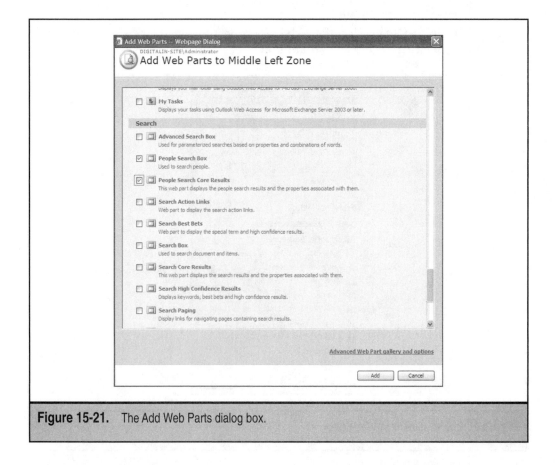

Figure 15-21. The Add Web Parts dialog box.

5. Click on the Add button to add the Web Parts selected. Your My Site page will reload and the Search Web Parts are added in the Middle Left Zone.

6. Click on the Edit Menu of the People Search Web Part and select the Modify Web Part option.

7. Expand the Miscellaneous Node in the Web Part panel and uncheck the Show Search Options checkbox, as shown in Figure 15-22.

8. Click the Apply button.

   Notice that the Search Options portion of the Web Part has been removed (see Figure 15-23). Next, you need to configure the People Search Web Part for where it is to display the search results. In most cases, you'd display the search results on the same page.

9. In the the Miscellaneous node of the Web Parts panel, scroll down to locate the Target Search Results Page URL property.

10. Enter the URL of the page on which you wish to display the search results in the Target search results page URL field.

11. Click on the OK button to set this property.

12. Click on the Exit Edit Mode button in the upper right corner of the page to view the Web Parts page in its display mode.

Figure 15-22. The People Search Box window.

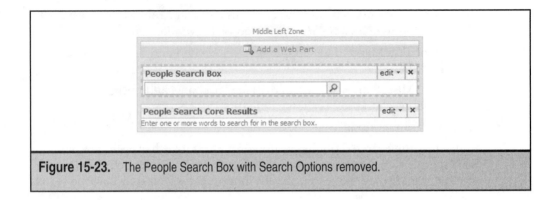

Figure 15-23. The People Search Box with Search Options removed.

Site Directory Web Parts

The Categories, Sites in Categories, and Top Sites Web Parts allow you to quickly build dynamic site-based navigation into your Web Parts page. New categories will automatically appear in the Categories Web Part, as will new sites assigned to categories.

Default Web Parts

The Default Web Parts group contains some Web Parts that are, by default, published to specific Web Parts pages. For instance, the "I need to…" Web Part contains a list of tasks and tools that should be used by the Web Parts page administrator to complete the setup of their new page. Other Web Parts include a Really Simple Syndication (RSS) Viewer, and This Week In Pictures. RSS is an XML-based method of feeding information from one web site to another. Blogs and news web sites often make an RSS feed available for subscribers to receive web site updates automatically.

This Week In Pictures is an interesting Web Part that could easily be categorized as a content rollup Web Part. This Week In Pictures summarizes pictures recently published to SharePoint and makes that picture a link to the original Picture Library Web Part.

Filter Web Parts

Filters reduce the amount of data displayed on your Web Parts page. The filter criteria may come directly from the user—for example, through the use of a Choice Filter, or by entering a date using the Date Filter Web Part. Or, filter criteria may be automated through the use of a hidden Web Part filter such as the Current User Filter. The Current User Filter automatically detects the current user, as well as any properties from that user's profile that you determine useful for filtering data.

Filtering is especially effective when creating digital dashboards. By filtering data, your digital dashboard can present different sets of data that are meaningful to different groups of users. Filters are used in combination with other Web Parts by connecting the filter results to another Web Part.

Business Data Web Parts

Business Data Web Parts allow you to leverage SharePoint to create rich data-driven content. The business data can come from multiple sources, including other SharePoint Web Parts through connections, Excel, SAP portals, or any other portal that supports the Web Services for Resource Portals (WSRP) standard. The IView Web Part lets you integrate SAP portal servers.

Business Data Web Parts include:

▼ Business Data Actions

■ Business Data Item Builder

■ Business Data List

■ Business Data Related List

■ Excel Web Access

■ IView Web Part

▲ WSRP Consumer Web Part

Dashboard Web Parts

The forte of a dashboard is its ability to effectively summarize a large volume of data and allow key actionable data to rise to the top. A key maxim of building an effective dashboard is "bad news should travel fast."

SharePoint contains a group of Web Parts for creating dashboards, including Key Performance Indicators (KPI) and KPI Details. KPIs visually display quantitative goal-based data in a manner that makes analysis quick and easy. Clicking a KPI allows you to investigate additional information associated with that KPI by viewing the KPI Detail Web Part.

NOTE For more information on Key Performance Indicators and other Business Intelligence elements and features in MOSS, see Chapter 21.

SUMMARY

It is important to understand that Web Parts are the functional building blocks of SharePoint. Web Parts are modular, reusable, and provide very specific functions. Web Parts pages host Web Parts within specific areas known as Web Parts zones.

All Web Parts share common properties associated to how the Web Part will be displayed, and how the user can interact with them. Custom properties expose specific features unique to each type of Web Part.

Web Parts can be visible to the user, display static or dynamic content, or be completely hidden, performing a valuable function behind the scenes, such as feeding data to another Web Part. Web Parts can be connected to other Web Parts for increased functionality. They can also be filtered to dynamically display content.

Web Part Galleries categorize Web Parts so they can be easily located when adding Web Parts to a Web Parts page.

Perhaps most importantly, Web Parts create a tremendous opportunity for creating feature-rich information-based web applications using nothing more than your browser and a mouse.

CHAPTER 16

SharePoint Views and Metadata

Perhaps the single most often used feature in an MOSS environment is a SharePoint view. A view presents a user with all or a portion of the content of a document, workbook, or data collection to satisfy a business-related or functional information need. In any MOSS environment, the number and flexibility of the views available can determine how effectively and efficiently the system supports users' needs.

Despite the efforts of forward-thinking Internet visionaries, most companies store their documents, business data, and records in a way that essentially follows the vertical structure of the organization. Within a typical organization, the departments tend to operate using their own proprietary procedures and information. This typically leads to the production of an ever-increasing number of documents, including redundant and duplicated information, which are stored vertically, corresponding to the organizational structure. The accounting department has its own information stored on the network, as does the marketing, production, and other departments of the company.

This chapter provides you with an approach to developing SharePoint libraries and their associated views, which help reduce information redundancies. In addition, using SharePoint libraries, views, and metadata, MOSS helps to flatten the information store so it can better serve the needs of the entire organization, with information shared across departmental lines.

To best understand how this approach is applied, you must first understand the difference between what has become the traditional approach to data storage and how in using SharePoint libraries and view you can flatten the data store. This is followed by a discussion of the role metadata plays in developing effective views of a SharePoint library and, finally, some tips on developing views that satisfy the needs of your users and the organization.

MOSS DATA ORGANIZATION

Since the time when the personal computer became interchangeable with a user's desktop, folders and subfolders (directories and subdirectories) have been used to organize files into hierarchies. Unfortunately, the structure and relationships of a hierarchical folder organization never quite makes sense to every user. The employees in a particular department may be able to navigate that department's folders, but should they need to find information in another department's folders, they can feel as if they are lost in a strange city without a roadmap.

Data organization standards seldom exist within a single department, let alone for an entire organization. When information must be shared across departments, the lack of data organization standards can make finding the information needed almost impossible, resulting in the redundant duplication of frequently accessed files. This situation can eat up available disk storage space, clog search inboxes, and require the manual merging of the various versions of key documents.

Without getting too deeply into MOSS document management benefits and techniques (for that, see Chapter 9), there are features and functions within MOSS to help users find the information they need and to prevent many other document issues common to the hierarchical folder approach, primarily SharePoint libraries.

SharePoint libraries are designed to make files easy to find and to facilitate the sharing of files. Of course, the ability for a user to find and access files is subject to the user's security permissions that control what the user can do with a file. SharePoint libraries also store metadata about each file separately within the library and can be displayed as configurable columns in a SharePoint view. A library can have multiple views to allow users to work with information in a variety of ways.

> **NOTE**   The SharePoint Search feature (see Chapter 8) is another tool that can help solve the problem of finding information when a user doesn't know where to look.

Metadata

Simply put, metadata is data about data. Metadata describe the data contained within a file and are stored separately from the file itself. Many applications of metadata are in use, but you shouldn't be confused by what may appear to be different applications. The metadata applied in a SharePoint library is very much like that included in the heading of a Hypertext Markup Language (HTML) document. In an HTML document, metadata describes a web page in terms of the topics included on that page using keywords and phrases that can be cataloged by a search engine for users looking for certain information. Search engines, at least those that use metadata to catalog web pages, index the words and phrases of metadata to list those web pages containing that information. This is essentially how SharePoint metadata works as well.

Metadata allows users to organize list and library content in a way that makes sense to them. Properly created metadata increases the accuracy of the search results returned by MOSS, which in turn improves the productivity of the users in the MOSS environment. Unfortunately, a great deal of time and effort is required to create a truly effective metadata scheme. However, over time, you should be able to develop your metadata scheme bit by bit.

Metadata Columns

Metadata is defined to a SharePoint library as an additional column that can be included in the views of the library. When a metadata column is added to a SharePoint library, it is assigned a word, topic, or other commonly sought after term. The documents in the library are then indexed on the data in the column, which enables fast and easy retrieval. As described more fully in Chapter 12, if a metadata column is added to a library of technical documents with a specific value in the metadata column, any of the documents in the library containing that value are indexed to the metadata. By selecting that metadata column, the library's contents are filtered and only those documents containing the given value are listed in the view. Figure 16-1 illustrates this example of a metadata application, where the "Topic" metadata column is filtered for the value "GPS."

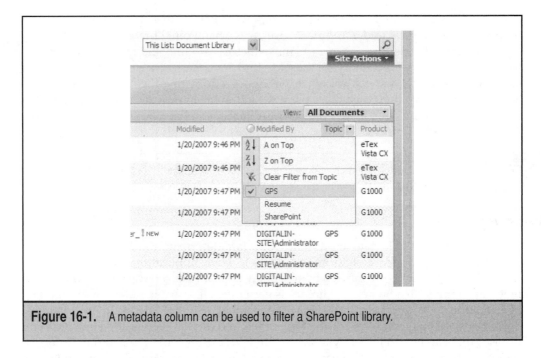

Figure 16-1.   A metadata column can be used to filter a SharePoint library.

When a SharePoint library is created, default metadata is also created that includes such information as the file's creation date, the file's creator, and the date on which a document was last modified. A SharePoint library can be configured to create additional metadata for its files, such as a project name, the purpose of a document, or any commonly accessed data, value, word, or phrase stored in its files.

A SharePoint library view can be customized to include a specific set of metadata. The customized metadata is then applied to the view and can also be used to filter the contents of the files in the library. MOSS only supports custom metadata columns on Microsoft Office documents, though. Users can then use the metadata to filter the library's columns to eliminate unwanted files and sequence the files meeting the metadata filter as they wish, with the file or files they need displayed at the top of the library's list.

It is important to understand that metadata is not stored in the files to which it is associated. However, if you should move a file (and its columns) from one library to another, the metadata associated with the columns that were moved is also transferred to the new library.

The filter options available for a metadata column should be simple enough for users to quickly scan the list visually. Also, if possible, you should limit the number of unique entries in any metadata column. Look for logical ways to group the data values in a metadata column to keep the list from becoming too long and nonproductive. For example, if a metadata column has 20 to 30 different data value entries, selecting a value to filter becomes fairly bothersome for users. However, if these values can be clustered into perhaps two or three common groupings, additional metadata columns can be added and the entries split across the columns.

Configure Metadata to a Library

SharePoint document libraries are configured with a set of default metadata columns. The standard set of default metadata is:

▼ **Title**   The title of the document. Remember that a document's title is different from its filename.

■ **Created By**   The user name of the document's author or the user that stored the document initially.

■ **Modified By**   The last user to modify the document.

▲ **Checked Out To**   The user who currently has the document open and locked for editing.

Additional metadata columns can be added to a library for inclusion and filtering of a view. We'll discuss views a bit later in the chapter (see 'Views' later in the chapter), but for now, let's work through the why and usage of metadata columns and their importance in creating user views. To help you understand the value of metadata columns, the following sections look at a basic flat view for a library, the various SharePoint column types, how to edit metadata columns and use application-supported metadata in a library.

A Flat View of a Library

A flat view of a library displays all of the elements in the library at the same level. If the library includes folders and subfolders, the folder hierarchy is dropped and all of the folder contents are displayed as if they were all in one big folder. A flat view of a library is the foundation from which customized views, which apply metadata, are created.

To have a SharePoint library display its contents in a flat view, perform the following steps:

1. Navigate to the site that contains the SharePoint library.

2. On the site's home page, click the View All Site Content link at the top of the Quick Launch menu.

3. On the All Site Content page, click the Title of the library you wish to modify.

4. On the Library page, click the Settings option to open its drop-down menu, and then click the Document Library Settings option, as shown in Figure 16-2.

5. On the Document Library Settings page, scroll down the page to the Views section (see Figure 16-3) and click the All Documents view to include all of the library's documents in the view.

6. Scroll down the page to the Folders section and click the plus-sign button to expand this node.

7. Select the Show All Items Without Folders option, as illustrated in Figure 16-4. The alternative selection, Show Items Inside Folders, would be the equivalent of the tree displayed in Windows Explorer, which is just what we are trying to avoid.

8. Click OK to save the library's settings.

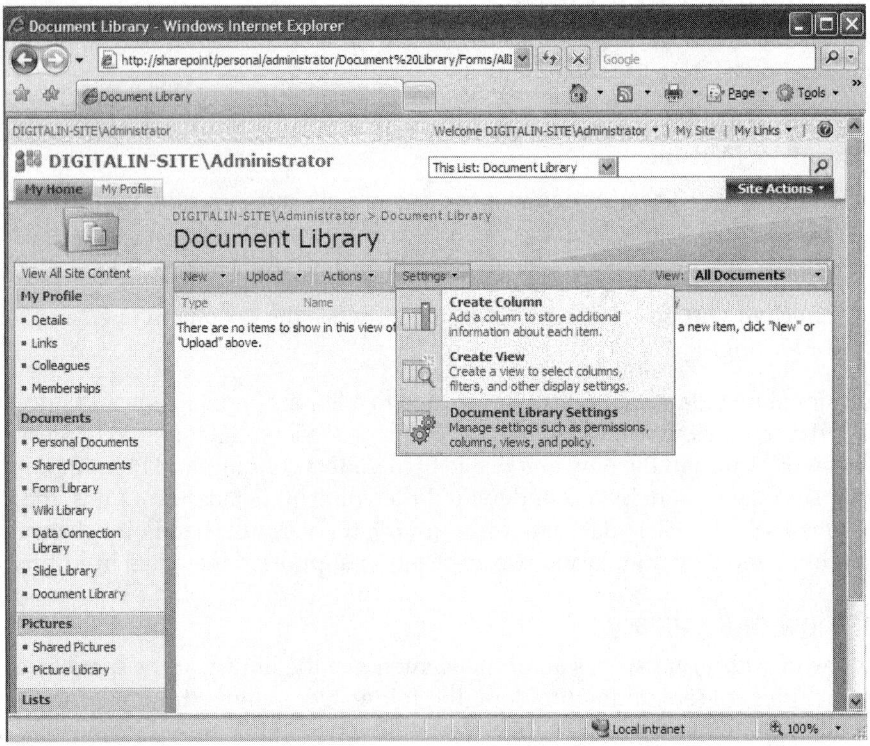

Figure 16-2. The Document Library Settings option on the Settings drop-down menu.

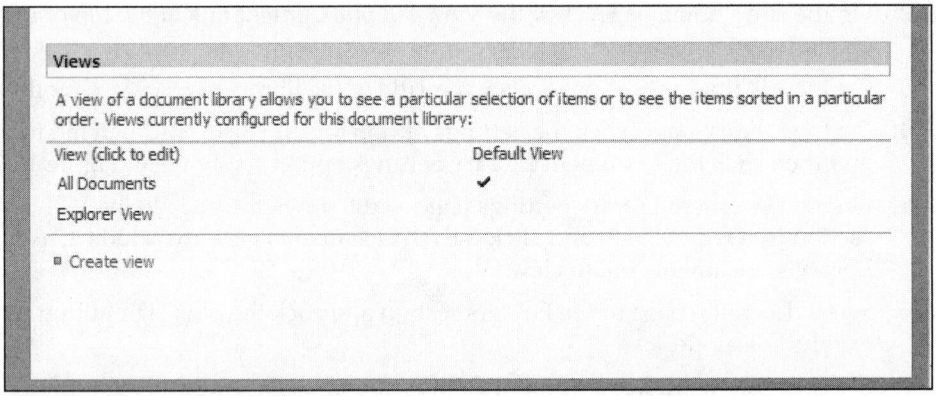

Figure 16-3. The Views section of the Document Library Settings page.

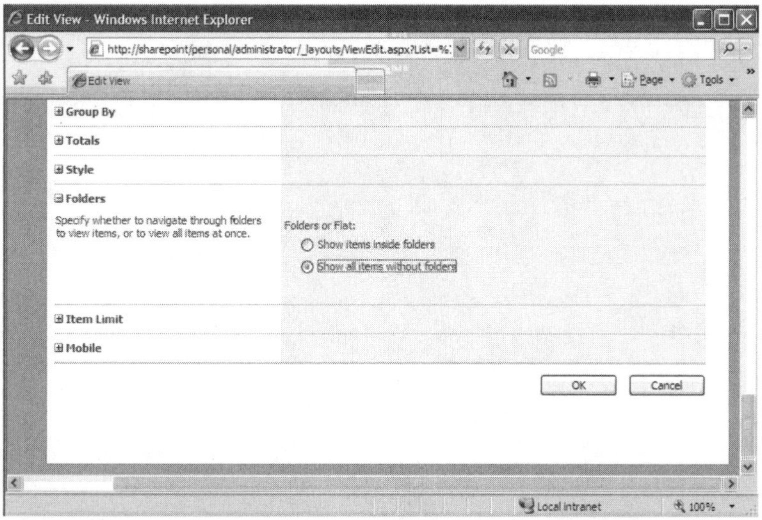

Figure 16-4.   The Folders section of the Document Library Settings page.

Figures 16-5 and 16-6 illustrate the differences between a flat view of a library and a view that displays the library's files inside their folders, respectively.

Add a Metadata Column

If you wish to create additional columns to a SharePoint library for more metadata, use the following procedure:

1. Navigate to the page that contains the SharePoint library and then click the View All Site Content link at the top of the Quick Launch menu.

2. Find the library you wish to modify and click its Title.

3. On the library's home page, click the Settings item to open its drop-down menu and then choose the Create Column option, as shown in Figure 16-7.

4. In the Name and Type section of the Create Column page (shown in Figure 16-8):

   a. Enter a descriptive and unique value for the column name.

   b. Choose a column type (the next section has more information on making this choice). The default is Single Line Of Text, which is the type most commonly used for a metadata column, but depending on the type of metadata you wish to designate, you may choose another column type.

5. In the Additional Column Settings area (see Figure 16-9), enter a description for the column being added, such as its purpose and the type of data the column should contain.

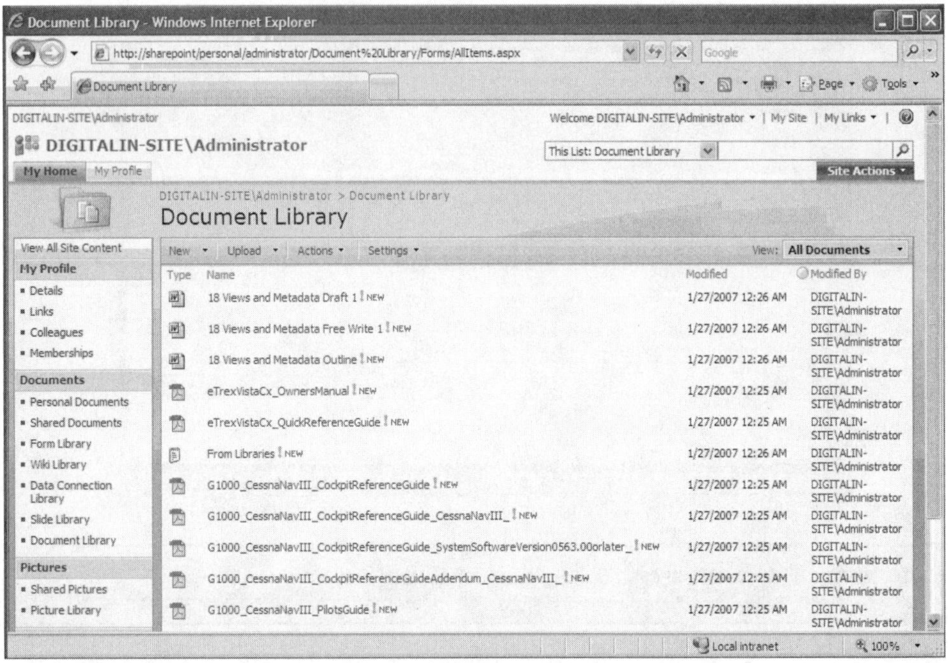

Figure 16-5. A flat view of a library's files.

6. If you wish the column to be included in the default view for the library, check the Add To Default View checkbox.

7. Click OK to create the library column.

SharePoint Column Types

Choosing an appropriate column type is vital to ensuring the validity of the metadata or content associated with a column. When creating a new column, you can choose from the following column types (see Figure 16-8):

▼ **Single line of text** This column type contains a few characters or words.

■ **Multiple lines of text** This column type contains a phrase or one or two sentences.

■ **Choice** This column type presents a list of values that you provide in the form of a menu.

■ **Number** This column type contains a numerical value. You may enter additional settings regarding minimum and maximum values and the number of decimals in the number.

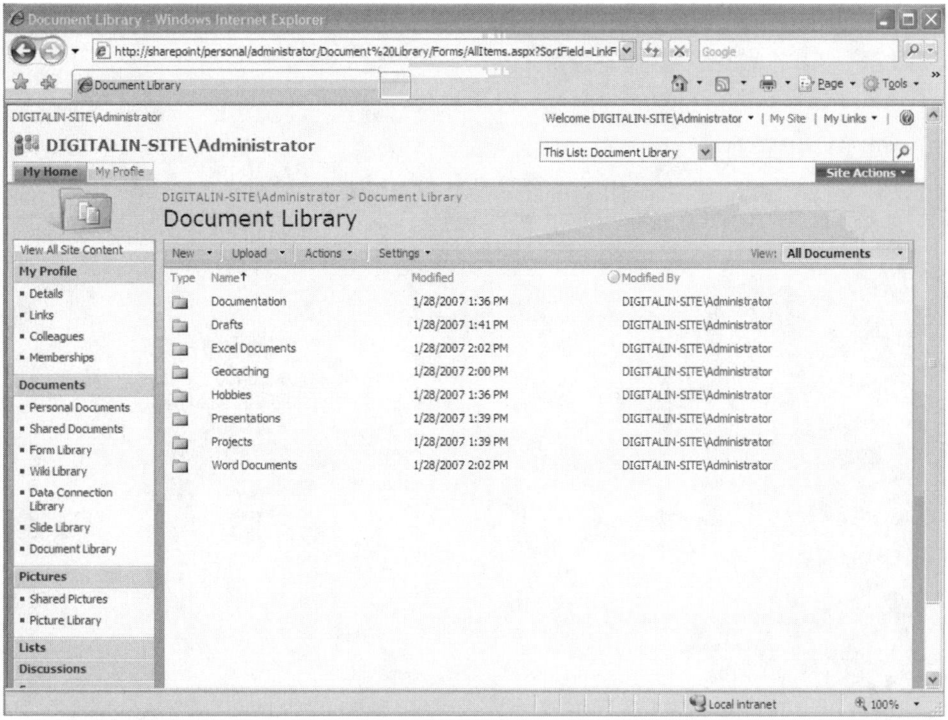

Figure 16-6. A library view that includes its files inside their folders.

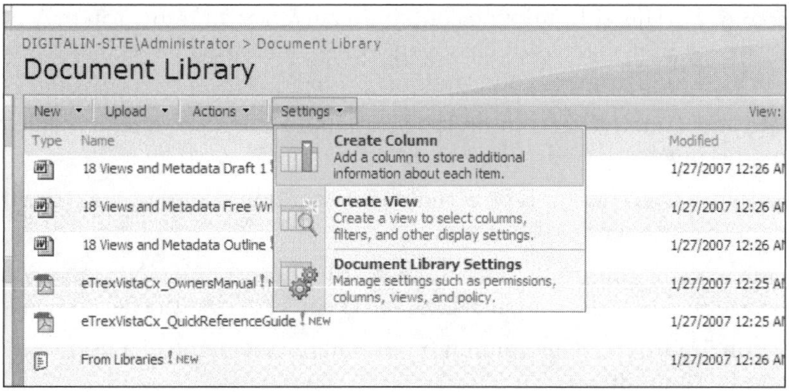

Figure 16-7. The Create Column option on the Settings drop-down menu.

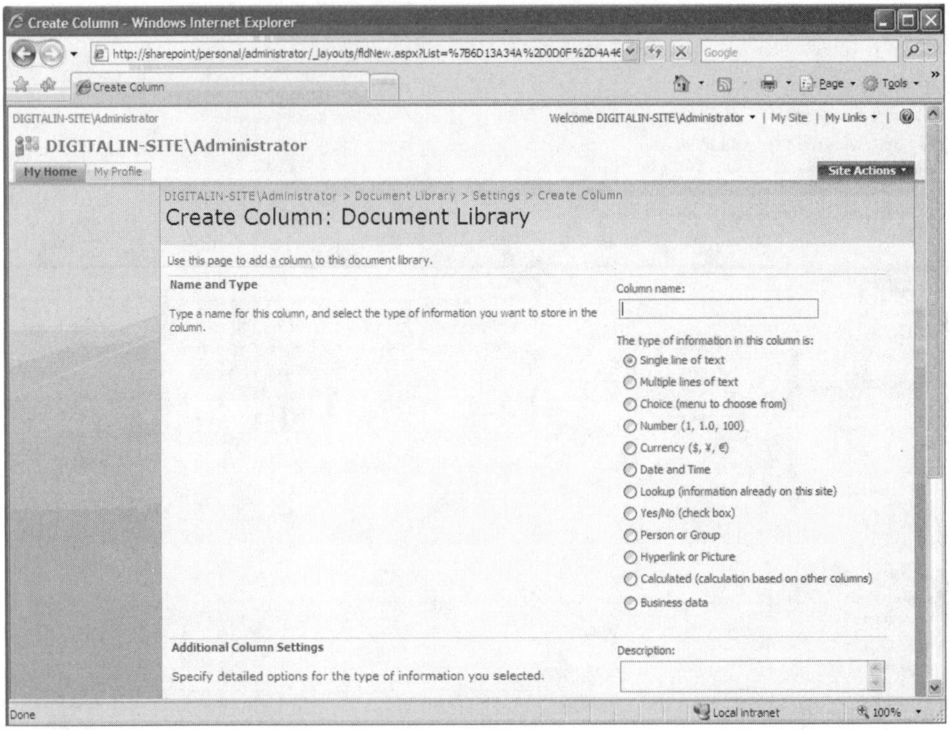

Figure 16-8. The Create Column page is used to define a column that is added to a library.

■ **Currency** This column type contains a currency amount. You may enter a currency unit, such as dollars, yen, euros, and so on, as well as the values indicated for a number column type.

■ **Date and Time** This column type contains a calendar date or a date and time-of-day.

■ **Lookup** This column type contains information stored in the current library or another library listed in the site collection.

■ **Yes/No** This column type contains a True/False or Yes/No value. A checkbox is presented to users in which checked means yes and unchecked means no.

■ **Person or Group** This column type contains the name of a user or a SharePoint group.

■ **Hyperlink or Picture** This column type contains a hyperlink or a link to a graphic. A picture or graphic is perhaps not the best choice for a metadata column, but a hyperlink that points to a picture can be used.

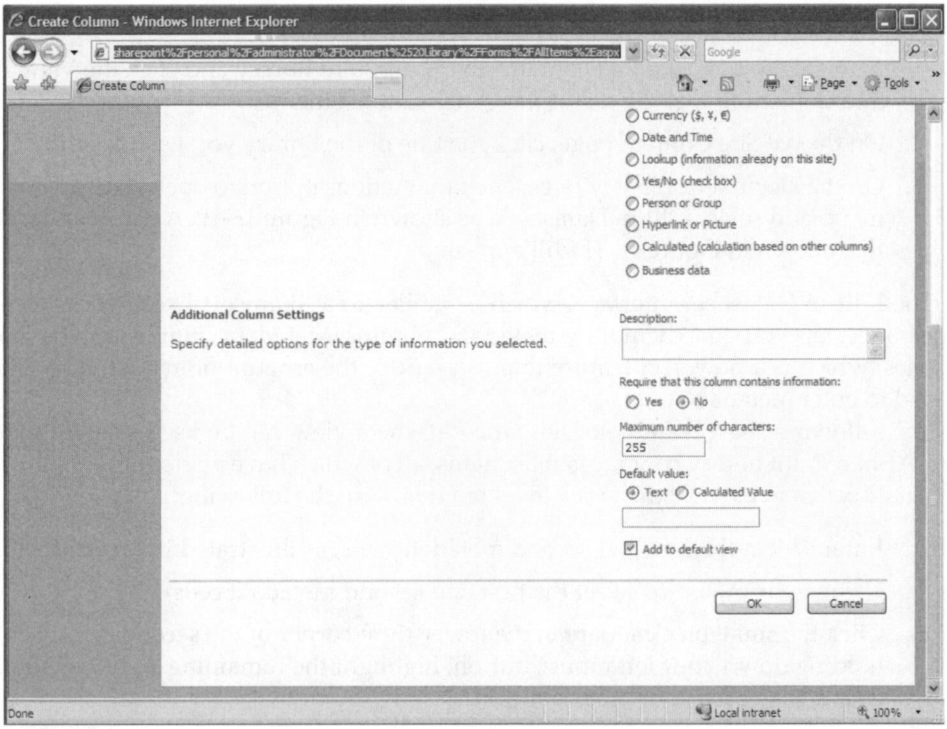

Figure 16-9.   The Additional Column Settings area of the Create Column page.

- ■   **Calculated**   This column type contains a calculation that uses any number of values from other columns of the same library.

- ▲   **Business Data**   This column type contains data provided from a business data application based on a business data profile.

Edit Metadata

The files stored in a SharePoint library are commonly a good starting place for identifying appropriate metadata for the library. After creating a new document library, publish a few representative files to the library and analyze the content for what they may have in common and what sets them apart. From this analysis, you should gain an idea of what metadata should be assigned to each file and you can proceed with creating the additional columns needed to support the metadata.

After creating your metadata columns, you should assign metadata to the library files. The most efficient way of assigning metadata to a large number of files is to edit the library using the datasheet view. To edit a library using the datasheet view, perform the following steps:

1. Navigate to the page that contains the SharePoint library and click the View All Site Content link at the top of the Quick Launch menu.

2. On the All Site Content page, click the title of the library you wish to edit.

3. On the Document Library page, click the Actions option to open its drop-down menu and select Edit In Datasheet, as shown in Figure 16-10. A page similar to that shown in Figure 16-11 will appear.

The Edit In Datasheet interface, which is similar to a Microsoft Excel worksheet in appearance, lets you quickly modify metadata columns. Metadata columns can be filled in series, which is a powerful feature that can reduce the amount of manual data entry needed to enter metadata.

The following is an example of how the datasheet view can be used to enter metadata. A SharePoint library contains ten list items, all of which have a price of $9.99. To use the datasheet view to enter this price to all ten items, do the following:

1. Enter 9.99 in the first and second metadata cells, as illustrated in Figure 16-12.

2. Using your mouse to select the first and second metadata cells.

3. Click the small black square in the lower right corner of the second cell. Then, holding down your left mouse button, highlight the remaining eight metadata cells and release your mouse button.

4. Each of the cells is automatically assigned a value of 9.99.

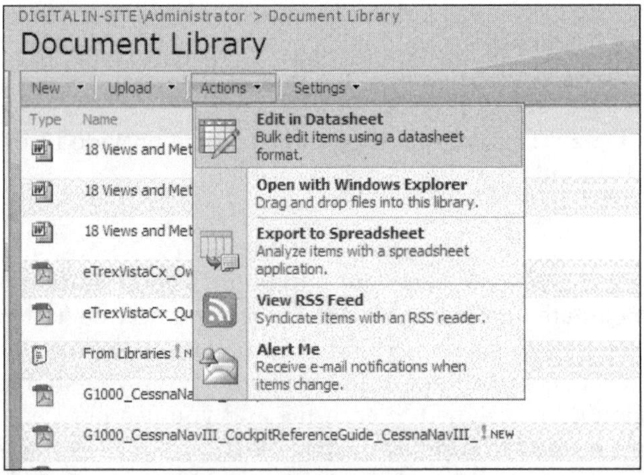

Figure 16-10. The Edit In Datasheet option on the Actions drop-down menu.

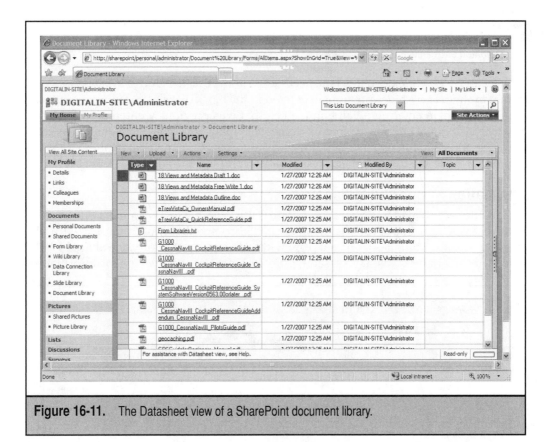

Figure 16-11. The Datasheet view of a SharePoint document library.

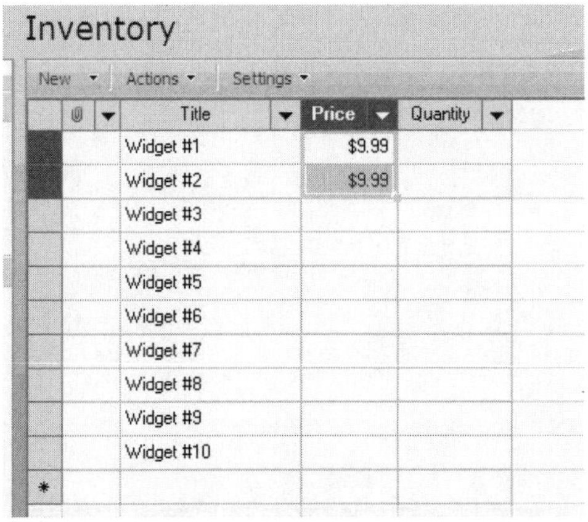

Figure 16-12. Data entered into the first two metadata cells of a library in datasheet view.

> **TIP**   It is not necessary to save the datasheet between entries. The datasheet is automatically updated each time you make a change to it.

Like an Excel worksheet, the datasheet view interface also includes IntelliSense. This feature monitors for values previously entered in the block of cells preceding the current cell. As you begin entering a value into a cell that was previously entered, IntelliSense displays a list of the previously entered values that match the data being entered as each character is typed. You can use the down arrow to select the metadata value you were entering, if it's in the list, and then press ENTER to complete the entry.

Application Supported Metadata

As new files are created in a SharePoint library, it is possible to assign metadata to a file from Microsoft Office applications and other MOSS-compatible applications. When a Microsoft Office application is launched from within a SharePoint library, the Shared Workspace window pane is displayed (see Figure 16-13). Select the Document Information

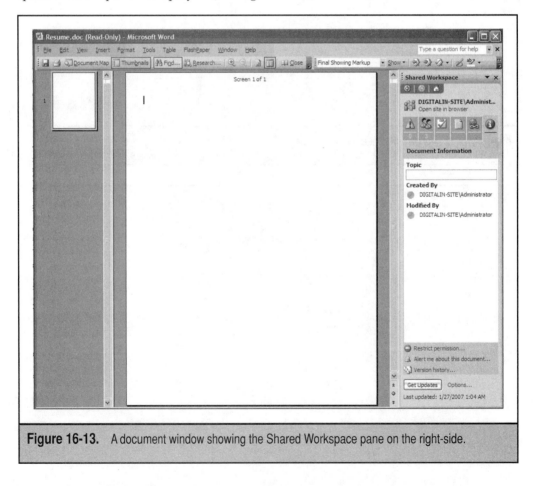

Figure 16-13.   A document window showing the Shared Workspace pane on the right-side.

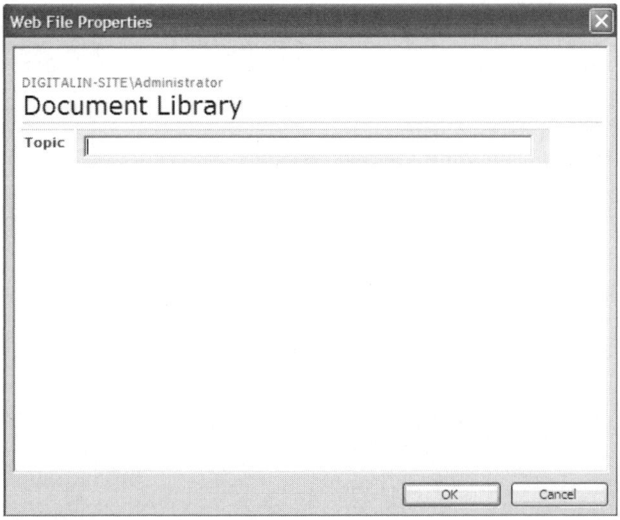

Figure 16-14.   The Web File Properties dialog box is used to assign metadata to a Microsoft Office document saved to a SharePoint library.

tab on the Shared Workspace page to display the file's associated metadata, if any. The Document Information tab can also be used to add or edit existing metadata. When you save a file to a SharePoint library, MOSS-compatible applications prompt you to assign metadata to the file using the dialog box shown in Figure 16-14.

TIP   You can display the Shared Workspace window by selecting Shared Workspace from the Tools menu on the SharePoint browser's menu bar.

Site Columns

The SharePoint Site Column feature lets you create a metadata scheme just once, and make it available to all libraries. Something to keep in mind about site columns is that they are built once, provide a single point of maintenance, and can be reused just about everywhere.

Site columns are not initially associated with any specific library, therefore they are created slightly different from library metadata columns. However, the process used to create a site column should be familiar by now. To create a site column, perform the following steps:

1.   Navigate to the top-level SharePoint site, click the Site Actions button to display its drop-down menu, and select Site Settings.

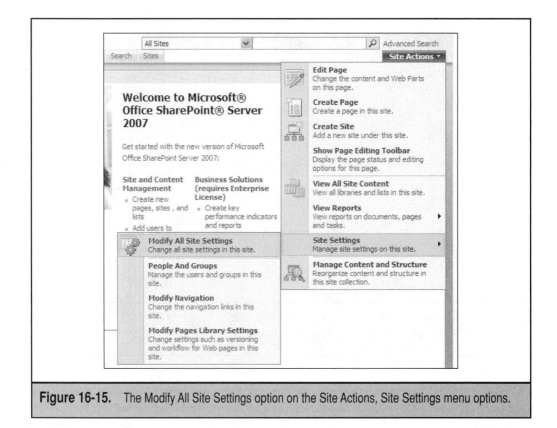

Figure 16-15. The Modify All Site Settings option on the Site Actions, Site Settings menu options.

2. On the Site Settings pop-up menu, select Modify All Site Settings, as shown in Figure 16-15.

3. On the Site Settings page, shown in Figure 16-16, click the Site Columns link under the Galleries heading.

4. On the Site Column Gallery page (see Figure 16-17), click the Create option on the blue horizontal bar.

NOTE Review the default site columns available before creating a new one. One of the default site columns may be able to meet your needs.

5. On the New Site Column: Home page (shown in Figure 16-18), enter a value or make an appropriate selection for each of the following fields:

   a. Enter a unique and descriptive column name.

   b. From the list provided, choose an appropriate Column type. (See the "SharePoint Column Types" section earlier in this chapter for information

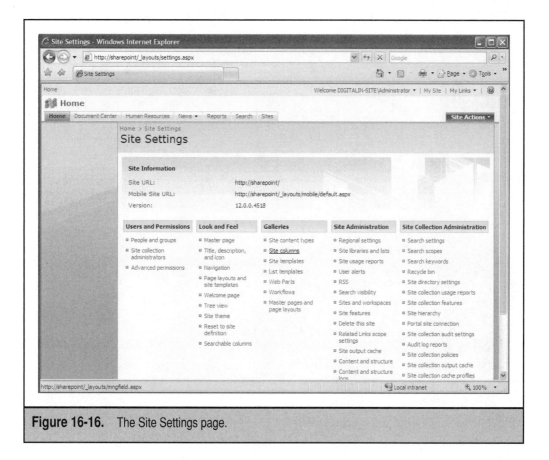

Figure 16-16.   The Site Settings page.

about each column type.) Depending on the column type selected, you may be required to enter additional column settings, such as the number of decimals in a number or currency column type.

c. Scroll down the page to the Group section (see Figure 16-19) and select an existing column group for the column. If none of the existing column groups are appropriate, you may create a new column group.

NOTE   To make your custom site columns easy for MOSS administrators or users to find, you may want to create your own column group or groups, rather than add them to one of the default or existing groups. It is unfortunate that Microsoft has chosen to use the term "group" for column groups, which are user-defined elements used as logical categories of custom site columns. No, you aren't setting permissions for a site column with the Group setting. You are merely categorizing like columns together so you can find them later.

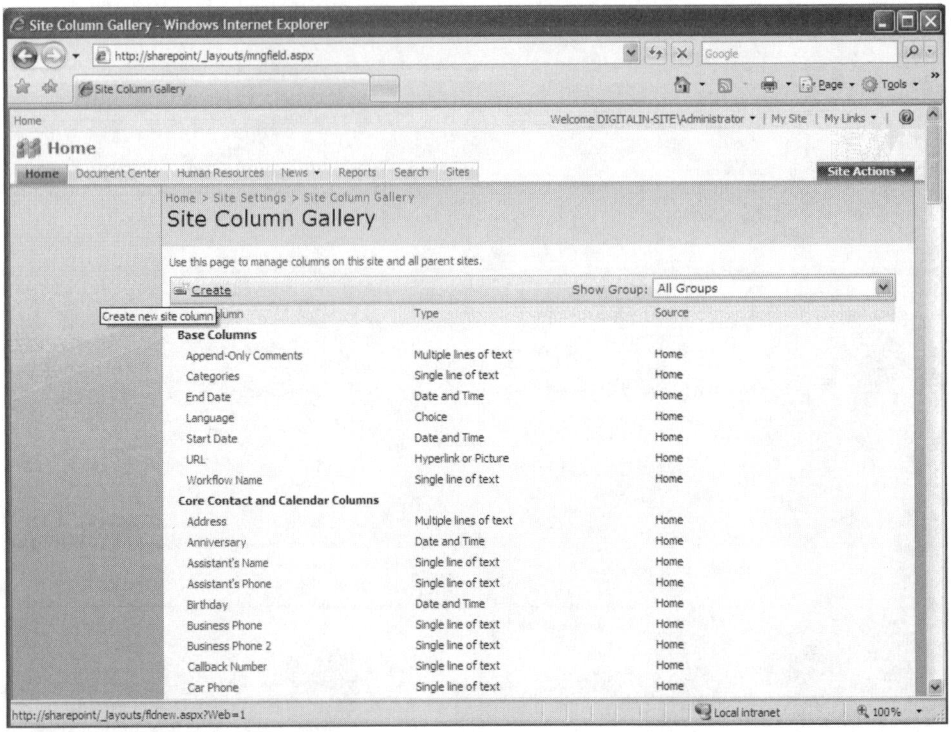

Figure 16-17.   The Site Column Gallery page.

6. Unless you chose a column type other than a single line of text and need to enter additional column settings, leave the remaining settings at their default values and click OK to create the site column.

7. If you did choose something other than the single line of text column type, fill in or select the appropriate settings in the Additional Column Settings section (see Figure 16-19) and then click OK to create the site column.

TIP   For easy site column maintenance, consider creating a custom list to store metadata values. Create a site column using the Lookup column type and reference the custom list. This approach allows you to rapidly update metadata for an entire SharePoint site simply by editing the custom list in the datasheet view.

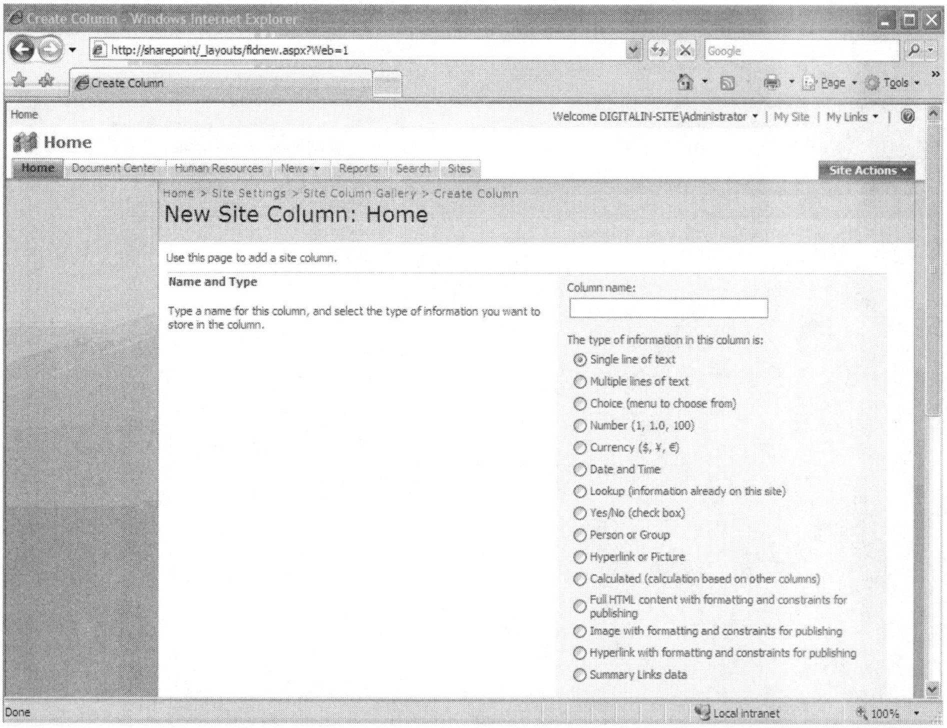

Figure 16-18.   The New Site Column: Home page.

VIEWS

As an MOSS or SharePoint library administrator, it is important to understand the files in your library as well as how users wish to access and use the information in those files. Although you may spend hours upon hours designing just the right views for a library, remember that no matter how much time you put into designing a library, it is almost never able to satisfy everyone, and it certainly won't be all things to all users.

If you are in a very large organization, you may want to create some basic views that satisfy most of what users have told you they need. Also keep in mind that users are able to create their own views for a SharePoint library—with your permission, of course.

Standard View Formats

A SharePoint library or list may have an unlimited number of views—public or private—assigned to it. However, one of its views must be designated as the list's or the library's default view, which is the view used when the library or list is initially displayed.

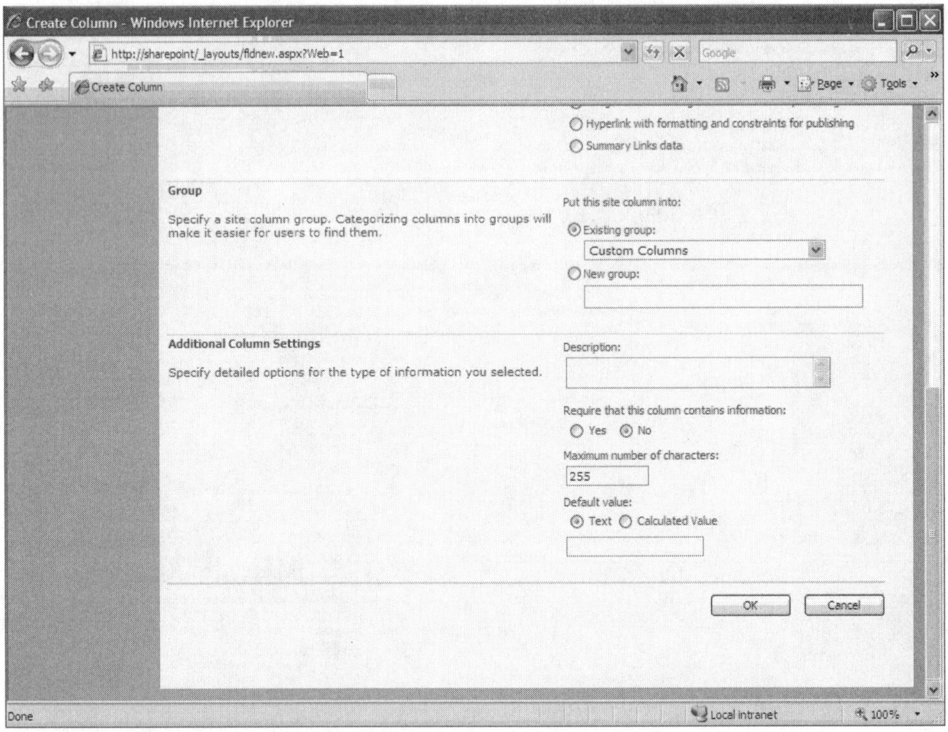

Figure 16-19. The Group and Additional Column Settings areas on the New Site Column page.

Views can be public, available to all users, or personal, available only to the creator. Typically, the SharePoint library administrator creates most of the public views, but users can also produce views if they have been granted the permission to do so. More commonly, users create personal views, which are available only to the creator. However, it is much better to have a few more public views of a library or list than it is to have each user with a dozen personal views.

A SharePoint library has two preconfigured views available:

▼ **All Items** This view displays every item in the library as a list and is the most commonly used view for the default view. In fact, as MOSS comes out of the box, this is the default view.

▲ **Explorer** This view is commonly used for managing library files displayed in a format very similar to that of Windows Explorer or My Computer.

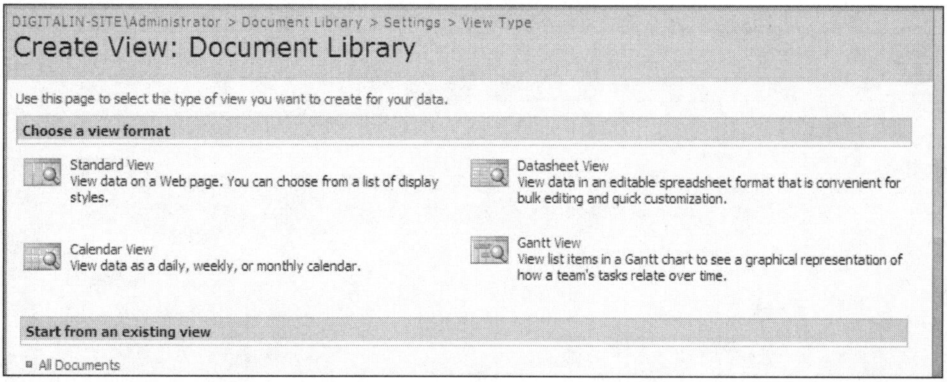

DIGITALIN-SITE\Administrator > Document Library > Settings > View Type

Create View: Document Library

Use this page to select the type of view you want to create for your data.

Choose a view format

Standard View
View data on a Web page. You can choose from a list of display styles.

Datasheet View
View data in an editable spreadsheet format that is convenient for bulk editing and quick customization.

Calendar View
View data as a daily, weekly, or monthly calendar.

Gantt View
View list items in a Gantt chart to see a graphical representation of how a team's tasks relate over time.

Start from an existing view

□ All Documents

Figure 16-20. The standard view formats for SharePoint libraries and lists.

New views for a SharePoint library or list can be created using one of four standard view formats (see Figure 16-20):

▼ **Standard** This is the default view format, if no other is selected. This view essentially displays data on a web page. However, you can pick from a list of display styles.

■ **Datasheet** This view format displays data in a spreadsheet format (see Figure 16-11 earlier in the chapter).

■ **Calendar** This view format displays event data using a daily, weekly, or monthly calendar format.

▲ **Gantt** This view format represents project or event data in the form of a Gantt chart that provides a graphical representation of tasks and how they relate to one another.

Create a View

To create a new view of a SharePoint library, perform the following steps:

1. Navigate to the page that contains the SharePoint library for which you wish to create a view and then click the View All Site Content link at the top of the Quick Launch menu.

2. On the All Site Content page, click the title of the Library.

3. On the Document Library page that displays, click the Settings option to open its drop-down menu and choose Create View.

4. On the Create View: Document Library page, select one of the four View Formats available (see Figure 16-20).

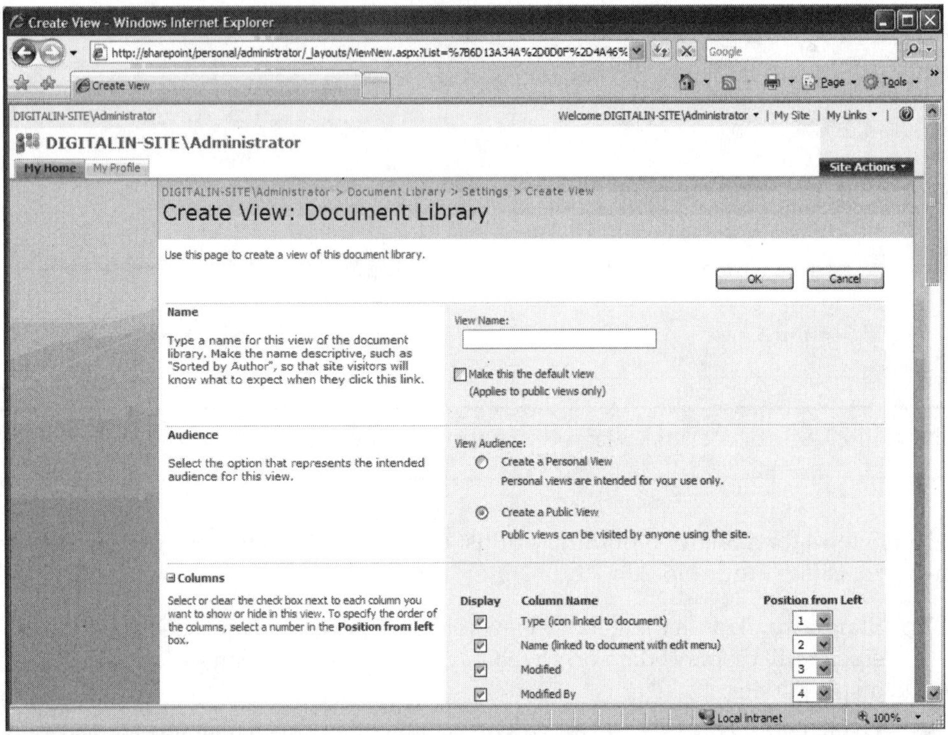

Figure 16-21.   The top portion of the Create View page.

NOTE   Most custom views are based on the Standard View format. But another format may be better suited to your needs, like a Calendar or Gantt view.

5. On the Create View page for the view format chosen (Figures 16-21, 16-22, and 16-23 show the Create View page for a standard view), enter a value or choose options for the following fields:

   a. Enter a unique and descriptive View Name. This is the name users see in the upper right corner of a library in a drop-down menu.

   b. In the Audience section, indicate whether you wish the new view to be public or private. The default selection is Create A Public View.

   c. In the Columns section, place a check in the checkboxes of the columns you wish to include in the new view. Use the Position From Left number list to position the column in the view left-to-right.

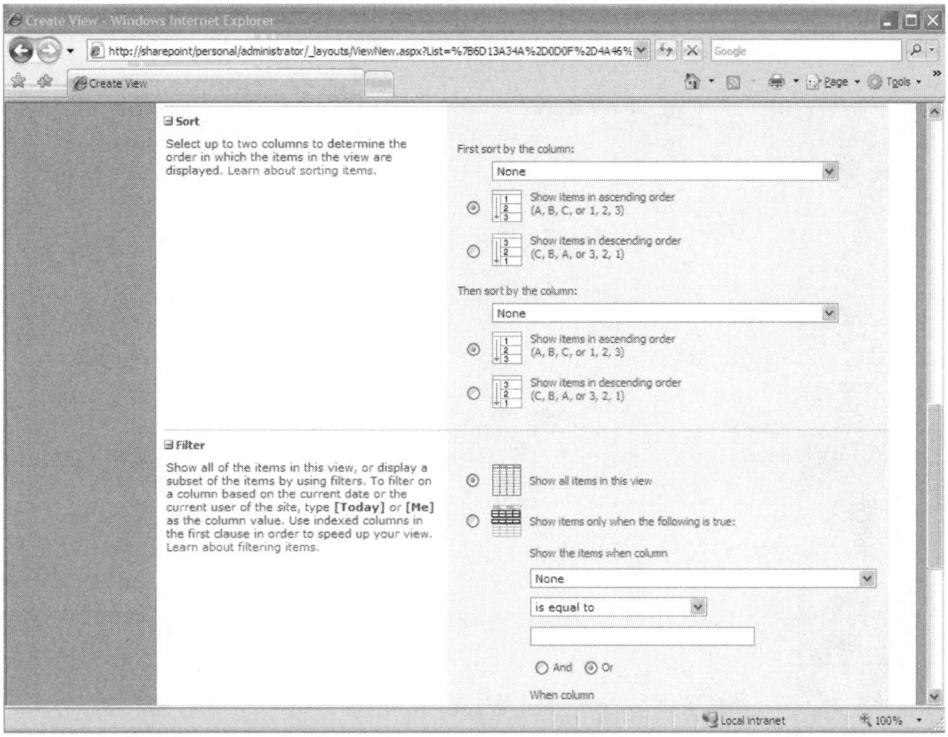

Figure 16-22. The middle portion of the Create View page.

d. Scroll down the page to the Sort section (see Figure 16-22) and, if desired, enter up to two columns in the First Sort By The Column and the Then Sort By The Column boxes to sequence the items displayed in the view, either in ascending or descending order individually.

e. Scroll down the page to the Filter section and choose whether you wish to display all content or to apply a filter to reduce the number of items in the display. If you choose to select the Show Items Only When The Following Is True option, you must do the following:

   i. Select the column name on which you wish to apply the filter from the pull-down box.

   ii. Select the conditional operator, such as equal to or greater than, from the next pull-down box.

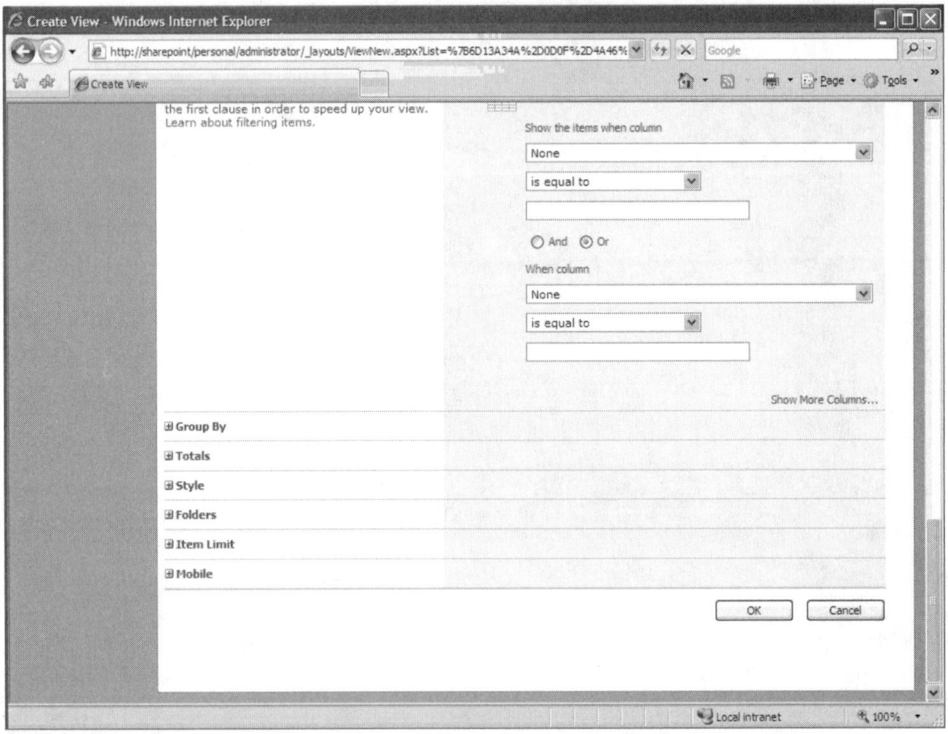

Figure 16-23. The lower portion of the Create View page.

    iii. If you wish to create a compound condition, select either the And or the Or option and fill in the second condition statement using the same process used in the two previous steps.

    iv. If you need to extend your compound condition to more columns, click the Show More Columns link to do so.

6. Scroll down the page until a list of other settings (see Figure 16-23), which are collapsed by default, are available for use in further defining your view. The most commonly used settings from this list are Group By and Totals. To add these options to your view definition, do the following:

    a. Groups are commonly included in views in which you expect a large number of items to be displayed. You may select up to two columns on which the items displayed are categorized into a group or a subgroup. If you wish to use this option, do the following:

       i. Select the column to be used as the major grouping and choose a sort order for the group, either ascending or descending.

    ii. If you wish to create a subgroup, select a second column and its sort sequence.

    iii. By default, groups are displayed in collapsed form. If you wish to display a group in expanded form, select the Expanded option.

    iv. If you want to limit the number of groups that display on each page of the view, enter a value in the Assign A Number Of Groups To Be Displayed Per Page field.

  b. Totals are commonly added to views that include columns that contain numbers or dollar amounts.

    i. If you wish to add one or more column totals to your view, select the columns for which a count, average, minimum, or maximum can be displayed.

7. Other settings available for use in your view are:

  a. Style options, which allow you to select a view style, and determine how the items are displayed for the view.

  b. The Folders option, which allows you to specify whether you wish to Show Items Inside Folders or Show All Items Without Folders.

TIP Applying a Folders option that shows items inside their folders may conflict with any groupings you may have included in a view.

  c. If you wish to limit the number of items displayed (say, the first one hundred in a sequence), use the Item Limit option and enter the maximum number of items to be displayed.

  d. If you wish a view to be available to mobile users and be optimized for mobile devices, use the Mobile option. Mobile settings are only available to public views.

8. Click OK to create the view.

Edit an Existing View

When you created a view in the preceding section, you, in effect, edited the view. Editing an existing view involves reviewing and altering the available settings used to create the view in the first place.

So why would you then edit a view? Well, perhaps you've learned which settings set up conflicts; or you need to change the view's name to better state the purpose of the view; or you wish to display additional metadata columns; or you want to change the display order of the metadata columns. Whatever your reason, to make a change to a view use the same procedure you employed to create it. There is one caveat, however. You must choose the view you wish to edit from the Views section of the Document Library Settings page (see Figure 16-3 earlier in the chapter).

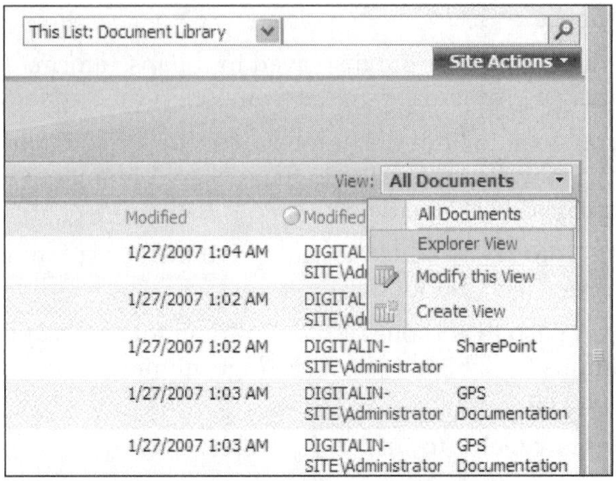

Figure 16-24. The All Documents drop-down menu lists any views available to the user in a library.

Selecting Views

Most SharePoint libraries, with the exception of the Wiki library, include an All Documents drop-down menu in the Library Web Part from which a user can select a view to be displayed. This drop-down menu, shown in Figure 16-24, enables users to select from the public views and any private views available for a library or list. The All Documents drop-down menu also includes links that can be used to modify the currently displayed view or create a new view.

Changing the Default View

As your MOSS environment and its users mature, it is common that the default view for a SharePoint library may no longer meet the needs of a majority of your users. Hopefully, the problem can be fixed though a minor adjustment to the view, but you should be careful about changing established views because some users may not appreciate your changes. A better and more user-friendly way to approach this issue is to keep the existing default view, create a new view that better serves the majority of users, and then designate the new view as the default view, leaving the original view available to those users who still want to use it.

To cancel out the designation as a default view for a SharePoint Library view, simply create a new view and designate it as the default view. The existing default view designation is overridden and cancelled.

SUMMARY

Doing away with folders and subfolders is a radical concept for many administrators new to MOSS. You may choose to ease your organization into the concept by initially creating non-native content sources to network shares. Once users are comfortable with MOSS and its features, you can migrate network share content into native SharePoint libraries and eventually switch the users to a flat library view. MOSS provides you with more than one way to view its content, which can be a valuable migration tool.

Good metadata improve search results, which leads to increased user efficiency. Users spend less time wading through lists of files when they are able to filter out unnecessary files and data from library lists. Metadata may be created from within MOSS-compatible applications, such as Microsoft Word and other applications in the Microsoft Office 2007 suite, when one of these applications is used to create and save (publish) a document to a SharePoint library. You can also use the Edit In Datasheet feature to quickly assign metadata to a large number of entries.

Metadata standards are an important organizational tool to ensure the effectiveness of metadata. Consider using site columns and custom lists to lower the administrative burden of implementing metadata.

PART III

MOSS and Office 2007

CHAPTER 17

MOSS and Outlook 2007

Perhaps of all of the Microsoft Office 2007 applications, Microsoft Outlook 2007 may provide you with the most benefit in terms of direct information. By enabling and utilizing the direct connection and synchronization features between Outlook and MOSS, your personal appointment calendar and address book contacts remain up-to-date in both applications. Linking a SharePoint meeting workspace to an Outlook meeting request or appointment enables the attendees of a meeting to access any associated documents, lists, or information relevant to the event from within Outlook.

In this chapter, we look at the ways in which MOSS and Outlook 2007 can be connected to share and maximize the capabilities of both applications. Our focus is on those SharePoint and Outlook features that you and your users are most likely to use in a new MOSS and Office 2007 installation.

OUTLOOK AND MOSS CONNECTIONS

Users can view MOSS resources using Outlook 2007, but the two applications must be connected first. The process detailed in this section can be used to establish the connection between MOSS and Outlook to provide your users with access to document libraries, task lists, discussion boards, contact lists, and other SharePoint elements. The MOSS elements for which a connection can be created in Outlook are listed in Table 17-1.

Connect MOSS Resources to Outlook

To create the connection between MOSS and Outlook 2007, use the following steps:

1. From the MOSS main page, open the Shared Documents library (or whatever element you wish to connect to Outlook) using its link in the Quick Launch navigation menu.

> **NOTE**   This example describes the process used to connect to a document library, but these steps can also be used for many other MOSS resources as well.

2. Click the Actions button and choose Connect To Outlook, as shown in Figure 17-1.

3. In the Connect This SharePoint Document Library To Outlook dialog box that displays (see Figure 17-2), click the Yes button.

> **NOTE**   If you are running on a Windows 2003 Server system, you may be prompted to download the Instant Search (Windows Desktop Search [WDS]) component as part of connecting your first SharePoint element to Outlook. WDS extends the search capability of your system to include e-mail, documents, and other files stored on the local computer. Windows Vista already includes this feature.

The connected MOSS resource should now be included in Outlook's Folders pane with the title SharePoint Lists (see Figure 17-3). Note that when you connect resources

Calendars	MOSS calendars can be displayed either adjacent to a user's Outlook calendar or as an overlay so both calendars are viewed as one calendar.
Contact List	An MOSS contact list is available in the Outlook Contacts.
Discussion Board	Allows a user to open and participate in a discussion forum from Outlook.
Document Library	MOSS document libraries can be viewed, searched, and edited from Outlook.
Task List	The tasks included in an MOSS task list are displayed in the Outlook Tasks and To-Do windows.

Table 17-1. The MOSS Elements that Can Be Integrated into Outlook 2007

to Outlook 2007, the resources appear in their respective sections of the Outlook 2007 navigation pane. Calendars appear in the Calendar pane, under Other Calendars; Tasks appear in the Tasks pane, under Other Tasks; Contact Lists appear in the Contacts pane, under Other Contacts. Discussion Lists are similar to Document Libraries and appear in the Mail pane, under SharePoint Lists.

Figure 17-1. The Connect To Outlook option on the Actions Menu.

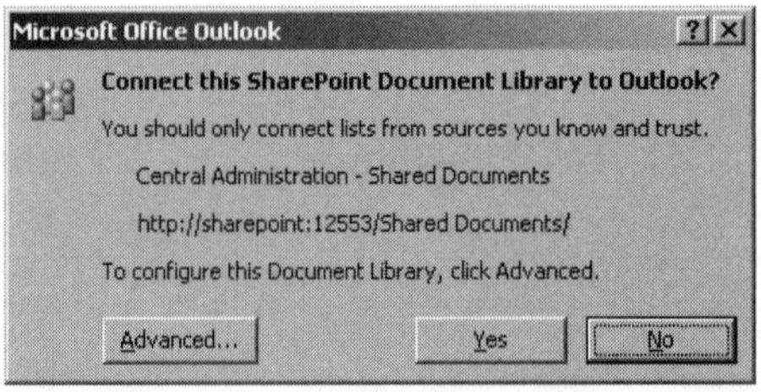

Figure 17-2. The Connect This SharePoint Document Library To Outlook dialog box.

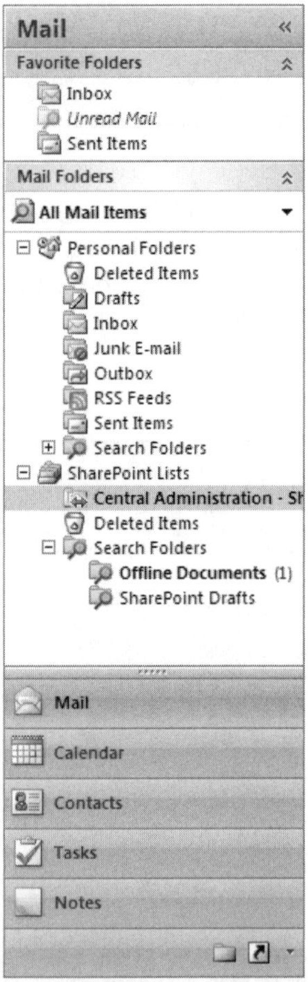

Figure 17-3. A connected MOSS resource included in the Outlook Folders list.

NOTE   Because the user permissions on an MOSS element carry over to Outlook, a user will have access only to those MOSS elements in Outlook to which she or he has access to in MOSS.

Share MOSS Resources through Outlook

Once a connection has been established between Outlook and an MOSS resource, the user can share the connection to the resource through a sharing message. Of course, this assumes the users with whom the connection is being shared have been granted the appropriate permissions by the resource's owner.

To share an MOSS resource connection to Outlook, do the following:

1. Under the SharePoint Lists heading in the Outlook Folders pane, right-click the resource for which you wish to share the connection.

2. From the pop-up menu, choose the Share *Resource Name* option, as illustrated in Figure 17-4, to open a sharing message that includes a link the message recipients can use to connect to the shared resource.

3. Add the e-mail addresses of the users with whom you wish to share the connection (see Figure 17-5) and click Send.

TIP   Should you be one of the addressees of a connection sharing message, use the Connect To This *Resource Name* option on the Open menu of Outlook to connect to the shared resource.

Edit Connected MOSS Resources in Outlook

Because a connected resource carries with it the permissions granted to the user in MOSS for that resource, any changes made to a calendar, task list, discussion board, or contact list in Outlook are automatically updated to the resource in MOSS, provided the user is

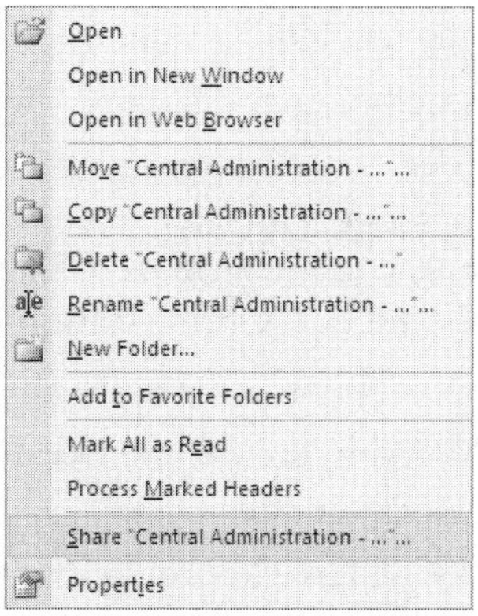

Figure 17-4.   The pop-up menu for an MOSS resource connected to Outlook.

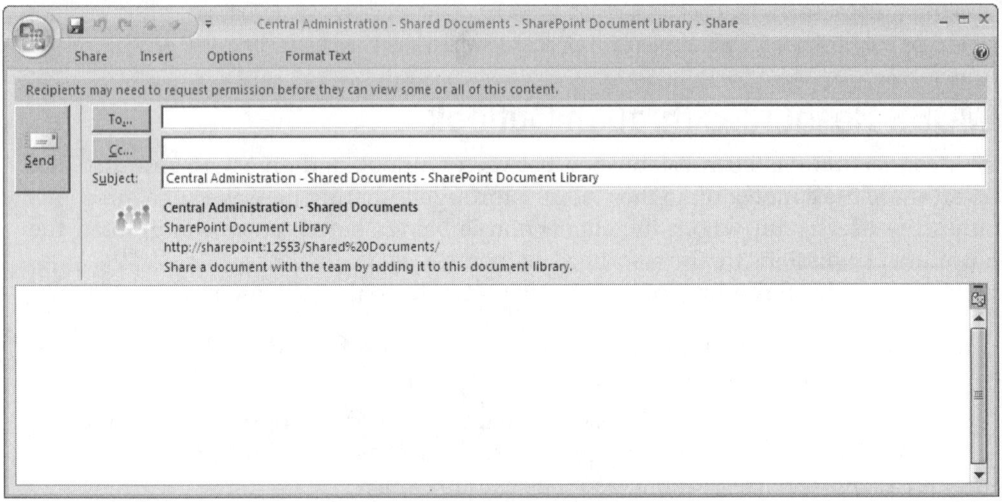

Figure 17-5. The e-mail message used to share a connection to a SharePoint document from within Outlook.

connected to the organization's network. However, to update changes made to a document library connected to Outlook, you must open the document, edit it offline, and then save it to the MOSS server after it is edited.

To open and edit a SharePoint document library file from within Outlook, do the following:

1. From the Outlook Folders list, double-click the document library file connection to open the connected document.

2. In the Opening File dialog box that displays, click the Open button.

3. When the document opens in its native application, such as Word, Excel, a web browser, and so on, a message bar (see Figure 17-6) is displayed advising you that to edit the document, you must do so offline. The document is opened as read-only until you click the Edit Offline button in the message bar.

4. An Edit Offline dialog box opens (see Figure 17-7). Click OK.

5. The file is copied and stored in the Offline Documents folder in the Search Folders of Outlook.

6. After you have made your edits, save and close the file. An Edit Offline dialog box opens (see Figure 17-8) giving you the option of updating or not updating the MOSS version of the document.

7. If you choose the Update option on the Edit Offline dialog box (see Figure 17-8), the master copy of the document is updated in MOSS during the next Send/ Receive process by Outlook.

TIP If you are concerned that others might try to modify a document while you are doing the same, before opening the document in Outlook, use the Check Out feature in MOSS to prevent others from accessing the document. You must also remember to use the Check In feature when finished.

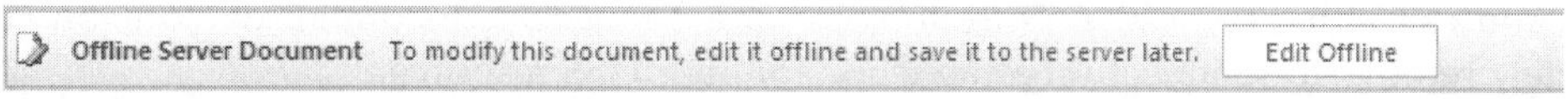

Figure 17-6. The message bar that displays when you open a connected MOSS document library file.

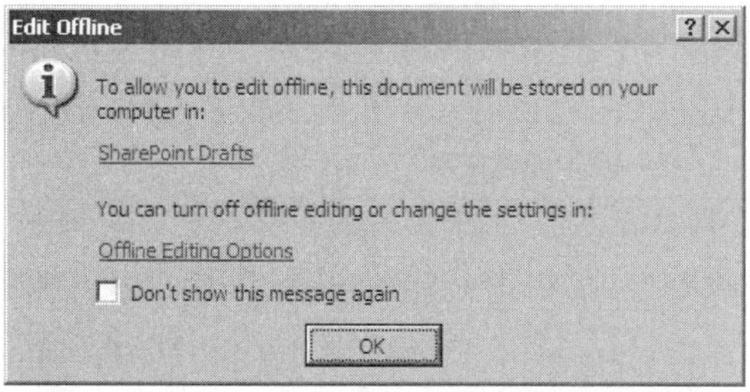

Figure 17-7. The Edit Offline dialog box used to indicate that a document is to be edited offline.

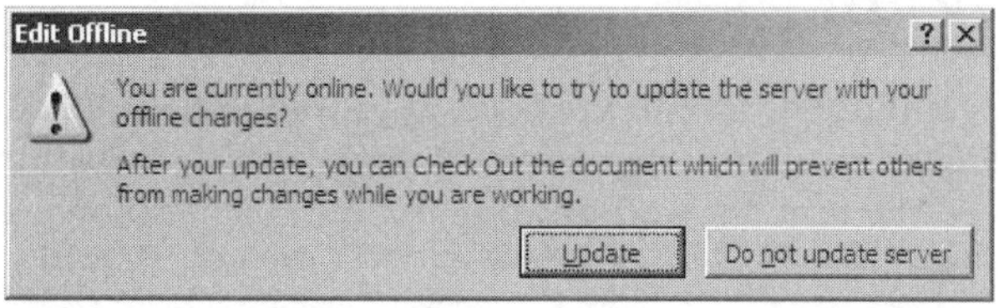

Figure 17-8. The Edit Offline dialog box used to indicate whether a document should be updated.

When you open a connected document in Outlook, it is stored in the SharePoint Drafts folder, which is a system folder located in the My Documents folder of the logged-in user. This means that after you have opened the document for editing, you can close the document, edit it offline, and update the MOSS version at a later time, when you have reconnected to the network.

Delete a Connected Document from Outlook

Unless you plan to frequently access and update a connected MOSS document from Outlook, you should remove the connection when you no longer need it. Otherwise, your Outlook SharePoint Lists folder can become cluttered and disorganized.

You can either remove an offline copy of a connected document or you can completely remove the connection established for an MOSS resource.

To remove an offline copy of a connected document from your Outlook SharePoint Lists folder, do the following:

1. Under the SharePoint Lists heading in the Outlook Folders pane, select the MOSS resource you wish to remove.

2. In the window to the right of the Mail navigation pane, select the file from the list of Downloaded Documents you wish to remove, as shown in Figure 17-9. To select multiple files, hold down the CTRL key while you click file names.

3. Right-click the selected file(s) and then click Remove Offline Copy from the pop-up menu. The document reference should move from Downloaded Documents to the Available For Download list.

To delete the connection for an MOSS resource from Outlook, do the following:

1. In the Outlook Folders pane, locate the resource in the SharePoint Lists folder or in the Calendars, Task Lists, and Contact Lists sections, as applicable, and select the resource connection you wish to delete.

2. Right-click the resource connection reference and click Delete *Resource Name* from the pop-up window that appears (see Figure 17-10).

MEETING WORKSPACES

MOSS, working in conjunction with Outlook 2007, has the ability to create a meeting workspace that can be used for the creation, storage, and distribution of meeting agendas, minutes, shared documents, and other general information about a meeting or series of meetings. A meeting workspace site in MOSS contains all of the documents, tasks, lists, and other resources needed for reference, edit, and update during a meeting that is held offline, such as in a teleconference, in person, or perhaps even e-mail. You can create a MOSS Meeting Workspace from an Outlook meeting request, which is likely the most commonly used method for doing so.

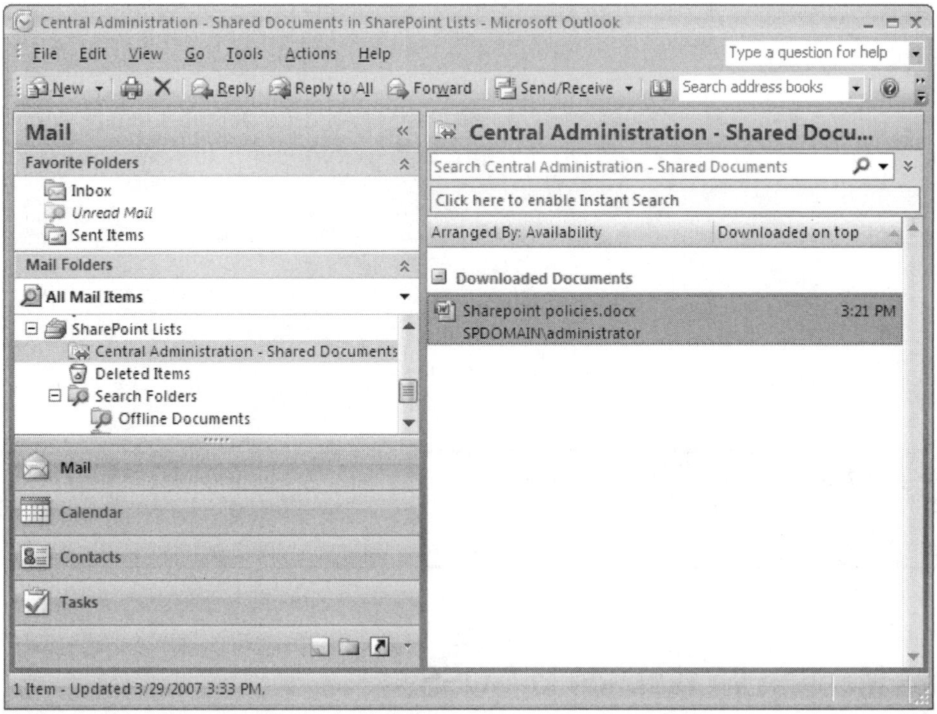

Figure 17-9.   A SharePoint resource selected for deletion from Outlook.

To create a Meeting Workspace from within Outlook 2007, you must first have Site Owner (full control) permissions for the meeting workspace site to be linked to the meeting request. The reason for this is that when a Meeting Workspace is created, the users listed as attendees must be granted access to the workspace, something typically reserved for the Site Owner or an administrator. For an administrator, this could possibly be any site within the MOSS environment, but for a user, it is likely to be his or her My Site site.

When a meeting is set up in Outlook, a link to the meeting workspace is included in the meeting request sent to each person invited. By clicking the link in the meeting request, the meeting workspace opens in the participant's browser, where he or she can read the agenda, documents, and relevant information for the meeting. Outlook also updates the meeting workspace site with the names of the meeting participants and the date, time, and location of the meeting. Outlook also posts any changes made to the meeting request at a later time to the meeting workspace.

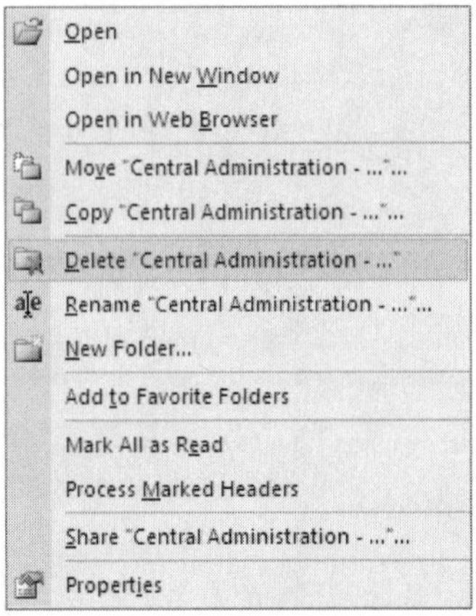

Figure 17-10. The Delete Resource option on the pop-up menu of a selected MOSS resource connection.

Create a Meeting Workspace in MOSS

To create a meeting workspace in MOSS, do the following:

1. Open the SharePoint site on which you wish to create a meeting workspace.

2. Click the Site Actions button and choose the Create option.

3. On the Create page, click the Sites And Workspace link under the Web Pages heading.

4. On the New SharePoint Site page, enter a title for the workspace that briefly describes the meeting to be held and a description that fully explains the purpose of the meeting.

5. In the Template Section on the New SharePoint Site page, click the Meetings tab and select the meeting workspace template most appropriate to the meeting to be held (see Figure 17-11).

   The meeting workspace templates provide a starting point for organizing the resources and information needed for your meeting. Remember that each of these templates can be modified to suit the specifics of your meeting. As shown in Figure 17-11, the meeting workspace templates available are:

   ■ **Basic meeting workspace** Includes elements (Objectives, Attendees, Agenda, and Document Library) to help plan, organize, and track a meeting (see Figure 17-12).

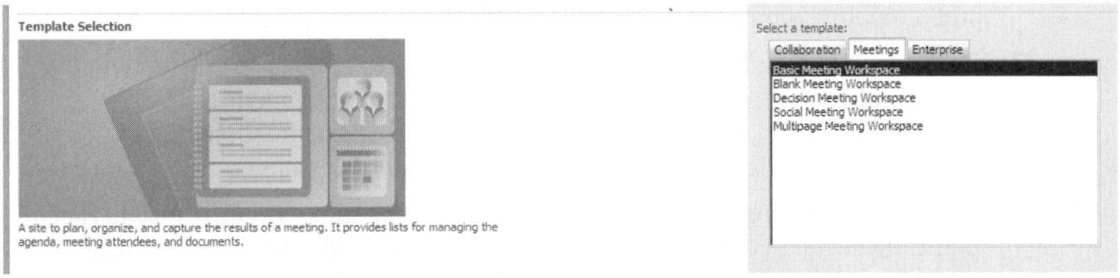

Figure 17-11. The Template Section of the New SharePoint Site page showing the available meeting workspace templates.

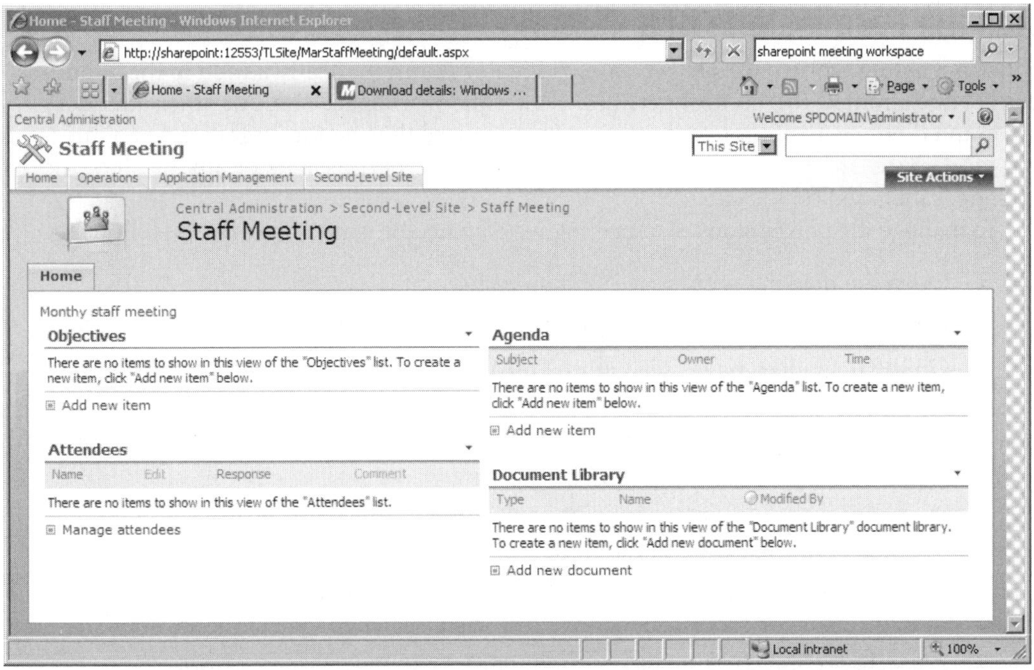

Figure 17-12. A meeting workspace created using the Basic Meeting Workspace template.

- **Blank meeting workspace** A blank workspace that can be customized to suit a meeting's particular needs and resources.

- **Decision meeting workspace** Creates a meeting workspace for reviewing documents and a record for any decisions made at the meeting. The elements included on the decision meeting workspace are Objectives, Attendees, Agenda, Document Library, Tasks, and Decisions.

- **Social meeting workspace** Creates a meeting workspace appropriate for planning social events that can be customized with elements that include Attendees, Directions, Images/Logo, Things to Bring, Discussions, and a Picture Library.

- **Multipage meeting workspace** Similar to the basic meeting workspace template, but allows for multiple pages on which meeting resources, such as Objectives, Attendees, and Agenda, can be included. The template creates two blank pages to allow for customization.

6. Click OK to create the meeting workspace using the template you've chosen.

Manage the Permissions of a Meeting Workspace Site

When a meeting workspace site is create, its creator is automatically added to the attendees list and granted full control permissions for the workspace site. All other attendees are granted only contributor permissions. However, as the creator (organizer) of a meeting workspace site, you have the ability to change the permissions of any or all of the attendees included on the site.

To manage the permissions of a meeting workspace site's attendees, do the following:

1. Open the meeting workspace's home page.

2. Under the Attendees heading, click the Manage Attendees link.

3. On the Attendees page (see Figure 17-13), click the Settings button and choose the List Settings option.

4. On the Customize Attendees page, click the Permissions For This List option under the Permissions and Policies heading.

5. On the Permissions: Attendees page, click the Actions button and select the Manage Permissions Of Parent link (see Figure 17-14).

6. On the Permissions page for the top-level site, select the check boxes associated with the users or groups for whom you wish to change permissions.

7. Click the Actions button and select the Edit User Permissions option.

8. On the Edit Permissions page for the user or group selected, modify the permissions assigned to the user or group as needed.

9. Click OK to store the modified permissions for the user or group.

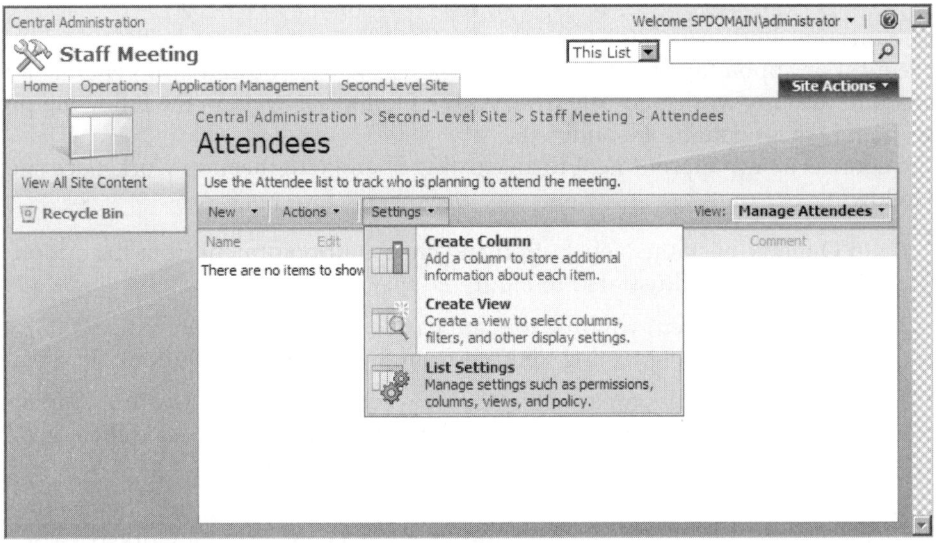

Figure 17-13. The Attendees page for a SharePoint meeting workspace site.

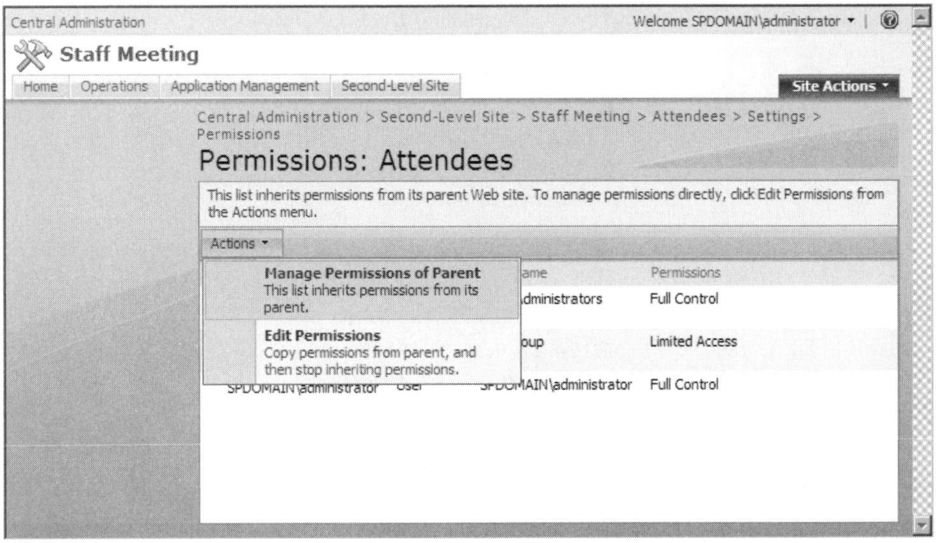

Figure 17-14. The Permissions: Attendees page.

Create or Link to a Meeting Workspace from Outlook

Once a meeting workspace has been created in SharePoint, its site can be linked to a meeting request or appointment created in Outlook. However, you can also generate a new SharePoint meeting workspace site from within Outlook as well. In the following procedure, both of these options are outlined.

To connect a new appointment to an existing SharePoint meeting workspace site, do the following:

1. In Outlook, click the New button and choose Appointment from the option list that appears, as illustrated in Figure 17-15.

2. In the Appointment window that appears, click the Microsoft Office 2007 button and choose Meeting Request from the Create New Outlook Item pane.

3. In the Meeting ribbon, find the Attendees section and click Meeting Workspace to open the Meeting Workspace panel (see Figure 17-16) on the right side of the window.

4. As shown in Figure 17-16, you have two options for connecting the meeting request to a meeting workspace site: creating a new meeting workspace or linking to an existing meeting workspace.

   - If you wish to create a new meeting workspace in SharePoint:
     a. Choose the Create a Workspace radio button.
     b. Choose the language you wish to use.

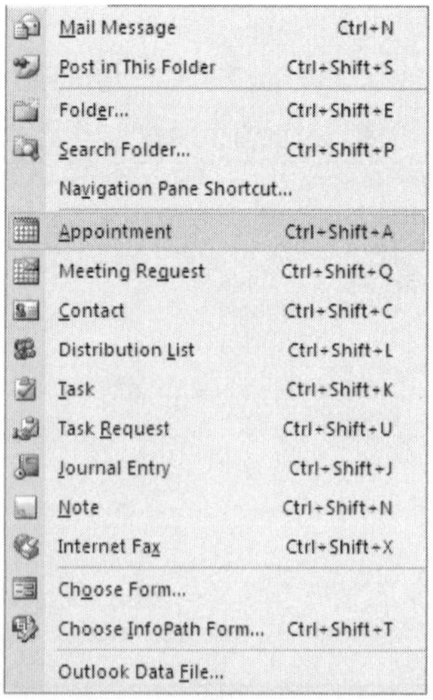

Figure 17-15. The New option list of the Outlook File menu.

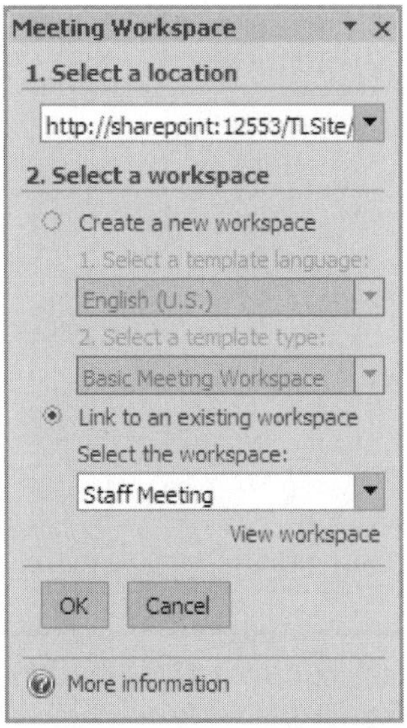

Figure 17-16. The Meeting Workspace panel on a new Meeting Request window.

c.   Choose the meeting workspace template you wish to apply to the meeting workspace site.

d.   Click the OK button to create the meeting workspace site.

e.   The Meeting Workspace panel's content changes giving you the option to change the existing or default settings for where the meeting workspace will be created (see Figure 17-17).

f.   If the settings listed are the ones you wish to use, click the Create button. Otherwise, click the Change Settings link to alter the location and template type for the new meeting workspace site. After changing the settings, click the Create button.

g.   The Meeting Workspace panel changes to show the progress of the create action, as shown in Figure 17-18.

h.   When the SharePoint meeting workspace site has been created, the appointment area and the Meeting Workspace panels will contain information regarding the new workspace site (see Figure 17-19).

■   If you wish to link the meeting request or appointment to an existing meeting workspace site:

a.   Choose the Link to an existing workspace radio button and select the workspace site from the pull-down list associated with this option.

b.   Click OK.

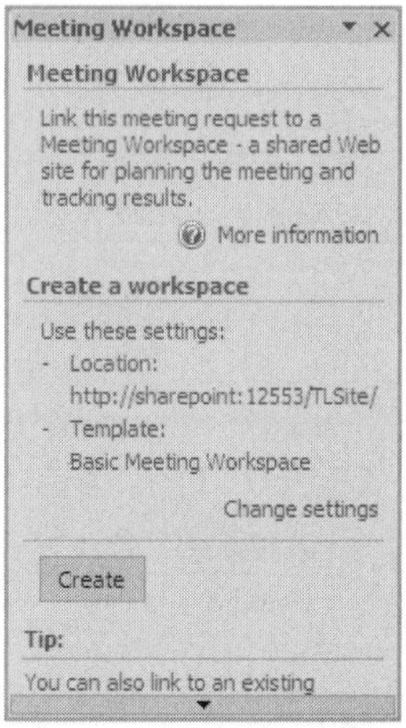

Figure 17-17. The Meeting Workspace panel showing the settings to be used to create a new SharePoint meeting workspace site.

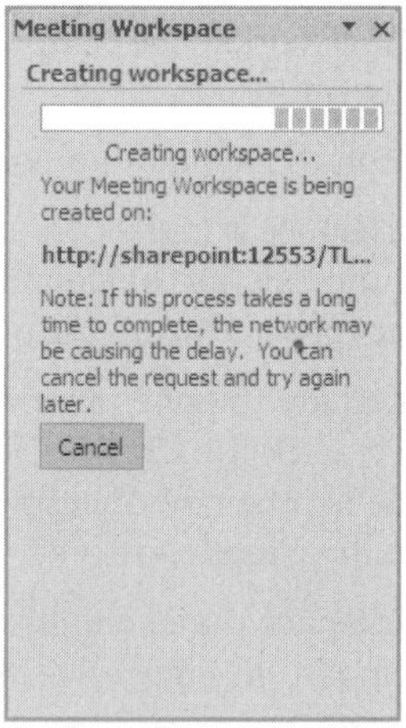

Figure 17-18. The Meeting Workspace panel showing the progress of the create action for a new SharePoint meeting workspace site.

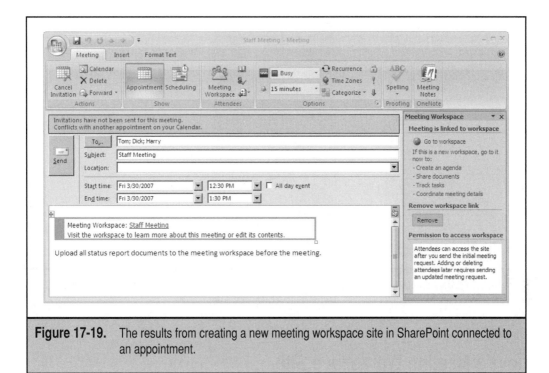

Figure 17-19. The results from creating a new meeting workspace site in SharePoint connected to an appointment.

c. The Meeting Workspace panel's contents change to display and confirm the location and site to which you wish to link the meeting request. If this information is correct, click the Link button (see Figure 17-20). Otherwise, click the Change settings link to modify the settings.

d. The results of the link action are displayed in the Meeting Workspace panel and the appointment pane, and are very similar to that used for the create workspace process.

View a Meeting Workspace from Outlook

SharePoint meeting workspace sites can be viewed from a variety of Outlook functions and features. From within Outlook, you can open and view a SharePoint meeting workspace site from a meeting request, a meeting reminder, or from your Outlook calendar. Table 17-2 lists how you can open and view a meeting workspace site from these Outlook features.

TIP You can also view a Meeting Workspace site from within MOSS by clicking the View All Site Content in the Quick Launch navigation pane and clicking the meeting workspace site's name under the Sites and Workspaces heading.

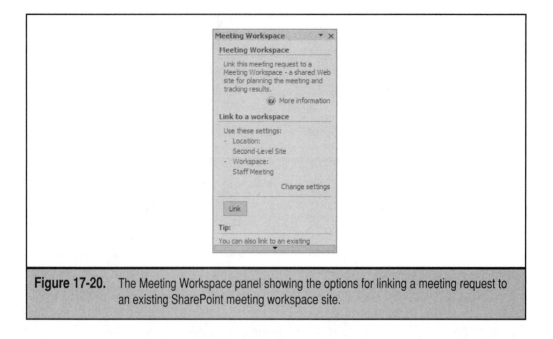

Figure 17-20. The Meeting Workspace panel showing the options for linking a meeting request to an existing SharePoint meeting workspace site.

Remove a Meeting Workspace Site

After a meeting has been held that was tied to a particularly unique meeting workspace site, you may wish to remove the meeting workspace site to free up the database space and to tidy up the attendees' Outlook links. However, a few considerations should be addressed before you actually remove the site:

▼ When you delete a meeting workspace, you delete all of the site's information from MOSS, but not any information regarding the meeting in Outlook. To remove the meeting from Outlook, you must open the appointment or meeting request and delete it specifically.

Outlook function	Steps used to open meeting workspace site.
Meeting reminder	Click the View Meeting Workspace link on the Meeting Services list (see Figure 17-21).
Meeting request or calendar appointment	Click the Meeting Workspace link or click the Go To Workspace link in the Meeting Workspace pane.
Outlook calendar	Right-click the meeting or appointment entry and select View Meeting Workspace from the pop-up menu.

Table 17-2. Open and View a Meeting Workspace Site from Outlook

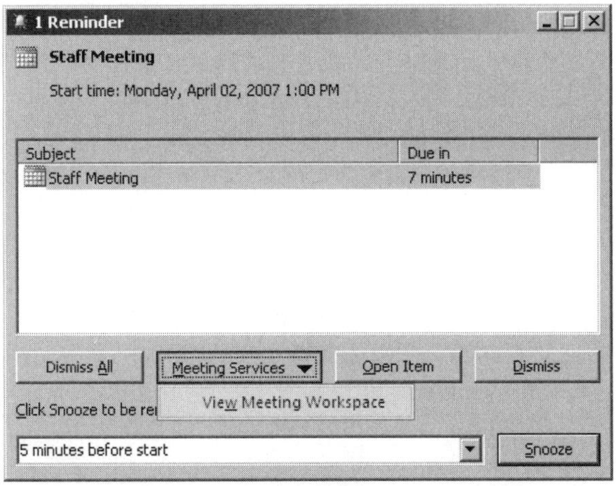

Figure 17-21.   Outlook Meeting Reminder.

- When you delete or cancel a meeting appointment in Outlook, the meeting workspace to which it may be linked is not affected.

- You don't need to delete a meeting appointment to change its details. You can send a meeting update to the attendees (including newly added attendees) that reflects the changes that have been made to the format, schedule, or location of the meeting. Sending an updated meeting request retains the meeting's link to a SharePoint meeting workspace site.

- ▲ If after you've deleted a meeting request or appointment, you wish to reestablish the meeting request, you must also reestablish the link between the meeting request and the SharePoint meeting workspace site to which it is associated.

To remove a SharePoint meeting workspace site, do the following:

1. Open the SharePoint meeting workspace site.

2. Click the Site Actions button and choose Site Settings from its menu.

3. On the Site Settings page, click the Delete This Site link under the Site Administration heading.

4. On the Delete This Site page that opens (see Figure 17-22), click the Delete button.

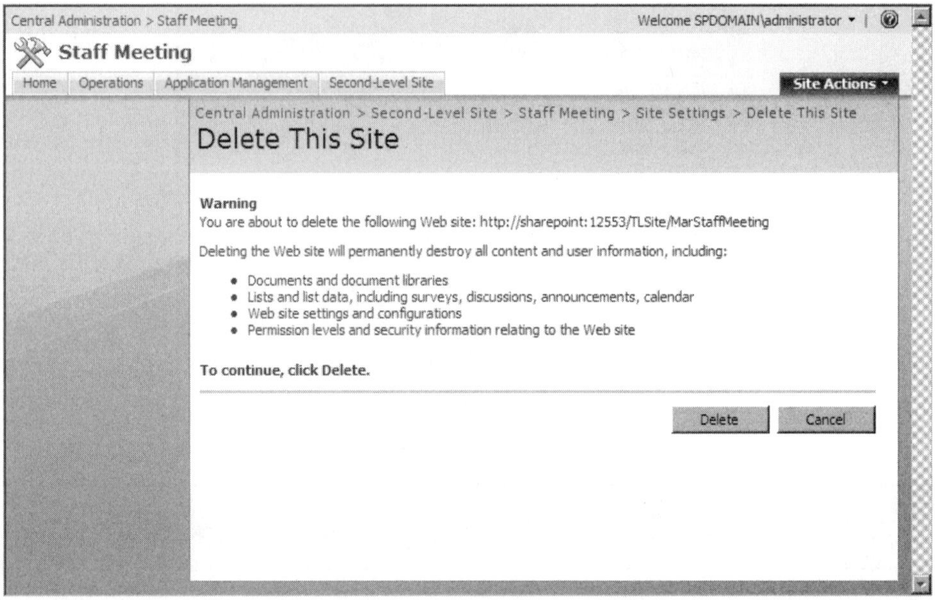

Figure 17-22.   The Delete This Site page.

Share an Agenda to Multiple Meetings

Meetings that are held regularly, such as a weekly staff, department, project, or team meeting, often have essentially the same standard agenda. In situations like this, rather than create separate copies of the agenda for each of a series of recurring meetings, it is far easier to simply share the agenda across all meetings associated with a particular meeting workspace site.

To use the same agenda document for a series of meetings, do the following:

1. Open the meeting workspace site's home page.

2. Click the Agenda heading.

3. On the Agenda page, click the Settings item and choose List Settings from the Settings menu.

4. On the Customize Agenda page, click the Advanced Settings link under the General Settings heading.

5. On the List Advanced Settings: Agenda page, choose the Yes radio button option in the Share List Items Across All Meetings (Series Items) section.

6. Click OK to link the agenda to all occurrences of the meeting.

CONTACTS

The people, organizational units, or distribution lists defined in Outlook and MOSS can be linked and synchronized so any changes made to the contact list in either application is automatically included in the other application. This allows you to create a contact or contact list within MOSS without the need to open Outlook and create the contact or contact list before referencing it in MOSS.

Create an MOSS Contact List and Add Contacts

To create a contact list in MOSS, do the following:

1. Open the home page of a SharePoint site.

2. Click the View All Site Content link in the Quick Launch navigation pane.

3. Click the Create button to open the Create page.

4. Under the Communications heading, click the Contacts link to open the New page (see Figure 17-23), which in this case is used to create a new list item.

5. As illustrated in Figure 17-23, enter a unique and descriptive name and description for the contact list and indicate whether you wish the contact list to be included in the Quick Launch menu.

6. Click Create to create the contact list.

Figure 17-23.   The New page is used to create a list item.

Once you've created a contact list, you can begin adding contacts to the list. To add a contact to a contact list, perform the following steps:

1. Open the SharePoint page where you have created your contact list.

2. Open the contact list (if you so chose, the list could be included in the Quick Launch menu).

3. Click the New button to open the contact list's new item page.

4. Enter the contact's data and click OK to create the contact (as shown in Figure 17-24). After the contact list item has been processed, it will appear on the list page.

TIP   If you don't have all of a contact's information available, only a Last Name is required to create the contact item.

Synchronize MOSS Contacts with Outlook

The contacts included in your Outlook address book can be synchronized into an MOSS contact list. To synchronize the two contact lists, do the following:

1. Open the SharePoint page containing the contact list with which you wish to synchronize your Outlook contacts.

2. Open the contact list.

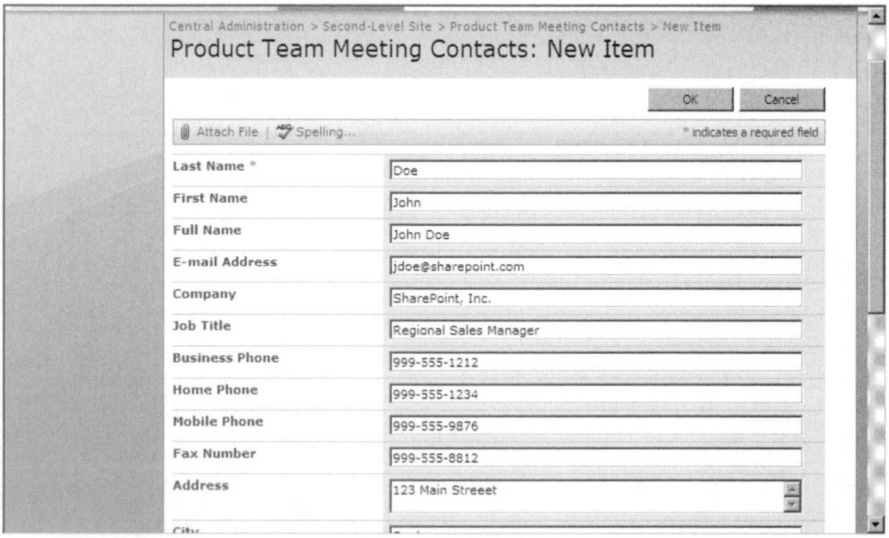

Central Administration > Second-Level Site > Product Team Meeting Contacts > New Item

Product Team Meeting Contacts: New Item

OK	Cancel

Attach File | Spelling... * indicates a required field

Last Name *	Doe
First Name	John
Full Name	John Doe
E-mail Address	jdoe@sharepoint.com
Company	SharePoint, Inc.
Job Title	Regional Sales Manager
Business Phone	999-555-1212
Home Phone	999-555-1234
Mobile Phone	999-555-9876
Fax Number	999-555-8812
Address	123 Main Streeet
City	

Figure 17-24.   Adding a new contact to a contact list.

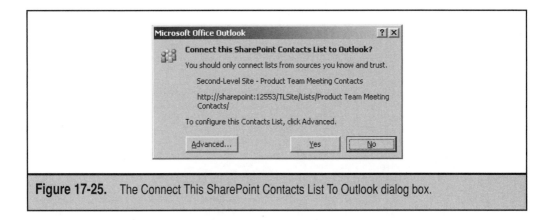

Figure 17-25.   The Connect This SharePoint Contacts List To Outlook dialog box.

3. On the contact list's page, click the Actions button and select Connect To Outlook from its drop-down menu.

4. Outlook displays an intercept dialog box (see Figure 17-25) to ensure that you truly wish to connect to Outlook. Assuming that you do, click the Yes button to proceed.

5. A new contacts group is displayed in the Outlook window (see Figure 17-26).

6. To verify that the two contact lists are in fact synchronized, access the contact list in Outlook and make a modification to one of the connected contacts. The modification should also appear in the SharePoint contact list entry after the next send/receive cycle of Outlook is completed. You may want to also verify that changes made to a contact on the SharePoint contacts lists are automatically updated into the Outlook contacts list as well.

CALENDAR LIST ITEMS

A SharePoint calendar list works very much like its Outlook counterpart and actually looks very much the same. A SharePoint calendar list, like the one shown in Figure 17-27, enables you to enter and track your appointments and meetings, as well as link directly to any meeting workspaces associated with an appointment or meeting.

Add a Calendar List Item

If you have created any meeting workspaces or connected an Outlook Calendar to a SharePoint site, a Calendar list should exist on that site and be listed in the Quick Launch menu under the Lists heading. To add an appointment or meeting to a SharePoint Calendar list, perform the following steps:

1. Open the site that holds the Calendar list you wish to update.

2. In the Quick Launch menu, under the Lists heading, click the link for Calendar.

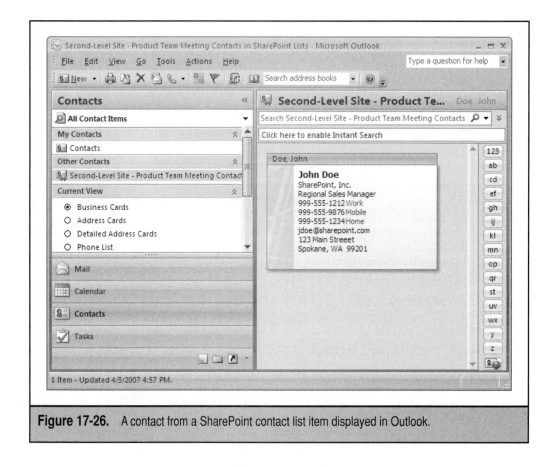

Figure 17-26. A contact from a SharePoint contact list item displayed in Outlook.

3. On the Calendar list page, click the New button and choose New Item.

4. On the Calendar: New Item page, enter the appropriate data into each of the calendar item's fields, as shown in Figure 17-28.

5. After filling in the form and checking any of the option checkboxes you wish to apply, click OK to create the Calendar list item and add it to the Calendar list.

Export a SharePoint Calendar List Item to Outlook

SharePoint Calendar list items can be exported to Outlook. To do so, do the following:

1. Open the Calendar list containing the item you wish to export.

2. Click the Calendar list item you wish to export to Outlook.

3. Click the Export Event link found on the item menu bar.

4. A dialog box is displayed that asks if you wish to save the new calendar event. Click OK.

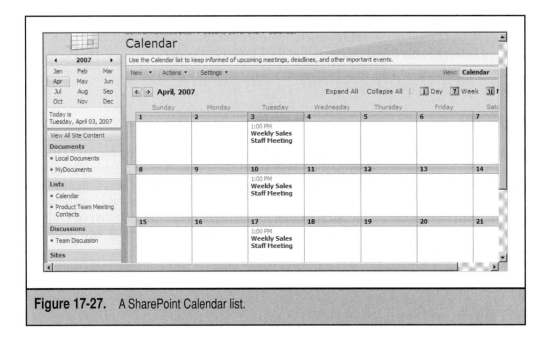

Figure 17-27.   A SharePoint Calendar list.

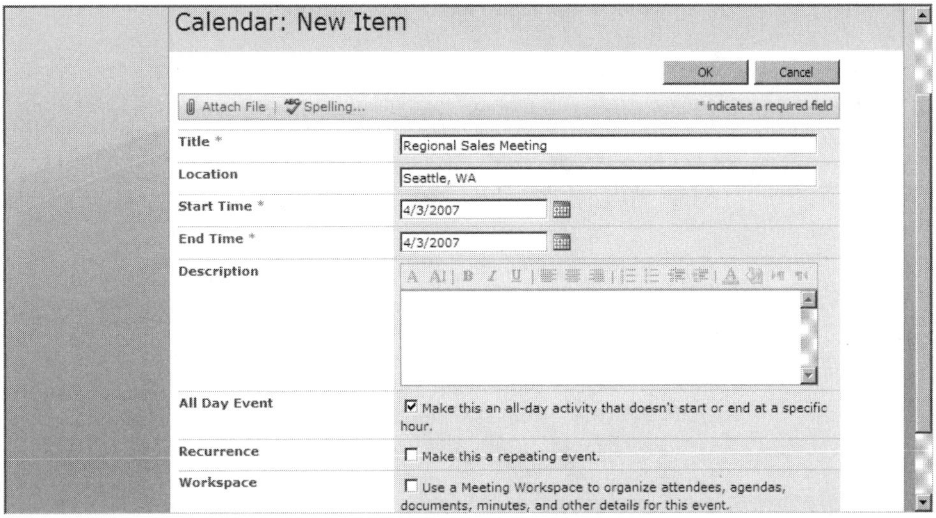

Figure 17-28.   Creating a new SharePoint Calendar list item.

5. An Outlook appointment window for this event is opened. Scan the information in the appointment window and if all is well, click Save and Close to save the appointment in the Outlook calendar.

6. Click back into the exported event's page and click Close.

SUMMARY

Because Microsoft Outlook provides portability for your e-mail, calendar, and tasks to mobile devices, creating a connection and synchronization between your SharePoint meeting workspaces and their associated documents, and your SharePoint Calendar lists and their events, provides a way for you to ensure that this information is current, up-to-date, and available in either application. The built-in connectivity between Outlook 2007 and MOSS can help enable you to manage your personal calendar appointments and meeting requests almost in real time.

CHAPTER 18

MOSS and Word 2007

It is a safe bet that the majority of an organization's documents are created using Microsoft Word. Most documents are created by a single individual, and do not require the collaborative features of a SharePoint document workspace. However, when a group of users needs to collaborate on a Word document, SharePoint greatly enhances the collaborative and document management possibilities.

Many SharePoint document workspace features can be accessed directly from Microsoft Word, including creating a document workspace, adding additional users to the workspace, and assigning tasks to each user. Clicking any Microsoft Office file in a SharePoint document library will launch the appropriate Microsoft Office application and open the file from the document library. If a user has sufficient permissions, any changes made to the file can be saved directly back to the SharePoint document library. Each SharePoint document library, if so configured, can maintain a document version history as each document is edited. Users may also check out a document to edit it exclusively, and then check it back into the document library when they have finished editing the document.

MS Word 2007 documents can be stored in a SharePoint library in a variety of ways. The two primary methods for including an MS Word document in SharePoint is through the creation of a document workspace, which stores the document in a SharePoint library, or by saving the document directly into a SharePoint library. This chapter discusses the various methods you can use to store, access, share, and control MS Word documents in SharePoint document libraries.

CREATE A SHAREPOINT DOCUMENT WORKSPACE USING MS WORD

A document workspace is a custom SharePoint site that contains one or more documents you wish to share with other users for collaboration or coordination. Because of the integration between the Microsoft Office 2007 applications, including Microsoft Word 2007 and Microsoft Office Server 2007, you can create a document workspace from within MS Word.

Of course, you can create a document workspace on a SharePoint site, but often it is much easier to do so right after you have created or edited a document in its source application, which in this case is MS Word. The ability to create a SharePoint document workspace allows you to immediately publish and share new and revised documents with others who need to view, add to, comment on, or modify the document's content.

> **TIP**   You must save your existing or new Word document before you can create a document workspace with it.

To create a SharePoint document workspace from MS Word 2007, do the following:

1. Click the Office button in the upper left corner of the MS Word window to open the Office functions menu (see Figure 18-1).

Figure 18-1. The MS Word 2007 Office Publish functions menu.

2. From the Office functions menu, select Publish to open its options pane.

3. Choose the Create Document Workspace option to open the Document Management pane on the left side of the Word document window (see Figure 18-2).

4. Enter a descriptive Document Workspace name in its text box.

5. Unless you enter the URL of another SharePoint site, the document workspace you create is placed on your MySite.

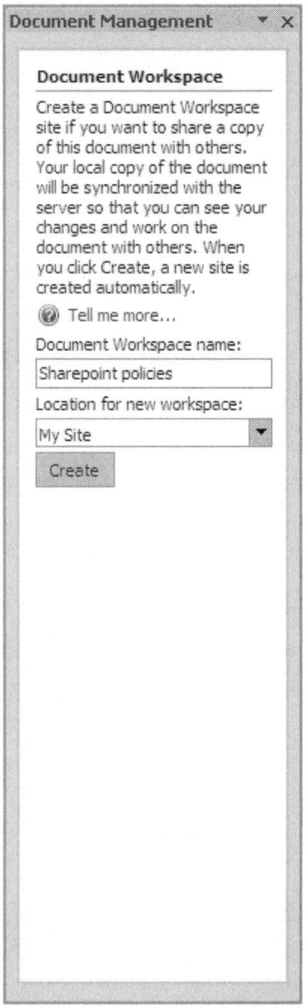

Figure 18-2. The MS Word Document Management pane.

Figure 18-3 illustrates a Download Sources document workspace created in a SharePoint site from MS Word. In this example, the URL of the SharePoint Users site was entered in the Location For New Workspace box.

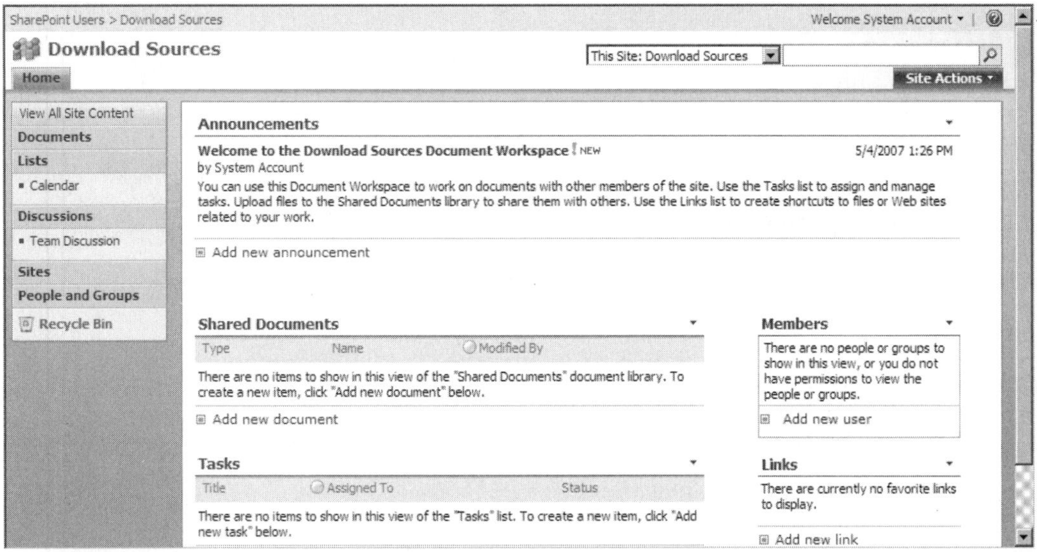

Figure 18-3. A new SharePoint document workspace created from MS Word.

UPLOAD AND SAVE DOCUMENTS TO SHAREPOINT

Once a document is added to a SharePoint document library, it can be opened for viewing or editing from a library view, such as that shown in Figure 18-4. Exactly which application is employed to open the document depends on the document template used to create the document originally, regardless of whether the document was created within SharePoint or of the application used to create the document in the first place. For example, as illustrated in Figure 18-4, this document library contains a variety of Microsoft Office documents, including a few Word documents, an Excel document, and a PDF document. These documents can all be opened from the document library using the application associated with the document template of each. Figure 18-5 illustrates a Word document opened from the document library view. Notice that the viewing window is different from a normal Word window (more about that in the following sections).

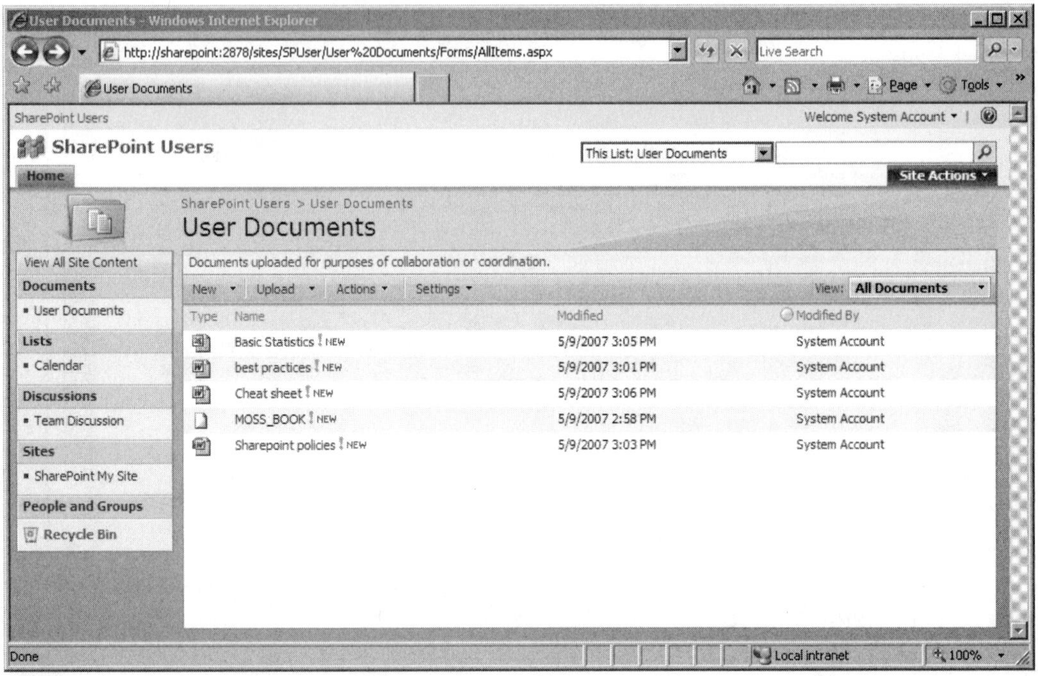

Figure 18-4. A standard view of a SharePoint Document Library.

The SharePoint Document Library Action Menu

The menu bar for the display area of the standard view of a document library, shown in Figure 18-6, contains selections for:

▼ **New** This choice opens a drop-down menu that allows you to either create a new document in the document library, using the default document template of the library, or creates a new folder in the library into which documents can be added.

■ **Upload** This choice allows you to upload one or multiple documents from your local computer or network into the current library.

■ **Actions** As shown in Figure 18-7, this choice includes options that allow you to:

  ■ Open the current library view in a datasheet view (see Figure 18-8) for editing purposes

  ■ Open the current view in a Windows Explorer view (see Figure 18-9), which allows you to drag and drop files into the library from other windows

  ■ Connect to Outlook to make documents available offline

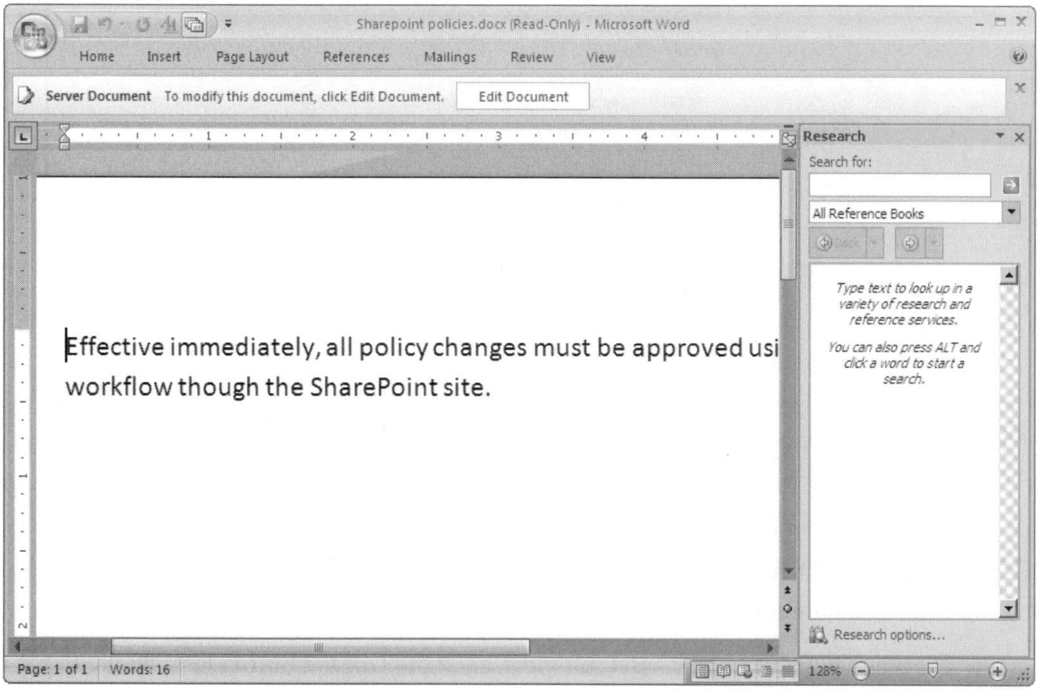

Figure 18-5.   A Word document opened from a SharePoint library.

- Open the current document library in an Excel spreadsheet (see Figure 18-10) so you can manipulate the document contents using Excel's analysis tools

- Use an Real Simple Syndication (RSS) feed to syndicate one or more of the library's documents

- Flag one or all of the documents in the library to alert you by e-mail when the document(s) are modified

▲   **Settings**   This choice provides options to add a column to the library, such as for metadata, create a new view for the library, and to manage the document library's settings.

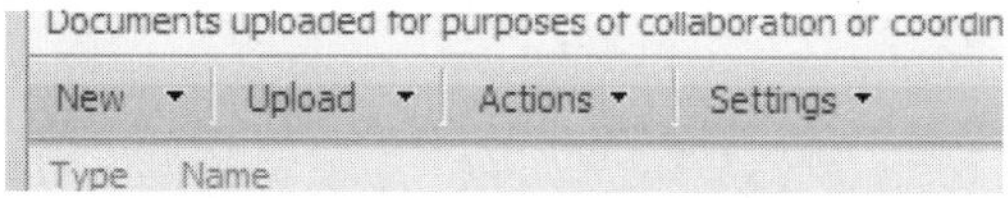

Figure 18-6.   The menu bar for the Standard View of a Document Library.

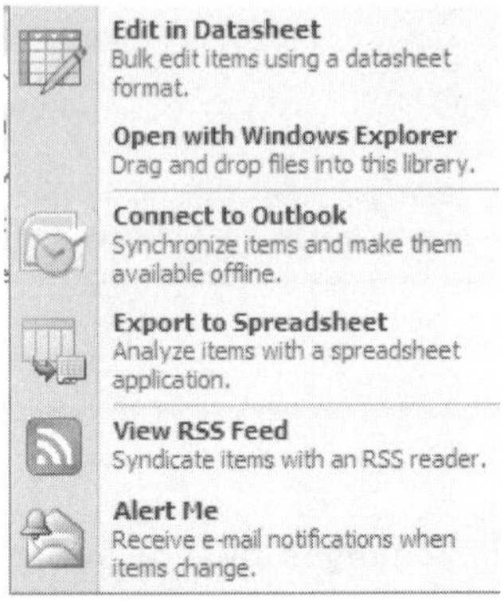

Edit in Datasheet
Bulk edit items using a datasheet format.

Open with Windows Explorer
Drag and drop files into this library.

Connect to Outlook
Synchronize items and make them available offline.

Export to Spreadsheet
Analyze items with a spreadsheet application.

View RSS Feed
Syndicate items with an RSS reader.

Alert Me
Receive e-mail notifications when items change.

Figure 18-7.   The drop-down menu of the Actions menu choice.

Upload Existing Documents to a SharePoint Document Library

To upload a document into a SharePoint library, use the following actions:

1. On the document library's default view, click the Upload button to open its drop-down menu.

2. Choose the option to upload either a single document or multiple documents. Depending on your choice, a different page appears:

   a. Single document:

      i. If your choice is to upload a single document, the page shown in Figure 18-11 displays.

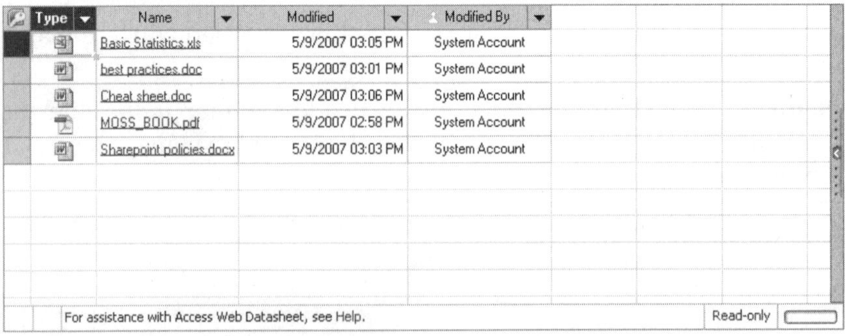

Type	Name	Modified	Modified By
	Basic Statistics.xls	5/9/2007 03:05 PM	System Account
	best practices.doc	5/9/2007 03:01 PM	System Account
	Cheat sheet.doc	5/9/2007 03:06 PM	System Account
	MOSS_BOOK.pdf	5/9/2007 02:58 PM	System Account
	Sharepoint policies.docx	5/9/2007 03:03 PM	System Account

For assistance with Access Web Datasheet, see Help.   Read-only

Figure 18-8.   A SharePoint Document Library shown in a datasheet view.

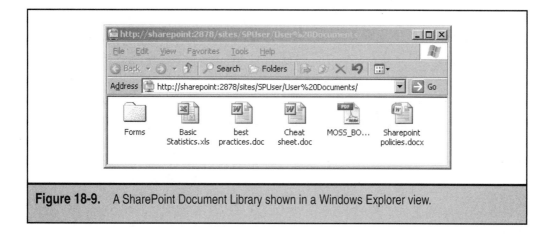

Figure 18-9. A SharePoint Document Library shown in a Windows Explorer view.

    ii. Using the Browse button, navigate to the folder containing the document and double-click the document name to start the upload process.

    iii. If you are possibly uploading a file that may already exist in the document library and you wish the new copy of the file to be added as a new version, ensure the checkbox associated with the Add As A New Version To Existing Files option is checked.

  b. Multiple documents:

    i. If your choice is to upload multiple documents, the page shown in Figure 18-12 displays.

    ii. Using the folder tree, navigate to the folder containing the documents you wish to upload and check the box corresponding to each document.

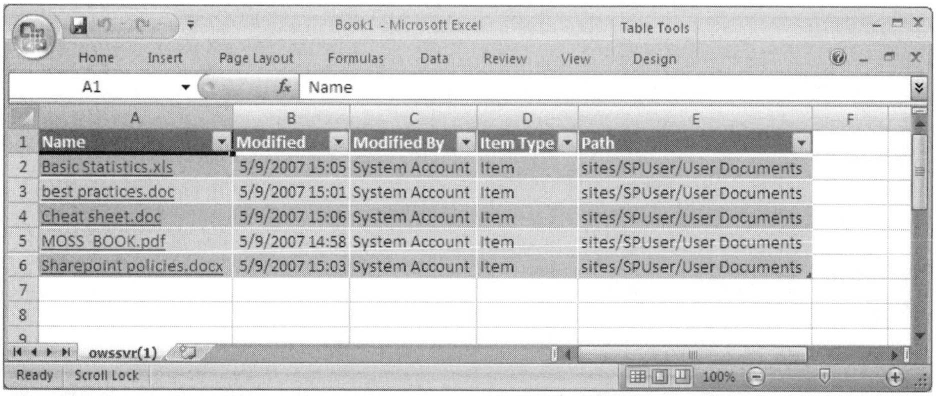

Figure 18-10. A SharePoint Document Library displayed in an Excel spreadsheet.

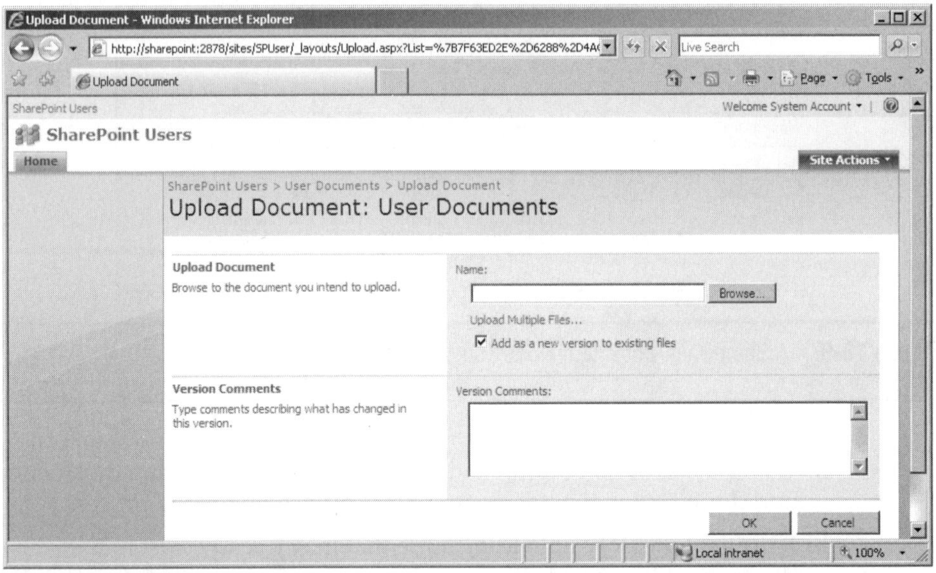

Figure 18-11. The Upload Document page used for uploading a single document.

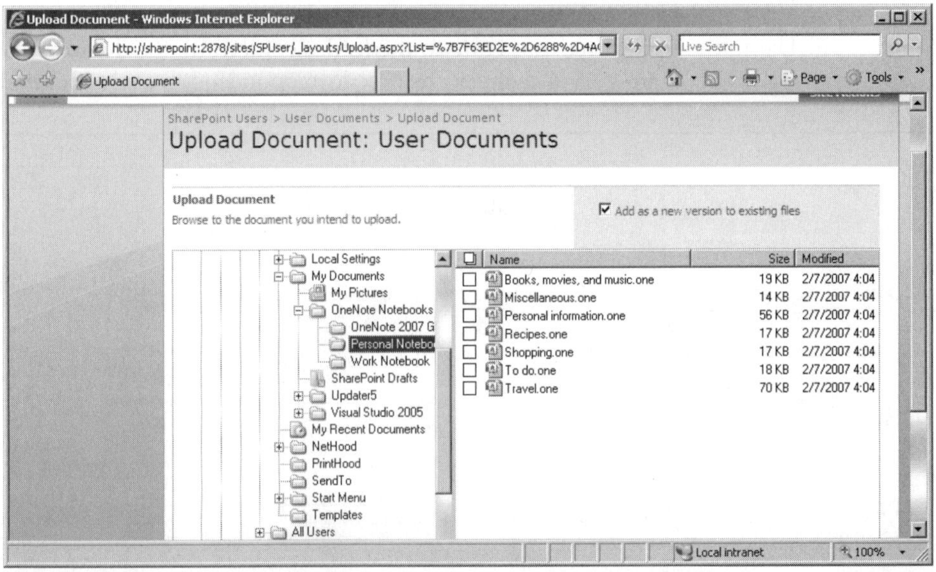

Figure 18-12. The Upload Document page used for uploading multiple documents.

NOTE You can only upload documents from one folder at a time.

iii. Click the OK button to start the upload.

3. When the upload action is completed, the default view of the document library is displayed with the uploaded documents shown as being in the library.

Set Alerts for Document Modifications

As an MOSS administrator or the administrator or owner of a document library, you may want to know when certain (or perhaps any) items in the library are modified. If this is the case, you can set an alert function on the entire library or on a particular file.

To set up an alert for the library or a single library item, do the following:

1. From any view of the library, click the Actions button to open its drop-down menu.

2. Choose the Alert Me option to display the New Alert page, the top of which is shown in Figure 18-13.

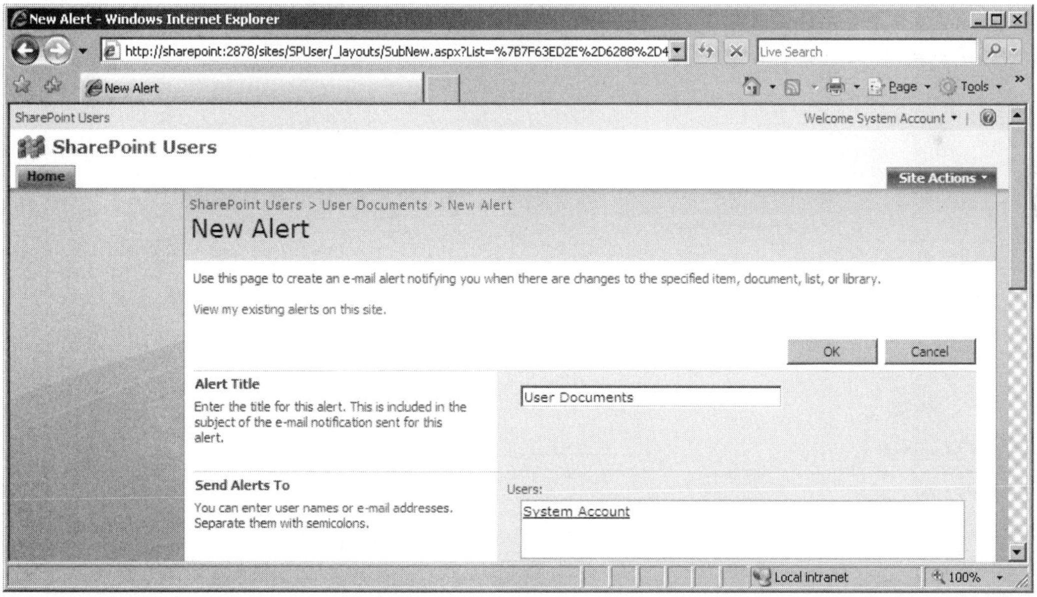

Figure 18-13. The New Alert page is used to set up an e-mail alert for modifications made to library items.

3. To create the new alert, enter the appropriate data into the following fields:

    a. Enter a title for the alert. This title will be included in the subject and text of the alert e-mail message.

    b. Enter the e-mail address or addresses to which you want the alert message sent.

    c. Click the radio button corresponding to the type of change for which you wish to be alerted. Figure 18-14 shows the various types of changes for which an alert can be issued. The types of changes include other discrete options, such as any modification made to an existing document, a new document added to the library, an existing document deleted from the library, or if the library contains a discussion forum, when messages are posted to the forum.

    d. You can have an alert sent when anything or anyone changes an item in the library or just when someone else makes the change. You may want to use

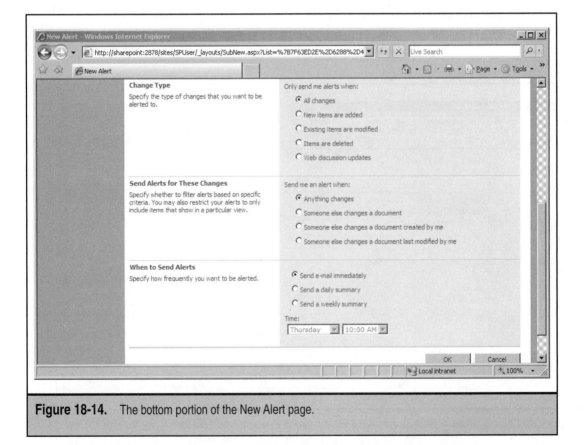

Figure 18-14. The bottom portion of the New Alert page.

this option to let you know a change was made (perhaps even those made by yourself) to notify you of any inadvertent changes that you, or someone else, has made.

e. Set the frequency for the alert and whether you wish to receive a summary of modifications, as well as when you wish to receive the alert. In a very active library, you may elect to use a summary message that is sent daily or weekly. However, with a new library in a MOSS installation, it may be better to have immediate alerts to avoid problems down-the-road.

VERSIONING

Each time you save a Word document (or any document for that matter) to a SharePoint document library, the previous version of the document is overwritten. If you require that the previous versions of a document are archived when a new version of the document is saved, a SharePoint document library can be configured to maintain a version history.

To configure versioning on a SharePoint document library, do the following:

1. Open the default view of the SharePoint document library on which you wish to configure versioning.

2. Click the Settings drop-down menu and choose the Document Library Settings option.

3. Under the General Settings column, click the Versioning settings link.

4. On the Document Library Versioning Settings page (see Figure 18-15), set the versioning configuration as follows:

   a. **Content Approval**   If you require content approval before new versions of the document are made available in the document library, select the Yes radio button.

   b. **Document Version History**   Use the radio button options in this section to select an appropriate level of versioning. Your choices are:

      i. **No versioning**   This is used to turn versioning off for a document library.

      ii. **Create major versions**   Use this setting if you wish to identify versions of a document as versions 1, 2, 3, 4, and so on.

      iii. **Create major and minor (draft) versions**   Use this setting if you wish to identify versions and drafts within versions—such as 1.0, 1.1, 1.2, 2.0, and so on—with the drafts being numbered within the major versions.

      iv. If you wish to limit the number of major and minor (draft) versions retained by the SharePoint document library, enter numbers in the

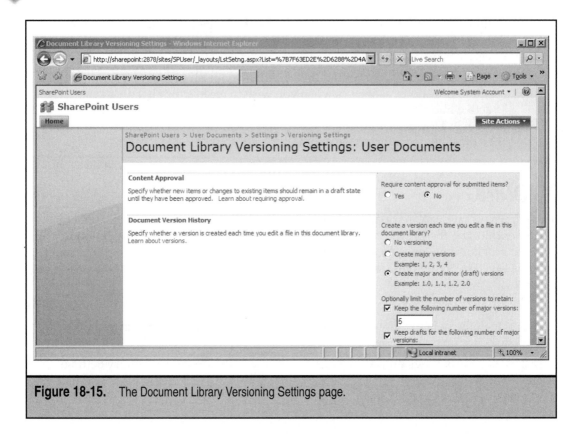

Figure 18-15.   The Document Library Versioning Settings page.

boxes associated with Keep The Following Number Of Major Versions and Keep Drafts For The Following Number Of Minor Versions. If you choose to keep ten major versions of a document, when the 11th version is created, the first version is dropped and versions 2 through 11 are retained for a total of ten major versions of the document. The versions are not renumbered. The same applies to the minor versions as well.

c. **Draft Item Security**   Only those who have the proper user security permissions can access a document library item for modification, but you can also control who has access draft versions specifically to only those users who are assigned edit permission (the default setting) or open-read access to drafts to all users.

d. **Require Checkout**   To ensure that multiple versions aren't being created at the same time, you can choose to require users to check out a document before they can modify it. When a document is checked out, SharePoint prevents other users with the edit privilege from editing the document.

Library Item Checkout

To avoid the issue or possibility of two (or more) users attempting to modify a document library item at the same time, items should be checked out by a user wishing to make modifications to it. Only one user can check out a library item at a time, much like a library book from a public library. Until the user checks the item back into the library, by saving it to the library, the document is unavailable to other users, except for read-only actions.

A user is required to check out a document before he or she can edit that document. Figure 18-16 shows the dialog box that appears when a document is opened from a library. If you are opening the library item to make changes to it, you must check the item out. This checkout status remains in effect until the document has been checked in or the checkout has been discarded.

TIP A document that has been checked out will have a padlock symbol added to its document template icon in the Document Library display.

Check In a Library Item

After you have made changes to a checked out document library item or have decided, for whatever reason, you no longer wish to keep the document checked out, you must either check in the document or discard the check out on the document. Either of these actions cancels the checked out status on the document, freeing others to access it for editing.

To check in a SharePoint library item from Microsoft Word 2007, do the following:

1. Click the Microsoft Office button in the upper left corner of the window to display the Office menu.

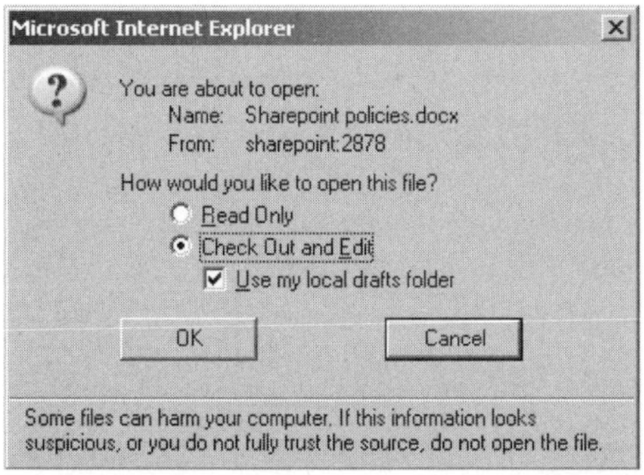

Figure 18-16. This dialog box appears when you open a document library item.

2. Move your mouse over the Server option to open its menu pane and click Check In, as shown in Figure 18-17.

3. A dialog box displays (see Figure 18-18) on which you indicate whether you wish to save the updated document as a major or minor version and whether you wish to keep the document checked out after saving it to the library.

4. You can now safely close the document or continue working on it to create an additional version or a new document.

After saving the document, you can use the pull-down menu for the item on the Document Library view to display its version history (see Figure 18-19).

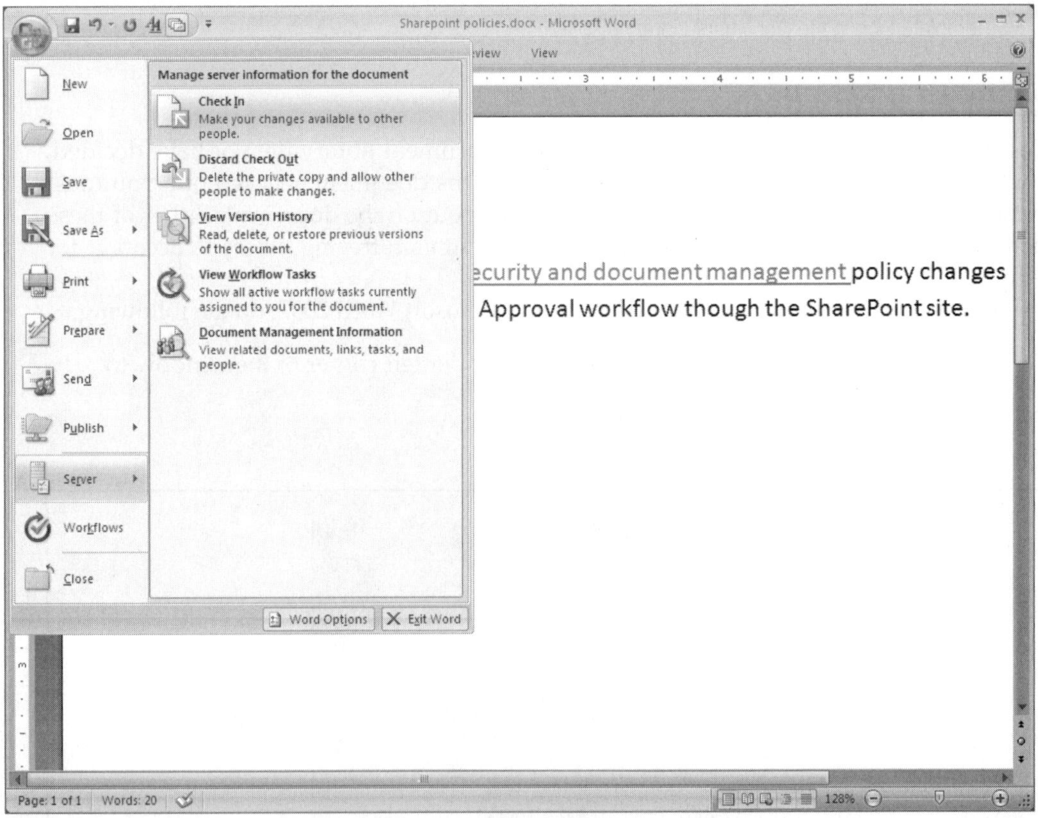

Figure 18-17.   The Server menu pane for a SharePoint Word document.

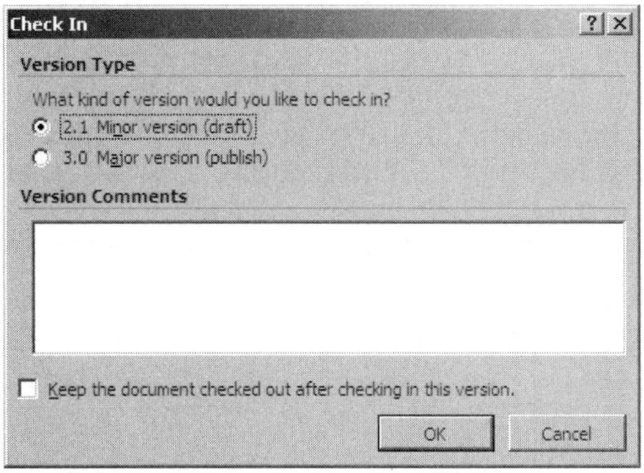

Figure 18-18.   The Check In dialog box.

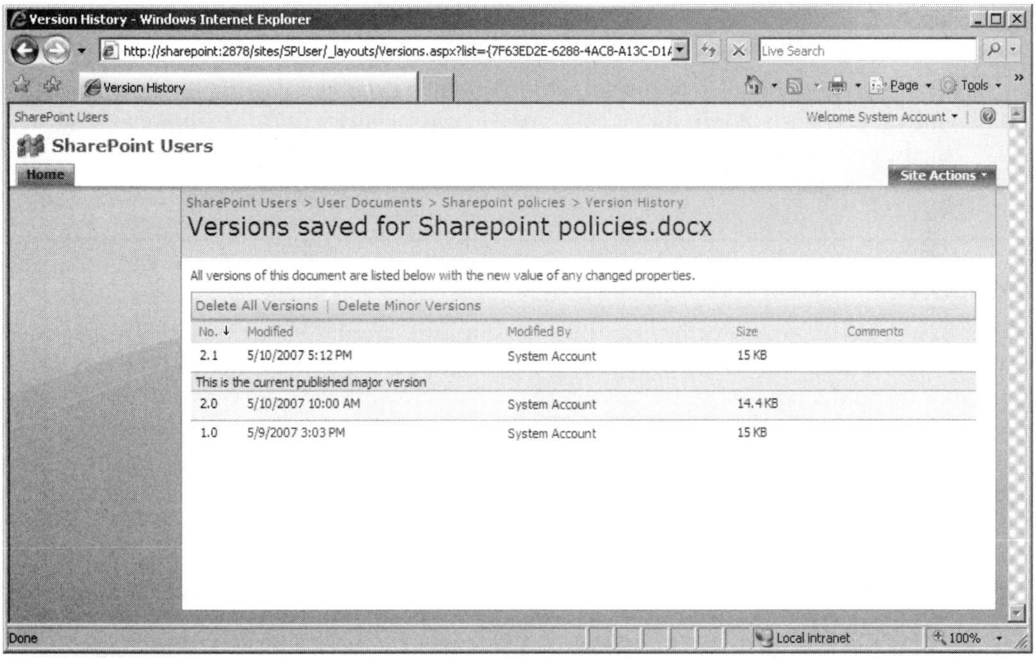

Figure 18-19.   The version history view of a SharePoint Document Library item.

ACCESS SHAREPOINT DOCUMENTS USING A URL

Document libraries in an MOSS environment are compatible with the Web-based Distributed Authoring and Versioning (WebDAV) protocol, which allows them to be accessed and be mapped as network drives. However, this process is fairly complicated and should be reserved for those users who author a great deal of content published to a SharePoint library.

A far simpler method to access a SharePoint Document Library is to use the URL of the library directly from within Microsoft Word 2007, or from any other Microsoft Office application. To access the page of a SharePoint Document Library from Word, do the following:

1. Launch Microsoft Word 2007.

2. Click the Office button in the upper left corner and choose Open on the Office menu.

3. Enter the URL of the SharePoint page you wish to open into the File Name field (as illustrated in Figure 18-20).

4. From the contents shown in the main pane of the Open dialog box, you can choose a document library to view its contents (see Figure 18-21) in that pane and choose the specific document you wish to open.

5. Double-click the Word document you wish to open.

6. The document opens in a special window that is used for viewing the document only. If you wish to edit the document, you must check out the document using the button located just below the menu bar (shown in Figure 18-22).

WebDAV

Web-based Distributed Authoring and Versioning (WebDAV) defines a group of extensions for the Hypertext Transfer Protocol (HTTP) that facilitates users to collaborate on documents stored on remote web servers. WebDAV was developed toward fulfilling the vision of making the Web a truly readable and writable resource that supports the ability of users to create, modify, and even move documents stored remotely on a web server or a web share.

WebDAV was officially implemented in March 2007 when Request for Change (RFC) 2518 was accepted by the Internet Engineering Steering Group. Nearly all operating systems included support for WebDAV. The features defined in the WebDAV protocol include overwrite protection; the capability to create, remove, or relocate documents; the capability to query author and document creation and modification information; and a collections function that allows documents to be referenced and managed as a group.

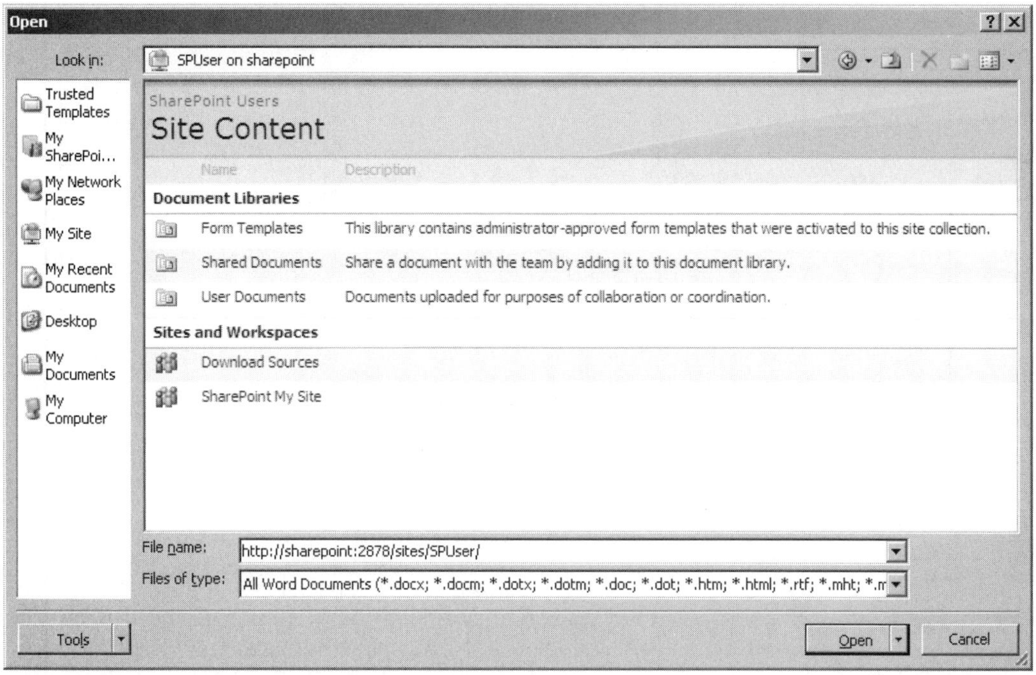

Figure 18-20.   Using a URL to access a SharePoint document library item.

7. If you have chosen to check out the document for editing, the procedure used to save the document and perhaps create a new version is the same as that described earlier in the section "Check In a Library Item."

DOCUMENT MANAGEMENT

Many SharePoint document tasks can be completed using the Document Management pane in Microsoft Word. The Document Management pane allows users to leverage the collaborative features of SharePoint from within Word without having to switch between two windows.

Before we begin discussing the Document Management pane, follow these instructions to display it.

1. You need to have already either opened a SharePoint document library item or created a document workspace (see the "Create SharePoint Document Workspace Using MS Word" section earlier in the chapter) for a new document.

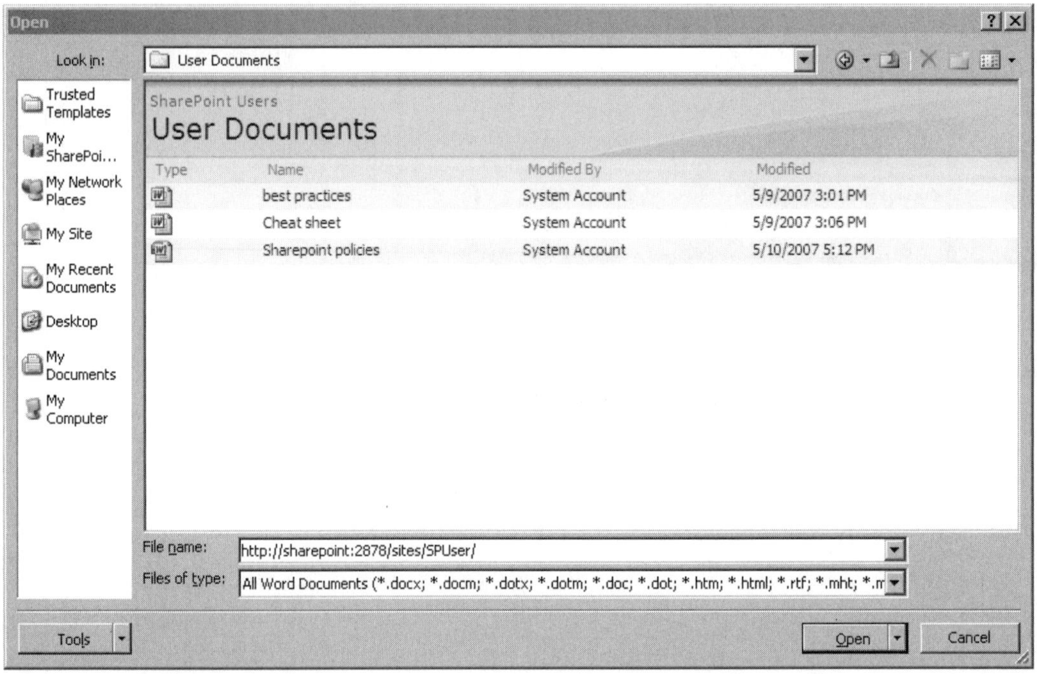

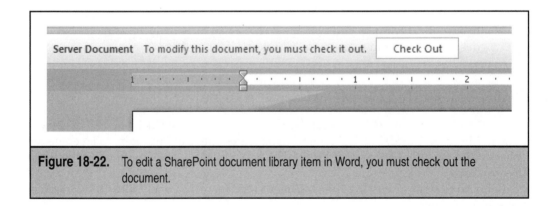

Figure 18-21. The contents of a SharePoint document library in the Word Open dialog box.

Figure 18-22. To edit a SharePoint document library item in Word, you must check out the document.

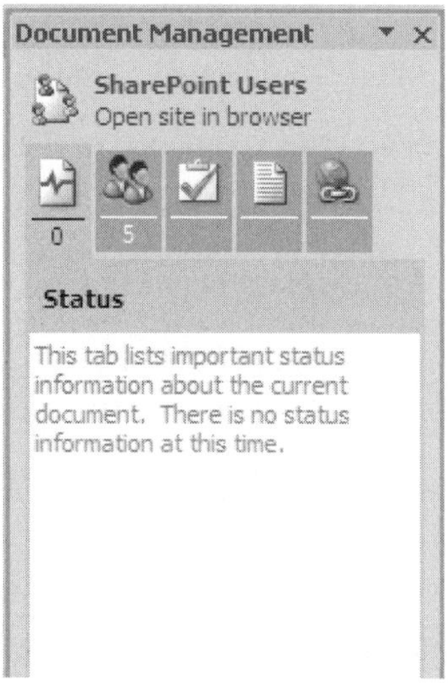

Figure 18-23.   The Document Management pane in a Word workspace.

2. Click the Office button in the upper left corner of the window to display the Office menu.

3. Select the Server option from the Office menu and click Document Management Information from its pop-up menu to open the Document Management pane on the right side of the document workspace, as shown in Figure 18-23.

The Document Management Pane

The Document Management pane includes five subpanes, which can be accessed using the grid at the top of the pane. The subpanes are:

▼   **Status**   Displays information, errors, or restrictions about the current document

■   **Members**   Displays a list of workspace members and their presence information, including online status if Live Communication Server is installed

■   **Tasks**   Displays tasks assigned to you, and may be used to assign tasks to other workspace members

- **Documents**   Displays additional documents saved to the workspace document library
▲ **Links**   Displays useful links associated with the document workspace

Each of the tabs and its functions are explained in the following sections.

The Members Subpane

The Members subpane is used to display the users who have been granted permission to the document workspace. If Microsoft Live Communication Server has been installed as a part of your MOSS environment, information about each user is displayed, such as the user's office location, telephone number, whether the user is currently in a meeting, and his or her availability to chat.

New members can be easily added to the workspace from Word by clicking the Add New Members… link at the bottom of the Members subpane and performing the following steps:

1. In the Add New Members dialog box (see Figure 18-24), enter member user names or e-mail addresses, separated by a semicolon (;).

2. Select a permission level to grant the users being added. All of the users added at one time are granted the same permission. If you wish to grant different permissions to different users, you need to repeat this step for each group of users with different permissions.

3. Click the Next button.

4. Click the Finish button to add the users to the workspace.

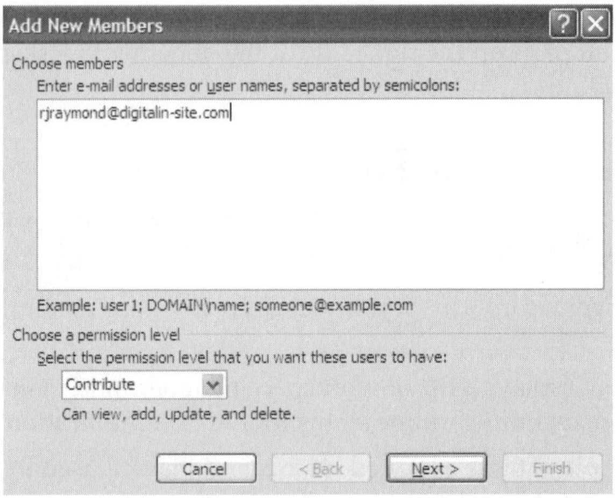

Figure 18-24.   The Add New Members dialog box.

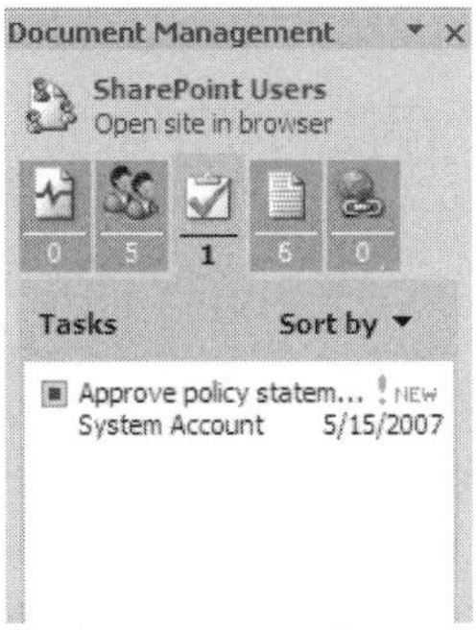

Figure 18-25. The Tasks subpane.

The Tasks Subpane

Using the Tasks subpane (shown in Figure 18-25) is a simple way to give visibility to any required actions individual members must accomplish. The Tasks tab displays any tasks that have been assigned to you and also allows you to assign tasks to other workspace members. Tasks can be assigned a status (not started, in progress, completed, deferred, or waiting on someone else), a priority (low, normal, or high), and a due date, among other properties.

As discussed earlier in the chapter (see the section titled "The SharePoint Document Library Action Menu"), you can set an alert to notify you by e-mail when the status of a task changes by clicking the Alert Me About Tasks… link at the bottom of the Tasks subpane.

The Documents Subpane

The Documents subpane (see Figure 18-26) displays other files that have also been saved to the workspace document library. Each file may be opened or deleted directly from the Document tab. Additionally, new documents may be added to the document library by clicking the Add New Document link found at the bottom of the subpane, and then browsing to the file. You can also use the Alert Me About Documents… link, which will allow you to configure e-mail alerts for the document library.

The Links Subpane

If your document collaboration includes online research, the Links subpane (see Figure 18-27) can be used to easily access associated URLs. Displayed links can be sorted by creation date, modified date, or URL using the Sort By drop-down list at the top of the Links tab. Links can also be edited or deleted directly from the Links tab by placing your mouse over the link, and clicking the drop-down menu when it is displayed.

The Add New link and the Alert Me About links options at the bottom of the subtab allow users to enter a URL, description, and notes for any link that may be useful to workspace members and to set an alert for the documents in the workspace.

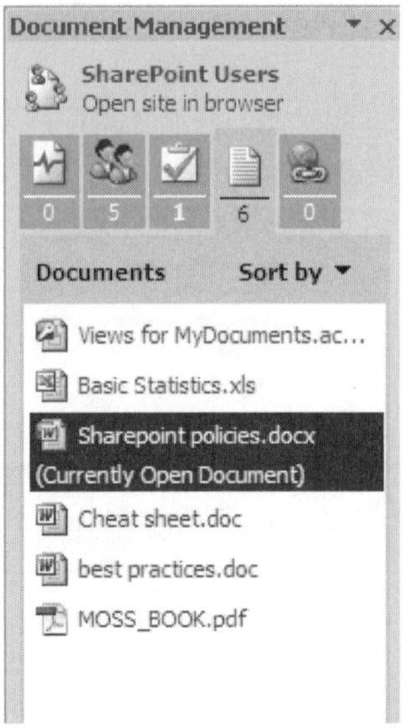

Figure 18-26. The Documents subpane.

Get Updates and Options

A Get Updates button and an Options link is included at the bottom of each of the Document Management subpanes. These two functions allow you to stay current and to control how and when the Document Management pane is used.

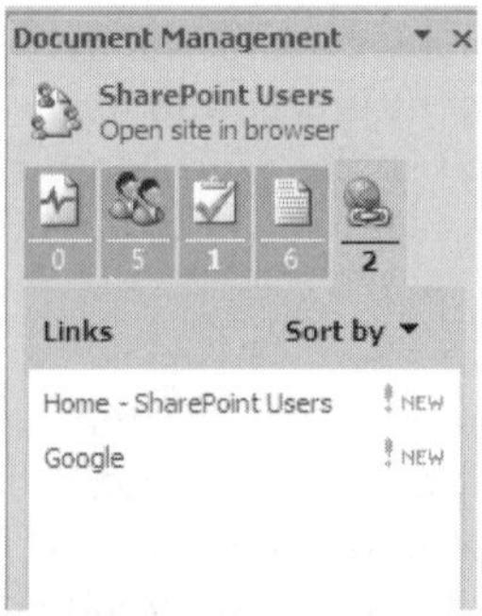

Figure 18-27. The Links subpane.

Get Updates   If you elect not to check out a document, and are concurrently editing the document with other workspace members, you may need to periodically get updates to your working copy of the document. Likewise, you may want to update the workspace copy of a document with local changes you have made to a document.

Options   The Options link can be used to automatically display the Document Management pane each time a workspace document is opened in Word, or only when important status information regarding the document becomes available. Clicking the Options link opens the Document Management Service Options dialog box (see Figure 18-28). The remainders of the options are dedicated to configuring how document updates are performed.

Document updates can be configured to occur automatically, periodically (configured in minutes), or never. Likewise, document updates can be configured to occur automatically, sometimes (you are notified when updates occur with a message box), or never. Whenever a copy of the same document is saved, the appropriate update option is triggered.

Workspace Commands

A collection of document workspace commands are available in a drop-down list that can be found on the workspace name at the top of the Document Management pane (see Figure 18-29). The Workspace commands included on this drop-down menu are:

▼   **Open Site in Browser**   Use this option to open the workspace site page in a Web browser

■   **Change Site Title**   This option opens a dialog box that allows you to change the title of the current workspace.

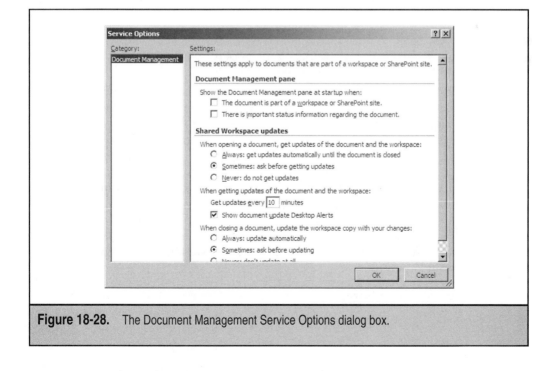

Figure 18-28.   The Document Management Service Options dialog box.

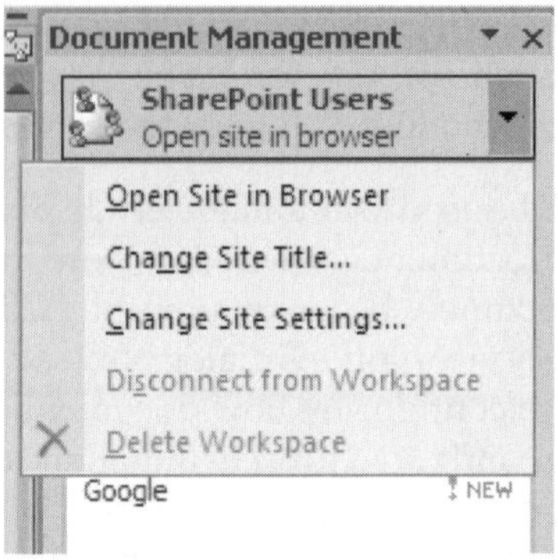

Figure 18-29.   The Document Management Workspace commands menu.

- ■ **Change Site Settings**   This option opens the site settings page for the workspace.

- ■ **Disconnect from Workspace**   If you are connected to the workspace, you can use this option to work offline.

- ▲ **Delete Workspace**   If you are connected to the workspace, meaning the SharePoint site, you can delete the workspace, provided you have the proper permissions.

LAUNCH A WORKFLOW FROM WORD

MOSS includes the capability for a document author to launch a workflow that includes a series of tasks that can be assigned to other users to accomplish a review of the document, collect signatures on the document (approvals), or merely collect feedback on the document. This process, which is an inherent MOSS feature can be launched from MS Word 2007, without requiring the document author to save the document, exit Work, and open the appropriate SharePoint site.

In general, to launch a workflow for a Word document, do the following:

1. From within Microsoft Word 2007, click the Office button in the upper left corner of the window.

2. Choose Workflows from the Office menu to display the Workflows dialog box shown in Figure 18-30.

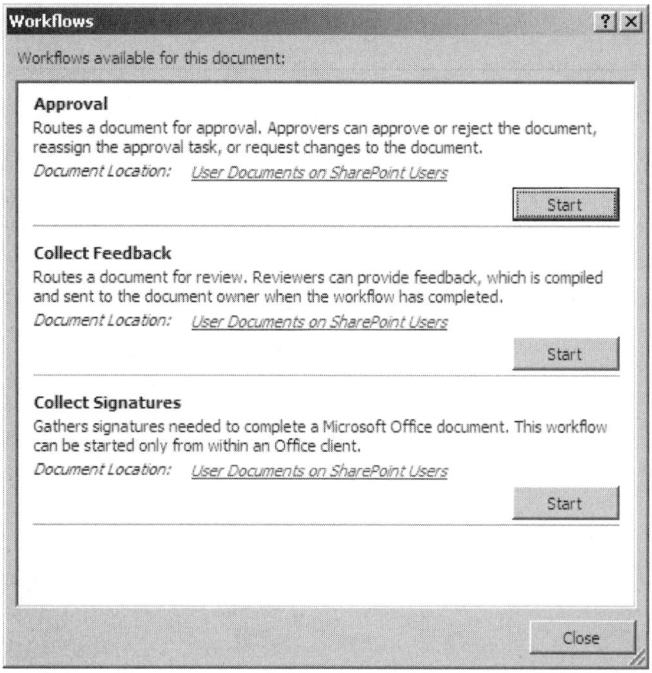

Figure 18-30. The Workflows dialog box opened from Word 2007.

As shown in Figure 18-30, the three types of workflows that can be launched from MS Word 2007 are:

▼ **Approval** Routes the document, as designated, so users can approve, reject, reassign this task, or request changes to be made to the document.

■ **Collect feedback** Allows users to whom the document is routed to provide feedback to the document. The feedback entered by the users to whom the document is routed is collected and provided to the document author when the workflow is completed.

▲ **Collect signatures** The document is routed to those users who must sign the document (in this case, electronically).

Each of these workflow options is discussed in the sections that follow.

NOTE MOSS workflows are covered in Chapter 10.

Document Approval Workflow

The approval workflow routes a Word document to those users or groups designated in the setup process for the workflow. To start an approval workflow from MS Word 2007, do the following:

1. Click the Start button associated with Approval Workflows on the Workflows dialog box (see Figure 18-30).

2. In the Select Names dialog box that appears (see Figure 18-31), enter the name(s) of the groups or users to whom you wish to route the document for approval.

3. Click OK when the list of users is completed.

4. In the Approval dialog box that appears (see Figure 18-32), you may choose to assign a task to all of the members of a group or just certain individuals in that group, enter a brief message to be included in the task created for each affected user, and set the number of days, weeks, and so on you wish to allow each user

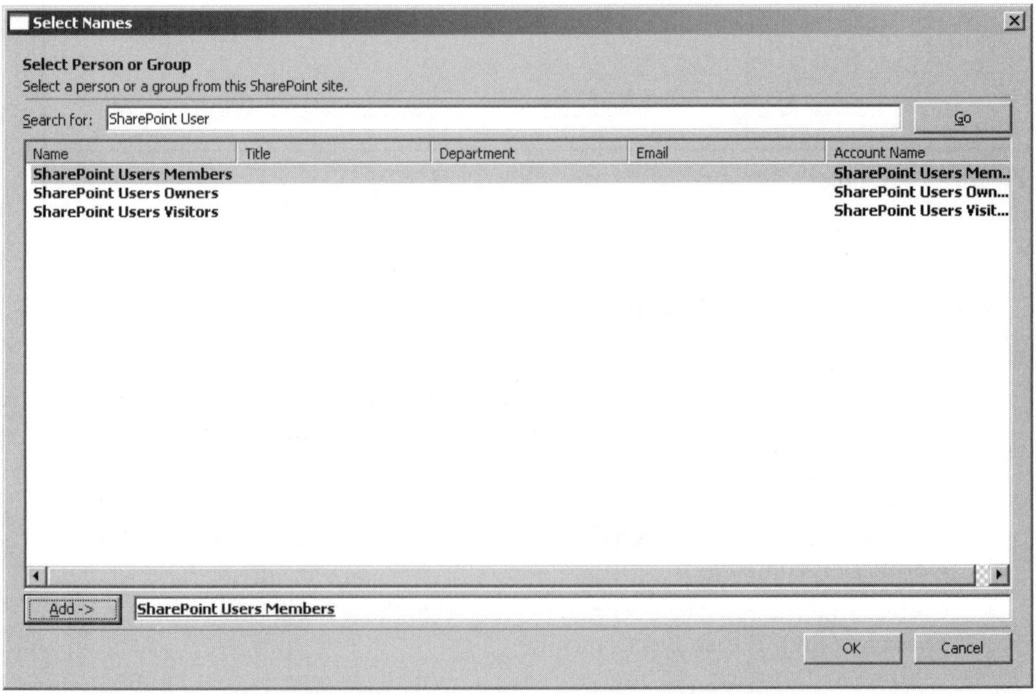

Figure 18-31. The Select Names dialog box is used to designate the users to whom an approval workflow is to be routed.

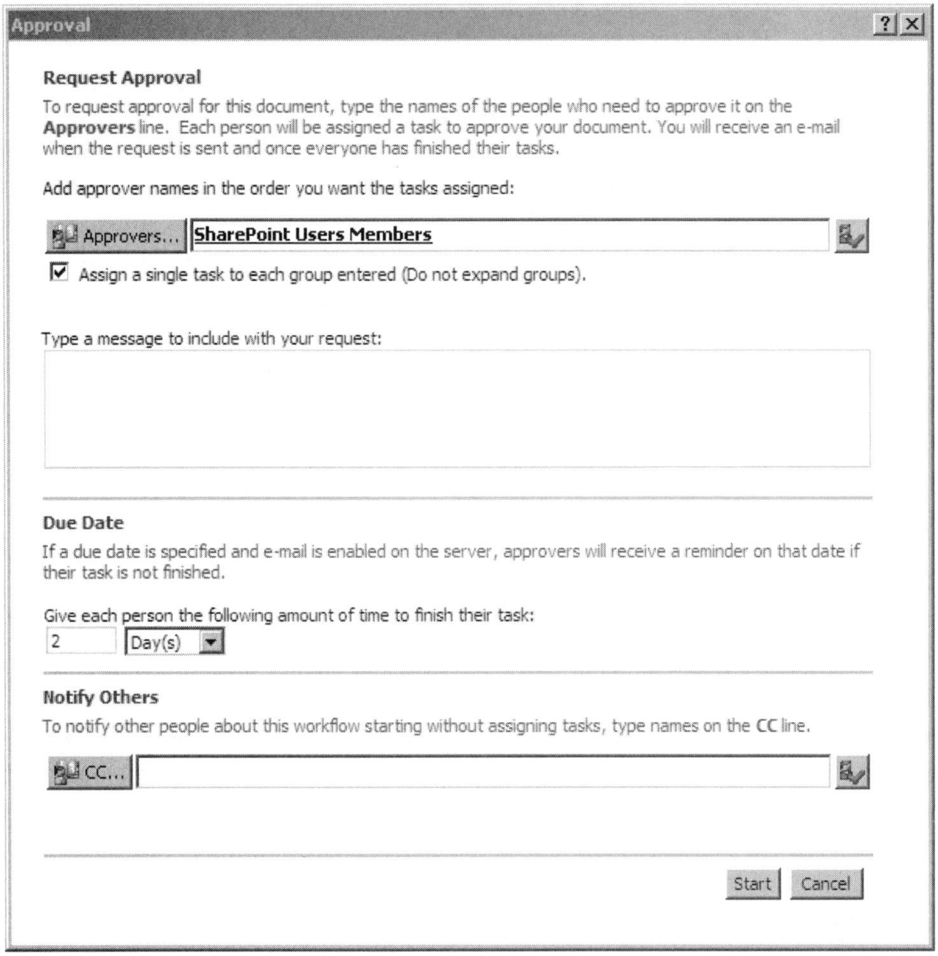

Figure 18-32.   The Approval workflow dialog box.

to complete the approval task. You may also add additional users you wish to receive a courtesy copy (cc) of the approval notification message.

5. Click the Start button to launch the Approval workflow.

As illustrated in Figure 18-33, each of the users included in the approval workflow has now been assigned a task to approve the document.

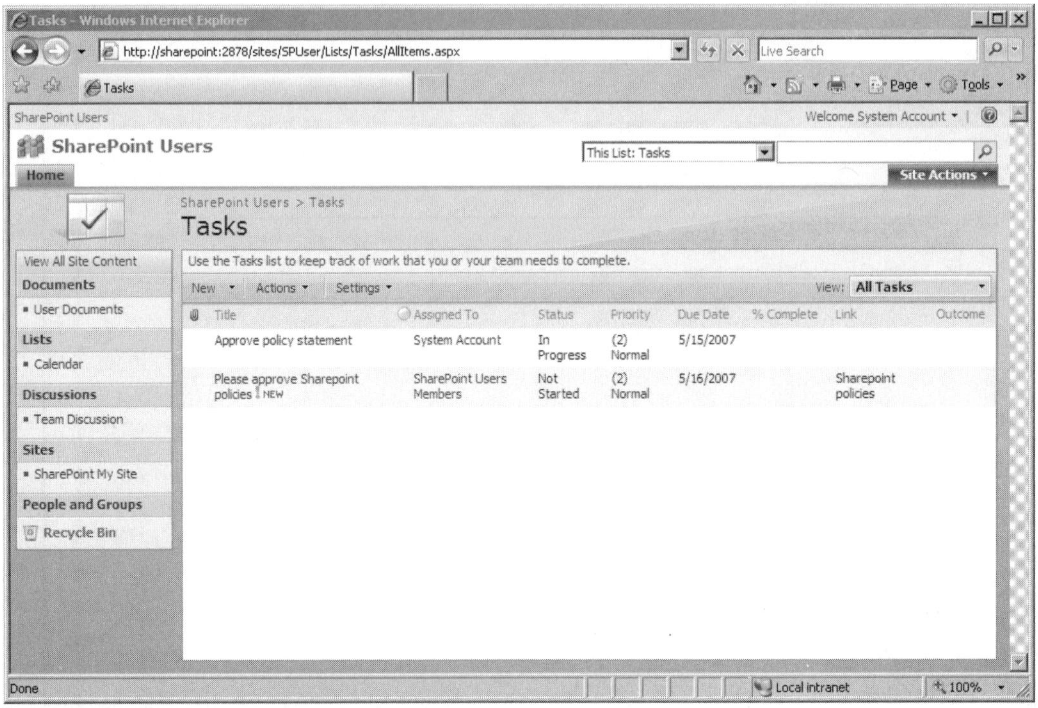

Figure 18-33. A task is assigned to each user or group included in the workflow.

Collect Feedback Workflow

The process involved to launch a collect feedback workflow is very similar to that used to launch an approval workflow. The primary difference is that instead of approvers, you designate reviewers on the Collect Feedback dialog box. The remainder of the process is the same as described in the preceding section.

Collect Signatures Workflow

There is a bit more setup that must take place before you can create a collect digital signatures workflow from Microsoft Word 2007. The primary action that must occur is that one or more signature fields must be inserted into the document.

Signature Line
Microsoft Office Signature Line...
Add Signature Services...
Symbols
at used to

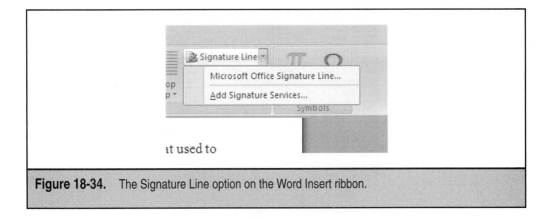

Figure 18-34. The Signature Line option on the Word Insert ribbon.

To configure a document for a collect digital signatures workflow and then launch the workflow, do the following:

1. Before concluding the document you wish to route for signature, insert at least one signature field into the document. To do this, use the following steps:
   a. Click Insert on the Word menu bar and choose Signature Line from the Insert ribbon (see Figure 18-34).
   b. A message box appears (see Figure 18-35) that allows you to designate the source you wish to use for your digital signatures. Normally, you will just click OK to use the signature services built into Office, but you can also use a third-party signature service from the Office Marketplace.
   c. Click OK to proceed with Office signature services and display the Signature Setup dialog box, shown in Figure 18-36.
   d. In the Signature Setup dialog box (see Figure 18-36), enter the name, title, and e-mail address for the person you wish to digitally sign the document.

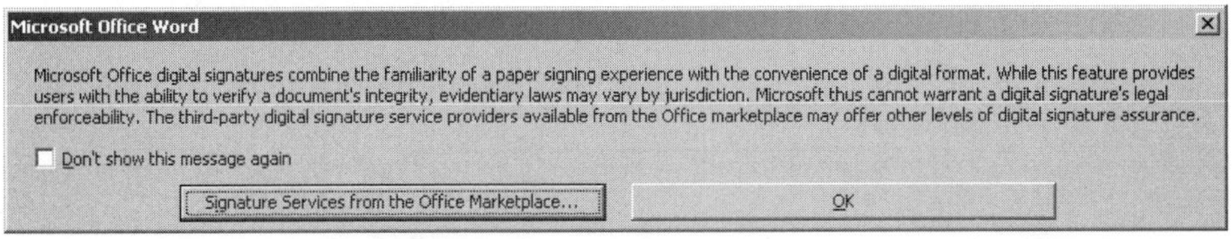

Microsoft Office Word
Microsoft Office digital signatures combine the familiarity of a paper signing experience with the convenience of a digital format. While this feature provides users with the ability to verify a document's integrity, evidentiary laws may vary by jurisdiction. Microsoft thus cannot warrant a digital signature's legal enforceability. The third-party digital signature service providers available from the Office marketplace may offer other levels of digital signature assurance.
Don't show this message again
Signature Services from the Office Marketplace...
OK

Figure 18-35. The digital signature message box.

Figure 18-36. The Signature Setup dialog box.

    e. To add multiple signatures to the document, repeat steps a through d for each.

    f. Each signature added to the document inserts a signature block like that shown in Figure 18-37.

2. After you have inserted the signature block(s) into the document, click the Office button in the upper left corner of the window and choose Workflows from the Office menu.

3. On the Workflows dialog box (see Figure 18-30 earlier in this section), click the Start button associated with the Collect Signatures option.

Figure 18-37. A signature block added to a Word document.

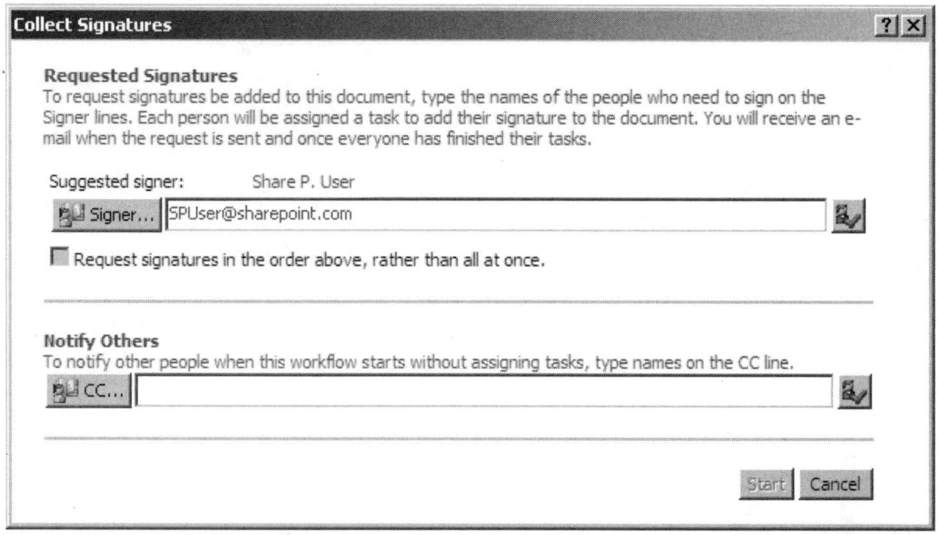

Collect Signatures   ? X

Requested Signatures
To request signatures be added to this document, type the names of the people who need to sign on the Signer lines. Each person will be assigned a task to add their signature to the document. You will receive an e-mail when the request is sent and once everyone has finished their tasks.

Suggested signer: Share P. User
 Signer... | SPUser@sharepoint.com |

☐ Request signatures in the order above, rather than all at once.

Notify Others
To notify other people when this workflow starts without assigning tasks, type names on the CC line.
 CC... | |

Start | Cancel

Figure 18-38.   The Collect Signatures workflow dialog box.

TIP   If you have checked out the document you're using, you are required to check it back in before proceeding with the next step.

4. The Collect Signatures workflow dialog box displays (see Figure 18-38) with the e-mail addresses supplied in the Signature Setup dialog box already loaded to the address area. Add any e-mail addresses for those users to whom you wish to provide a courtesy copy of the document and click OK.

5. A signature task is assigned to each designated user being requested to sign the document and added to the appropriate SharePoint site (as illustrated in Figure 18-39).

RESEARCH

The majority of Microsoft Office applications include a Research pane that can be used to look up information without leaving the current application. The research options include the Encarta English dictionary; the English, French, and Spanish thesauri; the Encarta encyclopedia; MSN Search; and other various research services.

By adding one or more SharePoint sites as a research resource, users can search SharePoint from within Word to locate company policy, forms, or any other information

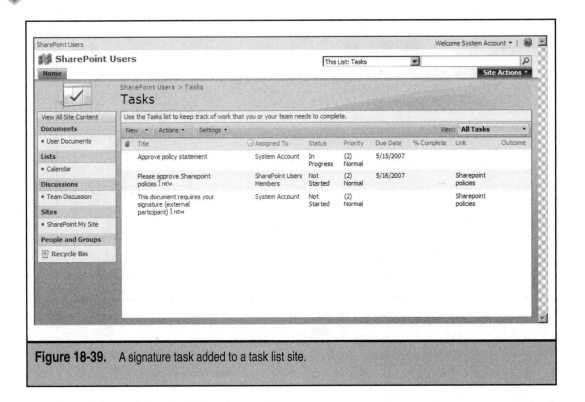

Figure 18-39.   A signature task added to a task list site.

that is required while collaborating on a document. To add a SharePoint site as a research resource, do the following:

1. From a Word 2007 document, click the Review option on the main menu bar to open its ribbon.

2. Click the Research option in the Proofing group to open the Research pane in the Word workspace.

3. Click the Research options link at the bottom of the Research pane to open the Research Options dialog box, which is used to indicate the research resources you wish to use (see Figure 18-40).

4. On the Research options dialog box, click the Add Services button to open the Add Services dialog box.

5. Enter http://[server]/_vti_bin/search.asmx, where [server] is the name of your SharePoint server (without the square brackets, of course). For example, enter http://sharepoint/_vti_bin/search.asmx. Then, click the Add button.

6. A dialog box appears requesting that you approve the installation of this search source. Click the Install button to complete the installation of the SharePoint Search service as a research option for this Word document.

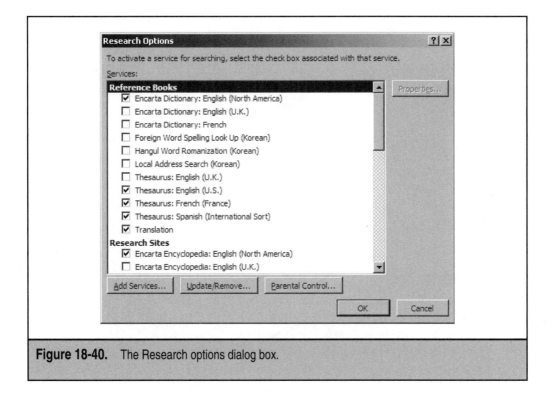

Figure 18-40.   The Research options dialog box.

7. Click OK when the installation is complete. The newly added resource location
    should now be listed under the All Intranet Sites and Portals section.

SUMMARY

The combination of Microsoft Office 2007, Microsoft Office SharePoint Server 2007, and
other Office 2007 applications provides a feature-rich suite of applications that are tightly
integrated, offering a compelling collaboration of features. In this chapter, you have learned
how many MOSS features can be used from within Microsoft Word 2007 to accomplish
tasks that in the past required the use of several discretely accessed applications and steps.

In Microsoft Word 2007, you have the capability of creating a SharePoint document
workspace from MS Word, which simplifies the process of sharing a document with other users on your network. You can also upload and save documents from Word directly
into a SharePoint library. You can control the version or revision-level of a document and
track who made modifications to it and when.

Working with the Workflows capability of MOSS, you can create a workflow for a document to seek approval, collect feedback, and have a document digitally signed by users.

SharePoint libraries and sites can also be included in the Research functions built into
all Office applications using the search capabilities inherent in MOSS.

CHAPTER 19

MOSS and Excel 2007

Microsoft Office Excel 2007 (and all previous versions of this electronic spreadsheet application) is arguably the most often used of the Microsoft Office suite of applications. Excel spreadsheets are used for the most basic of functions (such as creating a two-column reference list) as well as very complex multipage compilations of data and formula-based calculations (for example, comprehensive sales forecasts for multiple operating units).

With the release of the capabilities of the Microsoft Office SharePoint Server (MOSS) 2007 and the Excel Services, the ability to collaborate, share, extract, and report spreadsheet-based data and graphics has moved to the next level. Excel Services is comprised of service features of MOSS and the .NET Framework and provides MOSS users with a server-based calculation service and a web-based user interface. Because Excel Services is a part of MOSS it has the capability to apply many of MOSS's features, including document check-in and check-out, auditing, and versioning.

Excel Services includes two primary components: the Excel Calculation Server, the Excel Web Access Services, and the Excel Web Services. The Excel Calculation Server accesses and loads requested Excel workbooks, accesses any linked external data, and performs any required calculations. The Excel Web Access Services converts the Excel workbook (or worksheet) into Hypertext Markup Language (HTML) code and the Excel Web Services provides the interface needed for other applications to access Excel workbooks stored in a SharePoint document library.

In this chapter, we look at how Excel Services is used in conjunction with both the SharePoint document libraries and the Excel 2007 client. This discussion includes information on how to set up Excel Services in an MOSS environment, how to publish an Excel workbook to a SharePoint document library, and how to use Excel Web Access to view an Excel workbook.

EXCEL 2007 AND EXCEL SERVICES

Before you begin using Excel Services in an MOSS environment, you should understand that Excel Services and Excel are two entirely separate things. At the risk of oversimplifying their differences, essentially Excel is a document (workbook) authoring application and Excel Services is a reporting tool.

It is also important for you to understand how Excel Services and Excel 2007 co-exist in an MOSS environment. Figure 19-1 illustrates how Excel Services and Excel work together from both an administrator's and a user's points-of-view. Reference the numbered elements in Figure 19-1 to the following list of actions:

1. A user creates an Excel workbook using Excel.

2. The user publishes (saves) the Excel workbook to a SharePoint document library (or perhaps to a network file or web server).

3. Using Excel Services to access the workbook from the SharePoint document library, users are able to create reports, web pages, and dashboard elements.

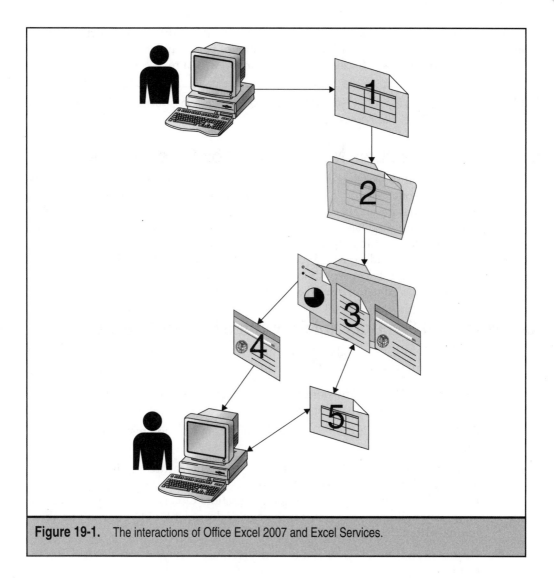

Figure 19-1.   The interactions of Office Excel 2007 and Excel Services.

4. Users can view a snapshot of all or part of the workbook in a browser through Excel Services.

5. Those users who have the appropriate permissions can access and save the workbook locally using the Excel application.

However, there are some significant differences between what Excel Services displays and what you may have experienced using Microsoft Office Excel 2007 (or any previous version). The primary difference is that Excel Services is a web-based reporting tool for

Excel workbooks that provides only a limited subset of the features and functions found in the Excel application. Another important difference between these two applications is that Excel Services displays Excel workbook contents with a read-only access.

NOTE It is possible, providing you have the appropriate permissions, to open a workbook for editing in Excel using Excel Web Access.

Excel Workbook Features Not Supported by Excel Services

Except for those features listed in Table 19-1, Excel Services supports the majority of date, cell, range, calculation, charting, formatting, external data connection, what-if analysis, and consolidation features available in an Excel 2007 workbook. However, some specific functions are not supported (see the "Excel Worksheet Features Not Supported by Excel Services" section later in this chapter). Excel Services will not load or display any Excel 2007 workbook that includes any of the unsupported features listed in Table 19-1. To avoid this problem, any Excel workbook you would later want to view through Excel Services should be saved using the Excel Services options on the Office menu.

Excel Worksheet Features Not Supported by Excel Services

Almost all Excel worksheet features are supported by Excel Services. However, the following features may not be fully functional:

▼ **Character (CHAR)** Any nonprinting characters specified with the CHAR function are displayed as a space.

■ **Cell information (CELL)** This Excel worksheet function results in a #VALUE! cell error.

■ **Hyperlink (HYPERLINK)** This Excel worksheet feature requires that the All Workbook Interactivity and the Workbook Navigation properties be enabled for Office Excel Web Access to properly function. Otherwise, the hyperlink will allow you to link to an external web page or document, but you won't be able to link within the same workbook.

■ **Information (INFO)** This Excel worksheet function results in a #VALUE! cell error.

■ **Computer date and time (NOW)** This function normally returns the date and time on the client computer, but Excel Services displays the date and time of the server.

■ **Real-time data (RTD)** Only RTD-generated values stored in the workbook are displayed. If the worksheet is recalculated, any RTD values will be displayed as a #N/A cell error.

Unsupported Feature	Description of Feature
Attached toolbars	Office Excel 2003 custom toolbars attached to the workbook
Comments	Comment display or adjustment
Controls	Form toolbar, Toolbox, and ActiveX controls
Data sources	Data retrieval services for Windows SharePoint Services (WSS) lists, tables linked to WSS lists, Microsoft SQL Server, and embedded query tables
Data validation	Prevents invalid data entry and creates drop-down lists
Displayed formulas	Workbooks saved with displayed formulas
Digital signatures	Visible and invisible digital signatures
External references	Linking a specific cell range in an external reference (workbook) that has been assigned a name
Images and objects	Linked or embedded objects or images, such as inserted pictures, AutoShapes, WordArt, and diagrams
Ink	All ink features, such as a drawing, hand writing, or notes and annotations
Legacy macro languages	Microsoft Excel 4.0 Macro Functions and Microsoft 5.0 dialog sheets
OLE and DDE	Object Linking and Embedding (OLE) objects and Dynamic Data Exchange (DDE) links
Queries	Web and text queries
Security and privacy	Workbooks, worksheets, or ranges with protection enabled
VBA	Visual Basic for Applications (VBA) coding, macros, add-ins, or user-defined functions (UDFs)
XML	XML maps and embedded smart tags

Table 1-1.   Office Excel 2007 Workbook Features Not Supported by Excel Services

- ■ **SQL request (SQL_Request)**   Only SQL_Request-generated values stored in the workbook are displayed. If the worksheet is recalculated, any SQL_Request values are displayed as a #N/A cell error.

- ▲ **Computer date (TODAY)**   This function normally displays the date on the client computer, but Excel Services displays the date on the server.

In addition, the following Excel worksheet visual features are not supported by Excel Services:

▼ **3-D charts and effects**   Excel Services does support the display of the 3-D graphic effects released in Excel 2007, including shadow, glow, warp, soft edges, and reflection. In addition, Excel Services doesn't support the display of the 3-D surface, wireframe 3-D surface, contour surface, and the wireframe contour surface 3-D chart formats included in Excel 2007.

■ **Line borders**   Triple and double lines, diamond, square, dotted, dash-short-dash, long-short-dash, and dash-short-dash-short-dash line borders are not supported by Excel Services. However, if the chart has been embedded (pasted) into a worksheet, Excel Services will display it as a graphic image.

■ **Text**   Any rich text features included in a worksheet, such as different fonts and font sizes, bullets, vertical text alignment, or superscript and subscript text are converted to plain text by Excel Services.

▲ **Page layout**   Excel Services doesn't display any page layout settings or custom page headers or footers configured on an Excel workbook.

CONFIGURE EXCEL SERVICES

To properly function with MOSS, Excel Services must be started in the MOSS environment. This action is performed from the Central Administration web site and you must have system administrator permissions to perform this task. Once Excel Services is started, you may need to configure trusted file locations, single sign-on (SSO), trusted data providers, trusted data connection libraries, and optionally user-defined functions. The process used to configure each of these areas is discussed in the following sections.

Start Excel Services

To start the Excel Services service or verify that it is already running, perform the following steps:

1. Open the Central Administration home page and click the Operations tab.

2. Under the Topology And Services heading, click the Services On Server link to open the Services On Server page (see Figure 19-2).

3. In the Start Services In The Table Below section of the page, find the information for Excel Services. Since this service is started by default in most installations, it is likely this service should show Started in the Status column. However, if the Excel Services service is not running (see Figure 19-3), click Start in the Action column to start Excel Services running.

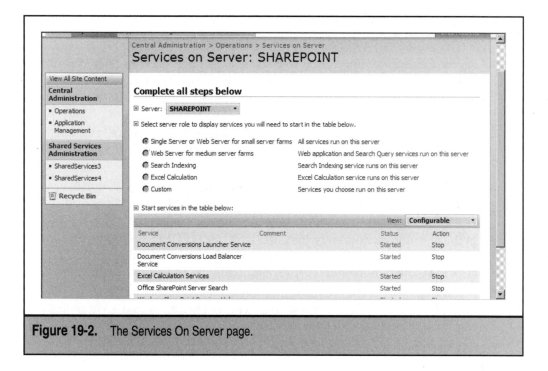

Figure 19-2. The Services On Server page.

Configure a Trusted File Location

Once you either started or verified that the Excel Services service is running, you next need to configure a trusted file location for your Excel workbook documents. This step is also performed from the Central Administration web page and you must have system administrator permissions to do this action.

Service	Comment	Status	Action
Document Conversions Launcher Service		Started	Stop
Document Conversions Load Balancer Service		Started	Stop
Excel Calculation Services	Required on Farm, not running	Stopped	Start
Office SharePoint Server Search		Started	Stop
Windows SharePoint Services Help Search		Started	Stop
Windows SharePoint Services Web Application		Started	Stop

Figure 19-3. An example showing the Excel Services disabled.

To configure a trusted file location for Excel workbook documents, perform the following steps:

1. On the Central Administration web site's home page, click the Shared Services link that is associated with the web application on which you wish to configure a trusted location. This link is in the Shared Services Administration section of the Quick Launch menu.

2. On the home page of the Shared Services Administration you've selected, locate the Excel Services Settings heading and click the link for Trusted File Locations.

3. On the Excel Services Trusted File Locations page (see Figure 19-4) that displays, click Add Trusted File Location to open the Excel Services Add Trusted File Location page (see Figure 19-5).

4. In the Location section, enter the URL, UNC, or HTTP address of the document library you wish to configure as a trusted location for Excel documents and click the radio button option corresponding to the address type you enter.

5. If you wish to extend the trusted location to include any child libraries created under the library located at the address you've entered in step 4, check the checkbox associated with Children Trusted.

6. Enter an optional description for the trusted location.

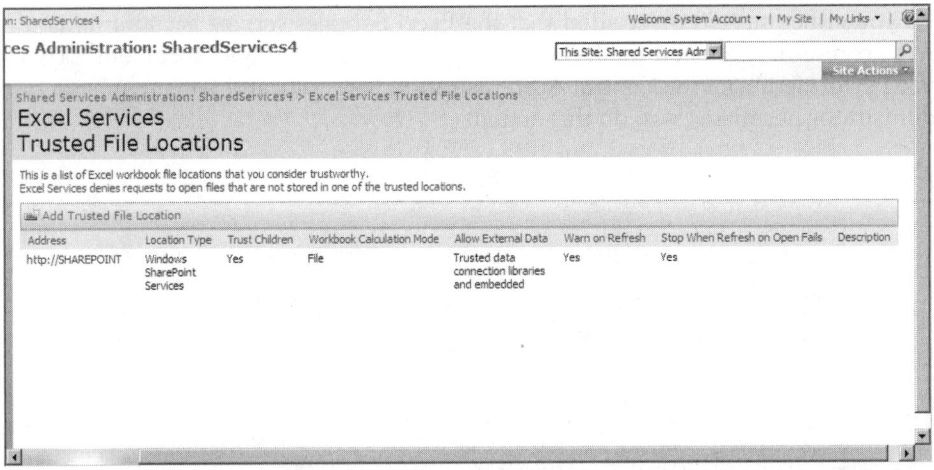

Figure 19-4. The Excel Services Trusted File Locations page.

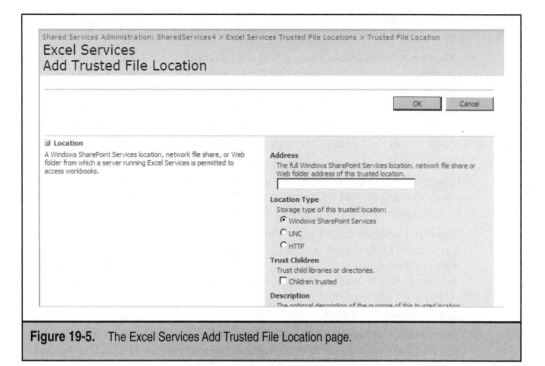

Figure 19-5.   The Excel Services Add Trusted File Location page.

7. Because many Excel workbooks can contain proprietary or sensitive information, you may want to control the length an Excel Services session can remain open and inactive by entering values in the Session Management section. The control settings available are:

   a. **Session Timeout**   Enter a value (in seconds) between 0 and 2073600, with 0 indicating that a session will last only for the duration of a single request and 2073600 indicating a session can remain open for 24 days. Enter the value –1 (minus 1) to remove the timeout limitation from Excel Services sessions.

   b. **Short Session Timeout**   The values used in step 7a can also be used to limit the amount of time (in seconds) an Excel Web Service session can remain open and inactive.

   c. **Maximum Request Duration**   Enter a value between 1 and 2073600 to set the maximum amount of time (in seconds) that a single request can be active within a session. Entering a –1 setting creates a no maximum duration limit condition.

8. In the Workbook Properties section, you can configure a maximum size limit for Excel workbooks and workbook-based charts. The two settings available are:

   a. **Maximum Workbook Size**   Enter the maximum size for an Excel workbook that can be opened by Excel Services in megabytes. The valid range of entries is from 0 to 2000, with 10 MB as the default value.

   b. **Maximum Chart Size**   Enter the maximum size for a chart created from an Excel workbook that can be opened by Excel Services in megabytes. The default value is 1 MB, but any positive integer value is valid.

9. In the Calculation Behavior section, you can configure the maximum amount of time a value computed from workbook data is to be cached for use in further calculations and the method you wish to use to override the workbook calculation settings. The settings available are:

   a. **Volatile Function Cache Lifetime**   Enter the maximum amount of time (in seconds) you wish to cache calculations made by Excel Services for any future recalculations. Enter a value of 1 to have calculations made only when the workbook is loaded, a 0 to automatically perform all calculations when a change is made to the workbook's data, and a value between 1 and 2073600 (24 days) to set a specific time in seconds to cache calculation-based values.

   b. **Workbook Calculation Mode**   Choose the radio button corresponding to the method you wish to use to perform calculations on workbooks loaded by Excel Services. The four options available are:

      i. **File**   Uses the settings of the workbook to control calculations.

      ii. **Manual**   Indicates that you wish to manually control when calculations are performed.

      iii. **Automatic**   Indicates that you wish to have calculations made automatically, should an individual workbook be configured to a manual calculation mode.

      iv. **Automatic except data tables**   Indicates that you wish to have all calculations made automatically except those included in the ranges of cells that have been defined as data tables.

10. In the External Data section, as shown in Figure 19-6, you configure the source for Excel workbooks that you wish to enable Excel Services to access and open. The following explains each of the settings in this section:

    a. **Allow External Data**   Assuming you wish Excel Services to include external (meaning data referenced in a workbook from a file source external to the workbook) data, your choices are whether you wish to also enable any hyperlinks embedded in a workbook. Choose the radio button corresponding to the setting you wish to make for the inclusion of external data in Excel Services workbooks. The choices are:

       i. **None**   Choose this option if you don't wish to include external data in workbooks accessed by Excel Services.

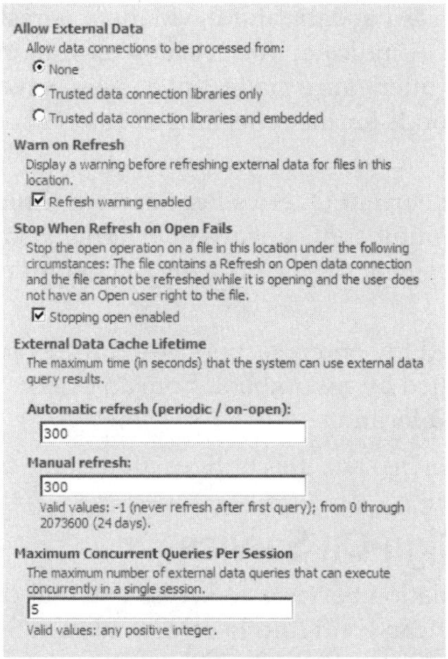

Figure 19-6. The External Data section of the Excel Services Add Trusted File Location page.

ii. **Trusted data connection libraries only**   This allows external data to be included, provided the source file is available through a trusted data connection library. However, this option omits any hyperlinks that may be embedded in the workbook.

iii. **Trusted data connection libraries and embedded**   This option includes the functions of the Trusted Data Connection Libraries Only option, but also enables the inclusion of any hyperlinks embedded in the workbook.

b. **Warn on Refresh**   Check the checkbox associated with this setting option if you wish a warning message to be displayed before any external data is refreshed from the active workbook.

c. **Stop When Refresh on Open Fails**   If a workbook file contains a Refresh On Open data connection and the workbook cannot be refreshed when it is opened, plus the user attempting to open the file doesn't have Open permissions for the file, checking the checkbox associated with the Stopping Open Enabled option, will cause the open operation to stop.

d. **External Data Cache Lifetime**   This setting controls how long (in seconds) a user can have any external data available for use. For both the Automatic refresh, which refreshes the external data upon open and sets up a periodic refresh of the external data, and the Manual refresh options, the settings are the same: a –1 indicates you wish no refresh operations to be performed after the initial queries are made, but a value between 0 and 2073600 set the time in seconds for the refreshing of external data either manually or automatically.

   e. **Maximum Concurrent Queries Per Session**   Enter a positive integer value to indicate the number of concurrent external data queries you wish to allow during a single session. The default value is five concurrent queries in a session.

11. In the User-Defined Functions section, you can choose to allow user-defined functions to be called by a workbook from an external data source also located in the same trusted location.

12. Click the OK button to save the configuration of the trusted location.

Configure the Single Sign-On Service

To enable the Excel Calculation Services to access external data from a source that requires authentication, you can configure Excel Calculation Services to access authentication credentials from the Single Sign-On (SSO) secure database. To enable SSO for an MOSS environment, there is a two-step process: start the SSO service and then configure its settings using the Central Administration web page.

Start the Single Sign-On Service

To start the SSO service, perform the following steps:

1. Open the Windows Start menu and click the Administrative Tools option.

2. On the Administrative Tools menu, click the Services option to open the Services dialog box.

3. Locate the entry for Microsoft Single Sign-On Service and double-click this service's name to open its Properties dialog box (see Figure 19-7).

Excel Data Tables

The capability to create a data table is one of the commands available in Microsoft Office Excel 2007 that can be used to perform a what-if analysis or make a side calculation. A data table, which is a range of cells set up as a one-, two-, or multiple-value data table, is used to determine the impact on a calculated amount using a formula without actually altering the primary data. In other words, you can test out how changing one or more values may affect a calculated amount.

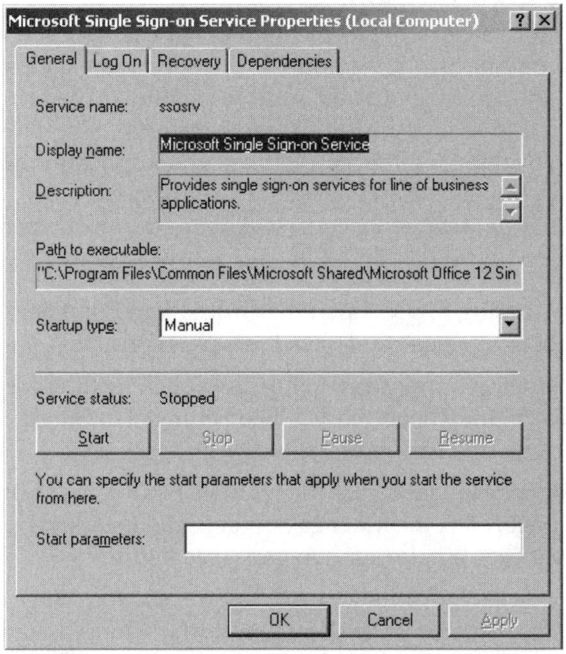

Figure 19-7. The Microsoft Single Sign-On Service's Properties dialog box.

4. If you wish this service to automatically start when the system is started, change the Startup Type to Automatic. If you do change the Startup Type, click the Apply button before proceeding.

5. If you wish to designate a single account log-on for the system, select the Log On tab and the This Account option. Enter the domain, username, and password you wish to configure.

6. Click the General tab to continue with the setup.

7. About two-thirds of the way down the General tab is the Service Status. If the service is stopped, click the Start button.

8. Click OK to close the properties dialog box and close the Services dialog box to return to the Desktop.

NOTE   You must start the SSO service on each farm server that will be running Excel Services.

Configure Single Sign-On Settings

Configuring the server settings for single sign-on in the MOSS environment requires that you specify the administrator accounts, the server on which the single sign-on database is located, and the time-out and audit log settings. The primary purpose of this configuration action is to assign the SSO administrator(s), who have the responsibility of creating, deleting, or changing the SSO settings and application definitions, as well as backing up the encryption key used with the SSO database.

To configure the SSO settings in your MOSS environment, perform the following steps:

1. On a server running MOSS, open the Office SharePoint Server Central Administration web page and click the Operations tab.

2. Under the Security Configuration heading, click the link for Manage Settings For Single Sign-On to open the Manage Settings For Single Sign-On For SharePoint page (see Figure 19-8).

3. In the Server Settings section of the Manage Settings For Single Sign-On For SharePoint page, click the Manage Server Settings link to open the Manage Server Settings For Single Sign-On page (see Figure 19-9).

4. In the Single Sign-On Administrator Account section, enter the domain and group or account name of the administrator(s) who is assigned as the SSO administrator. This entry should be in the form of either domain\group or domain\username. You can enter the name of the Windows security group of

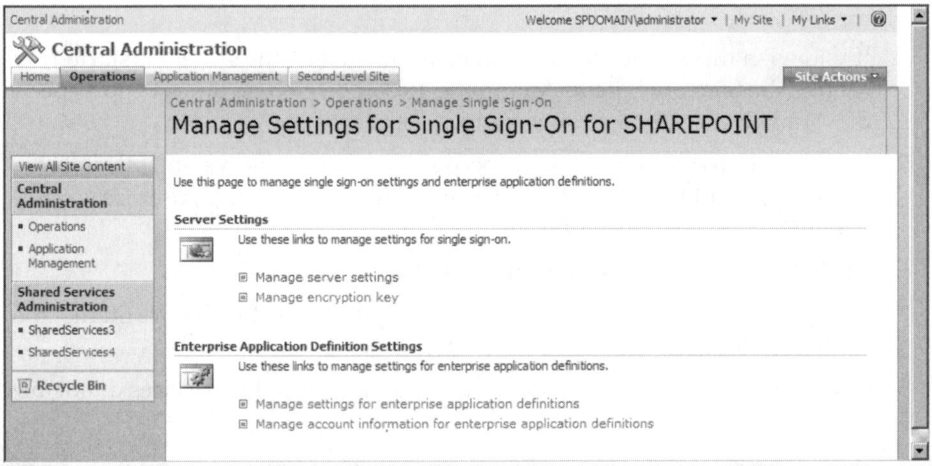

Figure 19-8.   The Manage Settings for Single Sign-On for SharePoint page.

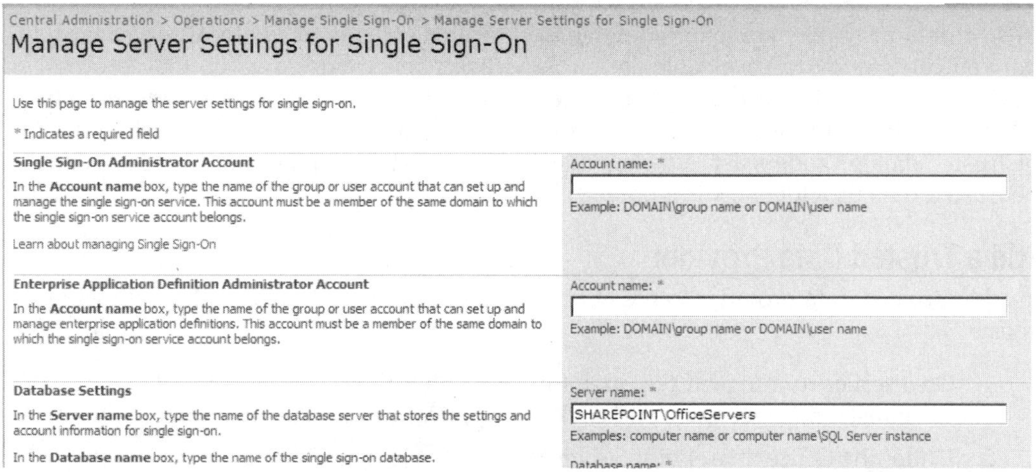

Figure 19-9. The Manage Server Settings for Single Sign-On page.

which the administrator is a member. The credential information entered here should be the same as that entered on the Log On tab of the Microsoft Single Sign-On Service dialog box (see the previous section).

5. In the Enterprise Application Definition Administrator Account section, enter the domain and group or username of the group or user who is assigned the responsibility for setting up and managing application definitions.

6. In the Database Settings section, enter the UNC (NetBIOS) name of the database server on which the SSO database (SQL server instance) is, or is to be located.

7. In the Database Name text box, either accept the default value or enter a name for the SSO database server.

8. In the Time Out Settings section, enter the number of minutes you wish to allow an SSO ticket to remain active before it times out. The default value is two minutes, which means that an application has two minutes from when the SSO ticket is issued to redeem it.

9. In the Delete audit log records older than (in days) text box, enter the number of days you wish to keep audit log records before they are deleted. The default value is ten days.

10. Click OK to save the SSO settings.

Configure Trusted Data Providers

Trusted data providers are external databases, located outside of the local server farm that you can specify to Excel Calculation Services as being trusted when they process the data connection links embedded in Excel workbooks. Excel Calculation Services will only process the data connections that point to a trusted data provider that is included in the trusted data providers list. A data connection to an external database not included in the trusted data providers list is ignored.

Add a Trusted Data Provider

To add a trusted data provider to the trusted data providers list, perform the following steps:

1. On a server running MOSS, open the Office SharePoint Server Central Administration web page and click the Applications Management tab.

2. Under the Office SharePoint Server Shared Services heading, click the Create Or Create This Farm's Shared Services link to open the Manage This Farm's Shared Services page (see Figure 19-10).

3. In the SSP and associated web applications list, click the Shared Services Provider on which you wish to configure Excel Services. In most installations, this will be the default: SharedServices1.

4. On the Shared Services Administration page, click the Trusted Data Providers link in the Excel Services Settings section to open the Excel Services Trusted Data Providers page (see Figure 19-11).

Figure 19-10. The Manage This Farm's Shared Services page.

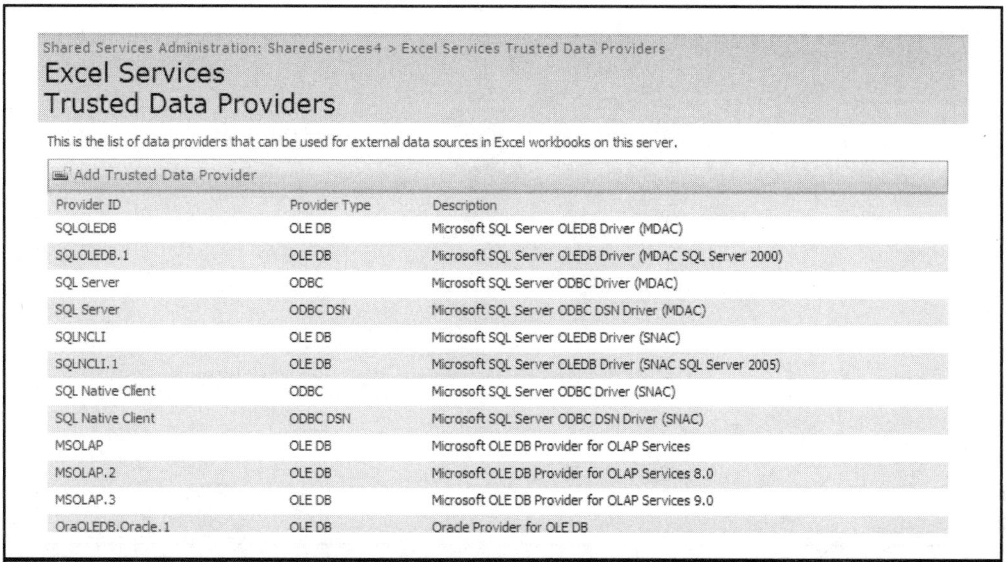

Shared Services Administration: SharedServices4 > Excel Services Trusted Data Providers

Excel Services
Trusted Data Providers

This is the list of data providers that can be used for external data sources in Excel workbooks on this server.

Add Trusted Data Provider

Provider ID	Provider Type	Description
SQLOLEDB	OLE DB	Microsoft SQL Server OLEDB Driver (MDAC)
SQLOLEDB.1	OLE DB	Microsoft SQL Server OLEDB Driver (MDAC SQL Server 2000)
SQL Server	ODBC	Microsoft SQL Server ODBC Driver (MDAC)
SQL Server	ODBC DSN	Microsoft SQL Server ODBC DSN Driver (MDAC)
SQLNCLI	OLE DB	Microsoft SQL Server OLEDB Driver (SNAC)
SQLNCLI.1	OLE DB	Microsoft SQL Server OLEDB Driver (SNAC SQL Server 2005)
SQL Native Client	ODBC	Microsoft SQL Server ODBC Driver (SNAC)
SQL Native Client	ODBC DSN	Microsoft SQL Server ODBC DSN Driver (SNAC)
MSOLAP	OLE DB	Microsoft OLE DB Provider for OLAP Services
MSOLAP.2	OLE DB	Microsoft OLE DB Provider for OLAP Services 8.0
MSOLAP.3	OLE DB	Microsoft OLE DB Provider for OLAP Services 9.0
OraOLEDB.Oracle.1	OLE DB	Oracle Provider for OLE DB

Figure 19-11. The Excel Services Trusted Data Providers page.

5. To add a new trusted data provider, click the Add Trusted Data Provider link on the navigation bar.
6. On the Excel Services Add Trusted Data Provider page (see Figure 19-12), enter the identifier for the external data source you wish to add and select the radio button corresponding to the file type. Enter an optional description for this new trusted data provider if you wish.
7. Click OK to add the trusted data provider.

Add a Trusted Data Connection Library

In lieu of embedded data connections in Excel workbooks, Excel Calculation Services can be configured to require the use of Office data connection (ODC) files. An ODC file, which has a .odc filename extension, contains trusted connections to external data sources and is stored in a data connection library. In order for Excel Calculation Services to be able to use the ODC files in the data connection library, it must be configured as a trusted source for the data connections.

Trusted Data Connection Libraries

The first step in the process of adding a trusted data connection library to Excel Services is to create a data connection library on a SharePoint site.

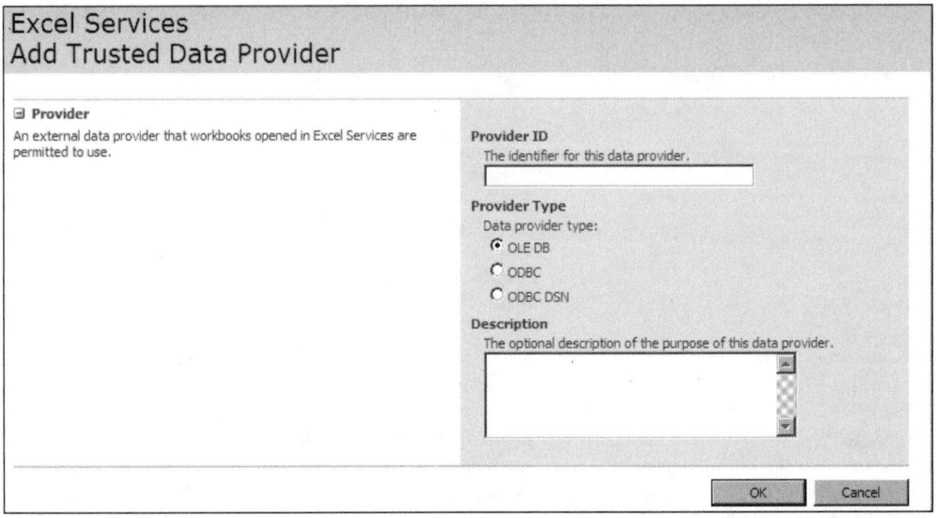

Figure 19-12. The Excel Services Add Trusted Data Provider page.

Create a Data Connection Library To create a data connection library in SharePoint, use the following steps:

1. Navigate to the top-level site on which you wish to create a data connection library and click the Site Actions button to open its drop-down menu. Click Create Site to open the Create page.

2. On the Create page, click the Data Connection Library link under the Libraries heading to open the New page.

3. Enter a name for the data connection library and complete the other settings as applicable.

4. Click the Create button to create the data connection library.

Add a Trusted Data Connection Library To add a trusted data connection library, perform the following steps:

1. On a server running MOSS, open the Office SharePoint Server Central Administration web page and click the Applications Management tab.

2. Under the Office SharePoint Server Shared Services heading, click the Create Or Create This Farm's Shared Services link to open the Manage This Farm's Shared Services page (see Figure 19-10).

3. In the SSP and associated web applications list, click the Shared Services Provider on which you wish to configure Excel Services. In most installations, this will be the default SharedServices1.

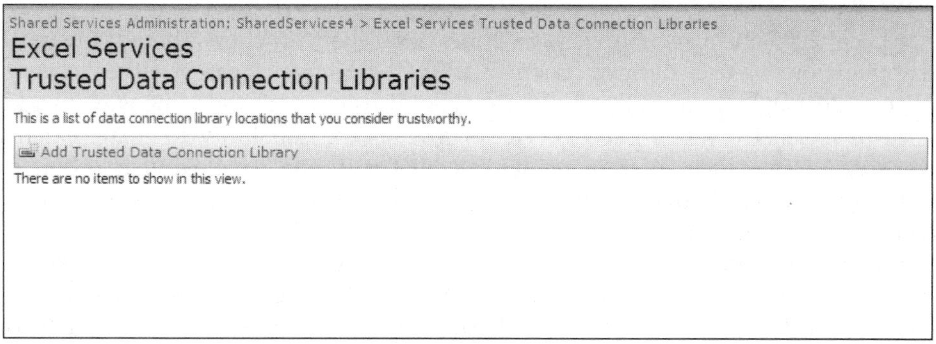

Figure 19-13.   The Excel Services Trusted Data Connection Libraries page.

4. On the Shared Services Administration page, click the Trusted Data Connection Libraries link in the Excel Services Settings section to open the Excel Services Trusted Data Connection Libraries page (see Figure 19-13).

5. To add a new trusted data connection library, click the Add Trusted Data Connection Library link on the navigation bar.

6. On the Excel Services Add Trusted Data Connection Library page (see Figure 19-14), enter the address for the data connection library you wish to add. Enter an optional description for this new trusted data provider, if you wish.

7. Click OK to add the trusted data connection library.

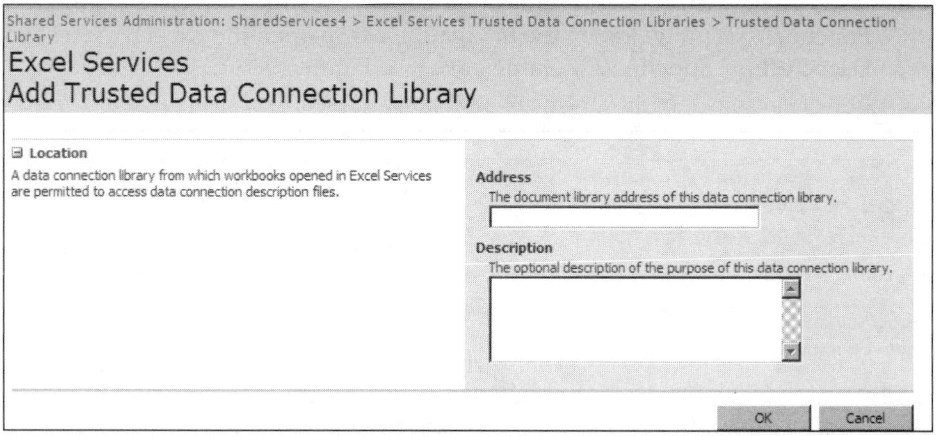

Figure 19-14.   The Excel Services Add Trusted Data Connection Library page.

User-Defined Functions

Office Excel 2007 and Excel Services let you extend their functions though the creation and application of a user-defined function (UDF). UDFs, which can be either server-side or client-side, can be used in Excel and Excel Services in much the same way an add-on is used in Excel. However, Excel services provides the capability to create extensible server-side UDFs, which are implemented as .NET methods. Excel Services orders must be configured for UDF functionality, and the individual UDFs you wish to use must be registered with Excel Services.

Enabling UDFs to work with Excel Services is a two-step process. The first step is to add the UDF assembly to the Excel Services' list in the Shared Service Provider, and the second is to also enable the use of the UDF for workbooks stored in trusted file locations.

Add User-Defined Function Assembly

To add a UDF assembly to Excel Services, do the following:

1. On a server running MOSS, open the Office SharePoint Server Central Administration web page and click the Applications Management tab.

2. Under the Office SharePoint Server Shared Services heading, click the Create Or Create This Farm's Shared Services link to open the Manage This Farm's Shared Services page (see Figure 19-10).

3. In the SSP and associated web applications list, click the Shared Services Provider on which you wish to configure Excel Services. In most installations, this will be the default SharedServices1.

4. On the Shared Services Administration page, click the User-Defined Function Assemblies link in the Excel Services Settings section to open the Excel Services User-Defined Functions page (see Figure 19-15).

5. To add a new trusted data connection library, click the Add User-Defined Function Assembly link on the navigation bar to open the Excel Services Add User-Defined Function Assembly page (see Figure 19-16).

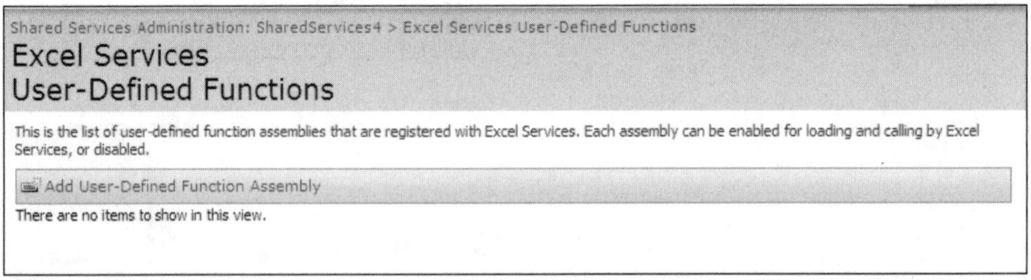

Shared Services Administration: SharedServices4 > Excel Services User-Defined Functions

Excel Services
User-Defined Functions

This is the list of user-defined function assemblies that are registered with Excel Services. Each assembly can be enabled for loading and calling by Excel Services, or disabled.

Add User-Defined Function Assembly

There are no items to show in this view.

Figure 19-15. The Excel Services User-Defined Functions page.

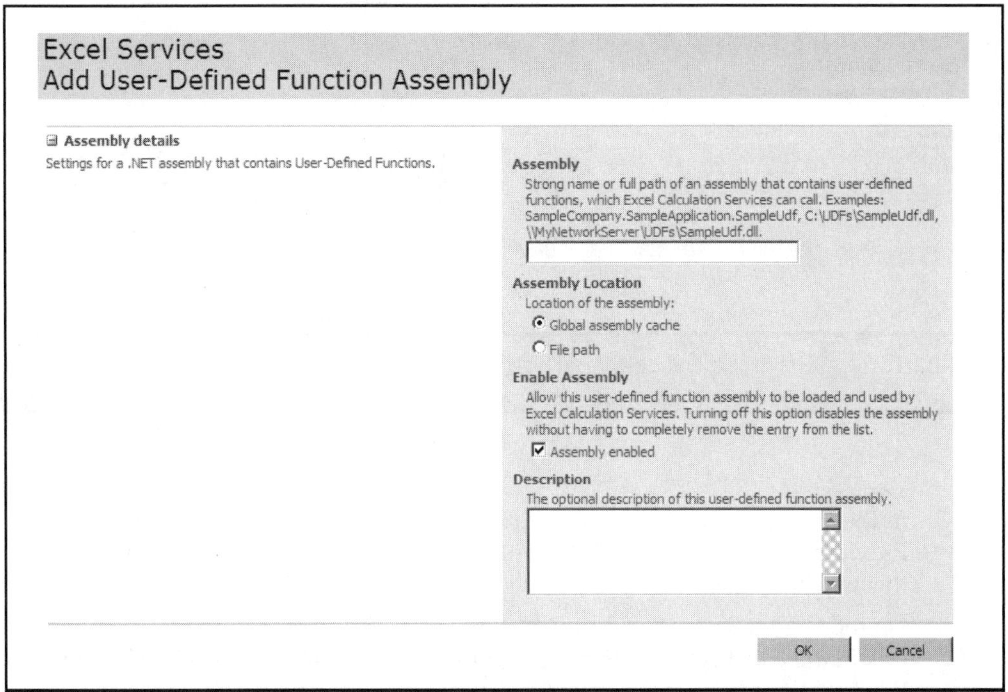

Figure 19-16. The Excel Services Add User-Defined Function Assembly page.

6. In the Assembly Details section, enter the full pathname of the assembly (DLL or XLL file) that contains the UDFs you wish to add and indicate whether this location is a global assembly area or a direct pathname by choosing the radio button corresponding to the appropriate type.

7. If you are adding a new UDF assembly, make sure the Enable Assembly checkbox is checked. This option can also be used to disable an assembly without deleting it.

8. Enter an optional description for the assembly if you wish.

9. Click the OK button to add the UDF assembly.

Enable User-Defined Functions for Workbooks

A UDF must be enabled for use by Excel workbooks stored in trusted file locations. To enable a UDF to a trusted file location, perform the following steps:

1. On a server running MOSS, open the Office SharePoint Server Central Administration web page and click the Applications Management tab.

2. Under the Office SharePoint Server Shared Services heading, click the Create Or Create This Farm's Shared Services link to open the Manage This Farm's Shared Services page (see Figure 19-10).

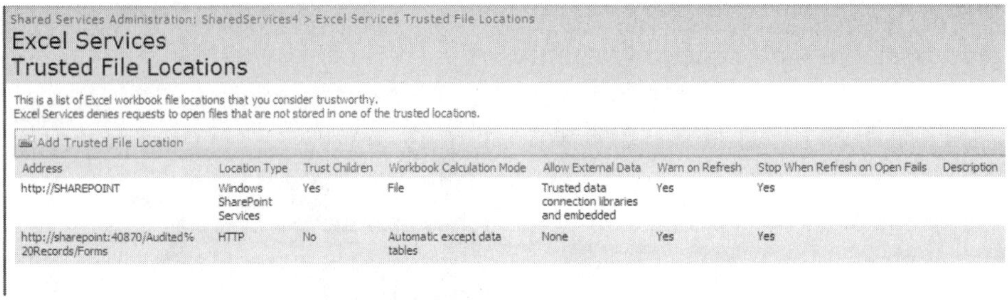

Figure 19-17. The Excel Services Trusted File Locations page.

3. In the SSP and associated web applications list, click the Shared Services Provider on which you wish to configure Excel Services. In most installations, this will be the default SharedServices1.

4. On the Shared Services Administration page, click the Trusted file locations link in the Excel Services Settings section to open the Excel Services Trusted File Locations page (see Figure 19-17).

5. Click the trusted file location for which you wish to enable UDFs to open the Excel Services Edit Trusted File Location page.

6. On the Excel Services Edit Trusted File Location page, scroll down to the User-Defined Functions section and check the Allow User-Defined Functions checkbox (see Figure 19-18) to enable UDFs for this trusted file location.

7. Click the OK button to save the trusted file location's settings.

Figure 19-18. The Excel Services Edit Trusted File Location page.

EXCEL 2007 AND MOSS

Like all Office 2007 applications, Excel workbooks can be saved to any SharePoint document library. If you are planning to use Excel Services to view Excel workbooks saved to a SharePoint document library, beyond creating the workbook and saving it to an existing or new document library, you must also add the document library to Excel Services as a trusted file location.

Perhaps during the planning of your MOSS environment, or whenever the need arises, you must start from the basics of enabling users to view Excel workbook documents using Excel Services. This means you must work backward from the actual document to its document library and on back to the Central Administration functions that enable the document library to be accessed by Excel Services.

In the following sections, we look at the processes used to create a SharePoint document library based on the Excel spreadsheet document template, add the new document library to Excel Services as a trusted file location, and publish an Excel workbook document to the document library and Excel Services.

Create a Document Library Using the Excel Spreadsheet Template

Creating a SharePoint document library as a repository for Excel workbooks is a fairly straightforward process that involves only a few decisions to be made. However, you must have a clear vision of whether or not the document library is to be used with Excel Services and in what manner.

To create a SharePoint document library based on the Excel spreadsheet document template, perform the following steps:

1. Navigate to the home page of the site collection to which you wish to add the document library and click the View All Site Content link at the top of the Quick Launch menu.

2. On the All Site Content page, click the Create button on the navigation bar to open the Create page.

3. Under the Libraries heading, click the Document Libraries link to open the New page.

4. On the New page, enter a name for the document library, an option description, and choose or enter the other settings as applicable.

5. In the Document Template section, use the list box to select the Microsoft Office Excel spreadsheet document template (see Figure 19-19).

6. Click the Create button to create the document library and open the home page of the new document library.

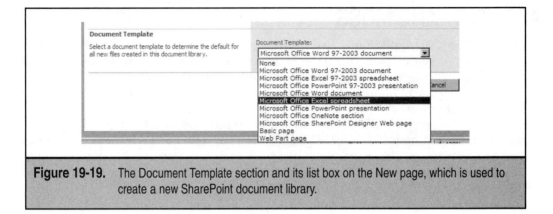

Figure 19-19. The Document Template section and its list box on the New page, which is used to create a new SharePoint document library.

Add Excel Workbook to a SharePoint Document Library

You can create a new Excel workbook document either from the document library's home page or from within the Excel application itself. We discuss the latter method later in the chapter, but first let's go over the process used to add an Excel workbook directly to a SharePoint document library.

To create a new Excel workbook document in a SharePoint document library, perform the following steps:

1. From the home page of the document library in which you wish to add an Excel workbook document, click the New option on the navigation bar and select New Document.

2. The Excel 2007 application starts up with a new document named template$n$. xlsx, where the n represents a sequence number.

3. Notice that on the right-side of the display is a Document Management pane that includes a Document Workspace panel (see Figure 19-20). Click the Create button, which will force you to save (and name) the document to a document workspace within the target document library. Understand that this step creates a new workspace site in the site from which you started this process. If you don't wish to create a document workspace on this site, skip this step.

4. You can now proceed with entering your data, formulas, and formatting into the worksheet.

5. When you have completed the document and are ready to save it, click the Office logo to open its menu and simply click Save to write the workbook to the document library.

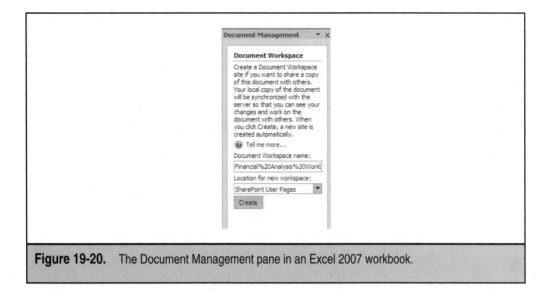

Figure 19-20.   The Document Management pane in an Excel 2007 workbook.

Publish Excel Workbook to Excel Services

When you publish an Excel workbook to Excel Services, you have the choice of allowing viewers to see the entire workbook or just parts of it. You can designate single worksheets, named ranges, or charts as the only part(s) of the workbook that can be viewed using Excel Services and a web browser. In addition, you can define parameters for the workbook that allow Excel Web Access viewers to enter data for purposes of a what-if analysis or special purpose calculation.

To publish an Excel workbook to Excel Services, including the features mentioned in the preceding paragraph, use the following process:

1. In the Office Excel 2007 application, either create a new workbook or open an existing workbook you wish to publish to Excel Services.

2. To define parameters for the workbook, follow these steps:

   a. In order to define parameters, you must first assign a name to each of the editable cells in the workbook. A parameter cell can only be a single worksheet cell, not a range of multiple cells.

   b. Select a cell you wish to use as a parameter cell, meaning cell users will be able to edit in their browsers using Excel Web Access.

   c. Click the Formulas tab to display the Formulas ribbon. In the Defined Names section (see Figure 19-21), click the Define Name option.

   d. In the New Name dialog box that displays (see Figure 19-22), enter the name for the cell, which should be something that clearly defines the use

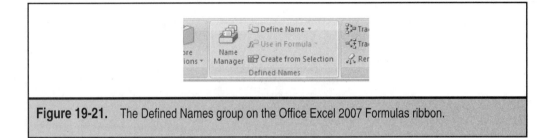

Figure 19-21. The Defined Names group on the Office Excel 2007 Formulas ribbon.

and purpose of the cell to the user. However, the name must begin with either a letter or an underscore character, it cannot include a space, and it cannot conflict with any predefined Excel names.

e. Select the Scope of the cell, meaning does this cell need to be available to all sheets in the workbook or only to a single worksheet.

f. Click OK to save the name definition.

3. Once you have entered the contents of the workbook and defined the parameters needed (if any) you are ready to publish the workbook to Excel Services. To publish the workbook to Excel Services, use the following steps:

a. Click the Office logo to open its menu and click the Publish option.

b. On the Publish menu that opens, click Excel Services.

c. Enter the path to the server on which you wish to save the workbook and enter a file name. For a SharePoint location, the pathname should be in the format of http://server/site/file name.

d. Set the Save As type to either the Excel 2007 XML-based format (.xlsx) or the Excel 2007 binary file format (.xlsb).

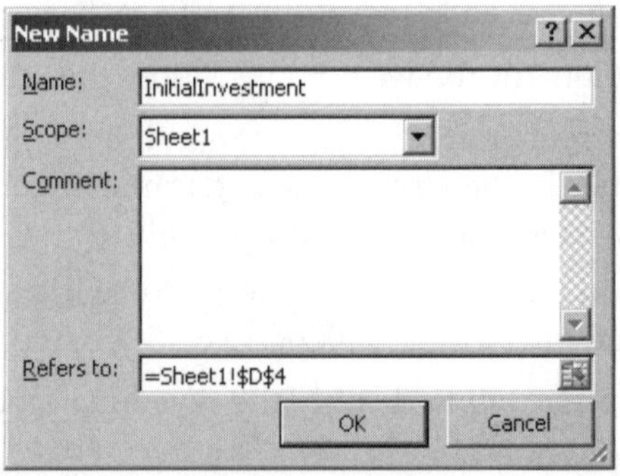

Figure 19-22. The New Name dialog box is used to define a name for an Excel cell or cell range.

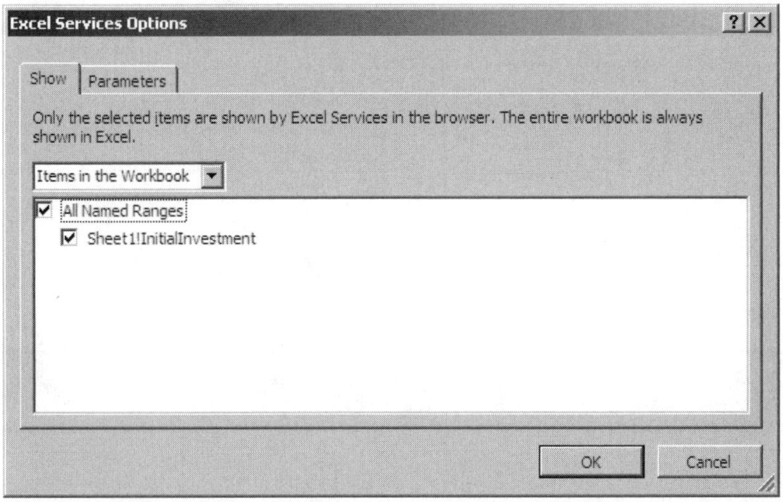

Figure 19-23.   The Excel Services Options dialog box.

   e. Click the Excel Services Options button to open the Excel Services Options dialog box (see Figure 19-23). On the Show tab, use the list box to select the appropriate display mode for the workbook in Excel Services:

      ■ Select Entire Workbook to have Excel Web Access display the entire workbook.

      ■ Select Sheets to limit the display to one or more worksheets.

      ■ Select Items In The Workbook to show only identified items defined in the workbook, such as parameters, named ranges, charts, and so on.

   f. If you wish to immediately view the document in a browser using Excel Web Access, check the checkbox associated with Open In Excel Services.

   g. Click the Save button to publish the document to Excel Services.

View an Excel Workbook in Excel Services

Typically, a user cannot modify the data of the Excel workbook source document displayed by Excel Web Access. However, a user can benefit from viewing a workbook in Excel Web Access in several ways. Among the benefits available to users are:

▼ View the latest values of the formulas and calculations in the workbook.

■ Use parameters to temporarily change the calculated values displayed from the workbook to perform a what-if analysis.

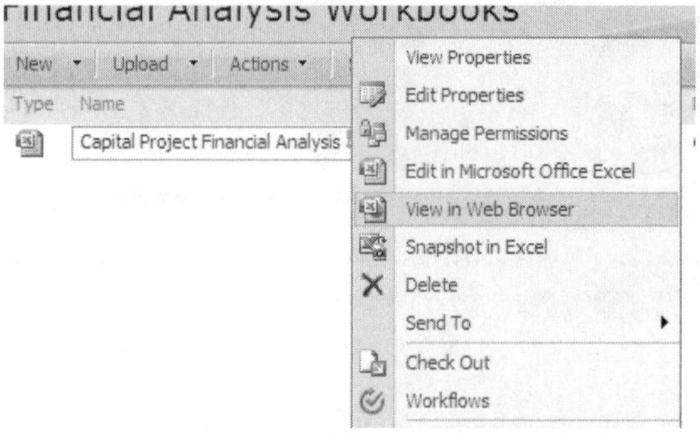

Figure 19-24. The drop-down menu of a document library item.

- Sort and filter data to address specific business questions.
- View different worksheets, named ranges, or charts in the workbook.
- ▲ Copy the workbook, or parts of the workbook, and create a new workbook in Excel 2007.

The primary benefit to the enterprise for using Excel Services to protect Excel workbooks and the data they contain is the controls that are in place to prevent the data from being manipulated, even inadvertently. Microsoft calls this "one version of the truth," which may or may not be factual, but the idea is sound that selected users can view a workbook without risk of the data becoming altered.

The process used to open an Excel workbook document using Excel Services is actually fairly simple. Providing the original document was published to Excel Services from the Excel 2007 application, in the worst case, all the user needs to do is navigate to the appropriate document library and use the drop-down menu of the document they wish to view to select View In Web Browser (see Figure 19-24). In the best case scenario, a Web Access Web Part can be added to a page and linked to a specific Excel workbook. In addition, Excel Services can be integrated into several business intelligence applications as well.

SUMMARY

Using the features of Excel Services, which is built upon MOSS and the .NET environments, users can share spreadsheet data securely. Excel Services includes two primary components: Excel Calculation Services and Excel Web Access. Excel Calculation Services provides a conversion of Excel workbooks and their data into web browser compatible formatting. Excel Web Access allows users to use a browser to display workbooks that have been published to Excel Services with support for parameters and recalculation.

CHAPTER 20

MOSS and Access 2007

In the past, before there was a SharePoint and MOSS, the Microsoft Access database management system was frequently used to track those data types that could be arranged into tables. At one time, Access was perhaps the most robust of the Microsoft Office applications in terms of its ability to organize, relate, present, and retrieve data in a variety of ways. However, it was somewhat difficult and problematic as to where the database files (the .mdf files) should be placed so they were available to be shared by all of the users who needed them and still be properly backed up.

In the Office 2007 applications suite, Access and the Office SharePoint Server work very well together in providing solutions not only to issues involved with database file usage and maintenance in the past, but to a host of newly discovered applications that center around shared data and multiple points of access. Access database files can be linked into SharePoint lists and SharePoint libraries and their contents can be cataloged in an Access view.

This chapter explores many of the more common ways to apply the linkage between Access and MOSS. The sharing ability of both Access and MOSS are demonstrated in the discussions on the ability to open SharePoint lists in Access, sharing Access database contents in SharePoint, and creating an Access view of a SharePoint library or list.

OPEN A SHAREPOINT LIST IN ACCESS

Perhaps the best demonstration of how MOSS and Access 2007 are integrated is the ability to create a SharePoint list and then open and view the list in Access. By performing the steps described in the following example, you should see first-hand how this capability works.

To demonstrate how a SharePoint list can be viewed in Microsoft Office Access 2007, do the following:

1. Navigate to the home page of a site on which you have user permissions to create a new list.

2. Click the List header in the Quick Launch menu to open the Lists page for the site. Click the Create button on the navigation bar to open the Create page.

3. Choose the Create A Custom List In Datasheet View link under the Custom Lists heading.

4. On the New page that opens, enter a title for the list, a brief description, and whether or not you want this list to appear in the Quick Launch menu (see Figure 20-1).

5. Click the Create button to create the list.

6. The new list opens in a datasheet view. Add some sample items to the view (see Figure 20-2).

7. Click the Actions button to open its drop-down menu and choose Open With Microsoft Office Access.

Figure 20-1.   The New page is used to create a new SharePoint list.

8. In the Open In Microsoft Office Access dialog box that appears (see Figure 20-3), select the radio button corresponding to the Link To Data On The SharePoint Site option.

9. Click the OK button to create a new Access database. The database should have at least two tables created (similar to the two shown in Figure 20-4).

The data displayed in Access is currently stored only in the SharePoint list. If you save the Access table, any changes you may have made while in Access are saved back to the SharePoint server. In fact, if you click the Refresh button on the Access Home ribbon, any changes that may have been made to the list on the SharePoint server are automatically updated in Access and reflected in the display of the list.

Although you are viewing the list in Access, the data is still stored in the SharePoint list. If you were to use the Take All Offline function on the External Data ribbon in Access, a local (Access) copy of the list would be created and saved. The Synchronize button on the External Data ribbon can be used to synchronize the data between the Access table and the SharePoint list, should changes have been made to either version.

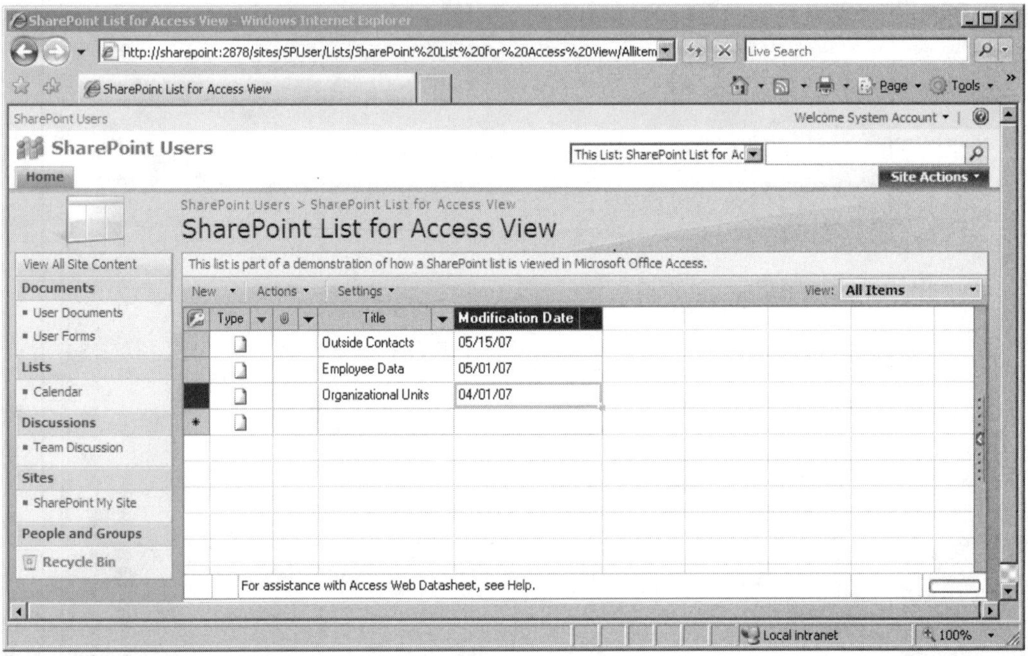

Figure 20-2. Sample items added to a list in Datasheet view.

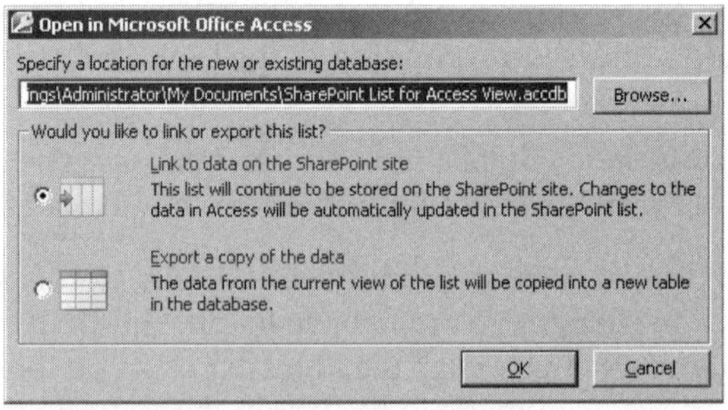

Figure 20-3. The Open In Microsoft Office Access dialog box.

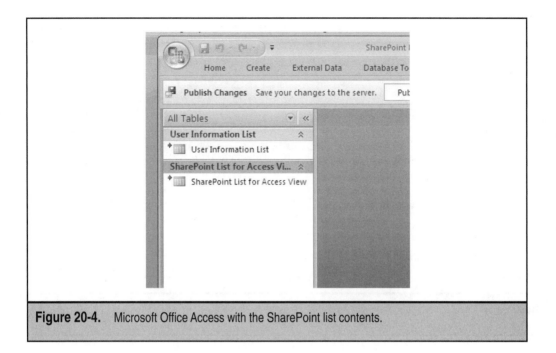

Figure 20-4. Microsoft Office Access with the SharePoint list contents.

ACCESS TEMPLATES AND SHAREPOINT

Microsoft Office Access 2007 features a variety of templates that can be used to create databases for a number of common business activities, such as asset records, contacts, sales data, projects, and more. These database templates include standard table, report, list, and, as applicable, charts appropriate to the application area each covers. For example, the Issues template includes the elements shown in Figure 20-5.

A very good feature of the Access templates is the ability to create SharePoint lists along with the local database when a template is applied. To create an Access database using a template and link it to a SharePoint site, do the following:

1. In Microsoft Office Access 2007, click the Office button in the upper left corner of the window and select New from the Office menu.

2. On the Getting Started With Access page that opens, choose Local Templates from the Template Categories pane on the left side of the window.

TIP Microsoft Office also provides a variety of templates in Business, Personal, Education, and a few samples that can be downloaded from the Microsoft Office templates web site.

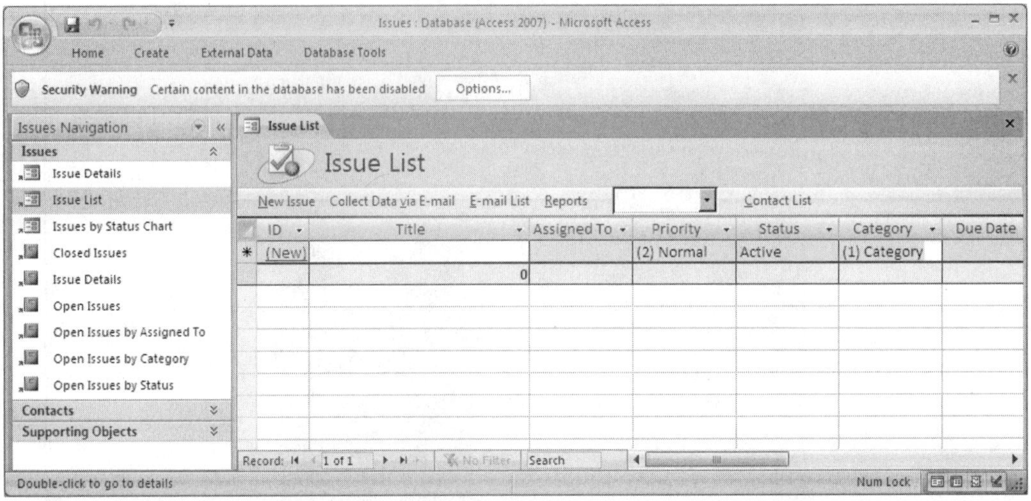

Figure 20-5.   An Access database created using the Issues template.

3. The center pane of the Access workspace changes to display an icon for each of the local templates available. Click the icon of the template you wish to apply. The right pane of the Access workspace changes to reflect the use of the template chosen (as illustrated in Figure 20-6).

4. Assign a name to the database to be created, or accept the default name, which is based on the name of the template to be applied.

5. Check the checkbox associated with the Create And Link Your Database To A Windows SharePoint Services Site (see Figure 20-6) to create lists in the SharePoint site and have the database tables created linked to them.

6. Click the Create button to apply the database template and create the elements of the Access database.

7. In the Create On SharePoint Site dialog box (see Figure 20-7), enter the URL of the SharePoint site you wish to link the Access database to, and then click the Browse button.

8. In the Location dialog box that appears, open the document library to where you wish to save the database tables and then click the OK button.

9. The Create On SharePoint Site dialog box reappears, containing the URL or pathname to the SharePoint site selected in the previous step. If this is the site you wanted, check the checkbox associated with the Save A Copy Of My Database… option and click the Next button. Otherwise, use the Browse button to reselect the SharePoint site and then complete this step.

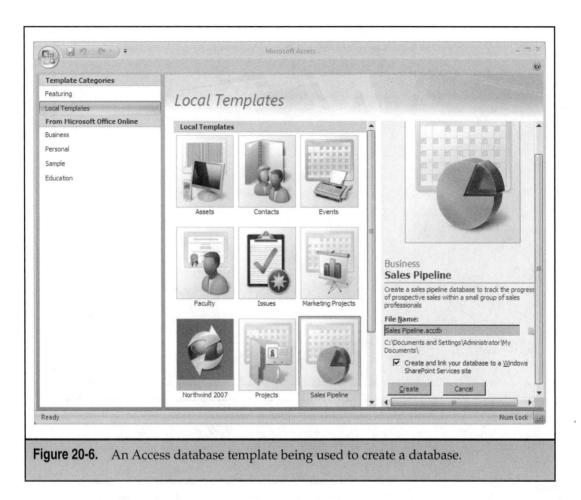

Figure 20-6. An Access database template being used to create a database.

10. The Access template wizard creates a link in the selected SharePoint site and displays a message indicating the success of this action (see Figure 20-8). If any issues occurred during this process, the details of these issues can be displayed, as shown in Figure 20-8.

11. Click the Finish button to complete the creation process and display the database in Access.

At this point, you should navigate to the SharePoint site on which Access has created its tables, lists, and other elements to verify this action. As shown in Figure 20-9, a link to the Sales Pipeline database now exists in the document library indicated during the creation of the template database. Clicking this database link on the SharePoint document page opens the database in Access.

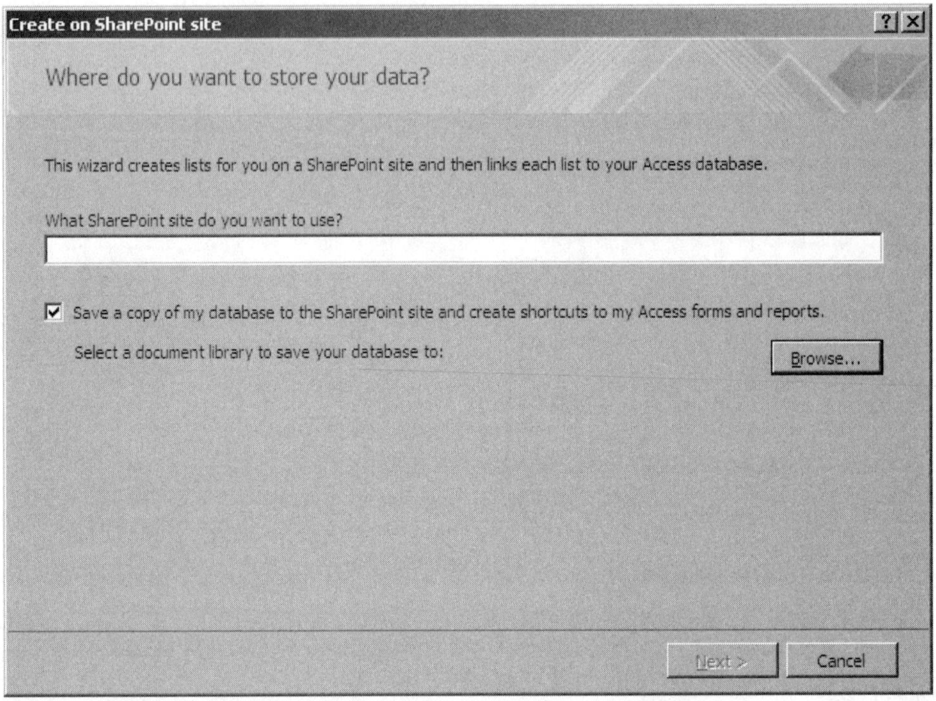

Figure 20-7. The Create On SharePoint Site dialog box.

> **TIP** If versioning is enabled on the site where the database has been added, the database is automatically checked out when it is opened and must be checked in at the completion of whatever action is taken on the database.

Access Views

Because the underlying structure of a SharePoint list is essentially much like that of a Microsoft Office Access 2007 table, it is fairly simple to create an Access-based view of a SharePoint library or list. The Access view of a list is stored in the MOSS database and included as a part of the library or list. Two configuration considerations must be addressed before this will actually work: Microsoft Office Access 2007 must be installed on the users' computers, and the users must have Manage Lists permission assigned.

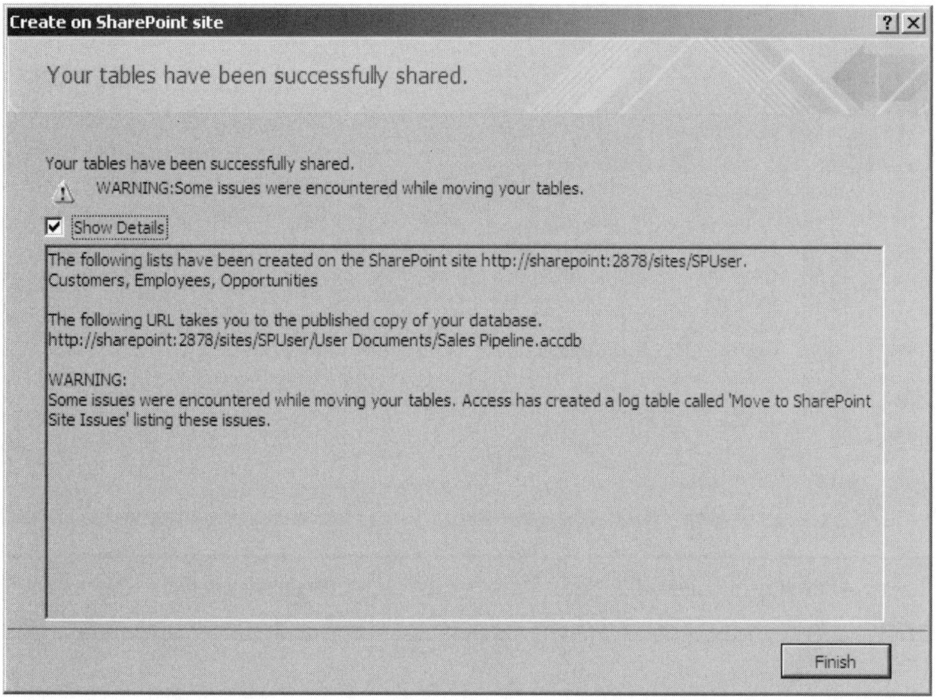

Figure 20-8.   The Create On SharePoint Site dialog box with end-of-process messages.

Create an Access View

To create an Access View of a library, do the following:

1. From the Create View page (see Figure 20-10) of the library, click the Access View link.

2. Access is automatically started and you are prompted to save a local copy of the Access database containing the library's Access views (as shown in Figure 20-11).

3. Accept the default name for the database, which is based on the name of the current SharePoint library, or assign your own name to the Access database being created.

4. Click the Save button to proceed. Access now saves the local copy of the database and displays the Create Access View dialog box (see Figure 20-12).

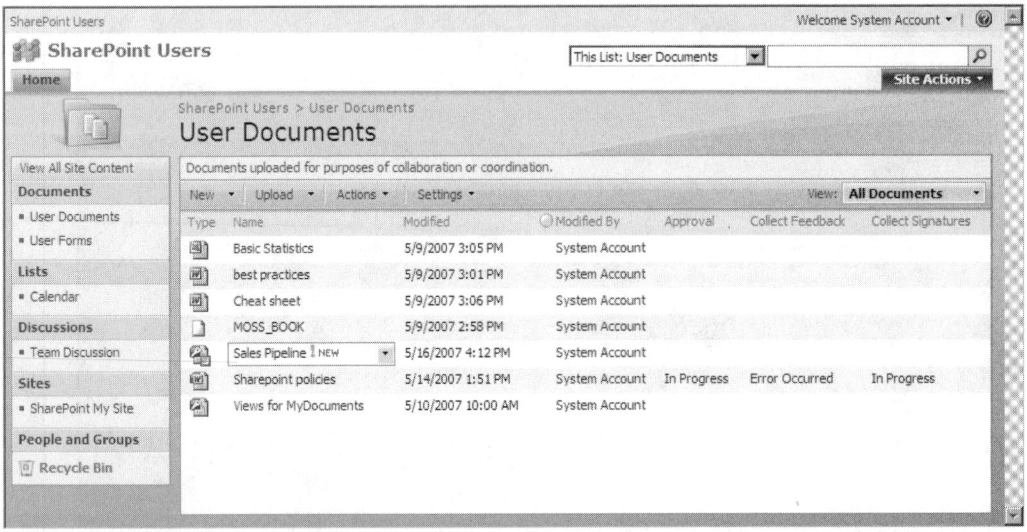

Figure 20-9. A new Access database link appears in the SharePoint document library.

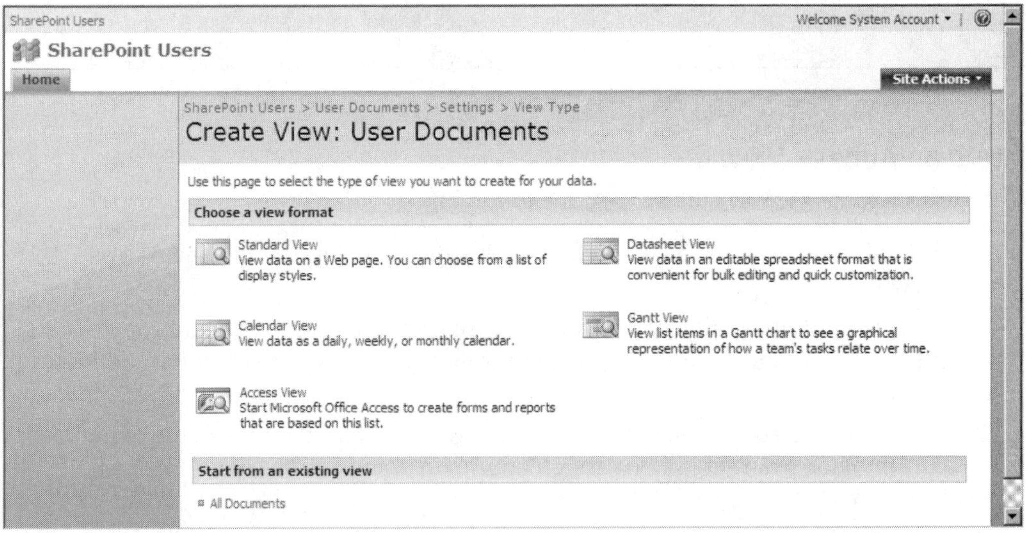

Figure 20-10. The SharePoint Create View page includes the option to create an Access view.

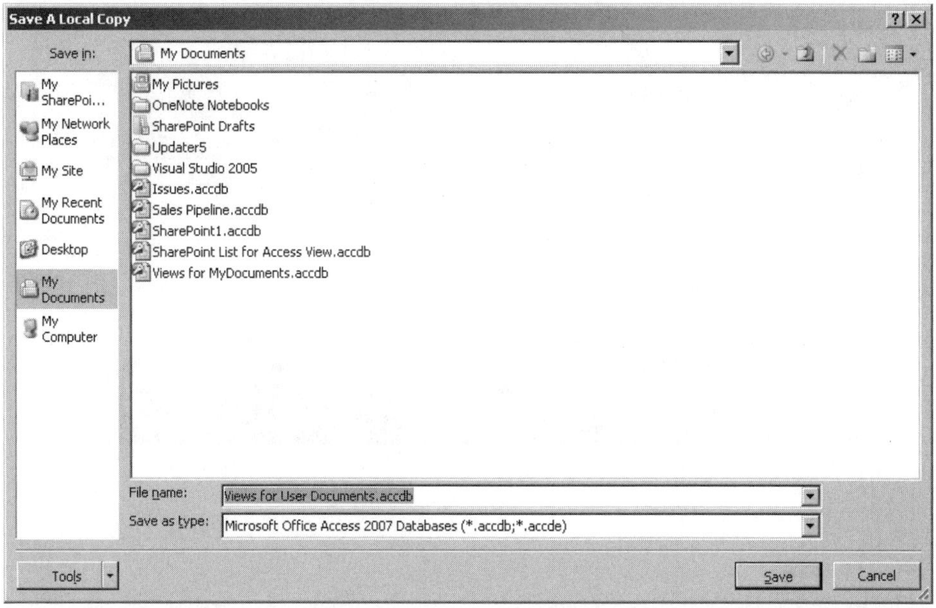

Figure 20-11.   The Save A Local Copy dialog box.

5. On the Create Access View dialog box, choose the view type you wish to create. The choices, as shown in Figure 20-12, are:

   ■ Form

   ■ Split Form

   ■ Multiple Items

   ■ Datasheet

   ■ Pivot Chart

   ■ Pivot Table

6. You can experiment with each of these table views to learn which best suits your particular needs. For this example, double-click the Split Form option.

7. The view option selected (Split Form in this example) is displayed in Access (as shown in Figure 20-13) in the Layout view.

Access has two view modes that can be used to customize a view: Layout mode and Design mode. Layout mode allows you to resize or move the controls, such as labels and

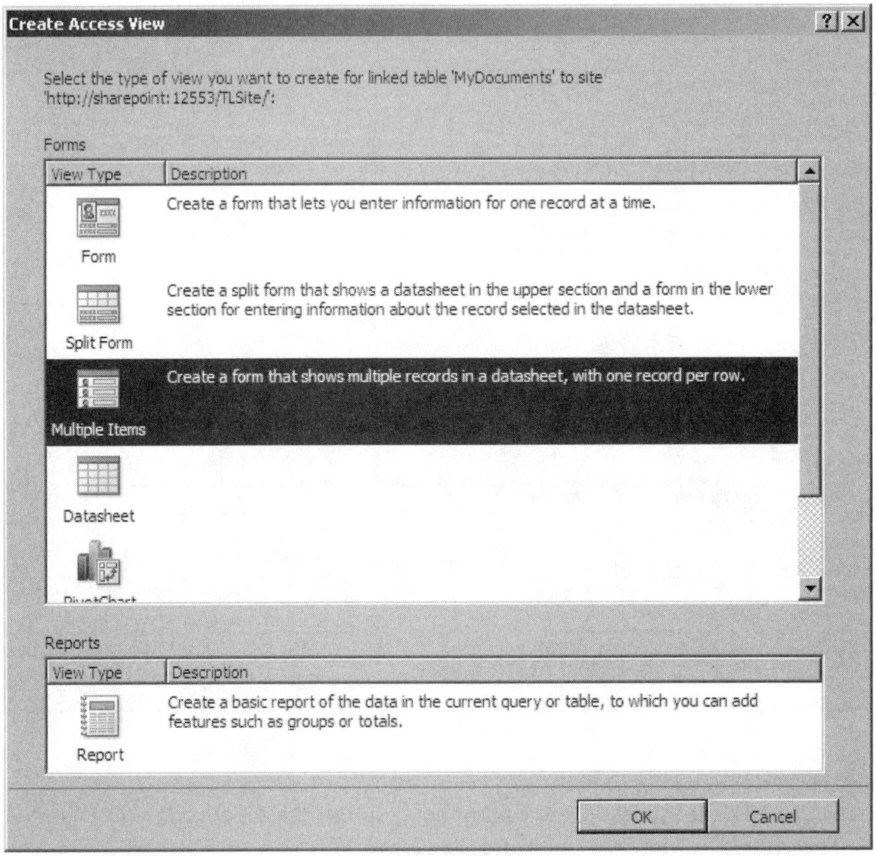

Figure 20-12. The Create Access View dialog box.

fields, in the view. Layout mode allows you to see how the data in the view will appear after your changes are made. However, Layout mode doesn't allow you to add controls to the view.

Design mode also allows you to resize or rearrange the controls in the view, but it does allow you to add additional controls to the view. Design mode doesn't provide a preview of how the view will look as a result of the changes, but you are able to switch between Design and View modes as needed.

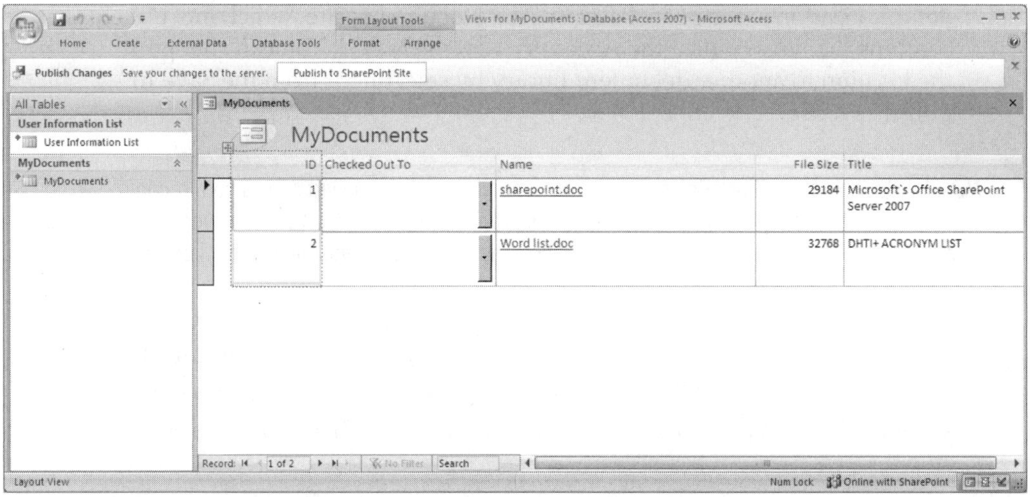

Figure 20-13.   The Split Form Access View of a SharePoint document library.

Publish Changes to SharePoint

Any changes made to a SharePoint Access view in Microsoft Office Access must be published to the SharePoint site for them to be in effect. To publish any format changes made to the view or data added to the list in Access, do the following:

1.   Click the Publish To SharePoint Site button on the Access message bar (see Figure 20-14).

TIP   If the Access message bar isn't displayed, click the Database Tools menu choice, select the Hide/Show option, and then click Message Bar.

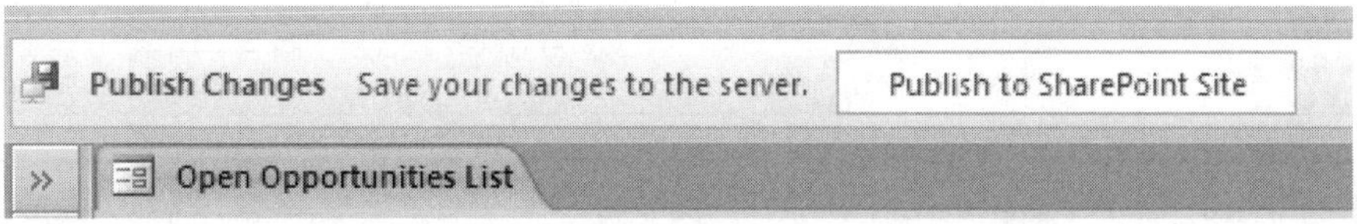

Figure 20-14.   The Publish To SharePoint Site button on the Access message bar.

2. In the Publish To Web Server dialog box that appears (see Figure 20-15), the default location is the SharePoint Shared Documents site, which most likely contains the list in which the Access view was created. You can change the location to another document library by selecting it from the Save In pull-down list.

NOTE Changing the SharePoint site to which the view is to be saved allows you to control which users are able to open the view and what they are able to do with the list. You may even wish to create a specific SharePoint library just for Access views and then publish the view to that library.

3. Access generates a name for the database in the File Name text box that is derived from the name of the database saved as a local copy. You can change this name, but for the most part it is safer to accept the name provided.

4. Click the Publish button to save the database to the SharePoint site entered in step 2.

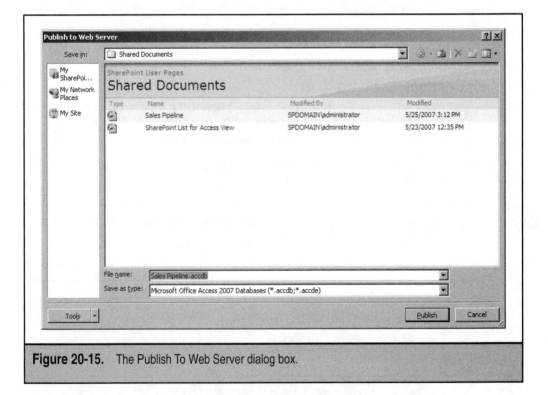

Figure 20-15. The Publish To Web Server dialog box.

SUMMARY

Microsoft Office Access 2007 has many built-in features that allow it to seamlessly integrate to an MOSS environment. Perhaps the best demonstration of this is the ability to create a SharePoint list in a document library and then open and view the list in Access. Access and SharePoint libraries are able to synchronize the data stored in shared and linked databases and views.

Microsoft Office Access 2007 supports a variety of templates that can be used to create SharePoint lists along with the local database when a template is applied. Because the underlying structure of a SharePoint list is essentially like that of a Microsoft Office Access 2007 table, it is fairly simple to create an Access-based view of a SharePoint library or list. The Access view of a list is stored in the MOSS database and included as part of the library or list. However, before any changes made to a SharePoint view in Access can be viewed in SharePoint, they must be published to the SharePoint site from Access.

CHAPTER 21

MOSS Business Intelligence

Especially for the larger business or enterprise, one of the better sets of features in Microsoft Office SharePoint Server (MOSS) 2007 is the tools that can be used to access, extract, display, and report a variety of business information in a usable and decision-supportive way. MOSS, working through a number of its own built-in features and those of the Microsoft Office 2007 applications, provides the means for SharePoint users to locate and display business information for analysis and decision-making purposes. Prior to the release of the Office 2007 suite of applications, the ability to combine data from a variety of sources into a single presentation of business intelligence existed only in power users, programmers, and the occasional consultant. If properly configured, your MOSS environment can give this ability to each of your SharePoint users.

To this end, this chapter focuses on the processes used to configure, create, and use the tools that combine to create a business intelligence reporting and analysis capability that is available to all of your users, at least those with the appropriate security permissions anyway.

CONFIGURE ACCESS TO THE BUSINESS DATA CATALOG

Before you can access business data in an MOSS environment, you must first configure the environment to include the building blocks required. Configuring MOSS to support business intelligence is a five-step process that includes configuring the Shared Service Provider (SSP) for access to the Business Data Catalog (BDC), ensuring access to pages within the SSP, securing the database store of business data, and granting permissions to the users authorized to access it. In detail, the five steps you must perform to complete this configuration are:

▼ Configure the SSP administrator with rights to the Business Data Catalog

■ Configure access to pages within the SSP

■ Configure the Business Data Catalog for Single Sign-On (SSO) service

■ Configure the data security settings for the data store

▲ Configure user security permissions for access to the appropriate business data

Each of these steps is discussed more fully in the following sections. However, before we get into the configuration of the BDC and the SSP, let's take a quick look at the BDC itself.

The Business Data Catalog

The BDC is a shared service feature introduced in MOSS 2007 that provides the capability for MOSS to access server-based business application data without the need for interface programming. BDC provides a linkage between a SharePoint portal site and business applications through which key business data can be brought into a SharePoint list or Web Part.

The BDC is the foundation element for the business data features built into MOSS, including business data elements such as Web Parts, lists, search, and user profiles. The BDC includes support for the display of data extracted from a database or a web server, through the use of a metadata model, including data drawn from a number of enterprise CRM (such as SAP or Siebel) systems or other line-of-business (LOB) applications.

Business Data Actions

A Business Data Action (BDA) is associated with an entity that has been registered in the BDC. A BDA is commonly used to create a link to the application data source to write updated data back to the database, to send an e-mail message, or to open a web page, such as a vendor's home page. If a BDA is associated with a BDC entity, it becomes a part of the entity's definition and is available anywhere the entity is displayed, including Business Data Web Parts or Business Data columns.

Business Data Lists

A Business Data list is created when a special type of column is added to a SharePoint list. This column, a Business Data column, allows a user to include data extracted from a business application that has been registered in the BDC in the list. A Business Data column can be used to tag a document included in a list to link the document to additional information about its creator, subject, or other related information. A Business Data column can be used to track data not included in a particular application without the need to customize the application. A Business Data column can also be used to include certain data in Office applications.

When a Business Data column is added to a list, the field(s) to be brought into the list from a server-based application is specified. The data in the field(s) is then displayed in the list. If you were to add a Business Data column for the vendor (entity) to a list of purchase orders forms, you have the capability of also including the vendor's name, address, phone, and email in the list.

A Business Data column carries the same features of any SharePoint column, including workflows, versioning, check in, and checkout. A list that includes a Business Data column can also be refreshed to resynch the column with its application data source to bring in any recent changes made in the application data as well.

Business Data Search

The Enterprise Search function of MOSS is able to crawl, gather, index, and perform a search on the entity instances of server-based applications defined in the BDC. This feature can be used to create customized search functions in the SharePoint Search Center for users who must access a variety of data from an application.

User Profiles

In many situations, depending on the software in use, gathering the information about each user may or may not be practical or even possible. If the enterprise has a human resource application running on a server, its data can be brought into a user profile for display as a single source of such information. Of course, you want to limit the users who could view such information, but creating user profiles from the application entities registered in the BDC can provide an efficient way for a user to view information about a user in one consolidated display.

Business Data Web Parts

MOSS includes five standard Business Data Web Parts:

▼ **Business Data Actions** This Web Part displays a list of the actions available to a user to perform on an entity instance entity (business data object), based on the definition entered into the BDC for the entity.

■ **Business Data Item** This Web Part displays the details of an entity instance from a business application, such as the details for a particular purchase order from a LOB application's database.

■ **Business Data Item Builder** This Web Part creates an entity instance using a query string and makes the data object available to Web Parts in Business Data profile pages.

■ **Business Data List** This Web Part displays a list of entity instances, such as a vendor number and a purchase order number, extracted from an LOB application that has been registered in the BDC.

▲ **Business Data Related List** This Web Part displays a list of related entity instances from a business application registered in the BDC. For example, you could list all of the pending orders placed with a single supplier.

Configure the SSP for the Business Data Catalog

MOSS's Business Data Catalog enables users to find and analyze business data. Because business data and its by-product, business intelligence, are commonly sensitive and proprietary in nature, it is very important that it be secure, and that only those users who require access to it are allowed access. If you intend to link business applications to the BDC, you must also ensure the integrity of their data is maintained as well.

Grant Access to the Business Data Catalog

The initial step in providing access to business data is to grant access to the administrator of the Shared Services Provider (SSP) under which the BDC is to be created. The SSP administrator requires permission to access the SSP administration pages for the BDC as well as the BDC itself. To configure administrator permissions to the BDC service, perform the following steps:

1. From the Windows Server desktop, open the SharePoint 3.0 Central Administration web page.

2. Click the Application Management tab.

3. On the Application Management page, click the Create Or Configure This Farm's Shared Services link under the Office SharePoint Server Shared Services heading.

4. On the Manage This Farm's Shared Services page, click the link for the SSP you wish to configure.

TIP   You can also access the Shared Services Administration page for a particular SSP by clicking the link for the SSP in the Quick Launch menu in the Shared Services Administration section.

5. On the Shared Services Administration page of the SSP you selected, click the link for Business Data Catalog permissions under the Business Data Catalog section to open the Manage Permissions: Business Data Catalog page (see Figure 21-1).

6. If the administrator you wish to assign to the SSP is not already listed, click the Add Users/Groups option on the navigation bar to open the Add Users/ Groups: Business Data Catalog page (see Figure 21-2).

7. Enter the username of the administrator you wish to grant permissions to and check the checkboxes corresponding to the permissions levels you wish to grant to this administrator.

8. Click the Save button to save the permissions and add the administrator to the BDC permissions list.

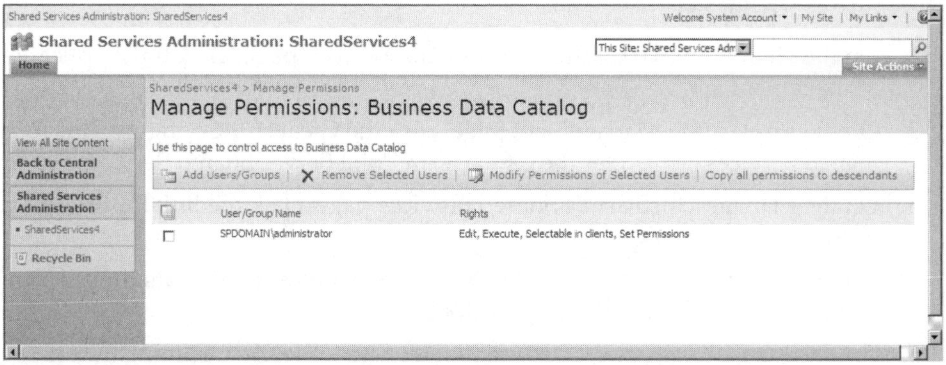

Figure 21-1.   The Manage Permissions: Business Data Catalog page.

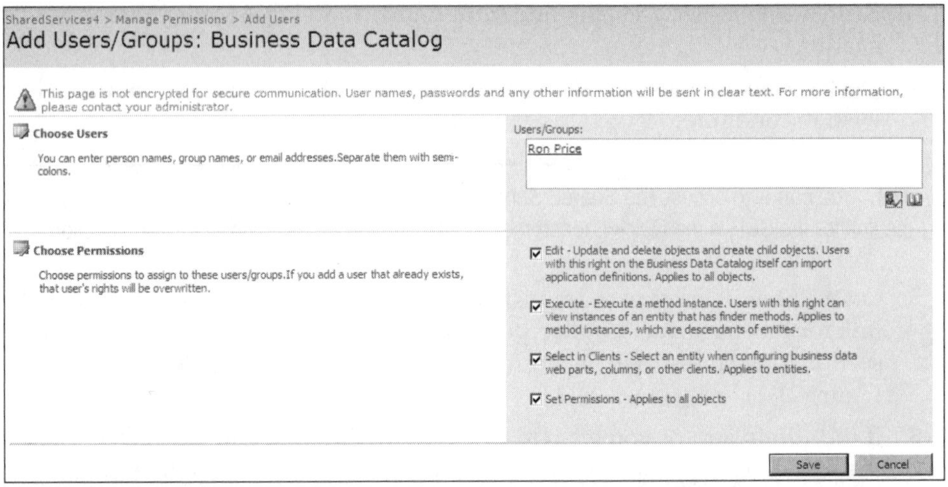

Figure 21-2.   The Add Users/Groups: Business Data Catalog page.

Grant Access to SSP Pages

While it may seem like we just accomplished this task in the preceding section, granting access to the pages within an SSP is separate from granting a user administrative rights to the BDC. In most new installations of MOSS, this step may not be required, given that the administrator who installed the system is already granted these permissions. However, should you wish to grant this access to another user with administrative rights, perform the following steps:

1. On the SharePoint 3.0 Central Administration web page, click the Application Management tab.

2. On the Application Management page, click the Create Or Configure This Farm's Shared Services link under the Office SharePoint Server Shared Services heading.

3. On the Manage This Farm's Shared Services page, click the link for the SSP you wish to configure.

4. On the SSP's home page, click the Site Actions button to open its drop-down menu and click the Site Settings option.

5. On the Site Settings page, click the link for Site Collection Administrators under the Users And Permissions heading to open the Site Collection Administrators page (see Figure 21-3).

6. In the Site Collection Administrators section, enter the user name(s) of the administrators to whom you wish to grant access to the pages of the SSP.

7. Click the OK button to save the administrators assigned to the SSP content.

Figure 21-3. The Site Collection Administrators page.

Configure Single Sign-On

Like other MOSS services, like Excel Services, the BDC can be included under the control of the Single Sign-On (SSO) service. SSO is able to grant a user access to multiple data sources and services without the need of the user having to log in to each data source or service individually. SSO credentials can be created for individual applications defined in the BDC, which is discussed later in the next section.

NOTE See Chapter 19 for a detailed description of the process used to configure SSO.

Configure Application Definitions

In order to access information from an external application through MOSS, the application information must be registered in the BDC. Once an application is registered in the BDC, MOSS is able to include the registered data in SharePoint lists, Web Parts, and sites. The process used to register an external application in the BDC involves four steps:

▼ Create an application definition for each external application

■ Import the application definitions into the BDC

■ Enable SSO for the applicable applications

▲ Configure business data types

Create Application Definitions An application definition is an Extensible Markup Language (XML) file that defines the data structure and business data schema of a database or a web service in use by the enterprise. An application definition must be created for each external application to be integrated into the MOSS environment.

An application definition file includes information related to three primary areas:

▼ Connection information

■ Authentication methods

▲ Business data type (entity) definitions

The application definition can also include other information related to the application on a case-by-case basis. The resulting application definition file, which is also called an application metadata file, is typically created by a programmer or database administrator who is familiar with the application database being defined. The application metadata file essentially contains information about the application programming interface (API) files of the application being defined to the BDC.

TIP MOSS includes a schema definition file (.XSD) for the BDC that prescribes what should be included in the application definition XML file. This file (BdcMetadata.XSD) is located in the \bin directory of the MOSS installation.

The following is an excerpt of an application definition file (this one taken from the Microsoft SQL Server AdventureWorks sample database):

```
...
<Entities>
 <Entity EstimatedInstanceCount="10000" Name="Product">
   <!-- EstimatedInstanceCount is an optional attribute-->
    <Properties>
     <Property Name="Title" Type="System.String">Name</Property>
    </Properties>
    <Identifiers>
     <Identifier Name="ProductID" TypeName="System.Int32" />
    </Identifiers>
    <Methods>
     <!-- Defines a method that brings back Product data from the
     back-end database.-->
     <Method Name="GetProducts">
       <Properties>
         <Property Name="RdbCommandText" Type="System.String">
          SELECT ProductID, Name, ProductNumber, ListPrice FROM Product
                WHERE (ProductID &gt;= @MinProductID) AND (ProductID &lt;
                = @MaxProductID) AND (Name LIKE @Name) AND (ProductNumber
                LIKE @ProductNumber)
         </Property>
         <Property Name="RdbCommandType"
                Type="System.Data.CommandType">Text</Property>
         <!-- For database systems, can be Text, StoredProcedure,
         or TableDirect. -->
       </Properties>
...
```

TIP   For more information and instructions on how to create an application definition file, visit the Business Data Catalog site at: http://msdn2.microsoft.com/en-us/library/ms563661.aspx.

Import Application Definition   Once the application definition has been created, it can be added (imported) to the BDC. To import an application definition to the BDC, perform the following steps:

1. From the SharePoint 3.0 Central Administration home page, open the administration page of the SSP on which the BDC has been configured.

2. On the Administration page of the SSP, click the Import Application Definition link under the Business Data Catalog heading.

3. On the Import Application Definition page (see Figure 21-4), use the Browse button to locate the XML file containing the XML code for the application definition.

4. In the File Type section, choose the radio button corresponding to the type of definition included in the metadata file, either Method or Resource. The creator of the file should provide this information.

SharedServices4 > Import Application Definition

Import Application Definition

Application Definition

An application definition describes a database or web service. It includes connection settings, authentication mode, definitions of available entities, and other information. After you upload an application definition to the Business Data Catalog, you can use its entities in lists, web parts, search, user profiles and custom applications.

Uploading a new application definition will overwrite any existing settings and changes you have made to the application. This includes security settings and actions. Before uploading a new version, you should export the current state of your application definition.

Choose an application definition file and click Import.

Learn about writing application definition files

Application Definition File:

`C:\Documents and Settings\Administrator\My Docume` | Browse... |

File Type

Choose the type of application definition file to import

○ Model
● Resource

Resources to import

Choose resources to import

☑ Localized Names
☑ Properties
☑ Permissions

| Import | | Cancel |

Figure 21-4.   The Import Application Definition page.

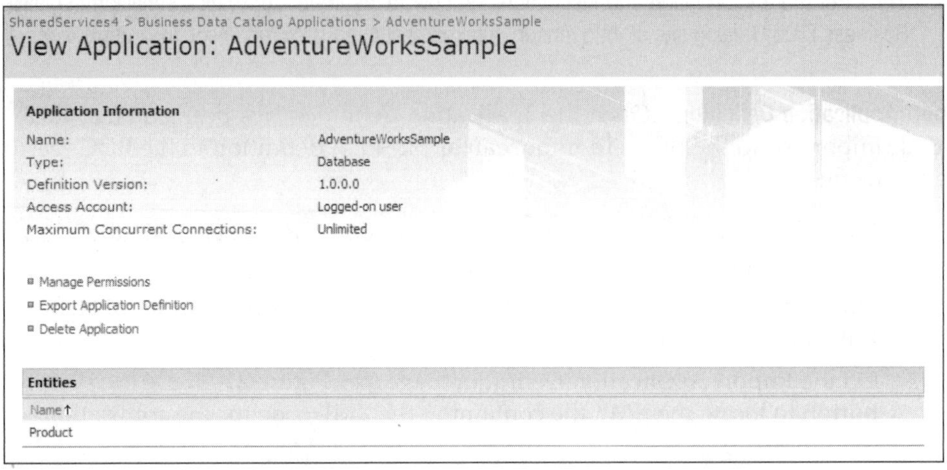

Figure 21-5. The View Application page.

5. In the Resources To Import section, check the checkboxes corresponding to the resource definitions you wish to import to the BDC.

6. Click the Import button to import the application definition and add it to the BDC.

7. If the import action is unsuccessful, you'll see a page explaining this and allowing you to either Retry The Import Or Start Over (OK). Commonly an import failure is the result of trying to import a Method file as a Resource, or vice versa.

8. If the action is successful, a page displays informing you of the success. Click the OK button to open the View Application page for the imported application definition (see Figure 21-5).

9. To view the entities created, in the Entities section of the page, click the name of each entity created to view its properties (see Figure 21-6).

Add Data Actions to an Entity   To add a business data action to an entity, use the following process:

1. From the home page of the SSP in which the BDC resides, click the View Entities link under the Business Data Catalog heading.

2. On the Business Data Catalog Entities page (see Figure 21-7), click the entity to which you wish to add a business data action.

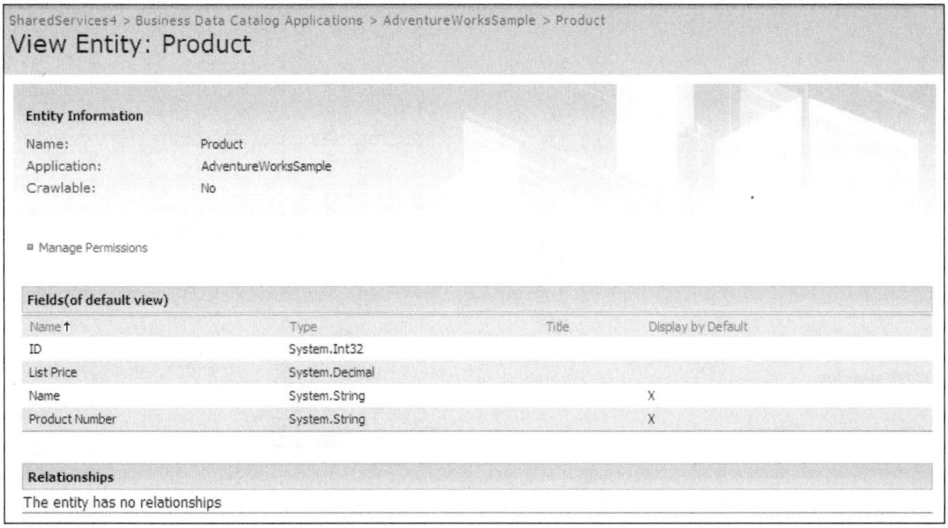

SharedServices4 > Business Data Catalog Applications > AdventureWorksSample > Product

View Entity: Product

Entity Information

Name: Product
Application: AdventureWorksSample
Crawlable: No

⊡ Manage Permissions

Fields(of default view)

Name ↑	Type	Title	Display by Default
ID	System.Int32		
List Price	System.Decimal		
Name	System.String		X
Product Number	System.String		X

Relationships

The entity has no relationships

Figure 21-6.   The View Entity page.

3. On the View Entity page (see Figure 21-6), click the Add Action link in the Actions section to open the Add Action page (see Figure 21-8).

4. In the Name section, enter a name for the action in the Action Name text box.

5. Enter the URL you wish the action to display in the browser when this action is chosen in the Navigate To This URL text box in the URL section.

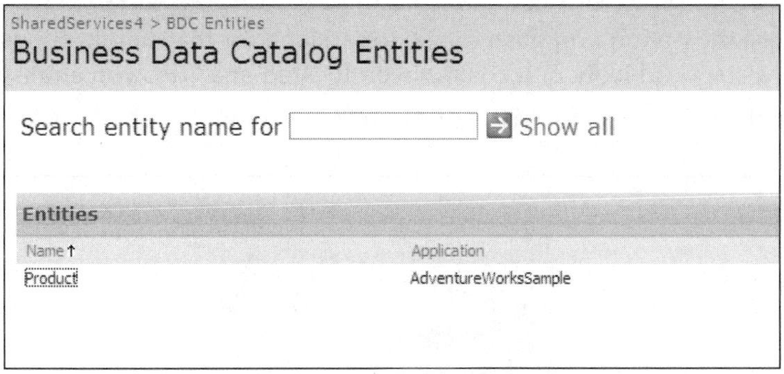

SharedServices4 > BDC Entities

Business Data Catalog Entities

Search entity name for [   ] ➔ Show all

Entities

Name ↑	Application
Product	AdventureWorksSample

Figure 21-7.   The Business Data Catalog Entities page.

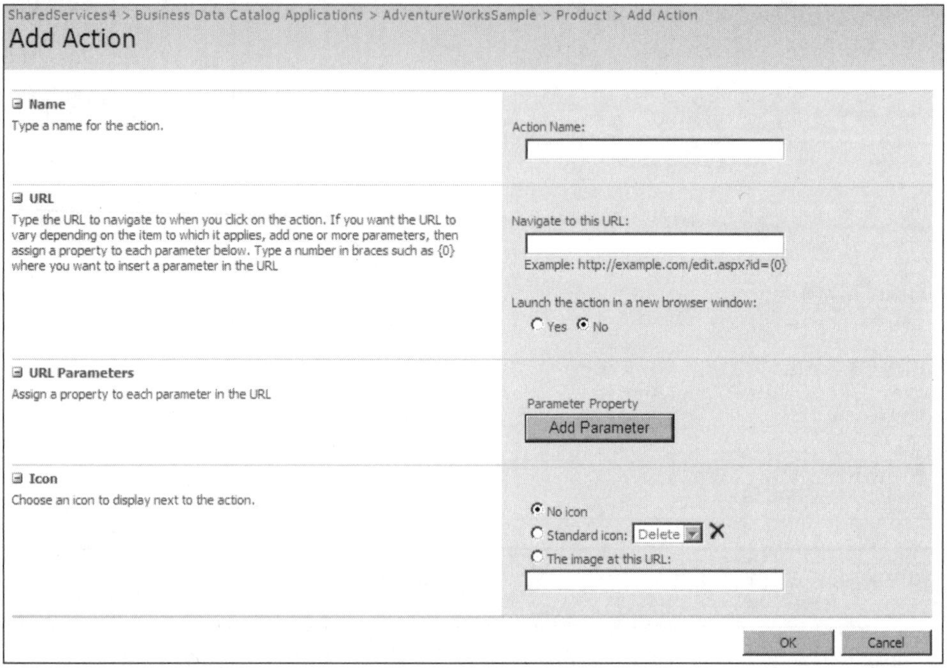

Figure 21-8. The Add Action page.

6. If you wish to pass parameters along with the URL, which are preprocessed by the associated Web Part, click the Add Parameter button to change the display of the URL Parameters section to that shown in Figure 21-9.

7. Use the list box to choose the field you wish to use as a parameter.

8. Choose the option you wish to use for an icon for this action, choosing from no icon, a standard icon, or a custom icon located at a URL you enter.

9. Click the OK button to save the action.

Figure 21-9. The URL section of the Add Action page after the Add Parameter button has been clicked.

Configure Application Definition for SSO   To configure SSO to access application data through the BDC, perform the following steps:

1. On the SharePoint 3.0 Central Administration home page, click the Operations tab.

2. In the Security Configuration section of the Operations tab, click the Manage Settings For Single Sign-On link.

3. On the Manage Settings For Single Sign-On page, click the Manage Settings For Enterprise Application Definitions link to open the Manage Enterprise Application Definition page.

4. Click the New Item option on the navigation bar to open the Create Enterprise Application Definitions page.

5. Under the Application And Contact Information heading, enter the name users will see for the application.

6. In the Application Name box, enter the name entered in the BDC for the application definition. This is the name that Web Parts will use to link to the enterprise application definition being created.

7. Enter the e-mail address users should use for assistance with the application in the Contact E-mail Address text box.

8. Select the option corresponding to the SSO login account type being created in the Account type section. The choices are Group, Individual, or Group using restricted account.

9. Click the OK button to save the application definition information.

SHAREPOINT BUSINESS INTELLIGENCE

Starting from their basic definitions, data are raw facts, statistics, numbers, or text that don't necessarily mean anything on their own, and information is data that have been processed, labeled, or manipulated into something meaningful. My rule of thumb is that information answers a question, while data cannot. For example, a field containing the text Blue means nothing, but this value displayed with the label Eye Color becomes information. This is essentially the basis of the relationships between data, information, and intelligence. Information may provide me with an answer, but intelligence can help me form the question.

MOSS provides a wide array of tools, features, and applications to report information, which, if filtered correctly, can provide business intelligence. The key elements of the MOSS environment for both information and intelligence are the Report Center, Excel Services, the Business Data Catalog, Key Performance Indicators (KPI), filter Web Parts, and Dashboard portals. These elements, which are discussed in this section, provide, separately—and in some cases together—an enterprise with a customizable reporting environment that can be tailored specifically to the needs of the organization.

The BDC contains an inherent hierarchy of registered application definitions. Applications, which can include SQL Server 2005 database elements and possibly line-of-business (LOB) applications from third-party vendors, define business data objects—otherwise known as business data entities. The application entities defined and registered in the BDC are the key objects used to create business data lists, KPI lists, Web Parts pages, and other SharePoint business data elements.

NOTE Excel Services is not discussed in this chapter. For more information on Excel Services, see Chapter 19.

The Report Center

The Report Center is an out of the box SharePoint site that is intended to provide a central repository for reports that are commonly used by a group of users, a team, or even the entire company. Because of its basic purpose, the Report Center can also be the central location for business reports, specialized document libraries (such as Excel workbooks), lists, and custom pages.

A Report Center subsite is created for each top-level site based on one of the Enterprise site templates, but additional Report Centers can be created within a site collection on team and organization sites. Figure 21-10 shows the default form of the Report Center in a top-level site. Lists are the primary organizing element in a SharePoint Report Center. In the sections that follow, we take a look at Report Center lists and the various tools available to help you create the lists and reports you need, including KPI, filter Web Parts, and dashboards.

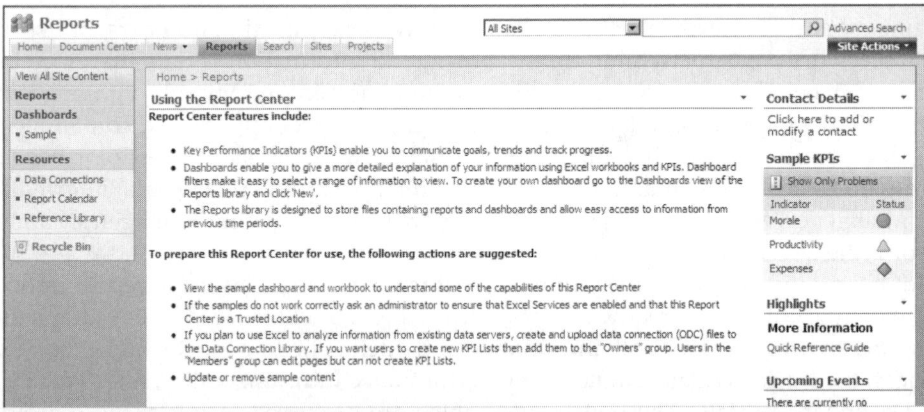

Figure 21-10. The Report Center on a SharePoint site.

Add Business Data to a List

How you go about adding a list to a SharePoint site has been discussed in this book in numerous places, but how to incorporate certain SharePoint business intelligence features in a list has not. Perhaps the most important action you can take to customize a standard SharePoint list is to add a business data column to a list.

Add a Business Data Column to a List

Adding a business data column to a list allows users to see, sort, or filter a list using relevant data pulled into the list from an external database. To add a business data column to a list, perform the following tasks:

1. Navigate to the list to which you wish to add a business data column by clicking its name in the Quick Launch menu or choosing it from the View All Site Content page for its site.

2. Click the Settings option on the navigation bar and choose Create Column from its drop-down menu to open the Create Column page.

3. On the Create Column page, shown in Figure 21-11, enter a name for the column and then select the Business Data option for The Type Of Information In This Column Is: setting.

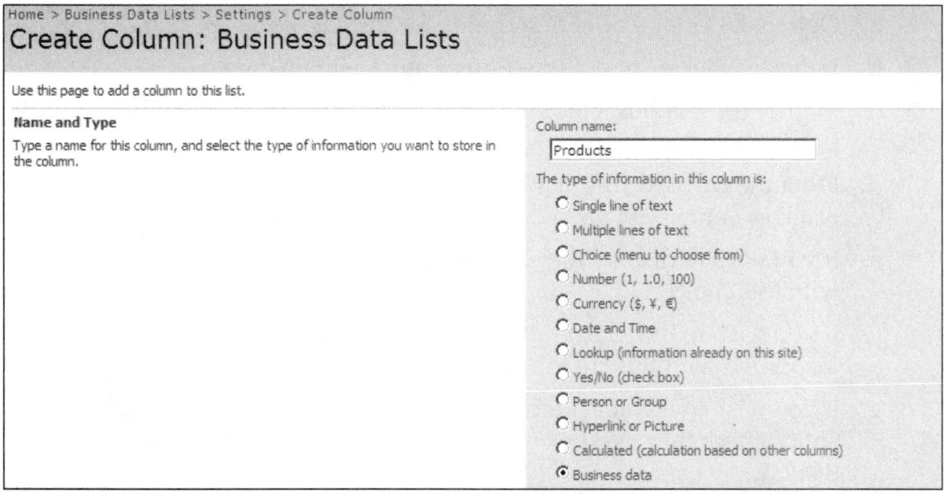

Figure 21-11.   The Create Column page with the Business Data option selected.

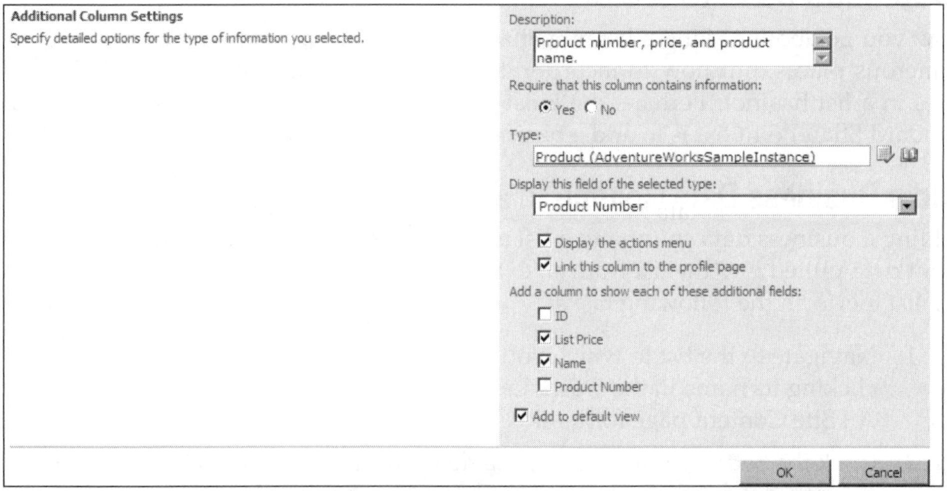

Figure 21-12. The Additional Column Settings section of the Create Column page.

4. In the Additional Column Settings section (see Figure 21-12), configure the following settings:

a. Optionally enter a brief description for the column.

b. Indicate whether or not the column must contain data.

c. In the Type text box, enter the name of the business data entity you wish to link to the column.

d. From the Display This Field From The Selected Type list box, choose the primary entity field you wish to display in the column.

e. If you wish to display the Actions menu, check the checkbox associated with this choice.

f. If you wish to link the new column to a profile page, check the checkbox associated with this choice.

g. If you wish to include additional columns to display other fields of the entity, check the checkbox associated with each entity field you wish to display.

h. Finally, if you wish to have this column included in the default view of the list, check the checkbox associated with this choice.

5. Click the OK button to add the column to the list.

Add Business Data Items to a List

After you have added a business data column to a list, you can then add a business data item (entity) to the list. The business data item is associated with the column to which it was identified.

To add a business data item to a business data list, perform the following steps:

1. Navigate to the Lists page and click the name of the list to which you wish to add a business data item.

2. On the page for that list, click the New option on the navigation bar and choose the New Item option.

3. On the New Item page (see Figure 21-13), enter a Title for the business data item.

4. In the search box for the primary business data item associated with the list, you have some options you can use to find the data value you wish:

   a. If you know the value of the item you wish to associate to the list, enter it in the item text box.

   b. If you aren't sure of the item's exact value, you have two options:

      ▼ Enter as much of the item as you know and then either click the Search button (the magnifying glass icon) or press CTRL+K. When the search results appear, select the value you wish to use.

      ▲ Click the Browse button (the open book icon) to display the Choose Item dialog box (see Figure 21-14) to search for the item value you wish to use.

5. After you have chosen the value you wish to use, click the OK button to add the item value to the list.

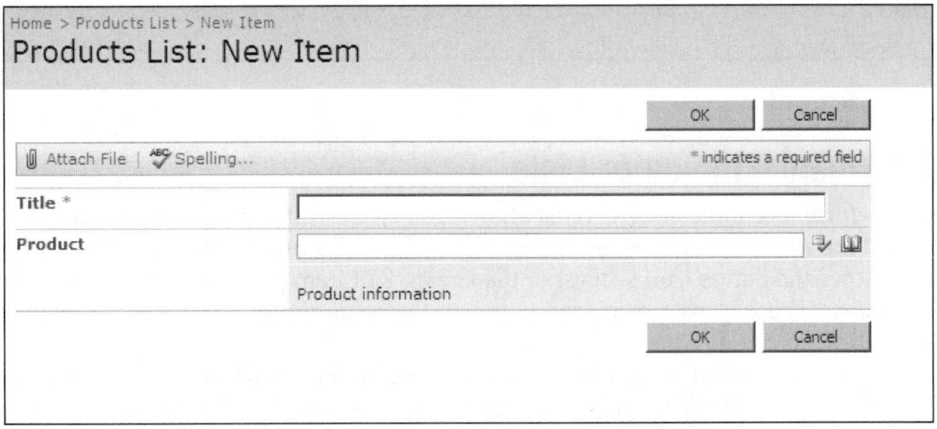

Figure 21-13.   The New Item page is used to associate a business data item to a list.

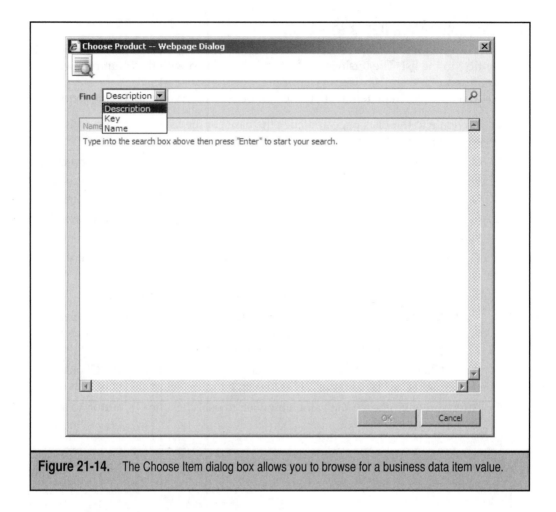

Figure 21-14. The Choose Item dialog box allows you to browse for a business data item value.

Key Performance Indicator Lists

A key performance indicator (KPI) list allows you to use different colored icons (KPIs) to represent the status, value, percentage, or a calculated amount. As shown in Figure 21-15, which shows the Status Icon section of the Create KPI item page, three status indicators are available. These icons are colored to match the colored lights in a traffic signal, with green, yellow, and red representing best to worse.

A KPI list is different from other SharePoint lists in that its KPI items can only be displayed using a KPI Web Part (more on that later in this section). KPI lists can be stored in the Report Center or included on any other site in the MOSS environment.

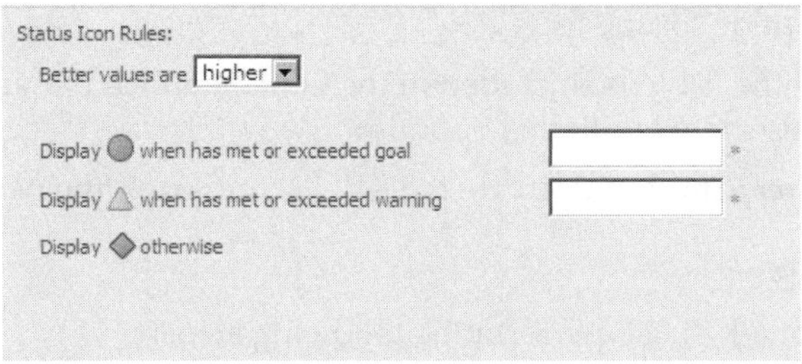

Figure 21-15. The Status Icon section of the Create KPI Item page.

Create a KPI List

To create a KPI item for inclusion in a KPI list, perform the following steps:

1. From the home page of the site to which you wish to add a KPI list, click the Lists heading in the Quick Launch menu to open the All Site Content page for lists.

2. Click the Create option on the navigation bar to open the Create page.

3. Click the KPI List option under the Custom Lists heading to open the New Item page (see Figure 21-16).

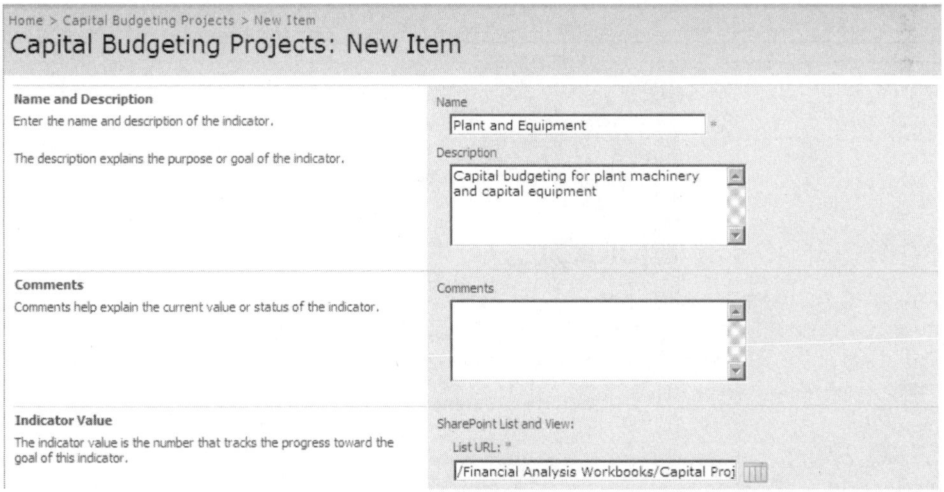

Figure 21-16. The Create KPI Item page.

4. On the New Item page, enter a name for the KPI list and optionally enter a brief description for the list.

5. If you wish the list to be included in the Quick Launch menu, mark the checkbox associated with this option.

6. Click the Create button to create the KPI list and open the new list's page.

Create KPI Items

To add a KPI item to a KPI list, perform the following steps:

1. On the main page of the newly created KPI list, click the New option on the navigation bar. As shown in Figure 21-17, you have four choices for the type of KPI item you wish to create:

   a. **Indicator using data in SharePoint list**   Use this option if you wish to base the indicator's status on data included in an existing SharePoint list.

   b. **Indicator using data in Excel workbook**   Use this option if you wish to base the indicator's status on data included in an existing Excel workbook, which can be in a SharePoint document library or stored outside of the MOSS environment.

   c. **Indicator using data in SQL Server 2005 Analysis Services**   If the SQL Server 2005 Analysis Services is installed in your MOSS environment, you can link a KPI directly to the business intelligence features supported in this product.

   d. **Indicator using manually entered information**   If you wish to create a KPI item to reflect information you enter yourself, use this option for the KPI item.

Figure 21-17.   New KPI item options.

Indicator Value

The indicator value is the number that tracks the progress toward the goal of this indicator.

For example, the indicator value may be:

The number of issues that are currently active

Or

The percentage of tasks complete

To specify the indicator value:

1) Select the SharePoint list that contains the information for calculating the value of this indicator.

2) Select the view of the list that contains the items for calculating the value of this indicator. Views can be used for selecting a subset of items.

3) Specify the calculation to perform for the value of this indicator. Choose summary calculation to set the goal to be the total, average, minimum or maximum of a numerical column.

SharePoint List and View:

List URL: *

Examples:
     http://portal/site/list/AllItems.aspx
  or /portal/site/list/AllItems.aspx

View: *

Value Calculation: *

  ◉ Number of list items in the view

  ◯ Percentage of list items in the view where

    Select column...
    is equal to

    ◯ And ◉ Or

    Select column...
    is equal to

    Show More Columns...

  ◯ Calculation using all list items in the view

    Sum

    of

    Select column...

Figure 21-18. The Indicator Value section of the New Item page for the Indicator using data in the SharePoint List option.

2. Depending on the option you choose for the new KPI item, a different version of the New Item page displays. The primary difference between the different options is in the Indicator Value section of the New Item page. Figures 21-18 through 21-21 show the Indicator Value sections and the SQL Server 2005 Analysis Services KPI section of each of the new KPI item options listed in the preceding step. The steps used to configure each of these KPI item types is covered in the following sections.

Create an Indicator Using Data in SharePoint List KPI To configure a KPI using a SharePoint list as its data source, perform the following steps:

1. Enter a name and an optional description for the KPI item in the Name and Description section and optionally enter any comments about the KPI in the Comments section.

2. In the Indicator Value section (see Figure 21-18), enter the appropriate values for each of the following settings:

    a. Enter the URL address for the SharePoint list you wish to use. You can select the Browse button (the gold icon) to look up the list's URL. Clicking

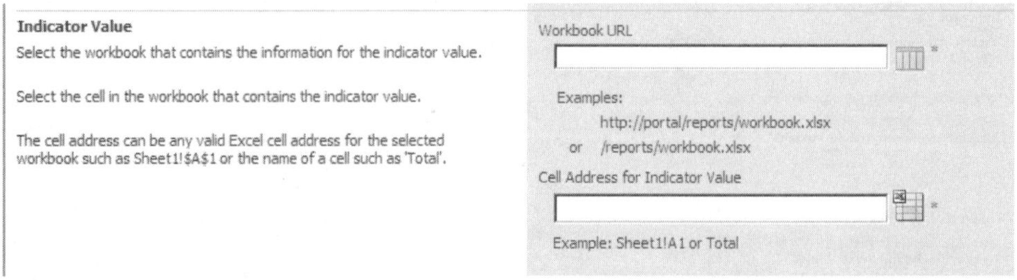

Indicator Value

Select the workbook that contains the information for the indicator value.

Select the cell in the workbook that contains the indicator value.

The cell address can be any valid Excel cell address for the selected workbook such as Sheet1!A1 or the name of a cell such as 'Total'.

Workbook URL

Examples:

    http://portal/reports/workbook.xlsx

  or /reports/workbook.xlsx

Cell Address for Indicator Value

Example: Sheet1!A1 or Total

Figure 21-19.   The Indicator Value section of the New Item page for the Indicator using data in the Excel Workbook option.

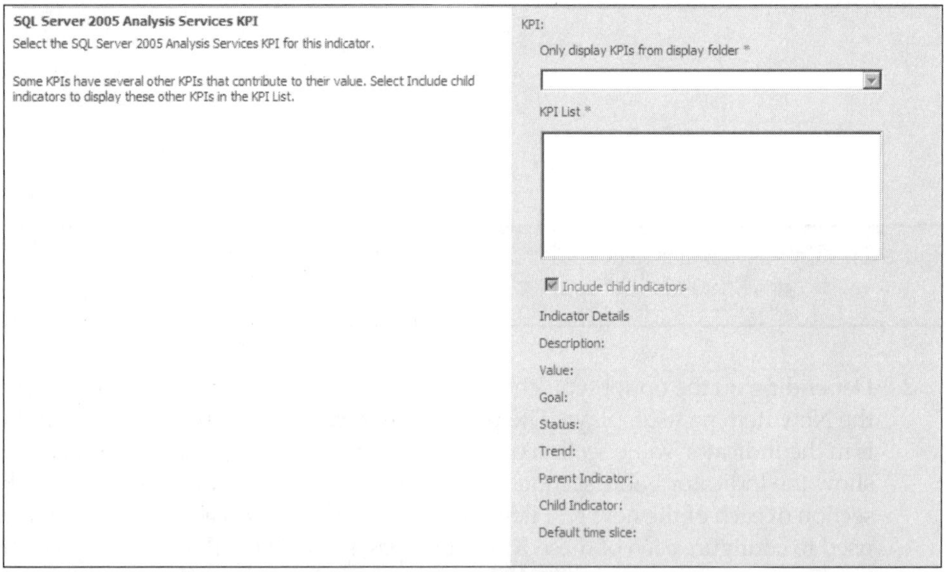

SQL Server 2005 Analysis Services KPI

Select the SQL Server 2005 Analysis Services KPI for this indicator.

Some KPIs have several other KPIs that contribute to their value. Select Include child indicators to display these other KPIs in the KPI List.

KPI:

Only display KPIs from display folder *

KPI List *

☑ Include child indicators

Indicator Details

Description:

Value:

Goal:

Status:

Trend:

Parent Indicator:

Child Indicator:

Default time slice:

Figure 21-20.   The SQL Server 2005 Analysis Services KPI section of the New Item page for the Indicator using data in the SQL Server 2005 Analysis Services option.

Indicator Value

Specify the current value for the indicator

Value:

Figure 21-21.   The Indicator Value section of the New Item page for the Indicator using manually entered information option.

the Browse button opens the Select a Link – Webpage Dialog box, shown in Figure 21-22. You can use the contents in this dialog box to navigate to the list you wish to use.

b. After you have entered or selected the SharePoint list you want, choose the type of view you wish to use for the KPI. Your choices are most commonly either All Documents or Explorer view.

c. In the Value Calculation portion of the Value Indicator section, you can choose to use the number of items in the list as the value for the KPI or you can create Boolean selection criteria using a full range of conditions on one or two of the columns in the list chosen.

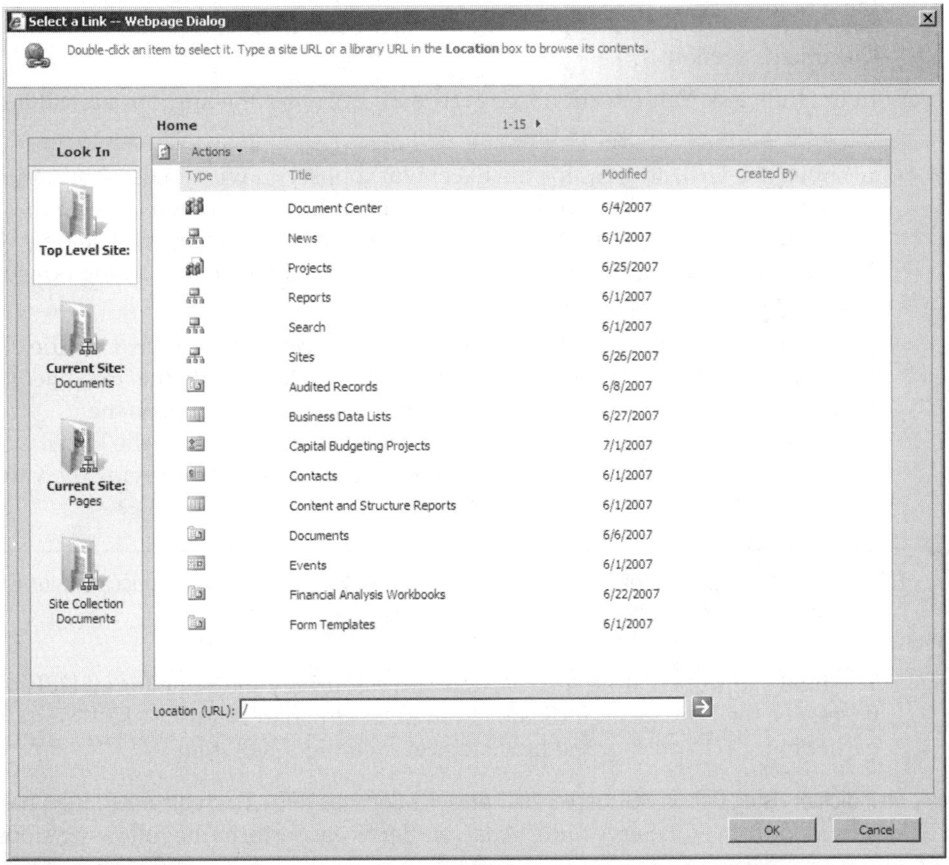

Figure 21-22.   The Select A Link—Webpage Dialog box is used to locate a SharePoint list.

NOTE   The following steps apply to creation of any of the four KPI item types.

3. In the Details Link section, found on the Create Items pages for all four KPI item types, enter the URL address for the page containing the detail data behind the KPI's status.

4. In the Update Rules section, which is not included on the Indicator Using Manually Entered Information creation page, select the radio button corresponding to the option you wish to use to update the KPI value, which can be either every time the KPI is viewed or manually.

Create an Indicator Using Data in Excel Workbook KPI   To create a KPI item based on data in an Excel workbook, perform the following steps:

1. Enter a name and an optional description for the KPI item in the Name And Description section and optionally enter any comments about the KPI in the Comments section.

2. In the Indicator Value section (see Figure 21-19), enter the appropriate values for each of the following settings:

   a. Enter the URL address for the Excel workbook you wish to use. You can select the Browse button (the gold Excel icon) to look up the list's URL. Clicking the Browse button opens the Select a Link – Webpage Dialog box, shown in Figure 21-22. You can use the contents in this dialog box to navigate to the list you want.

   b. Enter the worksheet and cell reference for the cell that is to provide the indicator value. If you wish to use the workbook to locate this reference, click the Excel worksheet icon to open a dialog box that opens the workbook using Excel Services. From the displayed view of the Excel workbook, choose the worksheet and the cells that are to provide the values for the value, goal, and warning levels of the KPI.

TIP   The location address of the Excel workbook you enter must be a trusted location for Excel Services in the appropriate SSP for the workbook to open.

3. The final steps in creating the KPI item are essentially the same for all KPI types. See the "Create an Indicator Using Data in SharePoint List KPI" section earlier in this chapter for the final steps in creating a KPI item.

Create an Indicator Using Data in SQL Server 2005 Analysis Services KPI   To create a KPI item based on data provided from SQL Server 2005 Analysis Services, perform the following steps:

1. Enter a name and an optional description for the KPI item in the Name and Description section and optionally enter any comments about the KPI in the Comments section.

2. In the SQL Server 2005 Analysis Services KPI section (see Figure 21-20), enter the appropriate values for each of the following settings:

   a. Enter the URL for the location of the SQL Server 2005 Analysis Services KPI you wish to associate with the new KPI item in the Data Connection section. Use the Browse button (database icon) to navigate to the .ODC file to which you wish to connect.

   b. Choose the display folder from which you wish to select the KPI using the Only Display KPIs From Display Folder list box. From the list displayed in the KPI list, choose the KPI you wish to use.

   c. If you wish to include the children indicators for this item, leave the Include Child Indicators checkbox selected. Otherwise, uncheck the checkbox associated with this option.

3. The final steps in creating the KPI item are essentially the same for all KPI types. See the "Create an Indicator Using Data in SharePoint List KPI" section earlier in this chapter for the final steps in creating a KPI item.

Create an Indicator Using Manually Entered Information KPI   To create a KPI item based on data entered manually, perform the following steps:

1. Enter a name and an optional description for the KPI item in the Name And Description section and optionally enter any comments about the KPI in the Comments section.

2. In the SQL Server 2005 Analysis Services KPI section (see Figure 21-21), enter the appropriate values for each of the following settings:

   a. In the Indicator Value section, enter the value to be used for the KPI in the Value text box.

   b. In the Status Icon section, use the Better Values Are list box to indicate whether the values higher or lower than the value entered in the Indicator Value section represent a better situation than that value.

   c. In the text box associated with When Has Met Or Exceeded Goal, enter the value at or above the KPI goal icon that is to be displayed.

   d. In the text box associated with the When Has Met Or Exceeded Warning, enter the value at or above the KPI warning icon that is to be displayed. Figure 21-23 shows sample values for these entries.

3. The final steps in creating the KPI item are essentially the same for all KPI types. See the "Create an Indicator Using Data in SharePoint List KPI" section earlier in this chapter for the final steps in creating a KPI item.

Figure 21-24 shows the All Items view of a list named Sample KPIs that includes the details for each KPI item included on the list. Figure 21-25 shows the resulting display for the KPI items included on the list in the list's primary view.

Indicator Value	Value:
Specify the current value for the indicator	100

Status Icon

Specify the icon rules that are used to determine which icon to display to represent the status of the indicator

Status Icon Rules:

Better values are higher ▼

Display ⬤ when has met or exceeded goal   100
Display △ when has met or exceeded warning   50
Display ◇ otherwise

Figure 21-23. A sample entry for a KPI item based on manually entered data.

Home > Reports > Sample KPIs
Sample KPIs

Sample Key Performance Indicators which are displayed by default on the home page of this Report Center.

View All Site Content
Reports
Dashboards
• Sample
Resources
• Data Connections
• Report Calendar
• Reference Library
Business Data Reports
🗑 Recycle Bin

New ▼   Actions ▼   Settings ▼   View: **All Items** ▼

Title	KPI Description	KPI Value	KPI Goal Threshold	KPI Warning Threshold	Content Type
Customer Ratings	The average customer rating sampled from end of sale questionnaires.	10	8	5	Indicator using manually entered information
Capacity Utilization	The production capacity used in production over the past month as a percentage of total production capacity.	85	90	75	Indicator using manually entered information
Overtime Expenses	The premium portion of overtime wages paid over the past two week period as a percentage of budgeted amounts.	81	60	75	Indicator using manually entered information

Figure 21-24. An All Items view of a KPI list.

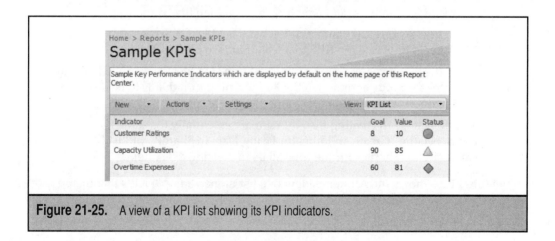

Home > Reports > Sample KPIs
Sample KPIs

Sample Key Performance Indicators which are displayed by default on the home page of this Report Center.

New ▼   Actions ▼   Settings ▼   View: KPI List ▼

Indicator	Goal	Value	Status
Customer Ratings	8	10	⬤
Capacity Utilization	90	85	△
Overtime Expenses	60	81	◇

Figure 21-25. A view of a KPI list showing its KPI indicators.

Business Data Web Parts

As discussed in Chapter 15, Web Parts are used to include certain types of data in a SharePoint web page, and business data Web Parts are really no different functionally. However, where they do differ from other Web Parts is in how they can be combined to create business intelligence. Business data Web Parts can be used in SharePoint lists and pages and provide users with data directly from a connected data source that is updated automatically.

MOSS includes six business data Web Parts:

▼   Core business data Web Parts

■   Filter Web Parts

■   KPI Web Parts

■   Specialized business data Web Parts

▲   SQL Server 2005 Analysis Services Web Parts

These Web Parts are explained and their use is outlined in the following sections.

Core Business Data Web Parts

Core business data Web Parts are a family of Web Parts that can be used to display information from data sources such as SQL Server 2005 and the database of any line-of-business (LOB) application registered in the BDC. The core business data Web Parts are:

▼   **Business data actions**   This Web Part is used to add a link to a SharePoint page that allows the user to view additional information on a particular topic. For example, if another Web Part is showing a sales summary, a business data actions Web Part can display a bulleted list of links to the details sales by region or salesperson.

■   **Business data association**   This Web Part displays a list of data related to information presented in another Web Part or a different business data type. For example, a list of salespersons that represent a particular product line or are based in a particular region.

■   **Business data catalog filters**   This Web Part is used to filter the information of one or more other Web Parts included on a page using values found in the SQL Server 2005 Reporting Services or the BDC.

■   **Business data details**   This Web Part is used to display the details of a single business data item, such as a single purchase order in the orders database.

▲   **Business data lists**   This Web Part displays business data in a list that can include one or more business data items from a single type of business data, as defined in the BDC. Business data list Web Parts can be connected to a filter Web Part to display only information for the current user or a specific value of an item in a registered business application.

The business data actions, business data associations, business data details, and the business data lists Web Parts are specifically used to display information from the SQL Server 2005 Reporting Service and LOB applications registered in the BDC. In addition, the business data associations, business data details, and the business data lists Web Parts can be included in a Report Center report or on other pages that include business data.

Filter Web Parts

Filter Web Parts have the capability of filtering the information displayed by one or more other Web Parts. In fact, a filter Web Part can be used to filter the displays of all of the Web Parts on a page (commonly referred to as a Dashboard) using the same business data item properties and values, resulting in a particular subset of the data available for one or all users.

MOSS includes a variety of filter Web Parts that can be used to limit the data displayed. As shown in Table 21-1, two of the filter Web Parts allow users to manually enter the value

Filter Web Part	Action Type	Description
Business Data Catalog Filter	List	Allows the page creator to select one business data entity from the Business Data Catalog and specify a Value column.
Choice Filter	List	Users select one of the values configured to the Web Part by the creator from a drop-down list.
Current User Filter	Automatic	Uses either the login name or the current user, or a selected SharePoint profile property.
Date Filter	Manual	Users can either select a date from a calendar or enter a date.
Page Field Filter	Automatic	Uses a value from a column on the list row to which the current page is associated.
Query String Filter	Automatic	Passes one or more values entered by the page creator to a URL.
SharePoint List Filter	List	Allows users to open a SharePoint list and choose a specific value in the column specified by the page creator.
SQL Server 2005 Analysis Services Filter	List	The page creator selects a data connection from one of three sources: a Web Part on the current page, a SharePoint Data Connection library, or an Office Data Connection library.
Text Filter	Manual	Users can accept a default value configured by the page creator or enter a text value.

Table 21-1. MOSS Filter Web Part Types

used to filter the information, four allow users to pick a filtering value from a list of available values, and three are configured with values to automatically filter the information.

Configure and Connect a Filter Web Part on a Web Part Page   Adding a filter Web Part to a Web Part page employs the same process used for virtually all Web Parts (see Chapter 15 for more information on Web Parts). The difference between a filter Web Part and other Web Parts is in how they are configured. Each filter Web Part uses a tool pane through which it is configured (see Figure 21-26).

The tool pane for each filter Web Part has a unique group of settings and options that can be used to configure its particular user interface, filtering options, and display. One of the settings available in several of the filter Web Parts is the ability to connect the Web Part to other Web Parts on the same page.

To connect a filter Web Part to another Web Part on the same page, it first must be a Web Part that allows connections to other Web Parts. This may sound somewhat obvious, but not all filter Web Parts allow these connections. A filter Web Part that does allow connections to other Web Parts will include a Connections option on its Edit menu, as shown in Figure 21-27. In many cases, the Connections option of the Web Part displays a dialog box in which the type of connection you are trying to create is configured. Figure 21-28 shows the dialog box displayed for the Connection option of a Current User filter Web Part.

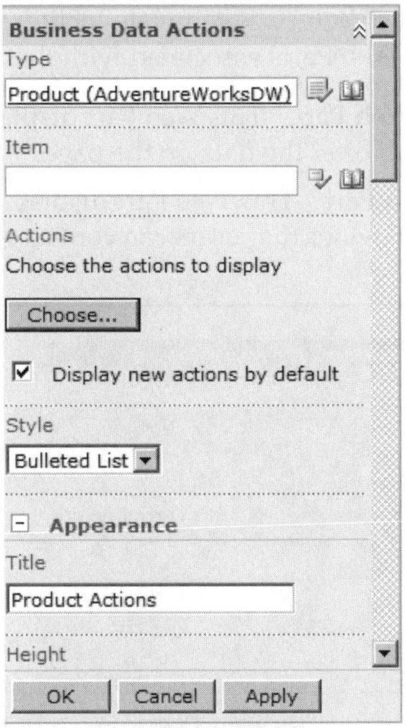

Figure 21-26.   The tool pane of a filter Web Part.

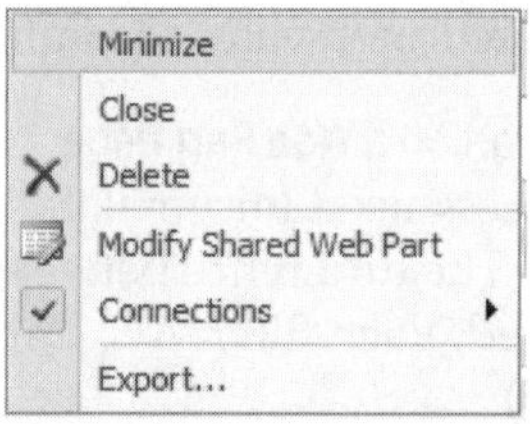

Figure 21-27. The Edit menu of a filter Web Part that allows connections to other elements.

Dashboards

A SharePoint dashboard is a specialized web page that is used to display the status of projects, budgets, and activities and provide users with links to other information. In effect, a dashboard is a summarized information web page that provides a quick look at where things are. A SharePoint dashboard can be created from scratch if you know the Web Parts needed and can be arranged as you wish. However, the dashboard web page template includes most of the Web Parts you need to build a good starting point dashboard.

The SharePoint dashboard web page template includes the following Web Parts, in addition to the related filter Web Parts associated with them:

▼ **The Apply Filters Web Part** This Web Part displays an Apply Filters button that users can click to filter the data on the page.

■ **Contact Details Web Part** This Web Part displays the contact information of the administrator or owner that users can contact regarding the page.

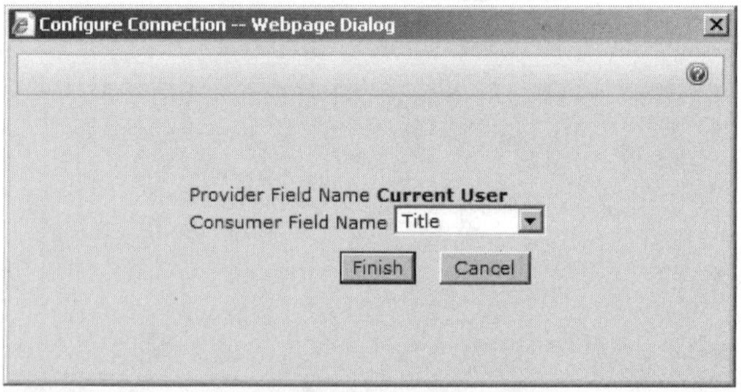

Figure 21-28. The Connection dialog box of a Current User filter Web Part.

- ■ **Excel Web Access Web Part**   This Web Part lets you add an Excel workbook, worksheet, or a range of cells from a worksheet to the page.

- ■ **KPI List Web Part**   This Web Part lets you display a KPI list on the page.

- ■ **Related Information Web Part**   This Web Part displays links to information related to other Web Parts on the page.

- ▲ **Summary Web Part**   This Web Part provides you with the capability to explain the information on the page.

Like virtually all SharePoint pages, a dashboard page is created by adding and configuring the Web Parts needed to provide users with relevant information. To create a SharePoint dashboard web page, perform the following steps:

1. Navigate to the home page of the Report Center site to which you wish to add a dashboard web page.

2. On the Report Center's home page, click the Dashboard heading in the Quick Launch menu to open the Reports Library page (see Figure 21-29).

3. Click the New button on the navigation bar and choose Dashboard Page from its drop-down menu.

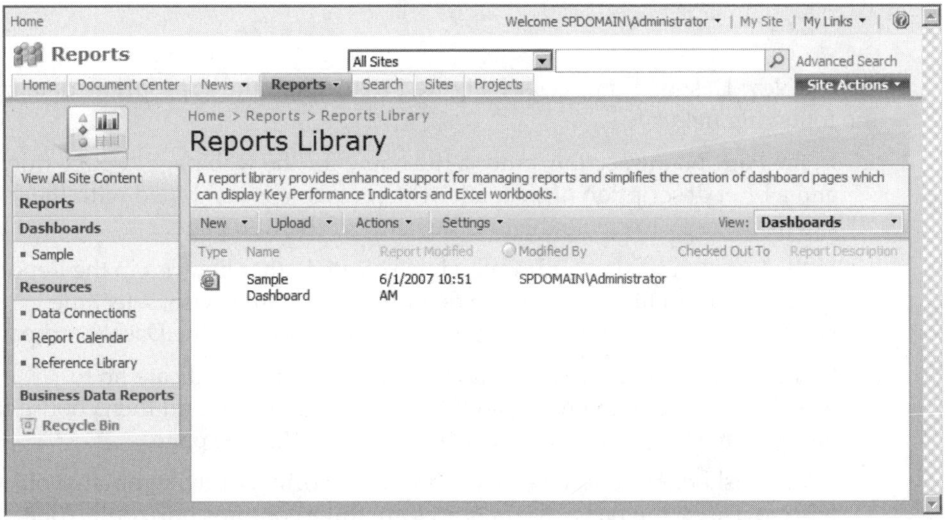

Figure 21-29.   The Reports Library page.

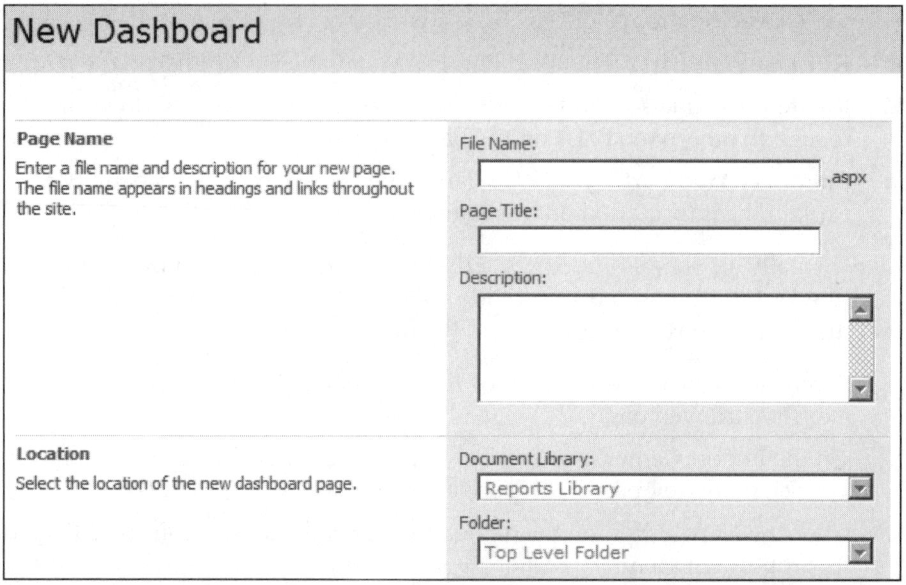

New Dashboard

Page Name

Enter a file name and description for your new page. The file name appears in headings and links throughout the site.

File Name:

[   ] .aspx

Page Title:

[   ]

Description:

[   ]

Location

Select the location of the new dashboard page.

Document Library:

[Reports Library   ▼]

Folder:

[Top Level Folder   ▼]

Figure 21-30.   The New Dashboard page.

4. On the New Dashboard page (see Figure 21-30), enter the appropriate data in the following fields:

   a. In the Page Name section, enter a file name for the web page, a page title, and a brief description of the page. The file name is combined with the file extension .aspx to create the full file name of the web page.

   b. In the Location section, unless you have created other libraries in the Reports Center, you can likely accept the default values. Otherwise, select the Document library and folder in which you wish to store the Dashboard page.

   c. In the Create Link In Current Navigation Bar section, indicate no to including a link on the navigation bar, or designate yes and then choose the navigation bar option under which you wish to list the page.

   d. In the Dashboard Layout section, choose the format of the template you wish to use on the page. Your choices are three columns horizontal, one column vertical, or two columns vertical.

   e. In the Key Performance Indicators section, choose the radio button option corresponding to whether or not you wish to include a KPI list on the page. If you do wish to include a KPI list on the page, choose the option for either

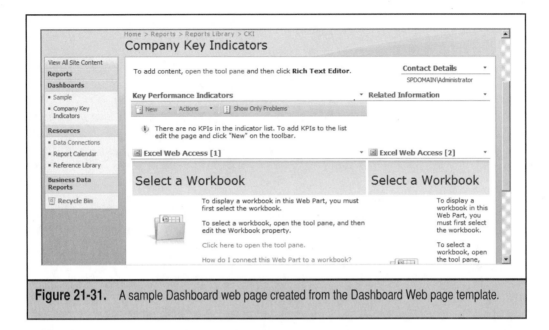

Figure 21-31.   A sample Dashboard web page created from the Dashboard Web page template.

Create A KPI List Automatically or Allow Me To Select An Existing KPI List Later. If you don't wish to include a KPI list, select the Do Not Add A KPI List To This Dashboard.

f.   Click the OK button to create the Dashboard page.

Figure 21-31 shows a sample of a Dashboard page created from the Dashboard Web page template.

SUMMARY

You aren't limited to only the data stored within your MOSS environment for reporting, tracking, and referencing business data. Through the configuration of the SSP and the Business Data Catalog, you can access data and information stored in external files, SQL Server 2005 databases, and even the databases of line-of-business applications, such as SAP and Siebel.

SharePoint sites can be configured specifically to include lists, dashboards, and reports that show business data in summary, detail, or using conditional status indicators. A variety of Web Parts are available to help you create meaningful, efficient, and current indications of the state of the business.

CHAPTER 22

MOSS and XML

The Extensible Markup Language (XML) is everywhere these days. XML is a flexible markup language that provides structure and context to data. XML is also text-based. It easily crosses application, platform, and network boundaries, making it ideal for integrating dissimilar systems.

This chapter will introduce you to what is possible with XML and MOSS, including the use of the XML Web Part. A wide variety of books have been written on XML and XSL. Hopefully, by the end of the chapter you will have a basic understanding of XML and XSL and continue your exploration of these topics in order to fully leverage them.

This chapter also introduces you to the SharePoint Form Library and Microsoft Info-Path. InfoPath is used to create and deploy XML forms in the MOSS environment.

AN OVERVIEW OF XML

XML is a text-based coding scheme for describing data. XML, based on the Standard Generalized Markup Language (SGML), which is itself based on the Generalized Markup Language (GML), was developed by IBM in the 1960s. Markup languages, such as XML, SGML, and GML, are used to describe, comment on, and format text-based communications.

XML uses a standardized set of encoding rules to describe the content and structure of data. XML was created to provide a vehicle that allows for easy sharing of data between applications, networks, operating systems, and hardware platforms. However, XML doesn't describe how data should be displayed. How best to display the data contained in an XML document is left up to the user or the receiving system.

Sample XML Document

To gain an understanding of what XML is and why it can be useful. Let's look at a short example of an XML document. The following is a simple recipe for pizza represented as an XML document:

```xml
<?xml version="1.0" ?>
<recipe name="pizza" prep_time="10 minutes" cook_time="18 minutes">
  <title>Pepperoni Pizza</title>
  <ingredient amount="1" unit="package">Pizza dough</ingredient>
  <ingredient amount="1" unit="package">Pizza sauce</ingredient>
  <ingredient amount="1" unit="package">Pepperoni</ingredient>
  <ingredient amount="2" unit="cups">Cheese</ingredient>
  <instructions>
   <step number="1">Prepare pizza dough according to package</step>
   <step number="2">Spread sauce on pizza dough</step>
   <step number="3">Cover sauce with cheese</step>
   <step number="4">Place pepperoni on top of cheese</step>
   <step number="6">Cook for 18 minutes at 425 degrees</step>
  </instructions>
</recipe>
```

Notice that the pizza recipe has been structured and encoded into a hierarchy of XML tags. These tags are actually different types of XML statements. The two primary XML statements are XML declarations and XML elements.

The XML Declaration

The XML declaration (<?xml version="1.0" ?>) is the first line of the XML document shown in the preceding section. It is an optional statement, but if included, it declares the document to be an XML document. The declaration may also contain additional attributes such as character encoding and more.

XML Elements

All of the XML statements that follow the XML declaration are called XML elements. Each XML element consists of a beginning and ending tag. For example, in the first statement after the XML declaration:

```
<recipe name="pizza" prep_time="10 minutes" cook_time="18 minutes">
```

The tag assigned to the element is "<recipe." XML tags are defined on-the-fly. Unlike Hypertext Markup Langauge (HTML), which is used to code web pages, XML tags are made up of the name of the hierarchical element (in this case, the record name recipe) and its attributes. Each attribute is made up of a name and a value, such as name="pizza," or prep_time="10 minutes." In each attribute, the name of the attribute is separated from its value by an equal sign and the value is enclosed in quotation marks. The recipe tag, in the example document, contains three attributes: the name attribute with the value "pizza," a prep_time attribute with the value "10 minutes," and a cook_time attribute with the value "18 minutes."

The first element of an XML document, which is called the root element, is the container for all of the other elements in the document. For each opening tag, such as the <recipe> tag, there is a corresponding closing tag. In the sample document, the last element in the sample document is the </recipe> tag. All of the other elements, including title, ingredient, instruction, and step, are contained within the recipe element.

Take a moment to examine how the <step> elements are nested within the <instructions> element. It is the combination of nested elements, along with element attributes and content that defines the structure of XML data.

XML APPLICATIONS IN AN MOSS ENVIRONMENT

XML has a variety of applications that can be implemented in an MOSS environment, including Really Simple Syndication (RSS) feeds, leveraging SQL data, and XML-based web services. RSS (also known as Rich Site Summary) feeds use XML to publish content that is frequently updated. Users can subscribe to an RSS feed using an RSS reader and receive regular updates of certain information at an interval each user defines. Microsoft SQL Server 2005, as well as SQL Server 2000, has the capability to output results in an XML format. This is accomplished by simply adding the two words FOR XML to the end of an SQL query.

Really Simple Syndication (RSS)

RSS is an information formatting scheme used primarily for syndicating (sharing) news, electronic magazines (e-zines), and personal weblogs (blogs). However, any information that can be structured into an XML-style format can be syndicated using an RSS feed and read using a news aggregator. A news aggregator is any program that is RSS-compatible, including most web browsers.

RSS began life as the Rich Site Summary in early 1999 for use with the Netscape web browser. From 1999 to 2002, several versions of RSS were released between competing groups attempting to establish the standard. Finally, in 2004, *The New York Times* provided its subscribers with the ability to use an RSS feed to download news content from its web site, establishing RSS as a viable tool and making RSS version 2.0 the de facto standard.

Information syndication, which is what RSS does, continues to evolve. A new standard, known as the Atom Syndication Format, is under development by the Internet Engineering Task Force (IETF).

TIP To produce XML output from a legacy database or an application that doesn't support XML, you can use a helper application, such as a web service or a third-party add-on or application. You can find ample information on these services on the Internet by searching for XML web services.

NOTE Microsoft InfoPath 2007, which is a separate application available in the Microsoft Office 2007 suite, can be used to quickly create XML-based forms. For more information on using InfoPath to create MOSS-compatible forms, see Chapter 24.

RSS Feeds

In a growing number of instances, information that is constantly (or at least frequently) updated, and must be distributed to a large number of subscribers, is being made available as an RSS feed. It is common for a news web site or a weblog (blog) to make its updated content available through an RSS feed.

RSS Viewer Web Part on a SharePoint Page

A SharePoint page can include an RSS viewer, which enables it to display RSS feeds. Before you begin the process of adding an RSS viewer to a SharePoint page, access the site settings and those of the library in which you wish to add an RSS viewer to ensure RSS has been enabled on the site and in the library.

To add an RSS viewer to a SharePoint page, do the following:

1. Navigate to the SharePoint page on which you wish to display an RSS feed and click the Site Actions button to open its drop-down menu.

2. On the Site Actions menu, click the Edit Page option.

3. On the Edit Mode page (see Figure 22-1), click the Add A Web Part button in the Web Part Zone in which you wish to place the RSS viewer.

4. On the Add Web Parts To Body dialog box (see Figure 22-2), click the Advanced Web Part Gallery And Options link at the bottom of the page.

5. The Advanced Web Part gallery opens in a window pane on the right side of the display (see Figure 22-3). Search through the list using the Next link until the RSS Viewer Web Part is displayed.

6. Drag the RSS Viewer Web Part into the Web Part zone where you wish to place it (as shown in Figure 22-4).

Now that an RSS Viewer Web Part has been added to the page, the next task is to assign an RSS Feed to the RSS Viewer Web Part. The next section continues this process.

Assign an RSS Feed to the RSS Viewer Web Part

Once an RSS Viewer Web Part is added to a SharePoint Web page, the RSS Viewer must be configured with the Internet address (URL) of an RSS feed and its options set. The options you can configure for the RSS Viewer include how many feed items to display, feed

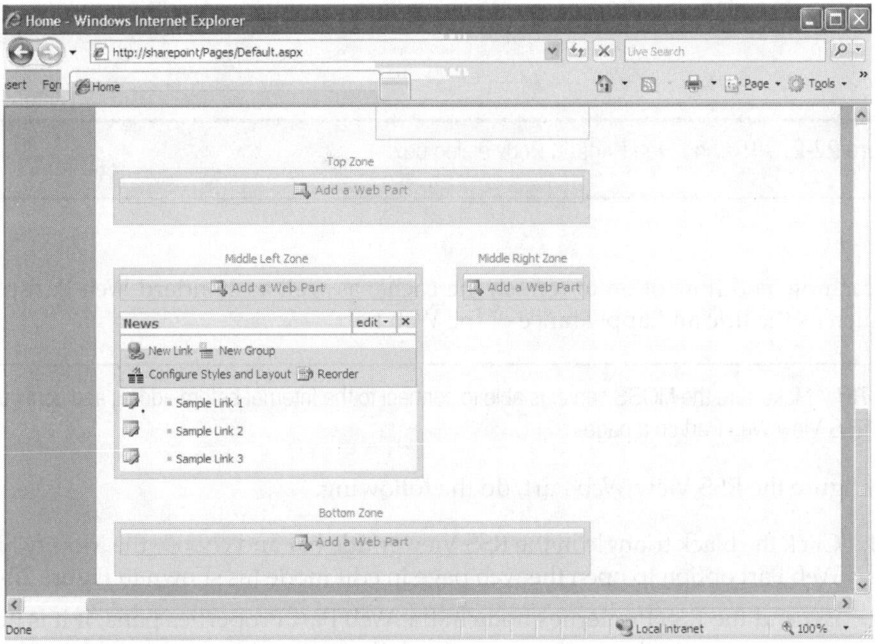

Figure 22-1. The Add A Web Part application is used to add an RSS viewer to a SharePoint page.

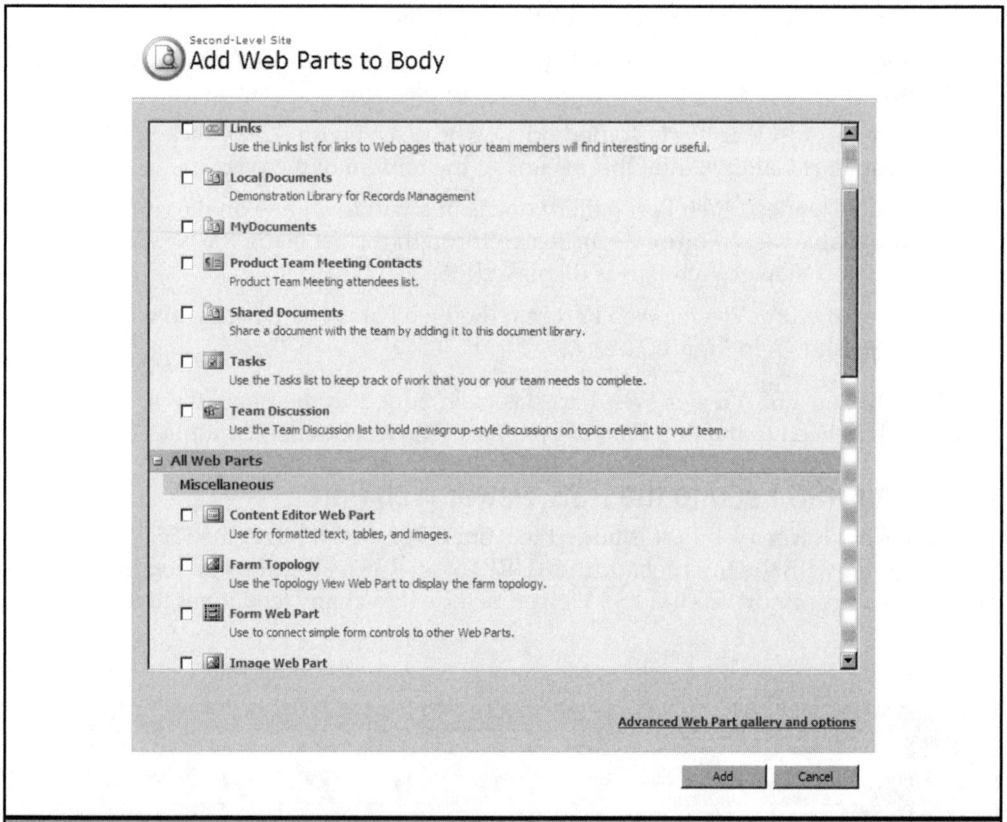

Figure 22-2. The Add Web Parts To Body dialog box.

item caching, and how often to refresh the cache, as well as standard Web Part properties, such as the title and appearance of the Web Part.

TIP Make sure the MOSS server is able to connect to the Internet before adding and configuring an RSS View Web Part on a page.

To configure the RSS View Web Part, do the following:

1. Click the black triangle in the RSS Viewer title bar and choose the Modify Shared Web Part option to open the web page in edit mode (as shown in Figure 22-5).

2. Expand the RSS Properties node in the Web Part Properties pane, if it is not already expanded, and then enter the URL for the RSS Feed to which this Web Part is to be linked (see Figure 22-5).

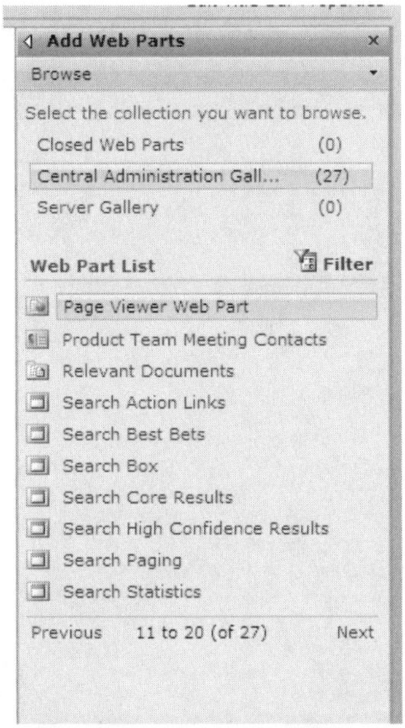

Figure 22-3. The Advanced Web Part gallery.

TIP It is usually best to cut and paste the URL of the RSS Feed into the RSS Feed URL text box to avoid mistakes.

3. By default, MOSS limits RSS feeds to five items. So, if you'd like to increase this number for most news-related feeds, such as to 20 items, enter this value in the Feed Limit box.

4. Scroll down in the Web Part Properties pane and expand the Miscellaneous node (see Figure 22-6).

5. If you wish to have the RSS Feed updated more frequently (or less) than every 10 minutes (600 seconds), change the value in the Data View Caching Time-Out box.

6. To give your RSS Viewer Web Part a title for display on the web page, open the Appearance node and enter a descriptive title, such as the "Top Sites" title shown for the Google News RSS Feed in Figure 22-7.

TIP Many RSS feeds already provide a title, so assigning and displaying a Web Part title can be redundant. To hide the RSS Viewer title, edit the RSS Viewer Shared Web Part Properties, and set the Chrome Type to None in the Appearance section.

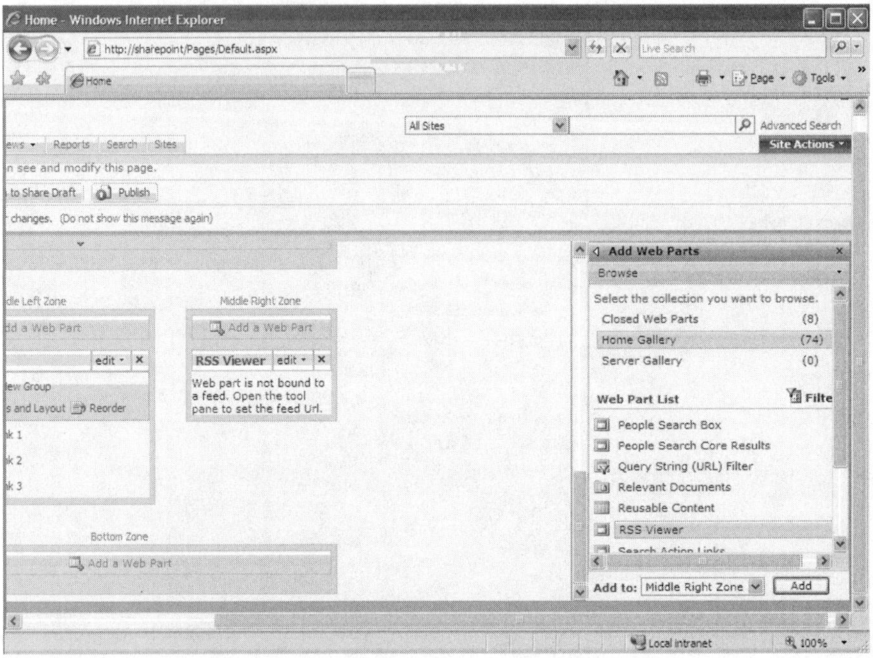

Figure 22-4. The RSS Viewer Web Part added to a Web Part zone.

7. Click the OK button to save your configuration settings and after the display is returned to Edit mode for the web page, click the Exit edit mode link to display the page as it is now configured.

XML Web Part

MOSS includes an XML Web Part that can be used to display virtually any XML document, which includes most Microsoft Office 2007 documents saved as XML by default. Other documents that can be displayed in an XML Web Part include query results from Microsoft SQL Server that can be configured to be produced as an XML document and an increasing amount of data available from a variety of web services that use XML for both requests for data and information responses. XML can also be manipulated using the Extensible Stylesheet Language (XSL). XSL can be used to convert an XML document into another XML document, an HTML document, or into a file format such as a Portable Document Format (PDF) or Scalable Vector Graphics (SVG). Because XML separates the data itself from its structure and presentation, these conversions are possible.

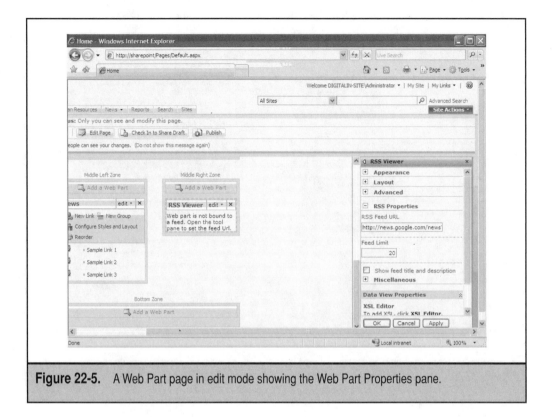

Figure 22-5.   A Web Part page in edit mode showing the Web Part Properties pane.

The SharePoint XML Web Part can be used to display a variety of XML data from a number of sources, including data from database tables and queries, XML documents, and XML forms (such as those created in InfoPath). Data content can be displayed through an XML Web Part using either the XML and XSL editors included in the Web Part, or by entering hyperlinks to text files that contain the XML and XSL source code. Only HTTP and HTTPS (HTTP with Secure Sockets Layer [SSL] encryption) URLs can be used with the XML Web Part though. The hyperlink addresses can be either absolute or relative URLs, but file pathnames cannot be used.

XML data is available from a variety of Internet sources. For example, the National Oceanic Atmospheric Administration (NOAA) produces a large volume of weather data for the United States using an XML web service. How this data is used, presented, or manipulated is up to the requesting site, but because it is in XML format, it can be used in a variety of ways.

The following example details the steps used to add and configure an XML Web Part on a SharePoint web page. In this example, we use XML data from the NOAA web service to add information to a web page.

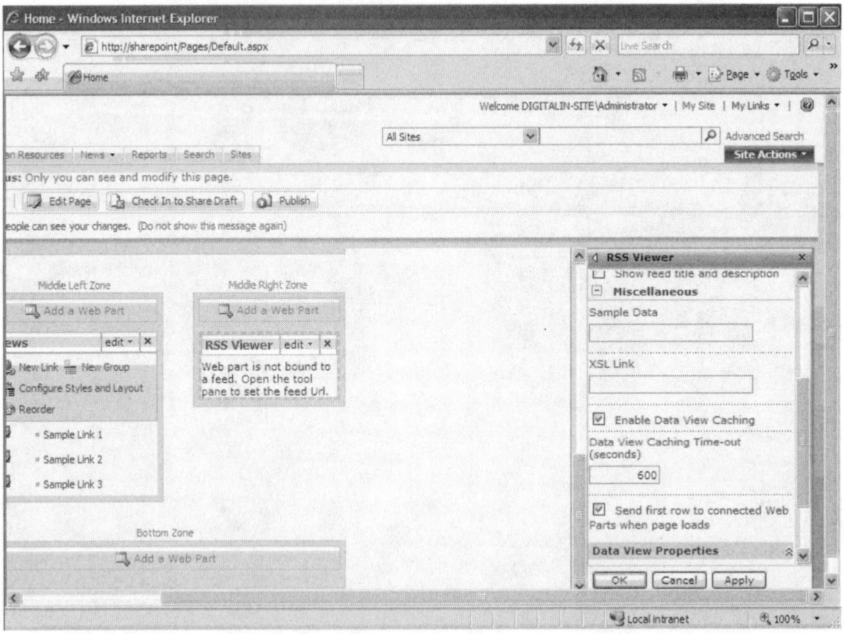

Figure 22-6.   The Miscellaneous properties node of the Web Part Properties pane.

Adding the XML Web Part to a SharePoint Page

To display an XML document on a Web Parts page, add the XML Web Part to the page. To do this, perform the following steps:

1. Navigate to a SharePoint Page on which you wish to display an XML document, click the Site Actions button to open its drop-down menu, and choose Edit Page.

2. Click the Add A Web Part button at the top of the Web Part Zone in which you wish to place the XML display.

3. On the Add Web Parts dialog box that opens, scroll down to the Miscellaneous section and check the box corresponding to the XML Web Part.

4. Click the Add button to add the Web Part and display the page in Edit mode (as shown in Figure 22-8).

As illustrated in Figure 22-8, the XML Web Part is now included on the page. However, at this point, the Web Part won't actually do anything until it has been configured with XML and XSL documents. Before we can assign these settings, however, we must first generate a Hypertext Transfer Protocol (HTTP) request for the data.

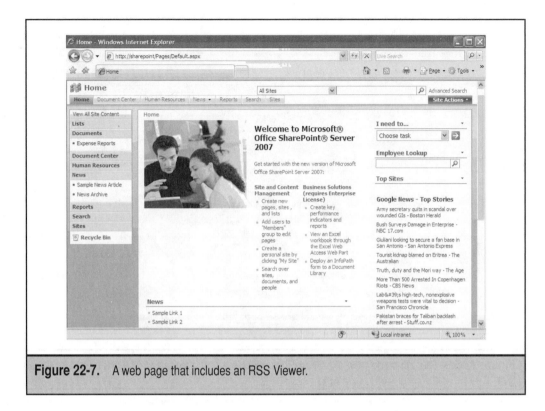

Figure 22-7. A web page that includes an RSS Viewer.

Obtaining and Entering an XML Link

To generate an HTTP request for XML data, in this case from the NOAA web service, do the following:

1. Navigate to the National Digital Forecast Database XML Generator web site at www.weather.gov/forecasts/xml/SOAP_server/ndfdXML.htm (see Figure 22-9).

2. On the web site, you can either accept the default latitude and longitude values, which represent the NOAA headquarters location, or you can use the Internet to find the latitude and longitude for your location.

3. For this example, set the variables on the NOAA web site you wish to include in the generated XML file.

4. Click the Submit Button to make an HTTP request to the web service. The web service then sends an HTTP response in the form of an XML document.

NOTE   More information about the National Digital Forecast Database, including detailed instructions, can be found at www.weather.gov/xml.

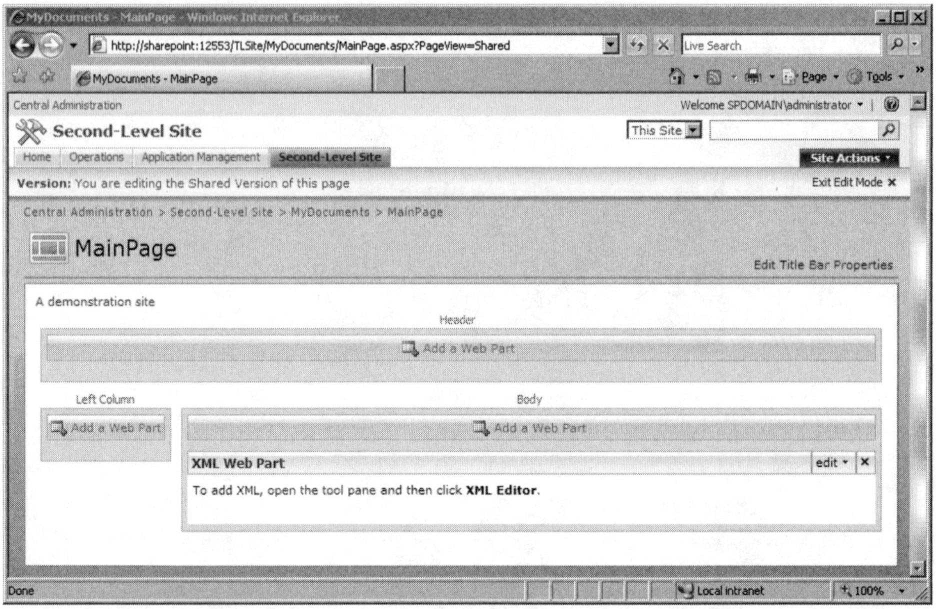

Figure 22-8. The edit mode view of a SharePoint web page that includes an XML Web Part.

5. After a few moments, an XML document appears in the web browser. The first line of code identifies the data as XML. The root element is <dwml> with several attributes in the form of a name=value pair. The plus and minus signs to the left of each element can be used to expand or contract each element. You should be able to identify a few weather details, such as the daily minimum temperature, cloud cover, or wind speed in the XML data.

6. In the browser's location or address bar, highlight and copy the URL. The URL is used to configure the XML Web Part to request the XML document.

7. Now that you've identified a source for an XML document, you must enter it into a SharePoint XML Web Part.

8. Open the SharePoint web page that contains the XML Web Part added earlier (see the "Adding the XML Web Part to a SharePoint Page" section earlier in this chapter).

9. Click the small black triangle for the XML Web Part and choose Modify Shared Web Part from the menu that drops down.

10. Paste the URL copied from the XML source (see step 6) into the XML Link property of the XML Web Part.

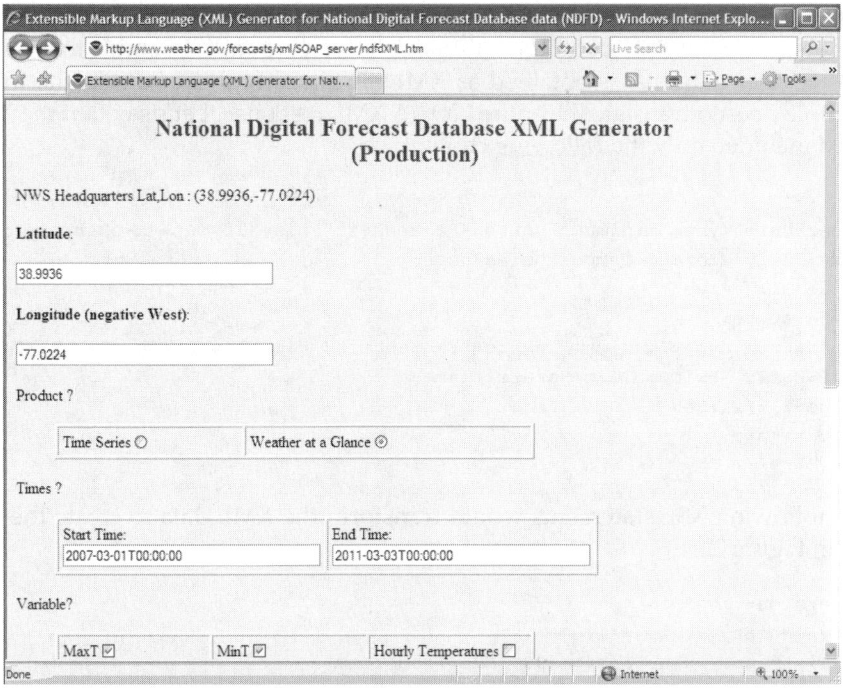

Figure 22-9. The National Digital Forecast Database XML Generator web site of the National Oceanic Atmospheric Administration (NOAA).

11. Click the Test link item to verify the validity of the URL entered.

12. Click the Apply button to save the XML Link property.

At this point in the process, the XML Web Part displays the weather data requested from the NOAA web site, but it is not necessarily presented in a format easily read by users. The next action in this process is to create an XSL filter for the XML data.

Use XSL to Format an XML Document

With the XML Link added to the Web Part configuration, you now must provide an XSL link that can be used to translate the XML data into the form you wish to display on the web page. Like XML, XSL can appear somewhat complex at first, but it is actually very similar to XML in form.

Like XML, XSL is a markup language. XML is the markup language used to provide structure to the data, and XSL provides the means to translate the XML into Hypertext

Markup Language (HTML) statements that can be interpreted by the web browser for display.

To illustrate what XSL is and how it's used, let's create an XSL sample to use with the NOAA weather data that is obtained as XML. To simplify this example, the following XSL sample doesn't translate the entire NOAA XML response. Let's say that the XML file obtained included only the following content:

```
<data>
  <temperature type="minimum" units="Fahrenheit" time-layout="k-p24h-n1-1">
   <name>Daily Minimum Temperature</name>
   <value>31</value>
  </temperature>
  <temperature type="maximum" units="Fahrenheit" time-layout="k-p24h-n1-1">
   <name>Daily Maximum Temperature</name>
   <value>51</value>
  </temperature>
</data>
```

The following XSL statements would transform the XML data to create the display shown in Figure 22-10:

```
<?xml version="1.0" ?>
<xsl:stylesheet version="1.0"
xmlns:xsl="http://www.w3.org/1999/XSL/Transform">
  <xsl:output method="html" />
  <xsl:template match="temperature">
     <xsl:value-of select="@type" />: <xsl:value-of select="value" /><br />
  </xsl:template>
</xsl:stylesheet>
```

In plain English, these XSL statements translate the XML weather data example like this:

▼ Find each "temperature" element.

■ Display the "temperature" element's "type" attribute.

■ Display the "temperature" element's "type" attribute.

▲ Display the content of the "value" element, which is nested inside the "temperature" elements.

Unless you purchase a third-party XSL editor, you will likely need to learn XSL coding if you plan to display XML data, regardless of its source (including InfoPath forms) using an XML Web Part.

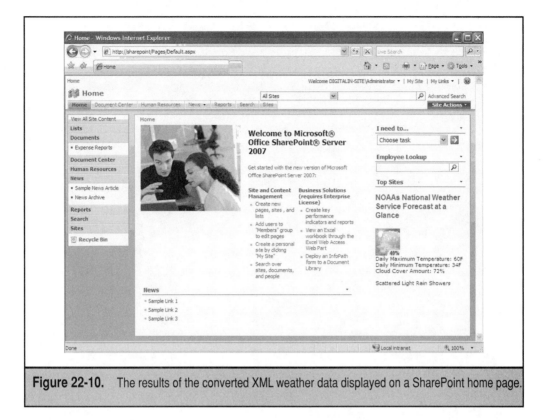

Figure 22-10.   The results of the converted XML weather data displayed on a SharePoint home page.

SUMMARY

XML is here to stay and it's become an integral part of the Microsoft Office environment. It is the de facto data format for transferring and storing information among and between the various Microsoft Office applications. In fact, several Internet technologies, such as Really Simple Syndication (RSS), rely on XML to exchange data between sources and requestors. Many relational database systems (RDBMS), including Microsoft SQL 2005, can be configured to produce XML output for reports and queries.

MOSS provides a variety of ways in which XML can be used, most of which are covered in other chapters of this book (see Chapter 20 for information on Excel Data Services and Chapter 24 for information on InfoPath forms). However, MOSS supports the use of two Web Parts that can be used to directly import and display XML data on web pages: the RSS Viewer Web Part and the XML Web Part.

The RSS Viewer Web Part allows a web page to include an RSS feed from an external source to be displayed and updated on a SharePoint web page. The XML Web Part is capable of storing an XML document, or requesting XML through a URL and including it as a part of a web page's display filtered though XSL statements contained within the XML Web Part or requested from an Internet site using a URL.

INDEX

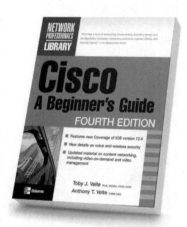

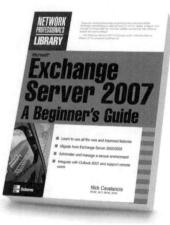